TRIPOLITANIA
IN THE ROMAN EMPIRE AND BEYOND

I0893463

British Institute for Libyan and Northern African Studies Open Access Monograph 4

TRIPOLITANIA
IN THE ROMAN EMPIRE AND BEYOND

Edited by
Niccolò Mugnai

BILNAS
BRITISH INSTITUTE FOR LIBYAN
& NORTHERN AFRICAN STUDIES

This publication has been supported by a grant from the Leverhulme Trust.

LEVERHULME
TRUST

British Institute for Libyan and Northern African Studies Open Access Monograph 4

Published in 2024 by
The British Institute for Libyan and Northern African Studies
c/o The British Academy
10–11 Carlton House Terrace
London SW1Y 5AH
www.bilnas.org

Copyright © 2024 British Institute for Libyan and Northern African Studies

This work is licensed under a Creative Commons Attribution – NonCommercial – ShareAlike 4.0 International (CC BY-NC-SA 4.0)
The text of the license is available at
https://creativecommons.org/licenses/by-nc-sa/4.0/

ISBN: 978-1-915808-10-3

Cover and interior design by Chris Bell, cbdesign

TABLE OF CONTENTS

ACKNOWLEDGEMENTS

This volume is the outcome of a long process that involved the work of many people. I would like to express my gratitude to all the Officers and Council Members of the British Institute for Libyan and Northern African Studies (BILNAS) for believing in this project and for publishing it in their Open Access Monograph Series. In times of financial restraints and budget cuts across the humanities and social sciences, it is heart-warming to see how the commitment of this group of people can generate such valuable scholarly outputs. A special thanks is due to Victoria Leitch, BILNAS' Publications Manager, for her constant assistance throughout the steps of this publication, and to Chris Bell for producing such an attractive book. I also wish to thank all the contributors to this volume for their enthusiastic work and patience – I hope they will be pleased with the final result of their efforts.

Work on this volume was undertaken as part of a Leverhulme Trust Early Career Fellowship held at the Faculty of Classics, University of Oxford in association with Wolfson College. The final part of this publication was completed following my move to the Institute of Classical Archaeology, University of Tübingen, where I am currently based. I would like to thank all these institutions for their various forms of support. The Leverhulme Trust also provided generous financial assistance towards the publication costs of the book.

The volume has greatly benefitted from the scientific advice of a team of scholars who offered comments, feedback, and constructive critiques to improve each contribution and the book as a whole. To all of them goes my sincerest thanks: Jonathan Bloom, Stefano Camporeale, Elizabeth Fentress, Bruce Hitchner, Philip Kenrick, David Mattingly, David Stone, Anna Walas, and Susan Walker. I would also like to thank Ahmed Buzaian and Muna Haroun Abdelhamed for providing the Arabic summary included at the end of this book.

Finally, my warmest thanks should go to my family, friends, and colleagues in different parts of the world. Without their encouragement through the years, I would not have been able to complete this or indeed any other projects.

Niccolò Mugnai
Tübingen, October 2024

LIST OF FIGURES

Chapter 3

Chapter 4

Chapter 5

Chapter 6

Chapter 7

Chapter 8

Chapter 9

Chapter 10

Chapter 11

LIST OF TABLES

Chapter 1

Chapter 7

LIST OF ABBREVIATIONS

AE	*L'Année Épigraphique (1888–).*
CIL	*Corpus Inscriptionum Latinarum (1863–).*
EDCS	*Epigraphik-Datenbank Clauss/Slaby.*
ILAfr	Cagnat, R., Merlin, A. and Chatelain, L. 1923. *Inscriptions latines d'Afrique (Tripolitaine, Tunisie, Maroc).* Paris: Éditions Ernest Leroux.
ILT	Merlin, A. 1944. *Inscriptions latines de la Tunisie.* Paris: Presses Universitaires de France.
IPT	Levi Della Vida, G. and Amadasi Guzzo, M.G. 1987. *Iscrizioni puniche della Tripolitania (1927–1967).* Rome: 'L'Erma' di Bretschneider.
IRT	Reynolds, J.M. and Ward-Perkins, J.B. 1952. *The Inscriptions of Roman Tripolitania.* London-Rome: British School at Rome.
IRT2021	*Inscriptions of Roman Tripolitania (2021)*, by J.M. Reynolds, C. Roueché, G. Bodard, C. Barron and others, available at: https//irt2021.inslib.kcl.ac.uk.
RIC	*Roman Imperial Coinage (1923–1967)*, by H. Mattingly, E.A. Sydenham and others.

Chapter 1

APPROACHING ANCIENT TRIPOLITANIA: AN INTRODUCTION

Niccolò Mugnai

Archaeological research and publications

The archaeology of the sector of Tripolitania corresponding to western Libya has been shaped to a large extent by the modern history of this country. Extensive excavations started under Italian colonial rule (1911–1943) and brought to light impressive remains of ancient monuments, especially at urban sites such as Lepcis Magna and Sabratha.[1] This colonial-era legacy has left some archaeological areas unpublished or only partly published, with preservation and conservation issues; however, post-colonial works by Libyan and international researchers abound, including fieldwork reports and more in-depth studies of specific buildings and sites. Those who are starting to familiarize themselves with the archaeology, history, and heritage of Libya can find a wealth of material in three dedicated journals: *Libyan Studies*, published yearly since 1970 by the British Institute for Libyan and Northern African Studies – BILNAS (formerly the Society for Libyan Studies); *Libya Antiqua*, the official journal of the Department of Antiquities of Libya – DoA, with a new series launched in 2010; and *Quaderni di Archeologia della Libya*, which was established in 1950 to continue the series of reports of the later decommissioned 'Ufficio Studi del Ministero dell'Africa Italiana' and its regular publication by 'L'Erma' di Bretschneider resumed in 2018. Important information can also be found in older, colonial-period publications, such as *Africa Italiana*, and in current academic journals focusing on North Africa and beyond: *Antiquités Africaines*, *Karthago*, *Azania*, and the *Journal of African Archaeology* are some examples. Significant archaeological, historical, and art historical studies on sites of Tripolitania have appeared in the *Papers of the British School at Rome*, the *Journal of Roman Studies*, the *Journal of Roman Archaeology*, *Archeologia Classica*, and other journals.

Studies on the architecture, art, and urbanism of ancient Libya (Tripolitania and Cyrenaica), among other topics, have appeared regularly in Italian in the book series 'Monografie di Archeologia Libica' ('L'Erma' di Bretschneider) since 1948. More works on similar subjects can be found in Italian and other languages in the (now discontinued) series of supplements to *Libya Antiqua*. To these one should add archaeological works that have been published in English as monographs and edited volumes in the BILNAS publication series, including the three most recent instalments dedicated to Tripolitania: Ahmed 2019; Sheldrick 2021; and the present volume. One should also acknowledge the painstaking work of scholars in the immediate post-Second World War and subsequent periods who contributed to enhancing our understating of ancient Tripolitania. Among these a special place must be reserved for John Bryan Ward-Perkins – see especially his work on the Severan buildings of Lepcis Magna (Ward-Perkins 1993) and references to his other studies in this volume – and for Antonino Di Vita, whose principal (published and unpublished) papers on Tripolitania are now conveniently collected in Rizzo and Di Vita-Évrard 2015; Rizzo 2017.[2]

There have been valuable attempts to offer syntheses of this rich material and to produce dedicated collections of studies that readers could use as a starting point for their own work. A case in point is represented by the volume *Town and Country in Roman Tripolitania* (Buck

[1] The literature on Italian colonial archaeology in Libya is vast, reflecting the vivid debate on its pitfalls and merits from historical, political, and social standpoints; for a recent review of the topic see Munzi 2012, with bibliography.

[2] For a detailed account of the life, work, and achievements of Ward-Perkins and Di Vita, one can look at the respective obituaries published in *Papers of the British School at Rome* 48, 1980 (by M. Pallottino and J.M. Reynolds) and *Libya Antiqua* n.s. 7, 2013–14 (by G. Rocco).

and Mattingly 1985), which brings together papers on the archaeology of Tripolitania – from the urban centres of the coastal region to the more remote desert areas. Similarly, a themed section in *Libyan Studies* 20, 1989 collects papers by an international team of scholars who outline the development of research in Libya from 1969 to 1989, focusing on archaeology (from prehistory to the Islamic period), history, epigraphy, art and architecture. These works served as a prelude to the publication of David Mattingly's *Tripolitania* (1995), which remains a fundamental reference study for anyone interested in this subject. Through engagement with a broad range of topics – geography, ethnicity, history, culture, urban and landscape archaeology, the army and frontiers, economy and trade – the book provides a comprehensive account of this North African region in Roman and late Roman times.

Archaeological studies on Tripolitania, as well as on Libya and North Africa more broadly, have much progressed since then (for a comprehensive assessment of the state of research see Mattingly, Chapter 11). Following the final publication of the UNESCO Libyan Valleys Archaeological Survey – ULVS (Barker 1996; Mattingly 1996), new projects have been developed to investigate societies, especially the Garamantes, at the fringes and beyond the borders of the Roman Empire: the Desert Migrations Project; Fazzan Project; Peopling the Desert Project; and Trans-Sahara Project (for an overview see Mattingly 2019; 2022, with references). The activity in the field of the French Archaeological Mission in Tripolitania and Cyrenaica has produced important scientific outputs, an outline of which can be found in Michel 2011–12; 2015. The fieldwork conducted by the German Archaeological Mission has provided a wealth of new data on Tripolitanian military structures in the Roman and Late Antique periods (Mackensen 2021; 2024; see also Mackensen, Chapter 6). A useful guide to the numerous archaeological projects undertaken as part of Libyan-Italian partnerships was published recently in a bilingual, Italian and Arabic, volume: Musso and Turjman 2022. It is also important to mention the recent work of international teams in the Tunisian sector of Tripolitania, especially on the Island of Jerba: Drine *et al.* 2009; Ritter and Ben Tahar 2022 (for a discussion of research in this area see Mattingly, Chapter 11). Reports of international events and projects on the preservation of Libya's cultural heritage can be found in themed sections of *Libyan Studies* 48, 2017 and *Quaderni di Archeologia della Libya* 21, 2018. Finally, a major advancement has been the creation of an online, freely available edition of the standard epigraphic corpus *Inscriptions of Roman Tripolitania – IRT* (originally published by Reynolds and Ward-Perkins in 1952), which incorporates hundreds of newly discovered texts: *Inscriptions of Roman Tripolitania (2021) – IRT2021*.

In addition to these publications, most of which are specifically aimed at the scholarly community, it is worth taking into proper account those works that have offered an overview of the archaeology and history of Tripolitania to broader audiences. There is quite an assortment of this kind of literature, starting with Denys Haynes' *Archaeological and Historical Guide to the Pre-Islamic Antiquities of Tripolitania* (fourth edition published in 1981); though outdated, there is still plenty of useful information one can gather from it.[3] Written by leading scholars, *Libya: The Lost Cities of the Roman Empire* (Di Vita *et al.* 1999, also available in French, German, and Spanish) provides an account of the archaeology, urbanism, art and architecture of Roman-period Libya, focusing mostly on Tripolitania with a shorter section on Cyrenaica. The most recent, and most welcome, addition to this series of publications is Philip Kenrick's *Libya Archaeological Guides: Tripolitania* (2009, also available in Arabic). With its critical assessment of scholarship and archaeological evidence dating from Phoenician/Punic times through to the early Islamic era, this is an indispensable resource for both general readers and established scholars, and it has inspired the present volume in many ways.

Tripolitania: a new regional study

Until very recently, the overwhelming majority of handbooks, syntheses, and collective studies on North Africa in the Roman period was available mostly in French and Italian,[4] while English-language works tended to be more limited in scope. Given the current structure of university courses in the Anglophone world, in many instances this has proved to be a severe limitation to the choice of items one could include in reading lists. The situation is now rapidly changing: the publication of Bruce Hitchner's *Companion to North Africa in Antiquity* (2022) has been a milestone to start addressing this imbalance. The inclusion of essays covering the archaeology, history, culture and geography of various areas of the Maghreb and beyond provides a valuable overview of the subject, encompassing a broad time frame from the first millennium BCE to the eighth century CE. This was followed by the timely publication of David Mattingly's *Between Sahara and Sea: Africa in the Roman Empire* (2023) – a book that offers a renewed, long-awaited insight

[3] There are also books, popular readings, and guidebooks to individual sites of Tripolitania, published at different stages and available in various languages, many of which are cited in chapters of this volume.

[4] Examples include, among many others: Romanelli 1970; Briand-Ponsart and Hugoniot 2006; Lassère 2015. See also the 22 volumes of *L'Africa Romana* conference proceedings published since 1984.

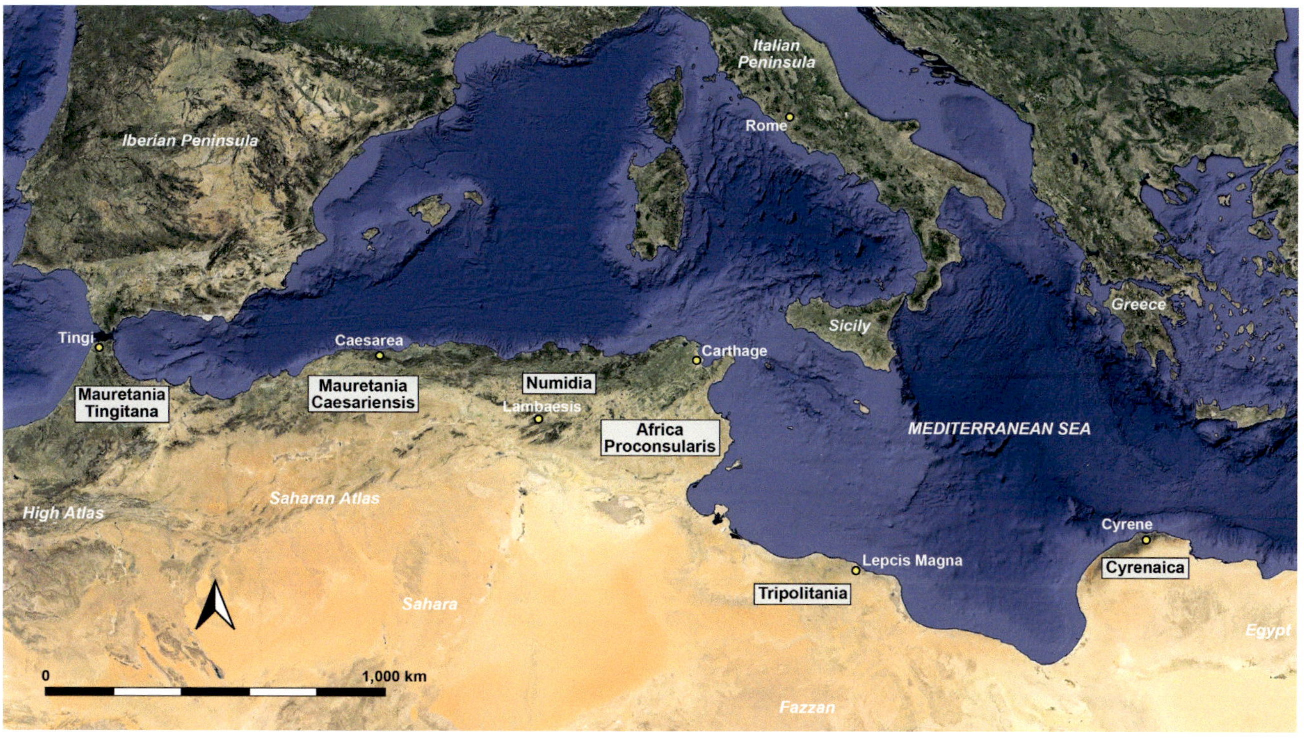

Fig. 1.1. Map of the North African region in the Roman period (basemap Google Earth, data SIO, NOAA, US Navy, NGA, GEBCO, image Landsat/Copernicus).

into the life of urban, rural, and military communities across North Africa from the first century BCE to the third century CE. By focusing on how the local inhabitants experienced imperial rule under Rome, this study moves away from old-fashioned (colonial) perspectives that shaped a substantial portion of past scholarship on ancient North Africa and proposes ideas and new directions for future research.

In the light of these developments, it seems appropriate to start thinking of region-focused studies that can complement and supplement these two more general works.[5] Given its rich archaeological heritage and the availability of new data thanks to the progress of research, Tripolitania represents an excellent case study in this context. The choice to dedicate a new volume to this region was therefore motivated by the desire to offer an up-to-date picture of aspects of the archaeology of this important territory of North Africa, building upon the solid corpus of literature discussed in the section above and attempting to incorporate at least some of the most recent advancements. The proposal was met with enthusiasm by BILNAS, and its Open Access Monograph Series was identified as a suitable venue for publication to make the volume easily accessible. Hopefully our friends and colleagues across the Maghreb will benefit from this choice above anyone else. Beyond this volume on Tripolitania, the intention is to encourage a continuation of the publication project through future collections of archaeological and historical studies on Cyrenaica (eastern Libya), as well as on the regions corresponding to present-day Tunisia (including the Tunisian part of Tripolitania), Algeria, and Morocco.

The principal aim of the volume is to look at Roman-period Tripolitania within its broader North African setting (Figs 1.1–2). The title '*Tripolitania in the Roman Empire and Beyond*' has a twofold meaning. The first refers to the geographical framework. This corresponds to the boundaries of the region as they were established under Roman imperial rule – essentially the territory of the three emporia (Lepcis Magna, Oea, and Sabratha) that formed a sub-provincial entity of Africa Proconsularis, before becoming an autonomous province around 303 CE; but at the same time the discussion in some of the essays extends to areas beyond Roman control, especially in the desert zone. The second meaning is chronological: the time frame under consideration spans mainly from the first century BCE to the fourth century CE, but earlier and later periods are also included. Authors were presented with the challenging task of writing a piece that was both authoritative and accessible. This reflects the broad readership of the volume, which is intended to encompass university students at different levels, younger and more senior scholars, as well as general readers. Hopefully each of these groups will find something of interest among the contents of this book.

[5] Current scholarship is also proposing a 'micro-regional' approach to North Africa, as shown by case studies in Numidia (Ardeleanu 2021) and Africa Proconsularis (Scheding 2019).

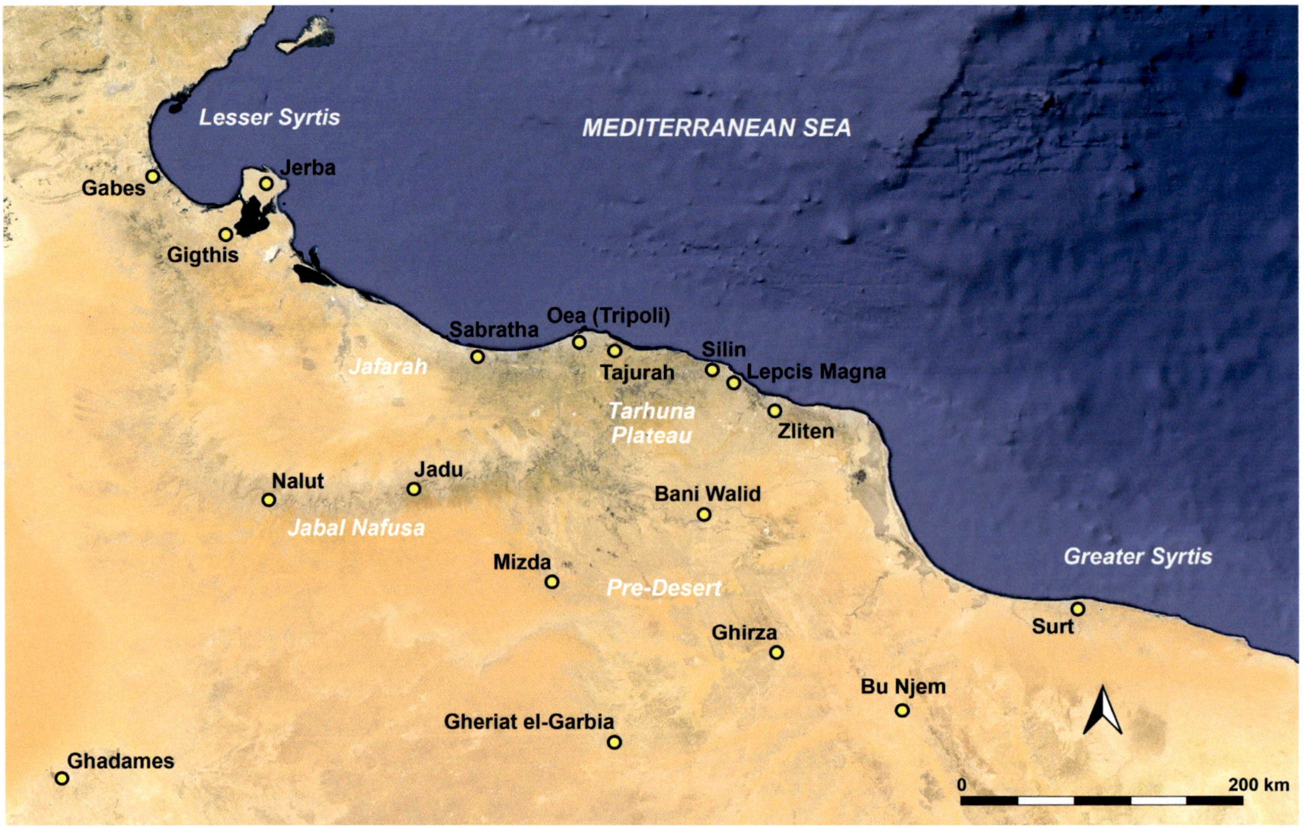

Fig. 1.2. Map of Tripolitania with main sites cited in the volume (basemap Google Earth, data SIO, NOAA, US Navy, NGA, GEBCO, image Landsat/Copernicus).

The main type of evidence under examination is archaeological, but textual and epigraphic sources are also considered. No claim is made to encompass all aspects of the archaeology of Tripolitania, and the selection of topics was influenced by the authors' personal expertise and research interests, allowing a plurality of voices, as well as different opinions in some instances, to emerge.[6] It should also be noted that the principal focus is on the (western) Libyan part of Tripolitania, while the region in antiquity extended into south-eastern Tunisia to the west and beyond Surt to the east. The first part of the volume (Chapters 2–4) is concerned with urban sites and villas on the coastal area. Aiosa (Chapter 2) offers new hypotheses on the urban development of Sabratha from pre-Roman to late Roman times. By challenging earlier views and traditional interpretations, the author's reappraisal of much of the extant archaeological evidence has far-reaching consequences with regard to the chronology or identification of both individual monuments and entire districts of the ancient city. Mugnai (Chapter 3) looks at the transformation of Lepcis Magna in the Severan period. Starting with a review of the 'traditional' Severan buildings that were central to Ward-Perkins' studies, the essay also examines smaller construction projects in the city that were undertaken alongside larger, imperial enterprises. A wealth of evidence is examined: design and construction features, building materials, architectural ornament and sculpture, and the monuments' epigraphic apparatus. In Chapter 4, Wootton gives a wide-ranging overview of Tripolitanian decorated pavements and mosaics from the Punic/Hellenistic era through to the Byzantine period. Matters of style, iconography and craftsmanship are addressed, examining these Tripolitanian productions within their broader Mediterranean context. Importantly, the essay engages with issues of conservation of this exceptional, yet fragile, heritage.

In the second part (Chapters 5–10), attention shifts to the hinterland and to the more remote, pre-desert and desert areas of Tripolitania. Nikolaus and Sheldrick (Chapter 5) provide a comprehensive overview of rural and funerary landscapes in the pre-desert, building upon the results of the ULVS Project and incorporating the latest research. The careful use of archival materials and satellite imagery among other resources allows the authors to investigate the life and death of those who inhabited these zones in the Roman and Late Antique periods. The following three essays deal

[6] One must be aware of an ongoing imbalance in the scholarship, where external, non-African voices are still predominant, but it is to be hoped that future instalments in this and other publication series will manage to invert the trend (on the need to 'decolonize' North African studies see Mattingly 2023, xvii–xxi, 3–8).

with complementary aspects of the army at the border. Through a detailed assessment of archaeological evidence, Mackensen (Chapter 6) outlines the development of military installations on the *limes Tripolitanus* across modern-day Libya and Tunisia from the second to the fifth century CE. This includes data from recent excavations at the fort of Gheriat el-Garbia, which are contributing significantly to our understanding of Tripolitania's frontier zone. These new datasets, along with the evidence collected in previous studies and fieldwork in the region, enable Schimmer (Chapter 7) to examine the food supply of the army, looking in particular at amphora content and circulation, epigraphic sources, archaeobotanical and faunal evidence. In Chapter 8, Schmid looks at cults and the religious practices of soldiers. The layout of buildings identified during past and current research is connected to their specific religious use, while inscriptions complement this picture through the information they provide on worshipped deities and the identity of worshippers.

The section is concluded by two essays that look at the post-Roman phases. Welsby Sjöström (Chapter 9) compiles a gazetteer of sites in Jabal Nafusa where future field surveys could confirm the presence of Roman/Late Antique archaeological remains. This includes previously surveyed sites, such as those that were recorded in the 1920s by Italian army officers, and places where the presence of Roman-period spolia in Islamic buildings (especially mosques) was noticed in more recent years. In Chapter 10, Prevost draws attention to the cultural connections between the Island of Jerba (Tunisia) and Tripolitania. While it is known that these territories were part of the same (sub)provincial entity in Roman times, the essay highlights important architectural links between some Islamic mosques of Jerba and examples from Jabal Nafusa, which speak of a continuous interconnectivity of these areas into the Islamic period. Finally, in Chapter 11, Mattingly provides a series of thoughts and reflections on the archaeology of Libyan and Tunisian Tripolitania. Themes explored in the various chapters are critically reviewed, while recent advancements as well as gaps in our knowledge are pointed out, which can be used to develop future research projects and approaches.

Two points merit attention. The subject of Tripolitanian economy and trade is addressed in more than one paper (see especially Chapters 5, 7, 11), with particular emphasis on the economic life of rural settlements and the circulation of goods at infra- and cross-regional level. Further in-depth studies on these topics exist; with regard to Anglophone scholarship, first and foremost, readers are referred to the fundamental works by Mattingly (1995, 138–59; 2023, 529–59, with references to previous works). On urban production at Sabratha, for example, see also Wilson 1999; 2002, 241–50. A detailed assessment of the 'economic boom' in Africa Proconsularis (Tunisia and Libya) can be found in Hobson 2015 (in particular 95–99 on olive oil/wine pressing installations in Libyan Tripolitania, and 119–23 on amphora production sites in the region). To these studies one should add the important results of a recent field survey carried out in the Tarhuna Plateau, which has provided new, first-hand data on olive oil, wine, and amphora production (Ahmed 2019).

With regard to Late Antiquity and the subsequent transition into the Islamic period, the evidence discussed in this volume comes mainly from rural and hinterland/pre-desert sites (see Chapters 5–6, 9–10), with references to buildings or public areas from urban contexts on the coast where relevant. Readers who would like to delve deeper into the transformation of cityscapes across these historical phases will find a wealth of information (in English) in Leone 2007 and 2013, whose analysis incorporates data from major sites of Tunisia and Libya. A comprehensive collection of studies (in Italian) on the inscriptions and urban features of Lepcis Magna from the late third to the fifth century CE can be found in Tantillo and Bigi 2010. Archaeological evidence for the transition of Tripolitanian rural and urban sites from the Byzantine to the Islamic era is further explored in Leone 2019 (see also the gazetteer in Sjöström 1993). For an accessible, up-to-date reading on early Islamic North Africa, including evidence from Tripolitania, see Fenwick 2020.

A final note concerns the transliteration of Arabic names. This is often a thorny subject given that it varies significantly in past and current academic works, with different spellings being used in English, French, and Italian scholarship for example. Efforts have been made to adopt a spelling consistency for the names of the main sites and those that are cited more frequently throughout the volume. Readers may notice more variability in the case of smaller sites – this is in part due to the fact that in some instances authors refer purposefully to particular spellings that were adopted in previous scholarship.

Chronological table

Table 1.1 overleaf provides a selection of key dates and historical events for Tripolitania and the broader North African region, from Phoenician/Punic times through to the early Islamic period. This is intended to point out potential links between some of the major events and the archaeological evidence discussed in the volume. Additional chronological information on specific sites, as well as on issues about the date of textual or material sources, is provided in the respective chapters.

Table 1.1. Tripolitania: chronological table with key dates and historical events (after Kenrick 2009, 215–16; Mattingly 2023, 573–87).

Date	Events
814/813 BCE	Conventional date for the foundation of Carthage by Phoenician settlers from Tyre
Seventh century BCE	First archaeological evidence of occupation at Lepcis Magna (Phoenician/Punic emporium)
Fifth century BCE	First archaeological evidence of occupation at Sabratha (Phoenician/Punic emporium)
264–241 BCE	First Punic War: Rome conquers Carthaginian territories in western Sicily, Sardinia, and Corsica
218–201 BCE	Second Punic War: Scipio Africanus defeats Hannibal at Zama (Tunisia) and Carthage surrenders
149–146 BCE	Third Punic War: destruction of Carthage and annexation of its territory by Rome (Africa Vetus)
48–46 BCE	Civil war between Pompey and Caesar: annexation of Numidia (Africa Nova)
31 BCE	Roman civil war and ultimate victory of Octavian (Augustus) against Mark Antony at Actium
27 BCE	Africa Vetus and Africa Nova formally united as the senatorial province of Africa (Proconsularis)
20–19 BCE	Expedition of L. Cornelius Balbus against the Garamantes of Fazzan: triumph celebrated in Rome
17–24 CE	Revolt of African chief Tacfarinas: final Roman victory celebrated at Oea and Lepcis Magna
69 CE	Land dispute between Oea and Lepcis Magna involving the Garamantes and Rome respectively
c. 73–74 CE	Lepcis Magna acquires the status of Roman *municipium*
109/110 CE	Lepcis Magna becomes an honorary *colonia*, Oea and Sabratha probably become *municipia*
c. mid-second century CE	Oea and Sabratha become *coloniae* probably under Antoninus Pius or Marcus Aurelius
193 CE	Septimius Severus (native of Lepcis Magna) becomes emperor
c. 201 CE	Construction of legionary vexillation forts at Bu Njem, Gheriat el-Garbia, and Ghadames
211 CE	Death of Septimius Severus at Eboracum (York, Great Britain)
235 CE	End of the Severan dynasty with assassination of Severus Alexander
238 CE	Disbandment of the *legio III Augusta* by Gordian III after its involvement in succession disputes
253 CE	Reconstitution of the *legio III Augusta* by Valerian I
259–263 CE	Withdrawal of military garrison from Bu Njem and (partly?) from other desert forts
293–305 CE	Reorganization of the Empire: Lepcis Magna becomes capital of the new province of Tripolitana
365 CE	Historical accounts of devastating earthquake and tsunami across the eastern Mediterranean
429–439 CE	Invasion of North Africa via Spain by the Vandals, moving from central Europe: fall of Carthage
455 CE	Annexation of Tripolitania and Numidia into the Vandal kingdom
533 CE	Reconquest of North Africa by Belisarius under the Byzantine emperor Justinian
642–645 CE	Conquest of Cyrenaica (eastern Libya) by the Arabs: advent of Islam in North Africa (Ifriqiyah)
670 CE	Foundation of Arab capital at Kairouan (Tunisia) and start of new administrative structure in Ifriqiyah
800 CE	Establishment of Aghlabid dynasty at Kairouan: beginning of extensive building programme in Tunisia
909–969 CE	Overthrow of the Aghlabids by the Fatimids in Tunisia and subsequent expansion as far as Egypt
1051 CE	Invasion of the Bani Hilal ('Children of the Moon'): end of urban life at many sites in Tripolitania

References

Ahmed, M.A.M. 2019. *Rural Settlement and Economic Activity. Olive Oil, Wine and Amphorae Production on the Tarhuna Plateau during the Roman Period.* London: Society for Libyan Studies.

Ardeleanu, S. 2021. *Numidia Romana? Die Auswirkungen der römischen Präsenz in Numidien (2. Jh. v. Chr. – 1. Jh. n. Chr.).* Wiesbaden: Reichert Verlag.

Barker, G. (ed.) 1996. *Farming the Desert. The UNESCO Libyan Valleys Archaeological Survey. Volume 1: Synthesis.* London: Society for Libyan Studies.

Briand-Ponsart, C. and Hugoniot, C. 2006. *L'Afrique romaine de l'Atlantique à la Tripolitaine (146 av. J.-C. – 533 ap. J.-C.).* Paris: Armand Colin.

Buck, D.J. and Mattingly, D.J. (eds) 1985. *Town and Country in Roman Tripolitania. Papers in Honour of Olwen Hackett.* Oxford: British Archaeological Reports.

Di Vita, A., Di Vita-Évrard, G. and Bacchielli, L. 1999. *Libya: The Lost Cities of the Roman Empire.* Cologne: Könemann.

Drine, A., Fentress, E. and Holod, R. (eds) 2009. *An Island through Time: Jerba Studies, Volume 1. The Punic and Roman Periods.* Portsmouth, RI: Journal of Roman Archaeology.

Fenwick, C. 2020. *Early Islamic North Africa: A New Perspective.* London: Bloomsbury.

Haynes, D.E.L. 1981. *An Archaeological and Historical Guide to the Pre-Islamic Antiquities of Tripolitania (4th Edition).* Tripoli: Department of Antiquities.

Hitchner, R.B. (ed.) 2022. *A Companion to North Africa in Antiquity.* Hoboken, NJ: Wiley-Blackwell.

Hobson, M.S. 2015. *The North African Boom. Evaluating Economic Growth in the Roman Province of Africa Proconsularis (146 B.C. – A.D. 439).* Portsmouth, RI: Journal of Roman Archaeology.

Kenrick, P.M. 2009. *Libya Archaeological Guides: Tripolitania.* London: Silphium Press.

Lassère, J.-M. 2015. *Africa, quasi Roma (256 av. J.-C. – 711 apr. J.-C.).* Paris: Éditions du CNRS.

Leone, A. 2007. *Changing Townscapes in North Africa from Late Antiquity to the Arab Conquest.* Bari: Edipuglia.

Leone, A. 2013. *The End of the Pagan City: Religion, Economy, and Urbanism in Late Antique North Africa.* Oxford: Oxford University Press.

Leone, A. 2019. Cultural transitions in archaeology: from Byzantine to Islamic Tripolitania. In R. Bockmann, A. Leone and P. von Rummel (eds), *Africa – Ifrīqiya. Continuity and Change in North Africa from the Byzantine to the Early Islamic Age. Papers of a Conference Held in Rome, Museo Nazionale Romano – Terme di Diocleziano (28 February – 2 March 2013).* Wiesbaden: Harrassowitz Verlag, 265–78.

Mackensen, M. 2021. *Das severische Vexillationskastell Myd(---)/Gheriat el-Garbia am limes Tripolitanus (Libyen), I: Forschungsgeschichte, Vermessung, Prospektionen und Funde 2009–2010.* Wiesbaden: Reichert Verlag.

Mackensen, M. 2024. *Das severische Vexillationskastell Myd(---) und die spätantiken castra Madensia/Gheriat el-Garbia am limes Tripolitanus (Libyen), II: Ausgrabungen und Untersuchungen im Kastell, im Steinbruch, in den Heiligtümern und am Beobachtungsturm 2009–2010.* Wiesbaden: Reichert Verlag.

Mattingly, D.J. 1995. *Tripolitania.* London: Batsford.

Mattingly, D.J. (ed.) 1996. *Farming the Desert. The UNESCO Libyan Valleys Archaeological Survey. Volume 2: Gazetteer and Pottery.* London: Society for Libyan Studies.

Mattingly, D.J. 2019. A road less travelled? The Society for Libyan Studies and the landscape archaeology of Libya's early civilisations. *Libyan Studies* 50: 35–46.

Mattingly, D.J. 2022. Beyond barbarians: the Garamantes of the Libyan Sahara. In R.B. Hitchner (ed.), *A Companion to North Africa in Antiquity.* Hoboken, NJ: Wiley-Blackwell, 64–80.

Mattingly, D.J. 2023. *Between Sahara and Sea: Africa in the Roman Empire.* Ann Arbor, MI: University of Michigan Press.

Michel, V. 2011–12. L'activité récente de la Mission Archéologique Française en Libye pour l'Antiquité, 2007–2012. *Libya Antiqua* n.s. 6: 103–24.

Michel, V. (ed.) 2015. *De Leptis Magna à Derna, de la Tripolitaine à la Cyrénaïque. Travaux récents sur la Libye antique.* Paris: Riveneuve Éditions.

Munzi, M. 2012. Italian archaeologists in colonial Tripolitania. *Libyan Studies* 43: 81–110.

Musso, L. and Turjman, M.A. (eds) 2022. *Libia – Italia. Un'archeologia condivisa (Castello Rosso, Tripoli, 22 settembre – 22 dicembre 2021).* Rome: 'L'Erma' di Bretschneider.

Ritter, S. and Ben Tahar, S. (eds) 2022. *Studies on the Urban History of Meninx (Djerba). The Meninx Archaeological Project 2015–2019.* Wiesbaden: Reichert Verlag.

Rizzo, M.A. (ed.) 2017. *Antonino Di Vita. La Tripolitania antica, scritti inediti.* Rome: 'L'Erma' di Bretschneider.

Rizzo, M.A. and Di Vita-Évrard, G. (eds) 2015. *Antonino Di Vita. Scritti Africani, I–II.* Rome: 'L'Erma' di Bretschneider.

Romanelli, P. 1970. *Topografia e archeologia dell'Africa romana.* Turin: Società Editrice Internazionale.

Scheding, P. 2019. *Urbaner Ballungsraum im römischen Nordafrika. Zum Einfluss von mikroregionalen Wirtschafts- und Sozialstrukturen auf den Städtebau in der Africa Proconsularis.* Wiesbaden: Reichert Verlag.

Sheldrick, N. 2021. *Building the Countryside. Rural Architecture and Settlement in Tripolitania during the Roman and Late Antique Periods.* London: Society for Libyan Studies.

Sjöström, I. 1993. *Tripolitania in Transition: Late Roman to Early Islamic Settlement.* Aldershot: Avebury.

Tantillo, I. and Bigi, F. (eds) 2010. *Leptis Magna. Una città e le sue iscrizioni in epoca tardoromana*. Cassino: Edizioni dell'Università degli Studi di Cassino.

Ward-Perkins, J.B. 1993. *The Severan Buildings of Lepcis Magna: An Architectural Survey (published by P.M. Kenrick)*. London: Society for Libyan Studies.

Wilson, A.I. 1999. Commerce and industry in Roman Sabratha. *Libyan Studies* 30: 29–52.

Wilson, A.I. 2002. Urban production in the Roman world: the view from North Africa. *Papers of the British School at Rome* 70: 231–73.

Chapter 2

THE URBAN DEVELOPMENT OF SABRATHA: OLD THEORIES AND NEW PERSPECTIVES

Sergio Aiosa

Introduction

The publication of the results from the excavations conducted by John Bryan Ward-Perkins and Kathleen Kenyon, edited by Philip Kenrick (1986), represents a milestone for our knowledge of the city of Sabratha (Fig. 2.1). These works (1948–51) mostly focused on the forum area, including the surrounding blocks of houses as well as the Byzantine defensive wall, although the book also provides some information about the harbour, the Severan Monument, and the series of surveys carried out to the south of the theatre. The editor's personal considerations and contributions emerge with clarity even when they disagree with the excavators' opinions, and the limitations and difficulties related to the revision of old data are highlighted in the text.

Equally significant are the various contributions by Antonino Di Vita for the reconstruction of the main urban phases of Sabratha and for the understanding of specific archaeological contexts and monuments.[1] Both the archaeological and architectural studies on Mausoleum B and the extensive excavation of the so-called 'Punic district'[2] south of the forum revealed an impressive stratigraphic sequence, spanning from the times of the Punic emporium (fifth century BCE) to the very end of the history of Sabratha around the eighth century CE (on these works see in particular Di Vita 1976; Di Vita *et al.* 2006).

There are several points of convergence between these research lines. As Kenrick highlights, his volume is significantly influenced by Di Vita's (1990) theories about the series of five earthquakes that in some way marked, if not influenced, the urban development of Sabratha (for a useful summary of these events at Sabratha and in Tripolitania, see Kenrick 2009, 10–13). Kenrick (1986, 5) takes into account especially two of these seismic events: the one of the Flavian, or late Neronian, period and the one dated to 365 CE. These two earthquakes respectively marked the beginning of a new phase of embellishment of the city and the destruction of the main buildings, which were not rebuilt afterwards with the exception of the most functional ones, such as the curia and the baths.

It would be impossible not to notice that some major urban phases, which at Lepcis Magna are represented by the erection of important monuments such as the Arch of Trajan on the main *cardo* or the Hadrianic Baths along the southern stretch of the (later) Colonnaded Street, are virtually absent at Sabratha. These phases are only documented by some layers in the stratigraphic sequence that was identified during the excavation of Mausoleum B. After the Severan period, evidence of third-century CE building activities remains entirely unknown, while what we know about the fourth century mostly concerns two earthquakes that almost caused the end of the Roman city. The fifth and sixth centuries are represented by the erection of Christian buildings and by some tombs whose chronology is only rarely provided by coins found inside them (in most cases these tombs did not yield any significant objects or were looted in antiquity). The last series of tombs dates to the period immediately preceding the Arab conquest of the seventh century CE.

All these studies and field research have provided an important contribution to our knowledge of Sabratha. One certainly cannot blame Kenrick or Di Vita if the image of the city has since remained 'crystallized' in the form that was presented at the time. The aim of this chapter is therefore to outline an up-do-date history of Sabratha's urban development, in particular by providing an in-depth analysis of the city's extension towards

[1] For a wide selection of Di Vita's works on Sabratha, see Rizzo and Di Vita-Évrard 2015.

[2] I am aware of the difficulties related to the use of the term 'Punic' instead of 'Western Phoenician': see Prag 2014.

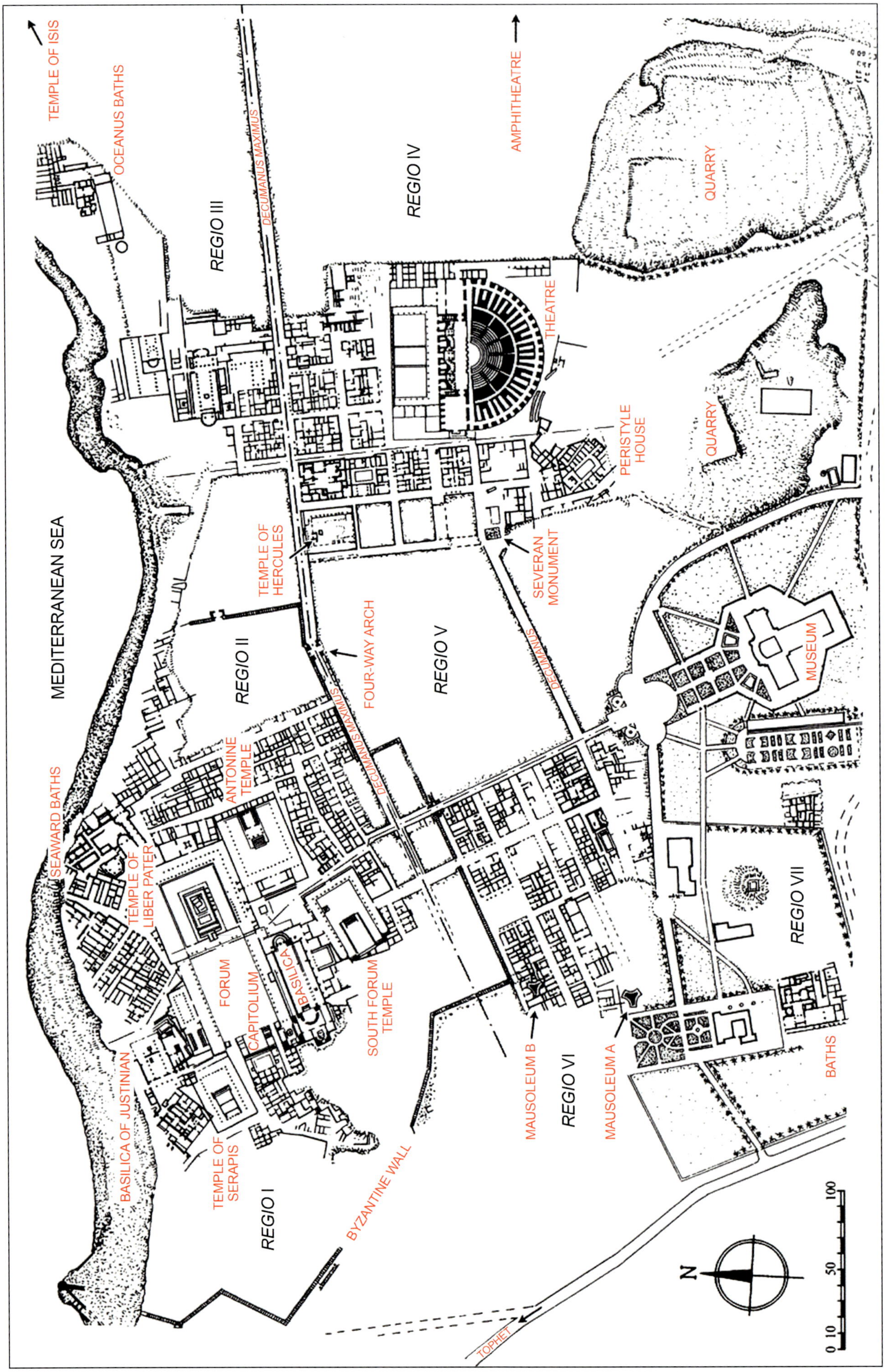

Fig. 2.1. Sabratha: general map with main monuments cited in the text (after Aiosa 2014, fig. 4).

the east, where the old sondages by Giacomo Caputo at the Temple of Hercules in 1938 and the excavation and restauration of the theatre by Giacomo Guidi remained for a long period the last archaeological interventions.

Some of the most important questions about Sabratha's urban development are related to the history of archaeological research carried out by Italian archaeologists since the 1920s. The aim of these excavations was to bring to light the ancient city in its entirety, starting from two sand dunes at the opposite sides of the site which covered two of Sabratha's most significant architectural remains: the ruins of the forum and those of the theatre. Moving on from these two areas, Italian archaeologists continued their research along the so-called 'main *decumanus*'. The forum and theatre districts are physically separated by large areas that are still unexplored – occasionally they have even been regarded as two distinct sites rather than two parts of the same ancient city. The location of Sabratha's Museum reveals how improperly the limits of the excavated site were thought to correspond to the edges of the Roman city itself. For this reason, buildings such as the baths of *Regio* VII (Fig. 2.2) at the south-western limit of the excavated area and the 'Peristyle House' ('House of the Swimming Pool') south-west of the theatre (Fig. 2.3) were considered suburban or extra urban structures. Indeed, the latter was frequently labelled 'villa' instead of 'house' in past scholarship (see Aiosa 2011).

The monuments and finds that were brought to light by old Italian investigations (mostly still unpublished) inspired the new 50-year series of studies and research by the Archaeological Mission of the University of Palermo at Sabratha.[3] Since 1977, the year when the work of the mission formally started, researchers have not explored any new areas of the city, with the exception of small surveys within or near previously excavated monuments in order to refine their chronology. The most extensively investigated building was the Temple of Serapis through a series of small-scale surveys that took place from 2003 to 2010. Starting from the results of my personal studies, the aim is to provide here a renewed image of Sabratha's urban development.

Pre-Roman evidence: new data

When the ancient city disappeared under the sand dunes, even its name was forgotten. The old Italian and Catalan maps from the thirteenth century onwards labelled the ancient ruins 'Tripoli Vecchio', Old Tripoli (Montali 2014) – a confusion that would last until the

Fig. 2.2. *(above)* Baths of *Regio* VII, *frigidarium* (photo S. Aiosa).

Fig. 2.3. *(left)* Peristyle House, view from south (photo S. Aiosa).

[3] For an almost complete list of publications and a synthesis of the works by the University of Palermo, see Bonacasa and Aiosa 2017.

end of the nineteenth century. Yet Tripoli was not the only city whose name was duplicated. Before the start of the Italian excavations, the Vicomte de Mathuisieulx (1904, 737), while recording the temples, circuses, and amphitheatres of both Lepcis Magna and Sabratha, distinguished a 'maritime Sabratha' – the site we can still observe alongside the coast – from an inland one, which would have served as a gathering point for the caravans transporting goods from central Africa (Merighi 1940, I, 17–18). The existence of this 'double' was argued on the basis of literary sources and on the local toponym *Sabra*, or *es-Sabria*, known from medieval cartography.[4] A map illustrating an old Italian translation of Ptolemy's *Geographia* locates the site just to the north of the Tropic, much more to the east of the actual Sabratha. Its position corresponds to that of the Abraham Ortelius map (1598), where another site labelled 'Tripoli Vecchio' also appears to the west of Tripoli.

The hypothesis of an 'inland' Sabratha did not leave any trace in subsequent scholarly literature. In the same way, even the meaning of the Greek name of the city, *Abrotonon*, has never been investigated in any detail. It remained unclear whether it was just a transliteration of the Punic name *Sbrth*, which would have translated as 'grain market' (Ward 1970, 19), or whether the Greek word had another specific meaning. A plant named *abrotonon*, corresponding to the contemporary 'abrotanum', is a variety of the artemisia, an essence similar to wormwood. Mostly used to flavour wine, it was known as a powerful aphrodisiac that increases sexual power.[5] It is also mentioned as an antidote to snakes' poison (Dioscorides and Nicander). In Lucan's *Pharsalia* (9.890–937), the Psylli, a North African people said to be the only one able to survive a snake's bite, burned the abrotonon during rituals celebrated to ward off venomous snakes. According to tradition, the Psylli settled in front of the Greater Syrtis, also named *Psyllikos Kolpos*, which means 'Gulf of the Psylli'. It is worth remembering that the region of the two Syrtes was called 'Earth of Snakes' in ancient sources – a name that was also applied to the attitude of its inhabitants due to a form of 'proto-racism' (Isaac 2006). We could therefore consider the Greek name of Sabratha a phytonym (a name derived from the name of a plant), as already argued about the Punic *Sbrth*. In addition to his other attributes, the god Bes granted protection against snake bites; a small limestone statue from Sabratha showing the god holding a snake could support this interpretation. This statue was recovered near Mausoleum B, where the depiction of Bes appears again on a metope of this monument grabbing two lions by the tail, in accordance with the most common iconography of the god.

The weighing of silphium at Cyrene under the king's control was depicted in a famous Laconian plate and we know that until the age of Caesar large quantities of this precious essence were kept in the public *aerarium* (Theophrastus reports that the Cyrenaican plateau, where silphium was harvested, was infested by a variety of artemisia very similar to the abrotanum). Even if the abrotanum was a less precious essence, its trade could have been subjected to the control of Sabratha's central authorities. Even though their architectural similarity to Numidian monumental tombs has been acknowledged, neither Mausoleum B nor Mausoleum A have ever been considered to have belonged to a Numidian prince – not even when, after the fall of Carthage, the Numidians took control of the region of the Tripolitanian emporia. It is more than probable that not all of the Numidian-style tombs belonged to members of the royal family (Quinn 2013, 186, 194), but it is clear they should be linked to very wealthy members of the elites. This could have been the case of the owner of the Sabratha tomb – a wealthy person who was responsible for the commerce of the abrotanum, although this is just a speculative hypothesis.

A specific research project on Punic Sabratha has never been carried out, neither by Italian nor British archaeologists. Our knowledge of the Punic emporium comes mostly from scanty evidence intercepted by the British excavation trenches – a methodology that did not allow a detailed reconstruction of the different chronological phases. These works did not solve the discrepancy between the archaeological record and the literary sources on the chronology of the first settlement of Sabratha. The most ancient traces of occupation in *Regio* II have been interpreted as the remains of 'one of those seasonally occupied trading posts situated in protected anchorages' (Howard Carter 1965, 130; Kenrick 1986, 11, 125), which predated the foundation of a permanent settlement. This must have been established to the west of the Roman-period city. More specifically, the little bay known as 'Marsa Sabratha' might have been the Hellenistic-period port of the city, which was protected by a *clausura* (a sort of defensive wall), while the harbour on the seafront of the actual site was built in Roman times. In contrast, a 3 m thick wall, interpreted as part of a mole, would show that the harbour of Lepcis Magna was at that time located alongside the coast, west of the ancient site, towards the modern town of Homs (Di Vita 1974). If this hypothesis is correct, the difference of scale between Lepcis Magna and Sabratha would have been evident already in the Hellenistic period. Only later, during the reign of Nero, would the harbour of Lepcis Magna be transferred to the bay where

[4] Similarly, the frequent occurrence of the name 'Newport' in the USA is pointed out in Ward 1970, 19–20.

[5] In his description of the properties and varieties of this plant, Pliny (*Naturalis Historia*, 14.105; 19.100; 21.59–61, 92, 160–62, 168) does not pay attention to the similarity of its name with that of the North African city, which he mentions as well (5.27).

Fig. 2.4. *(right)* Temple of Serapis, Hellenistic-period building underneath the court in front of the temple (photo S. Aiosa).

Fig. 2.5. *(below)* Temple of Serapis, plan showing Hellenistic-period structures under the Roman building (University of Palermo).

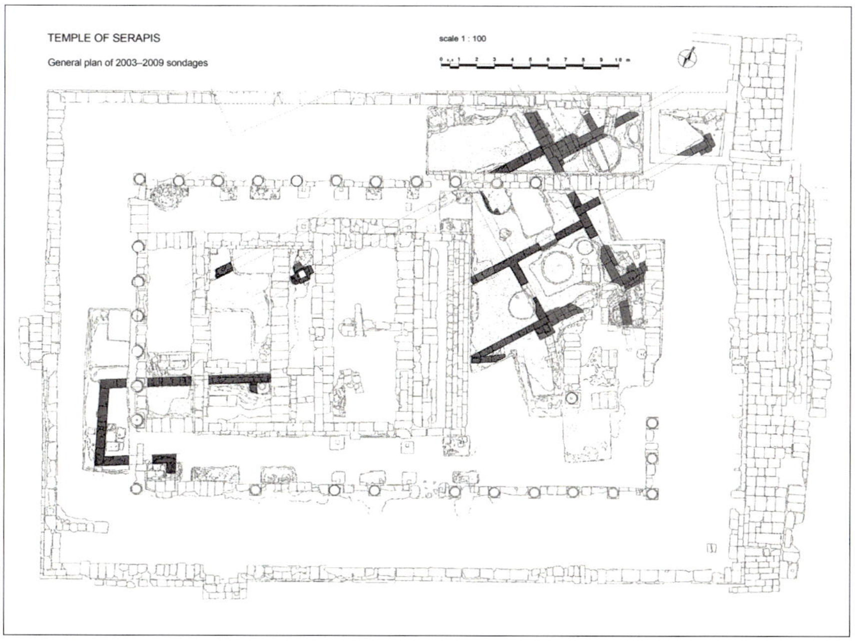

we can currently observe the impressive remains of the Severan-period harbour (on some of the dating issues see Mugnai, Chapter 3).

The excavations by the University of Palermo at the Temple of Serapis, directed by the late Nicola Bonacasa from 2003 onwards, attempted to reconstruct the main building phases of the Roman-period edifice, but they also determined a considerable improvement of our knowledge about the history of Hellenistic-period Sabratha. The orientation of the temple is slightly different from the other buildings of the Roman period and from the layout of the houses in *Regio* II.[6] The main analyses were initially conducted inside the temple's precinct, especially within the court (Figs 2.4–5) in front of the actual temple and along the north portico. During the subsequent years further research was carried out inside the *cella* itself and in the west portico, including a small extension onto the street behind the temple.[7] Excavations brought to light the remains of an earlier building that was probably constructed in the second century BCE and whose orientation, which strongly differs from that of the Roman temple, almost coincides with that of the Punic houses identified in the British trenches underneath the forum levels. A coin of the Numidian king Micipsa (148–118 BCE), which seems to have been found in the building's foundation trench, suggests a chronology after the fall of Carthage (Bonacasa 2016, 43–44).

The chronology of the pre-Roman edifices previously intercepted by the British excavations under the forum is still debated. It is probable they should be assigned to the second century BCE, rather than to the fourth century (Kenrick 1986, 8). Due to their size and careful execution, the identified structures surely belong to a public building. Despite the long, narrow plan and the presence of a sequence of rooms (until now four of them have been excavated: Mistretta 2016, 130), an interpretation as a stoa is unsupported by the evidence. Some rooms could have been warehouses while other spaces, which appear to have been carefully decorated with paintings imitating marble slabs, might have had a public function as administrative offices, as stated by the excavators. Nothing allows us to postulate the presence

[6] This 'suggests adherence to an earlier layout and which may be the Temple of Serapis known from coins of Sabratha of the second-first centuries B.C.': Kenrick 1986, 7. On the coinage of Sabratha see also Aiosa 2016, 314–19.

[7] A surface of 280 m² was cleared over 18 excavation seasons: Mistretta 2016, 125. However, we are still waiting for the final results of these works, given that the reports published to date are far from exhaustive.

of a religious space within this building,[8] and the subsequent edification of an Augustan-period (?) temple indicates a change of use of this area.

According to Di Vita, the north-west–south-east orientation of the first settlement in the Hellenistic period, as reflected by the houses of *Regio* II north of the forum, was replaced by a new urban layout influenced by the model of Alexandria.[9] Very narrow house blocks divided by large *plateiai* with an east–west orientation occupied some terraces sloping down towards the sea. Only three of them would have survived in the area to the south of the Antonine Temple. Moreover, their east–west orientation contrasts with that of *Insula* X, the so-called 'Casa Brogan'. Given that this *insula* predates the Roman era, its alignment on a north–south axis that was not affected by the (later) forum layout could be interpreted as evidence for a different urban grid that is otherwise unattested by other archaeological remains. Di Vita's hypothesis is based on two different assumptions. The first is that the Punic edifices revealed by the British trenches under the forum belong to a phase that predates the above-mentioned urban layout (fourth century BCE). The second assumption concerns the fact that the model of Alexandria's regular urban grid could have still inspired the urbanism of a city that was being reshaped in the second century BCE. This proposal would imply that the design of the agora should have corresponded to a multiple of a modular unit, which is normally constituted by a single block of houses.

It is also evident that the space between the westernmost Punic structure identified by the trenches and the Capitolium is far too small to have hosted an agora. Moreover, the existence of unidentified structures further to the west might have made this area even smaller (see Kenrick 1986, fig. 1). Equally, the arrangement of the sector that was later occupied by the Capitolium is unknown. Excavations on the front of the temple revealed some large jars set in holes in the ground (Kenrick 1986, 19–20, fig. 17b, section AN–NM). Together with a number of other holes interpreted as traces of tents, the whole context was interpreted as a marketplace, but it is also possible to suggest a different function. South of this area, a pit filled with at least 14 Punic amphorae Maña D (the so-called 'torpedo amphorae') was uncovered by the British archaeologists. According to the finds, two possible dates can be proposed: the first half of the second century BCE or the early first century BCE (depending on the exclusion or inclusion of some ceramic sherds labelled as intrusions). The amphorae were mostly intact and some of them were sealed with a stone slab on the top. This means that the amphorae were put into the pit intentionally rather than being casually thrown there; it is thus reasonable to think of a religious purpose, such as a votive deposit. Furthermore, Kenrick (1986, 46, fig. 9) clarifies that 'the excavation and filling of the pit [...] does not bear any relationship to the use of the area at any time as an open marketplace' (see also Eingartner 2005, 132). An amphora of the same type, containing ashes and animal bones, was found at the north-west corner of the Antonine Temple. These remains were interpreted as the traces of a ritual within an open-air religious space of the Punic period.[10]

Even though there are some doubts about the interpretation of the pre-Roman remains, the discovery of the Hellenistic-period building has not enlightened the debate on a potential location of the marketplace. From the Hellenistic era onwards, economic transactions and public administration were carried out in the same location. Among the edifices identified under the Roman forum levels, some structures can be assigned to two buildings which must have had a public function, as suggested by their large size; towards the west, a series of layers without any traces of constructions may represent 'an open space, a predecessor in function to the forum' (Kenrick 1986, 8, 12). In my opinion, both the shape and the location of the new building suggest that the 'agora' might have been further to the north-west, thus being more closely connected with these structures. Immediately to the north of these, a large house was built when the Temple of Serapis was already dismantled or, at least, had ceased its original function, as shown by the fact that the south corner of this house partially encroaches the north foundation wall of the temple's precinct.

The remains of the Basilica of Justinian are located next to this late house and might be related to it. This monument is described as 'a building which in the final period was a church containing a very fine Justinianic mosaic, but on the earlier history of which nothing is known' (Kenrick 1986, 7). It is impossible to say whether this area was previously occupied by Roman-period buildings and whether these in turn may have replaced some earlier Punic structures. Since the Roman houses of *Regio* II adjacent to this area have the same orientation as the previous Punic houses, both the house and the church could have occupied the space of an earlier open area. Its location facing the sea, close to the harbour and to a suburban road, appears to be functional to the trade activities managed by the city

[8] A stuccoed limestone column drum was found inside a room of this building, but its interpretation as an altar is entirely speculative: Bonacasa and Mistretta 2011, 94, fig. 20.

[9] For a detailed assessment of this hypothesis, see Aiosa 2014, 22 ff.

[10] Bartoccini 1964, 37–42, pl. 16. Some structures identified inside the foundations of the Temple of Liber Pater are oriented coherently with these remains, but their walls are considerably thicker. Together with the pottery deposits, this would suggest the presence of a Punic religious building that might have preceded the Temple of Liber Pater: Tomasello 2010, 8.

and might have even replaced a Hellenistic-period area that served the same function. Indeed, a forum placed 5 m above the sea level and separated from the sea by a series of house blocks appears to be rather unfunctional to the commerce of Sabratha both in Hellenistic and Roman times, while a political function was evidently predominant.

The Hellenistic building would be eventually obliterated by the Temple of Serapis, which marks the beginning of a new urban organization of this public area. The temple is still unpublished and one must rely on the brief syntheses of about 10 years of investigations by Bonacasa (2016) and Mistretta (2016). Both authors agree that the first-phase temple dates to the Augustan era. This chronology (already proposed by Kenrick) requires stronger evidence, however. In the reports, the only dating element mentioned for this phase is a coin bearing the head of a god interpreted as Serapis on the reverse and the head of Augustus with the *lituus* on the obverse (Bonacasa 2016, 43, fig. 19; Mistretta 2016, 132). If not even minted under Tiberius, these coins were still circulating for most of the Julio-Claudian period anyway,[11] and therefore they cannot support a date in the Augustan era.

Bonacasa and Mistretta abandoned their previous hypothesis of a Hellenistic phase of the temple.[12] This chronology had been already suggested by Philip Ward (1970, 34) and Denys Haynes (1981, 118) on the basis of the orientation of the temple which differs from that of the forum (see also Eingartner 2005, 132, note 1157). The position of the *cella* in the middle of the precinct was also considered a common feature of the Hellenistic period. If the coin of Micipsa mentioned above was to date the construction of the previous Hellenistic building, a subsequent Hellenistic phase for the Temple of Serapis would have been short-lived. Whether the collapse of the Hellenistic public building should be connected to the same earthquake which, according to Di Vita, caused the destruction of Mausoleum B or to another event, remains an open question. In the first case, the life of the public building would have been very short.

The eastward extension of the city

The Roman city extended beyond the limits of the Hellenistic emporium as it is shown by the remains of the two mausolea, which had been presumably erected along an inland road leading into the town. After their collapse, and following the beginning of the new expansion of the site towards the south, the area of these tombs was surrounded by houses. Less evident are the eastern limits of the city. Some aerial photographs show the traces of a regular urban grid more to the east than previously believed (Wilson 2001). The western limit has been inferred by the presence of the tophet, which was afterwards occupied by a necropolis. Another element which may help define the city extension might come from three villas that have been identified around the site. Their architectural features show they are suburban dwellings rather than urban residences (Montali 2018). Two of them are located along the coast, respectively to the east not far from the amphitheatre, and to the west close to the bay nowadays called Marsa Sabratha.

The (modern) subdivision of Sabratha into *Regiones* (Fig. 2.1), although very useful to locate the various sectors of the site on the plan, appears to have hindered research on the city as a whole, as most scholars have tended to focus on the different quarters of the town regarding them as independent units. The houses in *Regio* VI, immediately south of the forum, would have replaced the tombs of the Hellenistic necropolis at the same time as the creation of the forum itself or shortly after. The eastern limit of Sabratha, on the other hand, would have remained identical to that of the Hellenistic emporium until the beginning of the second century CE, when new quarters were created filling the empty space between the forum and the Flavian-period Temple of Isis. Also the theatre has traditionally been regarded as a late insertion within a pre-existing urban grid.

The city blocks of *Regio* V have been attributed to the post-Trajanic period, because of their similarity to the urban plan of Thamugadi (Timgad, Algeria), which clearly derived from the layout of a legionary fortress (Caputo and Ghedini 1984, 10). In my opinion, if one considers both layouts in their entirety, this analogy – far from being so evident – appears to be limited to the square shape of each house block, which can hardly be regarded as a specific feature of Trajanic-period urbanism. Moreover, the design of legionary fortresses shows similar characteristics even before the reign of Trajan. Equally, the size of the house blocks in *Regio* V and *Regio* VI at Sabratha is quite similar.[13] This concept of a city extension only towards the south, along a strip of land of the same width as that of the forum, would provide a picture of an unplanned expansion of the site and does not correspond to what we know about Roman urbanism. Even though it may not have been extensively occupied, the layout of the eastern part of Sabratha must have been, at least, planned.

There are also various traces of a previous occupation of the eastern sector already in the Hellenistic

[11] A dupondius of Caligula would provide a date for the destruction of the Hellenistic public building: Bonacasa and Mistretta 2011, 98, fig. 24.

[12] Also a cursory reference to a putative refurbishment of the temple after the earthquake of the Neronian-Flavian period disappeared: see Bonacasa and Mistretta 2011, 85.

[13] The two *Regiones* would have been planned and partially built in the first century BCE: Di Vita 1990, 432.

period. The isolated discovery of black-gloss fineware (*vernice nera*), when it is not related to any built structures, cannot be used to confirm this assumption. A report on the investigations around the Severan Monument provides information on a cocciopesto floor associated with some structures, yet these finds do not offer precise evidence for an absolute chronology (Kenrick 1986, 217–19). In contrast, the remains identified within the Temple of Hercules are more significant. The foundation of the western precinct wall overlies an earlier structure that probably belonged to a house, as shown by a wall composed of several courses of stone blocks. This wall is related to a cocciopesto floor located about 1.2 m below the level of the temple (Aiosa 2013, 197). The first phase of the temple should date to sometime before its refurbishment in the late second century CE, when a new façade encroached the *decumanus*, as it was evident already at the moment of the excavation. Furthermore, the street immediately south of the temple was partially encroached by the apses and the south portion of the *cella*. This determined a sort of 'chain reaction': also the eastern stretch of this street between the so-called 'theatre baths' and the Peristyle House would be occupied by later structures, and the two respective *insulae* appear to create a narrow rectangular block instead of a square one. Unfortunately, the chronology of the temple's first phase has not been established with certainty, and I can only point out the large quantity of black-gloss ware that was recovered in the sondages excavated by Caputo in 1938. The Peristyle House and the theatre baths have revealed some traces of a previous building that could belong to the first century CE. Finally, the Peristyle House partially obliterates the remains of an undated metal furnace, which was conveniently located at the edge of the site. The review of old data together with new research therefore seems to add further elements to hypothesize an extension of the city in this sector during the first century CE.

A new forum at Sabratha

The Temple of Hercules belongs to a category of religious edifices that is widespread across the whole of North Africa: the so-called '*templa cum porticibus*' (Eingartner 2005; Aiosa 2013, with bibliography). The building faces a large unexcavated area to the north of the *decumanus*. The actual temple, of the Romano-Italic type, had a tetrastyle front and was set on top of a podium abutting the rear wall of the precinct. Two apses at the ends of the side porticoes flank the main structure (Fig. 2.6). Due to this characteristic of its plan, the temple is usually grouped together with two other Tripolitanian religious buildings: the 'Temple of the Unknown Deity' (South Forum Temple) at Sabratha, which might even have been designed by the same architect, and the 'Anonymous Temple' along the *decumanus maximus* at Lepcis

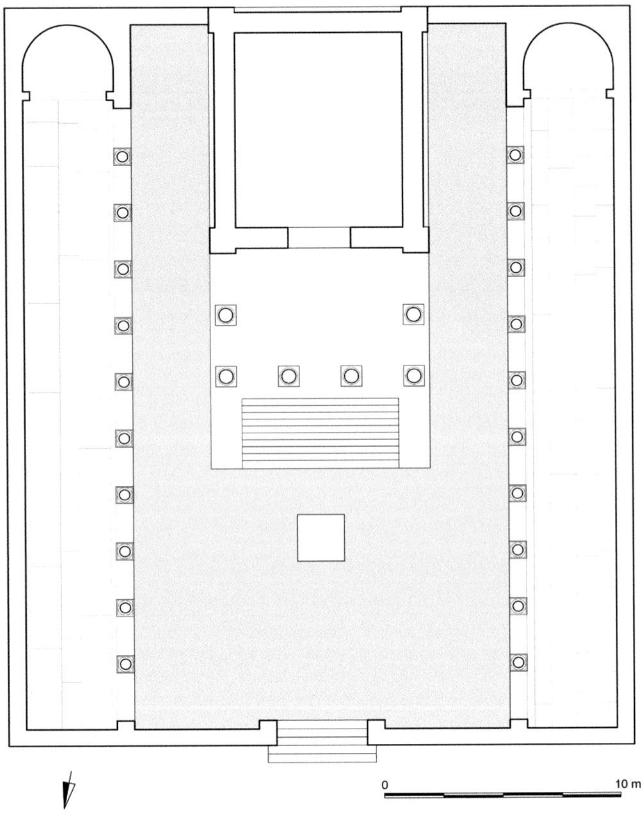

Fig. 2.6. Temple of Hercules, restored plan (drawing S. Aiosa).

Magna (on the latter building see Mugnai, Chapter 3). These two edifices add a transversal portico on the precinct's front side.

In my opinion the apses, which represent the main feature in all three temples, have a specific geometric relationship with the temple *cella*. They would represent one of the reasons why they cannot be considered as a simple variant of the more common rectilinear end of porticoes. They appear to function as actual *cellae*, or shrines, dedicated to minor deities associated with the cult of the god worshipped in the main building at the centre of the precinct. This is in some way proved by the paintings on the vault of the apses in the Temple of Hercules. The painting in the east apse shows a goddess with a shield and a spear, which was previously interpreted as the goddess Roma, but should be rather interpreted as an (African?) Minerva. The west apse depicts the apotheosis of the emperor Marcus Aurelius, according to the typical iconography of the second century CE with the emperor's bust placed on an eagle. An inscription running on the marble frieze of the porticoes (*IRT2021* 29) provides a chronology for the dedication of the temple in 186 CE, the year when Commodus held his fifth consulate.

In the case of the Temple of the Unknown Deity the apses are entirely made of stone blocks from the foundations upwards, instead of concrete. Such an effort in their execution appears to be out of proportion for a simple compositional variation. Moreover, the thresholds with holes for hinges indicate that a door separated each apse from the rest of the porticoes. This suggests a special use for these two spaces. Even if it was modified in a subsequent phase, the Temple of Serapis at Lepcis Magna also would have had two apses at the end of the side porticoes (although the east apse is hypothetical), and the Greek inscriptions recovered in the building mention the main deity along with the *synnaoi theoi* (associated deities). However, this example is probably less significant since similar inscriptions come from many other temples of Isis and Serapis, independently from the shape of their plan.

The relative chronology of the two temples at Sabratha was not determined archaeologically, but was simply based on their location: since the whole of the forum was already occupied by civic and religious buildings, the Temple of Hercules had to be built in the new district. According to a different theory, the more elaborate plan of the Temple of the Unknown Deity suggests this building was built after the 'experimental' design of the Temple of Hercules, which presents some incongruities in its plan. The location of the Temple of Hercules calls for a different explanation, however. In the central decades of the second century CE, the *tabernae* on the north and south sides of the forum were dismantled and replaced by two porticoes with granite columns, in order to obtain a new celebrative public space in a spot that was previously used for economic and administrative activities, which must have thus been transferred elsewhere. Along the flanks of the *decumanus*, the presence of a rectilinear perimeter wall in all the city blocks occupied by houses or public buildings is clearly visible, even in those parts where only the foundations are preserved. It is only in correspondence with the unexcavated area to the north of the Temple of Hercules and of the two streets at its sides that all traces of this wall disappear. This suggests the presence of an area free of buildings opposite the temple (Figs 2.7–8). The religious and civic spaces of the forum were separated by the main street of Sabratha (the *decumanus*), as is largely attested in many Roman cities. A four-way arch along the *decumanus* (only the plinths of the gateposts and one capital survive), hiding the change of direction of the street, might have functioned as a monumental entrance to the new public area. The 'old' forum of Sabratha was accessed through an arch as well whose gateposts abutted the façades of the Temple of the Unknown Deity and of the

Fig. 2.7. *(above)* Location of the 'new' forum along the *decumanus maximus* (photo S. Aiosa).

Fig. 2.8. *(right)* Area of the 'new' forum (in purple) with Temple of Hercules in the background (photo S. Aiosa).

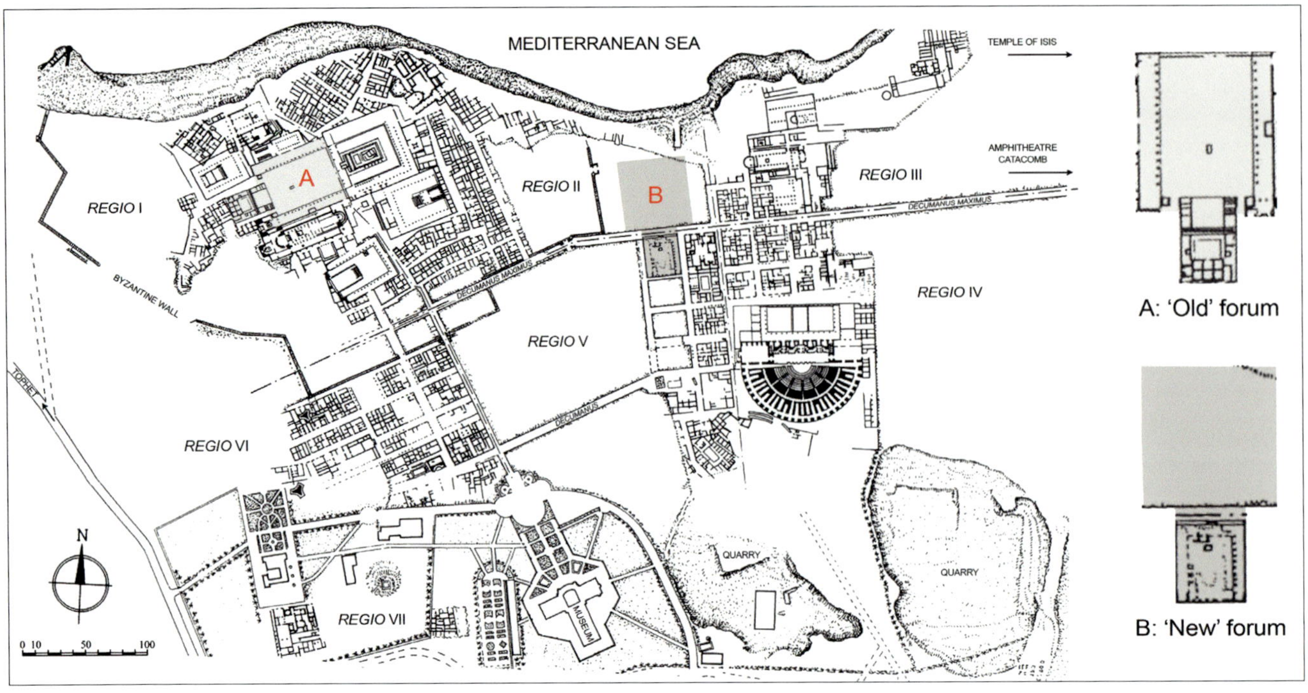

Fig. 2.9. A comparison of the surface of the 'old' and 'new' forum (after Aiosa 2014, fig. 4).

Antonine Temple. Also the size of the 'old' and of the 'new' fora is comparable (Fig. 2.9).

If the hypothesis of a sequence of earthquakes affecting the urban development of Sabratha has been accepted by scholars to some extent, the consequences of the last of these events over the whole Mediterranean basin in 365 CE have been much more debated. A recent paper goes back to Lepelley's arguments against Di Vita's reconstruction of those events (Fentress and Wilson 2021). The idea of a single, large-scale disaster that would have hit the cities of Asia Minor, Greece, Egypt as well as all the North African coast and Sicily is considered unacceptable on the basis of geological or seismological considerations. Focusing on Tripolitania and on the last two earthquakes of Di Vita's proposed sequence, a first disastrous event would have damaged many civic and religious buildings in this region at the beginning of the fourth century CE, while the second earthquake would have determined their definitive collapse. Some finds from various contexts at Sabratha and Lepcis Magna are considered dating elements for the buildings' destruction. Among them are some *Aes* III coins of Valent (364–78 CE) or Valentinianus (364–75 CE) and Tripolitanian lamps (Di Vita 1990, 458, 463). Therefore, the start of the production of these lamps should have predated the earthquake, although this is a circular argument that cannot be discussed in detail here.

Looking at the Temple of Hercules, both apses of the lateral porticoes show traces of ancient restoration (for a detailed discussion see Aiosa 2013, 11–17). Furthermore, a small coin hoard and a Tripolitanian lamp were found under the stone blocks of the western precinct wall, which had collapsed on the street flanking the temple.[14] These finds could confirm Di Vita's hypothesis in general, without attempting to propose an exact date for the destruction. What we could still consider as plausible is the occurrence of an earthquake in the second half of the fourth century CE, probably as part of a series of seismic events, which caused the collapse of many buildings at Sabratha and Lepcis Magna. Regrettably, it is difficult to find precise references to these events in the epigraphic record, since earthquakes as well as other calamities were rarely referred to with their specific names and only generic, less distressing phrases were used. This is also the case with the word '*ruina*' mentioned in *IRT* 103 (*IRT2021* 103), and it is worth commenting on the heated debate on the meaning of this term. Its interpretation as 'disaster' – thus recording the occurrence of an earthquake – seems more reasonable than a putative invasion of desert peoples, such as the Austuriani/Laguatan, as previously proposed. Di Vita (1990, 452–65) pointed out that there is no evidence these peoples assaulted the coastal cities rather than just pillaging the farms in the countryside around them, especially in the region of Lepcis Magna. Without over-stressing this argument, I take the 365 CE earthquake as a 'symbol' of the last, to some extent documented, destruction of the main monuments of Sabratha.

Some 20 years ago, I went back to the inscription *IRT* 7 (*IRT2021* 7) naming Constantius II and Constans, the two sons of the emperor Constantine who are also

[14] Aiosa 2013, 105, 120. In addition to coins of Constantius II and Constans, there is a fragmentary *Gloria Romanorum* coin, but unfortunately its size cannot be determined nor can the issuing authority be recognized.

mentioned in *IRT* 55 (*IRT2021* 55), which honours them for the restoration of the Temple of Liber Pater in the forum of Sabratha (Aiosa 2003). The latter inscription mentions an '*antiqua ruina cum labe*' that caused damage to this building and, after a considerable hiatus, required the intervention of the two Augusti in 340 CE. Thus, the inscription provides a second occurrence of the term '*ruina*' that also appears in *IRT* 103. In *IRT* 7, the incomplete word HORRO[---] was considered a mistake in the engraved text, and this was therefore restored as HORREO (warehouse), since *horror*, the only Latin word starting with those letters, would not theoretically have made sense. Rejecting the proposed solution of an engraver's mistake, which is too often advocated to solve problematic inscribed texts, I proposed a new reading of the inscription that confirms in part the hypothesis of an earthquake at the beginning of the fourth century CE. To fill the lacuna at the end of the word HORRO[---], I suggested a more metaphoric phrase, which is never attested on inscriptions, but which does occur in ancient sources to avoid using the dreadful expression '*terrae motus*'. This phrase is '*horror soli*', and one could therefore integrate the text with *horro[re soli dilapsum]*. This new reading of the inscription suggested to me that the restoration by Constantius II and Constans of the Temple of Liber Pater in 340 CE (*IRT* 55) would thus find a parallel in *IRT* 7, which attests to an intervention of the two Augusti in the Temple of Hercules. This could allow us to consider that Hercules and Liber Pater might have been also the two *dii patrii* of Sabratha, not only of Lepcis Magna. Di Vita highlighted the long span of time between the earthquake and the restoration of the two Augusti of the Temple of Liber Pater. If one goes back to the text of *IRT* 7, after the word *Herculis* there is another incomplete word: LO[---], which I proposed to restore as *lo[nga maiorum incuria]* – a phrase that occurs frequently in building inscriptions.

According to Di Vita (1982), with the Augustan-period expansion of Lepcis Magna the trajectory of the so-called '*cardo maximus*' changed in order to make it cross the main *decumanus* orthogonally.[15] The latter is considered to be the urban section of the cross-regional road connecting Alexandria with Carthage. This idea that a cross-regional road could reach the very centre of all the cities and towns along its path, thus continuously deviating from its main route, is traditionally applied to Sabratha, where it is particularly evident how this assumption is wrong. Even at Lepcis Magna a recent topographical survey has revealed the existence of a network of secondary routes departing from the main road to connect it with all the urban centres along the coast (Zocchi 2018), and it is therefore logical to assume the same applies to Sabratha. Here the *decumanus maximus* passes between the area of the emporium and that of the quarries. Its eastward extension along a hypothetical straight line (Fig. 2.10) would reach a small bay well

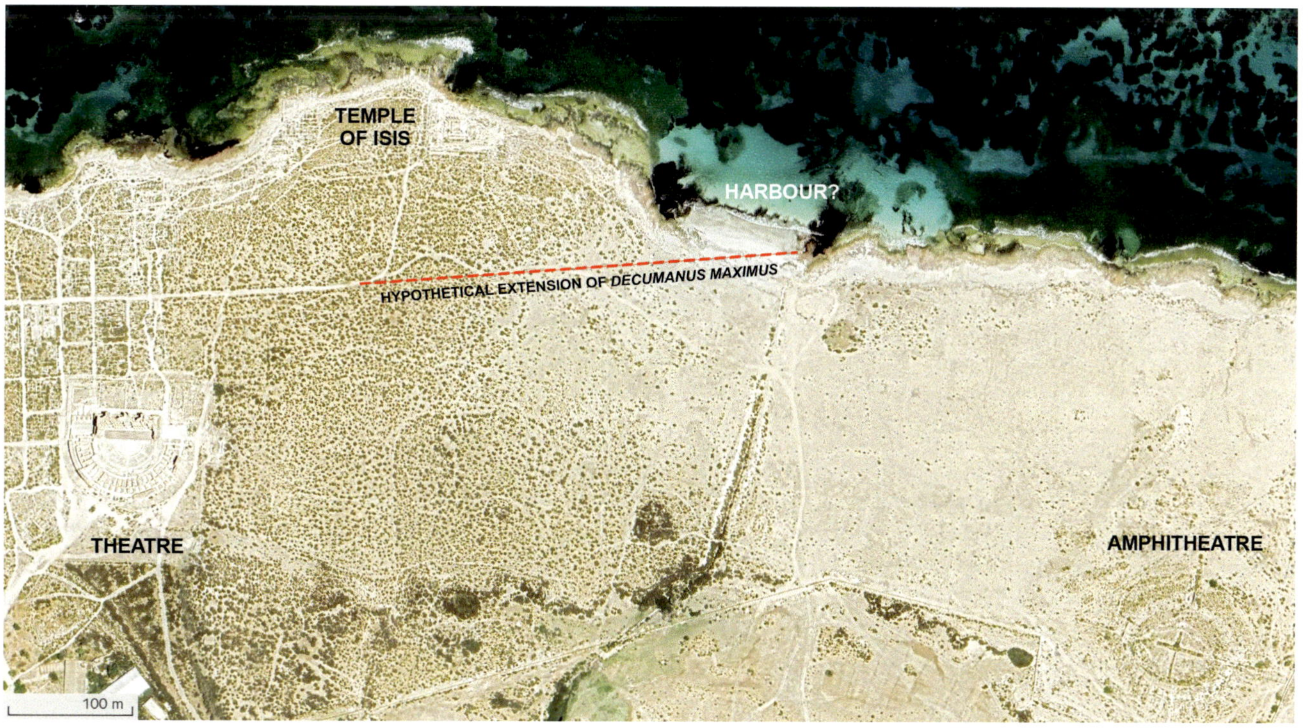

Fig. 2.10. Bay to the east of the Temple of Isis and hypothetical extension of the *decumanus maximus* (basemap Google Earth, image Airbus, Maxar Technologies).

[15] This was one of the points of disagreement between Di Vita (1982) and Ward-Perkins (1982) on the early imperial urban development of Lepcis Magna.

protected from the winds, which is located just after the promontory where the Temple of Isis stands, thus assuring the goddess' protection. Isis' Greek epiclesis '*euploia*', as well as '*limnesia*', '*pharia*', etc., attests to her role as a protector of maritime routes and harbours. The temple faces eastwards, as usual, but one could also argue that it faces this small bay. Regardless of whether the *decumanus* corresponded with the urban section of the above-mentioned road or not, it is evident that it had to change its direction again to continue its path eastwards.

The harbour

The coastline in front of Sabratha must have changed over the centuries.[16] The so-called 'Seaward Baths' as well as part of the precinct of the Temple of Isis have collapsed into the water, while along the area between the two buildings the sea appears to have receded. The water level in the bay facing the city must have been deeper in antiquity and should have hosted, if not a harbour proper, at least some wharfs. Ancient sources use an accurate terminology to indicate the various possibilities of docking that were offered by the Mediterranean centres, distinguishing between simple stopovers and actual ports. In the *Stadiasmus Maris Magni*, Sabratha is referred to as a 'city without a port, having just a stopover' (99: *salon*), while the *Periplus* of Pseudo-Scylax (c. fourth century CE) mentions the city and the port (110: *polis kai limen*) of *Abrotonon*, the Greek name of Sabratha. This contradiction could be explained by the fact that the ships' tonnage and draught was greater in the early imperial period, when this section of the *Stadiasmus* was presumably written.

According to a report on the underwater survey of the seabed on the coast of Sabratha, the harbour was sheltered by two submerged natural rocks which were reinforced with concrete. The space between these rocks corresponded with the entrance to the port. Closer to the coastline, the presence of a harbour should have been revealed by the 'piles of sherds' that remained unaltered in the same position over the centuries (see Robert Yorke's report in Kenrick 1986, 243–45). However, I would like to point out that hundreds of *decauville* wagons full of sand, debris, and pottery discharged their contents in the sea in front of the city during the archaeological excavations. Also the presence of marble columns that was recorded by the divers could have belonged to the Seaward Baths rather than to the harbour structures. At Lepcis Magna, some column drums and other architectural elements were recovered from the sea. The limestone elements were attributed to some structure of the harbour itself, while those of marble were supposed to have fallen into the water from a ship transporting architectural elements to the city (Laronde 1988; but see also the remarks in Beltrame 2012 and Mugnai, Chapter 3).

Sabratha is among the Mediterranean centres that had a *statio* (i.e. an office) in the so-called 'Square of the Corporations' at Ostia, the ancient port of Rome. Each *statio* was paved with a black-and-white mosaic depicting a subject related to the respective site; in the case of Sabratha, this symbol was an African elephant. The *statio Sabrathensium* thus attests to the extensive trade and economic exchanges managed by this city. It should follow that the harbour infrastructures along the coast of Sabratha, even if not comparable with the impressive remains of the Severan harbour of Lepcis Magna, must have been suitable for such activities.

Related to this topic is the caravan roads that transported the *ferae libicae* to the coast – the beasts coming from Central Africa that were shipped to Rome for amphitheatre games. The Great Hunt mosaic at Piazza Armerina (Sicily) gives an idea of the infrastructures that were necessary to embark an elephant onto a ship. Also the tons of decorative marble, which in the second century CE was widespread in the city, must have reached Sabratha from the sea; this would imply the presence of a harbour equipped with large and sturdy moles where the lifting machinery could be positioned. It does not seem plausible that the transport and movement of such bulky items was managed by employing *naves caudicariae*, small boats shuttling from the main ship anchored off the coast to the moles of the harbour.

No investigations have been carried out in the bay east of the Temple of Isis to verify its possible pertinence to a harbour system. Directly connected to the city centre by the *decumanus maximus*, this bay is also close to the amphitheatre, which could have served as a space to gather the caravans that transported goods and animals from Central Africa. Further to the east, on a small promontory closing off this bay, the remains of a suburban villa were partially investigated. The private anchorages of these *villae maritimae* could have contributed to the management of goods reaching the main harbour, as happened at Lepcis Magna. This suggestion requires further investigations and is not in contrast with the existence of a port on the front of the city, nor with Di Vita's hypothesis which locates the Hellenistic harbour at Marsa Sabratha, to the west of the city. Here the shallow water of the seabed was probably sufficient to host the small ships of that period, but it must have become insufficient for the size and quantity of Roman-period ships. Also the communication between this small bay and the supposed harbour in front of the city was impossible, since the water between the two areas is less than 1 m deep. It is also evident that this subject can only be properly evaluated through a comprehensive core sampling of the seabed.

[16] For a more detailed discussion of the issues around Sabratha's harbour, see Aiosa 2014, 11–22.

The theatre

The front of the theatre's stage building, or *pulpitum* (Aiosa 2020), is composed of seven alternating (four rectangular and three semicircular) recesses, with the central one being larger than the other two flanking it (Fig. 2.11). Each recess is separated from the next by a projecting rectangular element bearing a relief on the front that depicts a deity framed by two columns at the sides. At the right- and left-hand edges of the *pulpitum*, two parapets decorated with couples of dancing Maenads conceal from view two small staircases leading up to the stage. These are accessible from the first and the last rectangular recess, respectively. The subjects represented in each recess are heterogeneous. The central scene appears to be the only one depicting an historical subject (Fig. 2.12), while the others are believed to represent several theatrical genres without any specific relationship between them. This opinion has affected the interpretation of the first scene. Apart from an old hypothesis according to which the relief depicts a double representation of Aeschylus, Sophocles, and Euripides, which was advanced to justify the presence of six figures instead of three, the scene is now more cautiously described as a theatre academy (Fig. 2.13).

Each rectangular recess hosts a relief on the front side, depicting the main subject. At the two sides are represented some elements that add meaning to the main scene. The front side of the third rectangular recess hosts a tragedy scene (Fig. 2.14) (the actors wear masks and the *cothurni*), while the two side reliefs represent respectively tragedy and comedy masks: a sort of generic reference to theatre plays. Less straightforward is the interpretation of the objects on the second rectangular

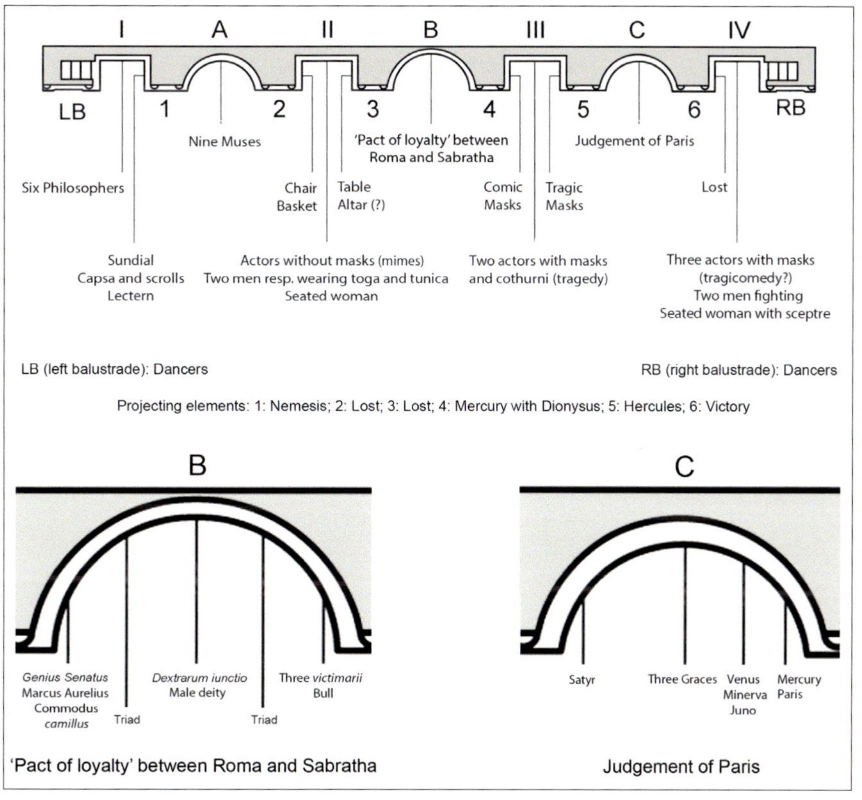

Fig. 2.11. *(right)* Reconstruction of the scenes depicted on the theatre's *pulpitum* (drawing S. Aiosa).

Fig. 2.12. *(below)* Theatre, *pulpitum*: central semicircular recess (photo S. Aiosa).

Fig. 2.13. *(top left)* Theatre, *pulpitum* (first rectangular recess): savants/theatre academy (photo S. Aiosa).

Fig. 2.14. *(top right)* Theatre, *pulpitum* (third rectangular recess): tragedy scene (photo S. Aiosa).

Fig. 2.15. *(left)* Theatre, *pulpitum* (second rectangular recess): mime scene (photo S. Aiosa).

recess: a wooden box or cist, and a wicker basket. A passage of Apuleius' *Metamorphoses* (9.23–24) alludes to similar objects inside which the lovers of married women could rapidly hide to avoid being seen by the husbands. This was the subject of many so-called '*fabulae Mylesiae*', a literary genre also explored by Apuleius, and this could indeed be the subject of this relief (Fig. 2.15).

With regard to the sundial on the right-hand side of the first recess (Fig. 2.16), this brings to mind the Torre Annunziata (Fig. 2.17) and Sarsina mosaics depicting the Seven Savants. Almost at the very centre of both mosaics a sundial is depicted to indicate a specific scene setting: the Academy at Athens. Several other iconographic details of these mosaics are very similar to those of the relief. This has led us to recognize the six old men wearing the Greek *pallium* as philosophers, rather than actors or poets, as was previously believed. In the relief there is no room for a seventh philosopher, but the list of Seven Savants was often modified in its order and composition, changing the names of some of them or reducing their number, especially in the case of philosophers whose behaviour was unethical, such as the tyrant Kleobulos.

The assumption that the gods depicted on the projecting elements of the *pulpitum* are the most important divinities of Sabratha – even if partially justified by the presence of Hercules and Mercury (Figs 2.18–19), who also occur on the local issues of Sabratha's coins (together with Serapis, who is not among the gods represented on these reliefs) – is far from certain. For instance, Victory and Nemesis are frequently represented together in theatres and they do not have any specific relationship with this city. One would have also expected Liber Pater to be placed at the side of the central recess, given that his temple occupies the entire east side of the forum. Even Hercules, a good candidate to be the patron god of Sabratha, appears much more to the right on the *pulpitum* instead of being placed in a prominent position. Furthermore, the loss of some of the reliefs makes a comprehensive reading of the entire composition and iconography impossible. It is clear that each relief bears its own meaning and can or cannot be related to the other scenes of the *pulpitum*. The ascertained connection between the recess with the six philosophers and the second one with the nine muses does not necessarily imply similar relationships among the other recesses.

Depictions of philosophers and muses occur on numerous marble sarcophagi of the imperial period, but in the case of the Sabratha reliefs the connection between these two subjects seems to derive from a passage of Apuleius' *Florida* (20). Here the author advocates his intellectual affinity with all the nine muses instead of a single literary genre, as is the case with each of the six savants he names in the same passage. Sabratha was

Fig. 2.16. *(top left)* Theatre, *pulpitum* (first rectangular recess): sundial (photo S. Aiosa).

Fig. 2.17. *(top right)* Naples, National Archaeological Museum: mosaic with the 'Seven Savants' (photo S. Aiosa).

Fig. 2.18. *(right)* Theatre, *pulpitum*: projecting element with depiction of Hercules (photo S. Aiosa).

Fig. 2.19. *(far right)* Theatre, *pulpitum*: projecting element with depiction of Mercury with little Dionysus (photo S. Aiosa).

the place where Apuleius defended himself, delivering his famous *Apologia* when he was put on trial with the charge of practising sorcery – a crime that was punished with the death penalty, as stated by a senatorial decree that extended to this category of offences the penalties prescribed by the *Lex Cornelia de sicariis et veneficis*. Once he was acquitted from this charge, immediately before becoming *sacerdos Africae*, Apuleius could have decided to express his personal gratitude to the judges and to the city by refurbishing the local theatre and embellishing the stage building with marbles. Moreover, while holding this priesthood, he would have had to pay for *munera gladiatoria* and *venationes* in honour of the emperor.[17] Similar acts of euergetism were common among the Roman elite and may have contributed to increasing Apuleius' personal prestige; for instance, we know that he was honoured with the dedication of a statue in Carthage, the metropolis of Africa Proconsularis (*Florida*, 16).

As Apuleius specifies in his *Apologia* (23.1), he inherited the sum of 1,000,000 sesterces from his father and considered this as a demonstration that he did not

[17] Saint Augustine, *Epistulae*, 26. However, the exact nature and duties of this priesthood are debated: Rives 1994; *contra* La Rocca 2005, 21–22.

Fig. 2.20. Theatre, stage building (photo S. Aiosa).

need the money of his wife Pudentilla, whose financial assets amounted to about 4,000,000 sesterces (71.6; 77.1). He therefore had sufficient means to be a magistrate, and most of all *sacerdos Africae*. Apuleius would not necessarily have been the only sponsor of the refurbishment of the theatre's stage building (Fig. 2.20): another wealthy donor, or perhaps even the entire city municipality, could have contributed to this enterprise, but he could definitely have afforded to pay for the new marble *pulpitum*. His personal assets and the *pecunia publica* he administered as *flamen perpetuus* would have provided the funds required for this enterprise. To try to estimate the approximate sum required for these works, one can look at some examples from the same region and period. As shown by the text of the dedicatory inscription (*IRT2021* 534), for the refurbishment of the theatre's stage building at Lepcis Magna the two donors paid respectively 200,000 (Marcius Vitalis) and 300,000 (Junius Galba) sesterces, although these funds did not come from their private assets but from the city's finances (*pecunia publica*). The construction of the theatre of Madauros, Apuleius' hometown in present-day Algeria, required 375,000 sesterces and this sum was provided by M. Gabinius Sabinus as *flamen perpetuus*. Finally, the almost contemporary Arch of Marcus Aurelius at Lepcis Magna required an investment of 120,000 sesterces for its construction (*IRT2021* 1011; Pensabene 2003, 357).

It cannot be said with certainty how many years Apuleius lived, and what we do know about his life comes from his own works. Some believe he died before the Severan era, which is traditionally regarded as the date for the completion of Sabratha's theatre and its sculptural decoration. My interpretation of the sacrifice scene on the central recess of the *pulpitum* might solve this apparent problem. The relief shows an emperor and other figures on the left-hand side (Fig. 2.21), separated from the animal sacrifice scene at the opposite end (Fig. 2.22) by the group of divinities represented at the centre. The most widespread opinion is that this scene depicts the emperor Septimius Severus, although there are uncertainties about the identification of the other figures at his sides. Starting from the left, I propose to identify: the Genius of the Senate; the emperor Marcus Aurelius; and his son Commodus with the *toga virilis*, which he took on when he joined his father on the throne. The fourth figure could represent an assistant to the sacrifice (*camillus*), which is very common on reliefs depicting the same subject.[18] This hypothesis would also fit with the idea that the central scene with the *dextrarum iunctio* between the goddess Roma and the personification of Sabratha in front of seven 'soldiers' (or, more plausibly, planetary gods) should be related to the moment when Sabratha acquired the status of *colonia*, which, according to several scholars, took place in the Antonine period.

[18] The two moments of the sacrifice are depicted together on the relief with Marcus Aurelius *sacrificans* in the Capitoline Museums, Palazzo dei Conservatori in Rome (inv. MC0807); the figures in the foreground are almost identical to those that appear at the two ends of the Sabratha relief.

Fig. 2.21. Theatre, *pulpitum* (central semicircular recess, left-hand side): sacrificing emperor (photo S. Aiosa).

Fig. 2.22. Theatre, *pulpitum* (central semicircular recess, right-hand side): sacrifice of a bull (photo S. Aiosa).

Fig. 2.23. Theatre, *pulpitum* (semicircular recess): judgement of Paris – the Three Graces (photo S. Aiosa).

Fig. 2.24. Theatre, *pulpitum* (semicircular recess): judgement of Paris – Venus, Minerva, and Juno (photo S. Aiosa).

The most evident reference to a work by Apuleius is the relief with the judgement of Paris in the semicircular recess on the right-hand side of the *pulpitum*. In the central part of the recess, the three Graces (Fig. 2.23) are depicted according to their common iconography, which is well-known through different media, such as the painting in the Museum of Naples or the marble statuary group from Cyrene, just to mention two of the most famous examples.[19] The main scene with the three goddesses, Mercury, and Paris appears on the right end of the relief (Figs 2.24–25). A single figure carrying an oblong object in his hand is at the opposite end of the recess (Fig. 2.26). This figure has been traditionally interpreted as a 'fat satyr' and the irregular surface of the landscape behind him should have represented Mount Ida, where the judgement took place. The obvious relationship between the three Graces and Venus, the winner of the competition, does not explain their prominent position in the central part of the semicircular recess. That this relief could represent a theatrical scene instead of a mythological episode has

Fig. 2.25. Theatre, *pulpitum* (semicircular recess): judgement of Paris – Mercury and Paris (photo S. Aiosa).

[19] The same subject occurs on a Roman lamp in the Sabratha Museum, which has been attributed to a local workshop: Joly 1974, 28, 72, 138, pl. 20, no. 512.

Fig. 2.26. Theatre, *pulpitum* (semicircular recess): judgement of Paris – child with a torch (?) (photo S. Aiosa).

been already hypothesized, but without attempting to recognize a specific play. I would mention a passage of Apuleius' *Metamorphoses*, in which Lucius attends the performance of the judgement of Paris at the theatre of Corinth. The play was preceded by a procession involving many actors interpreting various characters. Among them are the three Graces and some plump and sweet children dressed up with wings, recalling as many cupids carrying torches. The figure on the Sabratha relief, previously interpreted as a satyr, could thus have represented one of these children. In conclusion, I suggest reading all the three sections of this relief as a single composition.

The visit of Septimius Severus to Lepcis Magna, his hometown, coincided with the initial phases of an impressive building programme that saw the erection of the new Severan Forum and Basilica, the Great Nymphaeum, and the magnificent Colonnaded Street leading to the harbour (see Mugnai, Chapter 3). At the intersection of the *cardo maximus* and *decumanus maximus*, a tetrapylon (four-way arch) celebrated the emperor's victories against the Parthians as well as his visit to Lepcis Magna. For the year of this visit two dates are the most probable: 202/203 or 205/206 CE. A sacrifice scene among the reliefs decorating this arch is intended to represent one of the religious events of those days and a specific location within the city has been proposed. Nothing comparable to this happened at Sabratha. Here the only monument one can surely refer to Septimius Severus is a large inscribed podium, known as the 'Severan Monument', which would have served to support a statue of the emperor on a quadriga (Fig. 2.27). It was built with blocks of the same variety of yellowish limestone that was sourced from the local quarries exploited during the Severan period.

One should also assume that the 'Severan' sacrifice scene on the *pulpitum* in Sabratha's theatre was made within the context of the imperial family's visit. Since there is no representation of any buildings which could suggest a specific setting in the city, and the figures are carved against a neutral background, this sacrifice has been considered to be a generic (metahistorical) scene rather than a real episode that took place specifically at Sabratha. One cannot fail to notice how the same event, at Lepcis Magna and Sabratha, would have been depicted in two very different ways, not only with regard to how the figures were displayed on the relief but also in terms of the portrait types adopted (leaving aside the presence/absence of certain members of the imperial family). Even attributing them to two separate workshops, the discrepancy of style between the Lepcis Magna and Sabratha reliefs is notable, and so is the iconographic difference between the presumed portraits of Septimius Severus and Caracalla on the Tetrapylon of Lepcis Magna and those of the Sabratha relief, where Julia Domna and Geta are absent. Guidi (1930, 50), who first investigated the theatre and its sculptural decoration, did not propose any precise identification for the main figure of the sacrifice scene, although he pointed out a presumed stylistic correspondence with the Severan reliefs from Lepcis Magna – an interpretation that has been generally followed by later scholars (including Caputo 1959, 19). To my knowledge, Ward-Perkins was the only scholar who clearly rejected any stylistic parallel between the Sabratha reliefs and those of the Severan Tetrapylon at Lepcis Magna.[20]

Among the elements that can lead us to reconsider the chronology of the theatre there is a monumental inscription attributed to the *porticus post scaenam* (*IRT* 973; *IRT2021* 973). The text is for the most part fragmentary, but the name *Flavi*[*us*] can be read on it. Both this name and the chronology of the text, probably to be assigned to the end of the first century CE, led Caputo (1959, 28) to believe that the theatre superimposed a previous public building of the Flavian period. The possibility that the present theatre could be the result of a late Antonine or Severan refurbishment of a Flavian edifice was never contemplated, however. The oddity is that Caputo himself noticed that a circle traced with its centre on the orchestra would have

[20] With regard to the theatre, he simply concluded that 'the building can hardly be earlier than the middle of the second century': Kenrick 1986, 224. On the disagreement about the date of the Sabratha reliefs between Ward-Perkins (Antonine) and Caputo (Severan), see also Kenrick 2009, 65.

included both the cavea and the *porticus post scaenam*. The coherence of this design should have suggested the same chronology for the theatre and the *porticus*. However, the theatre was considered to be the last relevant architectural enterprise in a city that was almost ignored by the African emperor, with the sole exception of the Severan Monument located at the very centre of the so-called 'Theatre Street', almost to block access to that road. The chronology to the second century CE of the whole theatre quarter is what has contributed to this assumption.

Apart from the inscription, there are other details that should be considered. The decorative analogies between the astragal on the entablature of the Temple of the *Genius Coloniae* at Oea and the one we can observe on the marble door frame of the Sabratha scene building would suggest the presence of the same workshop operating in both cities. A distinctive feature of the products of these artisans would be their inspiration from models of the Flavian period, whose influence is still recognizable in the second half of the second century CE. In my opinion an earlier chronology for the occurrence of their first productions is not to be excluded; equally, this could also be suggested for the cornice of the *pulpitum*. The stylistic differences between the high relief of some scenes of the *pulpitum* and the flat relief of others, which are commonly described as a sign of eclecticism, pose the question of whether they all belong to the same period and were thus executed by the same workshop, or whether some new reliefs might have repeated (or changed) the subject of a previous set. Together with the small differences noticed in the architectural decoration, all these elements might suggest a first Flavian-period phase for both the ornamentation of the scene building and the *pulpitum*, and their replacement about a century later.

To add a further, significant, clue to this discussion we must look at the amphitheatre. As a result of his accurate study of this monument, Gilberto Montali (2015, 295–97) has proposed a chronology in the Flavian period. The extensive spoliation of the building makes a close comparison with the theatre difficult; however, some architectural elements together with historical considerations leave room for the possibility that both edifices might have been built at the same time. One should remember that Kenrick (1986, 223; see also Aiosa 2016, 349) had already suggested conducting some surveys south of the cavea to ascertain the chronology of the theatre, whose construction was believed to have started at the very end of the second century CE, most likely under the emperor Commodus, to be completed under Septimius Severus. In conclusion, a complete revision of the relative chronology traditionally assigned to the theatre and to the quarter – at the very end and at the beginning of the second century CE, respectively – could be proposed. One should also keep in mind the slightly different orientation of the blocks of houses and the theatre. As mentioned above, the latter building was long considered to be the last architectural enterprise in this district, but it now appears that both the theatre and the district might be assigned to the end of the first century CE.

I am aware that each of the arguments that may lead us to review the chronology of the (first-phase) theatre is far from being indisputable, but there are many clues that do seem to point in this direction. An example can

Fig. 2.27. Severan Monument, view from east (photo S. Aiosa).

Fig. 2.28. Decorated soffit of architrave blocks. A: Temple of Hercules, portico; B: Theatre, stage building, ground-floor order (photos S. Aiosa).

be useful to clarify this hypothesis: the barrel vaults of the theatre galleries are made of sandstone ashlar blocks rather than concrete. One could regard this technological feature as the survival of a local, Hellenistic-period building tradition that lasted until the latter half of the second century CE; however, we should also remember that tons of concrete were used for the Antonine-period refurbishment of the Augustan theatre of Lepcis Magna, as is normal after the Trajanic period (see, for example, the vaults of the baths to the northwest of the theatre at Sabratha). In this latter case, we could consider this masonry technique as a further element to propose a chronology of the theatre within the first century CE. Even if it does not allow us to solve the problems about the chronology of the theatre stage building, it is important to point out a decorative detail that occurs in the porticoes of the Temple of Hercules. The soffit of the architrave features a braiding pattern, which is identical to that on the entablatures of the stage building (Fig. 2.28a–b). This comparison shows that the architectural ornament of both edifices was produced by the same workshop. Obviously, the date of 186 CE deriving from the inscription *IRT2021* 29 of the temple's porticoes cannot be extended automatically to the theatre, since the activity of the workshop could have lasted many years. Also the presence of an earlier group among the different series of the theatre's marble capitals is not a conclusive proof, since some capitals could have been stored for several years before their use.

Conclusions

All the new hypotheses discussed here need further field research to be confirmed and to make us achieve a better understanding of the main urban phases of the city. The duplication of the main public square (forum) is a common phenomenon in several Roman cities and towns across North Africa as well as in other provinces (Kleinwächter 2001). In the case of Sabratha, the existence of a second forum is more than probable, and the University of Palermo has been planning to carry out additional fieldwork at the site to confirm this hypothesis. Research in the eastern part of the city is allowing us to reconstruct in more detail the history of Sabratha's urban expansion and is revealing the specific role of the Flavian emperors in the embellishment of the city, which was not restricted to the refurbishment of the 'old' forum area but also involved the erection of two of the most impressive spectacle buildings across the whole of North Africa: the theatre and the amphitheatre. The latter monument is located at the edge of the city, close to a bay that could have been used as part of an articulated harbour system. Even if this aspect – which would require a comprehensive underwater survey to be better assessed – cannot be confirmed, there is no reason to exclude this section of the city from an overall appraisal of the urban development of Roman-period Sabratha.

The considerable efforts by the Flavians to embellish the whole city would not have been limited to the refurbishment of the Temple of Liber Pater and Temple of Isis, or to the addition of a basilica on the forum's south side. In addition to these edifices,[21] the impressive spectacle buildings would have transformed Sabratha well before the architectural enterprises of the Antonine period. From what has been discussed above, it is evident that only a fragmentary dedicatory inscription survives which we can use to attempt to connect the new stage building to a given ruler, to establish a date for its refurbishment, and to identify the patron of these works. However, the sacrifice relief on the *pulpitum* shows a mature man whose iconography is

[21] I do not include the Seaward Baths, since a putative Flavian date for the first construction phase of this building is not well documented.

much more similar to Marcus Aurelius than Septimius Severus (although the portraits of the latter emperor were inspired by those of his predecessor), and a young prince of the Antonine dynasty instead of a young Caracalla, as the comparison with the reliefs on the Tetrapylon of Lepcis Magna shows. If this identification is correct, the time span for the scene depicted on the relief can be reduced to the years between Commodus' acquisition of the toga virilis in 175 CE – or at the latest when he gained the role of co-ruler with his father in 177 CE (*Historia Augusta, Commodus*, 12.4) – and 180 CE, when he became emperor.

Finally, although the proposed identification of Apuleius as the patron who sponsored the *pulpitum*'s marble refurbishment might seem purely speculative, the correspondences between the scenes depicted on the reliefs and some specific passages of his works are too numerous to be just a coincidence.

References

Aiosa, S. 2003. Un restauro antico al Tempio di Ercole a Sabratha: 'longa maiorum incuria' o testimonianza di un terremoto? *Quaderni di Archeologia della Libya* 18: 421–33.

Aiosa, S. 2011. La Casa della Piscina di Sabratha: anticipazioni e problemi. *Mare Internum: Archeologia e Culture del Mediterraneo* 3: 103–11.

Aiosa, S. 2013. *Il Tempio di Ercole a Sabratha. Architettura e contesto urbano*. Rome: 'L'Erma' di Bretschneider.

Aiosa, S. 2014. Rileggendo la Sabratha di Antonino Di Vita: riflessioni e proposte sul porto e la città. *Mare Internum: Archeologia e Culture del Mediterraneo* 5: 11–30.

Aiosa, S. 2016. Sabratha. Riflessioni sull'urbanistica e l'architettura religiosa della città punico-romana. In N. Bonacasa (ed.), *Giornate di studio: l'archeologia del sacro e l'archeologia del culto. Sabratha, Ebla, Ardea, Lanuvio (Roma, 8–11 ottobre 2013): Sabratha*. Rome: Bardi Edizioni, 301–413.

Aiosa, S. 2020. 'Un uomo di lettere'. Ipotesi sul programma figurativo dei rilievi scultorei del pulpitum del Teatro di Sabratha. *Libya Antiqua* n.s. 13: 39–85.

Bartoccini, R. 1964. Il tempio antoniniano di Sabratha. *Libya Antiqua* 1: 21–42.

Beltrame, C. 2012. New evidence for the submerged ancient harbour structures at Tolmetha and Leptis Magna, Libya. *International Journal of Nautical Archaeology* 41.2: 315–26.

Bonacasa, N. 2016. Sabratha. Il Tempio di Serapide. In N. Bonacasa (ed.), *Giornate di studio: l'archeologia del sacro e l'archeologia del culto. Sabratha, Ebla, Ardea, Lanuvio (Roma, 8–11 ottobre 2013): Sabratha*. Rome: Bardi Edizioni, 23–105.

Bonacasa, N. and Aiosa, S. (eds) 2017. *Sabratha. A Guide to the Studies and Investigations of the Past 50 Years*. Rome: Bardi Edizioni.

Bonacasa, N. and Mistretta, A. 2011. Il Tempio di Serapide a Sabratha. *Mare Internum: Archeologia e Culture del Mediterraneo* 3: 83–100.

Caputo, G. 1959. *Il teatro di Sabratha e l'architettura teatrale nordafricana*. Rome: 'L'Erma' di Bretschneider.

Caputo, G. and Ghedini, F. 1984. *Il tempio d'Ercole di Sabratha*. Rome: 'L'Erma' di Bretschneider.

Di Vita, A. 1974. Un passo dello Σταδιασμός τῆς μεγάλης θαλάσσης ed il porto ellenistico di Leptis Magna. In *Mélanges de philosophie, de littérature et d'histoire ancienne offerts à Pierre Boyancé*. Rome: École française de Rome, 229–49.

Di Vita, A. 1976. Il mausoleo punico-ellenistico B di Sabratha. *Mitteilungen des Deutschen Archäologischen Instituts, Römische Abteilung* 83: 273–85.

Di Vita, A. 1982. Entgegnung. In *150-Jahr-Feier Deutsches Archäologisches Institut Rom. Ansprachen und Vorträge (Rom, 4.–7. Dezember 1979)*. Mainz: Philipp von Zabern, 46–49.

Di Vita, A. 1990. Sismi, urbanistica e cronologia assoluta. Terremoti e urbanistica nelle città di Tripolitania fra il I secolo a.C. ed il IV d.C. In *L'Afrique dans l'occident romain (Ier siècle av. J.-C. – IVe siècle ap. J.-C.). Actes du colloque organisé par l'École française de Rome (Rome, 3–5 décembre 1987)*. Rome: École française de Rome: 425–94.

Di Vita, A., Bessi, B. and Manfredi, L.I. 2006. Il mausoleo punico-ellenistico B di Sabratha. La stratigrafia e i materiali delle fasi ellenistiche e protoromana. Monete puniche da Sabratha. *Quaderni di Archeologia della Libya* 20: 6 116.

Eingartner, J. 2005. *Templa cum porticibus. Ausstattung und Funktion italischer Tempelbezirke in Nordafrika und ihre Bedeutung für die römische Stadt der Kaiserzeit*. Rahden: Marie Leidorf Verlag.

Fentress, E. and Wilson, A.I. 2021. Terra septem diebus mugitus dedit: North African earthquakes revisited. In X. Dupuis, V. Fauvinet-Ranson, C.J. Goddard and H. Inglebert (eds), *L'automne de l'Afrique romaine. Hommages à Claude Lepelley*. Paris: Hermann, 133–54.

Guidi, G. 1930. Il teatro romano di Sabratha. *Africa Italiana* 3: 1–52.

Haynes, D.E.L. 1981. *An Archaeological and Historical Guide to the Pre-Islamic Antiquities of Tripolitania (4th Edition)*. Tripoli: Department of Antiquities.

Howard Carter, T. 1965. Western Phoenicians at Lepcis Magna. *American Journal of Archaeology* 69.2: 123–32.

Isaac, B. 2006. Proto-racism in Graeco-Roman antiquity. *World Archaeology* 38.1: 32–47.

Joly, E. 1974. *Lucerne del Museo di Sabratha*. Rome: 'L'Erma' di Bretschneider.

Kenrick, P.M. 1986. *Excavations at Sabratha 1948–1951. A Report on the Excavations Conducted by Dame Kathleen Kenyon and John Ward-Perkins*. London: Society for the Promotion of Roman Studies.

Kenrick, P.M. 2009. *Libya Archaeological Guides: Tripolitania.* London: Silphium Press.

Kleinwächter, C. 2001. *Platzanlagen nordafrikanischer Städte. Untersuchungen zum sogenannten Polyzentrismus in der Urbanistik der römischen Kaiserzeit.* Mainz: Philipp von Zabern.

La Rocca, A. 2005. *Il filosofo e la città. Commento storico ai Florida di Apuleio.* Rome: 'L'Erma' di Bretschneider.

Laronde, A. 1988. Le port de Lepcis Magna. *Comptes rendus des séances de l'Académie des Inscriptions et Belles-Lettres* 132.2: 337–53.

Mathuisieulx de, H.M. 1904. An expedition to Tripoli. *Bulletin of the American Geographical Society* 36.12: 736–44.

Merighi, A. 1940. *La Tripolitania antica. Dalle origini alla invasione degli Arabi, I–II.* Verbania: Airoldi Editore.

Mistretta, A. 2016. Sabratha: nuove ricerche e scoperte al Tempio di Serapide. In N. Bonacasa (ed.), *Giornate di studio: l'archeologia del sacro e l'archeologia del culto. Sabratha, Ebla, Ardea, Lanuvio (Roma, 8–11 ottobre 2013): Sabratha.* Rome: Bardi Edizioni, 107–87.

Montali, G. 2014. Da Sabratha a Tripoli Vecchio. L'identificazione dell'emporium tripolitano, la riscoperta dell'anfiteatro e le ragioni di un toponimo. *Mare Internum: Archeologia e Culture del Mediterraneo* 5: 57–76.

Montali, G. 2015. *L'Anfiteatro di Sabratha e gli anfiteatri dell'Africa proconsolare.* Rome: 'L'Erma' di Bretschneider.

Montali, G. 2018. La cosiddetta 'villa a mare' di Sabratha e le ville suburbane dell'emporio tripolitano. *Sicilia Antiqua* 15: 387–99.

Pensabene, P. 2003. La Porta Oea e l'Arco di Marco Aurelio a Leptis Magna: contributo alla definizione dei marmi e del loro costo, delle officine e delle committenze. *Quaderni di Archeologia della Libya* 18: 341–67.

Prag, J.R.W. 2014. Phoinix and Poenus: usage in antiquity. In J.C. Quinn and N.C. Vella (eds), *The Punic Mediterranean: Identities and Identification from Phoenician Settlement to Roman Rule.* Cambridge: Cambridge University Press, 11–23.

Quinn, J.C. 2013. Monumental power: 'Numidian Royal Architecture' in context. In J.R.W. Prag and J.C. Quinn (eds), *The Hellenistic West. Rethinking the Ancient Mediterranean.* Cambridge: Cambridge University Press, 179–215.

Rives, J.B. 1994. The priesthood of Apuleius. *American Journal of Philology* 15.2: 273–90.

Rizzo, M.A. and Di Vita-Évrard, G. (eds) 2015. *Antonino Di Vita. Scritti Africani, I–II.* Rome: 'L'Erma' di Bretschneider.

Tomasello, F. 2010. Tradizione locale e influssi esterni nell'architettura protoimperiale di Sabratha. *Bollettino di Archeologia Online* 1: 7–21.

Ward, P. 1970. *Sabratha. A Guide for Visitors.* Cambridge: The Oleander Press.

Ward-Perkins, J.B. 1982. Town planning in North Africa during the first two centuries of the Empire, with special reference to Lepcis and Sabratha: character and sources. In *150-Jahr-Feier Deutsches Archäologisches Institut Rom. Ansprachen und Vorträge (Rom, 4.–7. Dezember 1979).* Mainz: Philipp von Zabern, 29–46.

Wilson, A.I. 2001. Aerial photographs of Sabratha and Gharian. *Libyan Studies* 32: 107–13.

Zocchi, A. 2018. The periphery of Lepcis Magna: new data related to the ancient road network and land partition. *Libyan Studies* 49: 51–79.

Chapter 3

TRANSFORMING THE CITY: LARGE- AND SMALL-SCALE BUILDING ACTIVITIES AT LEPCIS MAGNA IN THE SEVERAN PERIOD

Niccolò Mugnai

The monumental enhancement of Lepcis Magna under the Severan dynasty is a subject that is almost inevitably touched upon in most handbooks of Roman history, archaeology, art and architecture. The grandiosity of this building programme and the outstanding archaeological remains it left are among the reasons why this site has always offered a unique experience to visitors, even in difficult times such as those of present-day Libya (Figs 3.1–2). As the birthplace of the emperor Septimius Severus, the city came to be at the centre of imperial attentions, as demonstrated by the award of the *ius Italicum* that was also bestowed on Carthage and Utica in the province of Africa Proconsularis. This status promotion probably took place at the time of the imperial family's visit to Lepcis Magna in 202–3 CE (on the date and controversies around this matter, see Birley 1999, 146–54; Cordovana 2007, 417–31, with references). Building activities, however, had started even before that date and

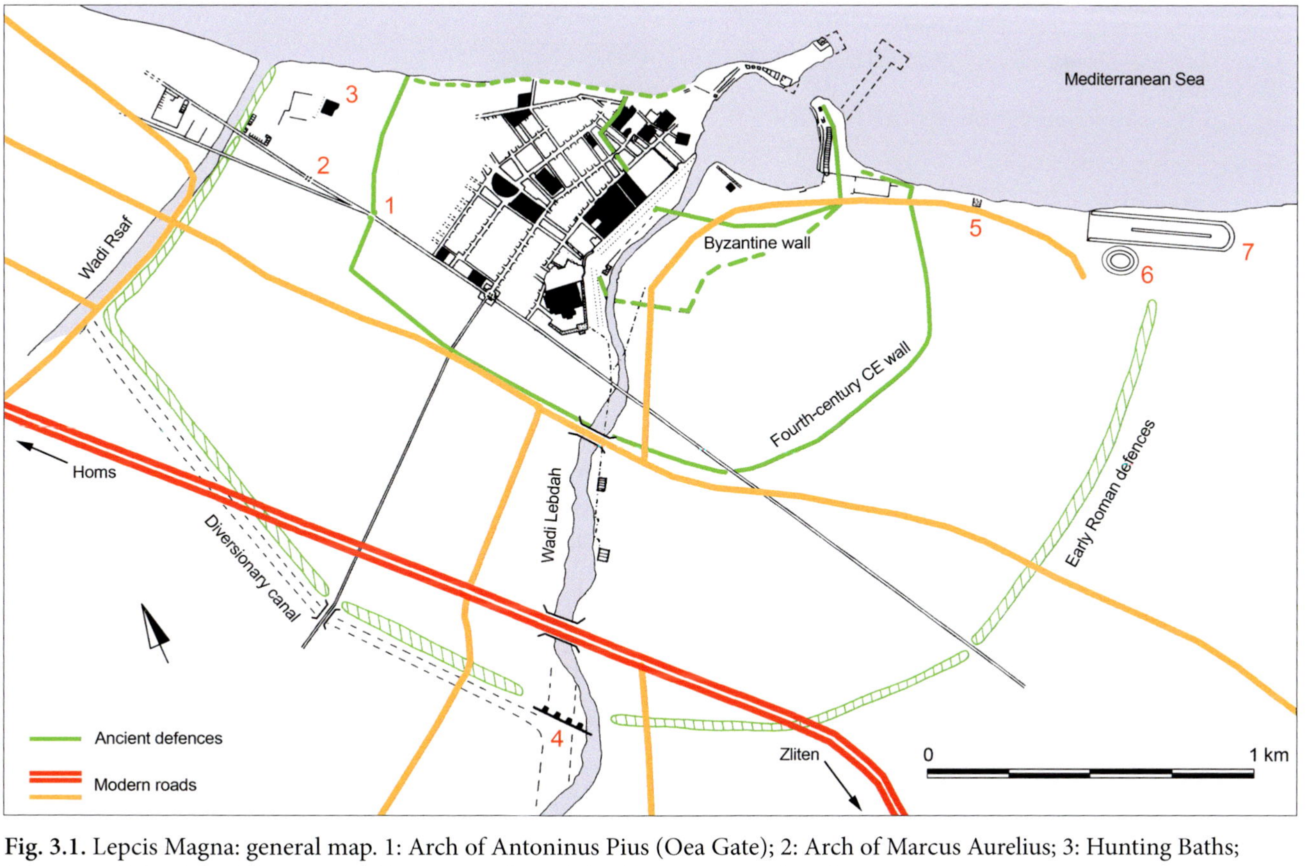

Fig. 3.1. Lepcis Magna: general map. 1: Arch of Antoninus Pius (Oea Gate); 2: Arch of Marcus Aurelius; 3: Hunting Baths; 4: Dam; 5: Villa of the Nile; 6: Amphitheatre; 7: Circus (after Kenrick 2009, fig. 31).

continued until the end of Caracalla's reign. Along with large-scale imperial constructions, a series of larger and smaller construction and restoration projects were carried out across the city, some of which have only been identified recently thanks to the progress of archaeological research.

This chapter aims to offer an up-to-date, critical review of the topic, taking into account the data provided by old and new studies on the architecture and urbanism of Severan-period Lepcis Magna, and addressing some of the issues that are still open to debate. The first section deals with the 'traditional' Severan buildings: the Severan Forum complex (piazza, temple, and basilica), the Colonnaded Street, the Great Nymphaeum and annexed piazza, and the Severan Tetrapylon. In the second section, the archaeological evidence and problems of interpretation about the reshaping of the city's harbour under the Severans are examined. The third section looks at the other buildings and renovations dating to this period, which complemented the imperial building projects and contributed to Lepcis Magna's embellishment. The analysis is based on the examination of the available archaeological datasets and on observations on the edifices' architectural features, sculptural and architectural ornamentation, building materials, and epigraphic apparatus. Hopefully this review will provide an account of the subject to be used as a starting point for future research.

An ambitious building programme: from the Severan Forum to the Tetrapylon

The core of the Severan building projects at Lepcis Magna is represented by the construction of a new forum complex in the sector of the city along the left bank of the Wadi Lebdah, the course of which had already been diverted probably at the start of the second century CE. This tripartite forum was composed of a large porticoed piazza (internal dimensions c. 100 × 60 m) with a temple on the south-west side and a civic basilica (c. 70 ×

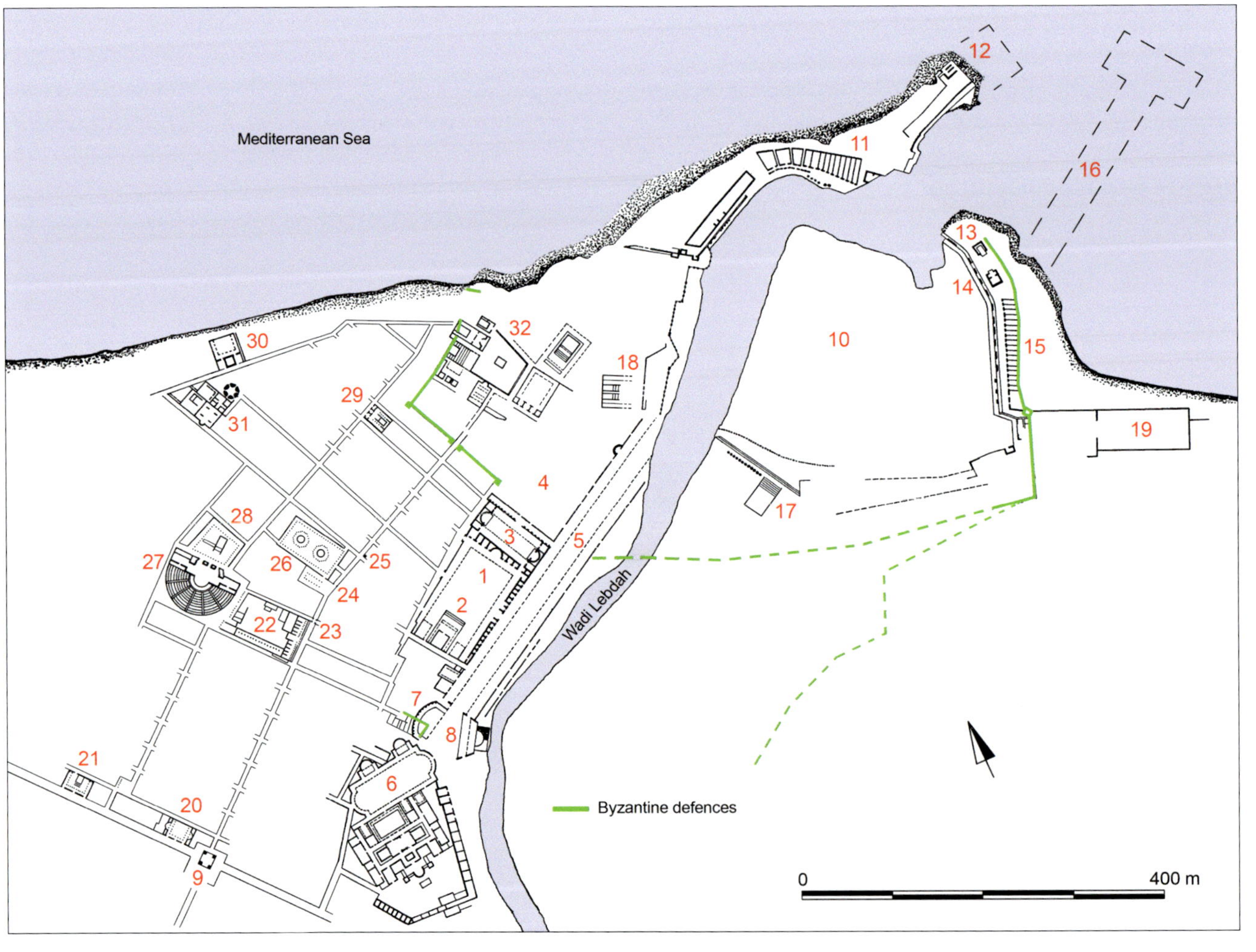

Fig. 3.2. Lepcis Magna: map of central area. 1: Severan Forum; 2: Severan Temple; 3: Severan Basilica; 4: Unfinished twin piazza (?); 5: Colonnaded Street; 6: Hadrianic Baths; 7: Exedra; 8: Great Nymphaeum; 9: Severan Tetrapylon; 10: Harbour; 11: North warehouses; 12: Lighthouse; 13: Signal-tower; 14: Doric temple; 15: East warehouses; 16: Submerged mole (?); 17: Temple of Jupiter Dolichenus; 18: Flavian Temple; 19: Eastern Baths; 20: *Schola*; 21: Anonymous Temple; 22: *Chalcidicum*; 23: Arch of Trajan; 24: Arch of Tiberius; 25: Nymphaeum of Hercules; 26: Market; 27: Theatre; 28: *Porticus post scaenam*; 29: Temple of Serapis; 30: Oriental sanctuary; 31: Unfinished baths; 32: Old Forum (after Kenrick 2009, fig. 32).

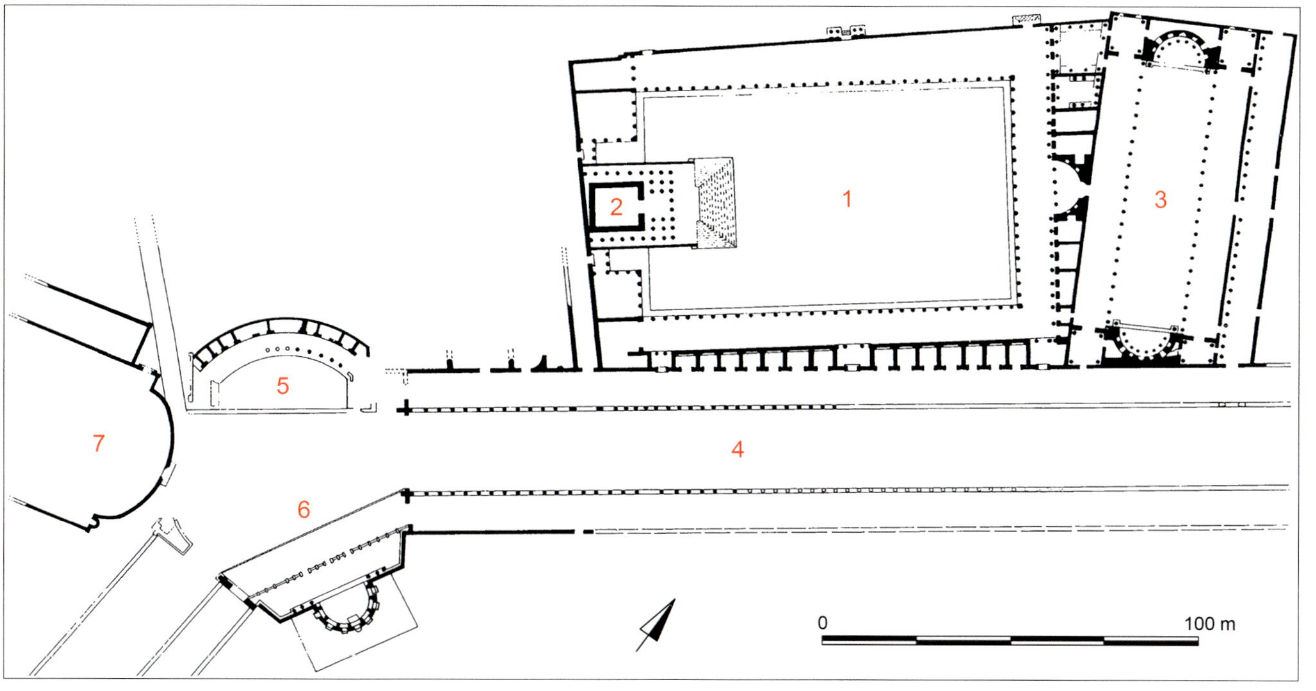

Fig. 3.3. Plan of the Severan Forum and annexed monuments. 1: Forum piazza; 2: Severan Temple; 3: Severan Basilica; 4: Colonnaded Street; 5: Exedra; 6: Great Nymphaeum; 7: Hadrianic Baths (*palaestra*) (after Ward-Perkins 1993, fig. 4).

36 m) attached to the north-east side (Fig. 3.3). According to Antonino Di Vita (1982), the project envisaged construction of a twin piazza to the north-east of the basilica, which was never implemented; this proposal has sparked debate in the scholarly community, but ultimately it remains difficult to prove one way or the other until further research is carried out on site.[1] The name *Forum Severianum / Forum Novum Severianum* is only found on later, fourth-century CE dedications that were set up in the piazza (*IRT2021* 562, 566). The text that was repeated on the three dedicatory inscriptions, placed on the exterior walls of the basilica's short sides and on the entablature of the nave's colonnade, records that work on the complex started under Septimius Severus (*coepit et ex maiore parte perfecit*) and was completed by Caracalla (*perfici curavit*) in 216 CE (*IRT2021* 427–28, 1018) (Fig. 3.4).[2] It is unanimously acknowledged that the emperors' names in the nominative in the text demonstrate that the construction of the forum was carried out through imperial agency and funding.[3] This is the only case of a large-scale building enterprise in this sector of the city where the emperors' sponsorship is confirmed directly by epigraphic evidence.

The architecture of the Severan Forum has been discussed extensively in the scholarship, from the work of the Italian teams that

Fig. 3.4. Severan Basilica, north side: remains of the dedicatory inscription *IRT2021* 427 (photo N. Mugnai).

[1] See some of the views in Ward-Perkins 1982; Jones 1989, 101; Mattingly 1995, 121; Mahler 2005, 7; Cordovana 2007, 343–44; Livadiotti and Rocco 2016, 142; Mazzilli 2016, 146–47.

[2] A block of black marble, probably meant to be used in the Severan Forum, bears a consignment note from the quarry to the praetorian prefect C. Fulvius Plautianus datable to between 202 and 205 CE; it shows that works in the forum must have been at an advanced stage by then (*IRT2021* 530; Ward-Perkins 1951b, 90–91, pl. 10.1; 1993, 100).

[3] On the recording of imperial agency and its phraseology in North African building inscriptions, see Saastamoinen 2010, 137–42.

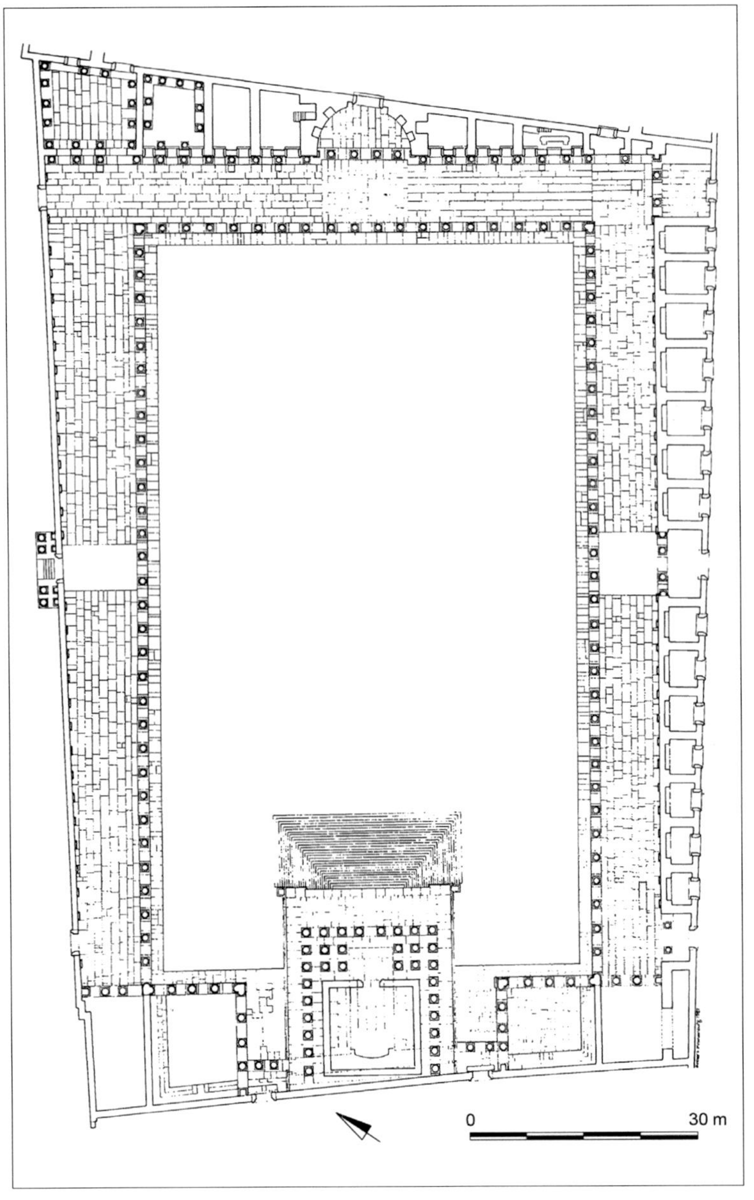

Fig. 3.5. Severan Forum, plan of the porticoed piazza (after Ward-Perkins 1993, fig. 5).

excavated the complex from the 1920s onwards (accounts can be found, among others, in Apollonj 1936; Bartoccini 1961; Mazzilli 2019; 2020) to the thorough studies by John Bryan Ward-Perkins (1948; 1951a; 1981, 384–91; 1993, 7–66). This is not the place to describe in detail all the features of these buildings, but it is worth commenting on certain architectural and decorative characteristics and issues of interpretation. The building project of the Severan Forum is an example of high-level Roman engineering and craftsmanship, starting with the planning of its layout that had to overcome several problems of the site's irregular topography. It is often described as a 'cosmopolitan' enterprise, where skilled architects and masons from the Italian Peninsula, the eastern Mediterranean, as well as local workforce collaborated to accomplish this grand project (Romanelli 1970, 105–8; Ward-Perkins 1981, 391; Livadiotti and Rocco 2016, 142).

This is also reflected in the range of materials that were used for construction and decorative purposes. Brown-yellowish and travertine-like varieties of limestone were sourced from newly opened quarries in the Ras el-Gadatza (Wadi es-Smara) district, c. 6.5 km south-west of Lepcis Magna (Bruno and Bianchi 2015a; 2015b, 3–4; Munzi *et al.* 2016, 79–80; Musso *et al.* 2018a, 114); these stones replaced the sandstone and the white limestone of Ras el-Hammam that were employed in buildings of the early imperial era.[4] At the same time, prestigious decorative stones were imported from abroad: pink Aswan granite from Egypt's eastern desert, Carystian green marble (*cipollino*) from Euboea, honey-white Pentelic marble from Attica, and white-greyish Proconnesian marble from the Sea of Marmara were some of the most commonly used materials.[5] The targeted use of brickwork, mortared rubble, and brick-stone masonry in specific sectors of the complex – such as the apses of the basilica, the exedra giving access to the basilica from the forum piazza, and the internal walls of the forum – indicates the presence of Italian masons who were familiar with materials and building technologies that are otherwise less frequently attested in Tripolitanian architecture (Ward-Perkins 1993, 90–91).[6] At the same time, there are various traces of afterthoughts and changes to the original design of these buildings, as well as evidence that the construction project had to be completed hastily to meet the deadline for its inauguration; this is shown, for instance, by the mouldings of the column bases of the basilica's nave, which were left roughed-out on the side facing the aisles (Ward-Perkins 1993, 101–3; Wilson 2007, 301; Kenrick 2009, 108–9).

The architectural grandiosity of the complex was further enhanced by the richness of its decoration. The inner walls of the forum precinct were veneered with coloured marbles; the piazza was paved with slabs of white Proconnesian marble, which have now almost entirely disappeared, and was surrounded on three sides by a portico with column shafts of Carystian green marble, matched with Attic bases and lotus-and-acanthus

[4] For a recent review of the evidence from the quarries of Ras el-Hammam, see De Simone and Tomasello 2014, with further references.

[5] Ward-Perkins 1993, 88–90; Bruno and Bianchi 2015b, 34–35; Musso *et al.* 2018a, 113–15. Greek signatures on architectural elements of Pentelic marble provide details about the workshops that produced them: *IRT2021* 799–803; Ward-Perkins 1951b; Bianchi *et al.* 2015.

[6] Scholarly attention has focused largely on local and imported decorative stones, while a comprehensive study of bricks and concrete masonry at Lepcis Magna (and in Tripolitania) is still lacking. For an outline of the brick types employed in some fountains of the city, see Tomasello 2005, 275–80.

Fig. 3.6. Severan Forum, view of the porticoed piazza from south-west (photo N. Mugnai).

capitals of Pentelic marble (Ward-Perkins 1993, 9–22; Kenrick 2008, 170–74) (Figs 3.5–6). Above the columns were set arcades surmounted by architraves, vegetal friezes, and cornices of white Gadatza limestone.[7] The decorative features and carving details of these elements reveal how the respective ateliers were influenced both by local traditions and by those that were transmitted by the workshops from the eastern Mediterranean that carved the marble components of the portico (Bianchi 2015) (Fig. 3.7).[8] The most striking feature of the portico's ornamentation is the series of roundels with heads of Gorgons (60 examples survive) and 'Nereids'/Sea Gorgons (13 examples), carved out of Proconnesian marble, which were inserted into the arcades (Floriani Squarciapino 1974, 65–90, pls 25–40). It is debated whether these roundels were purely decorative, or whether their iconography had a direct connection with the emperor's household and with Severus' self-legitimization to rule the Empire following the outcome of the civil wars. According to the latter hypothesis, the severed Gorgon (Medusa) heads should be linked to the act of decapitation of state enemies and the exposure of their heads in public places, with particular regard to the fate of Pescennius Niger and Clodius Albinus after they were defeated by Septimius Severus (Ensoli 1994, 734–50; Cordovana 2007, 377–94; 2012). To complete the decorative programme, the Forum piazza and annexed spaces were adorned with dedications and statues of emperors and notables, which were still set up here through to the fifth century CE.[9]

Equally outstanding was the ornament of the basilica (Figs 3.8–9), in particular the renowned 'peopled-scroll' pillars with vegetal motifs and human figures placed at the sides of the two internal apses. The marble pillars at the south-east end feature representations of the labours of Hercules, while those at the north-west end depict scenes of Dionysus/Liber Pater – the equivalents in the Roman pantheon of Lepcis Magna's patron gods, Milk'Ashtart and Shadrapa (Floriani Squarciapino 1974, 93–152, pls 45–75). The execution of these pillars was attributed for a long time to a 'School of Aphrodisias' on the basis of decorative comparanda from that city in the hinterland of Asia Minor, where also the marble would have been sourced (for instance, Floriani Squarciapino

[7] The hypothesis of a second storey above the ground-floor portico (Ensoli 1994, 719–27, figs 4, 6; Di Vita *et al.* 1999, 133) can now be rejected: see Livadiotti and Rocco 2016, 149–50, figs 20–22, and the previous reconstructions in Apollonj 1936, 6, pls 24–25; Bianchi Bandinelli *et al.* 1963, 94, fig. 240; Ward-Perkins 1993, 9–15, figs 6–7.

[8] On the hybridization of local and external carving styles in the architectural sculpture of Severan-period Lepcis Magna, see Walda 1985, 61–65, who uses the label 'Libyco-Roman art'.

[9] See Kleinwächter 2001, 252–53; Tantillo 2010, 176–78; Murer 2017, 100, with further bibliography.

Fig. 3.7. Severan Forum, decorated arcades of the portico (photo N. Mugnai).

1974, 137–52). Recent archaeometric analyses, however, have shown that the marble came from the quarries of Proconnesus and therefore the sculptors must have come from that area of the Mediterranean.[10] The choice of Proconnesian marble is consistent with the rest of the basilica's ornament, where this material is also used for the Attic bases, Corinthian capitals, and entablatures of the nave's colonnade (the column shafts are of Aswan granite: Ward-Perkins 1993, 57–62) (Fig. 3.10). Furthermore, the activity of specialized ateliers that were familiar with this type of marble and applied standardized blueprints has been recognized through the recent examination of the carving of the basilica's entablatures.[11] A peculiarity of the brickwork walls behind the 'peopled-scroll' pillars is the presence of decorative panels of limestone reticulate masonry, featuring pinecones, *kantharoi*, lozenges and other shapes, which were probably a 'factory mark' of Italian masons involved in the construction of the Severan Forum complex (Romanelli 1970, 53, pl. 33; Ward-Perkins 1993, 105; Wilson 2003) (Fig. 3.11). The panels are partly hidden by the pillars and the walls would have been veneered with marble, so it has been argued these were not meant to be seen, but they might have been part of a discarded decorative motif, perhaps marking the spots on the wall where coloured marble slabs were to be attached matching the shapes underneath.

The most prominent feature of the forum was the temple on the south-west side (c. 34/36 × 23 m). This has suffered greatly from spoliation; only the skeleton of the podium and the pyramidal staircase on the front survive *in situ*, but numerous elements of its architectural ornament have been found scattered around it and allow for a secure reconstruction of the elevation, although regrettably nothing survives of the pedimental sculpture (Floriani Squarciapino 1966, 99–104; Ward-Perkins 1993, 31–54) (Figs 3.12–14).[12] The temple was octastyle; the porch consisted of columns with monolithic shafts of Aswan granite, and Attic bases and Corinthian capitals of Proconnesian marble. To increase their heights even further, the columns rested on pedestals of Pentelic marble, some (not all) of which were elaborately carved with

[10] Bianchi *et al.* 2011; Pensabene 2006 proposes a workshop from Nicomedia. On archaeometric analyses of marbles from Lepcis Magna, see also Walda and Walker 1984; 1988; Musso *et al.* 2018b; Bruno *et al.* 2020.

[11] Ponti 2015; for an up-to-date assessment of the standardization of design and construction in the Severan Forum, see Toma 2018, 177–83.

[12] Architectural elements from the Severan Temple and Severan Forum complex, as well as from other buildings at Lepcis Magna, were shipped to Great Britain by H. Warrington and W.H. Smyth in 1816–17 and were incorporated in the folly at Virginia Water, Windsor Great Park: Lane 2004; 2012. Various sets of monolithic columns had already been sent to France by C. Le Maire between 1686 and 1708 and sold there: Romanelli 1925, 47–49, 58–60; Laronde 1995.

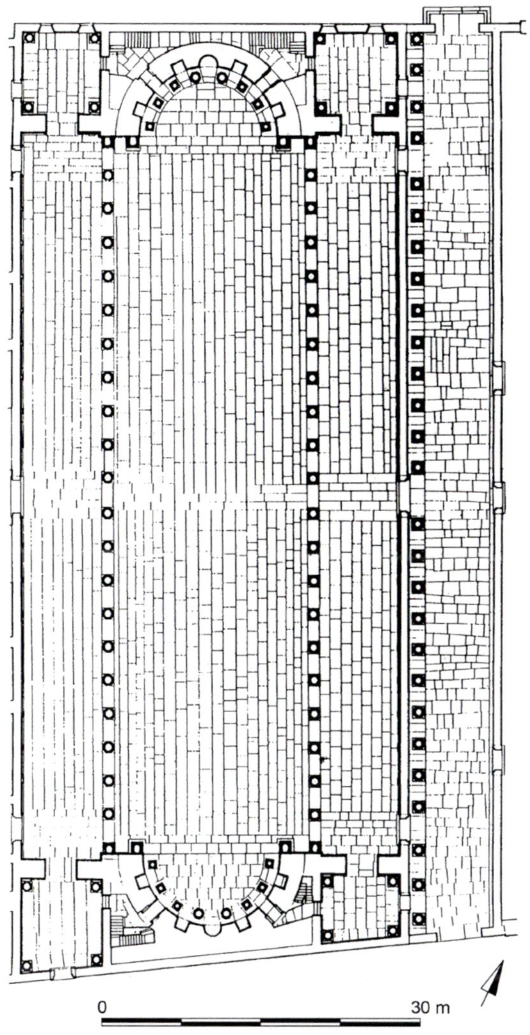

reliefs representing scenes of a Gigantomachy (Floriani Squarciapino 1974, 7–61, pls 1–21; Maderna 2005). The dedication of the temple is a debated subject, but most scholars connect it more or less directly to the deified Septimius Severus, the imperial family (*gens Septimia/divina domus*), and Concordia Augusta.[13] The theme of Augustan concord would create a link with the iconography of the Severan Tetrapylon (see below); the word [*c*]*onco*[*rdia* (?)] may appear on a fragment of the temple's dedicatory inscription, which must have run for a length of c. 17 m but of which very little survives (*IRT2021* 815). However, no photographs of this specific fragment exist and the other extant bits are too fragmentary to provide a meaningful restoration of the full text (cf. the different readings in Ward-Perkins 1993, 53 and Cordovana 2007, 375).

Another argument that has been used to support the identification of the Lepcitanian temple as a sanctuary dedicated to the Severan dynasty is its architectural similarity to the Temple of the *Gens Septimia* at Cuicul (Djémila, Algeria), which was erected at the expense of the local municipality in 229 CE (*AE* 1913, 120) (Fig. 3.15).[14] This may be plausible, but there are also notable differences between the two temples that are not always pointed out in the literature. At Cuicul,

Fig. 3.8. *(left)* Severan Basilica, plan (after Ward-Perkins 1993, fig. 24).

Fig. 3.9. *(below)* Severan Basilica, view over the north apse (photo R. Burns, Manar al-Athar).

[13]For instance: Bianchi Bandinelli *et al.* 1963, 95–97; Floriani Squarciapino 1966, 99–100; Brouquier-Reddé 1992, 97; Ward-Perkins 1993, 52–54; Ensoli 1994, 748–49; Di Vita *et al.* 1999, 136; Cordovana 2007, 366–77.

[14]On the architectural features and analogies between the two temples, see Pensabene 1992, 797; Gros 2011, 196; D'Alessio 2018, 104–5; Yegül and Favro 2019, 509, 532. But see also Gros 2008, 54–58 on the different layouts of the Severan piazza at Cuicul and the Severan Forum complex of Lepcis Magna.

Fig. 3.10. Severan Basilica, nave: ground-floor colonnade and entablature with part of the dedicatory inscription *IRT2021* 428 (photo N. Mugnai).

Fig. 3.11. Severan Basilica, north-west apse: 'peopled-scroll' pillar and *opus reticulatum* panels on the wall behind (photo N. Harris, Manar al-Athar).

the majestic staircase does not give access to the temple proper but to the portico that encloses it, while the temple itself is a rather small tetrastyle building (22.9 × 11.4 m) unlike the octastyle, peripteral *sine postico* Severan Temple of Lepcis Magna. The different settings of the two temples in the respective piazzas also created a different perception of their monumentality and relationship with the adjoining buildings (overall, the design of the Severan Forum of Lepcis Magna recalls the layout of the imperial fora in Rome). The smaller size of the Temple of the *Gens Septimia* at Cuicul could be explained by the more limited financial resources of the local *res publica*, but perhaps this may also have been perceived as more appropriate to the worship of the 'semi-divine' imperial household.[15]

The monumental size of the Severan Temple has led some scholars to propose an alternative identification with the 'excessively large' Temple of Hercules and Dionysus that was built by Septimius Severus and attracted Cassius Dio's criticism (*Historia Romana*, 76.16.3).[16] However, there is no evidence that Cassius Dio is talking about Lepcis Magna in this passage, and in all probability the city's patron gods Hercules/Milk'Ashtart and Dionysus (Liber Pater)/Shadrapa already had their respective temples in the city's Old Forum.[17] Another hypothesis that merits attention is that this temple could be a Capitolium, as was occasionally proposed in past scholarship (see Cordovana 2007, 367, 371, with references). We know that the Capitoline cult existed at Lepcis Magna, as attested by a late-second/early-third-century CE dedication on a votive tablet that was found (not *in situ*) in the Old Forum (*IRT2021* 209). The presence of a Capitolium on that piazza should probably be excluded, since the main forum temples were erected in the Augustan and early Julio-Claudian period, while none of the securely identified North African Capitolia predate the

[15] Even in the city of Rome it is hard to find evidence of octastyle temples dedicated to deified rulers. For instance, the Temple of Divus Julius, Temple of Divus Vespasian, and Temple of Antoninus and Faustina (and probably also the Temple of Divus Augustus, Temple of Divus Claudius, and Temple of Trajan and Plotina) were all hexastyle buildings.

[16] See Mattingly 1995, 121; Birley 1999, 151; Sanna 2005; Thomas 2007, 334, 363.

[17] Di Vita 1968; Di Vita *et al.* 1999, 75. On the architecture and dedication of the Old Forum temples, see Livadiotti and Rocco 2005; Masturzo 2005; Ricciardi 2005; Mugnai 2021, 103–7, with references.

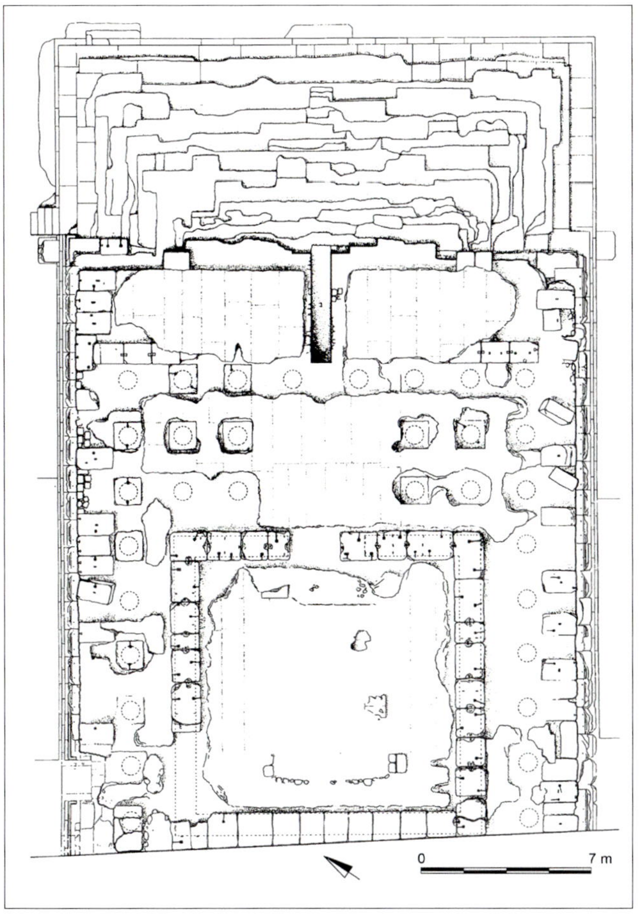

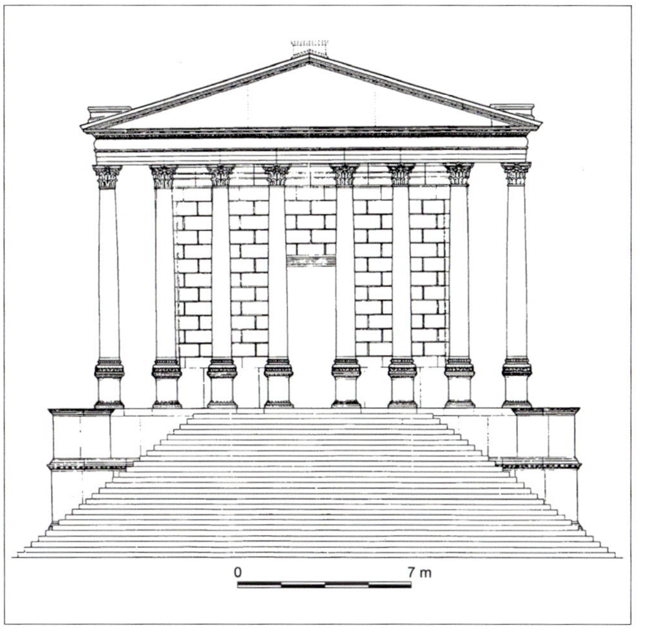

Fig. 3.12. *(left)* Severan Temple, plan of the extant remains (after Ward-Perkins 1993, fig. 14).

Fig. 3.13. *(above)* Severan Temple, restored elevation of the façade (after Ward-Perkins 1993, fig. 19).

Fig. 3.14. *(below)* Severan Temple, remains of the podium and scattered architectural elements (photo N. Mugnai).

second century CE (Gros 2011, 192–93; Quinn and Wilson 2013, 166–67).[18] It therefore seems that the Capitolium of Lepcis Magna should be sought outside the old civic centre, and indeed there is evidence of Capitolia in North Africa being built within newly created piazzas, as the examples of Thamugadi in Algeria (late Antonine or Severan period) and Volubilis in Morocco (dedicated in 217 CE) show. While the ideological meaning of the Gorgons' heads on the Severan Forum portico and the messages of military triumph that were conveyed by the Gigantomachy on the Severan Temple are seen as attributes of Septimius Severus and his dynasty, there

[18]The hypothesis that Temple A (Temple of Liber Pater) in the Old Forum could have been a Capitolium (Masturzo 2005, 128–31; Musso 2008, 182–89) does not rest on any solid evidence and has been challenged: see Di Vita 2005; Quinn and Wilson 2013, 154–55; Marmouri 2017; Mugnai 2021, 104–5, with references.

Fig. 3.15. Cuicul (Djémila, Algeria), Temple of the *Gens Septimia* (photo N. Mugnai).

is no reason to dismiss a connection between the imperial household and the Capitoline cult. In this regard, one could cite the example of the Capitolium of Thugga, Tunisia (dedicated under Marcus Aurelius and Lucius Verus in 166–69 CE), where the pediment of the temple was decorated with a sculptured relief depicting the apotheosis of Antoninus Pius (Aounallah and Golvin 2016, 175–81, figs 59–63). It is also known that Septimius Severus was often associated with Jupiter on coins and portraits as a way to strengthen his imperial rule through this powerful iconographic link.[19] Notably, the Capitoline triad appears on the smaller reliefs of the Severan Tetrapylon along with Lepcis Magna's patron gods, Liber Pater and Hercules; one of these reliefs depicts an enthroned Septimius Severus-Jupiter with Julia Domna-Juno standing to his right and a figure of Minerva on his left (La Rocca 1985; Cordovana 2007, 416–17, fig. 61; Faust 2013, 501–2, fig. 6).

With regard to the building process of the Severan Temple, it has been established that this was an integral part of the design of the Severan Forum from the start (Ward-Perkins 1993, 31, 52; *contra* Bartoccini 1961, 114), although it might have been completed at a late stage of the works and a series of structural changes occurred throughout its construction. The temple was initially meant to be c. 4 m shorter, as revealed by various details of the masonry in the portion of the pronaos between the front row of columns and the podium staircase (Ward-Perkins 1993, 33–34). At the same time, perhaps more speculatively, it has been argued that the two sets of tall Aswan granite columns decorating the central part of the basilica's apses might have been originally intended for use in the internal column rows of the Severan Temple's porch (Ward-Perkins 1993, 52–53; Kenrick 2009, 105–7). It is also notable that the pyramidal staircase on the front of the temple incorporates some recycled fragments of entablatures and other decorations, some of which would have been hidden by the marble veneer. These pieces are interpreted as rejects from other parts of the forum complex (Ward-Perkins 1993, 39), but a new detailed survey of the building could reveal whether any of these may actually belong to small repairs to the temple in later periods (before the Byzantine era). Severan-period inscribed bases were recycled for new dedications in the piazza, so it is plausible that some restoration of these edifices took place (Pentiricci 2010, 149–50; Tantillo 2010, 176–78).

The construction of the Severan Forum complex was complemented by the erection of an equally impressive Colonnaded Street (width of carriageway: 20.5 m; total width including lateral porticoes: 42.5 m), which ran for c. 400 m from the south-west edge of the harbour basin to the piazza where the Great Nymphaeum and Severan Exedra are located (Ward-Perkins 1993, 67–77) (Fig. 3.16); here, after a change of direction, it continued southwards to intersect the so-called '*decumanus maximus*' (also known as the 'Alexandria-Carthage road').[20] Scholars have pointed out frequently the design analogies with the colonnaded avenues of the East, making Lepcis Magna's thoroughfare a classic example of 'connective architecture' despite the limited spread of this architectural feature in the western Mediterranean (MacDonald 1986, 33–51; Gros 2011, 111–13; Yegül and Favro 2019, 531–32). It should be noted that no dedicatory inscriptions were recovered from the street and annexed monuments; however, their architectural – and ideological – relationship to the Severan Forum is beyond question. The lack of epigraphic evidence does not allow us to understand whether this construction enterprise was carried out entirely through imperial funds, as conventionally claimed on the basis of the dedication of the Severan Basilica/Forum (for instance: Ward-Perkins 1993, 104; Mahler 2005, 16–17; Wilson 2007, 297), or whether the city's elites and municipality could have contributed to it at least to some extent (as suggested in Jouffroy 1986, 281; Mattingly 1995, 121–22).

[19] *RIC* V, 31, no. 67; 356, nos 1–2; 360–61, nos 18, 25; Finocchi 2015, 132–34, with references. See also the iconography of Septimius Severus as Jupiter on a relief from Cyrene: Strong 1973; Cordovana 2007, 385–86, with bibliography.

[20] It is debated whether the southern stretch of the Colonnaded Street was already monumentalized in the pre-Severan period, perhaps in relation to the dedication of the Hadrianic Baths (137 CE): see Ward-Perkins 1951a, 298, note 27; Di Vita 1975, 24–26; Mahler 2005, 9–10, 13; Mazzilli 2016, 147, 250; Aiosa 2020, 296.

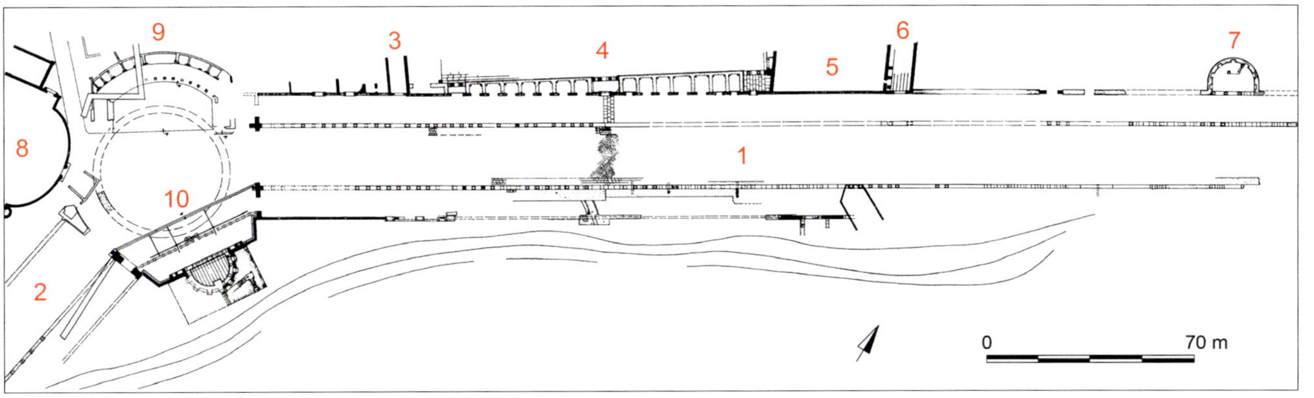

Fig. 3.16. Plan of the Colonnaded Street and annexed monuments. 1: North-west stretch; 2: South-east stretch; 3: South-east cross-street; 4: Severan Forum; 5: Severan Basilica; 6: North-east cross-street; 7: Small Nymphaeum; 8: Hadrianic Baths (*palaestra*); 9: Exedra; 10: Great Nymphaeum (after Ward-Perkins 1993, fig. 39).

Excavations in the Colonnaded Street in the 1950s and 1980–90s have revealed traces of the drainage system and of the massive mortared rubble foundations of the portico on the south-east flank (Bartoccini 1961, 118–19; Ward-Perkins 1993, 71; Ricciardi 2016), but the results of these works are still awaiting a full publication. The abundance of architectural fragments lying on the ground has enabled reconstruction of the layout of the porticoes that flanked the street on both sides (Figs 3.17–18). The colonnade recalled the portico of the Severan Forum with its monolithic shafts of Carystian green marble and the presence of arcades on top; like the porch of the Severan Temple, the height of the columns was increased through insertion of pedestals at the bottom. Attic bases and Corinthian capitals of Proconnesian marble decorated the north-east (and probably the southernmost) stretch of the street, while in the sector facing the Severan Forum these were replaced with bases and lotus-and-acanthus capitals of Pentelic marble, thus giving the portico a more elaborate appearance. The local Gadatza limestone was employed for the arcades and entablatures; these latter display a conspicuous Doric frieze that matches the one on the exterior of the Severan Forum's enclosure. This was a tribute to the local Lepcitanian taste, as attested by the continuity of use of Doric entablatures – often mixed with Ionic and Corinthian or Corinthianizing colonnades – in public and funerary architecture from the early imperial period

Fig. 3.17. *(above)* Colonnaded Street, fragments of Carystian green marble shafts and limestone Doric friezes (photo N. Mugnai).

Fig. 3.18. *(left)* Colonnaded Street, restored elevation of the section at the south-west edge of the Severan Forum (after Ward-Perkins 1993, fig. 37).

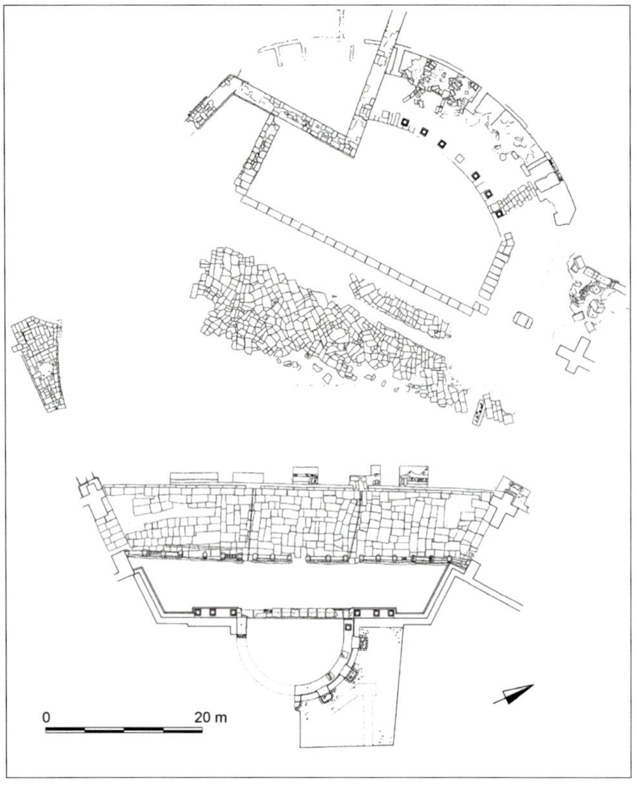

Fig. 3.19. Great Nymphaeum and Severan Exedra, plan of the extant remains (after Ward-Perkins 1993, fig. 40).

onwards.[21] Some details of the Colonnaded Street's construction project are debated; in his architectural survey, Claudio Parisi Presicce (1994) argued that the layout of the avenue was not part of the original design of the Severan Forum complex and must have been conceived at a later stage, probably after the death of Septimius Severus (*contra* Ward-Perkins 1993, 74–75, 104–7). A recent reassessment of the subject, however, has reinforced the idea of unity of the entire building project, according to which the Forum and the monumental avenue were intended as a single architectural/urban feature (Mahler 2005, 7–8).

Some 50 m to the south-west of the Severan Forum enclosure, the Colonnaded Street reached a junction that was marked on the opposite side by the eastern exedra of the *palaestra* of the Hadrianic Baths. According to Ward-Perkins (1993, 79, 105), this space was meant to take the shape of a circular piazza in the late Antonine period, but this layout was abandoned in favour of a trapezoidal piazza at the time of the Severan construction projects.[22] Two monuments were erected here to give the area a monumental façade: the Great Nymphaeum on the south-east side, and the Severan Exedra on the north-west side (Fig. 3.19).[23] The latter monument is poorly preserved and has never been studied in detail; it features a curvilinear structure faced by a portico with

Fig. 3.20. Great Nymphaeum, view from south-west (photo N. Mugnai).

[21] See von Hesberg 2005 (Severan-period Doric order) and Mahler 2006, 105–6, 231–34, nos 789–821 F, pls 102–5 (pre-Severan examples). Doric elements and mixed architectural orders spread to the hinterland and pre-desert of Tripolitania, where they were employed until later Roman times and beyond – a notable example is Tomb North A in the necropolis of Ghirza: Brogan and Smith 1984, 121–33, 208; Masturzo 2023, 18–20; Mugnai 2022, 275.

[22] It is difficult to understand whether the circular piazza was conceived as such in the late Antonine era, or whether it was an initial (discarded) design of the Severan-period project: see the remarks in Mazzilli 2016, 147–48.

[23] Another large fountain (diameter of basin 14.4 m), misleadingly labelled the 'Small Nymphaeum', was built at the opposite end of the Colonnaded Street between the Basilica and the harbour as a pendant to the Great Nymphaeum. This structure was incorporated into a church in the Byzantine period: Ward-Perkins and Goodchild 1953, 82; Ward-Perkins 1993, 76–77; Sandoz 2004, 1801–6; Lamare 2019, 346–47.

arcades on top, but this was altered in the Byzantine era. Caputo (1965) argued that it could have been a *Chalcidicum* with *stibadion*, similar to the one located on the city's '*cardo maximus*' (see below), but this does not rest on any evidence. Similarly, the suggestion that the structure was completed hurriedly at a late stage of the Severan works (Ward-Perkins 1993, 107) cannot be proved until further research is carried out.

The Great Nymphaeum on the opposite side of the piazza is better preserved and its architectural layout can be commented on with more confidence (Fig. 3.20).[24] It consists of a two-storey façade, c. 36 m in length, featuring a central hemicycle with a diameter of 17.4 m (Ward-Perkins 1993, 79–87; Lamare 2019, 343–46). The core of the structure was built with mortared rubble with levelling courses of bricks, framed on the front and sides by ashlar masonry. The walls would have been lavishly veneered with coloured marbles; the Corinthian columns of the ground-floor order had shafts of Carystian green marble, those of the upper storey were made of Aswan pink granite, which recalled closely the colour scheme of the Severan Forum. The hemicycle was provided with 14 niches (seven on each storey) that would have hosted as many statues. A series of sculptures of Lepcitanian notables and deities was recovered around the area of the Nymphaeum, but their original setting is uncertain and some of them may not belong to this building at all (Finocchi 2015, 83–138, nos 1–14, figs 64–92; Lamare 2019, 345–46). While it is commonly believed that statues of the imperial family would have been displayed in the Nymphaeum (Ward-Perkins 1993, 86; Wilson 2007, 297; Finocchi 2015, 130–37), the absence of any such finds should probably be taken into account.

With regard to the date of the building, the matrix of a lead pipe carrying the names of Septimius Severus, Geta and Caracalla was discovered *in situ* (*IRT2021* 398a), demonstrating that the construction was at a well-advanced stage by 211 CE at the latest, when Geta was murdered and his name suffered the *damnatio memoriae*. A base with a dedication to Septimia Polla, the aunt of Septimius Severus, was found in front of the Nymphaeum (*IRT2021* 607), but this may have been set up in the late Antonine period, thus predating the construction of the building. A third inscribed text on a fragmentary base records the donation of 16 statues by a local notable, Q. Furius Cerealis, and may date to the end of the second or early third century CE (*IRT2021* 706); the exact provenance of the base is not clear, but attempts have been made to connect this benefaction to the sculptural programme of the Nymphaeum and the Severan Exedra (Finocchi 2015, 118; Lamare 2019, 345). Should this connection be accepted, it would suggest that Lepcitanian sponsors were involved in this building enterprise along with the imperial household. A final note concerns the Nymphaeum's design and its visual impact. The superimposed orders of the façade are rightly likened to theatre scene buildings, and those of the Sabratha and Lepcis Magna theatres would have been obvious models. These, in turn, are often cited as references for the design of the *Septizodium* in Rome (dedicated in 203 CE), which served as a monumental façade of the imperial residence on the Palatine, 'greeting' those who entered the city from the Via Appia. A passage of the *Historia Augusta* (*Septimius Severus*, 24.3) claims that the *Septizodium* was meant to look familiar to travellers coming from North Africa; whether this is true or not, it does suggest some connection between Septimius Severus' building programmes in Rome and Tripolitania (Thomas 2007, 329–44, 363–64). The Great Nymphaeum of Lepcis Magna bore a resemblance both to the North African theatres and to the *Septizodium* in Rome, and its prominent position in the piazza served to 'greet' those who reached this central urban intersection when walking along the Colonnaded Street.[25]

The last monument to be discussed is the Severan Tetrapylon (four-way arch) located at the intersection of the *cardo* and *decumanus maximus* (Fig. 3.21). Its architectural and decorative features have been debated at length, but some issues remain unresolved; a new monographic study is in preparation (Di Vita *et al.* forthcoming b), which will discuss the construction features of the monument, its architectural and sculptural decoration, and the complex history of its restoration. Here it will suffice to point out the main characteristics and problems of this edifice. The date of construction is uncertain; some scholars argue that the arch was dedicated, perhaps only partly finished, by the time of Septimius Severus' visit to Lepcis Magna in 202–3 CE (Ward-Perkins 1948, 72; Cordovana 2007, 417–20; Mazzilli 2016, 254), while others claim that the hairstyle of certain figures and the absence of Plautianus and Plautilla from the reliefs would point to a later date around 205–9 CE (Strocka 1972, 169–70; Ghedini 1984a, 89–90; Mahler 2005, 10–11; Faust 2013, 493–94). Fragments of a monumental inscription (*IRT2021* 1009) bearing the words *divo* and *divae*, referring to a deified emperor and empress, were recovered in the so-called '*schola*' next to the Tetrapylon and were attributed to the arch (Ioppolo 1968; Bacchielli 1992, 765). These can now be seen reassembled on the north-west side of the monument (Fig. 3.22), but their association with it has been called into question, especially since the putative reference to the deification of Julia Domna would push

[24] Some test pits were opened in the Nymphaeum in the early 2000s to investigate the building's construction and later phases, but only preliminary reports have been published to date: Sandoz 2004, 1792–801; 2006, 403–7.

[25] The Great Nymphaeum is not included in the (small) group of *septizodia* attested by epigraphic evidence at Lambaesis (Algeria) and Cincari (Tunisia), but the presence of seven niches on each storey of the hemicycle may hint to a similar function. On the North African *septizodia* see Lamare 2019, 273–85, with bibliography.

the date of this text after 217–18 CE (Di Vita 1975, 3–11; Cordovana 2007, 409). On balance, one could argue that a dedication to the deified Septimius Severus and his wife might have been added on the Tetrapylon after its construction, but in the absence of any supporting evidence this can only remain a matter of speculation.

Honorific arches in the provinces were usually set up at the expense of the local city councils, and it is believed that the same applies to the Tetrapylon of Lepcis Magna (Wilson 2007, 295–97; Mazzilli 2016, 254; Musso *et al.* 2018a, 110–11). It is unquestionable, however, that the architectural and sculptural decoration was executed by the same workshops that were involved in the Severan buildings along the Wadi Lebdah. This is evidenced by the stylistic similarities, such as the carving of the Corinthian capitals and the vegetal scrolls of the corner pilasters that recall closely the

Fig. 3.21. *(right)* Severan Tetrapylon, view from south-west with *cardo maximus* in the background (photo N. Mugnai).

Fig. 3.22. *(below)* Severan Tetrapylon, detail of north-west side with controversial inscription *IRT2021* 1009 (photo N. Mugnai).

ornamentation of the Severan Basilica (Ward-Perkins 1948, 72–74; Musso *et al.* 2018a, 111–12), as well as by the combined use of Pentelic and Proconnesian marble.[26] A further connection between the arch and these edifices is to be sought in the position of the Tetrapylon at this road intersection. With its stepped base (width of each side c. 15.7 m), the arch made movement of wheeled traffic here almost impossible, diverting vehicles southwards on the *decumanus* to the junction with the southern stretch of the Colonnaded Street, from which they would have followed a route that led them to pass by the Great Nymphaeum, Severan Exedra, and Severan Forum complex (Mahler 2005, 10–14; Mazzilli 2016, 148–50; Aiosa 2020, 296). Di Vita (1975; 1977) argued that a previous (Trajanic?) arch stood in the spot that was occupied by the Severan Tetrapylon, but this suggestion was rejected by Stucchi (1976, 488–89; 1981) and the subject is still debated today.[27] The hypothesis rests mostly on the features of the limestone blocks that form the core of the arch underneath the marble veneer; this stone was traditionally believed to belong to the Ras el-Hammam variety, while more recently it has been suggested that it could be Severan-period Gadatza limestone instead (Bruno and Bianchi 2015a, 41; Mazzilli 2016, 254). Ultimately, the matter remains difficult to assess until a comprehensive study of the monument is published.

The current aspect of the Tetrapylon is the result of a long restoration process that was concluded in 2004, incorporating a large number of architectural and sculptural elements that were found in the area.[28] The most prominent decorative feature is represented by the four friezes that adorn the respective sides of the attic, in addition to the smaller reliefs on the gateposts. The friezes depict the Severan family, triumphal processions, gods of the Roman and Lepcitanian pantheon, battle scenes, and images connected to the celebration of pietas, *virtus*, and *concordia*.[29] However, there are some oddities in the layout of the monument – a 'very over-decorated structure, of interest more for the content and quality of its sculpture than for its architectural design' (Ward-Perkins 1981, 386). For instance, while the (re)positioning of the eight broken pediments on top of the projecting columns on each side seems secure, these compromise a full visibility of the sculptured friezes behind them (Kenrick 2009, 94–95). Because of its exuberant ornamentation, the Severan Tetrapylon is often regarded as a unique monument, but one should note that simple and four-way arches were a common feature of Lepcis Magna's cityscape – from the Arches of Tiberius (35–36 CE: *IRT2021* 330–31) and Arch of Trajan (109–10 CE: *IRT2021* 353, 523, 537) on the *cardo*, to the Arch of Antoninus Pius (the so-called 'Oea Gate') and Arch of Marcus Aurelius (173–74 CE: *IRT2021* 1011) on the *decumanus* – and therefore the builders of the Severan monument kept developing a well-known architectural type.[30]

Reshaping the harbour: architectural development and open questions

It is commonly believed that the Severan building projects discussed above were complemented by the remodelling and monumentalization of the city's harbour, which became one of the largest ports in the ancient Mediterranean.[31] The harbour was excavated mainly in the 1920s and 1950s by Renato Bartoccini (1958), who brought to light the structures one can see today; in more recent years, further accounts have been published especially on the port's (meagre) epigraphic dossier (Rosamilia 2021) and its architectural and topographic features (Feuser 2020, 188–228). One should observe that identification of a Severan-period redevelopment does not rest on any data from archaeological stratigraphy or inscriptions, but mostly on the types of building materials and stone masonry that were employed in the constructions in this area (Bartoccini 1958, 11; Ward-Perkins 1948, 65–66). In their study of Lepcis Magna's quarries, Bruno and Bianchi (2015a, 40; 2015b, 4) list the harbour buildings among those in the city that were built with Gadatza limestone, which is a strong clue in support of a date in the Severan era; a future, targeted survey of the buildings in the port will hopefully provide more information in this regard. For the time being, it seems safe to claim that building activities took place in the harbour to enhance its appearance under the Severans, but whether these involved a restructuring of the entire basin remains open to question.[32] It is also

[26] On the occurrence of Pentelic and Proconnesian marble in public buildings in Tripolitania before and during the Severan period, see Pensabene 2001.

[27] For instance, see the different views in Mahler 2005, 10–11; Cordovana 2007, 406–7; Mazzilli 2016, 148–49.

[28] On the history of excavations and the restoration of the Tetrapylon, see in particular Bartoccini 1931; Bacchielli 1992; Di Vita 2003; 2006. For a synthetic description of the monument, see also Mühlenbrock 2003, 212–16.

[29] On these reliefs see especially Ward-Perkins 1948, 75–80; Strocka 1972; Ghedini 1984a, 57–110; 1984b; Musso 1995, 341–42; Fähndrich 2005; Cordovana 2007, 409–32; Newby 2007, 206–11; Faust 2013.

[30] On the architecture and ideological function of Lepcis Magna's arches, see Romanelli 1940; Pensabene 2003; Mühlenbrock 2003, 205–16; Mazzilli 2016, 123–50, 249–56; Aiosa 2020; Mugnai 2021, 93–98.

[31] Di Vita *et al.* 1999, 112; Laronde and Degeorge 2005, 131; Cordovana 2007, 338; Kenrick 2009, 126.

[32] A first construction phase of the harbour in the Neronian period is confirmed by epigraphic and archaeological evidence from the west quay: *IRT2021* 341; Bartoccini 1958, 27–52; Feuser 2020, 193–204; Mugnai 2021, 100. Excavations around the Flavian Temple have also revealed traces of an earlier paving underneath the Severan-period street/quay level: Fiandra and Dolciotti 2010, 29–31, figs 7–11, with references. The diversion of the Wadi Lebdah through the construction of a dam seems to date to the late first or early second century CE (Pucci *et al.* 2011, 182–83), and it is entirely plausible that this determined some changes to the layout of the harbour before the Severan era.

Fig. 3.23. Harbour, signal-tower on the east mole and remains of lighthouse on the north mole in the background (photo N. Mugnai).

impossible to say whether these constructions were carried out through imperial funding or were paid for by the local city council, or both.

It is reasonable to suppose that any substantial modifications to the harbour should have been at a well-advanced stage of completion by the time work on the Severan Forum, Colonnaded Street, and annexed edifices started, in order for the port infrastructures to handle the enormous quantities of imported stone that were being shipped to Lepcis Magna for those building projects (Di Vita *et al.* 1999, 112; Mahler 2005, 10; Feuser 2020, 206). As to the basin layout, the existence of an extension to the harbour's east mole projecting into the sea is another debated subject. A submerged structure was identified by André Laronde (1988, 343–50) who interpreted it as a T-shaped jetty, c. 250 m long and 50 m wide. It is claimed that this underwater survey recorded *in situ* limestone blocks belonging to the foundations of this structure and scattered marble and granite architectural elements of uncertain provenance, which are comparable to those used in the Severan Forum complex. This putative jetty was considered to be contemporary to the Severan harbour (Laronde and Degeorge 2005, 127–30, figs 96–97). In contrast, a subsequent reassessment has concluded that all these submerged materials should be interpreted as spolia belonging to a Late Antique, c. fourth- to sixth-century CE, breakwater (Beltrame 2012, 320–25). The matter is not easy to resolve until a more detailed investigation of this structure is undertaken and a precise plan of the remains is drawn (Mahler 2005, 10; Stone 2016, 132–33).[33] With regard to the marble and granite elements, it would be useful to determine whether these are spolia or flawed pieces that were rejected during construction or even upon arrival in the port.

Most of the space on the harbour's west, north, and east sides was occupied, rather unsurprisingly, by warehouses. The most extensive remains are on the east side, and these have allowed reconstruction of two-storey porticoed buildings decorated with simple Tuscan columns (Bartoccini 1958, 116–22, figs 23–27, pls 60–65). At the extremity of the harbour's northern end one can see what is left of a lighthouse (width of square base: c. 21 m), while a smaller signal-tower (width c. 9.9 m) or similar building is close to the tip of the east mole (Fig. 3.23). The depiction of a (generic) three-storey lighthouse can be discerned in the background of a relief from the Severan Tetrapylon showing a procession with the imperial quadriga, and it is believable that this was meant to represent the lighthouse of Lepcis Magna (Bartoccini 1958, 63; Tuck 2008, 338–39; Kenrick 2009, 128). The fact that this edifice is shown in association with Septimius Severus and his family may be seen as a further hint to its construction, or renovation, in this period.

In addition to the utilitarian structures, the harbour was provided with sacred buildings as well. A Doric,

[33] See also the remarks in Feuser 2020, 206–7, note 923. The hypothesis by Salza Prina Ricotti (1972–73, 95–103) that Lepcis Magna's harbour had silted shortly after the time of Septimius Severus is now largely dismissed: Laronde 1994; Cordovana 2007, 338–40; Pucci *et al.* 2011, 182–83; Mazzilli 2016, 143–44; Rosamilia 2021, 283–85.

prostyle *in antis* temple (13 × 10.4 m) is located on the east mole facing the signal-tower (Bartoccini 1958, 123–25; Feuser 2020, 214–16) (Fig. 3.24). Ward-Perkins (1948, 65, fig. 9) pointed out the similarity between the ashlar masonry of this building and that of the outer wall of the Severan Forum. The 'old-fashioned' Doric order of the temple is consistent with the use of Doric entablatures on the forum complex wall and on the porticoes of the Colonnaded Street (von Hesberg 2005, 47–49, fig. 1). The dedication of the temple is regrettably unknown. Bartoccini (1958, 124) argued that traces for the lodging of three statues inside the *cella* could suggest worship of the Tyche of Lepcis Magna along with Hercules and Liber Pater, while von Hesberg (2005, 49) envisaged a potential relationship between the sculpted ribboned wreath in the middle of the temple's pediment and the imperial cult, but both suggestions are purely conjectural (see also Brouquier-Reddé 1992, 125 for additional proposals, including the unlikely hypothesis of a Capitolium).

On the south side of the basin, a majestic flight of 20 steps (width c. 25 m) gave access to a temple, the superstructure of which is poorly preserved and cannot be reconstructed (Bartoccini 1958, 94–95) (Fig. 3.25). An altar was recovered in front of it, bearing a dedication by a centurion to Jupiter Dolichenus on the occasion of the Severan emperors' return to their city, probably corresponding to the imperial visit to Lepcis Magna in 202–3 CE (*IRT2021* 292; see also Schmid, Chapter 8). The text confirms the dedication of the temple to this god but uncertainties remain as to the date of the building, since a fragmentary architrave with a bilingual, Latin and neo-Punic, inscription dedicated to Domitian was also recovered here (*IRT2021* 349; *IPT* 9). Some scholars have argued for a Domitianic date (Bartoccini 1958, 95; Dolciotti *et al.* 2012, 271–72), which would be further supported by the architectural analogies between this edifice and the Flavian Temple on the west side of the harbour erected in 93–94 CE (*IRT2021* 348). Others have preferred to interpret it as a Severan-period construction contemporary with the redevelopment of the harbour, hinting at a connection between the Syrian god Jupiter Dolichenus and the empress Julia Domna (Salza Prina Ricotti 1972–73, 88; Kenrick 2009, 130; Pentiricci 2010, 153).

Fig. 3.24. *(left)* Harbour, Doric temple on the east mole and warehouses in the background (photo P. Kenrick).

Fig. 3.25. *(below)* Harbour, staircase of the Temple of Jupiter Dolichenus (photo N. Mugnai).

Other construction and restoration activities in the city

In addition to the large imperial (and non-imperial) building projects along the Wadi Lebdah, on the *decumanus maximus*, and in the harbour basin, the progress of archaeological research at Lepcis Magna in recent years has allowed recognition of other construction and restoration activities that took place in the city during the Severan period. In most cases these were funded by individuals or by the city council, although epigraphic evidence is not abundant. These activities varied considerably in scale – from small building and restoration works, to the erection of larger edifices. Many of these can be interpreted as a further development of the extensive renovations that had already transformed Lepcis Magna's cityscape in the Antonine era, in particular through the introduction of marble ornamentation in public architecture and the embracing of Empire-wide decorative fashions.[34] Furthermore, dedications and statues of the emperors were set up by the city council and by Lepcitanian notables as homages to the Severan family; these are to be found in the main public buildings, including those that were erected in this period and pre-existing ones (Wilson 2007, 301–7, table 14.1). Wealthy individuals also set up personal dedications, portraits, and statues of gods in key areas of the city, attesting to the continuity of private euergetism as part of this programme of urban embellishment.[35]

New excavations in the so-called 'Anonymous Temple' on the *decumanus maximus*, c. 165 m north-west of the Severan Tetrapylon, have provided crucial information on the architecture and chronology of this sanctuary (Tomasello 2011). The building consists of a rectangular enclosure (28.6/29.2 × 22.7/22.8 m) with three arched entrances opening onto the street; the small temple inside the precinct sits on a stepped podium (12.1 × 6.8/7.3 m) and is surrounded on three sides by a colonnaded portico (Fig. 3.26). The stratigraphy and the materials recovered from a series of test pits indicate a construction date of this complex between the end of the second and the early third century CE (Tomasello 2011, 121–78, figs 52–61, pls 1–15). This proposed chronology is matched by the

Fig. 3.27. Anonymous Temple, one of the Asiatic Corinthian capitals from the portico (photo N. Mugnai).

Fig. 3.26. Anonymous Temple, general view from south-west (photo N. Mugnai).

[34] For an overview, see Pensabene 2001; Bianchi 2009; Bruno and Bianchi 2015b, 31–38; Mugnai 2021, 96–97, 109–12.

[35] For an outline of these activities, see Murer 2017, 91–110. A significant group of Severan-period dedications and statues was recovered in the Temple of Serapis, a building that had been erected around the mid-second century CE on a secondary *cardo* to the west of the Old Forum: Di Vita *et al.* 2003; forthcoming a; Kreikenbom 2005.

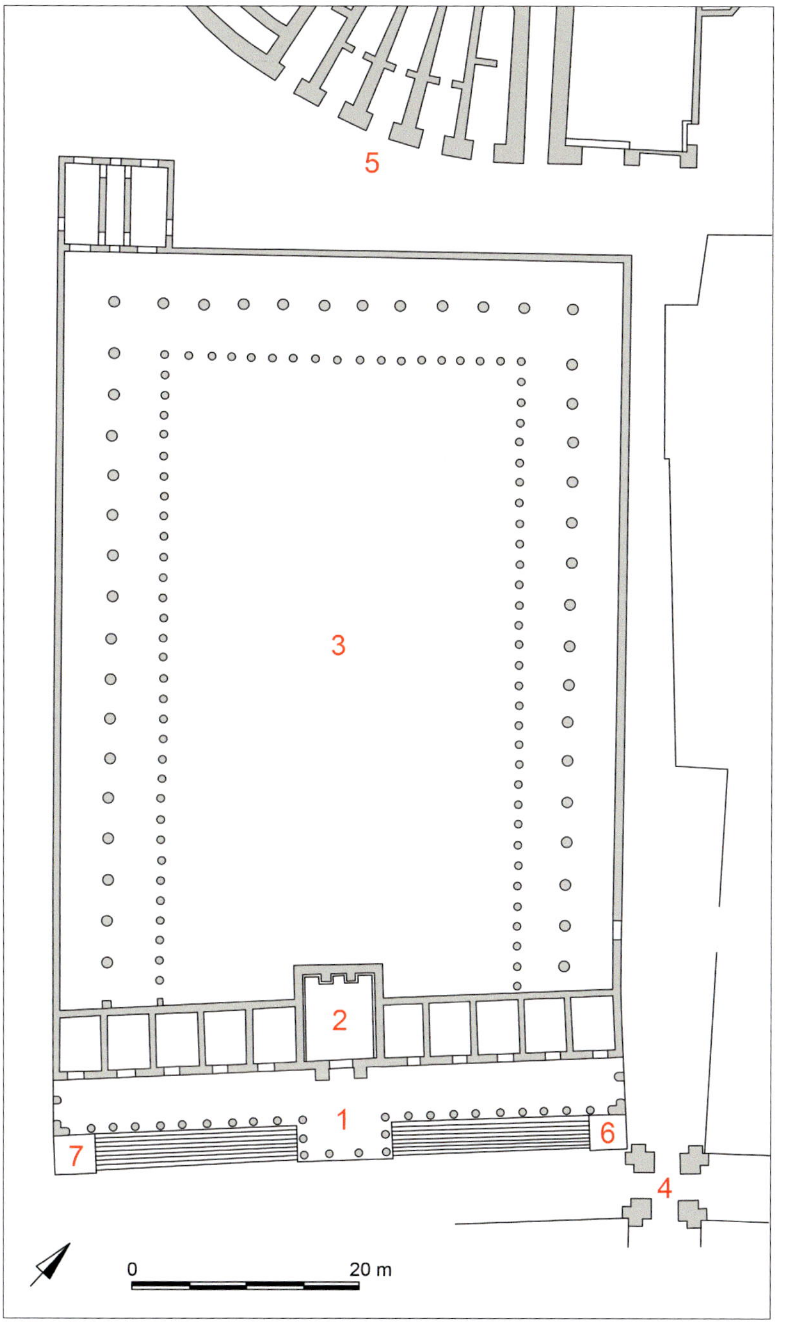

Fig. 3.28. *Chalcidicum*, plan (before Late Antique modifications). 1: Colonnaded front; 2: *Sacellum*; 3: Porticoed square; 4: Arch of Trajan; 5: Theatre; 6: Nymphaeum of the Lion and small fountain; 7: West Nymphaeum and small fountain (after Mugnai 2021, fig. 7).

features of the architectural decoration, in particular the Asiatic-style Corinthian capitals of Proconnesian and white Lesbos marble from the portico (Tomasello 2011, 102–5, 187–88, figs 45, 66, pl. 18), which are provided with prickly acanthus leaves and show an overall 'stylized' design that is typical of the productions of this period (Fig. 3.27).[36] This phenomenon of standardization was labelled 'marble style' by Ward-Perkins (1980, 40–54; 1981, 391). Originating in the eastern Mediterranean in the second century CE, these products became increasingly widespread across the Roman world as an imperial-style type of decoration, and their use reached a peak under the Severans – the marble architectural ornamentation of the Severan Forum and annexed buildings is the most conspicuous example of this trend at Lepcis Magna.

Not much of the superstructure of the Anonymous Temple survives, but it is possible to restore a tetrastyle front (Tomasello 2021, 73–85, figs 32–37). The columns have shafts of pinkish breccia from Skyros (Greece) and capitals of white (Proconnesian?) marble. It has been proposed that the two outermost columns featured Corinthian capitals, while the two in the middle had lotus-and-acanthus capitals – if correct, this layout would recall the design of the Colonnaded Street on a smaller scale. The extant blocks of the limestone entablature may suggest the presence of a 'Syrian arch' (a straight entablature with an arcade in the middle) decorating the temple front. Unfortunately nothing is known about the patronage of this building, and the deity to which it was dedicated is equally elusive. The fragment of an enthroned goddess and the iconography of some lamps recovered from the temple have been used to hypothesize the cult of Caelestis, hinting at a connection with Julia Domna and with the religious programme of the Severan dynasty (Tomasello 2021, 109–17). This needs further evidence to be confirmed, but for the time being it remains a valid suggestion that would fit well within the context of Severan-period building activities in this area (cf. the Tetrapylon).

The importance of water features in public architecture is clearly attested by the Great Nymphaeum and Small Nymphaeum at the two ends of the Colonnaded Street, and these large-scale building projects were complemented by smaller interventions in other parts of the city. A case in point is represented by the addition of fountains on the front of the *Chalcidicum* on the *cardo maximus*. This edifice is composed of a row of 10 rooms with a central shrine dedicated to the *numen* of Augustus and is faced by a colonnaded front with steps opening onto the street (length c. 51 m) (Fig. 3.28). It was

[36] Bruno *et al.* (2020, 75–76) propose a late Antonine date for these capitals on stylistic grounds, arguing they were stockpiled materials. The existence of a production-to-stock system in the Roman Empire based on the prefabrication of marble architectural elements at the quarries was first proposed by Ward-Perkins (1980) and has generated a variety of responses: see especially Pensabene 2001; Russell 2013, 201–55; Toma 2018; Bruno *et al.* 2020, 97–104.

Fig. 3.29. *Chalcidicum*, colonnaded front with small fountain at the south-west edge of the steps (photo A. Leone, Manar al-Athar).

built in 11–12 CE by a local notable, Iddibal Caphada Aemilius, and underwent subsequent modifications (*IRT2021* 324; Schippa 1981–82; Mugnai 2021, 89–92, 97, with bibliography). One of the most evident changes was the replacement of the original limestone colonnade with new columns with shafts of Carystian green marble, Attic bases and Corinthian capitals of white marble. Opinions vary on when this renovation took place; surely not before the late Antonine period, and a date of the architectural ornament on stylistic grounds to the end of the second or early third century CE seems the most probable.[37] Through a recent architectural survey and the opening of small test pits, new data have been gathered on the relationship between this renovation and the inclusion of a series of fountains along the front of the building (Tomasello 2005, 112–55, figs 47–66). The so-called 'Nymphaeum of the Lion', an apsidal structure (4.33 × 3.62 m) that filled the space between the south-east corner of the *Chalcidicum* and the north-west gatepost of the Arch of Trajan, was probably erected at the same time as the refurbishment of the colonnade. This was followed by the insertion of two small fountains at either end of the staircase (inner size of basins: 1.9 × 1.6 m and 1.68/1.77 × 1.03 m, respectively) (Fig. 3.29); the analysis of their architectural stratigraphy and the use of brown-yellowish Gadatza limestone suggest these were set up in the Severan period (Tomasello 2005, 121–26; Pentiricci 2010, 114; Mazzilli 2017, 142).[38]

The porticoed enclosure behind the colonnaded front of the *Chalcidicum* was also subject to significant alterations through time, including the transformation of the west side of the portico into a cistern perhaps at some point in the fourth century CE. Some have argued that the modification of the sector of the north portico through the erection of a series of rooms fronted by a colonnade overlooking the south side of the cavea of the theatre might date to the Severan era (Schippa 1981–82, 232; Caputo 1987, 114). These columns, provided with shafts of grey Mysian granite (quarried from the region around Pergamon) and white marble Attic bases and Corinthian capitals, rest on pedestals of white marble to increase their height – an architectural feature which may recall similar solutions adopted in the Colonnaded Street and Severan Temple. The date of this colonnade, however, is not clear (Bruno and Bianchi 2015b, 68–69, pl. 31.2 list it among the Antonine-period buildings in the area) and neither is that of the rooms behind it, which may be much later, so this hypothesis should be taken with caution.

[37] Floriani Squarciapino 1966, 71 (second to third century CE); Tomasello 2005, 120 (late Antonine); Kenrick 2009, 118 (late second or third century CE). A later date in the second half of the third century CE, as proposed by Schippa (1981–82, 225–26), should be discarded.

[38] The larger 'West Nymphaeum' of the *Chalcidicum* appears to date to the first half of the second century CE, as suggested by the type of brickwork masonry employed in this construction: Tomasello 2005, 127–55.

Fig. 3.30. *(above)* Nymphaeum of Hercules, restored elevation of north side (after Tomasello 2005, pl. 7).

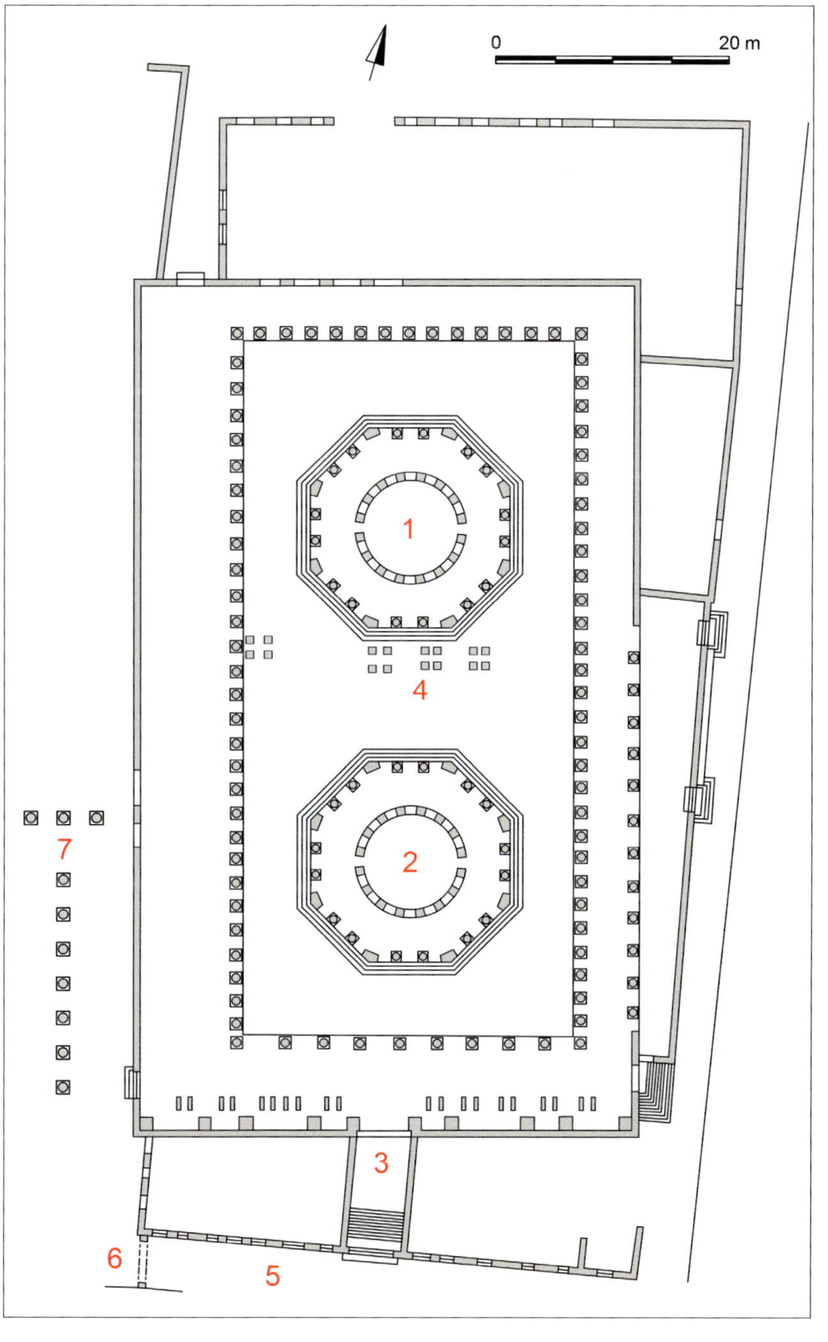

Fig. 3.31. *(right)* Market, plan. 1: North *tholos*; 2: South *tholos*; 3: South gate; 4: Miniature tetrapyla; 5: *Cardo maximus*; 6: Arch of Tiberius; 7: Early imperial stoa/ Late Antique portico (after Mugnai 2021, fig. 2).

A date in the Severan period is ascertained for the water features of the 'Nymphaeum of Hercules', which is located c. 100 m eastwards from the *Chalcidicum*, to the south-east of the market at the intersection between the *cardo maximus* and a secondary *decumanus* running towards the Severan Forum (Tomasello 2005, 57–111, 238–43, figs 20–46, pls 3–8; Lamare 2019, 347–50). This L-shaped monument (7.13 × 10.38 m) was decorated with a series of niches framed by columns of coloured marbles topped by arcades (including one example of a shaft of red marble from Iasos, Caria: Baldoni 2005). The first construction phase dates to the Antonine era, but recent excavations and architectural analyses have demonstrated the water basin along the front and the annexed hydraulic system were added under the Severans (Fig. 3.30). This was complemented by a renovation of the sculptural ornament, in particular the addition of a group of statues of Hercules (three are preserved), whose beard and hairstyle were clearly meant to imitate the Severan fashion of the time (Tomasello 2005, 162–63, 174–79, pls D–E). The patronage of the building and of its decorative programme is unknown, but the discovery of a fragmentary slab with the words *divi imp*[---] (not included in the *IRT2021* corpus) may suggest a dedication to some member(s) of the imperial family.

In this same area, the market was subject to transformations through time, at least some of which can be assigned to a phase of renovation in the Severan period, despite the lack of epigraphic evidence (Degrassi 1951, 45–50, 57–67; Mahler 2005, 15; 2011; Mazzilli 2017, 145–53). Construction of the building, a porticoed enclosure (c. 43.5 × 73.6 m) with two circular *tholoi* in the middle, was funded by Annobal Tapapius Rufus and dedicated in 9–8 BCE (*IRT2021* 319; *IPT* 21) (Fig. 3.31). Changes to the structure and ornamentation of the first-phase edifice occurred from as early as the Tiberian era.[39] The shape of the rectangular enclosure was modified through the addition of a row of *tabernae* on the south side opening onto the *cardo* perhaps already in the first century CE, while a trapezoidal space was built afterwards along the east side making ample use of spolia, including the recycling of a Tiberian inscription (*IRT2021* 332) on the stylobate of the annexed colonnade. Blocks of brown-yellowish limestone, likely of the Gadatza variety, were documented in these two sectors of the market during the 1920–40s excavations, and the *opus africanum* masonry of their walls may recall the technique employed in other Severan-period constructions/restorations in the city (Degrassi 1951, 47–48, fig. 17; Mahler 2011, 225–26, note 18), although a comprehensive survey of building techniques at Lepcis Magna remains a major desideratum. Analogous arguments have been used to suggest a date in the Severan era for the arched gateway fronted by a flight of steps on the market's south side (Fig. 3.32). An entrance there might have already existed before this period, so this phase could be a monumentalization of an extant feature. It has been observed that the gateway and staircase were oriented towards a *decumanus* that led southwards to meet the western outer wall of the Severan Forum and, consequently, the intersection with the Colonnaded Street (Mahler 2005, 17; 2011, 226).

In his recent study of the market, Karl-Uwe Mahler (2011) confidently attributed to the Severan period the renovation of the south *tholos*, whose limestone columns were replaced with marble ones (Fig. 3.33). In particular, the use of lotus-and-acanthus capitals is interpreted as a typical Severan feature (Mahler 2011, 227–33, figs 4–13; see also Ward-Perkins 1948, 66–70, figs 11–12; Kenrick 2009, 116), although the carving of the acanthus shows that the (local?) workshops that produced these pieces were different from those working in the Severan Forum complex. In this regard, Bianchi (2009, 57–58, figs 20–21) preferred a date in the Antonine period for these capitals, advancing the hypothesis of a previous restoration of the market in those years. The fact that the capitals were probably produced by local ateliers, however, may suggest that certain carving features remained in use for a longer span of time, thus making a distinction between Antonine- and Severan-period productions not always clear. Additional elements in support of a Severan date for the renovation of the *tholos* may be provided by some details of the Ionic capitals from the heart-shaped pillars of this edifice and by the shape of the Attic column bases (Mahler 2011, 228–39, figs 14–21; Mazzilli 2017, 147).

Another evident restoration concerned the portico of the market, which was refurbished with columns of grey Mysian and Troad granite from Asia Minor (Bruno and Bianchi 2015b, 66–69), matched with Attic bases

Fig. 3.32. Market, staircase and arched gateway on south side (photo N. Mugnai).

[39] On the pre-Severan architectural ornament of the market, see Bianchi 2005, 191–92, 211–13, figs 1–3, 23–26; Mahler 2006, 147, 153, nos 1–4 KK, 61–63 IK, pls 1, 16–17; Mugnai 2021, 88–89, 94–95, figs 2–4.

Fig. 3.33. *(above)* Market, south *tholos* with marble columns (photo N. Mugnai).

Fig. 3.34. *(right)* Market, shaft of grey granite and Corinthian capital of white marble from the portico (photo N. Mugnai).

and Corinthian capitals mostly of Proconnesian marble (Fig. 3.34). A close analysis of the capitals' carving features has revealed that the majority of them can be compared with the types IV–VI established by Moshe Fischer (1990, 46–55, nos 133–206, pls 24–37; Bianchi 2009, 55–57, figs 15–19), which often overlap with each other and provide a chronology between the late second and the mid-third century CE. This would be compatible with a renovation of the colonnades under the Severans, but it seems almost certain that the portico witnessed a further restoration in 324–26 CE under the initiative of the *praeses* of the province, Laenatius Romulus, as attested by an inscription recovered from the market: *porticuum macelli in ruinam [lab]emque conversam* (*IRT2021* 468; Pentiricci 2010, 121–23; Mazzilli 2017, 152–53).[40] On balance, one may wonder whether this intervention could have included, or should actually be referred to, the so-called early imperial 'stoa' (namely a portico) facing the south-west side of the market, which was entirely rebuilt with marble columns and capitals of various provenance probably in the fourth century CE (Di Vita 2017; Mazzilli 2017, 156–60).

Small-scale building activities carried out by individuals in the market can be recognized in the erection of four monuments in the form of miniature tetrapyla, which can be seen in the area inside the portico closer to the north *tholos* (Mühlenbrock 2003, 216–17, pl. 26; Bigi 2010, 229–32, figs 7.10–11; Feuser 2020, 225–26). These structures were meant to support honorific statues; a date in the Severan era is likely on the basis of the materials employed (limestone and recycled marble) and architectural characteristics, but they were kept in use in later periods. One of them bears an inscription recording the donation of four wild beasts for entertainment games by a Porfyrius, which is datable in the latter half of the third century CE (*IRT2021* 603; Tantillo *et al.* 2010,

[40] Laenatius Romulus also sponsored the restoration of the civic basilica (*basilica vetus*) in the Old Forum in those same years: *IRT2021* 467; Pentiricci 2010, 134–40; Tantillo *et al.* 2010, 451–56, no. 71.

Fig. 3.35. *(above)* Market, miniature tetrapylon with inscription *IRT2021* 603 (photo N. Mugnai).

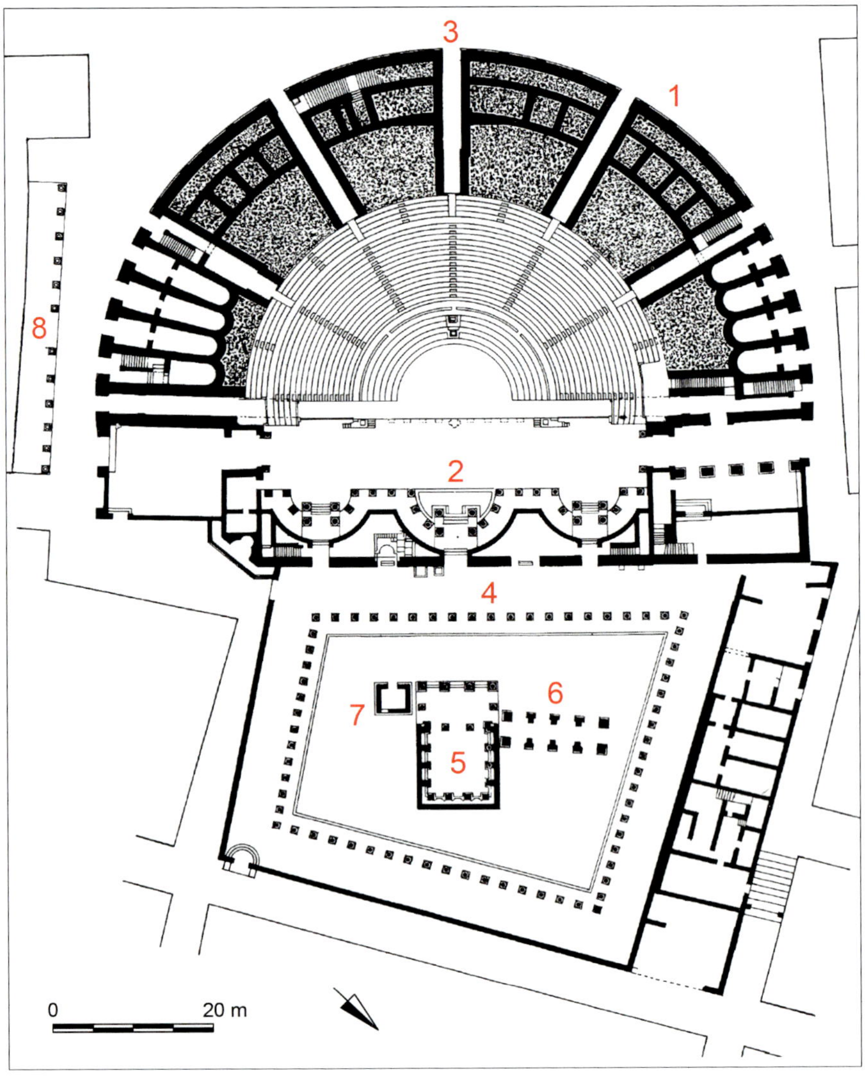

Fig. 3.36. *(right)* Plan of the theatre and adjoining buildings. 1: Cavea; 2: Scene building; 3: Temple in *summa cavea* (not shown on plan); 4: P*orticus post scaenam*; 5: Temple of the Augustan Gods; 6: Tetrapylon monument; 7: *Sacellum*; 8: Colonnade facing north side of *Chalcidicum* (after Bianchi Bandinelli *et al.* 1963, fig. 234).

408–12, no. 50) (Fig. 3.35). This text was engraved on the stone after erasing a previous inscription, and the two ships carved on the uprights of the tetrapylon strongly suggest this was originally a monument set up by a *navicularius* (Mühlenbrock 2003, 217; Feuser 2020, 226).

Renovations and the erection of new monuments under the Severans can be identified in the theatre and adjoining structures in the city area west of the *Chalcidicum* and market. The theatre, one of the largest in North Africa (diameter of cavea c. 87.6 m), was built in 1–2 CE at the expense of Annobal Tapapius Rufus, the same Lepcitanian notable who had donated the market a few years earlier (*IRT2021* 321–23; *IPT* 24a–b) (Fig. 3.36). Subsequent building phases are attested, the most substantial of which concerned the refurbishment of the *scaenae frons* with coloured marble columns in 157–58 CE – a costly enterprise of 500,000 sesterces that was financed by two wealthy donors, Marcius Vitalis and Junius Galba (*IRT2021* 534; see also Aiosa, Chapter 2). The construction history of the theatre is known thanks to the excavations and research by Giacomo Caputo (1987; on the various phases see also Di Vita 1990; Sear 1990; 2006, 281–82). Small restorations of the outer wall of the cavea and of the theatre paving can probably be attributed to the Severan period because of the use of brown-yellowish limestone (Caputo 1987, 30, 44, pl. 127.1–2). It is believed that the replacement of the original limestone columns of the shrine of Ceres Augusta at the top of the cavea with grey granite and Carystian green marble shafts should be assigned to the Severan era (Caputo 1987, 57, 62, pl. 152.2; Di Vita 1990, 138; Brouquier-Reddé 1992, 166; Mahler 2005, 15).[41] This

[41] The shrine was added to the cavea in 35–36 CE by a Suphunibal, the daughter of Annobal Ruso: *IRT2021* 269; Caputo 1987, 56–57; Brouquier-Reddé 1992, 164–66.

Fig. 3.37. Theatre, *porticus post scaenam*: general view from west (photo N. Mugnai).

intervention would have completed the theatre's renovation begun in the Antonine period, but the hypothesis rests solely on the types of marble employed and may thus be questioned. More remarkable is the number of dedications to the Severan family that were set up in the theatre by individual donors and by the *curiae* of Lepcis Magna between 198 and 203 CE (Wilson 2007, 305, table 14.1).[42] Among the numerous statues of gods, local notables, and emperors that adorned the building, one should list the head of a larger-than-life statue of Septimius Severus (Caputo and Traversari 1976, 98–100, no. 77, pls 85–87).

Severan-period building activities occurred in the *porticus post scaenam* attached to the north-east side of the theatre – a trapezoidal porticoed enclosure in the middle of which a small tetrastyle temple (9.5 × 16.5 m) had been set up by Iddibal Tapapius in 43 CE to honour the Augustan Gods (*Dii Augusti*: *IRT2021* 273). The limestone columns of the temple were replaced with marble ones and a polychrome marble veneer was added to the inner wall of the enclosure, probably at the same time as the refurbishment of the theatre's *scaenae frons* (Brouquier-Reddé 1992, 112–13; Kenrick 2009, 121). The portico colonnades (Fig. 3.37) were also upgraded with shafts of grey Mysian granite and white marble bases and Corinthian capitals (Bruno and Bianchi 2015b, 68). A Severan date has been proposed occasionally for this latter intervention (Sear 1990, 379; 2006, 282; *contra* Bianchi 2009, 61; Pentiricci 2010, 116); the capitals, or at least some of them, appear to be later than those employed in the *scaenae frons*, but only a detailed survey will provide a definitive answer. More secure is the date of the monument composed of a row of four tetrapyla (c. 13 × 4.6 m) abutting the temple's west side, although it is not perfectly aligned with it, and to which a fragmentary dedication to the Severan dynasty has been attributed (*IRT2021* 398; Caputo 1987, 127, pls 112.2–3, 121, 123.4; Mahler 2005, 15; Wilson 2007, 305) (Fig. 3.38). The monument's layout and its blocks of brown-yellowish Gadatza limestone further confirm this chronology (Bruno and Bianchi 2015a, 41). It is plausible that it served to host statues of the imperial family, and its prominent position at the side of the temple of the Augustan Gods was ideal to emphasize the 'divine' attributes of the dynasty. Additional statues of Septimius Severus, Julia Domna, and Caracalla were set up on inscribed pedestals by the procurator D. Clodius Galba in 203–4 CE on the south wall of the enclosure (IRT2021 395, 407, 424; Caputo 1987, 52, pl. 114.2; Bigi 2010, 224, fig. 7.6).[43] On the east side of the temple, there is a small square building (c. 4.3 × 4 m) probably serving as a *sacellum* (Fig. 3.39). Its construction date is unknown, but the heterogeneous limestone blocks of its masonry, some of which may belong to the Gadatza variety, suggest it was probably subject to restorations. Caputo (1987, 127, pls 112.1, 119) argued it may have been dedicated to Liber Pater, genius of the

[42] *IRT2021* 391–92, 399, 403, 405–6, 411, 413–14, 416–17, 420–22, 432, 434, 436.

[43] One should also record the dedication of a statue to the pantomime M. Septimius Aurelius Agrippa around 211–17 CE: *IRT2021* 606; Caputo 1987, 127, 139–40, pl. 64.4.

Fig. 3.38. *(above)* Theatre, *porticus post scaenam*: tetrapylon monument (photo N. Mugnai).

Fig. 3.39. *(right)* Theatre, *porticus post scaenam*: *sacellum* (photo N. Mugnai).

colony, on the basis of a fragmentary inscription that would fit with the size of the *tabula ansata* on the front of the building (*IRT2021* 296). The lettering of this text points to a date in the third century CE; if Caputo's hypothesis is correct, the erection or restoration of the *sacellum* might have occurred simultaneously with the construction of the tetrapylon monument on the other side.

Public honours to the Severan family are attested in the city's Old Forum, which continued to be used for civic and religious purposes alongside the new Severan Forum (Condron 1998; Kleinwächter 2001, 236–39). This trapezoidal piazza (c. 55 × 55.4 m) witnessed a first phase of monumentalization in the Augustan and early Julio-Claudian period with the construction of the three main temples (A–C) on the north-west side; this was followed by further building activities throughout the first century CE (Di Vita *et al.* 1999, 74–80; Mugnai 2021, 103–9; 2023, 160–66, with references) (Fig. 3.40). A major transformation of the Old Forum took place in the mid-second century CE, when the façades of Temple A (Liber Pater?), Temple B (Roma and Augustus), as well as the curia at the south-east edge of the piazza, were remodelled with new colonnades of white Proconnesian marble, echoing the stylistic upgrade of other public buildings across the city; this process was completed by the dedication of a shrine to an unknown Augustan deity on the forum's west side in 152–53 CE (*IRT2021* 370), which was adorned with columns of Carystian green marble.[44] The sides of the Old Forum were therefore saturated with buildings when Septimius Severus came to power, and for this reason a priest of the imperial cult, M. [---] Asper Aurelianus, chose a spot on the paving in the south-west sector of the piazza to set up an exedra

[44]On these renovations, see *IRT2021* 275; Masturzo 2005, 104–8, 123–28, figs 1.105–11; Livadiotti and Rocco 2005, 245–51, 296–98, figs 2.72–75, 2.109–10; 2018, 165–76, figs 152–64; Mugnai 2021, 102–3, 109–12, figs 48–52.

dedicated to Septimius Severus, Julia Domna, Caracalla, and Geta (*IRT2021* 397) (Fig. 3.41). The monument (c. 5 m in width) featured a moulded podium with a seating space inside the hemicycle and was meant to hold a set of statues of the imperial family on the top (Romanelli 1925, 127–30; Mahler 2005, 16, fig. 14). Four inscribed statue bases were recovered around the exedra, bearing dedications by M. Calpurnius Geta Attianus and M. Calpurnius Attianus to the respective members of the emperor's household (*IRT2021* 390, 402, 419, 433; Wilson 2007, 305). The presence of the exedra encouraged other donors to set up their dedications in this area, such as the one to Julia Domna-Juno by Q. Fulvius Dida Bibulianus that was found here (*IRT2021* 291), and perhaps also one to the deified Septimius Severus by the prefect of the *annona* Q. Marcius Dioga, which was recycled in the wall of the Christian baptistery nearby (*IRT2021* 401).

Dedications to Septimius Severus and his family were also discovered around Temple A.[45] This was an ideal setting given the presence of numerous other dedications and statues of emperors, which had been set up on that side of the forum – and particularly on the front of the adjacent Temple of Roma and Augustus – in the Julio-Claudian period (Aurigemma 1940; Musso 2008; Mugnai 2021, 105–7). It is possible that some restoration of the temple might have taken place along with these imperial honours. Recent observations on a fragmentary text found here suggest this recorded the restoration of the lower and upper parts of the building by two or more brothers: [---*infe*]*riorib*(*us*) *et superiorib*(*us*) (*IRT2021* 274). This surely occurred after the extensive renovation of the temple's façade in the mid-second century CE, but opinions diverge on whether it should be attributed to the Severan period (Marmouri 2017, 16–17) or to a later point in the third century CE (Tantillo *et al.* 2010, 443–45, no. 68). One may also be tempted to include in these works the erection of four columns of reddish limestone with (recycled?) Ionic capitals, which were inserted in the corridor between the podia of Temples A and B and may

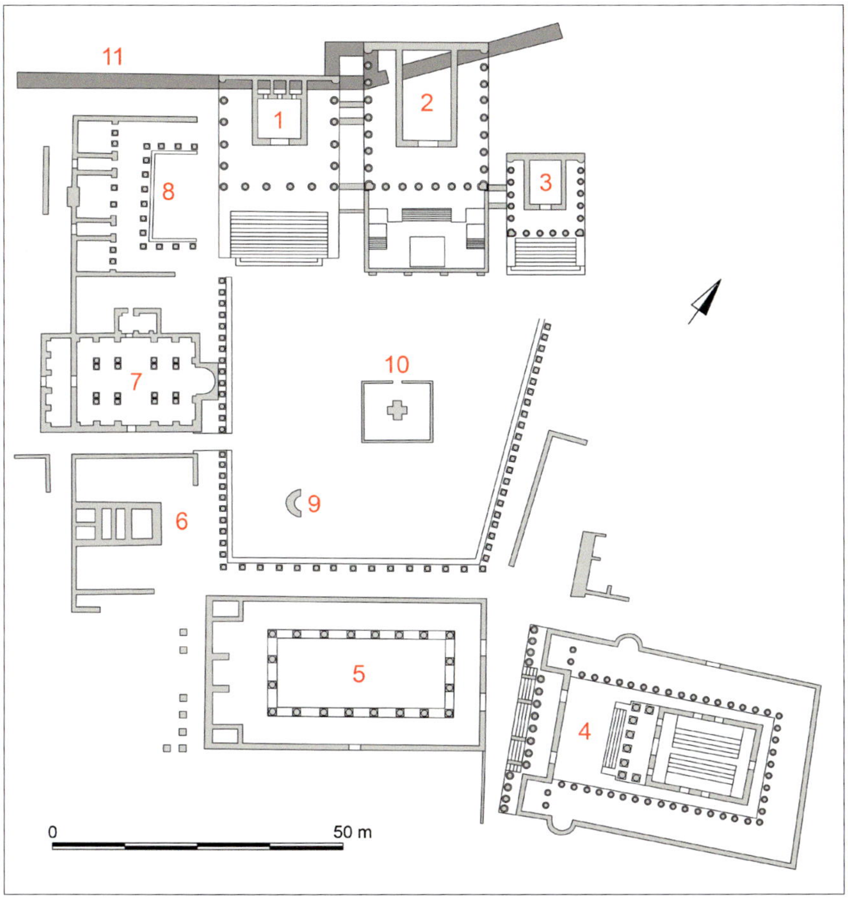

Fig. 3.40. *(above)* Old Forum, plan. 1: Temple A (Liber Pater?); 2: Temple B (Roma and Augustus); 3: Temple C (Hercules?); 4: Curia; 5: Basilica; 6: Temple of Magna Mater; 7: Early imperial building/church; 8: Antonine temple; 9: Severan exedra; 10: Baptistery; 11: Byzantine wall (after Mugnai 2021, fig. 37).

Fig. 3.41. *(right)* Old Forum, Severan exedra: view from south-east (photo N. Mugnai).

[45] *IRT2021* 387, 389, 399–400, 408, 410, 412, 415, 418; Wilson 2007, 305, table 14.1; Marmouri 2017, 14.

Fig. 3.42. *(left)* Old Forum, corridor between Temples A and B with columns of red limestone (photo N. Mugnai).

Fig. 3.43. *(below)* Old Forum, portico: Asiatic Corinthian capital with eagle motif (photo N. Mugnai).

have served as a support for a platform holding a statuary group, although their date is uncertain (Masturzo 2005, 85–87, figs 1.68–70) (Fig. 3.42).

A Severan-period intervention is recognizable in the colonnades of the portico that framed the piazza on three sides. The first phase of the portico dates to 53–54 CE, when this was erected along with the paving of the forum through the initiative of one Caius, son of Anno, and C. Phelyssam (*IRT2021* 338, 615; *IPT* 26a–b). Following the marble enhancement of the forum buildings, the original limestone columns were replaced with ones of Carystian green marble matched with Attic bases and Corinthian capitals of white marble, numerous examples of which are to be seen on the piazza. The portico has not been the subject of any detailed study, but scholars have commented on it occasionally (see Ricciardi 2005, 329–30; Montali 2016, 90). The stylistic features of the Asiatic Corinthian capitals are informative, with particular regard to those examples bearing an eagle in the middle of the abacus (Fig. 3.43) that recalls directly the decorative motif of some capitals from the Severan Tetrapylon and Severan Basilica (cf. Bartoccini 1931, 52–54; Ward-Perkins 1980, 52–53, no. 4, pl. 14; Pensabene 2001, 101, fig. 82).

The peripheral area of Lepcis Magna is less known because of the paucity of archaeological excavations, but some building activities pertaining to this period can be identified. In the north-west sector of the city close to the coastline, the 'Hunting Baths' were inserted within a pre-existing district at some point in the late second or early third century CE and underwent a series of structural and decorative modifications subsequently (Ward-Perkins and Toynbee 1949, 167–73, 191–95; Ward-Perkins 1981, 382–84; Musso 2012, 31–37) (Fig. 3.44).[46] Belonging to a category labelled 'neighbourhood bath complex', this building was probably meant for public use but was subject to private legislation. The baths are renowned for the good preservation of their concrete vaulted roofs and the pictorial decoration of the interior. Some of the paintings (landscape friezes) do not appear to predate the latter half of the third century CE, while

[46] Aerial photography has revealed the presence of large buildings (probably warehouses) to the west of the Hunting Baths: Jones 1989, 96–99, figs 4–5; Mattingly 1995, 118; Zocchi 2018, 73–74, fig. 20.

others (figurative friezes) show stylistic features typical of the late Severan period (Bianchi 2012, with references). In the opposite sector of the city, immediately eastwards of the harbour's east mole, a large public bath complex known as the 'Eastern Baths' was excavated by the French Archaeological Mission from 1994 to 2012. The data collected through this research have revealed that a first bath was established here in the first half of the second century CE; it was extensively enlarged and embellished with marble adornments under the Severans, although it seems that it fell into disrepair in the second half of the third century CE (Michel 2011–12, 114–17; Paulin and Dagnas 2012). Beyond the importance of the building itself, the location of a large bathing establishment in this area points to the existence of a large urban district of Lepcis Magna that awaits further investigation.

A final note concerns the information one can gather from two inscriptions. The first text comes from the Hadrianic Baths and refers to a substantial restoration of the *frigidarium* and annexed structures by the priest and magistrate [---] Rusonianus, probably to be identified with Q. Marcius Candidus Rusonianus (*IRT2021* 396) (Fig. 3.45).

Fig. 3.44. Hunting Baths, view from north-west (photo N. Mugnai).

Fig. 3.45. Hadrianic Baths, part of *frigidarium* with inscription *IRT2021* 396 (photo N. Mugnai).

Fig. 3.46. *(top left)* Amphitheatre, inscription *IRT2021* 1020 with names of the Severan emperors (photo N. Mugnai).

Fig. 3.47. *(bottom left)* Amphitheatre, upper cavea and remains of the *sacellum*: view from east (photo N. Mugnai).

The inscription bears the name and titles of Septimius Severus, but these were engraved on the marble slab after replacing Commodus' name and it is acknowledged that these works took place under Severus' predecessor (for instance: Di Vita-Évrard 1991, 37–38; Di Vita *et al.* 1999, 96; Laronde and Degeorge 2005, 114–15; Kenrick 2009, 96). Recent studies on the baths' architectural decoration have better defined the extent of the restorations, which seem to have involved the *natatio* and *palaestra* as well (Bianchi 2009, 51–55, figs 6–14; Bianchi and Bruno 2018, 128–34, figs 11–22). Some Corinthian capitals (see in particular Bianchi 2009, 53, fig. 13) show carving features that often overlap in date between the late Antonine and Severan periods (cf. Fischer 1990, 55, type IV), so one may wonder whether restorations might have continued to some extent after the reign of Commodus. If so, Septimius Severus' name could have been engraved not only because of Commodus' *damnatio memoriae*, but perhaps also to acknowledge further works.[47]

The second inscription was recovered in the amphitheatre (c. 1 km to the east of Lepcis Magna's harbour) and consists of a portion of a limestone entablature with the names of Septimius Severus, Julia Domna, Caracalla, and Geta (*IRT2021* 1020; Ricciardi 2018, 252–54, no. 3, fig. 321) (Fig. 3.46). It is especially significant since the names of the emperors are in the nominative, so the text should refer to a building initiative they sponsored directly. A first amphitheatre was built in this area under Nero in 56 CE (*IRT2021* 1013), but the remains of the building one sees today belong to a second monumentalization phase of the Antonine era, which probably took place around the same time as the construction, or renovation, of the adjacent circus in 161–62 CE (*IRT2021* 1014). It has been argued that the length of the entablature would be compatible with the shrine *in summa cavea* (width of front 7.7 m), which might have been dedicated to Ephesian Artemis (Fig. 3.47). This text could therefore refer to a renovation of the shrine or of the portico on the top of the cavea under the Severans, along with other structural changes and restorations that have been documented during a recent survey of the amphitheatre (Ricciardi 2018, 180, 187–88, figs 235–37). This would fit well with the possible existence of Severan-period construction phases in the circus that scholars have briefly commented on (see the observations in Humphrey *et al.* 1972–73, 90, with references), attesting to the attention for entertainment spectacles as part of the building and restoration projects across the city in this period.

Conclusion and further research

This review of construction activities at Lepcis Magna in the Severan period has revealed some patterns in the development of the cityscape at this crucial stage of its

[47] A third-century CE restoration phase of the baths is attested through a votive offering mentioning a *refectio thermarum tertium*: *IRT2021* 263; Pentiricci 2010, 144. One should also consider the presence of a marble head of Septimius Severus and fragments of a bronze imperial statue of this period: Finocchi 2012, 54–55, 139, no. 19, pl. 21, with references.

history. The impact of the new Severan buildings along the Wadi Lebdah has been widely acknowledged in the scholarship, with regard to their monumentality and decorative opulence, as well as in terms of ideological implications (for instance: Ward-Perkins 1948; 1993; Mahler 2005, 6–14; Cordovana 2007, 329–432; Wilson 2007, 295–301). Their location in this sector of the city determined a shift of previous routes towards this area, and the Colonnaded Street played an important role as an urban connector between the coast and the main inland road. Direct imperial patronage is evident in the case of the Severan Forum complex and this can be realistically extended to the annexed monuments, although it is possible that Lepcitanian notables participated in this enterprise at least to some extent (see, for instance, the sculptural ornamentation of the Great Nymphaeum and Severan Exedra). There are still some unresolved matters, such as the identification of the cult of the Severan Temple and that of other sacred buildings, and issues around the date of certain structures, which is exemplified by the case of the harbour and the edifices that were erected around the basin: how much of what we see today can be securely attributed to a Severan-period remodelling of the port? It is to be hoped that the progress of research will keep adding elements to clarify some of these points.

The re-examination of old data and new archaeological discoveries in recent years have been particularly valuable to assess the extent of Severan-period building and restoration activities in the city, in particular beyond the 'traditional' Severan (imperial) constructions. It is regrettable that, despite the extensive corpus of epigraphy of Lepcis Magna, only limited epigraphic evidence is available to ascertain the patronage of these building activities, although an active role of the municipality and of local wealthy individuals seems unquestionable. Some construction and renovation phases may not be securely datable, but the combined assessment of archaeological data, architectural characteristics, types of building materials, and stylistic features has proved to be effective to gain a better understanding of these matters (see Tomasello 2005; 2011; Mahler 2011; Bruno and Bianchi 2015a; Mazzilli 2017). It emerges that many building initiatives gave continuity to a large-scale phenomenon of urban embellishment that had started already in the Antonine period, particularly through the use of marble ornamentation (Pensabene 2001; Bianchi 2009). This is visible in the construction developments along the *decumanus maximus*, including the erection of a series of honorific arches as well as other types of buildings, and in the renovation of key public spaces such as the theatre with adjoining areas, the market, and the Old Forum.

There are also some gaps that need to be filled. For instance, our knowledge of domestic architecture at Lepcis Magna is extremely limited. This is unfortunate as it prevents us from appreciating how its inhabitants reacted to the architectural and decorative trends that were being introduced in the city, and how these elements were reinterpreted within the private sphere in elite and non-elite contexts. Some of the mosaics from the 'Villa of the Nile' (actually a domus located roughly halfway between the harbour and the circus) appear to date to the late second or early third century CE, which may point to a phase of decorative enhancement of the house in the Severan era, but many aspects of their architectural setting remain unclear (Kenrick 2009, 130; Rind 2009, 123–24, with references; on these and other Tripolitanian mosaics see Wootton, Chapter 4). More information is available on the maritime villas and other elite dwellings on the coastal strip to the west of Lepcis Magna, as several examples of such buildings in the areas of Homs and Silin show (Musso 1995, 344–45; Rind 2009, 119–26; Wilson 2018, 285–93). Within the city, excavations of a domestic context in an *insula* block located between the theatre and the Old Forum have revealed a succession of phases from Punic to Byzantine times, including construction activities datable to the first half of the third century CE (Calderone and Tramontana 2017, 14–18). Another house adjacent to the theatre has yielded evidence of Late Antique construction sequences (Walda *et al.* 1997). Hopefully the final publication of both excavations will set a new course for the study of domestic buildings at Lepcis Magna.

Finally, it is worth pointing out that any observations on the scale of public building projects in relation to the extent of the ancient city should consider the fact that only a portion of it is known archaeologically.[48] The urban area to the south of the *decumanus maximus* is unexplored, and the same applies to large parts of the city's eastern and western sectors beyond the central civic district. When visiting the site of Lepcis Magna, it would be impossible not to be captivated by the grandiosity of its monuments, which is even more striking in the case of the Severan buildings. These constructions are often regarded as 'out-of-proportion' to the actual needs of the city and it is ascertained that their completion required enormous financial efforts, thus speaking of their exceptionality – or extravagance – and their burdensome legacy (Barton 1977–78; Mattingly 1995, 121–22; Musso *et al.* 2018a, 113). However, broader considerations on their urban impact and their relationship to the rest of the city should probably remain provisional until future archaeological surveys and excavations can offer a better understanding of Lepcis Magna's layout in its entirety.

[48] Only a preliminary geophysical survey has been carried out in some of the areas beyond the central district of Lepcis Magna: Keay 2010, 333–34; Zocchi 2018, 71.

Acknowledgements

This chapter draws upon my studies on North African architecture, a topic I have familiarized myself with over the years. In this learning process I have greatly benefitted from the assistance of many colleagues who have shared with me their expertise and insights into ancient architecture and/or North Africa (especially Libya). I would like to thank in particular: Stefano Camporeale, Janet DeLaine, Philip Kenrick, David Mattingly, Dominik Maschek, Patrizio Pensabene, and Susan Walker. Sections of this chapter were presented at a seminar on Roman construction at the University of Padua; I am grateful to the organizers (Jacopo Bonetto, Caterina Previato, and Simone Dilaria) and all the participants for an engaging discussion that gave me the opportunity to improve many points of my arguments. My sincerest gratitude also goes to Luisa Musso who invited me to join her archaeological team in Libya, allowing me to spend time at Lepcis Magna. Of course, I alone remain responsible for any inaccuracies or errors that may appear in the text.

References

Aiosa, S. 2020. Questa è la città di Augusto: archi e processioni a Leptis Magna. In G. Mazzilli (ed.), *In solo provinciali. Sull'architettura delle province, da Augusto ai Severi, tra inerzie locali e romanizzazione.* Rome: Quasar, 285–300.

Apollonj, B.M. 1936. *I monumenti italiani: rilievi raccolti a cura della Reale Accademia d'Italia. Fascicoli VIII–IX. Il foro e la basilica severiana di Leptis Magna: rilievi eseguiti dalla Facoltà di Architettura della R. Università di Roma.* Rome: Libreria dello Stato.

Aounallah, S. and Golvin, J.-C. (eds) 2016. *Dougga: études d'architecture religieuse, 2. Les sanctuaires du forum, du centre de l'agglomération et de la Grande rue courbe.* Bordeaux: Ausonius Éditions.

Aurigemma, S. 1940. Sculture del foro vecchio di Leptis Magna raffiguranti la dea Roma e principi della casa dei giulio-claudi (pubblicazione provvisoria). *Africa Italiana* 8: 1–94.

Bacchielli, L. 1992. L'Arco Severiano di Leptis Magna: storia e programma del restauro. In A. Mastino (ed.), *L'Africa Romana. Atti del IX convegno di studio (Nuoro, 13–15 dicembre 1991).* Sassari: Gallizzi, 763–70.

Baldoni, D. 2005. Una colonna a Leptis Magna: alcune considerazioni sul marmor iassense. *Libyan Studies* 36: 101–10.

Bartoccini, R. 1931. L'arco quadrifronte dei Severi a Lepcis (Leptis Magna). *Africa Italiana* 4: 32–152.

Bartoccini, R. 1958. *Il porto romano di Leptis Magna.* Rome: Bollettino del Centro di Studi per la Storia dell'Architettura.

Bartoccini, R. 1961. Il Foro Severiano di Leptis Magna: campagna di scavo 1958. *Quaderni di Archeologia della Libya* 4: 105–26.

Barton, I.M. 1977–78. The effects of imperial favour: Septimius Severus and Lepcis Magna. *Museum Africum* 6: 60–63.

Beltrame, C. 2012. New evidence for the submerged ancient harbour structures at Tolmetha and Leptis Magna, Libya. *International Journal of Nautical Archaeology* 41.2: 315–26.

Bianchi, B. 2012. The pictorial decoration of the Hunting Baths and its chronological development. In B. Bianchi and L. Musso (eds), *Lepcis Magna, Hunting Baths: Building, Restoration, Promotion.* Florence: All'Insegna del Giglio, 55–72.

Bianchi, F. 2005. La decorazione architettonica in pietra locale a Leptis Magna tra il I e il II sec. d.C. Maestranze e modelli nell'architettura pubblica. *Archeologia Classica* 56: 189–223.

Bianchi, F. 2009. Su alcuni aspetti della decorazione architettonica in marmo a Leptis Magna in età imperiale. *Marmora* 5: 45–70.

Bianchi, F. 2015. Il complesso severiano a Leptis Magna: maestranze e modelli decorativi degli apparati architettonici in pietra locale. In P. Ruggeri (ed.), *L'Africa Romana. Momenti di continuità e rottura: bilancio di trent'anni di convegni L'Africa Romana. Atti del XX convegno internazionale di studi (Alghero, 26–29 settembre 2013).* Rome: Carocci, 235–55.

Bianchi, F. and Bruno, M. 2018. Le Terme di Adriano a Leptis Magna: fasi costruttive e decorazione architettonica. *Quaderni di Archeologia della Libya* 21: 117–39.

Bianchi, F., Bruno, M., Gorgoni, C., Pallante, P. and Ponti, G. 2011. The pilasters of the Severan basilica at Leptis Magna and the School of Aphrodisias: new archaeometric and archaeological data. In P. Jockey (ed.), *Interdisciplinary Studies on Mediterranean Ancient Marble and Stone. ASMOSIA VIII. Proceedings of the Eighth International Conference (Aix-en-Provence, June 12–18, 2006).* Paris: Éditions Karthala, 329–49.

Bianchi, F., Bruno, M. and Pike, S. 2015. L'apparato architettonico in marmo pentelico del complesso severiano a Leptis Magna alla luce di recenti indagini archeologiche, epigrafiche ed archeometriche. In P. Ruggeri (ed.), *L'Africa Romana. Momenti di continuità e rottura: bilancio di trent'anni di convegni L'Africa Romana. Atti del XX convegno internazionale di studi (Alghero, 26–29 settembre 2013).* Rome: Carocci, 215–34.

Bianchi Bandinelli, R., Caputo, G. and Vergara Caffarelli, E. 1963. *Leptis Magna.* Rome: Impresa Astaldi.

Bigi, F. 2010. I supporti epigrafici: tipi, decorazioni, cronologie. In I. Tantillo and F. Bigi (eds), *Leptis Magna. Una città e le sue iscrizioni in epoca tardoromana.* Cassino: Edizioni dell'Università degli Studi di Cassino, 219–52.

Birley, A.R. 1999. *Septimius Severus: The African Emperor (Revised Edition).* London: Routledge.

Brogan, O. and Smith, D.J. 1984. *Ghirza: A Libyan Settlement in the Roman Period.* Tripoli: Department of Antiquities.

Brouquier-Reddé, V. 1992. *Temples et cultes de Tripolitaine.* Paris: Éditions du CNRS.

Bruno, M. and Bianchi, F. 2015a. The limestone quarries of Wadi Gadatza in the territory of Leptis Magna. In P. Pensabene and E. Gasparini (eds), *Interdisciplinary Studies on Ancient Stone. ASMOSIA X. Proceedings of the Tenth International Conference (Rome, 21–26 May 2012).* Rome: 'L'Erma' di Bretschneider, 35–42.

Bruno, M. and Bianchi, F. 2015b. *Marmi di Leptis Magna: repertorio delle pietre bianche e policrome della città.* Rome: 'L'Erma' di Bretschneider.

Bruno, M., Bianchi, F., Attanasio, D. and Prochaska, W. 2020. Leptis Magna e il marmo di Lesbo. Cave, manufatti e distribuzione. *Quaderni di Archeologia della Libya* 23: 45–118.

Calderone, A. and Tramontana, E. 2017. Ricerche dell'Università di Messina a Leptis Magna. *Libya Antiqua* n.s. 10: 11–104.

Caputo, G. 1965. Spigolature architettoniche leptitane, I: tradizione interna nell'architettura di Leptis Magna. *Libya Antiqua* 2: 9–14.

Caputo, G. 1987. *Il teatro augusteo di Leptis Magna. Scavo e restauro (1937–1951).* Rome: 'L'Erma' di Bretschneider.

Caputo, G. and Traversari, G. 1976. *Le sculture del teatro di Leptis Magna.* Rome: 'L'Erma' di Bretschneider.

Condron, F. 1998. Ritual, space and politics: reflections in the archaeological record of social developments in Lepcis Magna, Tripolitania. In C. Forcey, J. Hawthorne and B. Witcher (eds), *TRAC 1997: Proceedings of the Seventh Annual Theoretical Roman Archaeology Conference (Nottingham 1997).* Oxford: Oxbow Books, 42–52.

Cordovana, O.D. 2007. *Segni e immagini del potere tra antico e tardoantico. I Severi e la provincia Africa proconsularis.* Catania: Edizioni del Prisma.

Cordovana, O.D. 2012. Between history and myth: Septimius Severus and Leptis Magna. *Greece & Rome* 59: 56–75.

D'Alessio, A. 2018. L'architettura: Roma, Leptis Magna e l'Oriente. In A. D'Alessio, C. Panella and R. Rea (eds), *Roma Universalis: l'impero e la dinastia venuta dall'Africa.* Milan: Electa, 90–107.

Degrassi, N. 1951. Il mercato romano di Leptis Magna. *Quaderni di Archeologia della Libya* 2: 27–70.

De Simone, R. and Tomasello, F. 2014. Dalla cava al monumento. Nuove considerazioni sui contrassegni punici di Leptis Magna. In J. Bonetto, S. Camporeale and A. Pizzo (eds), *Arqueología de la construccíon, IV. Las canteras en el mundo antiguo: sistemas de explotación y procesos productivos. Actas del congreso (Padova, 22–24 de noviembre 2012).* Merida: Consejo Superior de Investigaciones Científicas, 351–65.

Di Vita, A. 1968. Shadrapa e Milk'ashtart dèi patri di Leptis ed i templi del lato nord-ovest del foro vecchio leptitano. *Orientalia* 37: 201–11.

Di Vita, A. 1975. La ricostruzione dell'arco dei Severi a Leptis Magna in un disegno di C. Catanuso ed esistenza e significato di un tetrapilo preseveriano. *Quaderni di Archeologia della Libya* 7: 3–26.

Di Vita, A. 1977. Ancora del tetrapilo precedente l'Arco dei Severi a Leptis Magna. *Quaderni di Archeologia della Libya* 9: 135–43.

Di Vita, A. 1982. Il progetto originario del forum novum severianum a Leptis Magna. In *150-Jahr-Feier Deutsches Archäologisches Institut Rom. Ansprachen und Vorträge (Rom, 4.–7. Dezember 1979).* Mainz: Philipp von Zabern, 84–94.

Di Vita, A. 1990. Il teatro di Leptis Magna: una rilettura. *Journal of Roman Archaeology* 3: 133–46.

Di Vita, A. 2003. Leptis Magna. Tetrapilo dei Severi: filosofia e prassi di un restauro. *Quaderni di Archeologia della Libya* 18: 293–97.

Di Vita, A. 2005. Liber Pater o Capitolium? Una nota. In A. Di Vita and M. Livadiotti (eds), *I tre templi del lato nord-ovest del foro vecchio di Leptis Magna.* Rome: 'L'Erma' di Bretschneider, 14–21.

Di Vita, A. 2006. Leptis Magna. Tetrapilo dei Severi: dal rudere alla restituzione. In A. Akerraz, P. Ruggeri, A. Siraj and C. Vismara (eds), *L'Africa Romana. Mobilità delle persone e dei popoli, dinamiche migratorie, emigrazioni ed immigrazioni nelle province occidentali dell'Impero romano. Atti del XVI convegno di studio (Rabat, 15–19 dicembre 2004).* Rome: Carocci, 2305–12.

Di Vita, A. 2017. Tre nuovi monumenti leptitani: la fontana, la stoà aperta e il portico tardo ad ovest del mercato. In M.A. Rizzo (ed.), *Antonino Di Vita. La Tripolitania antica, scritti inediti.* Rome: 'L'Erma' di Bretschneider, 99–130.

Di Vita, A., Di Vita-Évrard, G. and Bacchielli, L. 1999. *Libya: The Lost Cities of the Roman Empire.* Cologne: Könemann.

Di Vita, A., Pugliese Carratelli, G., Di Vita-Évrard, G., Lazzarini, L. and Turi, B. 2003. Il Serapeo di Leptis Magna: il tempio, le iscrizioni, i marmi. *Quaderni di Archeologia della Libya* 18: 267–92.

Di Vita, A., Montali, G., Portale, E.C. and Rizzo, M.A. forthcoming a. *Il Serapeo di Leptis Magna.* Rome: 'L'Erma' di Bretschneider.

Di Vita, A., Rizzo, M.A. and Mazzilli, G. forthcoming b. *L'arco dei Severi a Leptis Magna.* Rome: 'L'Erma' di Bretschneider.

Di Vita-Évrard, G. 1991. Lepcis Magna: contribution à la terminologie des thermes. In *Les thermes romains. Actes de la table ronde organisée par l'École française de Rome (Rome, 11–12 novembre 1988).* Rome: École française de Rome, 35–42.

Dolciotti, A.M., Fiandra, E. and Mighetto, P. 2012. Il complesso templare della Gens Flavia a Leptis Magna (Libia) tra scenografia, funzionalità e colorismo. In L. Capogrossi Colognesi and E. Tassi Scandone (eds), *Vespasiano e l'impero dei Flavi. Atti del convegno (Roma, 18–20 novembre 2009).* Rome: 'L'Erma' di Bretschneider, 263–72.

Ensoli, S. 1994. Forum Novum Severianum di Leptis Magna: la ricostruzione dell'area porticata e i clipei con protomi di Gorgoni e 'Nereidi'. In A. Mastino and P. Ruggeri (eds), *L'Africa Romana. Atti del X convegno di studio (Oristano, 11–13 dicembre 1992).* Sassari: Editrice Archivio Fotografico Sardo, 719–51.

Fähndrich, S. 2005. Zum urbaner Kontext des severischen Quadrifrons in Lepcis Magna. In D. Kreikenbom, K.-U. Mahler and T.M. Weber (eds), *Urbanistik und städtische Kultur in Westasien und Nordafrika unter den Severern. Beiträge zur Table Ronde in Mainz am 3. und 4. Dezember 2004.* Worms: Wernersche Verlagsgesellschaft, 29–46.

Faust, S. 2013. Ideological messages and local preferences: the imagery of the Severan arch at Lepcis Magna. In T.C. Brennan and E.C. De Sena (eds), *The Roman Empire during the Severan Dynasty. Case Studies in History, Art, Architecture, Economy and Literature*. Piscataway, NJ: Gorgias Press, 493–514.

Feuser, S. 2020. *Hafenstädte im östlichen Mittelmeerraum vom Hellenismus bis in die römische Kaiserzeit. Städtebau, Funktion und Wahrnehmung*. Berlin: De Gruyter.

Fiandra, E. and Dolciotti, A.M. 2010. Missione archeologica congiunta italo-libica 'Tempio Flavio', Leptis Magna, Libia. Attività 1998–2007. *Libya Antiqua* n.s. 5: 25–36.

Finocchi, P. 2012. *Le sculture delle terme adrianee di Leptis Magna dagli appunti di M. Floriani Squarciapino*. Rome: Espera.

Finocchi, P. 2015. *Le sculture del ninfeo maggiore di Leptis Magna dagli appunti di M. Floriani Squarciapino*. Rome: Espera.

Fischer, M.L. 1990. *Das korinthische Kapitell im Alten Istrael in der hellenistischen und römischen Periode*. Mainz: Philipp von Zabern.

Floriani Squarciapino, M. 1966. *Leptis Magna*. Basel: Raggi Verlag.

Floriani Squarciapino, M. 1974. *Sculture del foro severiano di Leptis Magna*. Rome: 'L'Erma' di Bretschneider.

Ghedini, F. 1984a. *Giulia Domna tra oriente e occidente. Le fonti archeologiche*. Rome: 'L'Erma' di Bretschneider.

Ghedini, F. 1984b. Il pannello nord ovest dell'arco dei Severi a Leptis Magna: una proposta di lettura. *Rivista di Archeologia* 8: 68–87.

Gros, P. 2008. De Cyrene à Lepcis Magna. L'investissement des centres urbains par le pouvoir. In *Lieux de cultes: aires votives, temples, églises, mosquées. IXe colloque international sur l'histoire et l'archéologie de l'Afrique du Nord antique et médiévale (Tripoli, 19–25 février 2005)*. Paris: Éditions du CNRS, 47–59.

Gros, P. 2011. *L'architecture romaine du début du IIIe siècle av. J.-C. à la fin du Haut-Empire, 1. Les monuments publics (troisième édition mise à jour)*. Paris: Picard.

Humphrey, J.H., Sear, F.B. and Vickers, M. 1972–73. Aspects of the circus at Lepcis Magna. *Libya Antiqua* 9–10: 25–97.

Ioppolo, G. 1968. Una nuova iscrizione monumentale presso l'arco dei Severi a Leptis Magna. *Libya Antiqua* 5: 83–91.

Jones, G.D.B. 1989. Town and city in Tripolitania: studies in origins and development 1969–1989. *Libyan Studies* 20: 91–106.

Jouffroy, H. 1986. *La construction publique en Italie et dans l'Afrique romaine*. Strasbourg: AECR.

Keay, S. 2010. Research reports: the Ports Project. *Papers of the British School at Rome* 78: 330–34.

Kenrick, P.M. 2008. Sabratha and Lepcis Magna: two notes. *Libyan Studies* 39: 167–74.

Kenrick, P.M. 2009. *Libya Archaeological Guides: Tripolitania*. London: Silphium Press.

Kleinwächter, C. 2001. *Platzanlagen nordafrikanischer Städte. Untersuchungen zum sogenannten Polyzentrismus in der Urbanistik der römischen Kaiserzeit*. Mainz: Philipp von Zabern.

Kreikenbom, D. 2005. Zum Serapeion in Lepcis Magna. In D. Kreikenbom, K.-U. Mahler and T.M. Weber (eds), *Urbanistik und städtische Kultur in Westasien und Nordafrika unter den Severern. Beiträge zur Table Ronde in Mainz am 3. und 4. Dezember 2004*. Worms: Wernersche Verlagsgesellschaft, 83–99.

Lamare, N. 2019. *Les fontaines monumentales en Afrique romaine*. Rome: École française de Rome.

Lane, A. 2004. The ruins at Virginia Water (part 1). *Libyan Studies* 35: 67–94.

Lane, A. 2012. Emperor's dream to king's folly: the provenance of the antiquities from Lepcis Magna incorporated into the 'ruins' at Virginia Water (part 2). *Libyan Studies* 43: 67–80.

La Rocca, E. 1985. I rilievi minori dell'arco di Settimio Severo a Leptis Magna: una proposta di ricostruzione. *Prospettiva* 43: 2–11.

Laronde, A. 1988. Le port de Lepcis Magna. *Comptes rendus des séances de l'Académie des Inscriptions et Belles-Lettres* 132.2: 337–53.

Laronde, A. 1994. Nouvelles recherches archéologiques dans le port de Lepcis Magna. *Comptes rendus des séances de l'Académie des Inscriptions et Belles-Lettres* 138.4: 991–1006.

Laronde, A. 1995. Claude Le Maire et l'exportation des marbres de Lepcis Magna. *Bulletin de la Societé Nationale des Antiquaires de France*: 242–55.

Laronde, A. and Degeorge, G. 2005. *Leptis Magna, la splendeur et l'oubli*. Paris: Hermann.

Livadiotti, M. and Rocco, G. 2005. Il tempio di Roma e Augusto. In A. Di Vita and M. Livadiotti (eds), *I tre templi del lato nord-ovest del foro vecchio di Leptis Magna*. Rome: 'L'Erma' di Bretschneider, 165–308.

Livadiotti, M. and Rocco, G. 2016. Attività del Politecnico di Bari a Leptis Magna: i progetti di anastilosi del circo antonino e del foro severiano. In M.A. Rizzo (ed.), *Macerata e l'archeologia in Libia: 45 anni di ricerche dell'ateneo maceratese. Atti del convegno (Macerata, 18 marzo 2014)*. Rome: 'L'Erma' di Bretschneider, 131–50.

Livadiotti, M. and Rocco, G. 2018. *Exornata aedes. La curia del foro vecchio di Leptis Magna*. Rome: 'L'Erma' di Bretschneider.

MacDonald, W.L. 1986. *The Architecture of the Roman Empire, Volume II: An Urban Appraisal*. New Haven-London: Yale University Press.

Maderna, C. 2005. Zur Gigantomachie des sogenannten Tempels der Gens Septimia in Lepcis Magna. In D. Kreikenbom, K.-U. Mahler and T.M. Weber (eds), *Urbanistik und städtische Kultur in Westasien und Nordafrika unter den Severern. Beiträge zur Table Ronde in Mainz am 3. und 4. Dezember 2004*. Worms: Wernersche Verlagsgesellschaft, 61–82.

Mahler, K.-U. 2005. Stadtentwicklung und Stadtplanung der severischen Zeit in Lepcis Magna. In D. Kreikenbom, K.-U. Mahler and T.M. Weber (eds), *Urbanistik und städtische Kultur in Westasien und Nordafrika unter den Severern. Beiträge zur Table Ronde in Mainz am 3. und 4. Dezember 2004*. Worms: Wernersche Verlagsgesellschaft, 5–27.

Mahler, K.-U. 2006. *Die Architekturdekoration der frühen Kaiserzeit in Lepcis Magna*. Worms: Wernersche Verlagsgesellschaft.

Mahler, K.-U. 2011. Die severische Restaurierung des Macellums von Lepcis Magna. *Mitteilungen des Deutschen Archäologischen Instituts, Römische Abteilung* 117: 221–46.

Marmouri, K. 2017. Temple de Liber Pater ou Capitole? L'apport des inscriptions à l'identification d'un lieu de culte de Lepcis Magna. *Antiquités Africaines* 53: 5–21.

Masturzo, N. 2005. Il tempio occidentale – tempio di Liber Pater. In A. Di Vita and M. Livadiotti (eds), *I tre templi del lato nord-ovest del foro vecchio di Leptis Magna*. Rome: 'L'Erma' di Bretschneider, 35–163.

Masturzo, N. 2023. Modelli e ideologia nell'architettura funeraria di Ghirza in età imperiale (Tripolitania interna). *Libya Antiqua* n.s. 16: 11–33.

Mattingly, D.J. 1995. *Tripolitania*. London: Batsford.

Mazzilli, G. 2016. *L'arco di Traiano a Leptis Magna*. Rome: 'L'Erma' di Bretschneider.

Mazzilli, G. 2017. Appendice. Su alcuni temi di architettura e urbanistica leptitana: un aggiornamento bibliografico al contributo di Antonino Di Vita. In M.A. Rizzo (ed.), *Antonino Di Vita. La Tripolitania antica, scritti inediti*. Rome: 'L'Erma' di Bretschneider, 131–70.

Mazzilli, G. 2019. La basilica severiana di Leptis Magna: lo scavo, le indagini e i restauri degli italiani. Contributo alla storia delle ricerche e degli studi attraverso la documentazione d'epoca. Parte I: le ricerche di Romanelli e Bartoccini (1922–1928). *Libya Antiqua* n.s. 12: 11–41.

Mazzilli, G. 2020. La basilica severiana di Leptis Magna: lo scavo, le indagini e i restauri degli italiani. Contributo alla storia delle ricerche e degli studi attraverso la documentazione d'epoca. Parte II: le ricerche di G. Guidi e G. Caputo (1929–1938), con una postilla sulle prime indagini (1921–1923). *Libya Antiqua* n.s. 13: 11–38.

Michel, V. 2011–12. L'activité récente de la Mission Archéologique Française en Libye pour l'antiquité, 2007–2012. *Libya Antiqua* n.s. 6: 103–24.

Montali, G. 2016. Nuove ricerche sul tempio della Magna Mater a Leptis Magna. In M.A. Rizzo (ed.), *Macerata e l'archeologia in Libia: 45 anni di ricerche dell'ateneo maceratese. Atti del convegno (Macerata, 18 marzo 2014)*. Rome: 'L'Erma' di Bretschneider, 85–94.

Mugnai, N. 2021. A promenade at Lepcis Magna: experiencing buildings from the Augustan to the Antonine era. *Libyan Studies* 52: 87–118.

Mugnai, N. 2022. Architecture and art. In R.B. Hitchner (ed.), *A Companion to North Africa in Antiquity*. Hoboken, NJ: Wiley-Blackwell, 247–84.

Mugnai, N. 2023. Building and reshaping public spaces in North Africa in the early imperial period: the examples of Thugga, Lepcis Magna, and Cyrene. In N. Mugnai (ed.), *Architectures of the Roman World: Models, Agency, Reception*. Oxford: Oxbow Books, 153–78.

Mühlenbrock, J. 2003. *Tetrapylon. Zur Geschichte des viertorigen Bogenmonumentes in der römischen Architektur*. Münster: Scriptorium.

Munzi, M., Felici, F., Matoug, J., Sjöström, I. and Zocchi, A. 2016. The Lepcitanian landscape across the ages: the survey between Ras el-Maghreb and Ras el-Hammam (2007, 2009, 2013). *Libyan Studies* 47: 67–116.

Murer, C. 2017. *Stadtraum und Bürgerin. Aufstellungsorte kaiserzeitlicher Ehrenstatuen in Italien und Nordafrika*. Berlin: De Gruyter.

Musso, L. 1995. Leptis Magna. In *Enciclopedia dell'arte antica classica e orientale, II supplemento*. Rome: Istituto della Enciclopedia Italiana, 333–47.

Musso, L. 2008. La romanizzazione di Leptis Magna nel primo periodo imperiale: Augusto e Roma nel Foro Vecchio. In D. Kreikenbom, K.-U. Mahler, P. Schollmeyer and T.M. Weber (eds), *Augustus – Der Blick von außen. Die Wahrnehmung des Kaisers in den Provinzen des Reiches und in den Nachbarstaaten. Akten der internationalen Tagung an der Johannes Gutenberg-Universität Mainz vom 12. bis 14. Oktober 2006*. Wiesbaden: Harrassowitz Verlag, 161–96.

Musso, L. 2012. Hunting Baths/Terme della Caccia: topographical context, distribution of rooms, plan type. In B. Bianchi and L. Musso (eds), *Lepcis Magna, Hunting Baths: Building, Restoration, Promotion*. Florence: All'Insegna del Giglio, 21–39.

Musso, L., Buccino, L., Bruno, M. and Bianchi, F. 2018a. Leptis Magna colonia splendidissima: l'invenzione di una capitale. In A. D'Alessio, C. Panella and R. Rea (eds), *Roma Universalis: l'impero e la dinastia venuta dall'Africa*. Milan: Electa, 108–15.

Musso, L., Buccino, L., Bruno, M., Attanasio, D. and Prochaska, W. 2018b. Marble and sculpture at Lepcis Magna (Tripolitania, Libya): a preliminary study concerning origin and workshops. In D. Matetić Poljak and K. Marasović (eds), *Interdisciplinary Studies on Ancient Stone. ASMOSIA XI. Proceedings of the Eleventh International Conference (Split, 18–22 May 2015)*. Split: Arts Academy in Split, 481–90.

Newby, Z. 2007. Art at the crossroads? Themes and styles in Severan art. In S. Swain, S. Harrison and J. Elsner (eds), *Severan Culture*. Cambridge: Cambridge University Press, 201–49.

Parisi Presicce, C. 1994. L'architettura della via colonnata di Leptis Magna. In A. Mastino and P. Ruggeri (eds), *L'Africa Romana. Atti del X convegno di studio (Oristano, 11–13 dicembre 1992)*. Sassari: Editrice Archivio Fotografico Sardo, 703–17.

Paulin, M. and Dagnas, G. 2012. Les Thermes du Levant à Leptis Magna: présentation architecturale et périodisation générale. *Antiquités Africaines* 46–48: 99–145.

Pensabene, P. 1992. Il tempio della Gens Septimia a Cuicul (Gemila). In A. Mastino (ed.), *L'Africa Romana. Atti del IX convegno di studio (Nuoro, 13–15 dicembre 1991)*. Sassari: Gallizzi, 771–802.

Pensabene, P. 2001. Pentelico e proconnesio in Tripolitania: coordinamento o concorrenza nella distribuzione? *Archeologia Classica* 52: 63–127.

Pensabene, P. 2003. La Porta Oea e l'Arco di Marco Aurelio a Leptis Magna: contributo alla definizione dei marmi e del loro costo, delle officine e delle committenze. *Quaderni di Archeologia della Libya* 18: 341–67.

Pensabene, P. 2006. Le scuole di Nicomedia e Afrodisia e i pilastri della basilica severiana di Leptis Magna. *Marmora* 2: 41–58.

Pentiricci, M. 2010. L'attività edilizia a Leptis Magna tra l'età tetrarchica e il V secolo: una messa a punto. In I. Tantillo and F. Bigi (eds), *Leptis Magna. Una città e le sue iscrizioni in epoca tardoromana.* Cassino: Edizioni dell'Università degli Studi di Cassino, 97–171.

Ponti, G. 2015. Marble entablatures from the Severan basilica at Lepcis Magna: a working import model of materials from the Proconnesos quarries. In D.G. Favro, F.K. Yegül, J. Pinto and G. Métraux (eds), *Paradigm and Progeny: Roman Imperial Architecture and its Legacy. Proceedings of a Conference Held at the American Academy in Rome on 6–7 December, 2011 in Honor of William L. MacDonald.* Portsmouth, RI: Journal of Roman Archaeology, 15–26.

Pucci, S., Pantosti, D., De Martini, P.M., Smedile, A., Munzi, M., Cirelli, E., Pentiricci, M. and Musso, L. 2011. Environment-human relationships in historical times: the balance between urban development and natural forces at Leptis Magna (Libya). *Quaternary International* 242: 171–84.

Quinn, J.C. and Wilson, A.I. 2013. Capitolia. *Journal of Roman Studies* 103: 117–73.

Ricciardi, M. 2005. Il tempio di Milk'Ashtart Ercole. In A. Di Vita and M. Livadiotti (eds), *I tre templi del lato nord-ovest del foro vecchio di Leptis Magna.* Rome: 'L'Erma' di Bretschneider, 309–93.

Ricciardi, M. 2016. I lavori a Leptis Magna dal 1989 al 1996: le scoperte nella via Colonnata. In M.A. Rizzo (ed.), *Macerata e l'archeologia in Libia: 45 anni di ricerche dell'ateneo maceratese. Atti del convegno (Macerata, 18 marzo 2014).* Rome: 'L'Erma' di Bretschneider, 123–30.

Ricciardi, M. 2018. *L'anfiteatro di Leptis Magna.* Rome: 'L'Erma' di Bretschneider.

Rind, M. 2009. *Römische Villen in Nordafrika: Untersuchungen zu Architektur und Wirtschaftsweise.* Oxford: British Archaeological Reports.

Romanelli, P. 1925. *Leptis Magna.* Rome: Società Editrice d'Arte Illustrata.

Romanelli, P. 1940. Gli archi di Tiberio e di Traiano in Leptis Magna. *Africa Italiana* 7: 87–105.

Romanelli, P. 1970. *Topografia e archeologia dell'Africa romana.* Turin: Società Editrice Internazionale.

Rosamilia, E. 2021. Quando una città non parla del suo porto: Leptis Magna. In L. Chioffi, M. Kajava and S. Örmä (eds), *Il mediterraneo e la storia, III. Documentando città portuali – Documenting Port Cities. Atti del convegno internazionale (Capri, 9–11 maggio 2019).* Rome: Institutum Romanum Finlandiae, 265–89.

Russell, B. 2013. *The Economics of the Roman Stone Trade.* Oxford: Oxford University Press.

Saastamoinen, A. 2010. *The Phraseology of Latin Building Inscriptions in Roman North Africa.* Helsinki: The Finnish Society of Sciences and Letters.

Salza Prina Ricotti, E. 1972–73. I porti della zona di Leptis Magna. *Rendiconti dell'Accademia Nazionale dei Lincei. Classe di scienze morali, storiche e filologiche* 45: 75–103.

Sandoz, C. 2004. Les nymphées de Lepcis Magna: aperçu préliminaire. In M. Khanoussi, P. Ruggeri and C. Vismara (eds), *L'Africa Romana. Ai confini dell'impero: contatti, scambi, conflitti. Atti del XV convegno di studio (Tozeur, 11–15 dicembre 2002).* Rome: Carocci, 1789–808.

Sandoz, C. 2006. The Nymphaeum of Sabratha and the Great Severan Nymphaeum of Lepcis Magna (Libya): supply and hydraulic system. In G. Wiplinger (ed.), *Cura Aquarum in Ephesus. Proceedings of the Twelfth International Congress on the History of Water Management and Hydraulic Engineering in the Mediterranean Region (Ephesus, Selçuk, Turkey, October 2–10, 2004).* Leuven: Peeters, 401–8.

Sanna, A. 2005. L'attività edilizia di Settimio Severo: sulla ubicazione del Tempio di Eracle e Dioniso (Cassio Dione LXXVI, 16, 3–4). *Ostraka* 14: 187–99.

Schippa, F. 1981–82. Il calcidico di Leptis Magna: considerazioni preliminari. *Annali della Facoltà di Lettere e Filosofia, Università di Perugia. 1, Studi Classici* 19: 221–32.

Sear, F.B. 1990. The theatre at Leptis Magna and the development of Roman theatre design. *Journal of Roman Archaeology* 3: 376–82.

Sear, F.B. 2006. *Roman Theatres: An Architectural Study.* Oxford: Oxford University Press.

Stone, D.L. 2016. The jetty with platform: a distinctive port structure from North Africa. *Antiquités Africaines* 52: 125–39.

Strocka, V.M. 1972. Beobachtungen an den Attikareliefs des severischen Quadrifrons von Lepcis Magna. *Antiquités Africaines* 6: 147–72.

Strong, D.E. 1973. Septimius Severus at Lepcis Magna and Cyrene. *Libyan Studies* 4: 27–35.

Stucchi, S. 1976. Notiziario. *Quaderni di Archeologia della Libya* 8: 465–92.

Stucchi, S. 1981. Di un pre-arco insussistente: dialogo con le aquile leptitane. In S. Stucchi (ed.), *Divagazioni archeologiche.* Rome: 'L'Erma' di Bretschneider, 127–99.

Tantillo, I. 2010. I costumi epigrafici. Scritture, monumenti, pratiche. In I. Tantillo and F. Bigi (eds), *Leptis Magna. Una città e le sue iscrizioni in epoca tardoromana.* Cassino: Edizioni dell'Università degli Studi di Cassino, 173–203.

Tantillo, I., Bigi, F. and Del Corso, L. 2010. Catalogo dei monumenti iscritti. In I. Tantillo and F. Bigi (eds), *Leptis Magna. Una città e le sue iscrizioni in epoca tardoromana.* Cassino: Edizioni dell'Università degli Studi di Cassino, 313–493.

Thomas, E.V. 2007. Metaphor and identity in Severan architecture: the Septizodium at Rome between 'reality' and 'fantasy'. In S. Swain, S. Harrison and J. Elsner (eds), *Severan Culture*. Cambridge: Cambridge University Press, 327–67.

Toma, N. 2018. Standardization and mass customization of architectural components: new perspectives on the Imperial marble construction industry. *Journal of Roman Archaeology* 31: 161–91.

Tomasello, F. 2005. *Fontane e ninfei minori di Leptis Magna*. Rome: 'L'Erma' di Bretschneider.

Tomasello, F. 2011. *Il tempio sul decumano maggiore di Leptis Magna*. Rome: 'L'Erma' di Bretschneider.

Tuck, S.L. 2008. The expansion of triumphal imagery beyond Rome: imperial monuments at the harbors of Ostia and Lepcis Magna. In R.L. Hohlfelder (ed.), *The Maritime World of Ancient Rome. Proceedings of the Conference Held at the American Academy in Rome (27–29 March 2003)*. Ann Arbor, MI: University of Michigan Press, 325–41.

von Hesberg, H. 2005. Vergangenheit als Gegenwart – Die dorische Ordnung an Bauten severischer Zeit in Lepcis Magna. In D. Kreikenbom, K.-U. Mahler and T.M. Weber (eds), *Urbanistik und städtische Kultur in Westasien und Nordafrika unter den Severern. Beiträge zur Table Ronde in Mainz am 3. und 4. Dezember 2004*. Worms: Wernersche Verlagsgesellschaft, 47–59.

Walda, H. 1985. Provincial art in Roman Tripolitania. In D.J. Buck and D.J. Mattingly (eds), *Town and Country in Roman Tripolitania. Papers in Honour of Olwen Hackett*. Oxford: British Archaeological Reports, 47–66.

Walda, H. and Walker, S. 1984. The art and architecture of Lepcis Magna: marble origins by isotopic analysis. *Libyan Studies* 15: 81–92.

Walda, H. and Walker, S. 1988. Isotopic analysis of marble from Lepcis Magna: revised interpretations. *Libyan Studies* 19: 55–59.

Walda, H., Ashton, S.-A., Reynolds, P., Sidell, J., Welsby Sjöström, I. and Wilkinson, K. 1997. The 1996 excavations at Lepcis Magna. *Libyan Studies* 28: 43–70.

Ward-Perkins, J.B. 1948. Severan art and architecture at Lepcis Magna. *Journal of Roman Studies* 38: 59–80.

Ward-Perkins, J.B. 1951a. The art of the Severan age in the light of the Tripolitanian discoveries. *Proceedings of the British Academy* 37: 269–304.

Ward-Perkins, J.B. 1951b. Tripolitania and the marble trade. *Journal of Roman Studies* 41: 89–104.

Ward-Perkins, J.B. 1980. Nicomedia and the marble trade. *Papers of the British School at Rome* 48: 23–69.

Ward-Perkins, J.B. 1981. *Roman Imperial Architecture*. New Haven-London: Yale University Press.

Ward-Perkins, J.B. 1982. Commentary on Di Vita's paper. In *150-Jahr-Feier Deutsches Archäologisches Institut Rom. Ansprachen und Vorträge (Rom, 4.–7. Dezember 1979)*. Mainz: Philipp von Zabern, 100–1.

Ward-Perkins, J.B. 1993. *The Severan Buildings of Lepcis Magna: An Architectural Survey (published by P.M. Kenrick)*. London: Society for Libyan Studies.

Ward-Perkins, J.B. and Goodchild, R.G. 1953. The Christian antiquities of Tripolitania. *Archaeologia* 95: 1–82.

Ward-Perkins, J.B. and Toynbee, J.M.C. 1949. The Hunting Baths at Lepcis Magna. *Archaeologia* 93: 165–95.

Wilson, A.I. 2003. Opus reticulatum panels in the Severan basilica at Lepcis Magna. *Quaderni di Archeologia della Libya* 18: 369–79.

Wilson, A.I. 2007. Urban development in the Severan empire. In S. Swain, S. Harrison and J. Elsner (eds), *Severan Culture*. Cambridge: Cambridge University Press, 290–326.

Wilson, R.J.A. 2018. Roman villas in North Africa. In A. Marzano and G.P.R. Métraux (eds), *The Roman Villa in the Mediterranean Basin: Late Republic to Late Antiquity*. Cambridge: Cambridge University Press, 266–307.

Yegül, F.K. and Favro, D.G. 2019. *Roman Architecture and Urbanism from the Origins to Late Antiquity*. Cambridge: Cambridge University Press.

Zocchi, A. 2018. The periphery of Lepcis Magna: new data related to the ancient road network and land partition. *Libyan Studies* 49: 51–79.

Chapter 4

THE MOSAICS OF TRIPOLITANIA: HISTORIC VALUE AND FUTURE CHALLENGES

Will Wootton

Introduction

Mosaics are an excellent lens through which to understand the history, society and culture of Tripolitania. They range in date from Punic to late Roman and Byzantine phases, come from diverse contexts (whether in cities or the countryside), cover both domestic and public buildings, display an extraordinary decorative range, and evidence the high technical skill of the craftspeople. Not only do they offer insights into the preferences and fashions for interior embellishment but also how those mosaics have been excavated, studied and managed over the course of the twentieth and twenty-first centuries. Libya's mosaic heritage is extraordinarily rich but it faces many significant challenges and few quick fixes.

This chapter discusses some of those issues, looking at the causes and the ongoing work to provide solutions. It sketches some of what is known about these mosaics including their history and location, aspects of choice and intended meanings of the iconography, their craftsmanship and what this tells us about the clients who commissioned them. As such it aims for a contextual understanding of the artform. The focus is on floor mosaics, specifically tessellated pavements, of the Roman period when the wealth and demand resulted in some of the highest-quality mosaics known from around the Mediterranean. Some other flooring types are included where contextually important as well as decorative components such as mosaics and paintings on walls and vaults.

The core of the evidence, and hence the focus of the chapter, comes from two large coastal cities, Sabratha and Lepcis Magna, and the areas which surround and serviced them (Fig. 4.1). The third key emporium of this coastline, Oea, remains largely buried under the modern Libyan capital of Tripoli. The main concentration of mosaics in Tripolitania is along this coastline but occasional examples are encountered inland. The chapter begins with a survey of the surviving mosaics from the third century BCE to the sixth century CE. The organizing principle is broadly chronological, examining mosaics in urban contexts and then moving on to those from the countryside and extra-urban areas, in particular the villas in prime positions along the coastline. A brief overview of the technical aspects associated with these mosaics follows before the final section faces up to the conservation issues of the present.

An impressive and luxurious history: from the Punic to Byzantine worlds, and from cities to the countryside

The excavation of lavish villas along the Tripolitanian coastline has resulted in the associated mosaics becoming rightly famous.[1] Beginning with the earliest pavements, however, we encounter floors which are quite different in context and effect. Punic paving types survive in small numbers. Often referred to as *opus signinum*, they present a hard, flat and usually red-pink surface sometimes decorated with tesserae inserted at intervals to form a pattern. They are well known in Punic areas of North Africa, especially Carthage and the Cap Bon Peninsula as well as on Sicily (Vassal 2006; Tang 2018; Blanc-Bijon 2021). A small number of examples have been excavated along the coastline to the east, including the regions of Cyrenaica and Egypt (Wilson *et al.* 2004, 155–58; Guimier-Sorbets 2019, 16–19).

The scanty remains from Tripolitania indicate their use in both public and private contexts. The few examples from Sabratha include one with tesserae forming the

[1] Rind (2009, 114–33) brings together a catalogue listing some 28 villas, while Wilson (2018) gives an excellent overview of the villas of North Africa including those in Tripolitania.

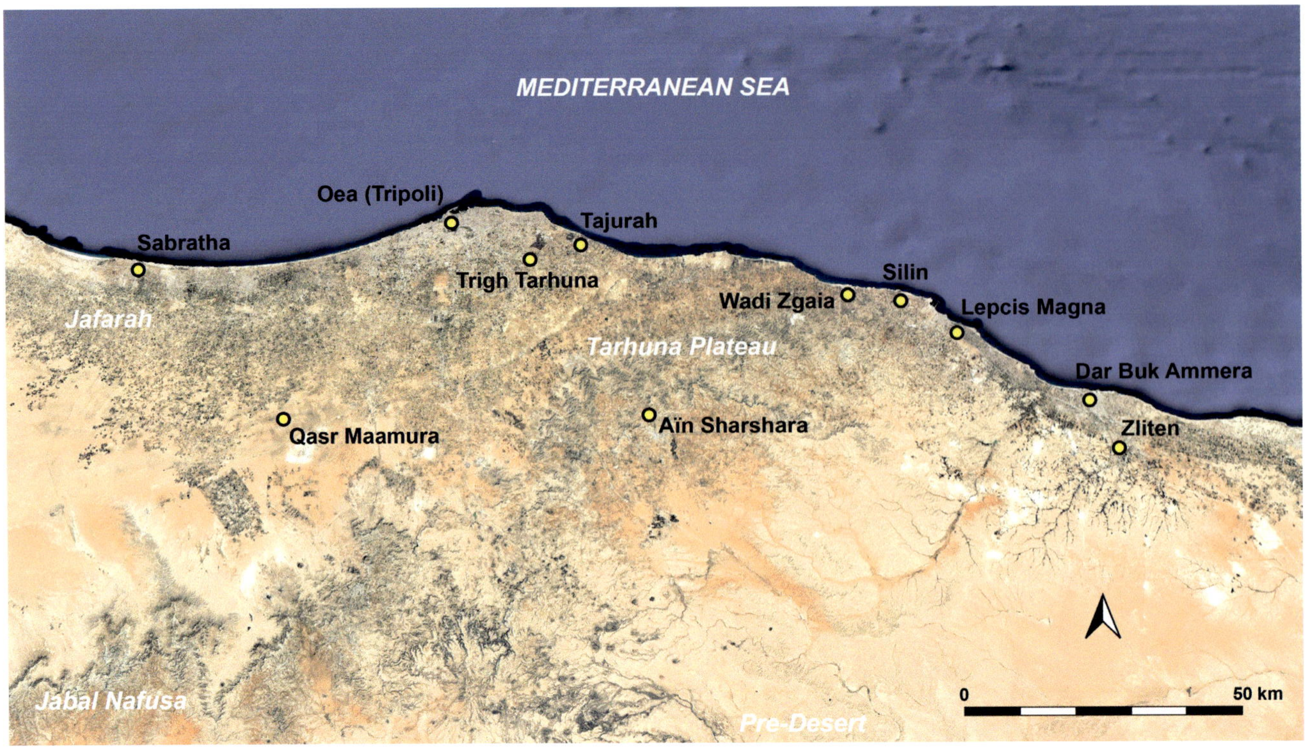

Fig. 4.1. Map of the region with sites mentioned in the text (basemap Google Earth, data SIO, NOAA, US Navy, NGA, GEBCO, image Landsat/Copernicus).

sign of Tanit which was recovered in the area between the theatre and the shore (Fig. 4.2).[2] This is listed as indirect evidence for the identification of an open-air sanctuary (tophet) located c. 300 m to the east of Sabratha's civic centre, along with the data provided by a series of decorated stelae found during the excavation of the sanctuary (Brouquier-Reddé 1992, 27–29, with references). At Lepcis Magna, the one published pavement is decorated with tesserae set in oblique lines forming a diamond pattern (Howard Carter 1965, 127–29, fig. 7; Vassal 2006, 82–83). It comes from pre-Roman levels on the eastern side of the Old Forum, although the sort of building it decorated is of unknown identification. At Sabratha, one example of *opus signinum* may date as early as the fourth century BCE but, for the large part, these floors probably belong in the second and into the first centuries BCE.[3] Similarly the pavement from Lepcis Magna dates between the mid-third and the late second century BCE.

Excavations in the region have not encountered mosaics in the Hellenistic or late Republican tessellated traditions as known on Sicily and in Italy or Cyrenaica and beyond into the eastern Mediterranean. The small number of mortar pavements evidence the close relationship between the Tripolitanian coastline and the Punic world around Carthage (Dunbabin 1999, 101–3, figs 100–1). The main series of mosaics begins in the first century CE when, following the outcomes of the Punic Wars and the civil war between Caesar and Pompey, this area had come under Roman rule as part of the province of Africa Nova, known as Africa (Proconsularis) from the Augustan period onwards. It is not until the late first and into the second century CE, however, that political stability, enhanced status, and increasing prosperity resulted in a vibrant and flourishing market for mosaics. This increase tracks closely the interventions by the Roman imperial administration, the most famous

Fig. 4.2. Mortar floor decorated in tesserae forming the sign of Tanit from Sabratha, on display in the Sabratha Museum (photo W. Wootton).

[2] For other examples of *opus signinum* floors at Sabratha, see Kenrick 1986, 127–28, 145–48; Dore and Keay 1989, 253–54.

[3] For example, phase IIIa (first century BCE) of the building under the so-called 'Casa Brogan' includes *signinum* floors being laid throughout: Kenrick 1986, 147–48.

Fig. 4.3. Detail of the amphitheatre scenes on a mosaic from the villa at Dar Buk Ammera, near Zliten, on display in the National Museum in Tripoli (photo W. Wootton).

being the arrival of the imperial legate Valerius Festus in 69 CE. He suppressed an incursion of the Garamantes, who had been invited by Oea from the interior during a land dispute with Lepcis Magna, and then he led an expedition south against them. It has been argued that the punitive measures against the Garamantian people are represented in the decorative boarder with amphitheatre scenes on a mosaic from a coastal villa at Dar Buk Ammera, near Zliten, to which we will return (Aurigemma 1926, 269–78) (Fig. 4.3).

Starting with our two main cities, they thrived through the course of the second century expanding and initiating major public building programmes (see Aiosa, Chapter 2 and Mugnai, Chapter 3, with bibliography). Black-and-white and polychrome mosaics survive from the first century CE onwards embellishing both public and private spaces. Most commonly mosaics are found decorating bath complexes, including their floors, walls and vaults.[4] Sabratha has a series of examples with such mosaics including the so-called 'Seaward Baths', 'Theatre Baths', 'Oceanus Baths' and 'Office Baths'. The Seaward and Theatre Baths have both black-and-white geometric and polychrome mosaics, and were probably established in the late first century CE (Figs 4.4–5). In the former a fragmentary hexagonal panel contained a scene of Pegasus being adorned by nymphs (Aurigemma 1960, 24–25, pls 7–8), while in the latter there are two evocative panels with inscriptions (*IRT2021* 170–71;

Fig. 4.4. Looking south-west over one of the mosaics of the Seaward Baths at Sabratha (photo W. Wootton).

[4]For wall and vault mosaics see, for example, the finds from the Hadrianic Baths at Lepcis Magna: Aurigemma 1960, 54–55, pl. 115.

Dunbabin 1989, 41; Kenrick 2009, 68). Both include representations of bathing equipment such as oil flasks, strigils and sandals, alongside inscriptions that exhort the users of the building to 'wash well' (BENE LABA) or remind them that 'it is well to have washed' (SALVOM LAVISSE).

The Oceanus Baths (Fig. 4.6) are named after a high-quality, long-haired and bearded bust in the *tepidarium* which belongs to a mid-second-century CE phase and is usually identified as Oceanus.[5] This mosaic was laid over an earlier level with another impressive and unusual head, this time of Diana or Luna, which is dated to the early second century by brick stamps, and has a black-and-white, rather than polychrome, geometric surround (Di Vita 1964, 316–18, pls 89.1, 90.1; Dunbabin 1978, 267). We will come back to this head below in this section on account of its stylistic similarity to the busts of Seasons from the villa at Zliten. The Oceanus

Fig. 4.5. *(above)* View of the display in the Sabratha Museum including one of the thresholds from the Theatre Baths (photo W. Wootton).

Fig. 4.6. *(left)* Overview of the Oceanus mosaic from the Oceanus Baths at Sabratha (photo W. Wootton).

[5] Aurigemma 1960, 23–24, pls 2–5. Dunbabin (1978, 151, note 73) suggests the figure might be Annus rather than Oceanus on the basis that the beard is made up of leaves, not seaward, and the wreath is fruit.

Fig. 4.7. *(left)* Detail of the *megalographia* in the Hunting Baths at Lepcis Magna (photo W. Wootton).

Fig. 4.8. *(below)* Detail of the Nilotic mosaic in the Hunting Baths at Lepcis Magna (photo W. Wootton).

Baths were probably private rather than public and connect with a large structure to the north. Similarly the highly decorated Office Baths were likely associated with a residential building. The fine geometric mosaics which decorate the floors and walls of the pools probably belong in the late second century, but unfortunately are now in poor state of preservation – an issue which will be discussed in the final section.

Under threat too are the lavishly decorated Hunting Baths from Lepcis Magna. These small baths, now located among the sand dunes close to the sea, were originally part of a western quarter of the city. Also likely to be private, some argue they serviced those involved in putting on the games, specifically the *venationes* (Ward-Perkins and Toynbee 1949, 191–95; Bianchi 2012, 68–69; Di Vita-Évrard 2012). This proposal is based on the interior decoration which includes a *megalographia* (a large-scale pictorial scene) in the *tepidarium* showing hunting scenes within the amphitheatre and other elements elsewhere referencing such activities (Fig. 4.7). Marble veneer and tessellated mosaic adorned the floors and walls. In one of the semi-domes there is a fine Nilotic scene (Fig. 4.8), while the smaller hot rooms have suspended floors with black-and-white geometric mosaics sometimes with the addition of yellow-brown decoration and further embellishment at the thresholds, such as a large drinking vessel or *kantharos* (Fig. 4.9). The overall impact is of a small, jewel-like complex whereas the Hadrianic Baths in the centre of Lepcis Magna are opulent on a grand scale (Bartoccini 1929; Finocchi 2012, 14–15). Decorated largely in imported marbles and integrated with a mythological sculptural programme, fragments of mosaic attest to the elaboration of the upper parts of the walls and into the vaults (Aurigemma 1960, 54–55, pl. 115) (Fig. 4.10).

The continuing popularity of scenes referring to Egypt and, in particular, the Nile – highlighting its significance and referencing fertility – can be found in other bathhouses such as the vibrant floors from Wadi Zgaia which date to the third or fourth centuries CE (Aurigemma 1960, 43–45, pls 71–73; Dunbabin 1978, 276; Johnston 1985, 195). Arranged across the mosaic, affording different viewpoints, human characters in black-and-white tesserae interact with polychrome animals; a hippopotamus swallows one of these figures and a long-beaked bird attempts to eat another while his companion tries to pull him out by his legs. Elsewhere fish and fowl abound alongside snakes, one of which reaches for a man who climbs a palm tree to escape and beats the serpent back. From the same building is a marine scene, in the same distinctive style and colour palette, with various types of fish and crustacea as well as

Fig. 4.9. *(left)* Detail of one of the thresholds in the Hunting Baths at Lepcis Magna (photo W. Wootton).

Fig. 4.10. *(below)* Fragment from the wall and vault mosaics decorating the Hadrianic Baths at Lepcis Magna (photo W. Wootton).

Fig. 4.11. *(left)* Fragment of the Nilotic mosaics from the baths at Wadi Zgaia, on display in the National Museum in Tripoli (photo W. Wootton).

fishing taking place from boats and the shore (Fig. 4.11). Two marine monsters inhabit the seascape, realized in different styles and colour schemes. The irregular frames are simple with regularly placed circles, indicating adaptation to the rooms and less skilled craftspeople. These energetic and busy scenes are appropriate to the context and evoke a humorous response at the expense of the caricatured figures.

Returning to the area around the theatre at Sabratha, and intentionally located within the cultural quarter and close to the bath complex, townhouses decorated with elaborate bichrome and polychrome mosaics have been found including the so-called 'Peristyle House' and those in other *Regiones* of the city (see Di Vita 1966, 51–61; Mandruzzato *et al.* 2017, 105–27, figs 95–122). These evidence the range of urban and suburban dwellings from the first into the late fourth century CE and include geometric decoration but also figurative mosaics and inscriptions. The Houses of Liber Pater and of the Tragic Poet offer two different takes on local preferences. The former property has a fine Dionysiac-themed mosaic with medallions containing the heads of a lion and leopard as well as Dionysus in triumph riding in a chariot (Aurigemma 1960, 25–26, pls 9–14) (Figs 4.5 and 4.12). The rectangular central field is surrounded by a complex bichrome mosaic of intersecting circles upon which couches would have been placed. As a triclinium, this room could be used for receptions. The decoration is appropriate to such activities, reminding the owner and guests of the god's power as well as that of the wine served. A popular theme, it echoes a tradition of representation known on mosaics from the Tunisian coastline and other media (Dunbabin 1978, 181–82).

In the other property, *emblemata* were inserted into the geometric surrounds. These extremely high-quality picture panels utilize tiny tesserae in a technique often termed *vermiculatum*. They depict foodstuffs in a *xenia* motif, speaking to hospitality and guest friendship, alongside amorous marine scenes between tritons and nereids accompanied by intricate paintings of the later first century CE with views of a busy coastline (Aurigemma 1960, 26–27, pls 15–17; Johnston 1985, 196). The so-called 'Casa Brogan' to the east of the forum offers insight into the later life of the city and the continuing production of mosaics. Four tessellated pavements were laid after the earthquake of 365 CE (on the effects of this event at Sabratha see Aiosa, Chapter 2, with bibliography). This includes a geometric floor with an inscription in a *tabula ansata* surrounded by a wreath, which appears to be some sort of invocation connected to fortune and fate but a satisfactory reading remains elusive (*IRT2021* 1074; Kenrick 1986, 158–62, fig. 74, pls 50–52; 2009, 59, 68).

The House of the Tragic Poet provides further evidence for the popularity and availability of these sophisticated *emblemata*. It was a fashionable choice which was particular prevalent in Tripolitania in the second century and is at its most visible in the sumptuous *villae maritimae* which lined the coast (Mattingly 1995, 161–62; 2023, 456–59; Wilson 2018, 285–97). These elite residences cluster around the three main emporia, usually within a day's journey overland and less than half a day by sea.[6] The extreme wealth of these villas, directly attested by the conspicuous consumption of the finest decorative displays, is based on the owners' exploitation of the fertile coastal plains. The mosaics, expensive marbles and wall painting demonstrate and declare their deep pockets and visually memorialize their public largesse, through the benefaction of games and other performances, and their private pleasures.[7] A handful of villas are known from around Sabratha and Oea but the largest group, more than twice their combined number, has been found in and around Lepcis Magna.[8]

The status of Lepcis Magna and the resources of its wealthiest citizens manifest in some of the most impressive architecture carefully integrated into the coastline.

Fig. 4.12. Detail of the Dionysus mosaic from the House of Liber Pater at Sabratha, on display in the Sabratha Museum (photo W. Wootton).

The villas are constructed over various levels affording interior and exterior views from long porticoes, large reception spaces and elaborate courtyards with gardens. The villa sites are usually situated on promontories with access to small harbours and incorporate a range of other facilities including baths, sunken gardens, loggia or even terraced seating areas as viewpoints or performance spaces. The mosaic decoration can be incorporated into these exterior locations, as at the Villa of the Bull at Silin (Wadi Yala) where low walls with mosaics run through one of the gardens (Fig. 4.13), or is used as a principal embellishment for corridors and rooms throughout the buildings themselves.

Starting with Lepcis Magna, the so-called 'Villa of the Nile' (actually an urban residence) is nestled between the port and the circus in the city's eastern sector. Combining a residential building with cryptoporticus and associated bath complex, it has a rich figurative mosaic decoration (Aurigemma 1960, 45–49, pls 75–97;

[6]On the road network and land partition around Lepcis Magna, see Zocchi 2018.

[7]For an overview of benefactions around Lepcis Magna, see Dunbabin 2016, 188–94.

[8]Rind (2009, 114–33) catalogues two villas around Sabratha, six around Oea and 20 around Lepcis Magna, although these figures include inland *villae rusticae* and other farm buildings.

Fig. 4.13. Overview of the garden at the Villa of the Bull near Silin (photo W. Wootton).

Fig. 4.14. Mosaics from the Villa of the Nile at Lepcis Magna, on display in the National Museum in Tripoli (photo W. Wootton).

Fig. 4.15. Detail of the amphitheatre mosaic from the villa of Wadi Lebdah near Lepcis Magna (photo W. Wootton).

Dunbabin 1978, 264; Kenrick 2009, 29, fig. 6). The baths have a *tepidarium* with a series of long rectangular panels containing vivid scenes of fishing and the sea, Pegasus once again being adorned and an allegory relating to the Nile (Fig. 4.14). All seem to have Alexandrian connections and are appropriate to their context with their watery associations. They belong to the latter part of the second or the early third century CE, but the corridor also shows phases into the later third and fourth centuries. Here we find panels concerned with mythological subjects and the prestigious activity of hunting.

One of the most important finds of recent years is a *villa suburbana* to the south of Lepcis Magna next to the Wadi Lebdah. Although the site and its structures have not been published, the mosaics have been (El Turki 2015; Musso *et al.* 2015; Dunbabin 2016, 193–94). They come from the *frigidarium* of the private baths of this residential building and consist of five adjacent rectangular panels representing the cycle of entertainment within the arena (Fig. 4.15). Gladiatorial combats were placed at either end, between are two scenes of hunting with a centrally placed chariot race around a spina which contains prisoners for execution and forms the stage for the performances of actors and acrobats. The mosaic, measuring over 11.5 m in length and nearly 5 m in width, is highly pictorial with the scenes represented vividly and with great technical assurance. Unusually it employs significant quantities of glass tesserae to supply a wide range of colour effects and create fully three-dimensional images at large scale. These are *megalographiae* like the paintings encountered at the Hunting Baths and those found on the upper walls of the internal court in the Villa of the Bull at Silin. They all date to the third century CE with the Wadi Lebdah mosaic probably produced early in that century.

The cycle is emotionally charged, in particular the large-scale gladiatorial contests evoke pathos in the viewer by selecting moments of reflection. There are no inscriptions to identify a specific event but that is no reason to assume they are generic images unrelated to real games. The desire of the local wealthy elite to commemorate episodes in the amphitheatre and circus is attested here and elsewhere. Patrons subscribed to the accepted social system of benefaction via public spectacles which were recorded in mosaic and painting to attest to such activities in the presence of visitors (Musso *et al.* 2015, 312–33; Dunbabin 2016, 193–94). At the Villa of the Bull, on the coastline to the west of Lepcis Magna, a traditional circus scene was commissioned in mosaic, perhaps alluding to the local circus of the city itself,[9] and another room had a scene of entertainment and/or execution. This latter mosaic has been much discussed with the one victim being offered up to a bull while two lie crumpled on the ground.[10] An inscription – *Filoserapis comp(osuit)* (*IRT2021* 1010) – refers either to the maker or, perhaps more likely, the organizer of the event (Kenrick 2009, 146).[11]

The property is an uncommonly well-preserved example of the coastal villa phenomenon (Al Mahjub 1983; Picard 1985; Dolciotti 2010; Wilson 2018, 289–93, figs 16.20–26). The two mosaics mentioned come from around a small, highly decorated internal court off of which are further rooms with mosaics including exuberant mythological scenes such as Lycurgus and Aion, and a rare example of a library paved with mosaic. This building is connected to a large peristyle courtyard, with another Nilotic mosaic covering the usual 'humorous' scenes, with rooms surviving along the south side (Fig. 4.16).[12] The marble decoration is lavish in some of the rooms with both floors in *opus sectile* and walls with butterflied *greco scritto* marble quarried from Cap de Garde near Hippo Regius, Algeria (Fig. 4.17). Moving to the east is a bath complex with an octagonal *frigidarium* and a mosaic of Oceanus on the floor. Boxers with referees were set in the semi-domes of the niches (Neira 2015;

[9] Dunbabin (2016, 149–50, and note 48) gives a brief overview of the arguments for and against this hypothesis.

[10] Dunbabin (2016, 192–93) notes an alternative interpretation that it represents the sport of bull-jumping rather than a scene of punishment.

[11] Wilson (2018, 291, note 157) discusses these possibilities, opting for the mosaicist on the basis of the name.

[12] For other examples of these scenes see Clarke 2007, 74–81, 87–107.

Fig. 4.16. *(above)* Detail of the Nilotic scene from the Villa of the Bull near Silin (photo W. Wootton).

Fig. 4.17. *(right)* Detail of the room with floor mosaics and marble veneer on the walls from the Villa of the Bull near Silin (photo W. Wootton).

Fig. 4.18. *(below)* Detail of the mosaic with boxers in the baths of the Villa of the Bull near Silin (photo W. Wootton).

Rossiter 2015) (Fig. 4.18). These are not only appropriate to context, reiterating the athletic nature of the baths and the aspirational nature of their desirable bodies, but may also record specific agonistic festivals put on by the owner and reiterate their civic generosity. There was a boom in these Greek-style contests in the late second and early third centuries CE. The villa, and its decoration, may signal the owner's early adoption and sponsorship of such events – the building and its decoration probably date in the second half of the second century (Wilson 2018, 293).

As mentioned, the garden area of the villa was also a place for pleasure with low walls covered in vegetal mosaic and wild animals. Looking over this outdoor space was an elegant dining room with *opus sectile* and tessellated mosaic communicating with another room, probably a cubiculum. Exterior garden mosaics of this kind are scarce but the interaction between landscape, gardens and architecture is common in these coastal villas; a couple of other examples around Silin are the Villa of the Maritime Odeon with its towers, porticoes and a rock-carved semi-circular seating area overlooking the sea, as well as the Villa of the Small Circus with panoramic views maximized by the addition of areas for

Fig. 4.19. *(above)* Overview of the villa at Tajurah (photo W. Wootton).

Fig. 4.20. *(right)* The mosaic with Amphitrite from the villa at Tajurah, on display in the National Museum in Tripoli (photo W. Wootton).

rooftop dining, a belvedere, and a large *ambulatio* around a fountained garden (Wilson 2018, 288–89, figs 16.18–19). These villas were all originally enhanced with mosaics, marble inlay and paintings.

It is worth mentioning two more lavish coastal villas at Tajurah and Zliten, whose mosaics were partially lifted and form an important part of the display in the National Museum in Tripoli (Aurigemma 1926; Di Vita 1966; Wilson 2018, 286–87, 293–97, figs 16.17, 16.27–32). The structures, and some of the mosaics, remain exposed *in situ* and are in a very poor state of preservation. Around 30 km east of Tripoli is the so-called 'Villa of the Nereids' at Tajurah (Fig. 4.19). It is named after the *apodyterium* decoration and is arranged over three interconnected terraces. The lowest, nearest the sea, is made up of a peristyle with reception and living spaces, then there is a colonnaded courtyard with dining rooms, followed by an upper terrace furnished with a bath complex. Decorated with paintings, sculpture and mosaics, it is dated by brick stamps to the middle of the second century CE (Di Vita 1966, 16–21, fig. 2, pl. 4a–e; Dunbabin 1978, 30). The mosaics are focused on marine themes. There is the mosaic with nereids racing sea monsters as well as two mosaics with Amphitrite (rooms 6 and 45), one of which is a huge rectangular floor with a central bust surrounded by personifications of the winds (Fig. 4.20).

Tajurah's mosaics are related iconographically to those known to the west in Byzacena and the villa itself is located to the west of Lepcis Magna, closer to ancient Oea.[13] The mosaics of Zliten, coming from the villa known at Dar Buk Ammera, are situated 20 km to the east of Lepcis Magna and have closer connections with Egypt and Alexandria in particular (Aurigemma 1926; Wilson 2018, 293–97). Zliten is central to arguments about the influences acting upon Tripolitanian mosaics and their chronology. They are the most hotly contested in terms

[13] Di Vita (1966, 43–51) argues for a close connection between Tajurah and Byzacena to the west, which Dunbabin (1978, 23, note 41) confirms with further comparison to the mosaics.

Fig. 4.21. General view of the Amphitheatre mosaic from the villa at Dar Buk Ammera, on display in the National Museum in Tripoli (photo W. Wootton).

of dating, varying from the late first to the third or even fourth centuries CE.[14] It seems that the earlier phase of the Oceanus Baths at Sabratha remains the key with the Diana/Luna mosaic offering a crucial stylistic comparison for the Seasons mosaic and thus placing Zliten in the first half of the second century CE. The mosaics of Zliten are also critical to the understanding of the distinctive decorative qualities of Tripolitania including style, design and technique.[15] Here one finds mosaics with interests in Egyptian themes,[16] such as the Nilotic scenes so popular in the region, as well as abundant use of *vermiculatum* and *emblemata*. The floors are laid out in eastern Mediterranean style with large panels surrounded by complex decorative bands rather than the well-known overall designs known to the west in Africa Proconsularis.

The villa is situated upon a rocky promontory, making the most of the views and sheltered bay. The building is organized around a 45 m long colonnaded corridor exhibiting high-quality figurative and landscape wall paintings in addition to stuccoed vaults with geometric floor mosaics to walk upon. Rooms line the south side including the famous gladiator mosaic, situated in a large room at the western end, with its opulent *opus sectile* panels interspersed with fine fish *emblemata* and surrounded by an extraordinarily detailed *vermiculatum* frieze recording the events at the amphitheatre (Figs 4.3 and 4.21). These include beast hunts, the *venationes*, musical interludes, gladiatorial fights with umpires and stretchers for the injured, and public executions. The latter may refer to real events, as seen elsewhere, but it may be hopeful to identify them as Garamantian prisoners who took part in the revolt recorded by Tacitus and the games as those celebrating the victory.[17]

The colonnade would have looked north over a large garden with fountains and on to the sea, although much of that side of the villa has been lost to erosion. Next to the room with scenes of the amphitheatre was the Seasons mosaic (Fig. 4.22). Again *opus sectile* panels alternate and then on either side are *emblemata* with Nilotic scenes and *xenia* motifs, laid side by side in a powerfully lavish manner. Their long oval heads evoke a particularly local style and fit closely with paintings in the villa and the Diana/

[14] See, for instance, the various views in Di Vita 1964; Dunbabin 1978, 235–37; 1999, 119, note 48; Johnston 1985, 196–204; Parrish 1985; Wilson 2018, 297.

[15] As argued, for example, by Dunbabin (1978, 23) and Mattingly (1995, 162) even if their opinion on dating is quite different.

[16] There has also been some interest in comparing materials and techniques between Tripolitania and Alexandria (see Abd El Salam 2009), but this approach is still at its early stages.

[17] As argued by Dunbabin (1978, 235; 1999, 120–21) in response to Aurigemma (1926, 269–78).

Luna mosaic from the Oceanus Baths at Sabratha. Moving back east, the ground rises and a series of rooms connect to a large upper courtyard and on to a bath complex. Here can be found what may have been a calendar mosaic with superb scenes of rural activities in tiny tesserae.

Other *emblemata* elsewhere, found in fragments, evidence highly decorated upper storeys with mythological scenes and those recording daily life. Next to the courtyard is a small room with a curved end wall which has puzzled and delighted scholars (Fig. 4.23).[18] The floor mosaic is of the highest quality, even if badly damaged, and enough survives of the exuberant composition of vegetal scrolls interspersed with animals and insects, sea creatures and garlands hung from *bucrania*. These latter give one indication of the intended sacred space which is assured by a second and most extraordinary feature: pairs of feet, one set human and one hooved, indicate Dionysian characters rooted in the mosaic and then rising up the walls, their bodies presumably painted on the plaster. It is a wonderful conceit harnessing the power of mosaic and painting to create a highly experiential environment for living as evidenced throughout the villa.[19]

Not far from the Villa of the Nereids at Tajurah is a simpler mosaic from a quite different context: a small shrine or temple located near a fort built at Trigh Tarhuna during the Italian military occupation of Libya. At either side of a rectangular niche, perhaps the location of the cult statue, were vestibules decorated with geometric mosaics and *tabulae ansatae* naming the dedicant as C. Calpurnius Candidus (*IRT2021* 245; Aurigemma 1960, 37–38, pls 56–57; Brouquier-Reddé 1992, 71–73, figs 27–28). This mosaic may date to the second half of the second century CE. Moving inland, the Jabal's rich soil for olive cultivation and the production of oil was the home of agricultural buildings focused on exploiting the land rather than conspicuous consumption, but there were luxury elements as well.[20] The best-known example is at Aïn Sharshara, around 50 km to the south-east of Oea and built probably in the second century CE. Here a luxury villa was carefully sited in the landscape. It features a long corridor with a fine geometric mosaic, which may have communicated between the main villa and some sort of lookout over a waterfall (Goodchild 1951, 56–59, fig. 5, pl. 11.2; Mattingly 1995, 141; Wilson 2018, 285–86).

Inscriptions on Tripolitanian mosaics are rare even on Christian tombs, which are well known to the west. They are usually painted or incised but one example has

Fig. 4.22. General view of the Seasons mosaic from the villa at Dar Buk Ammera, on display in the National Museum in Tripoli (photo W. Wootton).

[18] Aurigemma 1926, 205–32; Johnston 1985, 206; Dunbabin 1999, 121–22; Wilson 2018, 294.

[19] For the close connection between mosaic and painting elsewhere in the villa, see Johnston 1985 and Bianchi 2006.

[20] See, for instance, Mattingly 1995, 140–41; Ahmed 2019, 19–20, 47–59; Sheldrick 2021, 90–94, 100–5.

Fig. 4.23. *(left)* General view of the Dionysiac mosaic from the villa at Dar Buk Ammera, on display in the National Museum in Tripoli (photo W. Wootton).

Fig. 4.24. *(below)* Overview of the mosaic from the basilica of Justinian at Sabratha (photo W. Wootton).

a mosaic which speaks of Auguria who lived to the venerable old age of 65 (*IRT2021* 195; Kenrick 2009, 70). This comes from the catacombs near the theatre at Sabratha and belongs in the fourth century CE. Mosaics were used to decorate the pavements of churches, and wall or vault mosaics are known in other religious complexes such as the chapel of Qasr Maamura with a proposed dating in the fifth century.[21] Moving later, we finish this brief overview with a Justinianic mosaic belonging to the mid-sixth century CE (Fig. 4.24). It paves the nave of a church built on the location of earlier (residential?) buildings to the north of the Roman forum at Sabratha. Although the exterior and superstructure of the building may have been quite rough, including many reused materials, the interior was highly embellished with architectural elements in imported Proconnesian marble and an enormous and impressive mosaic floor, which Aurigemma (1960, 28) proposed to be 'the most beautiful Byzantine mosaic in the world' (see also Kenrick 1986, 316; 2009, 56–58, 69–70, figs 17, 22). The church is perhaps the one mentioned by Procopius in his list of buildings of the emperor Justinian (*De Aedificiis*, 6.4.13). Some scholars have argued that the mosaic was made by craftspeople from the eastern Mediterranean but it also has parallels to the west around Carthage (Ward-Perkins and Goodchild 1953, 15–18, 61; Duval 1971, 359–69; Dunbabin 1985, 13–14). It was lifted following excavation and is now redisplayed in a remarkable setting in the local museum.

[21] Aurigemma 1960, 27–29; Ward-Perkins and Goodchild 1953, 47; Oates 1954, 107–10; Rushworth 1992, 280–81; Mattingly 1995, 212.

The mosaic covered the entire floor with different decorative sections in the nave, the two side naves and the area behind the altar. In the central nave the mosaic consists of a huge and elaborate acanthus out of which grows an interlacing vine scroll. This is placed centrally with offshoots branching out towards the edges of the pavement. The vine is heavy with grapes and numerous species of recognizable birds – among them pheasants and ducks to eagles, swans and flamingos – peck at the grapes or vine. Within the oval shapes formed down the middle are a magnificent peacock towards the altar as well as a phoenix close to the lower part of the panel, and two caged birds in between. The other pavements are decorated with exquisite and complex geometric mosaics, one with roundels containing fish, which speak to the high production quality.

Materials and techniques

We know surprisingly little about the materials and techniques used in the production of mosaics in Tripolitania. There have been some recent attempts to characterize the mortars and tesserae but these exist largely in isolation (Abd El Salam 2009; El Turki 2015). In general, the mosaics' bedding layers are made up of a lime mortar, perhaps hydraulic, with various aggregates including beach sands, charcoal, terracotta and organic fibres. Variation has been noted across the coastline although it is not possible to make more precise observations about the meaning of these differences or to compare them with other areas of the Mediterranean, in particular Cyrenaica and Egypt to the east or Sicily and Italy to the north.

Similarly there is not much that we can say about the tesserae. Stone is commonly used but they have not been provenanced and so the quarry sites remain unknown. It cannot be said, therefore, with any certainty whether they are local or have been imported. If the latter, then it might be expected that the tesserae were produced from offcuts intended for buildings and their decoration, representing a form of recycling. There is considerable use of glass, for example at Wadi Lebdah where there is a wide-ranging colour palette including gold glass tesserae (El Turki 2015). Further research is needed to understand how and where the glass was produced and, hence, the mechanics of its acquisition. Initial observations, based on evidence from elsewhere, would suggest that local materials were used for tesserae (especially in stone) where available, but special colours in unusual materials, such as vitreous ones or particular metamorphic rocks such as marbles, may have been sought from further away. Crushed ceramic materials would have been used in the bedding mortars as a good sharp aggregate which also could modify its properties while cut cubes extended the colour palette when required.

The pavements themselves would have been made on site except in the case of the portable *emblemata*. These were laid into terracotta trays with lips to protect the very small tesserae laid in a *vermiculatum* technique and then set into the floor before the rest of the mosaic. In some instances a space may have been left for their subsequent installation. This type of mosaic was usually the most complex and skilled output. Mosaic quality has been assessed by measuring the density of tesserae in a set area, usually corresponding to a 10 cm square. The quality of the mosaics at Zliten is so high, however, that Aurigemma (1926, 244–49) used a 1 cm square instead as a reference. The *emblemata* have up to around 18 tesserae per cm^2 while the incredibly fine volute mosaic has more than 60 in places (Fig. 4.20). This latter mosaic is not an *emblema* and may have been made *in situ*, which is further testament to the very high levels of skill among the craftspeople working in the area. To learn more and understand better, a comprehensive programme of research is required which combines scientific, archaeological and art historical approaches with the aim of shedding light on the socio-economic history of the craft.

A challenging future? Conservation, management and engagement

Libyan mosaics in general face significant threats from a number of different sources, whether the recent or current socio-political situation, historic conservation decisions or their exposure to the environment (Wootton *et al.* 2015). Many mosaics along the coastline have already been lost to construction, theft and deterioration among other factors, especially from the 1960s onwards (Munzi and Zocchi 2017, 55–61). Tripolitanian mosaics which have been left *in situ* are particularly at threat from coastal erosion because of their location, which also brings with it saline conditions and high temperature fluctuations. A perfect storm is created when mosaics that have been lifted are relaid on iron-reinforced concrete – materials and method that were popular from the 1970s onwards. Unfortunately the country's political isolation did not save it from this misguided practice.

The mosaics at Tajurah, which were treated in this way and left on site, have been particularly badly affected (Figs 4.19 and 4.25). They are difficult to access and no conservation plan is currently in place. They are threatened with complete loss if action does not happen soon. The Villa of the Bull offers a good example of how such historic interventions have been remedied (Davidde Petriaggi *et al.* 2017). A project led by the University of Roma Tre has been active since 2012, studying and restoring the mosaics in collaboration with the Libyan Department of Antiquities (DoA). Work has focused on the Nilotic mosaics in the peristyle with some of the problematic panels being lifted and dismantled, and the

Fig. 4.25. Detail of the mosaics at Tajurah in a poor state of preservation and rapidly deteriorating (photo W. Wootton).

mosaics relaid and reinstalled. There remains much to do but the project has a clear strategy, financial support and the expertise to achieve its objectives.

Similar conservation work has taken place on the mosaic from Wadi Lebdah which, following excavation, was displayed vertically on the exterior walls of the 'Villas Museum' at Lepcis Magna (El Turki 2015). A plan was made to document, clean and consolidate the mosaic before it was relaid horizontally in its own purpose-built cover building. It currently resides there but the doors remain locked, awaiting a more stable time to open to the public. Some conservation work has also taken place around Lepcis Magna and Sabratha. Mosaics that remain *in situ* are at risk unless their condition is carefully and regularly checked as part of a management plan, which might include monitoring, cleaning, basic consolidation work or more complex interventions.[22] In 2012–13, a small project with archaeological, architectural, heritage and conservation expertise used Sabratha as the base for capacity-building workshops for DoA site managers and technicians from both Tripolitania and Cyrenaica (Fig. 4.26). The Conserving and Managing Mosaics in Libya Project (CaMMiL) was funded by the Getty Foundation and focused on assessing mosaics for condition, risk and significance before using such data to develop a site-wide management programme.

It was hoped to follow up that project with some practical interventions, but that proved difficult due to the situation in the country. However, subsequent projects such as Training in Action and now Managing Libya's Cultural Heritage (MaLiCH) have tried to follow up.[23] A recent visit to Sabratha in 2024, focused on vegetation control, resulted in the cleaning of the Office Baths. In 2013, a reburial plan was drawn up for this structure because it was rapidly deteriorating and rarely visited, and work is now being carried out towards completing that project (Fig. 4.27). Reburial is a cost-effective tool for conserving and managing mosaics on archaeological sites and has been used elsewhere in the country to great effect (Buzaian and Hashem 2014).

Building knowledge and skills is an important part of improving the future of Tripolitania's significant and valuable mosaic heritage. Over recent years international projects have supported such activities, carried out by the British, French and Italian archaeological missions. They aim at training local professionals at all career levels to increase understanding of materials, in particular encouraging the use of lime over cement, and the range of options available to them. A better knowledge of materials goes hand in hand with updated documentation and the larger challenge of prioritizing interventions based on a series of comparative assessments while

Fig. 4.26. Participants in the Conserving and Managing Mosaics in Libya Project (CaMMiL) working on a practical exercise at Sabratha (photo W. Wootton).

[22] For example, see Musso *et al.* 1997; Foschi 2003; Bonacasa 2004; Bonacasa Carra 2004; Wootton *et al.* 2015; Davidde Petriaggi *et al.* 2017.

[23] Leone *et al.* 2020. For MaLiCH, see the project's website at https://malichproject.wordpress.com (accessed on 01/02/2024).

Fig. 4.27. The Office Baths at Sabratha before and after the vegetation was cut back in 2024 (B–C), and what it looked like in 2013 (A) (photo W. Wootton).

also meeting budgetary constraints. Another step is combining new documentation with the extensive historical archives which the DoA looks after in order to create an inventory of Tripolitania's mosaics. This would be beneficial and a necessary update to the excellent research carried out during the twentieth century by Italian archaeologists such as Salvatore Aurigemma and Antonino Di Vita.[24]

It is important that these types of work are integrated with campaigns to engage and raise awareness.

The Tripolitanian coastline is naturally beautiful and ecologically diverse but is subject to the severe impacts of climate change. The two UNESCO World Heritage Sites of Lepcis Magna and Sabratha are popular destinations for the local population, playing a significant role in connecting people to their past and offering an enjoyable leisure destination in the present and for the future. Simple activities like managing vegetation can significantly improve that pleasure while also encouraging greater attachment to the sites with local people initiating their own cleaning activities, such as rubbish collection, or volunteering to take part in gardening activities.[25] Other events such as creative workshops around mosaic can prove valuable in helping people to understand the technical complexity of mosaic-making and hence give them a new respect for the craft.[26] A recent workshop with the London School of Mosaic, for example, raised awareness of the plight of Tripolitanian mosaics among craftspeople in the UK. Using Zliten as an example, a section of the famous small and curved room of Dionysian theme was remade in contemporary style and materials (Fig. 4.28).[27] The practical workshop was interspersed with classes on the history of these mosaics and the problems with safeguarding them. University students, both undergraduate and postgraduate, were involved and similar activities are incorporated into teaching and research (Wootton 2021).

Fig. 4.28. Participants in the workshop at the London School of Mosaic making a version of the Dionysiac mosaic from the villa at Dar Buk Ammera (photo W. Wootton).

[24] For an overview of Italian colonial archaeology, including a section on Aurigemma, see Munzi 2012.

[25] See, for example, the work carried out throughout 2024 by the MaLiCH Project.

[26] As part of the MaLiCH Project a workshop is being planned for architects, archaeologists and artists at Hosh al Saboun in collaboration with the Architectural Initiative (AI), which will also link between those living and working in different areas of Tripolitania.

[27] A short film about this workshop can be viewed here: https://vimeo.com/348609348 (accessed on 01/02/2024).

This region and its mosaics are an extraordinary survival from antiquity, and the Roman period especially. They speak to the embellishment of public and private structures both as a result of imperial and Mediterranean-wide networks but also through the agency and entrepreneurship of local actors. They evidence the natural resources of the region that were exploited agriculturally, creating the wealth necessary for these jewel-like coastal villas which belonged to a small elite, with Tripolitania being perhaps our best evidence of this Roman-period phenomenon. The mosaics offer evidence for the tastes of that group and also wider regional fashions, in particular relationships to Cyrenaica and Egypt in the east as well as the cities of Africa Proconsularis to the west. They also give us wide-ranging historical insights going beyond the elites, including those less fortunate people involved in public spectacles such as gladiators, venators, athletes, musicians, attendants or even prisoners. All of these mosaics were made by groups of craftspeople – consisting of men, women and children – who worked locally but may themselves have travelled to improve their work prospects or had connections along the Mediterranean coastline (see also Bianchi 2006). The mosaics therefore open up these different worlds and have significant potential for future research which will deepen our understanding of antiquity and of our cultural heritage. Crucially, however, we must act to ensure their long-term preservation for generations to come.

Acknowledgements

My thanks to Niccolò Mugnai for his vision in creating this volume and his endless patience, and to the anonymous reviewer for their helpful comments. My sincere gratitude to the Libyan Department of Antiquities for all their support over the years, in particular the current Chairman Dr Mohamed Faraj, as well as my friend and long-term collaborator, Mustafa Turjman, who has made working in Libya possible. I owe my research on Libyan mosaics to Hafed Walda, John Stewart, Bert Smith, Paul Bennett and Andrew Wilson. Of course, all errors are my own.

References

Abd El Salam, S. 2009. A comparative scientific study of mosaic fragments from Sabratha and Lepcis Magna, Libya. In M. Önal and M. Sait Yilmaz (eds), *Mosaic as Link among Cultures: The Proceedings of XIth International AIMC Congress of Mosaics (Ekim, October 7–10, 2008).* Gaziantep: Gaziantep Müzesi, 63–82.

Ahmed, M.A.M. 2019. *Rural Settlement and Economic Activity. Olive Oil, Wine and Amphorae Production on the Tarhuna Plateau during the Roman Period.* London: Society for Libyan Studies.

Al Mahjub, O. 1983. I mosaici della Villa Romana di Silin. In R.F. Campanati (ed.), *Atti del III colloquio internazionale sul mosaico antico (Ravenna, 6–10 settembre 1980).* Ravenna: Edizioni del Girasole, 299–306.

Aurigemma, S. 1926. *I mosaici di Zliten.* Rome: Società Editrice d'Arte Illustrata.

Aurigemma, S. 1960. *L'Italia in Africa: le scoperte archeologiche (a. 1911 – a. 1943). Tripolitania, vol. I: i monumenti d'arte decorativa. Parte prima: i mosaici.* Rome: Istituto Poligrafico dello Stato.

Bartoccini, R. 1929. *Le Terme di Lepcis (Leptis Magna).* Bergamo: Istituto Italiano d'Arti Grafiche.

Bianchi, B. 2006. Circolazione di maestranze e cartoni nell'occidente romano: esempi tripolitani. In A. Akerraz, P. Ruggeri, A. Siraj and C. Vismara (eds), *L'Africa Romana. Mobilità delle persone e dei popoli, dinamiche migratorie, emigrazioni ed immigrazioni nelle province occidentali dell'Impero romano. Atti del XVI convegno di studio (Rabat, 15–19 dicembre 2004).* Rome: Carocci, 1577–92.

Bianchi, B. 2012. The pictorial decoration of the Hunting Baths and its chronological development. In B. Bianchi and L. Musso (eds), *Lepcis Magna, Hunting Baths: Building, Restoration, Promotion.* Florence: All'Insegna del Giglio, 55–72.

Blanc-Bijon, V. (ed.) 2021. *Pavements et sols en béton et en mortier: vocabulaire, techniques, diffusion. Actes du colloque international (Aix-en-Provence, MMSH, 26–27 avril 2017).* Bordeaux: Ausonius Éditions.

Bonacasa, N. 2004. Sabratha: terme di Oceano, restauro dei mosaici: 1999–2002. In G. Meli (ed.), *Apparati musivi antichi nell'area del Mediterraneo: conservazione programmata e recupero, contributi analitici alla carta del rischio. Atti del I convegno internazionale di studi 'La materia e i segni della storia' (Piazza Armerina, 9–13 aprile 2003).* Palermo: Flaccovio, 328–31.

Bonacasa Carra, R.M. 2004. Il rilievo come strumento per la conoscenza e documento per la conservazione. In G. Meli (ed.), *Apparati musivi antichi nell'area del Mediterraneo: conservazione programmata e recupero, contributi analitici alla carta del rischio. Atti del I convegno internazionale di studi 'La materia e i segni della storia' (Piazza Armerina, 9–13 aprile 2003).* Palermo: Flaccovio, 191–97.

Brouquier-Reddé, V. 1992. *Temples et cultes de Tripolitaine.* Paris: Éditions du CNRS.

Buzaian, A.M.A. and Hashem, M. 2014. Reburial of a mosaic floor discovered at Tocra (Taucheira). *Libyan Studies* 45: 151–54.

Clarke, J.R. 2007. *Looking at Laughter: Humor, Power, and Transgression in Roman Visual Culture, 100 B.C. – A.D. 250.* Berkeley, LA: University of California Press.

Davidde Petriaggi, B., D'Angelo, C., Gennari, D., Angeletti Latini, V., El Turki, A., Santarelli, M.L., Bontempi, F., Arangio, S., Quattrociocchi, G. and Zuena, M. 2017. Innovative materials to restore mosaic pavements of the Roman villa of

Silin (Lepcis Magna – Libya). In J.M. Teutonico, L. Friedman, A. Ben Abed and R. Nardi (eds), *The Conservation and Presentation of Mosaics: At What Cost? Proceedings of the 12th ICCM Conference (Sardinia, October 27–31, 2014)*. Los Angeles: J. Paul Getty Trust, 270–77.

Di Vita, A. 1964. Questione di metodo. *Archeologia Classica* 16: 315–18.

Di Vita, A. 1966. *La villa della 'Gara delle Nereidi' presso Tagiura ed altri recenti scavi e scoperte in Tripolitania*. Tripoli: Directorate-General of Antiquities, Museums and Archives.

Di Vita-Évrard, G. 2012. What's in a name. Venatores and ferae Libycae. In B. Bianchi and L. Musso (eds), *Lepcis Magna, Hunting Baths: Building, Restoration, Promotion*. Florence: All'Insegna del Giglio, 73–75.

Dolciotti, A.M. 2010. Una residenza marittima in Tripolitania (Libia). Il programma decorativo della villa di Silin. In I. Bragantini (ed.), *Atti del X congresso internazionale. Association internationale pour la peinture murale antique (AIPMA) (Napoli, 17–21 settembre 2007)*. Naples: Università degli Studi L'Orientale, 659–70.

Dore, J.N. and Keay, N. 1989. *Excavations at Sabratha 1948–1951, Volume II. The Finds, Part 1: The Amphorae, Coarse Pottery and Building Materials*. London: Society for Libyan Studies.

Dunbabin, K.M.D. 1978. *The Mosaics of Roman North Africa: Studies in Iconography and Patronage*. Oxford: Clarendon Press.

Dunbabin, K.M.D. 1985. Mosaics of the Byzantine period in Carthage: problems and directions of research. *Cahiers des Études Anciennes* 7: 1–16.

Dunbabin, K.M.D. 1989. Baiarum grata voluptas: pleasures and dangers of the baths. *Papers of the British School at Rome* 57: 6–46.

Dunbabin, K.M.D. 1999. *Mosaics of the Greek and Roman World*. Cambridge: Cambridge University Press.

Dunbabin, K.M.D. 2016. *Theater and Spectacle in the Art of the Roman Empire*. Ithaca-London: Cornell University Press.

Duval, N. 1971. *Les églises africaines à deux absides: recherches archéologiques sur la liturgie chrétienne en Afrique du Nord*. Paris: De Boccard.

El Turki, A. 2015. The mosaics of the Roman villa at Wadi Lebda, Leptis Magna. In G. Trovabene (ed.), *Atti del XII colloquio AIEMA – Association internationale pour l'étude de la mosaïque antique (Venezia, 11–15 settembre 2012)*. Verona: Scripta Edizioni, 175–84.

Finocchi, P. 2012. *Le sculture delle terme adrianee di Leptis Magna dagli appunti di M. Floriani Squarciapino*. Rome: Espera.

Foschi, E. 2003. The mosaics of the Baths at Sabratha, in Tripolitania: a conservation methodology for an historical system. In P. Blanc (ed.), *Mosaics, Conserve to Display? Proceedings of the VIIth Conference of the International Committee for the Conservation of Mosaics (22–28 novembre 1999, Musée de l'Arles antique, Arles, Musée archéologique de Saint-Romain-en-Gal, France)*. Arles: Éditions du Musée de l'Arles et de la Provence Antiques, 265–71.

Goodchild, R.G. 1951. Roman sites on the Tarhuna Plateau of Tripolitania. *Papers of the British School at Rome* 19: 43–77.

Guimier-Sorbets, A.-M. 2019. *Mosaïques d'Alexandrie: pavements d'Égypte grecque et romaine*. Alexandria: Centre d'Études Alexandrines.

Howard Carter, T. 1965. Western Phoenicians at Lepcis Magna. *American Journal of Archaeology* 69.2: 123–32.

Johnston, D.E. 1985. Some mosaics and murals from Roman Tripolitania. In D.J. Buck and D.J. Mattingly (eds), *Town and Country in Roman Tripolitania. Papers in Honour of Olwen Hackett*. Oxford: British Archaeological Reports, 193–208.

Kenrick, P.M. 1986. *Excavations at Sabratha 1948–1951. A Report on the Excavations Conducted by Dame Kathleen Kenyon and John Ward-Perkins*. London: Society for the Promotion of Roman Studies.

Kenrick, P.M. 2009. *Libya Archaeological Guides: Tripolitania*. London: Silphium Press.

Leone, A., Alhddad, M.A., Alkhalaf, H., Belzic, M., Emrage, A., Fenwick, C., Jorayev, G., Nebbia, M., Othman, A., Siala, S., Voke, P. and Wootton, W.T. 2020. An integrated methodology for the documentation and protection of cultural heritage in the MENA region: a case study from Libya and Tunisia. *Libyan Studies* 51: 141–68.

Mandruzzato, A., Aiosa, S., Bonacasa, N. and Cipriano, G. 2017. La città e il suo porto. In N. Bonacasa and S. Aiosa (eds), *Sabratha. A Guide to the Studies and Investigations of the Past 50 Years*. Rome: Bardi Edizioni, 105–40.

Mattingly, D.J. 1995. *Tripolitania*. London: Batsford.

Mattingly, D.J. 2023. *Between Sahara and Sea: Africa in the Roman Empire*. Ann Arbor, MI: University of Michigan Press.

Munzi, M. 2012. Italian archaeologists in colonial Tripolitania. *Libyan Studies* 43: 81–110.

Munzi, M. and Zocchi, A. 2017. The Lepcitanian territory: cultural heritage in danger in war and peace. *Libyan Studies* 48: 51–67.

Musso, L., Baldoni, D., Felici, F., Fontana, S., Mallegni, F., Masturzo, N., Munzi, M., Pentiricci, M., Severini, F. and Usai, L. 1997. Missione archeologica dell'Università Roma Tre a Leptis Magna, 1996. *Libya Antiqua* n.s. 3: 257–72.

Musso, L., Matug, G. and Sandri, S. 2015. Leptis Magna, il mosaico delle terme dell'uadi Lebda: contesto, iconografia, valorizzazione. In G. Trovabene (ed.), *Atti del XII colloquio AIEMA – Association internationale pour l'étude de la mosaïque antique (Venezia, 11–15 settembre 2012)*. Verona: Scripta Edizioni, 305–17.

Neira, L. 2015. A pugilatum scene in the frigidarium's vault mosaic of the baths of the Roman villa at Silin (Tripolitania). In G. Trovabene (ed.), *Atti del XII colloquio AIEMA – Association internationale pour l'étude de la mosaïque antique (Venezia, 11–15 settembre 2012)*. Verona: Scripta Edizioni, 319–25.

Oates, D. 1954. Ancient settlement in the Tripolitanian Gebel, II: the Berber period. *Papers of the British School at Rome* 22: 91–117.

Parrish, D. 1985. The date of the mosaics from Zliten. *Antiquités Africaines* 21: 137–58.

Picard, G. 1985. La villa du Taureau à Silin (Tripolitaine). *Comptes Rendus des Séances de l'Académie des Inscriptions et Belles-Lettres* 129: 227–41.

Rind, M. 2009. *Römische Villen in Nordafrika: Untersuchungen zu Architektur und Wirtschaftsweise.* Oxford: British Archaeological Reports.

Rossiter, J. 2015. The 'Mosaic of the Boxers' in the Roman villa at Silin (Libya): its ludic and civic context. In G. Trovabene (ed.), *Atti del XII colloquio AIEMA – Association internationale pour l'étude de la mosaïque antique (Venezia, 11–15 settembre 2012).* Verona: Scripta Edizioni, 403–8.

Rushworth, A. 1992. *Soldiers and Tribesmen: The Roman Army and Tribal Society in Late Imperial Africa.* PhD Thesis: Newcastle University.

Sheldrick, N. 2021. *Building the Countryside. Rural Architecture and Settlement in Tripolitania during the Roman and Late Antique Periods.* London: Society for Libyan Studies.

Tang, B. 2018. *Decorating Floors: The Tesserae-in-Mortar Technique in the Ancient World.* Rome: Quasar.

Vassal, V. 2006. *Les pavements d'opus signinum: technique, décor, fonction architecturale.* Oxford: Archaeopress.

Ward-Perkins, J.B. and Goodchild, R.G. 1953. The Christian antiquities of Tripolitania. *Archaeologia* 95: 1–82.

Ward-Perkins, J.B. and Toynbee, J.M.C. 1949. The Hunting Baths at Lepcis Magna. *Archaeologia* 93: 165–95.

Wilson, A.I., Bennett, P., Buzaian, A.M.A., Fell, V., Found, B., Göransson, K., Guinness, A., Hardy, J., Harris, K., Helm, R., Kattenberg, A., Tébar Megías, E., Morley, G., Murphy, A., Swift, K., Twyman, J., Wootton, W.T. and Zimi, E. 2004. Euesperides (Benghazi): preliminary report on the spring 2004 season. *Libyan Studies* 35: 149–90.

Wilson, R.J.A. 2018. Roman villas in North Africa. In A. Marzano and G.P.R. Métraux (eds), *The Roman Villa in the Mediterranean Basin: Late Republic to Late Antiquity.* Cambridge: Cambridge University Press, 266–307.

Wootton, W.T. 2021. On the value of making and learning. In H. Hochscheid and B. Russell (eds), *The Value of Making: Theory and Practice in Ancient Craft Production.* Turnhout: Brepols, 235–47.

Wootton, W.T., El-Habashi, A., Stewart, J.D. and Walda, H. 2015. Conserving and Managing Mosaics in Libya (CaMMiL): the final project review. *Libyan Studies* 46: 103–13.

Zocchi, A. 2018. The periphery of Lepcis Magna: new data related to the ancient road network and land partition. *Libyan Studies* 49: 51–79.

Chapter 5

LIFE AND DEATH AT THE MARGINS OF THE ROMAN EMPIRE: RURAL SETTLEMENT AND FUNERARY LANDSCAPES IN THE TRIPOLITANIAN PRE-DESERT

Julia Nikolaus, Nichole Sheldrick

Introduction

The Tripolitanian pre-desert, south of the fertile coastal and mountainous Jabal regions, is a dramatic landscape formed primarily of a limestone and basalt plateau, crossed by a series of wide seasonal riverbeds, or wadis, fed by numerous tributaries (Fig. 5.1). The climate can be extreme, defined by very hot summers and cold winters, and in spring and autumn the *ghibli*, a strong and hot wind, blows from the desert, carrying sand that can damage crops and trees (Mattingly 1995, 8–9). Rainfall varies from about 25 to 150 mm per year and vegetation is sparse. Much of this limited rainfall occurs in torrential downpours, inundating the wadi channels in short, sudden events and causing dangerous flash floods. As a result, cultivation requires careful planning and water management, and a sophisticated understanding of what areas of the landscape are best suited for agricultural production (Barker 1996a, 5–13).

Due in large part to this extreme environment, today the pre-desert region of Tripolitania is sparsely populated and agricultural production is not common; however, this was not always the case. For centuries, visitors to the pre-desert have encountered the substantial remains of open farms, impressive fortified farms (qsur), hilltop settlements, huts, field systems, cemeteries and burials – evidence of rural communities who not only lived, but thrived, in this arid environment during the Roman and Late Antique periods. Their success was based on the use of sophisticated local water management techniques to make the most of the limited water resources for growing crops, coupled with long-standing traditions of raising livestock. The most successful members of the community were able to make a substantial profit that financed the construction not only of impressively large farm buildings, but also elaborate mausolea. The monumental tombs and farm buildings, particularly the qsur of the later periods, provided an ideal canvas to display the power, prosperity, and success of the elite, as well as acting as visual markers of property, ownership, and territorial boundaries in an otherwise rather stark landscape (Buck *et al.* 1983, 53; Nikolaus 2017). Furthermore, mausolea also offered an ideal way to create lasting memorials and places for ancestral worship, integral to North African funerary practices. In this chapter, we explore the different types of settlement and funerary structures that developed during the Roman and Late Antique periods in the pre-desert of Tripolitania, to bring to life some of the aspects of life and death at the margins of the Roman Empire.

Research methodologies and approaches: past and present

A combination of the use of stone as a primary building material, very little rainfall, and comparatively little modern development and agriculture has left us with an excellent level of preservation of a variety of rural structures in the pre-desert region, particularly from the Roman, Late Antique, and medieval periods. Many of these monuments were recorded by European explorers such as Heinrich Barth (1857) during the nineteenth century, but it was not until the mid-twentieth century that scholars such as Olwen Brogan, David Smith, and Richard Goodchild began to conduct detailed archaeological investigations of the Roman-period pre-desert

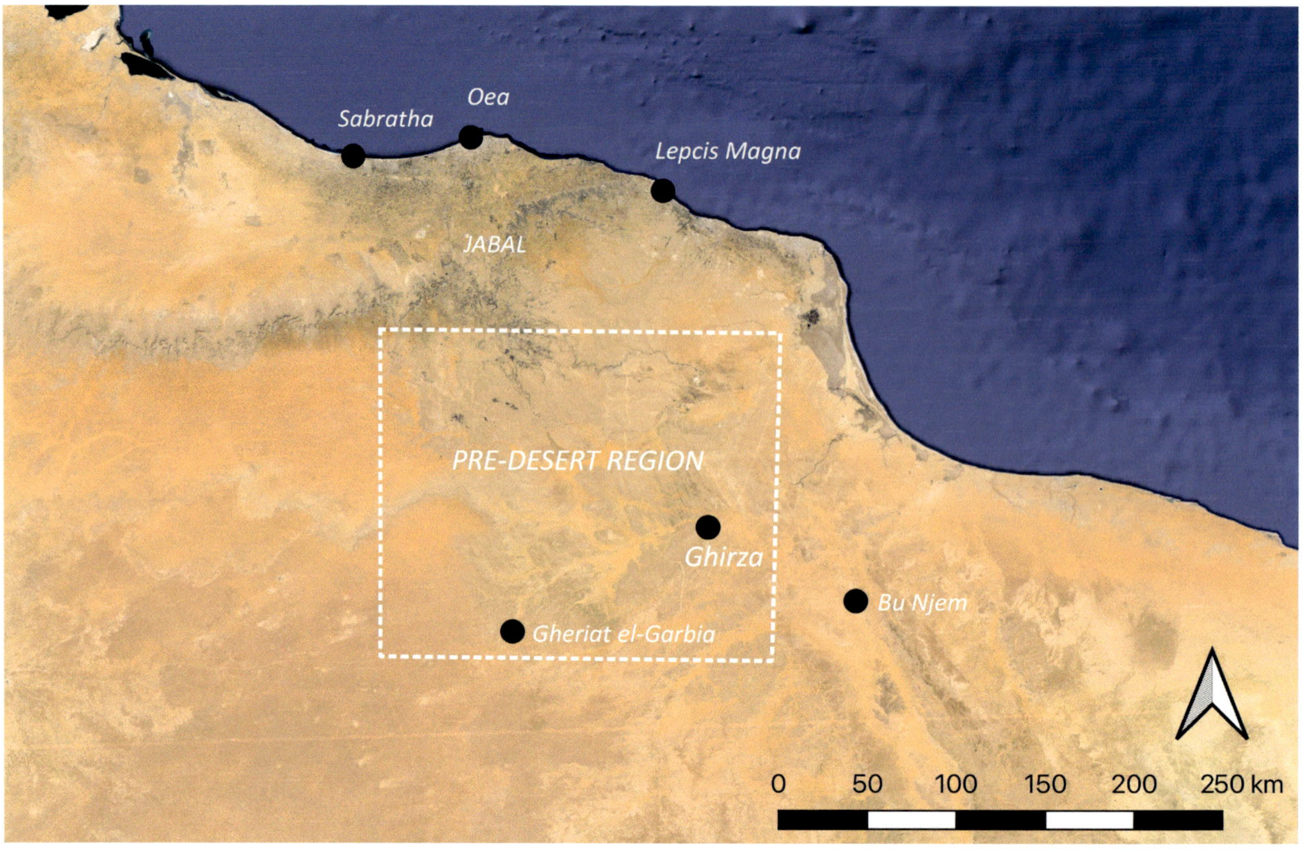

Fig. 5.1. Map of Tripolitania, showing the location of the pre-desert region. White box indicates approximate boundaries of the UNESCO Libyan Valleys Survey (satellite basemap copyright Google Earth, data SIO, NOAA, US Navy, NGA, GEBCO, image Landsat/Copernicus).

landscapes.[1] Brogan and Smith's work on the Roman-period settlement and cemeteries of Ghirza was especially important. They were among the first to conduct and publish an in-depth study of a large pre-desert settlement and its cemeteries in detail. They recorded five major cemeteries and several outlying graves and cemeteries, though the main focus of their work at Ghirza was the impressive, fortified buildings of the settlement and, in particular, the monumental tombs (Brogan and Smith 1957; 1984; Smith 1985).

In the 1980s, building on this previous work, the UNESCO Libyan Valleys Archaeological Survey Project (ULVS) conducted an extensive survey across nearly 75,000 km² of the Tripolitanian pre-desert, recording hundreds of rural settlements, structures, field systems, tombs and cemeteries (Barker 1996a; Mattingly 1996a6). They combined three survey methods to record the archaeological sites and features found across this vast and difficult terrain: rapid reconnaissance survey, systematic surveys of individual wadis and more detailed recording of selected sites (Barker *et al.* 1996, 27–32). Their aim was to record a representative sample of sites across the region in order to understand patterns in the wider landscape and through time, and the methods used meant that greater emphasis was placed on larger farms, settlements, mausolea and extensive field systems (wadi walls). While they certainly achieved these aims and more, the lack of systematic field walking has inevitably meant that certain types of structures and features, particularly those on the smaller and more ephemeral end of the scale, almost certainly went unrecorded.

Nevertheless, this ground-breaking survey pushed forward our understanding of many aspects of life in the pre-desert, bringing together a wealth of new data on settlement patterns and typologies, the chronological development of the region through detailed pottery analysis (Mattingly and Flower 1996), and monumental architecture (Welsby 1992), to present a cohesive picture of this complex landscape. They conducted the first in-depth investigations into the wadi walls and floodwater farming systems, providing new insight into how the ancient occupants of this region had managed to establish agricultural production in areas where this was no longer the case (Hunt *et al.* 1986; Gilbertson and Chisholm 1996). Furthermore, they investigated and

[1] Brogan 1964; 1971; 1976–77; Goodchild 1976; Brogan and Smith 1984. See Sheldrick 2021, 11–16 for a more detailed history of research on rural settlements in Tripolitania and Nikolaus 2017, 9–18 on funerary monuments.

published a number of cemeteries,[2] and many others which were recorded but not fully published.[3] This work was also complemented by additional surveys conducted to the east in Syrtica by a French team, who found similar patterns of settlement and subsistence (Reddé 1988).

In the last 20 years, the increasing availability of high-resolution satellite imagery via platforms such as Google Earth has changed the way many archaeologists are conducting survey. The pre-desert landscape of Tripolitania offers an ideal environment for remote sensing surveys thanks to the excellent preservation of stone buildings, lack of vegetation and development, and minimal cloud cover. Many projects are now using this method to geo-locate and enhance our understanding of previously recorded sites, as well as identify new ones, which has contributed substantially to our knowledge and understanding of rural buildings and landscapes.[4] There are many advantages to this type of survey. It provides the ability to survey remote areas quickly and efficiently and the aerial perspective can provide a clearer view of the layout of complex sites which can sometimes be difficult to understand on the ground.

However, there are also, inevitably, some limitations to this method which must be acknowledged. For example, even with high-resolution imagery, it can be extremely difficult to distinguish small tombs, cemeteries, huts, and small farm buildings from the surrounding landscapes, and conversely, natural geological formations can look deceivingly like cairns or other types of graves or structures. Furthermore, erosion and looting over the last two millennia have taken their toll on many smaller sites, graves in particular, often making them almost invisible both on the ground and in satellite imagery, as they blend into the arid landscape around them.[5] As a result, data collected from satellite imagery tends to be biased towards more substantial, sedentary settlement sites and buildings, and may not accurately reflect the full range of features in the landscape.

Another limitation of this method is that it is not normally possible to assign more than a tentative time period to features identified through satellite imagery. Comparison of sites identified on satellite imagery with previously known ones can indicate a probable period for more distinctive building forms. However, many simple rural building forms, such as small, one-roomed huts, enclosures, and field systems, have remained persistent with very little variation over centuries, so without on-the-ground survey and excavation, these forms can be very difficult or impossible to date with any accuracy from satellite imagery alone.

Problems with dating are not confined to data collected from satellite imagery. Previous surveys like the ULVS collected a great deal of surface material from pre-desert sites, which has provided us with a picture of the broad periods of occupation for many different sites and landscapes (Mattingly 1996a; Mattingly and Dore 1996). However, dwellings and other structures associated with farms that were constructed in long-lasting materials like stone tended to be used over much longer periods than many other kinds of material culture, and we cannot assume that surface finds are an accurate representation of an individual structure's period of construction, use, or abandonment. Unfortunately, few individual sites in Tripolitania's pre-desert have been excavated, and those excavations have tended to focus on large sites like Ghirza and other sites of elite occupation and production, rather than smaller, non-elite sites.[6]

Similarly, very few tombs and burials have been excavated and the very small number of excavated burials does not allow for wider interpretive studies.[7] Inscriptions and architectural features on mausolea can sometimes provide us with an indication of date for individual monuments, but we cannot necessarily assume that this extends to any other surrounding burial features. In most cases, we are reliant on pottery scattered around the graves and surrounding features in the vicinity, such as Roman-period farms and qsur, to give us an idea about their approximate dates, but this is not, for the same reasons just mentioned above, a completely reliable method. As a result, our understanding of the detailed development and phasing of individual sites and cemeteries is still limited for elite sites, and practically non-existent for non-elite ones.

Nevertheless, the extensive surveys that have been conducted in Tripolitania's pre-desert over the last century, both on the ground and via satellite imagery, have provided us with an incredible wealth of information on settlement patterns, building forms, funerary landscapes, and the wider chronological development of the landscape. In the following sections we investigate what this evidence tells us about how people lived in

[2] See, for instance: Buck *et al.* 1983, 45–51; Welsby 1992, 42–45; Mattingly 1996a, 48–55 (Bs010–12, Bs072), 78–79 (Dd001), 149 (Kh9511–15).

[3] These data are now held in the Archive of the British Institute for Libyan and Northern African Studies (BILNAS), currently housed at the School of Archaeology and Ancient History, University of Leicester. See Leitch and Nikolaus 2015 and Leitch *et al.* 2019 for more information about the BILNAS Archive.

[4] For example: LeQuesne *et al.* 2010; Mattingly *et al.* 2013; Nikolaus 2017; Rayne *et al.* 2017; Sheldrick 2021. See also Welsby Sjöström, Chapter 9, on the identification of archaeological sites in Jabal Nafusa.

[5] Olwen Brogan noted that they 'are extremely difficult to distinguish in so stony a landscape': Brogan and Smith 1984, 100. See also Mattingly and Flower 1996, 171.

[6] Brogan and Smith 1984; Barker and Gilbertson 1996, 36–38; Van der Veen *et al.* 1996, 227–29.

[7] Barker *et al.* 1991, 42–45 for a short summary on the excavations of four tombs in the Wadi Umm el-Kharab (Kh1007; 9512–14); Brogan and Smith 1984, 258–59 for the skeletal remains, and 236–37 for the pottery associated with the excavated tombs.

the Tripolitanian pre-desert during the Roman and Late Antique periods, and how they honoured and remembered their dead, exploring the traditions, beliefs and everyday lives of the people living at the southern edges of the Roman Empire.

Landscapes of the living

By the late first century BCE, agricultural production was already well-established in the areas surrounding the Libyphoenician coastal cities of Lepcis Magna, Sabratha, and Oea, particularly in the fertile, mountain regions of the Tarhuna Plateau. Evidence for permanent agricultural settlements in these regions dates back at least to the third century BCE, and probably even earlier (Munzi *et al.* 2004, 19–21; Ahmed 2019; Sheldrick 2021, 27–34). Far to the south in the oases of Fazzan, by the end of the first millennium BCE the Garamantes had also established several permanent settlements based around agricultural production, using sophisticated irrigation techniques (Mattingly 2022; 2023, 177–89).

In the pre-desert of Tripolitania, however, in the centuries prior to the first century CE, many, or perhaps most, of the peoples occupying the region, the Macae, seem to have been engaged in a type of transhumant pastoralism, moving between different areas with the seasons to pasture their animals. Stone huts, hilltop villages, rock art, lithic scatters, and cairn cemeteries, all attest to the presence of people moving across, living in, and utilizing the pre-desert landscapes in this way throughout the first millennium BCE.[8] Mattingly (2023, 189–90, 471–72) has convincingly argued that scholars have almost certainly underestimated the level of sedentary settlement and agricultural activity which had already been established by local peoples during this period. However, in the pre-desert zone, for the most part, this seems to have been restricted to oases and scattered hilltop villages, which probably acted as seasonal centres for pastoral groups.[9]

It was not until the mid-first century CE that growing numbers of people in the pre-desert began to adopt more sedentary lifestyles and increase their reliance on agricultural production, dramatically transforming the landscape. The timing of this change is undoubtedly connected to the period following a series of military campaigns against the Gaetuli and the Garamantes to the south, which asserted and consolidated Roman control over the pre-desert region.[10] However, while these actions were crucial in creating the circumstances which enabled this shift, there is no evidence to suggest that this change was driven by official mandates of any kind or by an influx of veterans or immigrants from other parts of the Empire, as was the case in other parts of Africa (Mattingly 1987; 1995, 160–70; 1996b).

Within a relatively short time frame, permanent farm buildings constructed in local stone began to appear along the edges of the wadis, close to the fertile wadi beds where their occupants could build field systems and continue to graze their animals (Mattingly and Flower 1996, 182–90). However, particularly in the early periods of the expansion of sedentary settlement to the wadis, the ULVS Project noted that the distribution of the earliest farms and the pre-existing hilltop settlements did not overlap, perhaps indicating that while clearly a portion of the population was adopting a new type of economy, others were continuing to maintain their traditional modes of subsistence, each within their own territories (Mattingly and Flower 1996, 160–62). The evidence for occupation at some of these hilltop settlements continues well into the Roman and Late Antique periods. It is clear therefore that while sedentary, agricultural settlements became increasingly the norm, the occupation of these hilltop settlements continued alongside them in the landscape, though more investigation is needed at these sites to understand how their function may have changed over time (Barker 1996b, 105; Mattingly and Flower 1996, 160).

The farm buildings that began to appear in the pre-desert in the first century CE are often characterized as open or unfortified farms, referring respectively to the fact that their primary feature was usually a large, open-air space, and that they had fewer features which can be considered as defensive in nature (as opposed to the more conspicuously fortified qsur which developed later on, as discussed below). These buildings varied widely in terms of their plan, size, and construction techniques, from small one- or two-room structures constructed in poorly coursed rubble, to large, multi-roomed complexes employing ashlar masonry techniques. However, broadly speaking, they can be divided into two basic forms: farmyard buildings and courtyard buildings (Sheldrick 2021, 63–71) (Fig. 5.2).

By far the most common form of open farm building recorded in the pre-desert is the farmyard building (Fig. 5.2a–b). These buildings were defined by a large, open-air farmyard, with one or more rooms usually found along one or two sides of the yard, but otherwise enclosed by a low stone wall. The majority of these farmyard buildings employed drystone construction techniques, the quality of which varied widely from irregularly coursed rubble to well-faced, carefully coursed masonry. In plan, they were often more or less rectilinear, but yards with curved or irregular shapes have also been recorded. While the

[8] Barker 1981; 1996b; Scheele 2017; Mattingly *et al.* 2020, 223–28; Mattingly 2023, 471–73.

[9] Barker 1996b, 105; Mattingly and Dore 1996, 117–18; Mattingly and Flower 1996, 160; Sheldrick 2021, 23–25.

[10] *IRT2021* 301; Pliny, *Naturalis Historia*, 5.35–38; Florus, *Epitome*, 2.31; Cassius Dio, *Historia Romana*, 55.28.3–4. See also Mattingly 1995, 68–77.

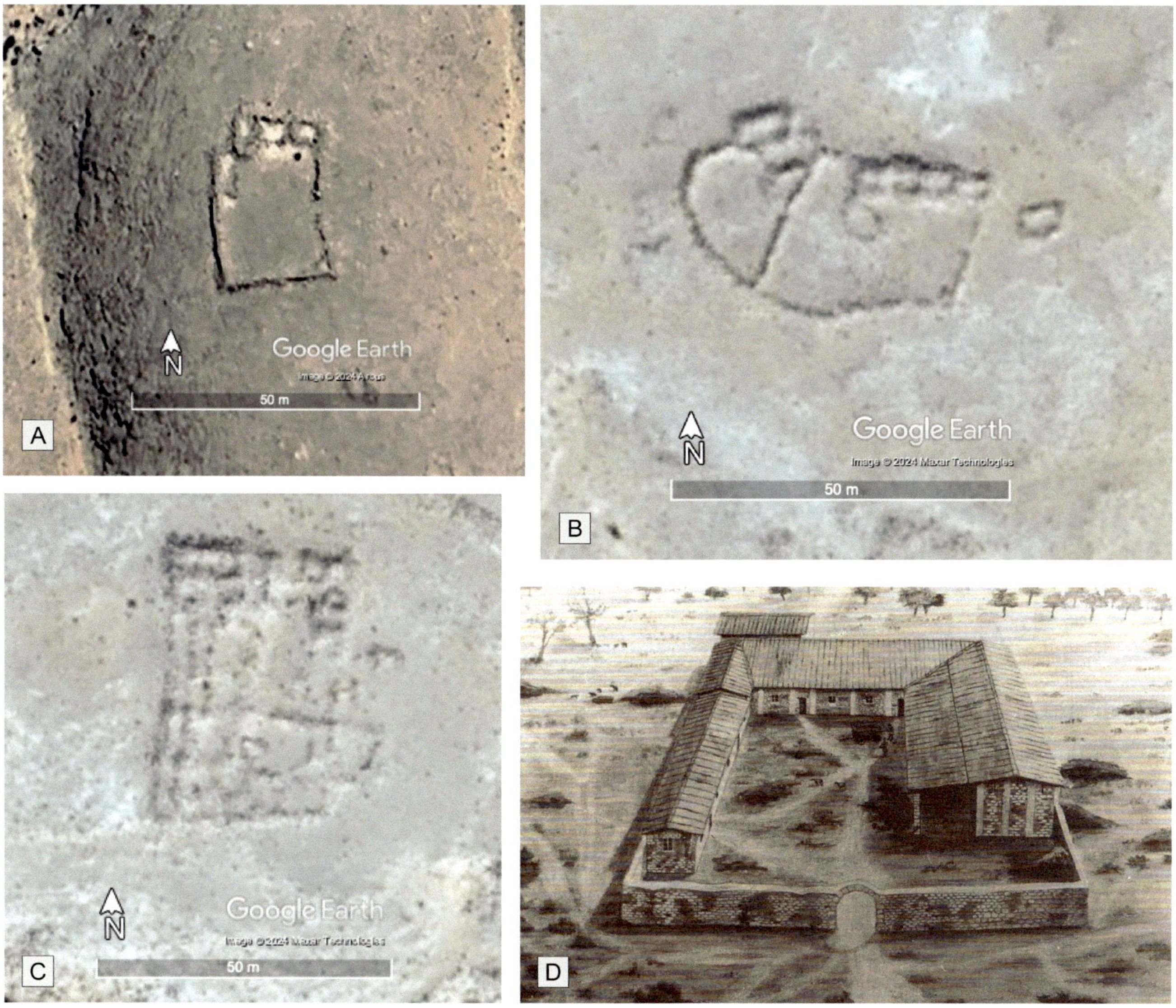

Fig. 5.2. Examples of farmyard (A–B) and courtyard (C–D) farms. A: Gh072, Wadi Ghirza (Mattingly 1996a, 112–13) (satellite image copyright Google Earth, Airbus); B: Mm070, Wadi Mimoun (Mattingly 1996a, 219) (satellite image copyright Google Earth, Maxar Technologies); C: Mm066, Wadi Mimoun (Mattingly 1996a, 219) (satellite image copyright Google Earth, Maxar Technologies); D: BUN007, Wadi Bani Walid (North) (reconstruction drawing: Mattingly 1996a, 58, fig. 5.4).

construction of stone buildings is clear evidence of the move to sedentary settlement, at the same time, the emphasis on the large farmyard was likely a reflection of the continued importance of pre-Roman traditions of subsistence, which focused on pastoralism and raising large herds of animals (Sheldrick 2021, 59–105). Excavations have shown that in this region, herding strategies focused primarily on sheep and/or goats, though other animals such as gazelle and camel were also exploited (Van der Veen *et al.* 1996, 249–53). Some scholars have even argued that the farmyard form was a kind of fossilization of the way in which pastoralist encampments would originally have been arranged, with lines of tents facing onto a corral (Liverani 2005, 397; see also Finkelstein 1995, 46–49).

Less common in the pre-desert were courtyard buildings (Fig. 5.2c–d). These structures were usually more strictly rectilinear in plan, with continuous ranges of rooms arranged around at least two sides of a well-defined courtyard. Although very large examples of the farmyard buildings just discussed certainly occurred, their mean size was around 500–600 m^2; on average, courtyard farms were almost twice this size (Sheldrick 2021, 73). Like farmyard buildings, courtyard buildings also employed a variety of construction techniques, but they were more likely than farmyard buildings to utilize ashlar masonry techniques in their construction, particularly *opus africanum* (Sheldrick 2021, 88). In contrast to the richly adorned mausolea discussed in the next section, figural decorations on open farm buildings were very rare, with the recorded instances found only at courtyard buildings. The known carvings were limited in variation, including a bull's head, a rosette, and phalli; these were not always found *in situ*, and it may be that they came from mausolea (Nikolaus 2017, 218–21; Sheldrick 2021, 90–94).

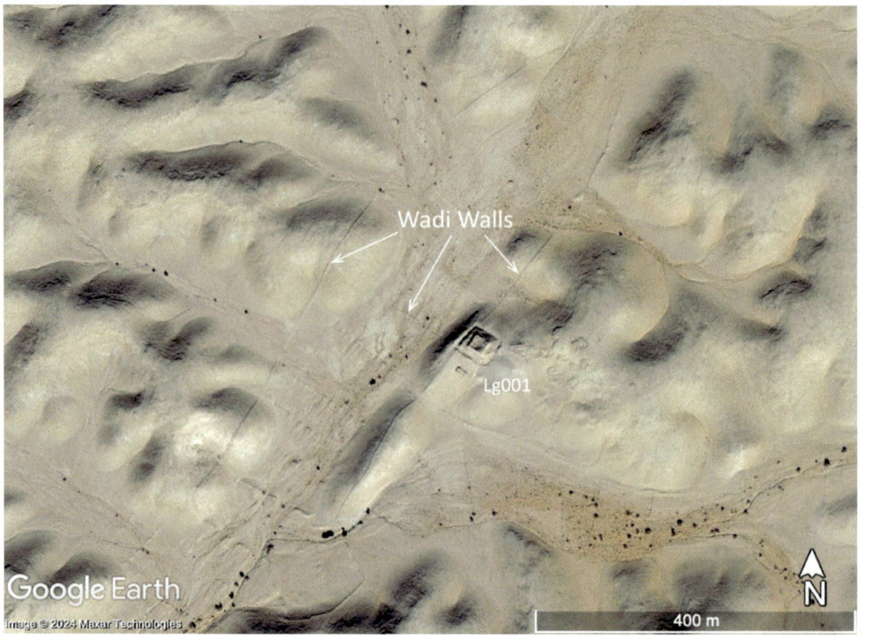

Fig. 5.3. Cross wadi walls and enclosures in the Wadi Legwais (Mattingly 1996a, 162–64) (satellite image copyright Google Earth, Maxar Technologies).

All of these features suggest that courtyard buildings were the building form associated with the elite, i.e. those with the means and wealth to construct these more substantial buildings. While it was suggested above that the farmyard building form reflected local traditions, the courtyard form had clear, and probably deliberate, similarities to the courtyard buildings around which the large olive oil producing estates were centred in the Jabal and closer to the coast (Ahmed 2019; Sheldrick 2021, 63–71). The pre-desert examples can thus be seen as a visible representation of the participation of elite members of pre-desert society in wider networks of contact and trade with the farming communities to the north and a conscious emulation of the forms used by the urban elite on their productive estates in the Jabal.

Excavations conducted by the ULVS Project at a few select pre-desert sites recovered evidence for the cultivation of a diverse range of cereals, pulses, and fruits, including barley, wheat, lentils, peas, grapes, figs, dates, and the exploitation of many other local plants.[11] However, like their neighbours to the north, one of the main ways in which the local elite of the pre-desert gained their wealth was through the production of olive oil (though not on the same scale); evidence for pressing facilities was recorded at 35 sites in the pre-desert.[12] Probably the most well-known, and best investigated of the pre-desert olive oil production sites was Lm004, a Romano-Libyan farm complex in the Wadi el-Amud, dating between the late first to third centuries CE.[13] With a potential capacity of more than 2,000 litres of oil per year, it is clear that this press and others like it were not used only for subsistence, but rather were designed for surplus production (Mattingly 1985; 1988; Barker *et al.* 1996). In the pre-desert, presses were recorded slightly more commonly at courtyard farm buildings, though not exclusively, but the pattern again suggests that it was those on the wealthier end of the scale who could afford the investment needed to construct and maintain an olive oil press, and then subsequently profited from the surplus production that it enabled (Sheldrick 2021, 75–80).

The majority of research into the farms of the pre-desert has tended to focus on these farm buildings themselves, but they would also have been surrounded by many other structures, many of which were probably related to the agricultural activities in which more and more people were now engaged. The ULVS Project recorded hundreds of small huts and enclosures, and satellite imagery has revealed hundreds more, many of which probably served as additional housing, storage areas, and animal pens. This almost certainly represents only a fraction of the structures which would have populated the landscape around the main farm buildings at the time, and we can imagine that even more structures constructed of less permanent materials and which no longer survive in the archaeological record would also have been present (Mattingly 1996a; Mattingly and Dore 1996, 133–42). Structures related to water management such as cisterns and wells were also recorded in many areas of the pre-desert by the ULVS Project (Mattingly and Flower 1996, 169–70), along with thousands of wadi walls, forming hundreds of kilometres of field systems (Hunt *et al.* 1986; Gilbertson and Chisholm 1996; Gilbertson and Hunt 1996) (Fig. 5.3). Further investigations into these other kinds of structures are sorely needed to help us better understand how individual farms functioned both as independent units but also as integral parts of wider landscapes of occupation and production.

Open farms could be isolated or occur in small groups or settlements. Sometimes multiple farms were constructed side by side to create extensive complexes, some reaching over 200 m in length (Sheldrick 2021, 67–69). There must have been many practical advantages to this arrangement, in that it provided greater

[11] Barker and Jones 1982; Hunt *et al.* 1986; Gilbertson and Hunt 1996; Van der Veen *et al.* 1996.

[12] Mattingly 1996a; Barker *et al.* 1996, 281–85; Sheldrick 2021, 76, table 5.10. Though cf. the more than 140 pressing sites recorded in the Jabal.

[13] Brogan 1964; Barker *et al.* 1984; 1996, 278–81; Mattingly 1996a, 167.

security and the possibility to take advantage of shared labour, but it was probably also related to family and community ties and obligations. In other parts of North Africa, historical sources and inscriptions have provided evidence for the existence of estate systems, in which wealthy landowners owned huge areas of lands, managed or rented out to tenant farmers (De Vos Raaijmakers 2013, 183–87; Mattingly 2023, 460–67). We have far less direct evidence about the extent to which a similar system may have operated in the Tripolitanian pre-desert, but there is some indication that elite families may have controlled large parts of certain wadis which were farmed by tenants or others with some level of cultural or legal obligation to the elite landowners (Mattingly 2023, 472).

Open farms dominated the rural landscape of the pre-desert through the first and second centuries CE, but starting in the third century, a new architectural form began to gain popularity. Fortified farm buildings, today known commonly in Libya as qsur, presented a stark contrast to the unfortified farms which preceded them. These imposing structures took the form of fortified towers, usually two to three storeys high, many of which still survive to great height (Fig. 5.4).

While the earlier unfortified farms were characterized by large, open spaces, most qsur were much smaller in plan, most averaging between c. 200–300 m^2, though their upper storeys would have added a certain amount of interior space (Fig. 5.5). They were more internally focused, often with only a single, highly defensible entrance, few and small windows, and only a small, internal courtyard or lightwell; they also commonly had

Fig. 5.4. Qasr BS004 in the Bir Scedua basin (BILNAS Archive, ULVS collection, D54/10/1/4).

additional features associated with defence or fortification, such as batters or surrounding ditches. They rarely used ashlar masonry, but it is clear that great care was taken in their construction, many of which were built with well-faced masonry and careful coursing, requiring skilled professionals, crucial for buildings of this size and height (Welsby 1992; Mattingly and Dore 1996, 127–33; Sheldrick 2021, 107–65).

Excavations have suggested that those who built and occupied the qsur were continuing to rely on most of the same species of plants and animals, and it seems likely that they simply continued to use many of the same enclosures and agricultural field systems that had been established previously. Fewer olive presses were found in direct association with qsur, but it is probable that some of the earlier presses remained in use (Sheldrick 2021, 133–37). However, while qsur were sometimes built directly over earlier farms (for instance, Ag001: Mattingly 1996a, 20), in many cases there appears to have been a desire to build these new structures and settlements in new locations. These tended to be both more defensible and more visible in the landscape, on hilltops and cliffs overlooking the wadis, rather than along their banks where the open farms had been located. Their size and prominent locations made the qsur significant focal points in the landscape, and more than a third of those recorded were surrounded by small clustered settlements, suggesting dependent communities (Sheldrick 2021, 155–56). Ghirza took this model to the extreme and was one of the largest known rural settlements in Tripolitania. Dating to Late Antiquity, the settlement was focused around six qsur, the largest of which, Building 34, was a massive fortified complex reaching nearly 50 m^2 (Fig. 5.5d) – one of the largest known in the region, surrounded by more than 30 smaller buildings (Brogan and Smith 1984).

There are two major factors which may have prompted this change in both the form and location of settlement during this period. The first is related to security. After a relative peace through the first and second centuries CE, there seems to have been increasing unrest in Tripolitania, with inscriptions from both military and civilian contexts recording 'barbarian' incursions (Mattingly 1995, 202–5; *IRT2021* 871, 880). This would explain both the increasingly defensive nature of the buildings themselves, but also the increasing number of settlements around these strongholds, with people clustering into larger communities for safety. At the same time, after two centuries of peace and productive activity, the leading families of the region had become well-established, amassing wealth and power. Many scholars have argued therefore that the construction of the qsur was representative of an increasing stratification of society and a desire on the part of the local elites to display and emphasize their status in dramatically visible ways (Mattingly 1996a, 326–31; Sheldrick 2021, 164–65).

The latter reason is also supported by the fact that whereas sculptural decoration was rarely found on open farms, some fortified farms began to display a wider range of decoration, particularly around doorways, as well as employing inscriptions which seem to have been completely absent at earlier farms. The sculpture often took the form of geometric patterns and rosettes, but also sometimes included figural decorations, of the kind which had previously been confined to funerary monuments, including animals, hunting scenes, and even a dolphin (Fig. 5.6). The limited figural decoration on domestic structures together with their prominent position above or near doorways suggests that the reliefs had a very specific protective function and were seen as powerful imagery to safeguard the building and its inhabitants. In some instances, in fact, it also appears that sculptural decoration and inscriptions incorporated into the qsur were reused from earlier mausolea, as in two instances where the inscriptions indicate that they were clearly dedications to the dead and their monument.[14] It may be that they simply desired to reuse the decoration, but it may also have been a deliberate act of invoking the protective power of their ancestors. It is clear, therefore, that the qsur developed to serve a dual purpose, of being both more physically secure but also acting as a conspicuous

Fig. 5.5. Examples of qsur. A: Kn077, Wadi Khanafes (Mattingly 1996a, 159) (satellite image copyright Google Earth, Maxar Technologies); B: BS003, Bir Scedua Basin (Mattingly 1996a, 45–46) (satellite image copyright Google Earth, Airbus); C: Kh014, Wadi Umm el-Kharab (Welsby 1992, 82, fig. 10; Mattingly 1996a, 133); D: Ghirza, Building 34 (Brogan and Smith 1984, 67, fig. 15) (satellite images copyright Google Earth).

[14] See the inscription integrated above the door at Qasr Elisawi in the Wadi Migdal (Mg006; *IRT2021* 1108) and at a qasr at Wadi el-Amud (Lm003; *IRT2021* 1012): Nikolaus 2017, 219–21.

Fig. 5.6. Sculptural decoration and inscriptions around doorways of qsur. A: Sf112, Qasr Nagazza East, Wadi Sofeggin (Mattingly 1996a, 290; BILNAS Archive, ULVS collection, D54/10/1/37); B: Kh014, Wadi Umm el-Kharab (Welsby 1992, 83, fig. 12; Mattingly 1996a, 133); C: Sf116, Wadi Sofeggin (Mattingly 1996a, 291; BILNAS Archive, ULVS collection, D54/10/1/37); D: Md028, Qasr Azziz, Wadi Merdum, *IRT2021* 893 (Mattingly 1996a, 182–84; BILNAS Archive, ULVS collection, D54/10/1/26).

display of the wealth and status which would have been necessary to build them.

Landscapes of the dead

Given the sheer amount of settlement and nomadic activity in this region, it is unsurprising that burial structures are numerous and span over a long period, from prehistoric to modern times. The grave types are varied in their form and size, ranging from simple graves marked by a line of stones to substantial mortuary structures built of ashlar masonry. The most common grave type was circular graves covered by a stone mound, a form widely represented across the Sahara. A variety of grave types in the same cemetery was not uncommon, including rectangular graves, circular cairns, mausolea, or rectangular platforms, as well as Islamic graves. Some burials had stelae (long limestone slabs), column drums, or offering tables associated with them (Mattingly 1996a, 144).

A good example of a complex cemetery that was used over hundreds of years can be found in the Wadi Antar (An001: Mattingly 1996a, 33–39; Ray and Nikolaus 2019, 94). Located on a prominent spur, the cemetery is visible from a considerable distance. Some features, such as flint scatters and hunting walls, most likely date to the prehistoric period. It comprised around 180 graves, including cist graves, eight tombs constructed of cut blocks, four rectangular 'platforms', two Roman-period mausolea and approximately 12 Islamic graves. The graves are largely simple piles of stones that range in size from c. 8 m^2 to an extremely large example measuring c. 400 m^2. The two mausolea were placed within sight of each other. The earliest mausoleum can be dated to the late first or early second century CE on the basis of the lettering of its Latin inscription (*IRT2021* 1137) and the *tria nomina* of the dedicatee, T. Flavius [---]ninus, which indicated that citizenship was received under the Flavian emperors (An001f: Mattingly 1996a, 35; for the translation of the inscription see Brogan and Reynolds 1985). The family lineage, including the names of the grandfather and father, and the names of the children, are stressed here, and all were of Libyan or Punic origin. A T. Flavius Capito was also mentioned on a building inscription of a nearby temple (Tininai) dating to the late second or early third century CE, and was probably a descendant of the same family (*IRT2021* 888; Brogan and Reynolds 1985, 13–15). The variety of grave types and furniture at this cemetery highlights its complexity, and perhaps can give indications about social hierarchies and family lineage among the local inhabitants (Brogan and Reynolds 1985, 29). As outlined in the introduction, very few cemeteries have been excavated and studied in detail and we still know relatively little about them. Because of this, the remainder of this section focuses mainly on the architecture and sculptural decoration of mausolea within their immediate and wider context, which have been studied and recorded in much more detail in the past.

Perhaps the most striking funerary structures of the pre-desert are the Roman-period mausolea, a type of burial monument that was previously unknown to the area. By the fourth century CE, over 100 such monumental structures dotted the pre-desert landscape (Nikolaus 2017). The majority are part of wider cemeteries of various sizes. The presence of libation channels and offering tables strongly suggests that mausolea (and indeed other burial types) were visited regularly by people who presented offerings to the deceased (Mattingly 1995; Stone and Stirling 2007, 22–23) (Fig. 5.7b–c). An offering table from the Wadi Tabuniyah displays a range of foods including fish and eggs (Tb045: Mattingly 1996a, 301–2) (Fig. 5.7a). Relief carvings on a mausoleum in the Wadi Lella likely depicts a range of offerings or a funerary feast, including a fish on a platter, fruits such as figs, vegetables, bread, as well as an amphora and a wine pitcher (Nikolaus 2017, 89–90) (Fig. 5.7d–e). Continuous rituals surrounding burial monuments were clearly important, so much so that an inscription from a mausoleum at Ghirza expresses the wish that the sons and grandsons shall visit the monument (*IRT2021* 898), and celebrations in honour of the ancestors are highlighted in another inscription from Ghirza (*IRT2021* 994). The ancient writers Herodotus and Pomponius Mela mention that the Augilae of north-east Cyrenaica slept outside burials to communicate with the powerful ancestors in dreams (Herodotus, *Historiae*, 4.172; Pomponius Mela, *Chorographia*, 1.46). Indeed, a similar practice was still carried out by the Berber and Tuareg of the Maghreb and Sahara in the late nineteenth and early twentieth centuries.[15] Women who wanted to know about the well-being of their absent husband would sleep on top of pre-Islamic tombs (Camps 1986, 163), and people would sleep in shrines (*koubba*) or caves where holy men were buried to receive revealing or premonitory dreams (Doutté 1909, 412; Basset 1920, 61).

Fig. 5.7. A–C: Offering tables, some with carved representations of offerings. A: Fish in the centre and dates in upper right bowl, Tabuniyah, found near mausoleum (BILNAS Archive, Olwen Brogan papers, D41/3/11/2/37); B: Offering table from Wadi el-Amud found near mausoleum Lm001 (BILNAS Archive, Olwen Brogan papers, D41/3/11/2/53); C: Offering table from Wadi Umm el-Agerem with libation channel and possible representation of bread found near Ag002-A (BILNAS Archive, Charles Daniels papers, D24/12/1/1, photo 1084). D–E: Mausoleum in the Wadi Lella depicting various foods including a basket of figs, a cup, vegetables, a fish on a tray atop a folding table and four loaves of round bread (BILNAS Archive, Olwen Brogan papers, D41/3/11/2/35).

[15] Duveyrier 1864, 415; Foureau 1902, 66; Foucauld 1918, 115; Camps 1986, 163.

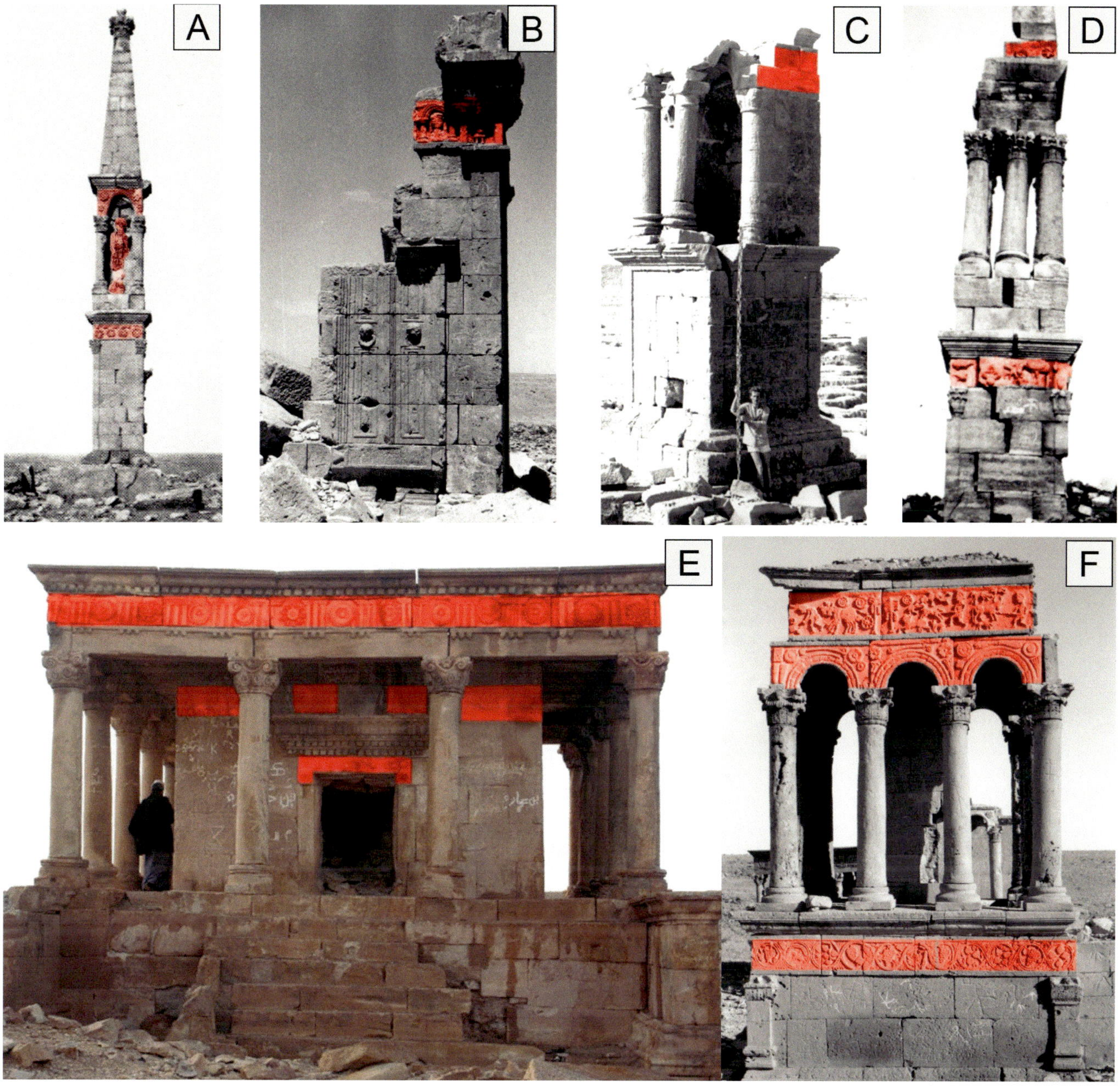

Fig. 5.8. Different architectural types of mausolea and the location of their decorations indicated in red (added by J. Nikolaus). A–D: Obelisk mausolea. A: Ghirza , Tomb South A (BILNAS Archive, Olwen Brogan papers, D41/2/7/8/9/1/1); B: Umm el-Agerem, Ag002 (BILNAS Archive, Olwen Brogan papers, D41/3/11/2/36); C: Wadi Migdal, Mg001 (BILNAS Archive, ULVS collection, D54/10/1/27); D: Wadi Mesueggi (BILNAS Archive, Olwen Brogan papers, D41/3/11/2/41). E–F: Temple mausolea. E: Ghirza, Tomb North A (photo P. Kenrick); F: Ghirza, Tomb North C (BILNAS Archive, Olwen Brogan papers, D41/2/7/8/3/1/24).

Mausolea started to appear in the pre-desert in the first century CE (Brogan 1971; Barker 1996a; Mattingly 1996a). The architectural types that first emerged were tower and obelisk mausolea, usually constructed of local limestone in ashlar masonry, occasionally with a rubble core and ashlar facing. Obelisk mausolea are unique to Tripolitania in that they are taller and thinner than other North African tower tombs, topped with a long and slender pyramidal roof (Fig. 5.8a–b). They typically consisted of two or three superimposed storeys, reaching a height of up to 18 m above the subterranean burial chamber.[16] Over time, preferences in design and form began to alter, giving each monument a very individual appearance. Indeed, the tall obelisk mausolea were so popular in Tripolitania that other architectural styles were adapted to fit within the architectural ideal of the tower and obelisk tomb, such as the integration of multi-storey aedicula tombs which were popular across the

[16] The earliest examples are still rather squat in appearance but already feature the distinct long obelisk roof, although they lack any figural or ornamental decorations such as Mausoleum A at Mselliten, in the Wadi Merdum. Pottery finds of first-century CE sigillata and Gaulish ware, as well as a neo-Punic inscription, suggest that this tomb was erected around that time: Brogan and Smith 1966–67, 141; Brogan 1971, 124–25; 1976–77, 104–6; Mattingly 1996a, 173.

Empire (Fig. 5.8c).[17] Another new sub-type integrated an open peristyle as the second storey, topped by a pyramid (for instance, at Wadi Mesueggi: Fig. 5.8d). Along with the various sub-styles that developed, figural and ornamental relief decorations became more popular in the second century CE. Typically, they were placed on top of the first and/or second storey under the cornice in highly visible positions.

At some point during the late second and the third century CE, new architectural styles emerged: the peripteral (Fig. 5.8e) and arcaded and tetrastyle temple mausolea.[18] These arcaded temple mausolea in particular displayed a high level of figural and ornamental decoration, predominantly placed on the monumental arches and on the friezes above (Fig. 5.8f). A third, and much rarer type of monumental tomb that appeared was the so-called rectangular mausoleum, which rose to only one storey and supported a flat roof. Only two of this type have so far been recorded in the pre-desert, both in the Wadi Mimoun (Mm091, Mm123: Mattingly 1996a, 220, 223).

What makes the pre-desert mausolea even more unique are their vivid stone-cut relief decorations displaying portraiture, agricultural scenes, hunting, religious practices, and symbols, and less commonly, free-standing sculpture. This stands in stark contrast to Africa Proconsularis where mausolea were not as heavily decorated and tended to be placed in more isolated, but visually prominent, positions within the landscape (Moore 2007, 89). In the pre-desert of Tripolitania, reliefs and statues were rendered in an abstract way, including figures with large heads, large almond-shaped eyes, small mouths and small torsos. This style drew heavily on Punic artistic traditions in appearance and symbology but also integrated Roman elements. Given that the majority of reliefs and statues were carved this way, even though craftsmen skilled in the 'classical style' were certainly available on the coast, it is very likely that this was a deliberate choice rather than a mere lack of available craftsmen or skill. Indeed, while the styles of carving display regional preferences, what the majority of them have in common is a remarkable attention to detail in their rendering (for example, see the observations on Ghirza by Zanker 2008, 217).

The iconography that was displayed was closely linked to regional and wider socio-cultural circumstances, while Greek and Roman mythological scenes, so popular elsewhere in the Roman Empire, are very rare (Nikolaus 2017, 79–82). A total of six such scenes have been noted, predominantly at Ghirza, some of which are rather ambiguous. For instance, Hercules may be represented on Mausoleum South D at Ghirza hunting a stag (Fig. 5.9a), and perhaps fighting a stag and a bull on Mausoleum North B (Fig. 5.9b). More convincing is the figure of Hercules on a mausoleum in the Wadi Ghalbun, where a standing male figure has a lion cloak thrown over the right shoulder while holding a club in the left hand (Fig. 5.9c). But are we really looking at an image of the Greek demi-god Hercules, or is the scene much more ambiguous? In North Africa, Hercules was syncretized with the Libyco-Phoenician god Melquart, called Milk'Ashtart at Lepcis Magna, where he was venerated as an important deity (Mattingly 1995, 167). Indeed, on Punic coins it is almost impossible to distinguish between Hercules and Melquart (Yarrow 2013, 357). Also known from Ghirza are two depictions of winged felines (sphinxes?) and winged females (victories?). The symbolism of the sphinxes was already an ancient one in the Roman period: guardians of temples and palaces in the Phoenician period, and tombs in the Greek and Roman world (Rösch-von der Heyde 1999).

The development of the iconography underwent four major phases: (1) the depiction of predominantly ornamental and vegetal decorations (if any) on late first-century and early second-century CE monuments; (2) a predominance of portraiture (depicted frontally, facing the viewer), symbolic and apotropaic imagery placed within a Doric frieze from the second century CE; (3) more complex imagery involving agricultural activities, hunting and a wider array of symbols on panels from the third century CE; and, (4) an increasing tendency towards power-related imagery such as ceremonial, religious and martial scenes from the mid- to late third century CE onwards (Fontana 1997; Mattingly 1999; 2011, 246–68; Nikolaus 2016; 2017). Portrait statues were rare, despite being so popular in neighbouring Africa Proconsularis (Moore 2007, 83). Only six examples have been found so far in the pre-desert, perhaps because sculpture in the round required specific skills of the craftsmen, which would have considerably increased the cost of the monument.[19]

[17] For Empire-wide examples see von Hesberg 1992, 121–58. For the pre-desert see Mattingly 1996a, 200 (Wadi Migdal, Mg001), 165 (Wadi el-Amud, Lm001).

[18] Peripteral temple mausolea: for instance, at Ghirza Tomb North A (Brogan and Smith 1984, 121–33; Masturzo 2023, 18–20); Qasr Banat (Nf038: Mattingly 1996a, 263); Kser Banat (Sf003: Mattingly 1996a, 280). Arcaded temple mausolea: for instance, at Ghirza (Brogan and Smith 1984, 134–77, 190–203; Masturzo 2023, 20–21); Bir Nesma (Sf092: Mattingly 1996a, 287); Wadi Khanafes (Kn005: Mattingly 1996a, 152–53). Tetrastyle temple mausolea: for instance, at Qasr Ajdab (Zenati 1997, 224–25). Temple mausolea became popular all across the Roman Empire from the first century CE onwards, especially in the western provinces. At Palmyra the number of temple mausolea rose dramatically from the second century CE, where they were chosen over the traditional tower mausolea: see von Hesberg 1992, 188.

[19] Two statues (male and female) were found at Mausoleum South A at Ghirza (Gh128); a male statue at the Wadi Khanafes (Kn005: Mattingly 1996a, 152–53); two statues (male and female) from two mausolea in the Wadi Antar (An001: Mattingly 1996a, 33–39); and a statue was seen by Brogan in the Wadi Ghurgar, but was later lost (see BILNAS Archive, Olwen Brogan papers, D41).

Fig. 5.9. The complexity of syncretism in pre-desert imagery on mausolea. A: Figure who may represent Hercules/Milk'Ashtart hunting a stag at Ghirza, Tomb South D (BILNAS Archive, Olwen Brogan papers, D41/2/7/8/12/10); B: Stag and bull hunt perhaps representing Hercules/Milk'Ashtart at Ghirza, Tomb North B (BILNAS Archive, Olwen Brogan papers, D41/2/7/8/2/2/15); C: Possible representation of Hercules/Milk'Ashtart on a tomb from the Wadi Ghalbun (photo P. Kenrick).

Stylistic changes over time range from figures placed onto a neutral background in early periods, to scenes populated with figures on different levels which created a *horror vacui* (the filling of the entire stone with figures) at some point in the third century CE, also visible in North African mosaics (Mattingly 2011, 251). The close relationship between trends in mosaic scenes and trends in the art of mausolea indicate that pattern books were used by the local sculptors and craftsmen, but only scenes that held some significance to the commissioner and the local audience were selected (on Tripolitanian mosaics see Wootton, Chapter 4). Indeed, these shifts in iconographic preferences do not exclusively imitate or emulate Empire-wide trends but reflect the ever-changing local realities and circumstances of life, social hierarchies and religious beliefs in the pre-desert.

Inscriptions associated with earlier mausolea frequently stress family lineage by mentioning the father of the deceased as well as their offspring to demonstrate the continuity of the family line. For instance, family trees can be established from groups of mausolea at the Wadi el-Amud, Ghirza and the Wadi Umm el-Agerem, demonstrating that cemeteries with multiple mausolea encompass a single elite family for several generations (Reynolds 1955; Brogan 1964; Mattingly 1995, 162–68). This was coupled with portrait imagery and images venerating the dead (Fig. 5.10a–b). It is clear that the patrons of earlier periods were particularly concerned with representing themselves and their ancestral lineage, stressing their Libyan and Punic names on the inscription. At the same time, they also emphasized their status within the Roman Empire by advertising their *tria nomina*, demonstrating that both a 'Roman' and a 'Libyan' identity could be displayed simultaneously, without causing any obvious conflict. This emphasis on portraiture and lineage reflects the realities of landowners who were establishing and reinforcing their influence over their territory when the area was intensively settled.

Over time the iconography grew increasingly complex, reflecting a wider spectrum of the social and ritual life of the region. Focus shifted from the representation of individual family members and ritual to other imagery. Everyday activities such as agricultural tasks and scenes of hunting became more prevalent in the late second and third centuries CE (Nikolaus 2017, 92–97, 98–106) (Fig. 5.10d, f). This was a trend across the Empire, and portraiture was frequently replaced by representations of the dead in the process of executing power (Fontana 1997; Mattingly 2011, 246–68). Several generations after the first intense settlement of the area, the territorial boundaries were well-established, and the need for self-representation in the form of portraiture and imagery was perhaps no longer as important. This trend can be observed on the later Ghirza mausolea, where Tombs B and C of the North cemetery lack portrait busts completely. Instead, the deceased can be

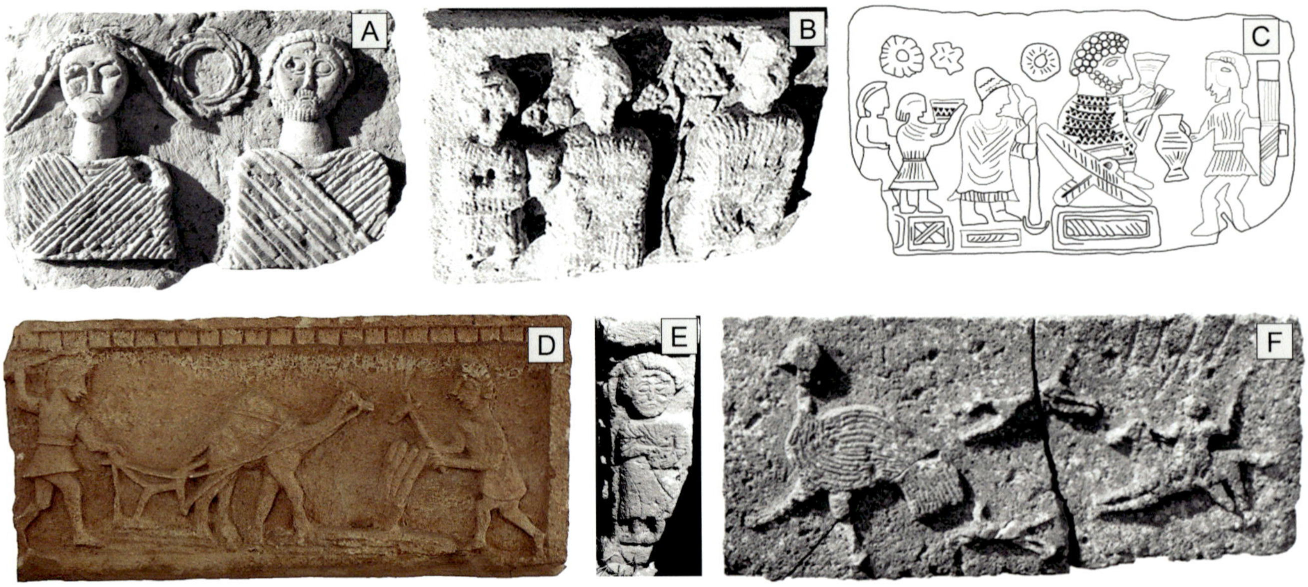

Fig. 5.10. Relief decoration on pre-desert mausolea. A: Portrait relief from Ghirza, Tomb South E (BILNAS Archive, Olwen Brogan papers, D41/2/7/8/13/33); B: Portrait relief of a man (right), woman (centre), child? (left), Wadi Khanafes, Kn005 (BILNAS Archive, ULVS collection, D54/10/1/23); C: So-called chiefdom scene from Tomb North C at Ghirza (drawing J. Nikolaus); D: Ploughing with a camel on a relief from the Wadi al-Binaya (photo M. al-Haddad); E: Bearded man holding an offering bowl, Ghirza Tomb North C (BILNAS Archive, Olwen Brogan papers, D41/2/7/8/3/2/13); F: Hunter on horseback pursuing an ostrich with his two hunting dogs, Ghirza Tomb South D (BILNAS Archive, Olwen Brogan papers, D41/2/7/8/12/9).

found sitting on a folding chair surrounded by a group of attendants (Fig. 5.10c). These individuals are clearly in a position of power, and most likely represented leading persons in the settlement. The Roman imperial authority gradually lost its power in the Libyan pre-desert, as well as in the mountainous hinterland of Numidia and Mauretania, resulting in the withdrawal of troops stationed in the pre-desert, and the local elite grew even more powerful (on changes to the military garrisons see Mackensen, Chapter 6).[20] This power shift is also reflected by an increase of martial scenes at Ghirza, depicting men garbed in military dress, and ceremonial scenes. Scenes of executions were also depicted at Nesma near Mizda and at al-Binaya, perhaps also alluding to the execution of regional power and the safekeeping of the former frontier zone. Despite the change in iconography, what remained important was the veneration of the dead, indicated by the continuous presence of libation channels and imagery depicting ritual practices (Nikolaus 2017, 173) (Fig. 5.10e).

Discussion and concluding thoughts

The pre-desert of Tripolitania changed drastically during the Roman period, with local peoples adopting new modes of settlement and subsistence, transforming the wadi basins of the arid pre-desert into productive agricultural landscapes. The primary drivers of these changes were the generations of leading Libyan families who were living in, and managing, their respective territories in the pre-desert and it was they who led the changes to this landscape over the centuries. Inscriptions associated with the largest pre-desert farms and burial monuments show that they were local residents and active participants in these new sedentary communities, in stark contrast to the neighbouring Jabal region, where the wealthy landowners lived far from their farms in the coastal cities. This rural setting, where monumentality and sculptural representation were almost absent before the Roman period (Nikolaus 2017, 171–73) offered an ideal opportunity to spend surplus wealth accumulated by their estates to create visible marks on the landscape. They laid claim to the land and reinforced their power by constructing massive courtyard farms, or later on, towering fortified farm buildings, and highly decorated mausolea, to show off their wealth and regional power.

In the first two centuries CE, the growing number of both substantial courtyard farms and monumental mausolea demonstrates the presence of several leading families in the area, and perhaps an increase of competition between them, as more and more families began to find success in this new economy. Portraiture and inscriptions displaying their likeness and family names on mausolea emphasized their (new) status. Indeed,

[20] Mattingly 1987; Merrills 2004, 3. See Nikolaus 2024 on Late Antique mausolea in North Africa and the role of shifting power relations and religion in this period.

both large farm buildings and mausolea provided one of the few opportunities to stand out and to highlight status and success in a progressively growing society. Mausolea in particular provided new focal points for communities to carry out long-established rituals and traditions across Tripolitania relating to the veneration of the dead, a tradition with which the growing population could identify (Assmann 2011, 149; Osborne 2014, 10, 13; Wendrich 2014, 412).

At the same time, it is clear that it was not only the elite families who were participating in the new modes of subsistence. The majority of stone buildings constructed during this period were not the massive courtyard farms, but rather those of the farmyard type, which speak to the clear continuation of the importance of animal husbandry and pastoralism. However, it is also clear that these stone structures, along with the investment in building wadi walls and other features to make the wadis agriculturally productive, represented a fundamental change in the ways in which the local population was supporting itself.

The funerary realm with its different grave types, libation channels, funerary stelae, and in particular mausolea, was perfectly suited to express the different levels of status. Many cemeteries were placed in highly visible locations, sometimes a considerable distance from the settlement, most likely to mark the boundary of the property of the elite families that owned the large farms along the wadis. The placement of mausolea amongst smaller burials further emphasized the power of the leading family, especially relative to the much humbler graves around them.[21] The presence of substantial rectangular graves and platforms in cemeteries may indicate further social differentiations among the burials. The abundance of smaller cairn burials reminds us that the leading families were only a very small part of the pre-desert community, and that their success was driven by a large community and workforce.

Cemeteries in general, and mausolea in particular, had highly religious and ritual functions as shrines to venerate the ancestors, offering protection of a different kind. Offering tables and libation channels associated with mausolea and other graves show that the population engaged actively with their burial monuments and their dead ancestors. They were places where social and communal identity could be created and maintained through acts of mourning and remembrance and through the practice of local ritual and religion in a region overshadowed by the Roman Empire. It appears that, for the local population at least, there was some distinction between imagery that was appropriate to decorate and safeguard the structures of the living, such as phalli and hunting scenes, and imagery that was fit to guard the structures of the dead – a distinction which was understood and differentiated by the local audience.

The style of decoration on both mausolea, and more rarely on farm buildings, conforms to what, in modern scholarship, is commonly broadly classed as 'provincial art', and in the pre-desert area constituted a novel form of visual expressions. The near absence of purely Greco-Roman conventions suggests that this 'un-classical' style of the imagery was seen as appropriate and suitable, or even desirable. Essentially, the imagery addressed a local audience that resided in, or around, the large farm buildings, not a global one. The aim was not to emulate Roman art and culture, but the visualization and (re)affirmation of local values, religion and social hierarchies in a way that was understood by the local community. However, the wide variety of architectural types found in mausolea construction, coupled with the decorations, emphasizes that a degree of individuality was also important, setting each monument apart from one another. The funerary realm in particular thereby created the opportunity to establish a visual distinction between the more powerful elite families themselves while, at the same time, creating a distinction between the elite and their subordinates. Coupled with the near-absence of distinctly Roman domestic architecture in the pre-desert and the continuous use of the indigenous Libyan and Punic spoken languages (mirrored in the presence of Libyan and neo-Punic inscriptions), a picture is painted of a fairly autonomous indigenous population that was led by elite family units that operated within the boundaries of Roman rule.

This autonomy is further emphasized by the apparent difference between the settlement landscape in Tripolitania's pre-desert and that found in the productive Jabal region nearer to the coast and other parts of Africa Proconsularis. North of Tripolitania's pre-desert in the Tarhuna Plateau, the courtyard farm, almost exclusively constructed in *opus africanum*, and almost always with one or more olive presses, was far more common (Ahmed 2019; Sheldrick 2021). Similar buildings were also recorded frequently by surveys in northern and central Tunisia where olive cultivation was common.[22] The widespread occupation of courtyard buildings constructed in *opus africanum* in these regions,[23] and the importance of pressing facilities in these areas of North Africa seems to reflect a continuation and further dispersion of a form that was probably already well-established in the region in Punic times. While similar courtyard buildings were present in Tripolitania's pre-desert, their

[21] See Quinn 2013, 197 for a similar observation on pre-Roman mausolea in Numidian territories, and Pollock 1999 for similar ideas in Mesopotamia.

[22] Kasserine: Hitchner 1989, 391–94, *et passim*. See also Hitchner 1988; 1993; Hitchner *et al.* 1990. Thugga: De Vos Raaijmakers 2000; 2013, 152–63, 183–89; De Vos Raaijmakers and Attoui 2013, for instance Site 49 (pl. 20) and Site 207 (pl. 80). Segermes: Carlsen and Tvarnø 1990; Dietz *et al.* 1995; Ørsted *et al.* 2000.

[23] See, for instance: Romanelli 1970, 56; Hanoune 2009; Adam 1994, 120–21. Though cf. also Camporeale 2016.

late appearance compared to other parts of North Africa, and the fact that they were normally adopted only by those in the upper classes, make it clear that these forms were a deliberate import into an area which had a very different socio-cultural background and tradition. The farmyard building, which better suited the environment and local traditions, remained the dominant form. In later periods, the distinction in the settlement landscapes between Tripolitania and its neighbours to the west widened. As described above, starting in the third century CE, fortified farm buildings began to emerge in Tripolitania as the primary form of elite residence, with settlements increasingly focused around these monumental structures. A similar pattern emerged in the Jabal to the north, and interestingly also in Cyrenaica to the east (Emrage 2015), but fortified buildings of this type so distinctive to Tripolitania have been much more rarely recorded in the regions to the west.

There are also clear distinctions in the funerary realm between Tripolitania and its neighbours. The rich figural and symbolic sculptural decoration found on funerary monuments and the wide variety of architectural sub-types is unique in the region. In neighbouring Cyrenaica and Africa Proconsularis such a variety of relief sculptures was rare. In Cyrenaica, portrait busts and statues were favoured, placed in niches of rock-cut tombs (Rosenbaum 1960, 13–28, 101–23; Cherstich 2011; Oldjira and Walker 2016). In Africa Proconsularis relief sculpture is much rarer, and primarily depicts scenes from the Greco-Roman repertoire, such as Cupids with downward-pointing torches, bull sacrifices, Dionysiac or zodiac themes, while free-standing sculpture was the dominant element (Moore 2007, 186). In modern Tunisia and Algeria, so-called 'Saturn' or 'Baal Hammon' stelae were much more widespread but, in turn, these are absent in Tripolitania (Wilson 2005, 403).

It is clear that during the Roman period, the rural pre-desert landscapes of Tripolitania underwent significant changes, made possible by the new economic circumstances and opportunities created by the region's incorporation into Roman imperial networks. These changes were driven from within by the pre-desert communities themselves, with the elite developing and enhancing the existing landscapes to establish and consolidate their position within the new regime of Roman imperialism. Nevertheless, the evidence shows that they did so through the integration of local methods of water management and pastoral economies with newly established agricultural settlement, and maintained their traditional customs and emphasis on ancestral worship through new forms of funerary monuments and landscapes.

References

Adam, J-P. 1994. *Roman Building: Materials and Techniques*. London: Batsford.

Ahmed, M.A.M. 2019. *Rural Settlement and Economic Activity. Olive Oil, Wine and Amphorae Production on the Tarhuna Plateau during the Roman Period*. London: Society for Libyan Studies.

Assmann, J. 2011. *Cultural Memory and Early Civilization: Writing, Remembrance and Political Imagination*. Cambridge: Cambridge University Press.

Barker, G. 1981. Early agriculture and economic change in North Africa. In J.A. Allan (ed.), *Sahara: Ecological Change and Early Economic History*. London: Menas Press, 131–45.

Barker, G. (ed.) 1996a. *Farming the Desert. The UNESCO Libyan Valleys Archaeological Survey. Volume 1: Synthesis*. London: Society for Libyan Studies.

Barker, G. 1996b. Prehistoric settlement. In G. Barker (ed.), *Farming the Desert. The UNESCO Libyan Valleys Archaeological Survey. Volume 1: Synthesis*. London: Society for Libyan Studies, 83–109.

Barker, G. and Gilbertson, D.D. 1996. The UNESCO Libyan Valleys Archaeological Survey: methodologies. In G. Barker (ed.), *Farming the Desert. The UNESCO Libyan Valleys Archaeological Survey. Volume 1: Synthesis*. London: Society for Libyan Studies, 21–48.

Barker, G., Gilbertson, D.D., Hunt, C.O. and Mattingly, D.J. 1996. Romano-Libyan agriculture: integrated models. In G. Barker (ed.), *Farming the Desert. The UNESCO Libyan Valleys Archaeological Survey. Volume 1: Synthesis*. London: Society for Libyan Studies, 265–90.

Barker, G., Gilberston, D.D., Jones, G.D.B. and Welsby, D.A. 1991. ULVS XXIII: the 1989 season. *Libyan Studies* 22: 31–60.

Barker, G. and Jones, G.D.B. 1982. The UNESCO Libyan Valleys Survey 1979–1981: palaeoeconomy and environmental archaeology in the pre-desert. *Libyan Studies* 13: 1–34.

Barker, G., Jones, G.D.B., Bennett, P., Burns, J., Dore, J., Fleming, A., Mattingly, D.J., Moffat, P., Ateyet Allah, M.A., Garsaa, J.S. and Zenati, M. 1984. The UNESCO Libyan Valleys Survey VI: investigations of a Romano-Libyan farm, part I. *Libyan Studies* 15: 1–44.

Barth, H. 1857. *Travels and Discoveries in North and Central Africa*. London: Longman, Brown, Green, Longmans & Roberts.

Basset, H. 1920. *Le culte des grottes au Maroc*. Algiers: Carbone.

Brogan, O. 1964. The Roman remains in the Wadi el-Amud. *Libya Antiqua* 1: 47–56.

Brogan, O. 1971. First and second century settlement in the Tripolitanian pre-desert. In F.F. Gadallah (ed.), *Libya in History. Historical Conference (16–23 March 1968)*. Benghazi: Faculty of Arts, University of Libya, 121–30.

Brogan, O. 1976–77. Some ancient sites in Eastern Tripolitania. *Libya Antiqua* 13–14: 93–129.

Brogan, O. and Reynolds, J.M. 1985. Inscriptions in the pre-desert of Tripolitania. In D.J. Buck and D.J. Mattingly (eds), *Town and Country in Roman Tripolitania. Papers in Honour of Olwen Hackett.* Oxford: British Archaeological Reports, 23–26.

Brogan, O. and Smith, D.J. 1957. The Roman frontier settlement at Ghirza: an interim report. *Journal of Roman Studies* 47: 178–84.

Brogan, O. and Smith, D.J. 1966–67. Notes from the Tripolitanian pre-desert. *Libya Antiqua* 3–4: 139–44.

Brogan, O. and Smith, D.J. 1984. *Ghirza: A Libyan Settlement in the Roman Period.* Tripoli: Department of Antiquities.

Buck, D.J., Burns, J.R. and Mattingly D.J. 1983. Archaeological sites of the Bir Scedua Basin: settlements and cemeteries. In G.D.B. Jones and G. Barker (eds), The UNESCO Libyan Valleys Survey IV: the 1981 season. *Libyan Studies* 14: 42–54.

Camporeale, S. 2016. Merging technologies in North African ancient architecture: opus quadratum and opus africanum from the Phoenicians to the Romans. In N. Mugnai, J. Nikolaus and N. Ray (eds), *De Africa Romaque: Merging Cultures across North Africa. Proceedings of the International Conference Held at the University of Leicester (26–27 October 2013).* London: Society for Libyan Studies, 57–71.

Camps, G. 1986. Funerary monuments with attached chapels from the northern Sahara. *African Archaeological Review* 4: 151–64.

Carlsen, J. and Tvarnø, H. 1990. The Segermes Valley Archaeological Survey (region of Zaghouan). An interim report. In A. Mastino (ed.), *L'Africa Romana. Atti del VII convegno di studio (Sassari, 15–17 dicembre 1989).* Sassari: Gallizzi, 803–13.

Cherstich, L. 2011. The changing funerary world of Roman Cyrene. *Libyan Studies* 42: 33–46.

De Vos Raaijmakers, M. 2000. *Rus Africum: terra, acqua, olio nell'Africa settentrionale. Scavo e ricognizione nei dintorni di Dougga (Alto Tell tunisino).* Trento-Tunis: Università degli Studi di Trento – Institut National du Patrimoine.

De Vos Raaijmakers, M. 2013. The rural landscape of Thugga: farms, presses, mills, and transport. In A.K. Bowman and A.I. Wilson (eds), *The Roman Agricultural Economy: Organisation, Investment, and Production.* Oxford: Oxford University Press, 143–218.

De Vos Raaijmakers, M. and Attoui, R. 2013. *Rus Africum, tome I. Le paysage rural antique autour de Dougga et Téboursouk: cartographie, relevés et chronologie des établissements.* Bari: Edipuglia.

Dietz, S., Ladjimi Sebaï, L. and Ben Hassen, H. (eds) 1995. *Africa Proconsularis: Regional Studies in the Segermes Valley of Northern Tunisia (Volume 1).* Aarhus: Aarhus University Press.

Doutté, E. 1909. *Magie et religion dans l'Afrique de Nord.* Algiers: Jourdan.

Duveyrier, H. 1864. *Les Touareg du nord. Exploration du Sahara.* Paris: Challamel Ainé.

Emrage, A. 2015. *Roman Fortified Farms (Qsur) and Military Sites in the Region of the Wadi al-Kuf, Cyrenaica (Eastern Libya).* PhD Thesis: University of Leicester.

Finkelstein, I. 1995. *Living on the Fringe: The Archaeology and History of the Negev, Sinai and Neighbouring Regions in the Bronze and Iron Ages.* Sheffield: Sheffield Academic Press.

Fontana, S. 1997. Il predeserto tripolitano: mausolei e rappresentazione del potere. *Libya Antiqua* n.s. 3: 149–63.

Foucauld, C. 1918. *Dictionnaire abrégé touareg-français.* Algiers: Jules Carbonel.

Foureau, F. 1902. *Mission saharienne Foureau Lamy, d'Alger au Congo par le Tchad.* Paris: Masson.

Gilbertson, D.D. and Chisholm, N.W.T. 1996. ULVSXXVIII: manipulating the desert environment: ancient walls, floodwater farming and territoriality in the Tripolitanian pre-desert of Libya. *Libyan Studies* 27: 17–52.

Gilbertson, D.D. and Hunt, C.O. 1996. Romano-Libyan agriculture: walls and floodwater farming. In G. Barker (ed.), *Farming the Desert. The UNESCO Libyan Valleys Archaeological Survey. Volume 1: Synthesis.* London: Society for Libyan Studies, 191–226.

Goodchild, R.G. 1976. *Libyan Studies: Selected Papers of the Late R.G. Goodchild (edited by J.M. Reynolds).* London: Elek Books.

Hanoune, R. 2009. La construction romaine en 'opus Africanum' et ses renaissances: innovation technique? Continuité accidentale? In J.-R. Gaborit (ed.), *Tradition et innovation en histoire de l'art. Actes du 131e congrès national des sociétés historiques et scientifiques (Grenoble, 2006).* Paris: Éditions du CTHS, 29–39.

Hitchner, R.B. 1988. The University of Virginia-INAA Kasserine Archaeological Survey 1982–1986. *Antiquités Africaines* 24: 7–41.

Hitchner, R.B. 1989. The organization of rural settlement in the Cillium-Thelepte region (Kasserine, Central Tunisia). In A. Mastino (ed.), *L'Africa Romana. Atti del VI convegno di studio (Sassari, 16–18 dicembre 1988).* Sassari: Gallizzi, 387–402.

Hitchner, R.B. 1993. The Kasserine Archaeological Survey 1982–1985. *Africa. Fouilles, monuments et collections archéologiques en Tunisie* 11–12: 158–98.

Hitchner, R.B., Ellis, S., Graham, A., Mattingly, D.J. and Neuru, L. 1990. The Kasserine Archaeological Survey 1987. *Antiquités Africaines* 26: 231–60.

Hunt, C.O., Mattingly, D.J., Gilbertson, D.D., Dore, J., Barker, G., Burns, J.R., Fleming, A.M. and Van der Veen, M. 1986. ULVS XIII: interdisciplinary approaches to ancient farming in the Wadi Mansur, Tripolitania. *Libyan Studies* 17: 7–48.

Leitch, V. and Nikolaus, J. 2015. The Society for Libyan Studies Archive: past, present and future. *Libyan Studies* 46: 151–57.

Leitch, V., Mattingly, D.J. and Mugnai, N. 2019. The Society for Libyan Studies Archive: history, organisation, recent and future developments. *Libyan Studies* 50: 81–85.

LeQuesne, C., Basell, L.S. and Sheibani, R. 2010. Archaeology in the Sirte Basin: preliminary results of mitigation surveys carried out for Shell 2007–2009. *Libyan Studies* 41: 7–32.

Liverani, M. (ed.) 2005. *Aghram Nadharif: The Barkat Oasis (Sha'abiya of Ghat, Libyan Sahara) in Garamantian Times.* Florence: All'Insegna del Giglio.

Masturzo, N. 2023. Modelli e ideologia nell'architettura funeraria di Ghirza in età imperiale (Tripolitania interna). *Libya Antiqua* n.s. 16: 11–33.

Mattingly, D.J. 1985. Olive oil production in Roman Tripolitania. In D.J. Buck and D.J. Mattingly (eds), *Town and Country in Roman Tripolitania. Papers in Honour of Olwen Hackett.* Oxford: British Archaeological Reports, 27–46.

Mattingly, D.J. 1987. Libyans and the limes: culture and society in Roman Tripolitania. *Antiquités Africaines* 23: 71–94.

Mattingly, D.J. 1988. Megalithic madness and measurement: or how many olives could an olive press press? *Oxford Journal of Archaeology* 7: 177–95.

Mattingly, D.J. 1995. *Tripolitania.* London: Batsford.

Mattingly, D.J. (ed.) 1996a. *Farming the Desert. The UNESCO Libyan Valleys Archaeological Survey. Volume 2: Gazetteer and Pottery.* London: Society for Libyan Studies.

Mattingly, D.J. 1996b. Explanations: people as agency. In G. Barker (ed.), *Farming the Desert. The UNESCO Libyan Valleys Archaeological Survey. Volume 1: Synthesis.* London: Society for Libyan Studies, 319–42.

Mattingly, D.J. 1999. The art of the unexpected: Ghirza in the Libyan pre-desert. In S. Lancel (ed.), *Numismatique, langues, écritures et arts du livre, spécificité des arts figurés. VIIe colloque sur l'histoire et l'archéologie de l'Afrique du Nord (Nice, 21–31 octobre 1996).* Paris: Éditions du CTHS, 383–405.

Mattingly, D.J. 2011. *Imperialism, Power, and Identity. Experiencing the Roman Empire.* Princeton: Princeton University Press.

Mattingly, D.J. 2022. Beyond barbarians: the Garamantes of the Libyan Sahara. In R.B. Hitchner (ed.), *A Companion to North Africa in Antiquity.* Hoboken, NJ: Wiley-Blackwell, 64–80.

Mattingly, D.J. 2023. *Between Sahara and Sea: Africa in the Roman Empire.* Ann Arbor, MI: University of Michigan Press.

Mattingly, D.J. and Dore, J. 1996. Romano-Libyan settlement. Typology and chronology. In G. Barker (ed.), *Farming the Desert. The UNESCO Libyan Valleys Archaeological Survey. Volume 1: Synthesis.* London: Society for Libyan Studies, 111–58.

Mattingly, D.J. and Flower, C. 1996. Romano-Libyan settlement: site distributions and trends. In G. Barker (ed.), *Farming the Desert. The UNESCO Libyan Valleys Archaeological Survey. Volume 1: Synthesis.* London: Society for Libyan Studies, 159–90.

Mattingly, D.J., Sterry, M. and Leitch, V. 2013. Fortified farms and defended villages of Late Roman and Late Antique Africa. *Antiquité Tardive* 21: 167–88.

Mattingly, D.J., Sterry, M., Al-Haddad, M. and Trousset, P. 2020. Pre-Islamic oasis settlements in the Northern Sahara. In M. Sterry and D.J. Mattingly (eds), *Urbanisation and State Formation in the Ancient Sahara and Beyond.* Cambridge: Cambridge University Press, 187–238.

Merrills, A.H. 2004. Vandals, Romans and Berbers: understanding Late Antique North Africa. In A.H. Merrills (ed.), *Vandals, Romans and Berbers: New Perspectives on Late Antique North Africa.* Aldershot: Ashgate, 3–29.

Moore, J.P. 2007. The mausoleum culture of Africa Proconsularis. In D.L. Stone and L. Stirling (eds), *Mortuary Landscapes of North Africa.* Toronto: University of Toronto Press, 75–109.

Munzi, M., Felici, F., Cifani, G., Cirelli, E., Gaudiosi, E., Lucarini, G. and Matug, J. 2004. A topographic research sample in the territory of Lepcis Magna: Silin. *Libyan Studies* 35: 11–66.

Nikolaus, J. 2016. Beyond Ghirza: Roman-period mausolea in Tripolitania. In N. Mugnai, J. Nikolaus and N. Ray (eds), *De Africa Romaque: Merging Cultures across North Africa. Proceedings of the International Conference Held at the University of Leicester (26–27 October 2013).* London: Society for Libyan Studies, 199–214.

Nikolaus, J. 2017. *Roman Funerary Reliefs and North African Identity: A Contextual Investigation of Tripolitanian Mausolea and Their Iconography.* PhD Thesis: University of Leicester.

Nikolaus, J. 2024. Changing funerary landscapes in Late Antiquity: mausolea in North Africa. In L. Lavan (ed.), *Burial and Memorial in Late Antiquity.* Leiden-Boston: Brill, 183–200.

Ørsted, P., Carlsen, J., Ladjimi Sebaï, L. and Ben Hassen, H. (eds) 2000. *Africa Proconsularis: Regional Studies in the Segermes Valley of Northern Tunisia (Volume 3: Historical Conclusions).* Aarhus: Aarhus University Press.

Oldjira, M. and Walker, S. 2016. Stones of memory: the presentation of the individual in the cemeteries of Cyrene. In N. Mugnai, J. Nikolaus and N. Ray (eds), *De Africa Romaque: Merging Cultures across North Africa. Proceedings of the International Conference Held at the University of Leicester (26–27 October 2013).* London: Society for Libyan Studies, 185–97.

Osborne, J.F. 2014. Monuments and monumentality. In J.F. Osborne (ed.), *Approaching Monumentality in Archaeology.* Albany: State University of New York Press, 1–19.

Pollock, S. 1999. *Ancient Mesopotamia: The Eden that Never Was.* Cambridge: Cambridge University Press.

Quinn, J.C. 2013. Monumental power: 'Numidian Royal Architecture' in context. In J.R.W. Prag and J.C. Quinn (eds), *The Hellenistic West. Rethinking the Ancient Mediterranean.* Cambridge: Cambridge University Press, 179–215.

Ray, N. and Nikolaus, J. 2019. Buried in the archives: cemeteries and mausolea in Tripolitania. *Libyan Studies* 50: 93–98.

Rayne, L., Sheldrick, N. and Nikolaus, J. 2017. Endangered archaeology in Libya: recording damage and destruction. *Libyan Studies* 48: 23–49.

Reddé, M. 1988. *Prospection des vallées du nord de la Libye (1979–1980). La région de Syrte à l'époque romaine.* Paris: Presses de l'École normale supérieure.

Reynolds, J.M. 1955. Inscriptions of Roman Tripolitania (IRT): a supplement. *Papers of the British School at Rome* 26: 124–47.

Romanelli, P. 1970. *Topografia e archeologia dell'Africa romana.* Turin: Società Editrice Internazionale.

Rosenbaum, E.A. 1960. *Cyrenaican Portrait Sculpture.* London: British Academy.

Rösch-von der Heyde, W. 1999. *Das Sphinxbild im Wandel der Zeit.* Rahden: Marie Leidorf Verlag.

Scheele, J. 2017. The need for nomads: camel-herding, raiding, and Saharan trade and settlement. In D.J. Mattingly, V. Leitch, C.N. Duckworth, A. Cuenod, M. Sterry and F. Cole (eds), *Trade in the Ancient Sahara and Beyond.* Cambridge: Cambridge University Press, 55–79.

Sheldrick, N. 2021. *Building the Countryside. Rural Architecture and Settlement in Tripolitania during the Roman and Late Antique Periods.* London: Society for Libyan Studies.

Smith, D.J. 1985. Ghirza. In D.J. Buck and D.J. Mattingly (eds), *Town and Country in Roman Tripolitania. Papers in Honour of Olwen Hackett.* Oxford: British Archaeological Reports, 227–39.

Stone, D.L. and Stirling, L.M. 2007. Funerary monuments and mortuary practices in the landscapes of North Africa. In D.L. Stone and L.M. Stirling (eds), *Mortuary Landscapes of North Africa.* Toronto: University of Toronto Press, 3–31.

Van der Veen, M., Grant, A. and Barker, G. 1996. Romano-Libyan agriculture: crops and animals. In G. Barker (ed.), *Farming the Desert. The UNESCO Libyan Valleys Archaeological Survey. Volume 1: Synthesis.* London: Society for Libyan Studies, 227–64.

von Hesberg, H. 1992. *Römische Grabbauten.* Darmstadt: Wissenschaftliche Buchgesellschaft.

Welsby, D. 1992. ULVS XXV: the gsur and associated settlements in the Wadi Umm el Kharab: an architectural survey. *Libyan Studies* 23: 73–99.

Wendrich, W. 2014. Visualizing the dynamics of monumentality. In J.F. Osborne (ed.), *Approaching Monumentality in Archaeology.* Albany: State University of New York Press, 409–30.

Wilson, A.I. 2005. Romanizing Baal: the art of Saturn worship in North Africa. In M. Sanader and A.R. Miočevič (eds), *Proceedings of the 8th International Colloquium on Problems of Roman Provincial Art (Zagreb 2003).* Zagreb: Opuscula archaeologica dissertationes et monographiae, 403–8.

Yarrow, L.M. 2013. Heracles, coinage and the West: three Hellenistic case-studies. In J.R.W. Prag and J.C. Quinn (eds), *The Hellenistic West. Rethinking the Ancient Mediterranean.* Cambridge: Cambridge University Press, 358–66.

Zanker, P. 2008. Selbstdarstellung am Rand der Libyschen Wüste. Die Reliefs an den Häuplings-Mausoleen in der Nordnekropole von Ghirza. In F. Pirson and U. Wulf-Rheidt (eds), *Austausch und Inspiration. Kulturkontakt als Impuls architektonischer Innovation. Kolloquium vom 28.–30.4.2006 in Berlin anlässlich des 65. Geburtstages von Adolf Hoffmann.* Mainz: Philipp von Zabern, 214–26.

Zenati, M. 1997. Recent finds and restorations, Department of Antiquities, Sabratha. *Libya Antiqua* n.s. 3: 223–26.

Chapter 6

MILITARY FORTIFICATIONS IN THE FRONTIER ZONE OF TRIPOLITANIA (*LIMES TRIPOLITANUS*) FROM THE MID-IMPERIAL PERIOD TO LATE ANTIQUITY

Michael Mackensen

Introduction

The military expansion of Rome in the province of Africa Proconsularis and the developments since the Julio-Claudian period can be traced through a temporally and regionally differentiated approach. Especially in Tripolitania, infrastructural development took place successively with the establishment and organization of frontier zones beyond the agriculturally usable areas of Jabal Garian and the adjoining pre-desert with Wadi Sofeggin as well as parts of Wadi Zemzem (Fig. 6.1). Information on the development of the Tripolitanian frontier zone is provided not only by written and especially epigraphic sources, but above all by archaeological sources, from fairly well-preserved monuments to small finds such as military equipment and chronologically relevant African red slip wares (ARS). This concerns not only the *limes Tripolitanus* road mentioned in the *Itinerarium Antonini Augusti* (73–77), the new so-called 'oasis forts' of 200 CE that advanced far to the south, and their abandonment during the third quarter of the third century; but also the Late Antique frontier sectors and forts of the newly established province of Tripolitana at the beginning of the fourth century, mentioned in the *Notitia Dignitatum Occidentis* (*Not. Dign. Occ.*), 31.2–31. The final abandonment of the military fortifications must be seen in the context of the Vandal conquest of the western part of the province in 442, or at the latest in 455 CE.

Apart from the forts at Bu Njem (1967–76) and Gheriat el-Garbia (2009–10), no modern fieldwork and interdisciplinary excavations with well-defined questions on the defences, the layout and the internal buildings of the forts, their civilian settlements, sanctuaries and cemeteries have been carried out at fort sites or on the *limes Tripolitanus* road in southern Tunisia and north-western Libya. Excavations carried out before the 1980s, including the terminology of the forts, were discussed by David Mattingly, who took into account the results of the UNESCO Libyan Valleys Archaeological Survey (ULVS) as well (see Mattingly 1995, 90–115; Mattingly and Dore 1996, 112–16; recently Sheldrick 2021, 35–58). Further results were obtained from a re-evaluation of the interior buildings of various forts such as Bu Njem and fortlets such as Qasr Duib, Qasr Wames and Ksar Rhilane, taking into account the garrisoned unit(s) and the officers commanding them. The barracks in particular allow conclusions to be drawn about the type and organization, the structure and the size of the garrisoned units (Mackensen 2008, 294–303; 2009; 2010a, 458–63).

Conquest campaigns and road building measures under Augustus

For the last decades of the first century BCE and the first half of the first century CE, the state of our knowledge of the frontier zone of the province of Africa, which was successively extended to the south-west and south of present-day Tunisia, remains modest (Mackensen 1997; 2000). The conquest campaigns under Augustus, which were aimed at gaining territory, cannot be documented at any site in southern and south-western Tunisia. Archaeological evidence of Roman troops in the form of temporarily-used marching camps of mobile battle-groups, or permanent forts of auxiliary units and legionary vexillations, still awaits discovery. In this context, the campaign of L. Cornelius Balbus mentioned in the triumphal records (*acta triumphorum Capitolina*) is of interest. In 21/20 BCE, the proconsul led a campaign

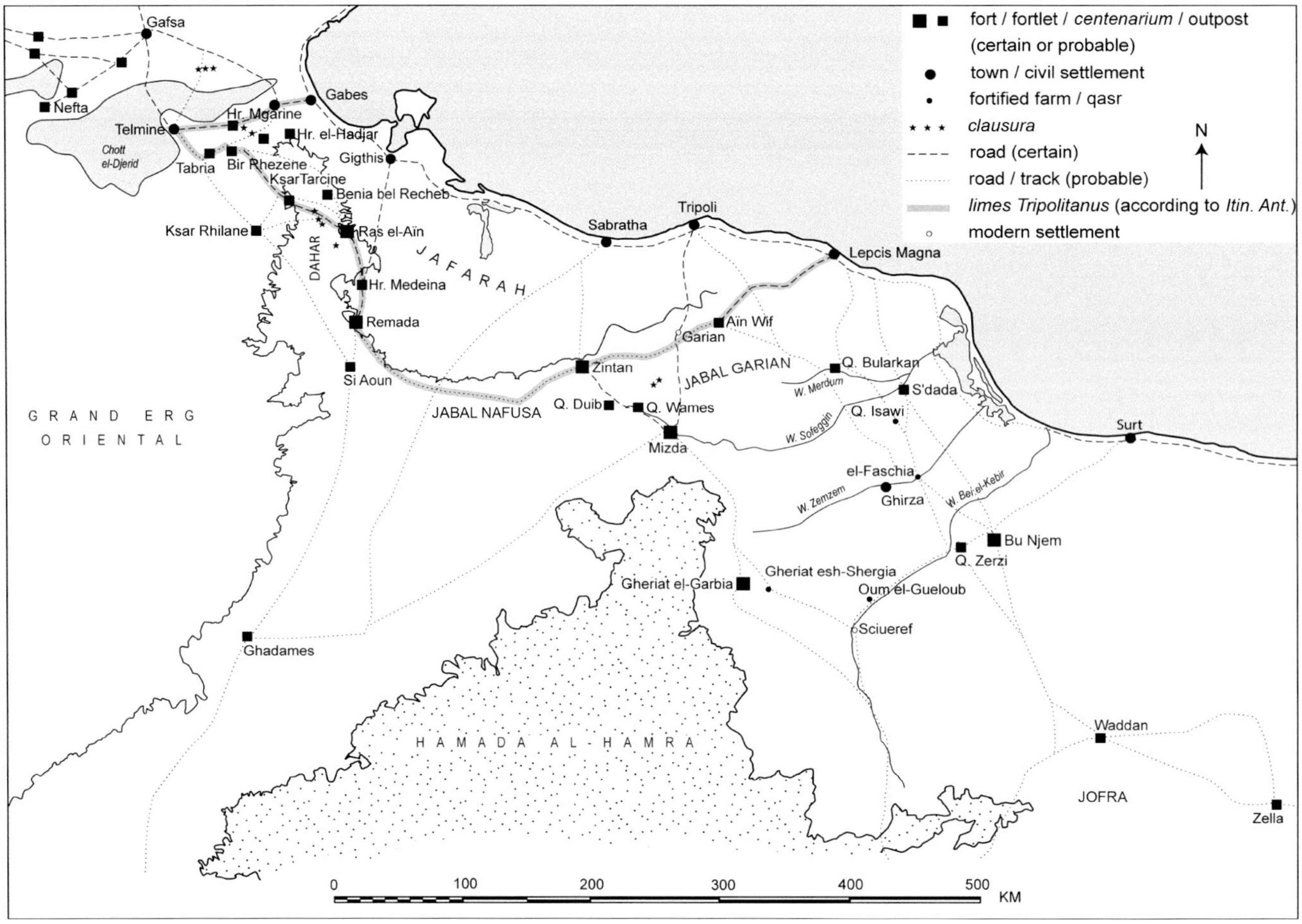

Fig. 6.1. Mid-imperial and late Roman military and civilian sites in Tripolitania (Mackensen 2021b, 113, fig. 1).

beyond the provincial borders into the land of the Phazanii with its capital Cidamus/Ghadames, and of the Garamantes with its capital Garama/Jarma-Zinchecra, for which he was awarded a triumph *ex Africa* in 19 BCE. The route of the successful expeditionary army from the Lesser Syrtis can roughly be traced due to the few localizable places.[1]

In 1953, Richard Goodchild recognized on an aerial photograph of Gheriat el-Garbia (Fig. 6.2) on the west side of Wadi Tula the course of a ditch at least 48 m long with a rounded corner, which he wanted to associate with a 'temporary marching camp' during a campaign in Fazzan (Goodchild 1954, 66; Jones 1983, 65 for GG17). Topography and the course of the ditch probably reveal only a small military post (c. 0.25 ha) which cannot be dated more precisely. Immediately to the north, the plateau top is occupied by a 0.3 ha promontory fortification of the autochthonous population (Jones 1983, 65 for GG15; Mattingly 1996, 105, fig. 14.11). This yielded a fragment of a bronze spiral brooch (type Feugère 1b2 or 2b), which can be dated around the mid-first century BCE (Mackensen 2021a, 223–24, pl. 24.13). However, it remains hypothetical to assume a connection between the Roman ditch and the brooch, which was most likely worn by a Roman soldier in the campaign of Cornelius Balbus, or with a flanking securing action.

Roman camps of the late first century BCE and the first and early second century CE could be proven neither in the eastern Jabal Nafusa and Jabal Garian, nor in the pre-desert or south of Wadi Zemzem or in the Wadi Bei el-Kebir. The same is true for the region south of the late Augustan road from Capsa/Gafsa to Tacape/Gabes. Recently, Nichole Sheldrick (2021, 46, fig. 4.6) pointed to a satellite image of an unclassifiable marching camp at Bir Umm el-Garanigh on the coast of the Greater Syrtis west of Arae Philaenorum/Ras el-Aali, showing a single ditch with an enclosed area of c. 142 × 234 m (3.8 ha); apparently it overlies a similar camp (Fig. 6.3). One could regard the ditch as a military building camp in connection with the construction of the coastal road in late Augustan or Tiberian times. For the coastal road between Sabratha and Oea/Tripoli, a milestone attests to an extension by the *legio III Augusta* in the years 8/9 CE at the earliest and 12/13 CE at the latest under the governor A. Caecina Severus (Di Vita-Évrard 1978–79, 9–16, 32–36, pl. 2; Mattingly 1995, 61, table 3.1). Likewise, the construction of the road from Ammaedara/Haïdra, the winter-quarters (*castra hiberna*) of the *legio III Augusta*,

[1] Pliny, *Naturalis Historia*, 5.34–38; Le Bohec 1989a, 338, with note 40; Mattingly 1995, 70; Guédon 2018, 43–60.

through the steppe highlands to Tacape/Gabes was completed in 14 CE as attested by numerous milestones, by soldiers of this legion under the governor L. Nonius Asprenas. This road, a *via militaris*, measured 197 miles in length and served to control the transhumance practiced by various nomadic peoples.[2]

Hadrianic auxiliary fort in Jabal Dahar

Almost 200 km south of Gabes, on the north–south route via Ghadames into the Fazzan desert, the auxiliary fort Tillibari/Remada was built for the auxiliary *cohors II Flavia Afrorum*.[3] Of the 157 × 124 m (1.95 ha) rectangular fort with rounded corners, the defence wall, the four multi-period gates and the area of the headquarters building have been partially excavated.[4] Trousset assumed a date of around 130 CE on the basis of the length-to-width ratio, which corresponds to that of the fort of Gemellae/El Kasbat on the *fossatum Africae* in eastern Algeria (Trousset 1974, 118; Euzennat and Trousset 1978, 140–42).

On the eastern north–south route via Mizda into Fazzan, one would expect a fort for a quingenary auxiliary unit built at about the same time between Jabal Nafusa and the fertile Jabal Garian, but there is no archaeological or epigraphic evidence for this (see Mattingly 1982, 78). Moreover, a secure dating into the second quarter of the second century CE is still pending for the fortified road station Thenadassa/Aïn Wif on the road to Lepcis Magna (Mattingly 1982, 73–77, figs 1–3; 1995, 99–100, fig. 5.9). At Mizda on the upper Wadi Sofeggin, too, there is no secure evidence for a postulated military presence in form of a fortlet or a fort around the middle of the second century (this could potentially be located at the southern edge of the modern village near the Italian *castello*). However, rural settlement and agricultural use in the pre-desert of the middle and lower Wadi Sofeggin, Wadi Merdum, and also Wadi N'f'd with Nf75 at Qasr Isawi (Nf37) (Fig. 6.1) had already begun in the late first century CE, as attested by Italian and South Gaulish sigillata.[5] Probably no further military protection and surveillance was required in the approaches to the Tripolitanian pre-desert during the second half of the first century until the late second century, with the exception of small road stations along the important traffic routes.

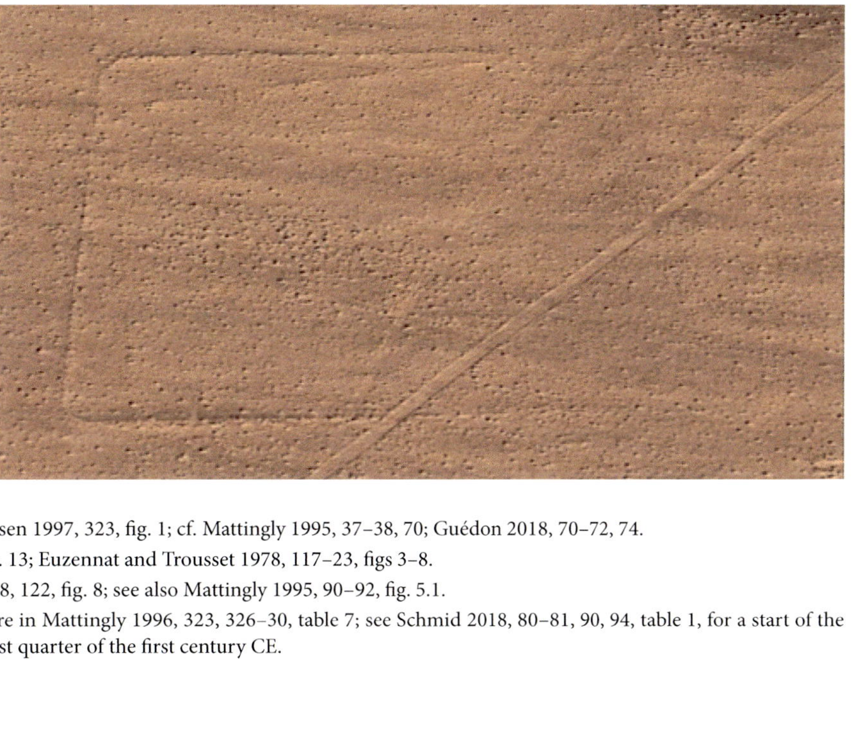

Fig. 6.2. *(top right)* Myd(---)/Gheriat el-Garbia, north-western Libya: aerial photograph (1950) of Severan fort (with Berber village) and vicus, oasis in Wadi Tula, and a linear structure of a military camp (GG17) in the left bottom corner (Goodchild 1954, pl. 10b).

Fig. 6.3. *(bottom right)* Bir Umm el-Garanigh, north-western Libya: early imperial (?) marching camp with two phases (Digital Globe via Google Earth Pro, 26/12/2011).

[2] *CIL* VIII, 10018; Le Bohec 1989a, 342; Mackensen 1997, 323, fig. 1; cf. Mattingly 1995, 37–38, 70; Guédon 2018, 70–72, 74.

[3] Le Bohec 1989b, 67; Trousset 1974, 114–18, fig. 13; Euzennat and Trousset 1978, 117–23, figs 3–8.

[4] Trousset 1974, 115; Euzennat and Trousset 1978, 122, fig. 8; see also Mattingly 1995, 90–92, fig. 5.1.

[5] Brogan and Smith 1966–67, 139–44, fig. 3; Dore in Mattingly 1996, 323, 326–30, table 7; see Schmid 2018, 80–81, 90, 94, table 1, for a start of the settlement Nf75 already during the second half or last quarter of the first century CE.

Fig. 6.4. *(left)* Tisavar/Ksar Rhilane, southern Tunisia: mid-imperial fortlet seen from the west (photo M. Mackensen).

Fig. 6.5. *(below)* Tisavar/Ksar Rhilane, southern Tunisia. 1: Plan of fortlet (*praesidium*), built in 184–91 CE, with buildings in front of the gate (Gombeaud 1901, pl. 16); 2: East wall with gate and tower, elevation and reconstruction (Mackensen 2010, 459, fig. 8); 3: East wall with gate (photo M. Mackensen).

Fortlets constructed under Commodus in Jabal Dahar

About 35 km west of the main road leading from Turris Tamaleni/Telmine to Tillibari/Remada, the fortlet of Tisavar/Ksar Rhilane was built on an isolated hill not far from an oasis in the middle of the Eastern Great Erg (Fig. 6.4). Based on the titles of the emperor Commodus on the building inscription, it can be dated to the years 184–91 CE.[6] The location beyond the main road was due to the nearby oasis and the spring. The ground plan of the rectangular fort measuring 28 × 37.5 m on the outside,[7] with rounded corners and a gate tower on the eastern side (Fig. 6.5.1), published by Gombeaud in 1901, shows the prototype of a fortlet of the late second century. The internal dimensions of 25.4 × 34.8 m, measured again in 2008, give an internal area of 860 m^2. The defence wall has survived up to a height of c. 4 m; the surrounding crenelated parapet is missing. The gate has slots in the door jambs for a portcullis (*cataracta*), for the operation of which a rope winch is to be postulated on the first floor of the c. 9 m high gate tower (Fig. 6.5.2–3). The installation of the portcullis was probably supervised by an engineer of the *legio III Augusta* stationed at Lambaesis. There is no other evidence of *cataracta* in the mid-imperial forts of Tripolitania and Numidia; rather, this is

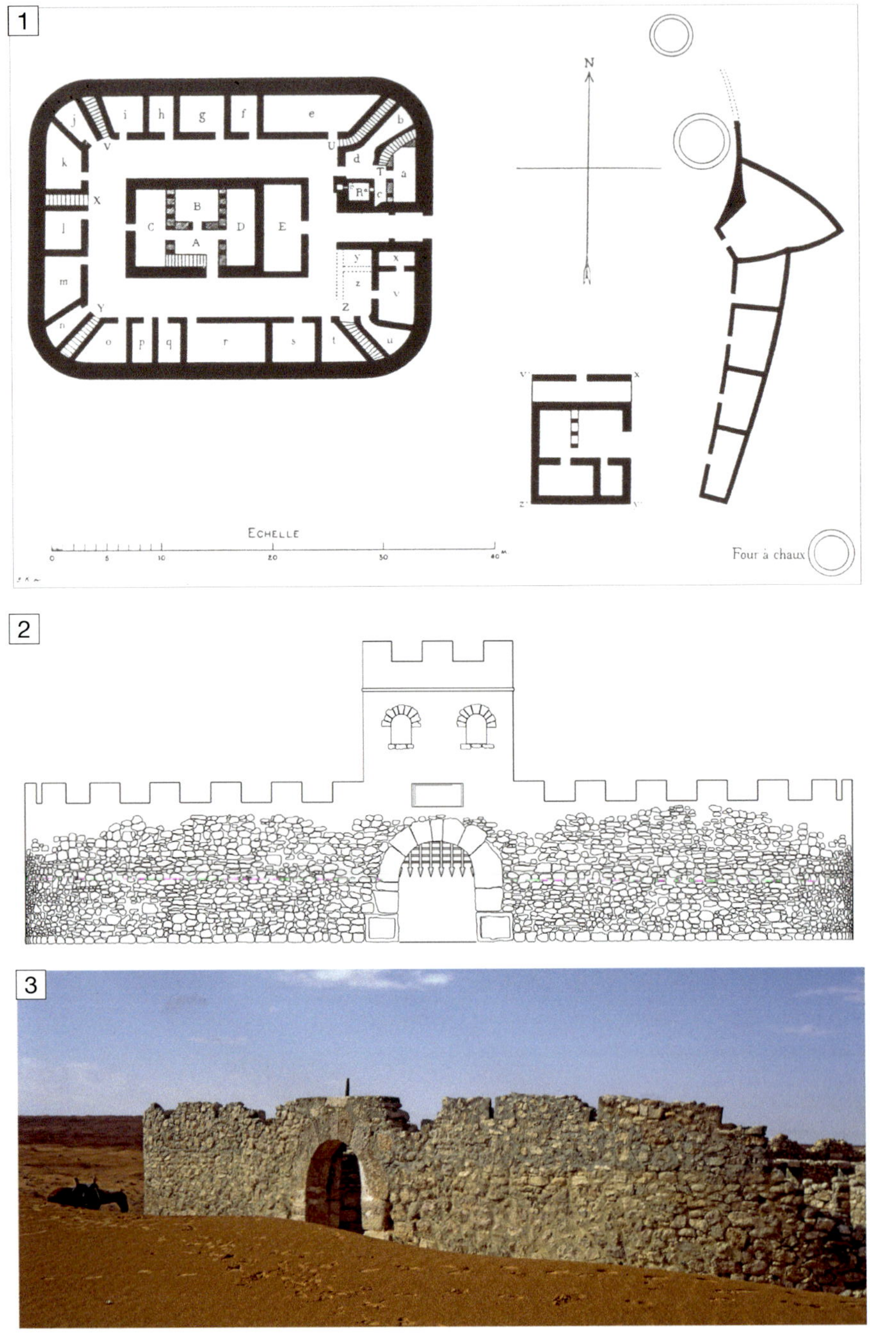

[6] *CIL* VIII, 11048; Le Bohec 1989a, 389 ff. on the possible construction period 183–85 CE; Mackensen 2015, 259, note 14.

[7] Gombeaud 1901, 83, pl. 16, with inaccurate measurements (30 × 40 m); see the detailed discussion in Mackensen 2010a.

Fig. 6.6. 1: Tisavar/Ksar Rhilane, southern Tunisia: central building of fortlet from west (photo M. Mackensen); 2–3: Vezereos/Sidi Mohammed ben Aïssa, southern Tunisia: plan of fortlet (*praesidium*), built in the 80s of the second century CE (Mackensen 2015, 261, fig. 3), and south wall with late Roman rectangular tower (photo M. Mackensen).

an exceptional transfer of technology from civil architecture of urban fortifications to a fortlet situated on the edge of the Sahara (Mackensen 2010a, 456–58, figs 7–8).

The barracks and larger storage rooms (E, R) were built along the inner side of the curtain wall and several staircases led up to the rampart-walk. Even if the use of the individual rooms cannot be clarified, with an average floor space of 3 m^2 per soldier (without distinguishing between legionaries or auxiliaries), the size of the (partial) unit stationed at Tisavar can be assumed to be 40–45 men (see in detail Mackensen 2010a, 459–62). It was not possible, however, to accommodate a legionary detachment of about 80 men here, i.e. in *centuria* strength, as suggested by Mattingly (1995, 85, 101, table 4.2). North of the alleyway leading into the fortlet is the cistern R, south of the commander's quarters with rooms U–Z. The total area of c. 50 m^2 could accommodate a non-commissioned officer (*principalis*), but by no means a legionary centurion. In the legionary fortress at Lambaesis, centurions were entitled to a 15 × 25 m (375 m^2) building as a centurion's quarter connected to the barrack with rooms (*contubernia*) for the soldiers. The 16.4 × 15 m (245 m^2) living quarters (*praetorium*) of the legionary centurion commanding the vexillation fort at Gholaia/Bu Njem can be compared to this as well (Mackensen 2010a, 461 ff.). These proportions show that only a non-commissioned officer commanded the small garrison of the fortlet at Tisavar.

The central building corresponds to a reduced headquarters building (*principia*) (Figs 6.5.1, 6.6.1). The entrance led into courtyard A; room B, located on the central axis, is to be regarded as a shrine (*aedes*) for the *vexillum* and the *imagines*, while the two lateral rooms C and D probably served as offices (*officia*) for administrative tasks. Later, a small sanctuary E was added for the victorious Jupiter (Mackensen 2010a, 463–65, figs 9–10). A rectangular building in front of the fort was regarded as a possible *statio* for the collection of customs duties (*portorium*: Mackensen 2010a, 465) (Fig. 6.5.1). Gombeaud (1901, 89 ff.) interpreted a series of five rooms with varied ground plans as stables and storerooms.

The fortlet of Tisavar is the best example of the military posts located along the supra-regional roads in the African frontier zone, which were erected in the 80s of the second century CE and in which legionary or auxiliary or mixed detachments, as a rule probably far below *centuria* strength, were stationed. The intention was to improve the security of the lines of communication in the frontier zone. The soldiers took over policing duties and were responsible for monitoring the traffic and checking the letters of consignment and passes, but probably also the safety of the caravans, which is why one should expect at least a dozen horses and/or dromedaries with corresponding *equites* and/or *dromadarii*. The civilian settlements (*vici*) belonging to the fortlets, with their oases, abundant perennial springs and wells, offered the caravans opportunities to rest and to take in water and food for men and beasts.

Another fortlet, built around the same time, is Vezereos/Sidi Mohammed ben Aïssa, which lies in the midst of shifting sand dunes on a flat hill on the main road leading from Telmine to Remada. The building inscription, which was renewed in 201 CE, suggests that it dates to the 80s of the second century.[8] For the time

[8] *CIL* VIII, 11048; *ILAfr* 26; Merlin 1921, 238 ff., 244 ff.; Trousset 1974, 75–77, no. 72, fig. 14.2 (50 × 65 m: 0.33 ha). Cf. Mattingly 1995, 80, who considered a construction before 180 CE possible; however, the corresponding red slip ware (ARS A^1 and A^2) is missing.

being, it is not possible to make any statements about the interior buildings of the fortlet, measuring c. 55 × 44 m (0.24 ha), with rounded corners, a (Late Antique?) gate tower in the south wall, a gate near the south-west corner, and a rear gate (Fig. 6.6.2–3). The barracks seem to have been attached to the inner walls. Based on the internal area, it can be assumed that in the late second century there was a legionary or auxiliary garrison, or possibly a mixed garrison of about the size of a *centuria* with an additional dozen cavalrymen (Mackensen 2015, 259–64).

The road from Turris Tamaleni/Telmine at Chott el-Djerid through Jabal Dahar via Tillibari/Remada and along the scarp of Jabal Nafusa to Tentheos/Zintan (Fig. 6.1) marked the southern frontier already in the late second century, which was mostly controlled only by the garrisons of fortlets such as Vezereos and Tisavar. However, it was not until the time of the *Itinerarium Antonini Augusti* (73–77), compiled between 211 and 235 CE, that this border was designated as *limes Tripolitanus* (Mattingly 1995, 62–66, 98, tables 3.3, 5.2). East of Remada, the military posts assumed on the east–west connection are not attested archaeologically, nor is the postulated auxiliary fort of Tentheos. This also applies to the military site postulated south-east of Zintan at Mizda, regardless of whether it was a fortlet or a fort (see above) (Mattingly 1995, 97; Schimmer 2012).

Territorial expansion under Septimius Severus and the construction of the so-called 'oasis forts' for legionary vexillations

Q. Anicius Faustus (196/197–201 CE), legionary legate and commander-in-chief of the *exercitus Africae*, was responsible for the territorial expansion of Tripolitania under the emperor Septimius Severus (193–211 CE), the *conservator orbis* ('defender of the world'), who was born in Lepcis Magna. The legate was responsible for the military security of the approximately 1,500 km long frontier and the protection of the province of Africa Proconsularis. The military building programme, an impressive demonstration of Rome's power, extended from Castellum Dimmidi/Messad (198 CE) in western Numidia to Gholaia/Bu Njem (201 CE) in eastern Tripolitania. But only in Tripolitania were three larger forts built in positions between 120 and 250 km to the south in an arid desert region with very low annual rainfall: at Gholaia/Bu Njem (Rebuffat 1972–73c, 135–45), Myd(---)/Gheriat el-Garbia (*IRT2021* 1135; Mackensen 2010b, 441–45, figs 68–71), and Cidamus/Ghadames (*IRT* 907; *IRT2021* 907) (Fig. 6.1). These places were situated near larger oases with perennial springs. They served as resting and supply places for the trade caravans and the transhumant nomads with their herds of cattle, sheep and goats. However, there was no need to build linear barriers here comparable with the Hadrianic *fossatum Africae*, as the traffic had necessarily to pass by the oases anyway.

The new forts functioned as logistical key points where mobility and transhumance could be controlled. Due to their location on the routes leading north from Fazzan, they served the associated control and security tasks of the garrisons for the cross-border movement of people and goods, far in advance of the agriculturally used, partly very fertile area of the province. The reason for this expansive policy was probably an increasing threat to the cultivated region from warlike nomads, as written sources suggest.[9] However, the increased control exerted on the semi-nomadic peoples by the new forts could also have been the cause of their hostile attitude and increasing conflicts. For the years 201–5 CE, Mattingly (1995, 80) also assumed active campaigning by the Roman troops stationed in Tripolitania, in addition to further building activities. Whether Septimius Severus took part in a campaign against the peoples not mentioned by name in the sources in the spring of 203 CE, or whether he reached as far as Gholaia or Myd(---), as Anthony Birley (1999, 153) considered, cannot be proven.

Geographically, Gheriat el-Garbia occupies the central position between the other two forts and lies on the main route leading from the three coastal cities of Oea, Sabratha, and Lepcis Magna via Mizda into Fazzan. At Bu Njem to the east, the routes bifurcated and led either south through the Wadi Bei el-Kebir or east via Waddan and Zella. The route coming from the heartland of Africa Proconsularis ran via the forts of Si Aoun and Ghadames on the western route towards Fazzan.

For Bu Njem, the arrival of the legionary vexillation on 24 January 201 CE and its mission – *at* (*sic!*) *castra Chol aedific*(*anda*) *venit* – are reported on an inscription.[10] At Gheriat el-Garbia, the building inscription dated to 199/201 CE also mentions a vexillation of the *legio III Augusta pia vindex*.[11] For Ghadames, a vexillation is only attested for the years 211–17 CE, although it can probably be assumed as early as 201 CE.[12] The commander (*praepositus*) of these legionary vexillations was a *centurio legionis III Augustae* in each of the three forts until 238 CE – in contrast to the equestrian *praefectus* of the auxiliary cohort in Tillibari/Remada. As a rule, the centurions (with their vexillations) were

[9] Aurelius Victor, *Caesares*, 20.19; *Historia Augusta, Septimius Severus*, 18.3; Rebuffat 2000, 235; Guédon 2018, 115, with note 145.

[10] *IRT2021* 1064; Rebuffat 1972–73b, 121–22, 132, pl. 47a; 1985a, 226.

[11] *IRT2021* 1110; Di Vita 1966, 107–11, fig. 12 (= Mackensen 2010b, 371, fig. 9; 2021a, 61, fig. 39; 2024, 313–15, fig. 193).

[12] *IRT* 907; *IRT2021* 907; Le Bohec 1989a, 403, note 326.

Fig. 6.7. Myd(---)/Gheriat el-Garbia, north-western Libya. 1: Severan fort defences with main gate (*porta praetoria*) and Berber village in the fort from north-east; 2: Severan fort defences on limestone plateau, in the foreground oasis in Wadi Tula seen from west (photos M. Mackensen).

ordered back to Lambaesis presumably after 15 to 18 months of service at a remote outpost such as Bu Njem (Speidel 1988, 99–102).

Myd(---)/Gheriat el-Garbia

The fort of Gheriat el-Garbia is situated on a rock plateau above the oasis (Figs 6.2, 6.7.2) and was visible from afar as a landmark from the south with its towers along the rear defensive wall. These towers had a maximum height of 8.8 m, of which the intermediate tower 4 has survived to a height of 7.2 m, and the curtain wall was built of white limestone ashlars, medium-sized squared stones and smaller rubble stones (Mackensen 2016, 89). North-east of the fort, about 20 m higher, is the so-called 'temple plateau' with several sanctuaries. To the west of the fort, the civil settlement (*vicus*) extends in the lower, gently sloping areas and at the foot of the plateau (Fig. 6.8). The 133 × 181 m (2.41 ha) fort (internally 128 × 176 m: 2.25 ha) with rounded corners corresponds to about one tenth of the area of the legionary fortress at Lambaesis (east Algeria). Here, as at Gholaia/Bu Njem, the Punic cubit served as the unit of measurement for distances and areas (Schimmer 2021, 86–91, figs 60–61; cf. Rebuffat 1989, 161–62).

The fort has preserved curtain walls up to 3.6 m high with corner and intermediate towers, as well as four gates with three different ground plans and a ditch in front of the north-east curtain wall (Fig. 6.7.1–2). Characteristic is the architecturally remarkable main gate (width 26.65 m), built mostly of ashlars or with larger and medium-sized stones, with a central carriageway and lateral passages as well as the characteristically shaped pentagonal towers with chamfered inner frontal corners (Figs 6.9–10). The ground plans of these towers are known from the two side gates of the legionary fortress at Lambaesis and were adopted for the main gate of the vexillation fort of Gholaia. The three-storey southern tower of the *porta praetoria* is still 10 m high and can be reconstructed with a

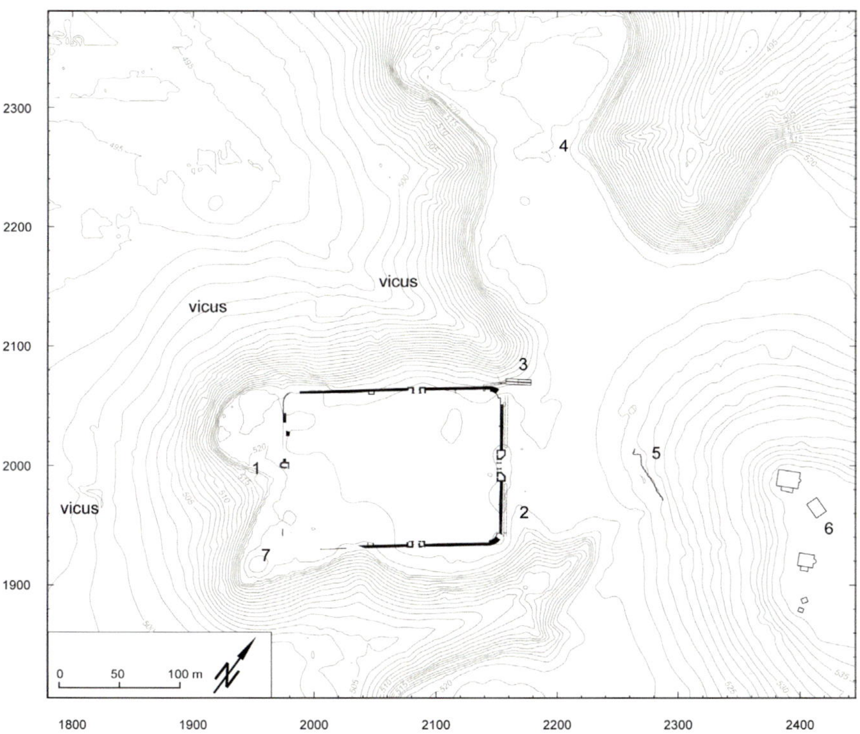

Fig. 6.8. Myd(---)/Gheriat el-Garbia, north-western Libya: topographical plan of Severan vexillation fort (*castra*). 1: South-west access; 2: East access; 3: Double cistern; 4: North access; 5: Limestone quarry; 6: Plateau with temples and sanctuaries (Mackensen 2016, 87, fig. 4).

Fig. 6.9. *(left)* Myd(---)/Gheriat el-Garbia, north-western Libya: main gate (*porta praetoria*) of Severan fort. 1: Gate towers with collapsed outer central arch, with Berber village in the fort's interior; 2: Excavations between the gate towers seen from the interior of the fort (photos M. Mackensen).

Fig. 6.10. *(below)* Myd(---)/Gheriat el-Garbia, north-western Libya: main gate (*porta praetoria*) of Severan vexillation fort. 1: Photogrammetry; 2: Documentation of elevated walls and reconstruction (Mackensen 2013, 99, fig. 15).

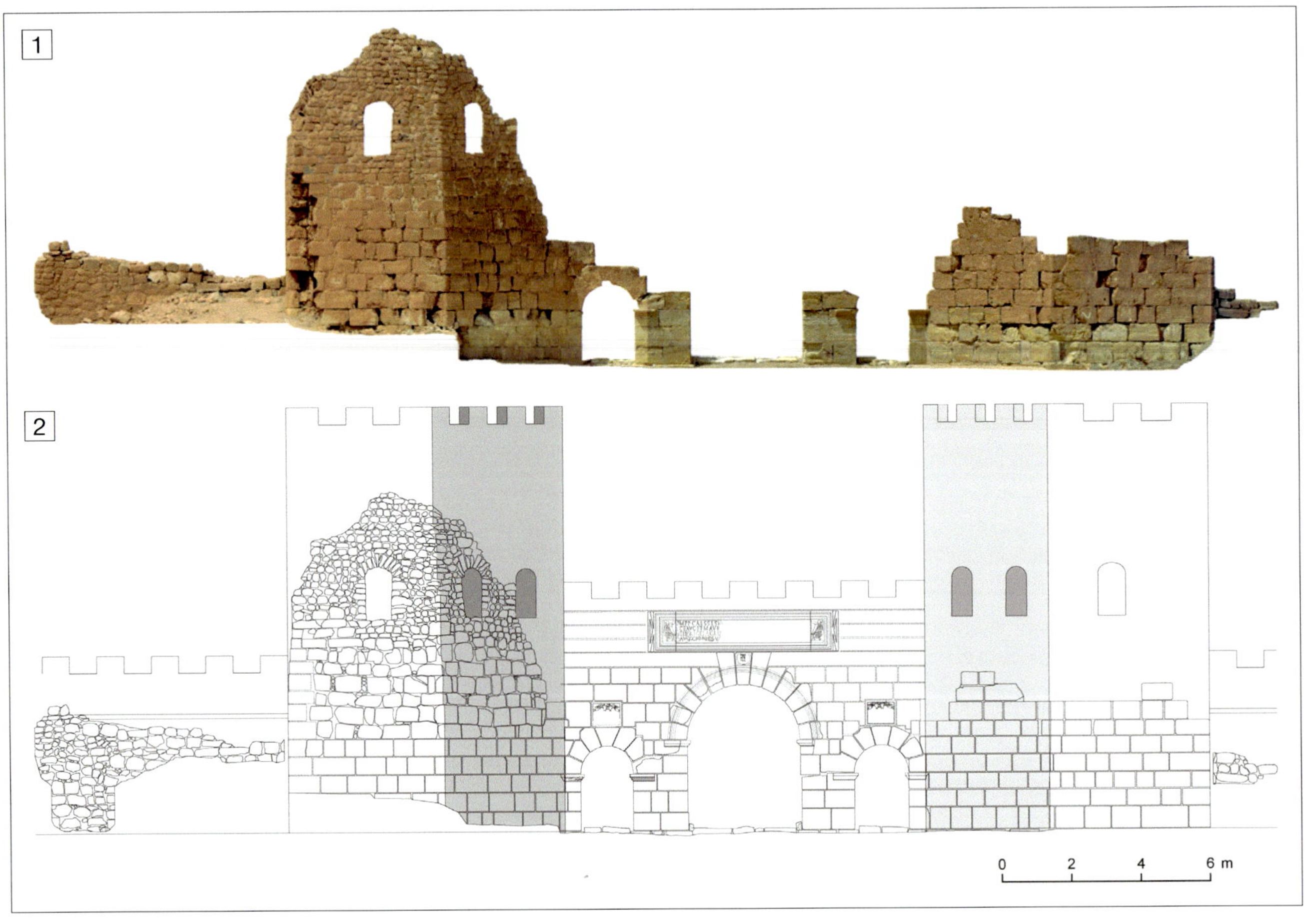

Fig. 6.11. Myd(---)/Gheriat el-Garbia, north-western Libya: plan of Severan vexillation fort (*castra*), built in 199–201 CE. 1–10: Interval towers; 11: Well; 12: Entrance to underground tunnel; 13: Cistern; 14: Ditch; 15: Headquarters building (*principia*); 16: Main gate (*porta praetoria*); 17–18: Lateral gates (*portae principales dextra et sinistra*); 19: Rear gate (*porta decumana*); 20: Storerooms (*horrea*); 21: Commander's living quarters (*praetorium*); 22: Bath building (*thermae*); 23, 25: Barracks; 24: *Groma* building (Mackensen 2024, 304, fig. 188).

crenelated platform at a total height of 12–12.5 m (Fig. 6.10.1–2); the adjoining curtain wall can be calculated at c. 4.8 m. Above the carriageway was a monumental building inscription with *tabula ansata* flanked by two antithetic victories.[13]

The interior buildings of the fort have been almost completely destroyed by a Berber village that had existed at least since the late seventeenth/early eighteenth century (Figs 6.2, 6.9.1). In the area of the headquarters building it has been possible to clear the dilapidated Berber houses and to excavate the central room of the rearward wing, the fort's regimental shrine (*aedes*), and an adjacent room without benches along the side walls (*officium*) as well as a corner of the building (Mackensen 2011, 302–10, figs 55–56; 2012, 51–52, fig. 11). On this basis, the *principia* could be reconstructed with a size of 36 × 36–40 m (Fig. 6.11.15), similar to the *principia* at Gholaia. A pedestal for a statue of the empress Julia Mamaea, reused in the blocked carriageway of the main gate, was consecrated by the soldiers (*milites praetendentes*) of the legionary vexillation garrisoned here, probably in 222/223 CE. It may be imagined that the pedestal with the statue had been erected in the courtyard of the headquarters building. The inscription mentions for the first time the fort's name Myd(---) and the otherwise unknown commander Aelius Crescentinus, a *centurio et praepositus* (*IRT2021* 1135; Mackensen 2010b, 441–45, figs 68–71).

On the basis of a fragment of a c. 8.4 m long, three-line inscription that was reused as spolia in a late Roman building (Fig. 6.21.1), a *groma* hall was assumed to have been constructed in front of the headquarters building above the intersection of the *via praetoria* and *via principalis* (Fig. 6.11.24). This would represent the adoption of a significant building type from the legionary fortress at Lambaesis, albeit with smaller dimensions (Mackensen 2011, 293–95, figs 45–46; 2021a, 251; *IRT2021* 1140). In the central area of the fort (*latera praetorii*), in addition to the headquarters building one can hypothesize the presence of the commander's residence (*praetorium*), a multi-aisled storage building (*horreum*), and a bath building (*thermae*) (Fig. 6.11.20–22).

The large number of decontextualized architectural elements is remarkable. On this basis, Johannes Eingartner reconstructed seven orders of columns of different heights;[14] their architectural use can be postulated for various large buildings (*principia*, *thermae*, *groma*?) and colonnaded porticoes along the *via praetoria*. The architectural decoration of the main gate and several central buildings of the fort is qualitatively more elaborate and sophisticated than that at Gholaia. The architecture conveys the impression of a scaled-down replica of the legionary fortress at Lambaesis. It underlines the prominent position and importance of the central Severan fort on the southern frontier of Tripolitania (Mackensen 2021a, 70, 253).

Only insignificant traces of the barracks in the northern *praetentura* have survived. The number of men in the legionary vexillation could be estimated from the available areas in the *praetentura* and the *retentura*.[15] Based on the accommodation for the soldiers in the *praetentura* of Gholaia, one can calculate 12 barracks for

[13] *IRT2021* 1110; Mackensen 2011, 280–85, fig. 36; 2012, 47–50, fig. 7; 2013, 96–107, figs 11–20; 2024, 130–35, figs 78–80.

[14] See Eingartner in Mackensen 2011, 327–36, esp. fig. 81; Eingartner 2021, 127–45, figs 96–98, pls 2.1–11, 4.1–11.

[15] Cf. Mattingly 1995, 91, table 5.1 (800–1,000 men); Mackensen 2021a, 251 (600–800 men).

a total of 576 men. In addition, there are probably two to four similar barracks in the *retentura* (Fig. 6.11.23, 25). This would result in a garrison of 772 soldiers plus 16 or 32 non-commissioned officers (*principales*). The individual barracks can be reconstructed with an officer's quarter for the non-commissioned officers, who were in command of sub-units of about 48 men each, and 12 rooms of four men each. In addition, one should assume a mounted sub-unit, perhaps in the strength of an auxiliary *turma*, i.e. 32 cavalrymen, who were accommodated in the rear part of the fort (*retentura*). A hint of the presence of cavalrymen (*equites*), or at least riding horses, is given by a pointed lens-shaped strap fitting that belonged to a (military) horse harness of the first half of the third century CE (Mackensen 2021a, 225–26, pl. 24.18). In addition to the postulated barracks for legionaries and cavalrymen (with additional stables), workshops (*fabrica*) and a hospital (*valetudinarium*) for sick and injured soldiers (*aegri*) can also be assumed in the *retentura*. The *aegri* probably accounted for 5% of the actual garrison, c. 40 men (Marichal 1992, 84–88).

Gholaia/Bu Njem

The fort of Gholaia/Bu Njem lies in the midst of shifting sand dunes, which have, after Rebuffat's excavations, again taken possession of large parts of the fort and the civil settlement (*vicus*) enclosed by a wall (Fig. 6.12). The fort's size is 93 × 139 m (1.28 ha). The curtain wall and especially the ashlar-built gates, and the central interior buildings as well, have suffered damage through stone robbing that was employed for the Italian fortress built within sight in 1927–29. The area of the fort (internally 87 × 133 m: 1.15 ha) (Fig. 6.13) is about half that of the fort Myd(---)/Gheriat el-Garbia (2.25 ha). The construction period, at least of the fortifications, was about one year from the arrival of the legionary vexillation at the end of January 201 CE until the setting of the four preserved building inscriptions of the gates (*IRT2021* 913–16). This is dated to the year 201 CE based on the indications of the tribunician power (TR POT IX), the imperatorial acclamations (IMP XI), and the second consulate (COS II) of the emperor Septimius Severus.[16]

The rectangular fort with rounded corners has four gates, with a single carriageway each, three of which have square towers. The main gate, on the other hand, has towers with a pentagonal ground plan with chamfered frontal inner corners. For the main gate (Fig. 6.14.1), which was built of rusticated ashlars with drafted edges, a total height of 8.5–9 m can be reconstructed for the three-storey towers with ground floor, first floor and crenelated tower platform. In a repair inscription by M. Porcius Iasucthan for the collapsed (south) side gate (*portam vetustate conlabsam lapidi quadrato arco curvato restituit*), which can be dated to 222 CE, the four-storey nature of the towers (*excelsae turres quater divisae*) is explicitly mentioned: see *IRT2021* 1091; Rebuffat 1995, 82, 87 (line 6), 93 (line 17). Therefore, only three-storey towers with a ground floor, first storey and crenelated tower platform should be assumed for the Severan foundation period. This is not altered by the incised drawing (graffito) from the *thermae* depicting an unidentified fort; however, it is

Fig. 6.12. Gholaia/Bu Njem, north-western Libya: plan of Severan vexillation fort (*castra*) with civilian settlement (*vicus*) and enclosure wall in 1972 (after Rebuffat 1976–77, 40–41, figs 2–3).

[16] Rebuffat 1972–73a, 104–6. Cf. Di Vita-Évrard and Rebuffat 1987, 110, who expected the building to take two to three years at the most, including the baths, which are probably the most recent major building complex. In 202 CE, Septimius Severus held the third consulate.

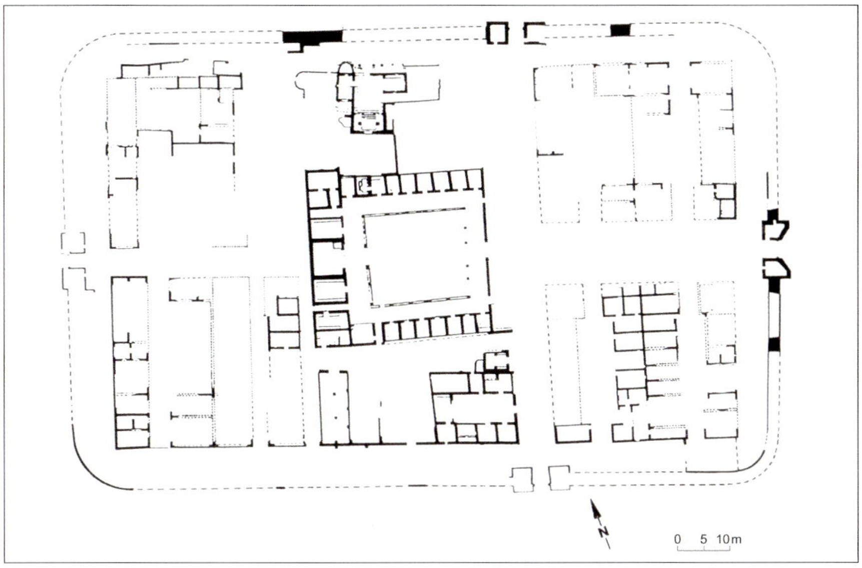

Fig. 6.13. *(left)* Gholaia/Bu Njem, north-western Libya: plan of Severan vexillation fort (*castra*), built in 201 CE (after Rebuffat 1989, 157, fig. 1).

Fig. 6.14. *(below)* Gholaia/Bu Njem, north-western Libya: Severan fort.
1: Main gate (*porta praetoria*);
2: Barracks of southern *praetentura* and headquarters building (*principia*) with elevated pillars (photos M. Mackensen).

hardly Gholaia – as is often assumed – since the foreground depicts galloping horses or exercises of two groups of cavalrymen together with two rows of soldiers as spectators.[17] A more probable alternative seems to me that the fort of Secedi with its partly mounted *cohors* was depicted here. The construction of four-storey towers around 220 CE in the Tripolitanian desert must be regarded as an innovative construction in terms of building technology (Mackensen 2013, 93–94).

Rebuffat concentrated his investigations on the central complex of the middle strip (*latera praetorii*). This proved to be a 36 × 34 m headquarters building with an inner courtyard enclosed by pillars (*porticus*) and rows of rooms behind it, a cross-hall with pillars and simple, trapezoidal capitals, a tribunal and a rearward range of rooms. This consists of the fort's regimental chapel (*aedes*), a sanctuary with a strongroom serving as the garrison's treasury (*aerarium*) in the basement, and two assembly rooms with benches (*scholae*) for the non-commissioned officers; also a northern double room used as an archive (*tabularium*). This is the prototype of a headquarters building for a vexillation fort of the early third century CE in Africa Proconsularis (Figs 6.13, 6.14.2). Of particular importance is the *scriptorium* discovered in the southern lateral row of rooms of the *principia*, which is unique throughout the Roman Empire. A plastered table with a gabled top has been preserved between two benches (Rebuffat 1974–75, 197–99, fig. 4, pls 59–61; cf. Walas 2022, 53–57) (Fig. 6.15). Obviously, there are no traces of a *groma* hall in front of the entrance to the *principia* (Mackensen 2008, 289–90). The c. 10 × 32 m large fore-hall suggested recently by Anna Walas (2022, 53–54, fig. 4) seems to be rather hypothetical.

[17] Rebuffat 1969–70b, 130, pl. 27d; 1989, 158, fig. 2; 2000, 238, fig. 5; cf. critically on this Mackensen 2008, 288, note 73.

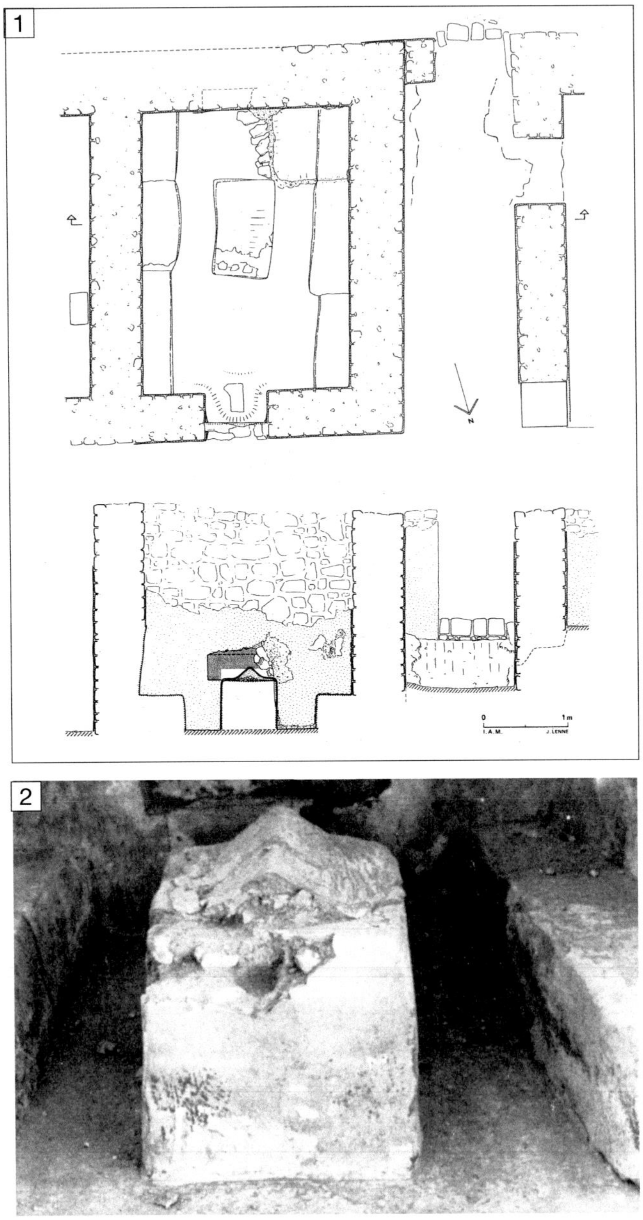

Fig. 6.15. Gholaia/Bu Njem, north-western Libya: Severan fort. *Scriptorium* in the headquarters building (*principia*) (after Rebuffat 1974–75, 206, fig. 4, pl. 59c).

South of the *principia* are the 16.4 × 15 m living quarters of the commander (*praetorium*) and next to it a small sanctuary with an altar consecrated in 201 CE to the *genius Gholaiae*, which served the *praepositus vexillationis* for his religious acts. At 245 m^2, the residential building is considerably smaller than normal centurions' quarters (375 m^2) in the *praetentura* of the legionary fortress at Lambaesis (Mackensen 2008, 292–93); however, they were designated for officers of equal rank. Behind it is a 12.5 × 15 m, two-aisled storage building (*horreum*) for grain and other foodstuffs (cf. Walas 2022, 54–56). To the north of the headquarters building is the bath building constructed in 202/203 CE with a complete sequence of bathing and recreation rooms, including a refreshing cold-water pool (Fig. 6.13). The dedicatory inscription to the goddess Salus described to the users of the bath in poetic form the strenuous climatic conditions in the sand desert, with extreme and fiery heat and sandstorms, as well as the care of the commander for his soldiers and their health, the team spirit, and the comradeship of the troops (*IRT* 918; *IRT2021* 918; Rebuffat 1978–79, 113–24; 1985a, 227).

Bu Njem is the only fort in the command area of Anicius Faustus whose accommodations for the soldiers (*centuriae*) have been partially investigated with their regular layout in the *praetentura*. The structure of two barracks is known, each with a quarter for the commanding officer, measuring 45–50 m^2, five or six rooms (*contubernia*) of about 15 m^2 for the soldiers and a double room at the end of the building (Figs 6.13, 6.14.2). The building scheme exemplifies the tactical structure of the legionary detachment, which was under the command of an experienced and reliable centurion of the *legio III Augusta*. The eight small sub-units, each commanded by a non-commissioned officer (*principalis*), comprised 24 men each – based on 4 m^2 floor space per legionary and four men per room. This results in 192 men and eight non-commissioned officers (see Mackensen 2008, 296–303, fig. 12). These figures are significantly (40%) below the estimates by Rebuffat (1989, 161–63: 320 men), who assumed standardized occupancies per room (eight men) without taking into account the available space and therefore equated two barrack blocks with a *centuria* of 80 men.

Rebuffat's plan shows in the southern half of the rearward area (*retentura*) four roughly equal-sized barracks, the tops of whose walls were partially uncovered; here a maximum of another 100 (and not 160) men could have been accommodated, possibly also some cavalrymen and their horses (Mackensen 2008, 295, 299–300). An actual troop strength of about 300 men seems more realistic in the early third century than Rebuffat's calculation of 480 men. For the years 236–38 CE, in addition to the legionary *vexillatio*, there is evidence for the first time of a *numerus conlatus* – a unit composed of soldiers from various (unknown) auxiliary units,[18] which could have been accommodated in the *retentura*. In the northern half of the *retentura* there would have been space for a workshop complex (*fabrica*) and a small hospital (*valetudinarium*).

Other forts and fortlets

In the first decade of the third century CE, about 27 km west of Bu Njem, the 12.8 × 9.2 m fortlet Gasr Zerzi with a 31.7 × 5.6 m cistern nearby was built to control an important crossing of traffic routes at the Wadi Bei el-Kebir.[19] Other outposts in the Wadi Bei el-Kebir have not been

[18] *IRT2021* 1059; Rebuffat 1978–79, 113–24; 1985a, 228; 1989, 162–63; 2000, 230–31.

[19] *IRT2021* 1226–27; Brogan and Reynolds 1964, 43–44, pl. 38a–b; Rebuffat 1969–70b, 136 ff., 163, fig. 6; 2000, 232.

confirmed archaeologically by characteristic structures. A 'fort vedette' (as referred to by Rebuffat) situated on a hilltop in Oum el-Gueloub is – contrary to what was originally assumed (Rebuffat 2000, 232: a 'camp miniature' for c. 30 soldiers) – an autochthonous fortification.[20]

Even though the vexillation fort of Cidamus/Ghadames has not yet been located at the edge of the vast oasis, one would like to assume a similar size as at Gholaia with a troop strength of about 300 men, knowing the central and the eastern forts. This would mean that around 200 CE c. 1,400 legionaries, including specialists (*immunes*) released from heavy service, would have been detached from their parent unit, the *legio III Augusta*, at Lambaesis.

Under Septimius Severus, building activities are recorded in western Tripolitania for the auxiliary fort of Tillibari/Remada: in 197 CE the *aedes*, which had collapsed due to age, was renewed (*annorum vetustate dilapsam a solo restitutit et perfecit*); this was not just any temple, but the regimental chapel of the headquarters building.[21] The fortlet of Si Aoun, built in 198 CE around 35 km south of Remada and measuring c. 30 × 40 m, has to be mentioned as well.[22] The fortlet is called a *praesidium* in the building inscription (*ILAfr* 269). It was built by a detachment of the *cohors II Flavia Afrorum* and a *numerus conlatus*. At least one building inscription also attests to repair work carried out by a legionary detachment in 201 CE at the fortlet of Vezereos (*CIL* VIII, 11048; see also note 8 in this chapter).

The extension of the *limes Tripolitanus* road, and of the traffic routes from Garian to Mizda and from Zintan to Mizda in 216 CE, documented by numerous milestones, should also be mentioned (Goodchild 1948, 7–24, esp. 14–23; *IRT*, maps 8–9). The round watchtower (*burgus*) of Gheriat el-Garbia, which lies 1 km north of the fort, is dated through an inscription to the time of Severus Alexander (222–35 CE); it provided a view of the caravans and of the marching route coming from the north through the upper Wadi Zemzem into the Wadi Tula (*IRT* 895; *IRT2021* 895; Mattingly 1985, 67–70; Schmid *et al.* 2019).

Reorganization of the *limes Tripolitanus* after the disbandment of the *legio III Augusta*

It is probable that the Tripolitanian legionary vexillations were not involved in the battle of the legionary legate Capelianus against the emperor Gordian II in January 238 CE in the hinterland of Carthage. The soldiers of the legionary vexillation stationed at Gholaia could therefore be reduced in rank only; the unit could have been demoted and renamed *vexillatio Golensis* (*IRT2021* 1053; Rebuffat 1985b, 137 ff.; Mattingly 1995, 83). The legionary vexillation stationed at Myd(---)/Gheriat el-Garbia was probably integrated into the *cohors I Syrorum sagittariorum*, which was now increased to a *cohors milliaria* of about 800 men, but it remained at its location.[23]

Whether the former legionary vexillations in Tripolitania now remained permanently on site with a changed status is not certain. For the *legio III Augusta*, loyal to emperor Maximinus I Thrax (235–38 CE), was dishonourably disbanded, the legate and other high officers probably executed in June/July 238 CE and the name of the legion erased from official inscriptions. At least some of the legionary detachments involved in the fighting were transferred to the provinces on the upper and middle Danube. In 253 CE, the emperor Valerian I (253–60 CE) reconstituted the remaining parts of the legion to the strength of a *vexillatio milliaria* and transferred them from Raetia to Gemellae in Numidia (*CIL* VIII, 2482, 17976; cf. Mackensen 2008, 286).

A heavily fragmented inscription from Gheriat el-Garbia mentions a local war (*bellum*) for the year 239 CE and the associated destruction of infrastructural installations.[24] The denomination of the structures that collapsed due to age, perhaps parts of the fort's defences, has not survived on the inscription, nor has the complete name of the military unit; it is uncertain whether the latter, perhaps the *cohors I Syrorum sagittariorum Gordiana* (Mattingly 1985, 70–72; Le Bohec 1987, 82–83), repaired a road from [---]atsa to Lepcis Magna.[25]

The two *burgus*-like fortlets Qasr Duib (Fig. 6.16.1–3) and Qasr Wames (Fig. 6.16.4), which lie on the Roman road from Zintan through the upper Wadi Sofeggin to Mizda, are military fortifications. Qasr Duib is referred to as *novum centenarium* [*Philippianum*] [*S*]*as* in the building inscription of the year 246/247 CE.[26] Both fortlets were built to protect the road and water points because of barbarian incursions (*incursiones barbarorum*). In addition, the inscription offers for the first time the hierarchy of the organizational structure of the *limes Tripolitanus*, which probably already existed in this form since 238/239 CE. The garrisons of the Tripolitanian frontier continued administratively to be under

[20] Mackensen 2009, 79, note 19 (with references); 2012, 42, fig. 2; 2021a, 43, with note 80, figs 23.1–2.

[21] Cf. Trousset 1974, 118; Euzennat and Trousset 1978, 134–35, 139; Le Bohec 1989a, 441; Mattingly 1995, 80.

[22] Trousset 1974, 118–20, no. 130; Mattingly 1995, 102; cf. Le Bohec 1989a, 393.

[23] *IRT* 896; *IRT2021* 896; Mattingly 1985, 70–72; 1995, 83, 87, table 4.2; Le Bohec 1989b, 88–90.

[24] *IRT* 896; *IRT2021* 896; Mattingly 1985, 70–72; Le Bohec 1989b, 89; Rebuffat 2000, 235.

[25] Cf. hypothetically Mackensen 2010b, 446–47. The [---]atsa in the inscription *IRT* 896 could also belong to the hitherto unknown name of Mizda, for from there a road led via Thenadassa/Aïn Wif to Lepcis Magna. South of Mizda, on the other hand, neither milestones nor a paved road are known.

[26] *IRT* 880; *IRT2021* 880; Di Vita-Évrard 1991, 427–44; recently cf. Mackensen 2009, 82–88, figs 3–6; Guédon 2018, 155–56, with note 159 (with references).

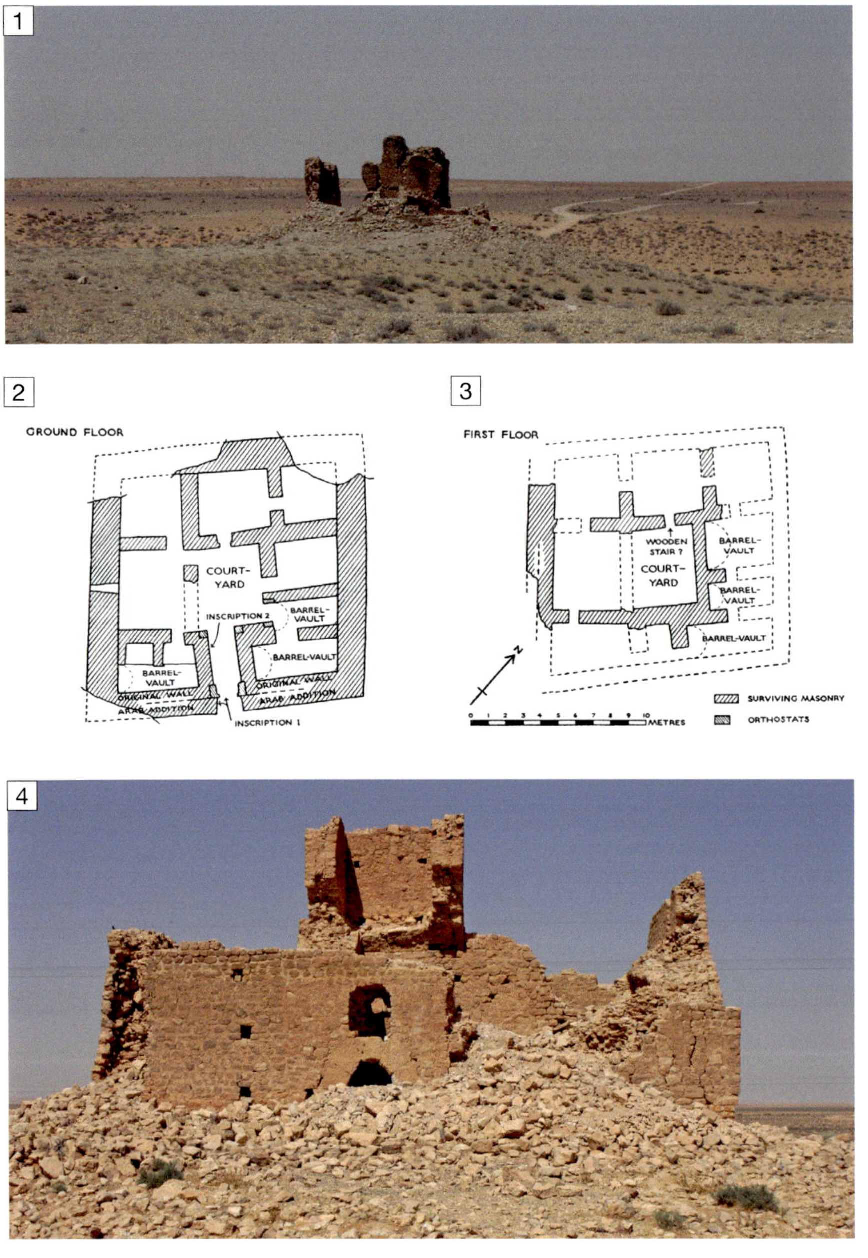

Fig. 6.16. 1–3: *Burgus*-like fortlet (*centenarium*) Sas(---)/Qasr Duib, north-western Libya, built in 246–47 CE. 1: South-east wall and rear wall of the lookout tower (photo M. Mackensen); 2–3: Plan of ground floor and first floor (after Goodchild and Ward-Perkins 1949, 89, fig. 17); 4: *Burgus*-like fortlet (*centenarium*) Qasr Wames, north-western Libya, with east wall and lookout tower above the buried entrance (photo M. Mackensen).

the supreme command of the governor (*legatus Augusti/Augustorum pro praetore*) of the province of Numidia, which had been established in the early third century CE, while an equestrian *procurator* was responsible as *praepositus limitis* (*regionis*) *Tripolitanae* for the entire frontier region. The *limes regionis Tripolitanae* was subdivided into individual frontier sectors; the *limes Tentheitanus* is mentioned, which probably extended from Tentheos at least to Mizda, and for which an equestrian tribune, the commander of the auxiliary cohort stationed in Tentheos, was responsible.[27]

The 15.5 × 15.5 m (240 m²) fortlet of Qasr Duib consists of two storeys (Fig. 6.16.2–3) with rooms arranged around a small courtyard and a flat roof with a crenelated parapet wall. The lookout tower built above the entrance area protrudes over the parapet and is a characteristic feature of military *centenaria* that the civil *centenaria*/qsur of indigenous Tripolitanian proprietors do not have (Mackensen 2009, 91–93, 100–1, figs 10–12). Among the rooms on the ground floor, accommodation for cavalrymen and stabling for three or four horses can be identified on the left side; behind the courtyard are an office and accommodation for the *praepositus*, a non-commissioned officer (*principalis*). On the first floor are the rooms for the soldiers. The strength of the small garrison was 30–40 men, including three or four cavalrymen (Mackensen 2009, 87–88, fig. 4). Qasr Wames measures 13 × 12.9 m (168 m²) and has only the ground floor with rooms arranged around a small courtyard, a flat roof with crenelated parapet wall, and the characteristic lookout tower (with still preserved climbing holds and footrests on the inner walls) (Fig. 6.16.4). The strength of the small garrison is estimated at six to 12 men (Mackensen 2009, 88–98, figs 8–16).

Further construction measures are attested in the regimental chapel (*aedes*) of the fort of Gholaia for 248 CE.[28] The inscription shows the same organizational structure of the *limes Tripolitanus* as that of Qasr Duib, but for the lowest level of command a *decurio* of the *ala Flavia* is named as commander (*praefectus*) of the *vexillatio Golensis* and of a second unit, probably a *numerus conlatus*.[29] A *limes Golensis* was also suspected (Rebuffat 1985b, 138), but this is not known to have existed in the middle of the third century.

[27] Di Vita-Évrard 1985, 149–56; Rebuffat 1978–79, 113–24; 1985b, 127–39; Mattingly 1991; 1995, 86–87.

[28] Rebuffat *et al.* 1966–67, 87–88, 90, pls 29c, 38a; 1987, 125–30; Guédon 2018, 156, with note 165.

[29] Rebuffat 1985b, 136–38; 2000, 230–31; Mattingly 1995, 86–87.

Among the several ostraca from Bu Njem, dated between 253 and 259 CE, seven different decurions (without naming their unit) are attested.[30] The ostraca served as semi-official documents for internal use of the garrison; they provide information about numerous activities and inform the *officium* of the *praepositus* about individual sub-units, their actual strength, the commanding non-commissioned officers (*principales*), those on sick leave (*aegri*), and the special tasks of the soldiers. Also of interest are the bills of lading for the delivery of wheat for the garrison. The command of the unit stationed at Gholaia, the *vexillatio Golensis*, was still in the hands of a *decurio* detached from his auxiliary unit after 253 CE. The ostraca show that some cavalrymen of the *cohors VIII Fida* (*equitata*)[31] were also seconded to Gholaia from the fort of Secedi, where their partially mounted auxiliary unit was stationed (Marichal 1992, 66, 200–3, nos 94–95; cf. nos 67–68). These cavalrymen served in part as dispatch riders (*dispositi*) to maintain communication between the various forts. The distance to the yet unlocated fort of Secedi was about two to three days' ride (Marichal 1992, 106–7, 202–3, no. 95). It is possible that Secedi was situated about 60 to 90 km north-east of Bu Njem at the lower reaches of the Wadi Bei el-Kebir, halfway to Macomades/Surt. Furthermore, it is conceivable that the decurions seconded to Gholaia as *praepositi* in the 50s of the third century also came from Secedi.

In addition to an unknown *ala Martia* (Marichal 1992, 66, 238, no. 143), an unnamed unit is mentioned on several ostraca with fluctuating strength between 42 and 96 men (Marichal 1992, 70–75, who speaks of a 'détachement', not a 'unité'). This cannot be identified as a sub-unit of the *vexillatio Golensis*. It is headed by a *librarius* (accountant) as commanding non-commissioned officer (*sesquiplicarius*), who is assisted by an *optio* as *adiutor* (scribe) as deputy; in addition, up to nine cavalrymen (*equites*) are listed (Marichal 1992, 68, 74, 76–77, 130–32, nos 12–13). The smaller military outposts Arnum, Boinag, Esuba, Hyeruzerian, and Galin[..]i listed in the ostraca, which belonged to the wide but geographically undefined command area of Gholaia (cf. Rebuffat 1985a, 234; 2000, 236), cannot be located in the field (Marichal 1992, 106; Rebuffat 2000, 232).

Despite the large number of written documents for the 50s of the third century CE, it is not possible to calculate the number of men of the *vexillatio Golensis* accommodated in the *praetentura* of the fort. It is likely to have been considerably lower than the approximately 200 men of the Severan period. For the unit mentioned above, which fluctuated greatly in numbers, with cavalrymen[32] and specialists – from various craftsmen to terrain experts (*proculcatores*) – barracks and stables were available in the *retentura*.

Abandonment of the advanced forts and military outposts and withdrawal of the units

The fort of Gholaia was evacuated by its troops in an orderly manner between 259 CE (the date of the latest ostraca)[33] and 263 CE.[34] This is indicated, for example, by the absence of statuary furnishings and their pedestals in the headquarters building – apart from the damaged, helmeted bust of a goddess from the strongroom underneath the regimental chapel (*aedes*) and a herm from the *principia* (Rebuffat 1969–70a, 48–49, pls 13–14; 1990, 125, pls 5–7). The decision must have come as a surprise, for the garrison had still participated in the *census* of 257/258 CE (Marichal 1992, 108, 152–53, no. 37). A military threat from outside is not recognizable. The date before 263 CE relates to the building inscription of the auxiliary fort of Talalati/Ras el-Aïn in the southern Tunisian Dahar (Figs 6.1, 6.17.1),[35] in which the emperor Gallienus *castra coh(ortis) / VIII Fidae opportuno loco a solo instituit / operantibus fortissimis militibus suis ex limi/te Tripolitano*. Accordingly, the fort of the *cohors VIII Fida* in south-eastern Tripolitania must have been disbanded and the unit moved from Secedi some 600 km to the western section of the *limes Tripolitanus* road. For the first time, the Talalati fort has an almost square ground plan (internally c. 88 × 90 m) with rounded corners and gates with semi-circular projecting towers; the internal buildings are largely unknown (Fig. 6.17.2).[36] The inside area of c. 0.79 ha makes it clear that the *cohors VIII Fida* (*equitata*) with a target strength of 480 soldiers (six *centuriae*) and 128 cavalrymen (four *turmae*) was already reduced to less than half at the time of its transfer from Secedi to Talalati and probably only had an actual strength of 250–300 men.[37]

Precisely because of the close connections with Secedi, a simultaneous withdrawal of the troops from Gholaia – and thus also an abandonment of outposts such as Waddan and Zella in the south-east, but also of those such as Qasr Zerzi in the Wadi Bei el-Kebir

[30] Marichal 1992, 67, 182–245, nos 75–79, 81–87, 92, 103, 107, 148; Rebuffat 2000, 230–31, 245–46.

[31] Cf. Le Bohec 1989b, 76, 79; Marichal 1992, 66; Mattingly 1995, 87–88.

[32] Cf. Marichal 1992, 200, no. 94, mentioning a [---]*atianu eq*(*ues*) · *n*(*umeri*).

[33] Marichal 1992, 65, 182–93, nos 76–85, esp. no. 81 (July 259 CE).

[34] Rebuffat 1989, 156–57; 2000, 235; Marichal 1992, 65–66; Mattingly 1995, 87–88, table 4.3.

[35] *CIL* VIII, 22765; Marichal 1992, 66; Guédon 2018, 157, with note 168.

[36] Boizot 1913, 261, fig. 1; Trousset 1974, 98–102, 132, fig. 14.4, no. 109; Mattingly 1995, 98, fig. 5.7 (external measurements 93 × 93 m = 0.86 ha).

[37] To be compared are Gholaia (internal area 1.15 ha/c. 300 soldiers) and Tillibari (internal area 1.90 ha/c. 600 soldiers); cf. Mattingly 1995, 90 ff., table 5.1.

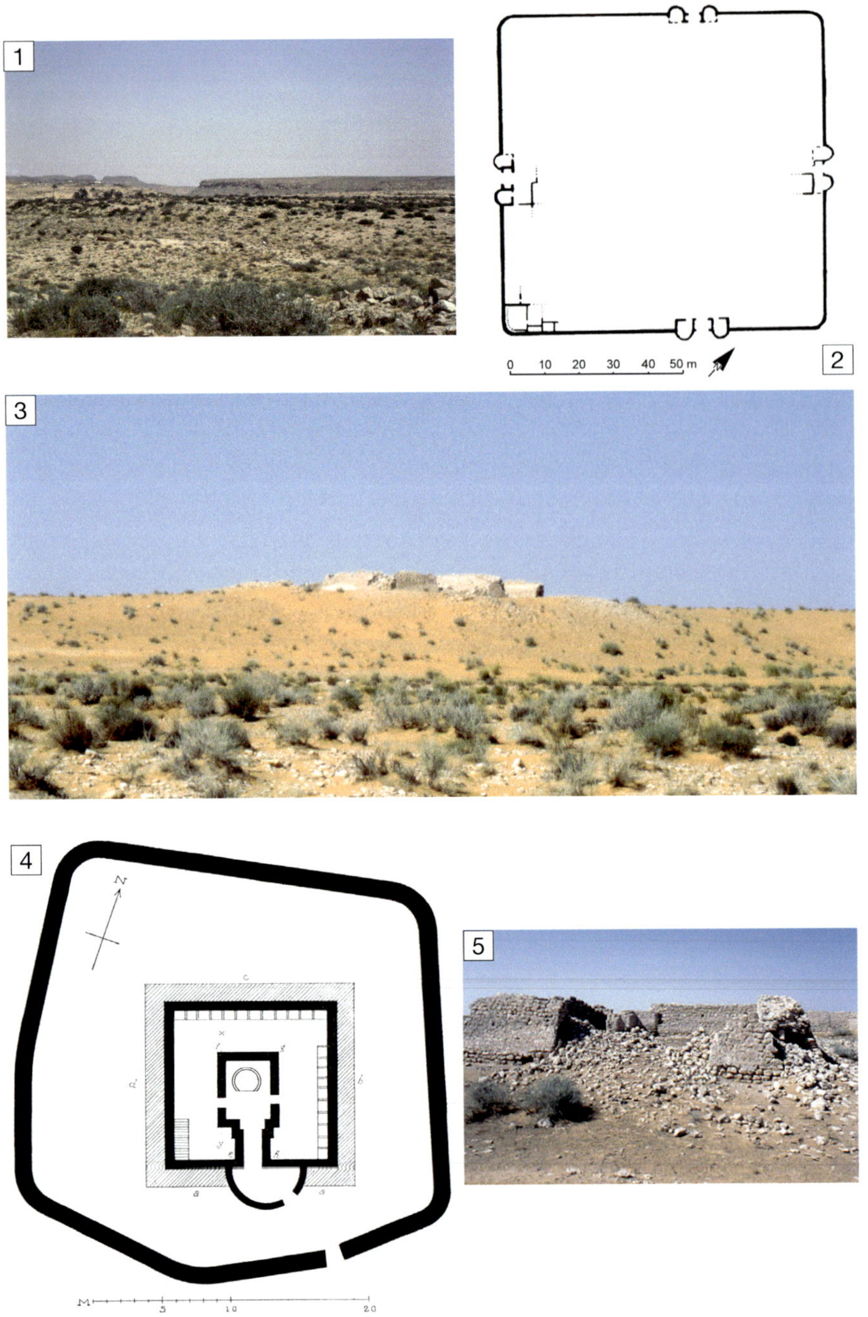

Fig. 6.17. 1–2: Talalati/Ras el-Aïn, southern Tunisia. 1: Auxiliary fort seen from the east (photo M. Mackensen); 2: Plan of auxiliary fort (*castra*), built in 263 CE (after Mattingly 1995, 98, fig. 5.7). 3–5: Tibubuci/Ksar Tarcine, southern Tunisia. 3: Tetrarchic *burgus*-like fortlet (*centenarium*) (photo M. Mackensen); 4: Plan of fortlet with surrounding wall, built in 303–5 CE (Gauckler 1902, 327); 5: South wall of fortlet with glacis-like reinforcement (photo M. Mackensen).

(Fig. 6.1) – around 260 CE, and before 263 CE, seems obvious. However, it cannot definitely be ruled out that reduced garrisons continued to exist at Gholaia and at some control posts until the middle of the 70s of the third century CE. This is probably indicated by an *antoninianus* for the deified Claudius II from the *praetorium* of Bu Njem, minted under the emperor Aurelian, 270–75 CE (Mackensen 2021b, 116, note 17). It is unknown where the *vexillatio Golensis* was transferred to, or whether it was integrated into another (auxiliary) unit along the *limes Tripolitanus* road or in the wider area of command of the governor of Numidia.

However, it can be shown by evidence from Myd(---)/Gheriat el-Garbia that the abandonment of the forts, which had been advanced far to the south, did not take place at the same time (as already suggested by Mattingly 1995, 83). On the basis of coins such as *antoniniani* of Claudius II Gothicus (268–70 CE), Tetricus I (270–73 CE), and Aurelian (270–75 CE) for the deified Claudius II, it can be assumed from the regular coinage of Claudius II Gothicus and Tetricus I that there was still a supply of coins and thus a presence of troops around 270–75 CE. The withdrawal of the garrison, whose strength had already been considerably reduced, most probably took place in 275–80 CE (Mackensen 2021a, 236–38). Whereto the unit was relocated and whether it was integrated into the units stationed at Mizda or Tentheos/Edref near Zintan cannot be said. This also applies to the situation at Cidamus/Ghadames, whose garrison was probably also withdrawn between 260 and 275–80 CE at the latest. It should be noted that the location of the hypothesized forts at these sites is a pending task for future archaeological research.

One should observe that the forts of Myd(---) and Gholaia with their associated military outposts and fortlets, as well as Cidamus and the auxiliary fort of Secedi, which has not been located yet in south-eastern Tripolitania, were cleared according to plan between 260 and 275–80 CE. The military units were relocated to rearward, mostly unknown positions, with the exception of Talalati/Ras el-Aïn. The south-east of Tripolitania with the middle and lower Wadi Bei el-Kebir and the lower Wadi Zemzem was obviously hardly under military control anymore. The central route via Myd(---)/Gheriat el-Garbia, on the other hand, was still monitored by the military there until 275–80 CE. The situation in western Tripolitania, on the other hand, was quite different. With the new construction work for the auxiliary fort of Talalati/Ras el-Aïn in 263 CE – and possibly the two fortlets of Henchir Mgarine and Henchir Medeina (cf. Trousset

1974, 132, fig. 14.5–6; Mattingly 1995, 99, fig. 5.8), which have square ground plans in contrast to the older forts and fortlets – there was obviously a reinforced protection of the main traffic routes in the Dahar.

The reasons for the orderly abandonment of the forts mentioned are unknown. However, it can be assumed that this was a decision made by the emperor Gallienus or his Numidian governor, in which both a lack of troops and the heavy losses at other imperial frontiers played a decisive role.[38] On a regional level, this meant that the enormous costs of supplying the garrisons could be dispensed with. The steady reduction in the actual strength of the vexillations and the auxiliary units such as the *cohors VIII Fida* (*equitata*) after 238 CE must also be considered; apparently its original strength of a *cohors quingenaria* had been more than halved by the time Secedi was abandoned. It is possible that there was a problem in recruiting new soldiers in Tripolitania in the 40s and 50s of the third century, too. It is not possible to prove whereto the withdrawn units – perhaps in the strength of only two to three quingenarian auxiliary cohorts in total, including two or three cavalry squadrons (*turmae*) – were relocated. Talalati is certain, Mizda and Tentheos might be candidates to strengthen their existing garrisons. Maybe they were sent to various sectors of the African frontier and the internal border between the provinces of Numidia and Mauretania as well.

The frontier of Tripolitania in late Roman times

The Tripolitanian frontier zone was considered as being unthreatened or a military backwater around the middle of the third century (Marichal 1979, 451; 1992, 61), but also in the following decades (Mattingly 1995, 192). However, in the spring of 298 CE, the emperor Maximian conducted a campaign against the alliance of the Laguatan/Ilasguas, although it is not clear in which part of Tripolitania the military conflict took place (Mattingly 1983, 97; Rebuffat 1992, 373–74). In the course of the Tetrarchic reorganization of the civil administration of the Empire and the military, the African provinces were reduced in size and in 303 CE the *regio Tripolitana*, which had hitherto belonged to Africa Proconsularis, was established as an independent *provincia Tripolitana* on its own (Mattingly 1995, 171–72). The governor (*praeses*) was also the military commander of the frontier troops (*limitanei*) until the appointment of his own *dux*, probably not until the end of the fourth century CE. In addition, there were numerous units of the mobile field army (*comitatenses*), mainly *legiones palatinae* (three) and *comitatenses* (eight), but also numerous mounted units (19), under the command of a *comes Africae* appointed around 330 CE (*Not. Dign. Occ.*, 7.140–52, 180–98; 25.21–36); the 16 border sectors of the provinces Byzacena, Numidia and Sitifensis adjoining Tripolitana to the west were also under his command.[39]

The division of the *limes Tripolitanus* into individual frontier sectors, which was already documented in the Qasr Duib inscription of 246/247 CE, is recorded in its entirety in the *Not. Dign. Occ.* (31.18–28, 31; see Mattingly 1995, 187–93, table 10.1–3, fig. 10.1). The Tripolitanian schedule was probably last updated in the early 20s of the fifth century (423 CE?). The identification of the individual frontier sectors, which were usually named after the most important larger fort, and the locations of the respective sector commanders (*praepositi limitis*) are still difficult or in many cases impossible to determine. In addition to the 12 *limes* sectors, there are two forts, the castra Leptitana/Lepcis Magna with the *milites fortenses* and the castra Madensia with the *milites munifices* (*Not. Dign. Occ.*, 31.29–30). Otherwise, there is a lack of information on the (at least partially mounted) units. Furthermore, it is not clear according to which criteria the individual frontier sectors were listed. In any case, the list is not based on a geographical sequence. However, the first four frontier sectors (*Not. Dign. Occ.*, 31.18–21) are those in which the toponymic adjective refers to auxiliary forts that already existed in the second half of the third century: Talalati, Tentheos, Vezereos, and Tillibari. Of the remaining sectors, only two can be located now: the limes Madensis with the castra Madensia between Gheriat el-Garbia and Mizda (see below), and the *limes Maccomadensis* (*Not. Dign. Occ.*, 31.22–23) in the region around Macomades/Surt.[40] After the repeated incursions of the Austuriani into the Jabal region and as far as Lepcis Magna and Oea in 363–66 CE (Mattingly 1983, 97–98; 1995, 176–78), the units of *milites fortenses* and *milites munifices* were interpreted by Mattingly as a counteraction of the years c. 375–78 CE. The first unit served for the immediate protection of the capital; on the other hand, the second unit was garrisoned at a still unknown location, perhaps adjacent to Sebkha Tauorgha on the Greater Syrtis.[41] With regard to the size of the garrisons stationed at a frontier sector (including the location of the *praepositus limitis*), Mattingly hypothesized c. 100–200 soldiers. In Tetrarchic times he estimated the total number of frontier troops

[38] Cf. Marichal 1979, 451–52; 1992, 114; Mattingly 1995, 83; Rebuffat 2000, 235–36; Mackensen 2008, 286, with note 65; 2021b, 120–21.

[39] See the detailed summary on the late Roman army in North Africa in Eger 2012, 171–76.

[40] In addition, the two frontier sectors of Talalati and Tillibari were also listed with the *comes Africae* (*Not. Dign. Occ.*, 31.33); the *limes Thamallensis* and the *limes Montensis* probably belonged to the province of Byzacena; see Mattingly 1995, 188.

[41] Mattingly 1995, 189, table 10.2; however, there is no evidence of the castra Madensia in this region.

at c. 1,500–2,000 men, which could have been reduced to c. 1,000 men (excluding the units of the castra Leptitana and castra Madensia) in the early fifth century (Mattingly 1995, 192–93).

New late Roman fort buildings

Due to the rarity of surviving building inscriptions for newly erected forts, a better understanding of the organization of the late Roman frontier sectors can only be achieved through a detailed analysis of the forts (size, ground plan, architectural innovations and construction of the fortifications, internal buildings). The topographical conditions and the location on the supra-regional traffic routes have to be considered as well. Military building activities can be observed increasingly in western Tripolitania due to the known monuments. Of note is the 15 × 15 m *burgus*-like, probably three-storey fortlet at Ksar Tarcine (Fig. 6.17.3–5), the *centenarium* Tibubuci, built in 303–5 CE next to the Wadi Hallouf, on the route between the fortlet Vezereos and the fort Talalati. Due to the presence of feeding troughs for 22 horses (Fig. 6.17.4), we may deduce that a small unit of 30–40 men, mostly cavalrymen (*equites*), took over the control and protection of the road between the two forts (Gauckler 1902; see recently Mackensen 2021b, 121, figs 7.1–2).

Most of the newly built small forts belong to a new type of fortification, which has a square ground plan with outwardly projecting square to rectangular corner and intermediate towers and only one gate protected by two projecting towers. The limited ground area of 0.1–0.35 ha suggests small, probably partially mounted units of 30–60 or at most 80 men. Due to the lack of building inscriptions and the unprocessed range of forms of African red slip ware, most of these small forts, built in ashlar masonry or roughly trimmed and coursed blocks of various sizes, cannot be chronologically classified more precisely. Nevertheless, it is probable that they were built during the second third of the fourth century CE (Rushworth 2015, 131). Most of these small forts, such as Benia Guedah Ceder near the *clausura* between Jabal Tebaga and Jabal Melab (Fig. 6.18.1), Benia bel-Recheb (Fig. 6.18.2–4), Henchir el-Hadjar, Henchir Temassine, and Henchir Rjijila are found in southern Tunisia,[42] whereas only one, Qasr Bularkan (Mselletin) on the Wadi Merdum (Fig. 6.19.1–3), is known from eastern Tripolitania. This last has a ground area of only

Fig. 6.18. 1: Benia Guedeah Ceder, southern Tunisia: late Roman fortlet with central building (photo M. Mackensen). 2–4: Benia bel-Recheb, southern Tunisia. 2: Plan of late Roman fortlet, built in the first half/mid-fourth century CE (after Trousset 1974, 134, fig. 15.2); 3: West wall with north-west corner tower (photo M. Mackensen); 4: Overview of fortlet (photo M. Mackensen).

[42] Trousset 1974, 133–35, figs 15.1–4; Mattingly 1995, 193–94, fig. 10.2; Rushworth 2015, 128–29.

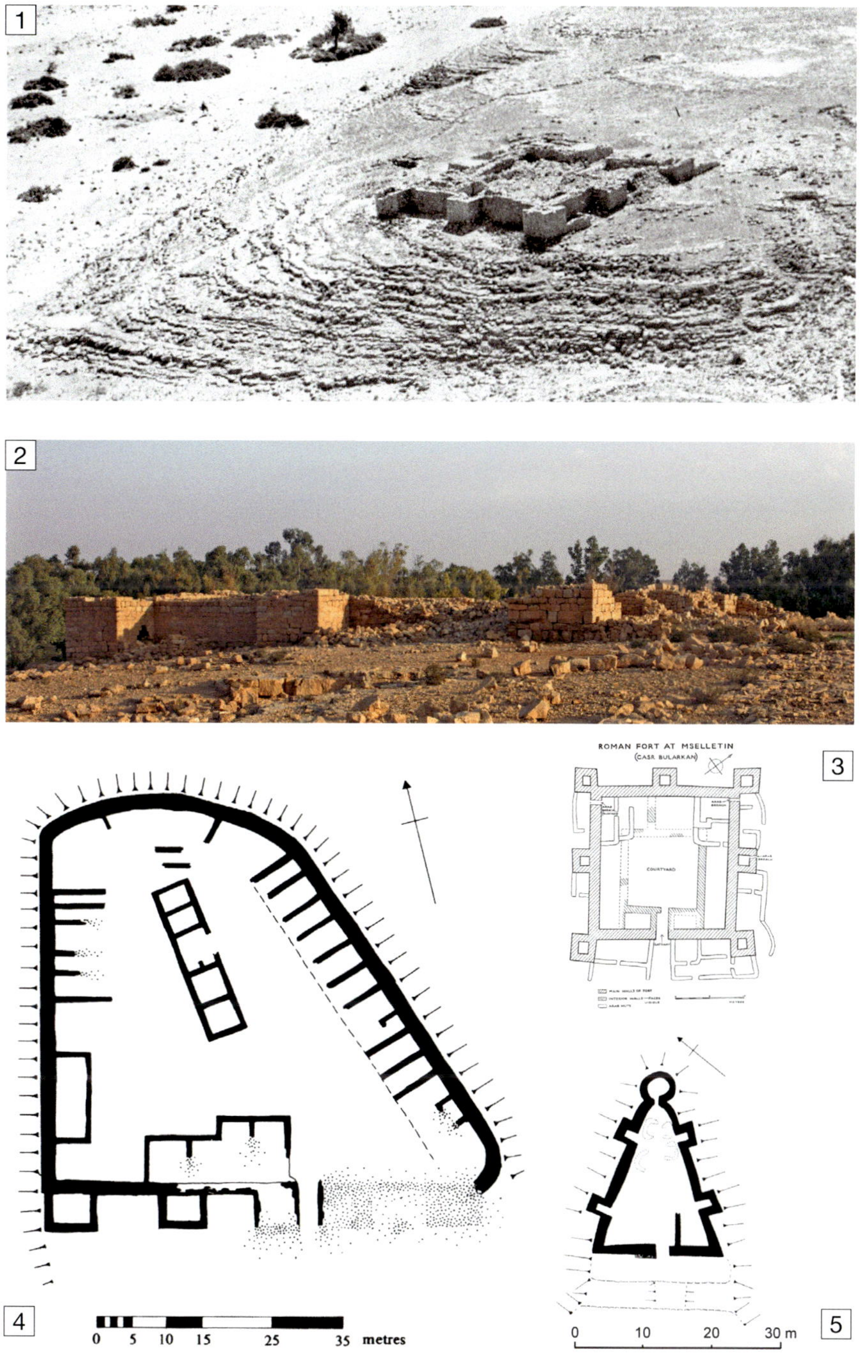

Fig. 6.19. 1–3: Qasr Bularkan (Mselletin), north-western Libya. 1: Aerial photograph of fortlet, 1949 (Goodchild 1950, 33, fig. 4); 2: South and east wall (photo M. Mackensen); 3: Plan of fortlet, built in the first half/ mid-fourth century CE (Goodchild 1950, 33, pl. 3.1); 4: Sdada East, Nf83, north-western Libya: plan of late Roman fortlet (after Mattingly 1996, 267, fig. 33.14); 5: Sdada East, Nf84a, north-western Libya: plan of late Roman fortlet (after Mattingly 1996, 259, fig. 33.15).

485 m^2, but the almost symmetrical ground plans of the rooms attached to the inner walls have been preserved; curiously, the ground floors of the towers are not accessible (see Mackensen 2021b, 126–28, figs 10.1–4 against a civilian use). The 0.36 ha large fort at Tabria, north-west of Vezereos, stands out because of its mudbrick construction and the semi-circular gate towers as well as the three-quarter round corner towers, which – as observed on site – are already accessible on the ground floor; here, too, construction in the second third of the fourth century CE is probable (Mackensen 2021b, 123–24, fig. 8). At Vezereos, a large gate tower (Fig. 6.6.3), built from spolia probably in the course of the last third of the fourth century, was observed; the Late Antique use of the fort is confirmed by the presence of African red slip ware which extends to c. 430–40 CE (Mackensen 2015, 263–69, figs 6–10; 2021b, 124–25, figs 9.1–3; 2022, 187–88, figs 2.4–12). However, it was not considered necessary to reinforce the defence walls with projecting square or three-quarter round corner towers here or at the larger mid-imperial *castra* such as Talalati/Ras el-Aïn (0.86 ha) (Fig. 6.17.2) and Tillibari/ Remada (1.95 ha) (Rushworth 2015, 126). At least at Talalati, two inscriptions attest to repair work in 355–60 CE, and the use of the fort has recently been proven by African red slip ware even up to the middle of the fifth century.[43] Due to the lack of excavations, however, it is not possible to judge whether only parts of the internal area of these two forts were used militarily in the fourth century by units of the frontier troops (*limitanei*), which were reduced in terms of their original strength, such as the *cohors VIII Fida* and the *cohors II Afrorum*.

The *propugnacula* mentioned in another inscription of 355–60 CE from Talalati/Ras el-Aïn are seen in the context of construction of three linear barriers (*clausurae*) in the Jabal Demmer mountains to the west.[44] At least for the command area of the *praepositus limitis Talalatensis* with its administrative and military centre at Talalati, the approximate extension can be assessed (see Rushworth 2015, 131–32, fig. 10.4) (Fig. 6.1). This commander was probably responsible not only for the three

[43] *CIL* VIII, 22766–67; *ILAfr* 2611; Trousset 1974, 101–2; Mackensen 2021b, 125; 2022, 188–93, fig. 3.

[44] *CIL* VIII, 22768; Trousset 1974, 102, 139–41, fig. 18; Mattingly 1995, 110–12, fig. 5.19.

western *clausurae*, but also for the section up to the fortlet of Benia bel-Recheb, c. 28 km to the north, and to the south a little more than halfway to Remada – perhaps as far as the Wadi Darcen with the fortlet of Henchir Medeina. The *centenarium* Tibubuci/Ksar Tarcine, on the other hand, already belonged to the command area of the *praepositus limitis Bizerentanae*. However, the length of individual sectors of the *limes*, the position of the eponymous fort in relation to the complete sector to be controlled – at the beginning, in the middle or at the end of the particular *limes* sector – and the subordinate new fortlets can rarely be determined with any degree of confidence. At least on the western part of the *limes Tripolitanus*, the mid-imperial forts were important as the bases of *praepositi limitis*, whereas the late fortlets were built as additions to the police surveillance of the routes (Rushworth 2015, 131–32, fig. 10.4).

The surprisingly small number of late Roman forts and outposts in eastern Tripolitania – especially in comparison to the unidentified sectors of the frontier – has been pointed out several times. Only the fortlet of Qasr Bularkan (Fig. 6.19.1–3) can be identified as a regular military fortification of the fourth century CE. In addition, there are the two fortifications of Sdada East on the Wadi N'f'd (Nf83–84a: Mattingly 1995, 194, fig. 10.2) with their irregular ground plans, each adapted to the topography of a promontory, which deviate from the known ground plans of late Roman fortlets in Tripolitania. The landward curtain wall of the trapezoidal, c. 66 × 55 m large fortification Nf83 (0.27 ha) (Fig. 6.19.4) is reinforced with several square towers projecting outwards, two of which flank the gate. A row of rooms is attached to the inner wall of the east side, and buildings of different sizes are attached to the west and south wall; in the centre is an elongated building with five rooms, which, like the one on the east wall, is to be regarded as accommodation for soldiers. The 22.8 × 19 m triangular enclosure Nf84a (c. 220 m^2) (Fig. 6.19.5) has square towers projecting outwards on the long sides and a round tower at the northern tip. The wall on the landward side is preceded by a wide ditch. The two fortifications of Sdada East, like Qasr Bularkan, are to be regarded as military fortifications for smaller garrisons, not least because of the outwardly projecting corner and intermediate towers and the regular internal buildings. Indications of the period of use are only available for Nf83, based on African red slip ware of the mid-fourth century (see at length Mackensen 2021b, 126–30, figs 10–11). However, it should also be noted that the *centenarium* Qasr Wames was probably used in the late fourth and early fifth centuries based on some fragments of Tripolitanian fineware (Mackensen 2009, 99–100, figs 18.1–4).

The Late Antique restoration of the fort at Gheriat el-Garbia (castra Madensia, *Not. Dign. Occ.*, 31.30)

The forts Gholaia/Bu Njem, Myd(---)/Gheriat el-Garbia, and Cidamus/Ghadames, placed far to the south, had been abandoned between c. 260 and 275–80 CE. Consequently, the regular control of the important east–west traffic routes along Wadi Bei el-Kebir and Wadi Zemzem was brought to an end. Military sites such as Tillibari/Remada and perhaps Mizda (Mackensen 2021b, 130; Schimmer 2012, 33–39) (or Tentheos/Edref near Zintan?) seem to have taken over the corresponding tasks in the last quarter of the third century and during the fourth century. In contrast, the situation east of the Mizda-Garian line can hardly be assessed, since there was apparently no larger mid-imperial (auxiliary) fort on any of the important traffic routes to which these tasks could have been assigned after the withdrawal of the garrisons from Gholaia and Secedi. In written sources, repeated incursions of the Austuriani/Laguatan into Roman provincial territory are mentioned several times after 360 CE, spreading fear and terror, culminating in the siege of Lepcis Magna in 365 CE. The countermeasures mentioned in several inscriptions for the late fourth/early fifth century are difficult to verify archaeologically (Mattingly 1995, 176–78). The new, permanent garrisoning of a frontier unit south of Wadi Sofeggin in one of the abandoned Severan oasis forts was not considered likely based on the then available archaeological evidence (Mattingly 1995, 187–93, fig. 10.1). Thus, although recent (probably pre-modern) structural alterations could be observed at two gates in the fort of Gholaia, Late Antique installations and layers of utilization (including garbage pits) in the central buildings are missing, apart from isolated fragments of late Roman pottery, which is insufficient as evidence for a military reoccupation of the fort (Mackensen 2021b, 130). This possibility was not even considered for Gheriat el-Garbia until the excavations in 2009–10.

From our investigations at Gheriat el-Garbia there is an extensive range of Late Antique forms of fine ceramics and amphorae of different provenances from the pottery survey in and around the fort, from sealed garbage layers, and from disturbed pottery deposits as well (see Mackensen 2024). Above all, a series of coins from the survey and the excavations reliably document the Late Antique reoccupation of the fort, which began after a hiatus of about 80–100 years around 360–80 CE or somewhat later.[45] As with other mid-imperial forts in Tripolitania, the rounded corners of the curtain wall were not reinforced by outwardly projecting towers (Fig. 6.20). Vertical cracks in the wall of the northern corner

[45] Mackensen *et al.* 2021, 177–82, 184–85, pls 20.1044–48, 21.1054–67, 23.1199–202; Mackensen 2021a, 215–22, 238–40, 254–55, pls 24.4–11; 2022, 184–87, figs 2.1–3; 2024.

tower cannot be related to a fourth-century earthquake. Reinforcement walls at two gate towers could also have been necessary due to earthquake damage or simply because of age-related dilapidation. For example, a massive wall reinforcement, obviously from Late Antiquity, was built around a corner at the west tower of the right lateral gate (*porta principalis dextra*). Even more impressive is the two-phase restoration of the north tower of the rear gate (*porta decumana*). A first 0.7 m wide retaining wall was reinforced by a second buttress wall, 1.3 m wide and still 2.2 m high, whose 70° steep, glacis-like outer shell consists of small- and middle-sized spolia blocks (Fig. 6.21.1). For the second phase the radiocarbon analysis gives a calibrated age (2σ) of Cal BP 420–97 CE. The *terminus post quem* for the construction of the second retaining wall is 420 CE; the first retaining wall should have been built around 380–400 CE, i.e. at the beginning of the renewed military occupation of the fort. Additionally, the central carriageway of the main gate (*porta praetoria*), but not the lateral

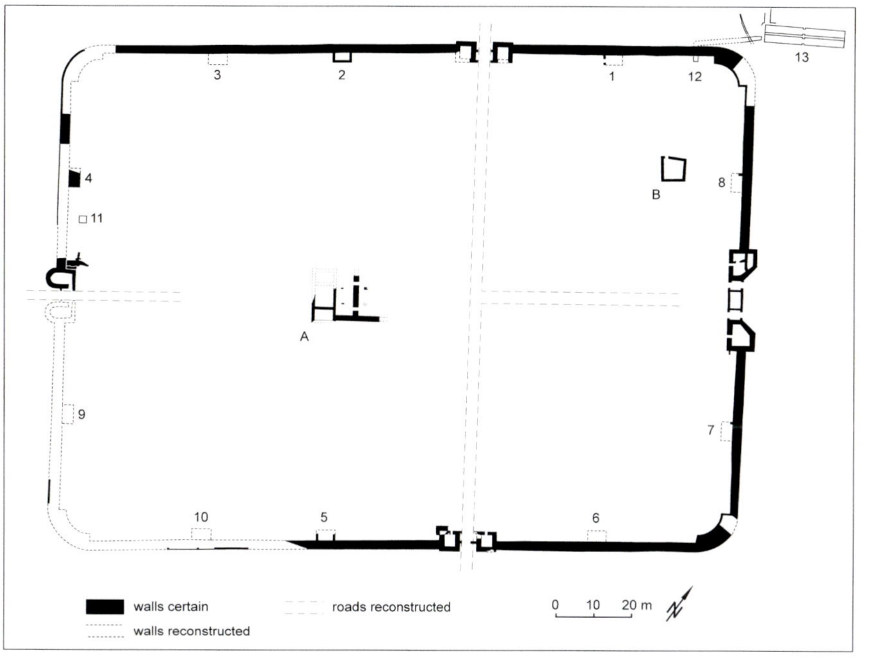

Fig. 6.20. *(above)* Castra Madensia/ Gheriat el-Garbia, north-western Libya: plan of the Severan fort, reused in 380–400 CE and in the first half of the fifth century CE, showing Late Antique restorations of the main gate (*porta praetoria*), the right lateral gate (*porta principalis dextra*), and the rear gate (*porta decumana*). 1–10: Interval towers; 11: Well; 12: Entrance to underground tunnel; 13: Double cistern; A: Late Antique headquarters building; B: Late Antique building (Mackensen 2021b, 131, fig. 12).

Fig. 6.21. *(left)* Castra Madensia/ Gheriat el-Garbia, north-western Libya. 1: North tower of rear gate (*porta decumana*), with Late Antique glacis-like reinforcement (phase 2); in the foreground Late Antique wall with reused fragment of Severan inscription (phase 3); 2: Rear range of the Severan headquarters building (*principia*) and Late Antique restoration with rooms R1 (*aedes*), R2 (*officium*), cross-hall and column base of courtyard (peristyle) (photos M. Mackensen).

passages, was blocked probably at the beginning of the Late Antique reoccupation of the fort (see Mackensen 2021b, 131–33, figs 12–15; 2021a, 245–48, table 9, on the radiocarbon data; 2024, 141–50, figs 86–91).

In the *praetentura* of the fort, only a 6.5 × 6.5 m residential building with a storage pit, but without internal partitioning, was investigated, which can be dated to the first half of the fifth century (Mackensen 2016, 98–99, fig. 16; 2021b, 137, fig. 17.1). In the centre of the fort, sections of the headquarters building (*principia*) were excavated, including the regimental chapel (*aedes*) and an office (*officium*). In the course of the Late Antique alterations, the rear row of rooms of the headquarters building was reduced to the three central rooms (R1, R2, and R4) and two massive, lateral longitudinal walls were added. In front of the three rooms a cross-hall measuring 4.5 × 11 m with two pillars and two lateral passages gave access to a colonnaded courtyard (Fig. 6.21.2). Unfortunately, the front with the entrance was not investigated in 2010. However, the symmetrical complex can be reconstructed as a tripartite building measuring c. 14 × 20 m with a colonnaded courtyard, a cross-hall and three rooms at the rear (Fig. 6.22.2). For the dating, two radiocarbon dates are available from the raised mortar floor of the central room R1 and from the mortar of a column base in the courtyard. The 2σ-values give a calibrated age of Cal BP 391–551 CE and 424–603 CE, or *termini post quos* of 391 and 424 CE. Major construction and repair work on this central building can hardly be dated before 424 CE, unless the portico was repaired or added later. Its ground plan suggests that this was a headquarters building adapted to the Late Antique requirements and appropriately reduced in size. On the one hand, attention was paid to functional and spatial continuity with the Severan *principia*, on the other hand, the essential rooms had to be available. This concerns the regimental chapel (*aedes*) for the standards and two rooms for administration (*officium*) and archives (*tabularium*), the roofed cross-hall (*basilica*), which served as assembly hall for meetings of officers and soldiers, as well as the courtyard (*peristylium*), which, due to the lack of a central visual axis, allowed indirect access to the cross-hall via the lateral passages (Mackensen 2021b, 133–37, figs 16–17.1; 2024, 250–62, figs 156–62).

In addition to the repair of the fortifications and the reduced but exceptional headquarters building, as well as the supply of large quantities of African and Tripolitanian red slip ware and cooking wares and amphorae for oil, wine and *garum* of various origins, there is also written evidence of the presence of Late Antique military personnel. In this context, eight ostraca fluently written in Latin italic characters, the official *scriptio continua*, in a hitherto unknown 'southern Punic' regiolect that is difficult to translate, but also partly in Latin, must be mentioned. The regional late Punic language was identified through a detailed linguistic analysis by Sabine Ziegler (see Ziegler and Mackensen 2014, esp. 318–35; see also Schimmer, Chapter 7). Of particular importance is a fragmentary official Late Antique building and repair inscription (Fig. 6.22.1), which mentions heavy rains (*ab impetu aquarum*) that caused regional flooding and marshes (*paludes*). Affected were numerous places (*multa loca*), probably mainly cisterns and wells, along a 107 mile (158 km) stretch to the *limes Tentheitanus* mentioned in the inscription (*IRT2021* 1122; Haensch and Mackensen 2011; Mackensen 2021b, 139, fig. 18.3). The route extends far beyond Mizda, where the *limes Tentheitanus* and the *limes* sector coming from Gheriat el-Garbia were to meet. The soldiers stationed at Gheriat el-Garbia were entrusted with the cleaning work, especially of the silted wells and cisterns, as was the case locally with the large double-chambered cistern (Fig. 6.20.13).

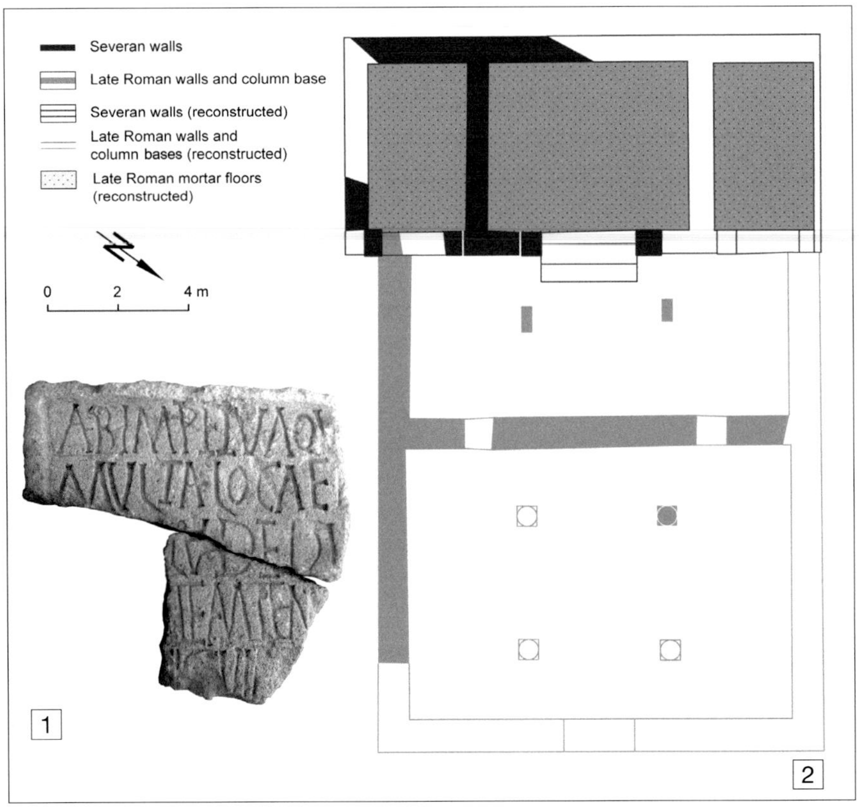

Fig. 6.22. Castra Madensia/Gheriat el-Garbia, north-western Libya. 1: Late Antique inscription (photo M. Mackensen); 2: Reconstructed Late Antique headquarters building (*principia*) with rear range of rooms, cross-hall and courtyard (peristyle), c. 425 CE (Mackensen 2021b, 138, fig. 17.1).

In the fort, which was probably repaired around 380–400 CE and occupied until the middle of the fifth century, the military commander of the province of Tripolitana probably stationed a partially mounted unit of *limitanei*. The largest Tripolitanian fort of the frontier zone, with an internal area of 2.25 ha, was a spectacular landmark with its gate and intermediate towers visible from a great distance. This fort could be classified as *castra*. For comparison, the *milites fortenses* (*Not. Dign. Occ.*, 31.29) were stationed within the Late Antique city walls of the provincial capital of Lepcis Magna in a yet unlocated area, the castra Leptitana. The term *castra* is otherwise only found in the province of Tripolitana in the castra Tillibarensia (*Not. Dign. Occ.*, 25.33). Based on Ziegler's linguistic expertise, the monosyllabic place-name Myd(---), attested for the first third of the third century CE in this abbreviated form, could have been changed into the similar name Mad(---). In the course of two centuries, this modification could have been a deliberate phonetic change of the consonant 'y' into the vowel 'a' or simply the result of an erroneous transcription. With the adjectival toponym, the new fort name castra Madensia (*Not. Dign. Occ.*, 31.30) would then result. Consequently, the unit of the *milites munifices* would have been garrisoned here and the *limes Madensis* (*Not. Dign. Occ.*, 31.22) would extend from Gheriat el-Garbia to Mizda (Mackensen 2021b, 139–41).

Even if this sounds conclusive and seems likely, there is ultimately no epigraphic evidence for the postulated Late Antique place-name Mad or Madi, based on which a location would be beyond doubt. It cannot be questioned, however, that the fort of Gheriat el-Garbia was repaired in the late fourth/early fifth century in the course of two phases (380–400 and c. 420–24 CE) by the Roman military because of the observed building techniques, which required skilled specialists with engineering knowledge. They must have been experienced with the use of pulleys for moving very large stone blocks for the foundation of a wall of the central building. In addition, this headquarters building of reduced size with the row of rooms at the rear, a cross-hall and a colonnaded courtyard was intentionally and functionally adapted in Late Antiquity. The entire fortification, no matter how much of the internal area was used by a unit of *limitanei*, probably partially mounted and about 200–400 men strong, corresponds to the term *castra* at least because of its impressive architectural appearance.

It is possible that the governor Silvanus (see *Codex Theodosianus*, 12.1.133), who is recorded as *dux et corrector limitis Tripolitanae* in 393 CE, was responsible for the restoration measures of the fort at Gheriat el-Garbia. In his official title the explicit mention of the provincial frontier within the scope of his duties as governor (*corrector*) and military commander (*dux*) is unique as far as we know. The repair and renewed stationing of a regular unit of *limitanei* in a far advanced position adjacent to an important oasis was obviously Rome's military response to the repeated invasions of the Austuriani/Laguatan between 363–67 CE and from the mid-80s of the fourth century onwards (Mackensen 2021b, 141; 2024, 602–3; cf. Tantillo and Bigi 2010, 25–26).

How long the individual sectors of the *limes Tripolitanus* with their forts and the units, which had probably been reduced in the meantime, lasted remains to be seen. There is no doubt that the governor (*comes et dux*) Flavius Ortygius fought the Austuriani quite successfully during the period 408–23 CE (*Austurianorum rabia ripraessa*), as can be deduced from the inscription on the pedestal of his statue at Lepcis Magna (*IRT* 480; *IRT2021* 480; Tantillo and Bigi 2010, 24–27, 370–71, no. 31).

African red slip ware offers the only reliable archaeological indicator for the occupation of the forts by frontier units. However, ARS and lamps are only available from a few forts such as Vezereos until c. 430–40 CE and Ras el-Aïn and Gheriat el-Garbia until the middle of the fifth century (Mackensen 2021b, 125, 137; 2022, 184–93, figs 2–3). How long the regular frontier units received their pay from the governor and what effects the capture of the provinces of Africa Zeugitana (429 CE) and Byzacena as well as the capital city Carthage (439 CE) by the Vandals had on the frontier units of the southern province of Tripolitana, their officers and their locations, remains obscure. However, at the latest with the Vandal conquest of western Tripolitania in 442 CE, or more than a decade later in 455 CE, the frontier units, which had been reduced in the last decades, would hardly have been able to fulfil their tasks of securing, surveillance and controlling the frontier zone and the most important traffic routes (cf. Mackensen 2024, 603–5).

Conclusion

It must be noted that there is hardly any archaeological evidence available for the Augustan campaigns of conquest in Africa Proconsularis – including the campaign of L. Cornelius Balbus in 21/20 BCE. The auxiliary fort of Tillibari/Remada in southern Tunisia, built around 130 CE, can be seen in connection with the military control and protection of the important trade routes leading to Fazzan and the transhumance routes of the semi-nomadic population. However, corresponding auxiliary forts have not yet been discovered in central and eastern Tripolitania and may never have existed. The two fortlets built under Commodus, Tisavar/Ksar Rhilane and Vezereos/Sidi Mohammed ben Aïssa, are located near oases. Their small garrisons controlled the traffic on the two western routes leading into the interior of Africa Proconsularis. In eastern Tripolitania there is no datable and secure evidence yet for fortlets (Aïn Wif?) or forts (Edref near Zintan, Mizda?)

(Fig. 6.1); these sites need urgently to be investigated archaeologically.

The legionary vexillation forts of the Severan period, Myd(---)/Gheriat el-Garbia, Gholaia/Bu Njem, and Cidamus/Ghadames, which were advanced far to the south, are in many respects outstanding testimonies to the Roman military garrisons living and working under extreme conditions. Bu Njem especially, with its exceptional number and quality of informative inscriptions and ostraca, offers fundamental insights into the history, organization, administration, tasks, and strength of changing garrisons between 201 and 263 CE at the latest, based on Rebuffat's campaigns of excavations (1967–76) in the fort, in the fortified civilian settlement (Fig. 6.12), and in the sanctuaries. In addition, the oasis fort, which was not built over by a pre-modern settlement but buried by shifting sand dunes, is impressive with its fortifications and the headquarters building with its unique *scriptorium* (Figs 6.13–15), the commander's residential building, and the baths. The repair inscription of the south gate attests to four-storey towers for the first time in 222 CE. Based on the eight barracks in the *praetentura*, the target strength can be calculated at 192 men – clearly below Rebuffat's assumption of 320 men – due to the number and the internal area of the *contubernia* as well as the floor space of approx. 4 m^2 per *contubernium* to which each legionary was entitled. Non-commissioned officers (*principales*) commanded the eight units of about 24 men each. Until 238 CE, a centurion of the *legio III Augusta* from Lambaesis acted as commander (*praepositus*) of the legionary vexillation and of a *numerus conlatus* attested for 236–38 CE; his residence (*praetorium*) corresponds only to about 60% of the area of the large centurion's quarters in the legionary fortress at Lambaesis. After 238 CE auxiliary decurions are attested as *praepositi* of the *vexillatio Golensis*; in 248 CE this is a *decurio* of an *ala Flavia* and in the 50s of the third century there are several *decuriones*, who were perhaps seconded from the still unlocated auxiliary fort Secedi of the *cohors VIII Fida equitata*, as well as some cavalrymen. I suspect that this fort, probably about 1.5–1.8 ha in size, should be located about 60 to 90 km north-east of Bu Njem on the Wadi Bei el-Kebir and might be hidden under sand dunes.

The investigations in the vexillation fort of Gheriat el-Garbia (2009–10) have not only provided clarity about the mid-imperial period of occupation (199/201 to 275–80 CE), but also revealed an unexpected Late Antique restoration and a reoccupation of the fort from c. 380–400 CE to the middle of the fifth century. The state of preservation of the fortifications is outstanding, allowing a reconstruction of the *porta praetoria* with three-storey towers (Figs 6.9–10). From the headquarters building only parts of the inner range of rooms with the regimental chapel (*aedes*) have survived. The layout of the accommodations for the legionaries in the *praetentura* was reconstructed based on the layout of the barracks of Bu Njem (Fig. 6.13) with 12 barracks containing 12 *contubernia* each for c. 576 men (Fig. 6.11); with four further barracks in the *retentura*, a garrison strength of c. 800 men in the early third century is probable. With its main gate, the postulated colonnaded porticoes along the *via praetoria* and probably also a *groma* hall in front of the headquarters building, as well as the seven different orders of columns with heights of up to 4.5 m, the Severan fort suggests a sophisticated architecture. This makes the largest Tripolitanian vexillation fort, with an internal area of 2.25 ha, appear to be a scaled-down replica of the legionary fortress at Lambaesis.

The *limes Tripolitanus* or *limes regionis Tripolitanae* had probably already been divided into different sectors since 238–39 CE – such as the *limes Tentheitanus* mentioned in an inscription from Qasr Duib (246–47 CE) – which were under the control of an equestrian *procurator* as *praepositus*. Whether his official military base was at Gheriat el-Garbia can only be assumed, but this would match the central geographical location, the outstanding architectural features, and the garrison strength.

The networks of small military outposts belonging to the oasis forts are at least partially known by name from the ostraca at Bu Njem, but the names cannot be reconciled with fortlets such as Qasr Zerzi or the military outposts at Waddan and Zella located even further south (Fig. 6.1). The so-called 'fort vedette' of Oum el-Gueloub in the Wadi Bei el-Kebir, in contrast, is not a Roman fortlet, but an indigenous fortification situated on a hilltop.

The withdrawal of the *cohors VIII Fida equitata* from Secedi for the construction of the auxiliary fort Talalati/Ras el-Aïn in southern Tunisia in 263 CE is also assumed to mark the end of Bu Njem. The partially mounted auxiliary unit was at this time – due to the size (0.79 ha) of Ras el-Aïn – already reduced to a strength of just 250–300 men. Nothing can be said about the whereabouts and new locations of the *vexillatio Golensis* and the *numerus conlatus* or of the units from Gheriat el-Garbia and Ghadames. This also applies to the continued existence of forts in eastern Tripolitania such as Mizda, Edref near Zintan, and Aïn Wif, where the archaeological evidence remains non-existent or rather modest.

With the establishment of the province of Tripolitana in 303 CE, the military fortifications were under the control of the governor (*praeses*), who was thus also responsible for the construction of new *burgus*-like fortlets (*centenaria*), linear barriers (*clausurae* and *propugnacula*), and small forts as well as for the repair of forts (*castra*). The appointment of a military commander (*dux*) is unlikely before about 390 CE. Especially in southern Tunisia, a series of new small forts can be observed, which were probably built during the second third of the fourth century. At least in and near the fort of Ras el-Aïn, restoration and construction measures under the *praeses et comes* Flavius Archontius Nilus in 355–60 CE are attested by two inscriptions. A few small forts with ground plans partly adapted to the topography, such as Sdada East Nf83 and Nf84a, also exist in the east of the province. However, all these late Roman fortifications have only been uncovered or the walls only superficially documented; modern excavations are lacking everywhere.

Based on the *Not. Dign. Occ.*, 31, the subdivision of the Tripolitanian frontier into 12 only partially identified frontier sectors is known for the early fifth century CE. Each of these was under the command of a *praepositus limitis*, but without naming the individual units or the rank of the officer in command. Only two sites are listed with their units of *limitanei*, the castra Leptitana/Lepcis Magna with the *milites fortenses* and the castra Madensia with the *milites munifices*. The castra Madensia can now probably be identified as the restored fort of Myd(---)/Gheriat el-Garbia. This is suggested by the massive restorations of the fort's defences and a reoccupation around 380–400 CE. In the case of the north tower of the *porta decumana*, two phases of repair can be observed, the more recent of which is radiocarbon dated to after 420 CE. The headquarters building was also rebuilt, reduced in size and reused for the same functions, either in two phases after 391 or 424 CE, or altogether after 424 CE.

The radiocarbon dates from Gheriat el-Garbia provide *termini post quos* that allow a connection with historical events. Thus, the reoccupation of the fort could have been the military response to the repeated invasions of the Austuriani between 363–67 CE and from the mid-80s of the fourth century onwards. Silvanus, who is recorded as governor and military commander (*dux et corrector limitis Tripolitanae*) for the year 393 CE, could have been responsible for this policy. However, Flavius Ortygius, also governor and military commander (*comes et dux*), is attested in an inscription of the period 408–23 CE, as having successfully fought the Austuriani. The castra Madensia/Gheriat el-Garbia may have played an important role as the most advanced and powerful revived military base. Ceramic surveys show that for a few forts such as Sidi Mohammed ben Aïssa and Ras el-Aïn as well as Gheriat el-Garbia, a military occupation until 430–40 CE, or around the middle of the fifth century, is most probable. It would therefore surely have been the Vandal conquest of the western part of the province of Tripolitana in 442 CE, or at the latest in 455 CE, which brought an end to the garrisons of the *limes Tripolitanus*.

References

Birley, A.R. 1999. *Septimius Severus: The African Emperor (Revised Edition)*. London: Routledge.

Boizot, Cap. 1913. Fouilles exécutées en 1912 dans le camp romain de Ras-el-Aïn-Tlalet (Tunisie). *Bulletin du Comité des Travaux Historiques et Scientifiques*: 260–65.

Brogan, O. and Reynolds, J.M. 1964. Inscriptions from the Tripolitanian hinterland. *Libya Antiqua* 1: 43–44.

Brogan, O. and Smith, D.J. 1966–67. Notes from the Tripolitanian pre-desert, 1967. *Libya Antiqua* 3–4: 139–44.

Di Vita, A. 1966. *La villa della 'Gara delle Nereidi' presso Tagiura ed altri recenti scavi e scoperte in Tripolitania*. Tripoli: Directorate-General of Antiquities, Museums and Archives.

Di Vita-Évrard, G. 1978–79. Le plus ancienne milliaire de Tripolitaine: A. Caecina Severus, proconsul d'Afrique. *Libya Antiqua* 15–16: 9–44.

Di Vita-Évrard, G. 1985. 'Regio Tripolitana' – a reappraisal. In D.J. Buck and D.J. Mattingly (eds), *Town and Country in Roman Tripolitania. Papers in Honour of Olwen Hackett*. Oxford: British Archaeological Reports, 143–63.

Di Vita-Évrard, G. 1991. Gasr Duib: construit ou reconstruit sous les Philippes? In *Histoire et archéologie de l'Afrique du Nord, II. L'armée et les affaires militaires. Actes du IVe colloque international (Strasbourg, 5–9 avril 1988)*. Paris: Éditions du CTHS, 427–44.

Di Vita-Évrard, G. and Rebuffat, R. 1987. La dédicace des thermes. *Karthago* 21: 107–11.

Eger, Ch. 2012. *Spätantikes Kleidungszubehör aus Nordafrika, I: Trägerkreis, Mobilität und Ethnos im Spiegel der Funde der spätesten römischen Kaiserzeit und der vandalischen Zeit*. Wiesbaden: Reichert Verlag.

Eingartner, J. 2021. Architekturglieder und Werksteine aus dem Kastellareal (ohne gesicherten Befundzusammenhang). In M. Mackensen, *Das severische Vexillationskastell Myd(---)/Gheriat el-Garbia am limes Tripolitanus (Libyen), I: Forschungsgeschichte, Vermessung, Prospektionen und Funde 2009–2010*. Wiesbaden: Reichert Verlag, 127–55.

Euzennat, M. and Trousset, P. 1978. Le camp de Remada. Fouilles inédites du Commandant Donau (mars-avril 1914). *Africa* 4–5: 111–75.

Gauckler, P. 1902. Le centenarius de Tibubuci (Ksar Tarcine – Sud Tunisien). *Comptes rendus des séances de l'Académie des Inscriptions et Belles-Lettres*: 321–40.

Gombeaud, Ltn. 1901. Fouilles du castellum d'el-Hagueff (Tunisie). *Bulletin du Comité des Travaux Historiques et Scientifiques*: 81–97.

Goodchild, R.G. 1948. *The Roman Roads and Milestones of Tripolitania (Discoveries and Researches in 1947).* Tripoli: Department of Antiquities – British Military Administration, Tripolitania.

Goodchild, R.G. 1950. The Limes Tripolitanus II. *Journal of Roman Studies* 40: 30–38.

Goodchild, R.G. 1954. Oasis forts of legio III Augusta on the routes to the Fezzan. *Papers of the British School at Rome* 22: 56–68.

Goodchild, R.G. and Ward-Perkins, J.B. 1949. The Limes Tripolitanus in the light of recent discoveries. *Journal of Roman Studies* 39: 81–95.

Guédon, S. 2018. *La frontière romaine de l'Africa sous le Haut-Empire.* Madrid: Casa de Velázquez.

Haensch, R. and Mackensen, M. 2011. Das tripolitanische Kastell Gheriat el-Garbia im Licht einer neuen spätantiken Inschrift: am Tag als der Regen kam. *Chiron* 41: 263–86.

Jones, G.D.B. 1983. The development of Gheriat el-Garbia. *Libyan Studies* 14: 64–68.

Le Bohec, Y. 1987. Les syriens dans l'Afrique romaine: civils ou militaires. *Karthago* 21: 81–92.

Le Bohec, Y. 1989a. *La troisième légion Auguste.* Paris: Éditions du CNRS.

Le Bohec, Y. 1989b. *Les unites auxiliaires de l'armée romaine en Afrique Proconsulaire et Numidie sous le Haut Empire.* Paris: Éditions du CNRS.

Mackensen, M. 1997. Die castra hiberna der legio III Augusta in Ammaedara/Haïdra. *Mitteilungen des Deutschen Archäologischen Instituts, Römische Abteilung* 104: 321–34.

Mackensen, M. 2000. Les castra hiberna de la legio III Augusta à Ammaedara/Haïdra. In M. Khanoussi, P. Ruggeri and C. Vismara (eds), *L'Africa Romana. Geografi, viaggiatori, militari nel Maghreb: alle origini dell'archeologia nel Nord Africa. Atti del XIII convegno di studio (Djerba, 10–13 dicembre 1998).* Rome: Carocci, 1739–59.

Mackensen, M. 2008. Mannschaftsunterkünfte und Organisation einer severischen Legionsvexillation im tripolitanischen Kastell Gholaia/Bu Njem (Libyen). *Germania* 86: 271–306.

Mackensen, M. 2009. Gasr Wames, eine burgusartige Kleinfestung des mittleren 3. Jahrhunderts am tripolitanischen limes Tentheitanus (Libyen). *Germania* 87: 75–104.

Mackensen, M. 2010a. Das commoduszeitliche Kleinkastell Tisavar/Ksar Rhilane am südtunesischen limes Tripolitanus. *Kölner Jahrbuch* 43: 451–68.

Mackensen, M. 2010b. Das severische Vexillationskastell Myd(---)/Gheriat el-Garbia am limes Tripolitanus (Libyen). Bericht über die Kampagne 2009. *Mitteilungen des Deutschen Archäologischen Instituts, Römische Abteilung* 116: 363–458.

Mackensen, M. 2011. Das severische Vexillationskastell Myd(---) und die spätantike Besiedlung in Gheriat el-Garbia (Libyen). Bericht über die Kampagne im Frühjahr 2010. *Mitteilungen des Deutschen Archäologischen Instituts, Römische Abteilung* 117: 247–375.

Mackensen, M. 2012. New fieldwork at the Severan fort of Myd(---)/Gheriat el-Garbia on the limes Tripolitanus. *Libyan Studies* 43: 41–60.

Mackensen, M. 2013. Baubestand und Rekonstruktion der porta praetoria des severischen Vexillationskastells Myd(---)/Gheriat el-Garbia am limes Tripolitanus (Libyen). Grundlage für die Rekonstruktion mittelkaiserzeitlicher Militärarchitektur in den Nordwestprovinzen? In Ch. Flügel and J. Obmann (eds), *Römische Wehrbauten. Befund und Rekonstruktion. Inhalte – Projekte – Dokumentationen.* Munich: Volk Verlag, 88–107.

Mackensen, M. 2015. Zur spätrömischen Nutzung des Kleinkastells Vezereos am limes Tripolitanus (Südtunesien). In P. Henrich, Ch. Miks, J. Obmann and M. Wieland (eds), *Non solum... sed etiam. Festschrift für Thomas Fischer zum 65. Geburtstag.* Rahden: Marie Leidorf Verlag, 259–70.

Mackensen, M. 2016. Survey and excavation of the German Archaeological Mission at the Roman Fort of Myd(---)/Gheriat el-Garbia and its vicinity, 2009/2010. *Libya Antiqua* n.s. 6: 83–102.

Mackensen, M. 2021a. *Das severische Vexillationskastell Myd(---)/Gheriat el-Garbia am limes Tripolitanus (Libyen), I: Forschungsgeschichte, Vermessung, Prospektionen und Funde 2009–2010.* Wiesbaden: Reichert Verlag.

Mackensen, M. 2021b. Observations and results of recent excavations and surveys of Late Roman military fortifications in the province of Tripolitana. *Libya Antiqua* n.s. 14: 111–45.

Mackensen, M. 2022. Late Roman African red slip ware from central Tunisia in Tripolitanian forts and fortlets. *Libya Antiqua* n.s. 15: 179–96.

Mackensen, M. 2024. *Das severische Vexillationskastell Myd(---) und die spätantiken castra Madensia/Gheriat el-Garbia am limes Tripolitanus (Libyen), II: Ausgrabungen und Untersuchungen im Kastell, im Steinbruch, in den Heiligtümern und am Beobachtungsturm 2009–2010.* Wiesbaden: Reichert Verlag.

Mackensen, M., Schimmer, F., Schmid, S. and Weber, M. 2021. Keramik-Survey. In M. Mackensen, *Das severische Vexillationskastell Myd(---)/Gheriat el-Garbia am limes Tripolitanus (Libyen), I: Forschungsgeschichte, Vermessung, Prospektionen und Funde 2009–2010.* Wiesbaden: Reichert Verlag, 155–214.

Marichal, R. 1979. Les ostraca de Bu Njem. *Comptes rendus des séances de l'Académie des Inscriptions et Belles-Lettres* 123.3: 436–52.

Marichal, R. 1992. *Les ostraca de Bu Njem.* Tripoli: Department of Antiquities.

Mattingly, D.J. 1982. The Roman road-station at Thenadassa (Aïn Wif). *Libyan Studies* 13: 73–80.

Mattingly, D.J. 1983. The Laguatan: a Libyan tribal confederation in the Late Roman Empire. *Libyan Studies* 14: 96–108.

Mattingly, D.J. 1985. IRT 895 and 896: two inscriptions from Gheriat el-Garbia. *Libyan Studies* 16: 67–75.

Mattingly, D.J. 1991. The constructor of Gasr Duib, Numisius Maximus, trib(unus cohortis I Syrorum sagittariorum). *Antiquités Africaines* 27: 75–82.

Mattingly, D.J. 1995. *Tripolitania*. London: Batsford.

Mattingly, D.J. (ed.) 1996. *Farming the Desert. The UNESCO Libyan Valleys Archaeological Survey. Volume 2: Gazetteer and Pottery.* London: Society for Libyan Studies.

Mattingly, D.J. and Dore, J. 1996. Romano-Libyan settlement. Typology and chronology. In G. Barker (ed.), *Farming the Desert. The UNESCO Libyan Valleys Archaeological Survey. Volume 1: Synthesis.* London: Society for Libyan Studies, 111–58.

Merlin, A. 1921. Le fortin de Bezereos sur le limes tripolitain. *Comptes rendus des séances de l'Académie des Inscriptions et Belles-Lettres*: 236–48.

Rebuffat, R. 1969–70a. Bu Njem 1968. *Libya Antiqua* 6–7: 9–105.

Rebuffat, R. 1969–70b. Bu Njem 1970. *Libya Antiqua* 6–7: 107–66.

Rebuffat, R. 1972–73a. Les inscriptions des portes du camp de Bu Njem. *Libya Antiqua* 9–10: 99–120.

Rebuffat, R. 1972–73b. L'arrivée des Romains à Bu Njem. *Libya Antiqua* 9–10: 121–34.

Rebuffat, R. 1972–73c. Gholaia. *Libya Antiqua* 9–10: 135–45.

Rebuffat, R. 1974–75. Bu Njem 1971. *Libya Antiqua* 11–12: 189–241.

Rebuffat, R. 1976–77. Bu Njem 1972. *Libya Antiqua* 13–14: 37–78.

Rebuffat, R. 1978–79. L'inscription du limes de Tripolitaine. *Libya Antiqua* 15–16: 125–38.

Rebuffat, R. 1985a. Les centurions de Gholaia. In A. Mastino (ed.), *L'Africa Romana. Atti del II convegno di studio (Sassari, 14–16 dicembre 1984).* Sassari: Gallizzi, 225–38.

Rebuffat, R. 1985b. Le 'limes' de Tripolitaine. In D.J. Buck and D.J. Mattingly (eds), *Town and Country in Roman Tripolitania. Papers in Honour of Olwen Hackett.* Oxford: British Archaeological Reports, 127–41.

Rebuffat, R. 1989. Notes sur le camp romain de Gholaia (Bu Njem). *Libyan Studies* 20: 155–67.

Rebuffat, R. 1990. Divinités de l'oued Kebir (Tripolitaine). In A. Mastino (ed.), *L'Africa Romana. Atti del VII convegno di studio (Sassari, 15–17 dicembre 1989).* Sassari: Gallizzi, 119–59.

Rebuffat, R. 1992. Maximien en Afrique. *Klio* 74: 371–79.

Rebuffat, R. 1995. Le centurion M. Porcius Iasucthan à Bu Njem. *Libya Antiqua* n.s. 1: 79–123.

Rebuffat, R. 2000. L'armée romaine à Gholaia. In G. Alföldy, B. Dobson and W. Eck (eds), *Kaiser, Heer und Gesellschaft in der Römischen Kaiserzeit. Gedenkschrift für Eric Birley.* Stuttgart: Franz Steiner Verlag, 227–59.

Rebuffat, R., Deneauve, J. and Hallier, G. 1966–67. Bu Njem. *Libya Antiqua* 3–4: 49–137.

Rushworth, A. 2015. Castra or centenaria? Interpreting the later forts of the North African frontier. In R. Collins, M. Symonds and M. Weber (eds), *Roman Military Architecture on the Frontiers. Armies and their Architecture in Late Antiquity.* Oxford: Oxbow Books, 123–39.

Schimmer, F. 2012. New evidence for a Roman fort and vicus at Mizda (Tripolitania). *Libyan Studies* 43: 33–39.

Schimmer, F. 2021. Metrologie des severischen Kastells Gheriat el-Garbia. In M. Mackensen, *Das severische Vexillationskastell Myd(---)/Gheriat el-Garbia am limes Tripolitanus (Libyen), I: Forschungsgeschichte, Vermessung, Prospektionen und Funde 2009–2010.* Wiesbaden: Reichert Verlag, 86–91.

Schmid, S. 2018. Gasr Isawi. Fortified farm and hilltop settlement in the Wadi N'f'd, Tripolitania. *Libya Antiqua* n.s. 11: 71–106.

Schmid, S., Mackensen, M. and Stephani, M. 2019. The Roman watchtower near Gheriat el-Garbia, Tripolitania. *Libya Antiqua* n.s. 12: 69–83.

Sheldrick, N. 2021. *Building the Countryside. Rural Architecture and Settlement in Tripolitania during the Roman and Late Antique Periods.* London: Society for Libyan Studies.

Speidel, M.P. 1988. Outpost duty in the desert. Building the fort at Gholaia (Bu Njem, Libya). *Antiquités Africaines* 24: 99–102.

Tantillo, I. and Bigi, F. (eds) 2010. *Leptis Magna. Una città e le sue iscrizioni in epoca tardoromana.* Cassino: Edizioni dell'Università degli Studi di Cassino.

Trousset, P. 1974. *Recherches sur le limes Tripolianus du Chott el-Djerid à la frontière tuniso-libyenne.* Paris: Éditions du CNRS.

Walas, A.H. 2022. New perspectives on the Roman military base at Bu Njem. *Libyan Studies* 53: 48–60.

Ziegler, S. and Mackensen, M. 2014. Spätantike Ostraka aus Gheriat el-Garbia (al-Qaryāt al-Garbīyah) in der Provinz Tripolitana (Libyen). Belege für eine regionale Variante des Punischen. *Mitteilungen des Deutschen Archäologischen Instituts, Römische Abteilung* 120: 313–40.

Chapter 7

FOOD SUPPLY OF THE *LIMES TRIPOLITANUS* IN THE THIRD CENTURY CE

Florian Schimmer

Introduction

Archaeological research of the past decades on the Tripolitanian pre-desert and on the forts of the *limes Tripolitanus* has significantly expanded our knowledge of the material culture, economic structures, trade networks, and commodity flows in this region.[1] This is all the more true for Fazzan, where recent intensive fieldwork has increasingly revealed the key role of the Garamantes in the network of ancient trans-Saharan trade.[2] From an economic point of view, in particular, this has opened up a new view of Roman Tripolitania from the south. Economically speaking, the pre-desert with the southern frontier zone of Tripolitania is at the interface between the Mediterranean market, with the coastal cities as hubs of maritime trade in the north, and the traffic routes of the trans-Saharan trade towards Fazzan in the south (Fig. 7.1). The three oasis forts of Cidamus/ Ghadames, Myd(---)/Gheriat el-Garbia, and Gholaia/ Bu Njem, built under Septimius Severus around 200 CE on the northern fringes of the Sahara, formed the southernmost military bases of the *limes Tripolitanus* (see Mackensen, Chapter 6). Due to their geographical key positions (oases) on the most important north–south routes from the Mediterranean to the Sahara, they were significant not only in strategic but also in economic terms.

The aim of this chapter is to provide an overview of the food supply of the Roman garrisons along the *limes Tripolitanus* during the third century CE based on archaeological data, above all amphorae, and epigraphic sources, as well as archaeobotanical and archaeozoological evidence (see also Mattingly 2023, 545–50). The focus is on the Severan oasis forts, whose state of research shows great differences: Bu Njem is still considered the best known military site in Roman-period North Africa, due to the extensive field research of the 1960–70s, the number of ostraca discovered at the site, and the exceptional state of preservation.[3] The latter also applies in part to the fort of Gheriat el-Garbia, which was the subject of extensive archaeological investigations in 2009–10, the results of which have shed new light on this site (Mackensen 2016; 2021a; 2024, with bibliography). In contrast, there is little information available on the fort of Ghadames (Mattingly 1995, 97), which has not yet been reliably located, and because of this it is excluded from the discussion.

All three forts were apparently abandoned in the course of the third century. At Bu Njem, the withdrawal of the troops is assumed to have taken place between 259 and 263 CE (or a decade later?), at Gheriat el-Garbia around 275–80 CE (Mackensen 2021b, 116–17), while the situation at Ghadames remains unclear. However, recent research has revealed that a Roman military unit was restationed at Gheriat el-Garbia between 390–400 and 430–55 CE (unlike at Bu Njem), and that an autochthonous civilian settlement was still occupied through to the mid-sixth century CE (Mackensen 2021b, 130–41). These Late Antique phases of occupation and the finds associated with them are not considered in this contribution, which focuses primarily on the third century.

[1] Dore 1996; Leitch 2014; Bonifay 2017; Leone 2017; Mackensen 2022. On specific sites see Schimmer 2012a (Mizda); 2012b; Weber and Schmid 2012; Mackensen 2015 (Vezereos); 2021a; 2024 (Gheriat el-Garbia); Leitch *et al.* 2018 (Ghirza); Schmid 2018 (Qasr Isawi). See also Guédon 2018; Ahmed 2019 (Tarhuna Plateau); Leitch *et al.* 2020 (re-examination of ceramics from the western Numidian *limes*).

[2] Garamantes/Fazzan: Mattingly 2003; 2007; 2010; 2013a; 2022, with bibliography; Liverani 2006; Mori 2013. On trans-Saharan trade see Dowler and Galvin 2011; Schörle 2012; Wilson 2012; 2017a; Mattingly 2013b; Mattingly *et al.* 2017.

[3] See the summaries in Rebuffat 1989; 2000; Mackensen 2008; Walas 2022; on the ostraca see below.

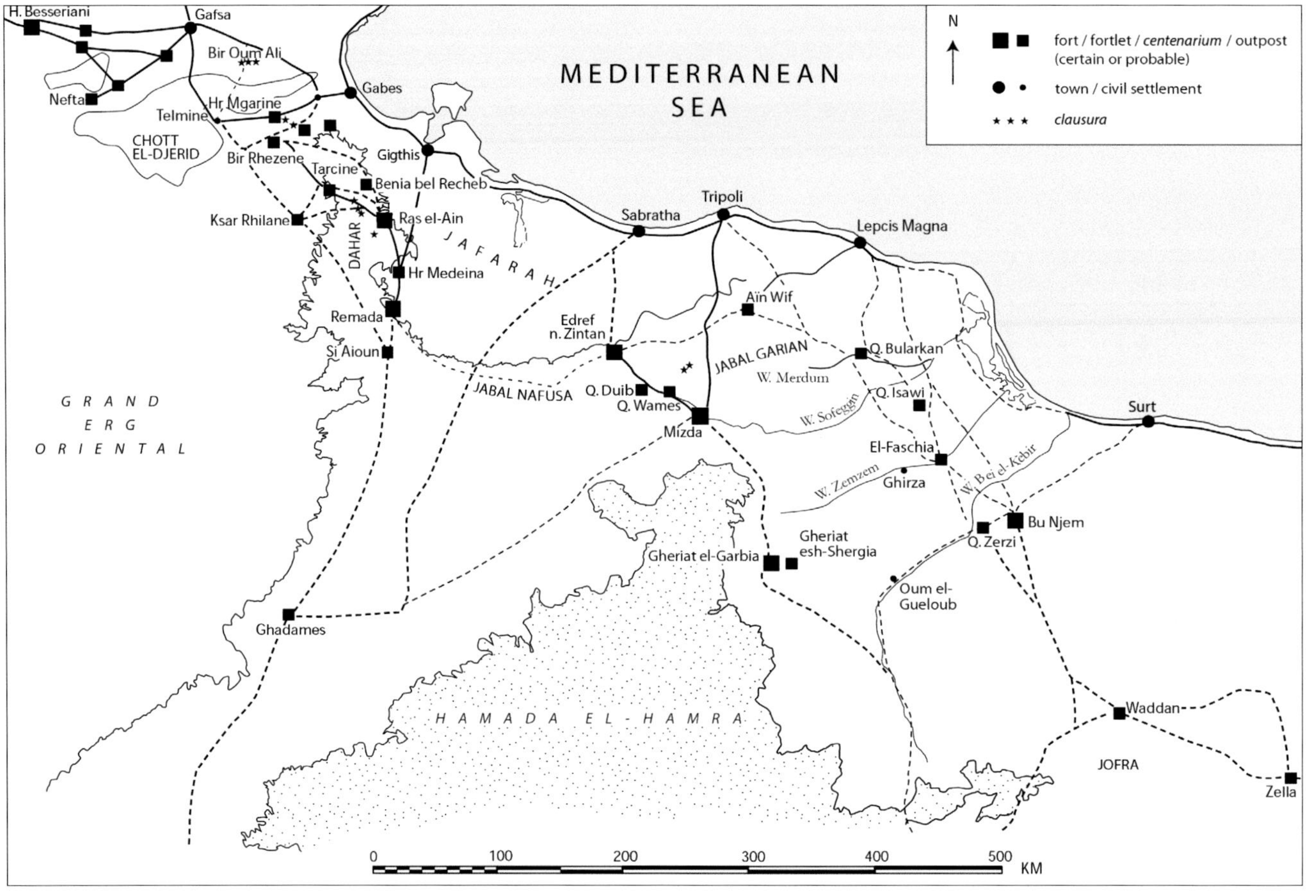

Fig. 7.1. Roman military installations in Tripolitania (after Mackensen 2016, fig. 1).

With regard to Bu Njem, the finds recovered during the excavations were presented as part of the series of published preliminary reports.[4] However, their evaluation remains difficult, and statistical studies based on the published data are problematic (Schmid and Weber 2010, 404, note 115). A comprehensive new study of these finds remains a major desideratum. In contrast, the recent excavations at Gheriat el-Garbia have yielded an extensive amount of materials whose chronology ranges from the late second to the mid-sixth century CE and beyond (Mackensen 2021a; 2024, with bibliography). At the moment it represents the most important reference collection of this period in southern Tripolitania. As to the other sites of the *limes Tripolitanus*, only sporadic finds have been published to date (see note 1).

In the following sections, the most important archaeological and epigraphic evidence on the food supply of the *limes Tripolitanus* is discussed. The focus then shifts on the individual commodities and their origins, followed by some remarks on the supply system and on the impact of the new military infrastructure on the pre-desert region and its inhabitants.

The evidence of the amphorae

Transport amphorae represent the most important archaeological source for information on the supply of olive oil, wine, and fish products to the garrisons of the *limes Tripolitanus*. However, it is well-known that the ceramic remains of these containers at a given site represent only a portion of the actual food supply in antiquity. In North Africa in particular, olive oil, wine and fish sauces were probably also transported in skins, and to a certain extent possibly also in wooden barrels, which have not been preserved in the archaeological record (Marlière and Torres Costa 2007; Leitch 2014, 123; Bonifay 2017, 354). In the present context it is not only the finds from the forts of the *limes Tripolitanus* that are relevant, but also those from the Libyan Valleys in the north and from Fazzan in the south.

Gheriat el-Garbia

In the Tripolitanian frontier zone, extensive collections of amphora types are only known from Bu Njem and Gheriat el-Garbia.[5] In addition, smaller assemblages

[4] Rebuffat 1966–67; 1969–70a–b; 1974–75; 1976–77; 1997.

[5] Bu Njem: Guéry in Rebuffat 1969–70a; 1997; further examples without illustrations are mentioned in the preliminary reports. Gheriat el-Garbia: Schimmer 2012b; Mackensen *et al.* 2021, 182–88, 210–14.

of finds from the area of the UNESCO Libyan Valleys Archaeological Survey (ULVS) have also been published (Dore 1996, 355–61; see also Schmid 2018, 85). The most extensive inventory is from Gheriat el-Garbia, where 212 diagnostic fragments were documented during a field survey conducted in the area of the fort and its surroundings in 2009 (Mackensen *et al.* 2021, 183) (Table 7.1). Further examples were found during the excavations in various parts of the fort, particularly in several Late Antique deposits.[6] Among the amphorae from the survey that have a reliably determinable provenance, by far the largest percentage can be classified as Tripolitanian,[7] followed by imports from the Tunisian part of Africa Proconsularis, other regions of North Africa, and Sicily; a single example can be attributed to the eastern Mediterranean. The finds from the excavations, where an amphora for fish products (*liquamen*, *muria* or *salsamenta*) from the southern coast of the Iberian Peninsula (type Dressel 14) was also recovered, show similar ratios (Schimmer 2012b, 322, fig. 4.17; on the Dressel 14 see Vaz Pinto *et al.* 2021).

Overall, it can be assumed that most of the amphorae from the survey can be attributed to the fort's first period of occupation (199–201 to c. 275–80 CE) and thus the distribution pattern described can essentially be attributed to the third century (Table 7.2). However, four Tunisian amphorae of the late third to sixth century (types Africana 3A, Spatheion 1, Keay 62Q/Albenga 11/12?) show that some vessels reached Gheriat el-Garbia in Late Antiquity. Furthermore, at least one fragment of a Late Antique wine amphora (Benghazi Late Roman Amphora/LRA 2), which was recovered during

Table 7.1. Gheriat el-Garbia: Roman amphorae (including Late Antique types) recovered during the surface survey in the fort and its surroundings (for information on provenance, content and date, see Bonifay 2016a–b).

Type	Provenance	Content	Date (c.)	Rims	Handles	Bases	total
Dressel 2–4/Schöne-Mau 35	Tripolitania (central)	Wine	15 – 180		1		1
Tripolitana 1/3	Tripolitania	Olive oil	-25 – 300?	1			1
Tripolitana 2	Tripolitania (central or eastern)	Fish products, Wine (?)	25 – 450+	8			8
Tripolitana 3		Olive oil	160 – 450+	72			72
Tripolitana 2/3	Tripolitania	?		3		5	8
Undetermined				10	19		29
Africana 1B-C	Tunisia (Byzacena, Zeugitana)	Olive oil	150 – 350+	2			2
Africana 2A	Tunisia (Sahel, Zeugitana)	Fish products, Wine (?)	150 – 270+	2*			0
Africana 2 (?)	Tunisia					1	1
Africana 3A	Tunisia (Byzacena, Zeugitana) Algeria?	Wine (?)	280 – 380+	1			1
Spatheion, Bonifay Type 1	Tunisia (Zeugitana, Nabeul, Byzacena)	?	400 – 500+	2			2
Keay 62Q/Albenga 11/12?	Tunisia (Nabeul, Byzacena?)	?	470 – 550+	1			1
Undetermined	Tunisia				7	1	8
Dressel 30	Mauretania Caesariensis Tunisia (Byzacena, Zeugitana)	Wine	150 – 300+	5	1		6
MRA 1a, Bonifay Var. 1		Wine	200 – 250	2			2
MRA 1a, Bonifay Var. 2/3	Sicily (?)	Wine	250 – 300+	1			1
Sicily (?) undetermined					7		7
Undetermined	North Africa			1			1
Kapitän 2	Aegean, Black Sea Region (?)	Wine	180 – 400	1			1
Undetermined	Undetermined			5	52	1	58
Total				117	87	8	212

* One rim Tunisia or Tripolitania.

[6] Schimmer 2011, 321–22, fig. 68; 2012b, 322, fig. 4.17. The materials from the Late Antique deposits are now discussed in Mackensen 2024.

[7] Archaeometric analyses indicate that most of these vessels come from the Jabal Tarhuna area.

Table 7.2. Gheriat el-Garbia: amphora types assigned to the third-century CE phase of occupation (surface survey and excavations) (amphora drawings after Keay and Williams 2005).

	Africa Proconsularis (Tripolitania)	*Africa Proc.* (Tunisia)	*Sicilia*	*Mauretania Caesariensis (?)*	Aegean/ Black Sea Region	Iberian Peninsula (south coast)
OLIVE OIL	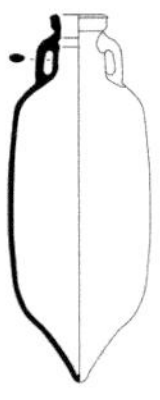 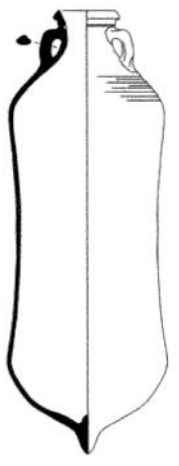 Tripolitana 1 Tripolitana 3	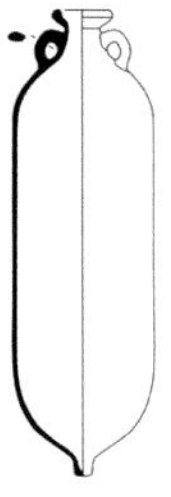 Africana 1				
WINE	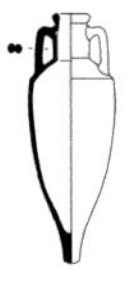 Dressel 2-4/Schöne-Mau 35	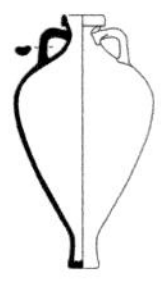 Dressel 30	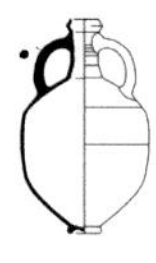 Mid Roman Amphora 1a	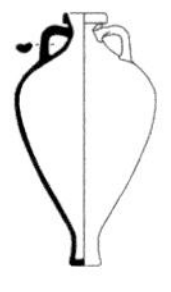 Dressel 30	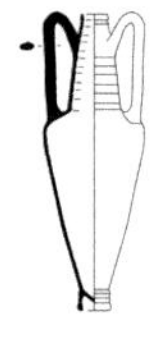 Kapitän 2	
FISH PRODUCTS	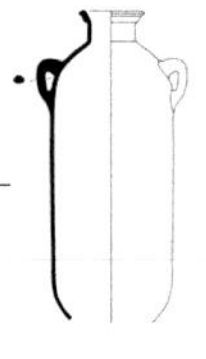 Tripolitana 2	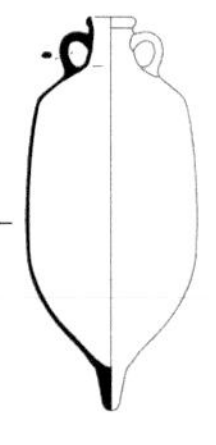 Africana 2A				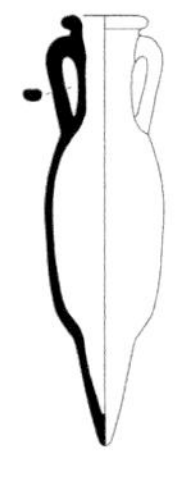 Dressel 14

the excavations, should be included here. These results are confirmed by the presence of Late Antique finewares and coins (Mackensen *et al.* 2021, 177–82; Noeske 2021). With regard to the Tripolitanian amphora types Tripolitana 2 and 3, a problem arises due to the fact that we do not know exactly how long they circulated in the region during the fifth century CE (Bonifay 2021, 290). It is therefore not possible to quantify exactly how many of these containers should be attributed to the fort's first period of occupation, and how many to Late Antiquity instead.

There is also some ambiguity concerning the transported goods. Especially with North African amphorae, the question of determining the contents is a long-known research problem that has received renewed attention in recent years (Bonifay 2021). In the case of the amphorae from the survey at Gheriat el-Garbia, there is little doubt that the vast majority were used to transport olive oil, as the numerous rims of Tripolitana 3 type, along with sporadic Tripolitana 1 type, show. In contrast, Tripolitana 2 amphorae are represented in much smaller numbers. These vessels were produced both on the coast and in the hinterland and carried fish products or wine (Bonifay 2021, 284). Wine imports from the Tripolitanian coastal zone are attested by Dressel 2–4 African/Schöne-Mau 35 type vessels (Mackensen *et al.* 2021, 184). However, in view of the well-represented, flat-bottomed containers Dressel 30 and Benghazi Mid-Roman Amphora/ MRA 1a, a larger percentage of the wine seems to have been shipped to Gheriat el-Garbia from Mauretania Caesariensis and Tunisia as well as from Sicily, at least in the third century. In addition, imports of oil (type Africana 1) and fish products or wine (type Africana

2A) from the Tunisian part of Africa Proconsularis[8] are attested in small quantities, as well as wine from the Aegean or the Black Sea region (type Kapitän 2: Mackensen *et al.* 2021, 184–86).

Bu Njem

Compared to Gheriat el-Garbia, the amphora types from Bu Njem are more difficult to identify. In the excavation report of the 1968 campaign, Roger Guéry (in Rebuffat 1969–70a; see also Rebuffat 1997) published a range of 119 amphora rims, distinguishing 83 'amphores à lèvre demi-ronde soulignée d'une moulure en forme de S' (types Tripolitana 2 and 3), two 'amphores à col évasé' (type Africana 1?) (cf. Rebuffat 1997, 165, 172), 13 'amphores de type divers', and 20 'amphores à rebord épaissi par un bourrelet externe' (type Africana 2A) (cf. Rebuffat 1997, 165–66). Further amphora fragments were recorded and briefly described in the finds catalogues of the excavation reports in the following years, but a precise classification is lacking and photographic documentation is only available in a few cases.[9] On the other hand, in 1997 René Rebuffat published no less than 28 amphora stamps (23 Tripolitanian and five Tunisian ones). Some of the Tripolitanian stamps could be traced to production sites in the Tarhuna area (Ahmed 2019, 150, 171, fig. 5.19). If one considers that only four amphora stamps have been found so far at Gheriat el-Garbia, this seems to suggest an extremely large quantity of amphora finds at Bu Njem. According to Rebuffat (1997, 163), two thirds to three quarters of all the amphorae recorded at Bu Njem can be interpreted as Tripolitanian, while the rest essentially consists of Tunisian vessels of the Africana 2(A) type and sporadic other types. According to the published rim profiles, around three quarters of the Tripolitanian amphorae can be identified as Tripolitana 3 oil containers and the others are primarily of the Tripolitana 2 type.[10] In the case of the latter type, the question again arises as to how many of these containers transported fish products or wine, which also applies to the Tunisian Africana 2A form (Bonifay 2021, 282–83, fig. 1). Nevertheless, the absence of any other wine amphorae is remarkable,[11] particularly with regard to the flat-bottomed containers from North Africa and Sicily. These are quite frequently documented at Gheriat el-Garbia, while MRA 1 also reached other places in the pre-desert, at least in small quantities (see below).

There is little doubt that the published amphorae from Bu Njem largely belong to the period between c. 200 and 260–70 CE, when the site housed a military garrison. Although some activities after the abandonment of the fort are attested, there is no evidence for a renewed military presence in Late Antiquity here, unlike Gheriat el-Garbia (on Late Antique terra sigillata from the area of the fort, see Mackensen *et al.* 2021, 179). It is noteworthy that among the Tripolitana 3 rims there are a number of examples with 'cap-shaped' profiles.[12] These are considered characteristic of the later Tripolitana 3 variants of the fourth century, but they are also attested as early as the third century at Monte Testaccio in Rome.[13] The question is therefore to what extent the multiple occurrence of these variants in the repertoire of Bu Njem is chronologically relevant, or whether it may reflect different production sites.

Libyan Valleys and Ghirza

In the catalogue of his ULVS report from 1996, John Dore listed 117 entries of amphora fragments, which he assigned to 32 different rim forms.[14] According to his description, the amphora repertoire is composed almost exclusively of Tripolitanian or Tunisian vessels. These cover a chronological range from the first to the seventh century CE, even though the dating possibilities in the sixth and seventh centuries are limited. Early on Dore observed a consistently high presence of Tripolitanian amphorae from the first to the fourth century, followed by a rapid decline from about the late fourth century. In contrast, a continuous influx of Tunisian amphorae can be noted from the third century onwards, which continued unabated in Late Antiquity (Dore 1996, 352–54, fig. 47.1). Apart from various Tunisian types, most amphorae from the pre-desert are represented by the 'classic' Tripolitanian containers, Tripolitana 1–3, including the type Benghazi LRA 7, which is probably to be regarded as a late variant of the type Tripolitana 2.[15] The series is completed by six rim fragments, published as 'flagons' from different sites, which can be identified as Sicilian wine

[8] It cannot be ruled out that there might be isolated Tripolitanian imitations among the Africana 2A: Mackensen *et al.* 2021, 184 (cat. no. 1196).

[9] Rebuffat 1969–70b, 166, pl. 37c–d; 1976–77, 60–63, 78, pls 22–23 (amphora stoppers).

[10] Victoria Leitch (2014, 121, note 54) identified 19 fragments as Tripolitana 2 and four as Tripolitana 2/3.

[11] Rebuffat 1997, 167. Some of the amphora profiles published by Guéry in Rebuffat 1969–70a, 102 might be possible candidates for flat-bottomed amphorae, such as A86 (Keay 1A/Dressel 30?).

[12] For instance, Guéry in Rebuffat 1969–70a, 99–101, figs 17–19, A21–22, A31, A33, A70; see also Bonifay and Capelli 2013, 120–22, fig. 29.

[13] Bonifay 2004, 105; Revilla 2010, 398–99; see also Bonifay and Capelli 2013, 83 (a context of the late third/early fourth century CE at Lepcis Magna).

[14] Dore 1996, 355–61. However, the total number of documented amphora fragments must be estimated higher, since '(...) the total number of examples of particular forms is not always given (...)': Dore 1996, 355. Overall, relatively few amphorae were documented as surface finds during the ULVS: Leitch 2014, 122.

[15] Tripolitana 1–3: Dore 1996, 356, fig. 47.3, nos 3–7, of which 4, 6, and 7 are Tripolitana 2 (Leitch 2014, 122). LRA 7: Dore 1996, 356, nos 8–10; Bonifay *et al.* 2010, 155–56, figs 6.9–11.

amphorae MRA 1a, Bonifay variant 1 (Dore 1996, 362, 368–69, fig. 47.5, no. 56). The small amphora assemblage from Qasr Isawi recently presented by Sebastian Schmid (2018, 85), where the Tripolitana 1, 2 (?), and 3 types as well as MRA 1a were documented, fits well with the supply pattern shown by the ULVS.

The amphora repertoire from Ghirza remains largely unknown. This site was the most important civilian settlement in the pre-desert, whose heyday was in the late third and fourth centuries CE (Brogan and Smith 1984, 230; Mattingly 2011, 2). John Hayes (in Brogan and Smith 1984, 237, no. 26) mentioned two amphora fragments that can probably be identified as Late Antique type Antique British B ii (Benghazi Late Roman Amphora 1) from the eastern Mediterranean. Particularly noteworthy is a relief built into a monumental tomb of the local elite dating to the first half of the fourth century,[16] which seems to illustrate either a festive event including the corresponding preparations or a market scene where agricultural products (grain, oil, and wine) from the rural settlements of the wadis were sold (Zanker 2008, 219–21, fig. 10; Mattingly 2011, 259–60). In the centre of the relief, a person carries a large amphora, possibly to be identified as a Tripolitana 2 vessel. Regarding the content, the context in this case may suggest wine rather than fish products (Leitch 2014, 121–22; on depictions of food on these funerary reliefs see also Nikolaus and Sheldrick, Chapter 5).

Fazzan

Thanks to the intensive research of the past few decades, we now have a fairly precise idea of the more or less intensive trade relations between Roman-period Tripolitania and Fazzan. This can also be applied to the imports of olive oil, wine, and fish products in amphorae (Dore *et al.* 2007, 336–63; Leone *et al.* 2013, 334–38; Leitch *et al.* 2017, 291–94). The following developments, among others, have emerged:

- Most of the Roman fineware and amphora imports into Fazzan occurred between the later first and third centuries CE (Leitch *et al.* 2017, 292–93, figs 11.3–4).
- Just as in the Libyan Valleys and in the Severan oasis forts, the majority of the amphorae documented in Fazzan originate from Tripolitania, with fewer amphorae coming from the Tunisian part of Africa Proconsularis. However, according to Michel Bonifay (2013, 540, note 38; 2017, 361), most of the Tripolitana 1–3 vessels documented at Jarma predate the third century CE. On the other hand, Victoria Leitch pointed out that most of the amphorae there identified as Tripolitanian have a small and squat shape, which distinguishes them from the 'classical' Tripolitanian types. She argued that these small containers, which have not yet been attested either at the *limes Tripolitanus* or further north, were made specifically for desert transport. It is possible that they provided better protection for contents such as fish products or wine from the heat and were used several times (Leitch 2014, 122–23; Leitch *et al.* 2017, 297; 2020, 56; Bonifay 2017, 362). The production sites of these vessels have not yet been located.
- Many of the Roman finewares and amphorae from Fazzan are of a conspicuously poor quality with traces of over-firing, cracks, etc. and may therefore be regarded as 'seconds'. This may have been the result of a deliberate selection by the caravan traders in view of the special risks of long-distance transport across the desert (Leitch *et al.* 2017, 297–98).
- From the late second and third centuries Fazzan seems to have been disconnected, to a certain degree, from the Mediterranean trade along the *limes* zone. It is interesting to note that flat-bottomed wine containers from Sicily and Mauretania or Tunisia attested at Gheriat el-Garbia and in the pre-desert (MRA 1 and Dressel 30) apparently did not reach south beyond the *limes Tripolitanus* (Bonifay 2017, 362). In contrast, the role of the *limes* from Numidia to Tripolitania and its possible continuation into Cyrenaica and the Western Desert of Egypt as a trade and supply route during the first half of the third century CE has been discussed extensively in recent years (Ballet *et al.* 2012; Bonifay 2017, 362–63; see also Mazou 2017).

The epigraphic evidence

Ostraca

The importance of the ostraca from Bu Njem as an epigraphic source for the organization and everyday life of a garrison on the North African desert frontier and beyond need not be emphasized here (Marichal 1979; 1992). They also shed a unique light on the supply of goods and trade at this peripheral military site. Various texts explicitly or implicitly mention the delivery of foodstuffs, including wheat and oil (Marichal 1992, 99–106, ostraca nos 75–81, 88). As an example, several deliveries of wheat are attested for the year 259 CE, which were arranged by a soldier named Aemilius Aemilianus, who was specially commissioned for this purpose by the *praepositus* Octavius Festus (ostraca nos 76–80). The transport of these relatively small cargoes

[16] Tomb North C, garden scene, stone 7: Brogan and Smith 1984, 154, 223, no. 7, pl. 82a.

was carried out by Libyan *camellarii*, apparently the producers of the wheat or their representatives, who in this way presumably sold their agricultural surpluses directly to the garrison. Both the Libyan and Punic names of the *camellarii* and the use of local units of measurement indicate that these people belong to the Libyan wadi communities of the pre-desert.[17] However, these deliveries may only have met a part of the wheat demand of the soldiers at Bu Njem, and in a sense may have been a 'supplement'. Instead, the regular supply of wheat and oil according to Robert Marichal (1992, 103; see also Guédon 2018, 206) is likely to have come from the state *horrea* on the coast. Ostracon no. 75, which attests to the provision of oil (?) for the soldiers at Bu Njem by a *procurator Augustorum*, is probably best understood in this context.[18]

It is noteworthy that the Garamantes are mentioned frequently on the ostraca. They seemed to have played a central role in the Saharan trade, and in many cases they were apparently also directly involved in the transport of trade goods (Broekaert and Vanacker 2016; Guédon 2018, 233). For example, there is little doubt that they conducted the transport of barley on four donkeys and three mules, as is probably documented on ostracon no. 72.[19] We do not know where the barley came from, but the apparently small size of the load makes a source in the immediate vicinity plausible (Wilson 2017b, 201). The Garamantes were probably also involved in the transport of *suriacae*, which are mentioned as the cargo of a donkey on ostracon no. 73 (Marichal 1992, 179–80). The meaning of the word *suriacae* remains unclear; textiles from Cappadocia, Syria or Egypt,[20] or the fruit of the *myrobalanum*[21] have been suggested. In addition, reference should also be made to ostracon no. 71, according to which Garamantes accompanied by four donkeys and two Egyptians brought to the fort both a letter (*litterae*) for the *praepositus* and a fugitive enslaved person whom they possibly wanted to sell there (Marichal 1992, 109, 177–78; Guédon 2018, 170–71). According to Wim Broekaert and Wouter Vanacker (2016, 105–12), the Garamantes, as trading partners, made an essential contribution to the supply of the Roman garrisons. The authors assume that they delivered not only food (barley, salt, fruits?, meat?) and livestock (mules, donkeys), but perhaps also military equipment (armour and weapons) and other products (hides and leather).

In contrast to Bu Njem, only nine ostraca of Late Antique date have been found at Gheriat el-Garbia. They were recently studied by Sabine Ziegler and come from two find deposits in the area of the (former) *porta praetoria*, which are dated to the first half and to the middle of the fifth century CE respectively. Unlike the Bu Njem ostraca, which are almost exclusively written in Latin, the ones from Gheriat el-Garbia show a regional southern variant of Punic ('southern Punic'). Two of the ostraca appear to be southern Punic-Latin bilinguals (Ziegler and Mackensen 2014, 325–27, nos 1–2). The exact content of these texts remains unknown. However, it is interesting that on ostracon no. 3 the terms 'protection', 'grain', 'Fazzan', 'oxen' and 'labourer' apparently appear together with a date (Ziegler and Mackensen 2014, 327–30). Also noteworthy is the bilingual ostracon no. 2, where Ziegler identified the Latin verb *pedatur*, which is possibly to be understood in the sense of 'to untie, to prop up (a plant in vegetable or vine cultivation)'.[22] It is conceivable that this text refers to the cultivation of the nearby oasis, which probably played a role in supplying the garrison by the third century.

Customs tariffs

Two sources of particular importance that are frequently referred to in connection with trade in the hinterland of the North African *limes* in the second and early third centuries CE, are two customs inscriptions from Numidia, one from Lambaesis (second century) and another from Zaraï (202 CE), which is located about 60 km to the north-west.[23] These inscriptions list a number of foodstuffs that are also attested in Tripolitania through archaeological and archaeobotanical evidence, such as wine and fish products as well as dates and figs. With regard to wine, the inscription from Lambaesis distinguishes between different types, namely products from Italy (*vinum Ammin(eum)*) and Greece (*vinum Graecum*) as well as a presumably African table wine (*vinum Cibarium*) (Léquement 1980, 187; Bonifay 2017, 358, note 61). On the inscription from Zaraï, *garum* is also found alongside wine, both in combination with the term *amphora*, which presumably does not refer to the container itself here but to the unit of capacity (Bonifay 2013, 553). The two inscriptions shed light on the

[17] Marichal 1992, 57–63, 99–106; Mattingly 1995, 151–52; 2023, 546–49 (with analysis of the load capacities and animals involved in table 12.1); Mitthoff 2001, 48–50; Guédon 2018, 205–6.

[18] Marichal 1992, 104; Rebuffat 1997, 165; Mitthoff 2001, 50; Guédon 2018, 207; Mattingly 2023, 549.

[19] Marichal 1992, 104, 178–79, no. 72; cf. Guédon 2018, 170. Of the name [*Garaman*]*tes* at the beginning of the second line, however, only the last three letters are preserved.

[20] Marichal 1992, 111; Rebuffat 2000, 236, note 65; Guédon 2016, 250; 2017, 272; 2018, 174–75.

[21] Broekaert and Vanacker 2016, 109–10. According to Pliny (*Naturalis Historia*, 12.101), the fruit of the Arabian kind of this tree is called *syriaca*.

[22] Ziegler and Mackensen 2014, 326–27; in contrast, De Simone (2018, 360–61) suggested a reading as *pedatur*(*a*).

[23] France 2014. On the inscription from Lambaesis see also Cagnat 1914; Schallmayer *et al.* 1990, 603–5, no. 781; Le Bohec 1989, 537, note 52; on the inscription from Zaraï see Trousset 2002–03; Morizot 2009; Guédon 2018, 186.

movement of goods in this section of the African frontier zone and provide an interesting comparison to the *limes Tripolitanus*, even if practices in these two areas might not have been necessarily identical.

Archaeobotanical and faunal evidence

The archaeobotanical and faunal record also provides important information on food consumption in the pre-desert and on the *limes Tripolitanus*.[24] At Gheriat el-Garbia, archaeobotanical investigations by Jacob Morales documented a wide range of cereals, fruits, and wild plants (Morales and Mackensen 2020) (Table 7.3). It has to be stressed that this evidence comes from Late Antique find deposits from the second half of the fourth to the mid-sixth century. However, there seems to be no evidence that agriculture in the Tripolitanian pre-desert changed significantly from the third century to Late Antiquity. Since it is also unlikely that the range of plants at Gheriat el-Garbia was more reduced during the first phase of military occupation than during the fourth and fifth centuries, the results of the investigations can probably be largely applied to the third century.[25]

In the case of cereals, similarities can be observed with finds from other late Roman sites in the pre-desert as well as with settlements in Fazzan (Morales and Mackensen 2020, 215). Barley seems to have played a particularly important role, which is confirmed in the ostraca from Bu Njem (see above). It was used in the Roman army primarily as animal feed, but was also consumed by soldiers, especially in regions with specific cultural traditions.[26] However, it was also one of the crops that thrived well in the dry landscape of the pre-desert and could have been used more frequently as food here. This may also explain the significantly higher proportion of hard wheat compared to bread wheat in the archaeobotanical record (Morales and Mackensen 2020, 215) (Table 7.3). The sporadic occurrence of pearl millet, which originates from the sub-Saharan regions and is widespread in Fazzan, is noteworthy as it has not yet been documented at the sites of the pre-desert (Pelling 2013; Morales and Mackensen 2020, 215). Pearl millet obviously arrived at Gheriat el-Garbia as part of the south–north trade. The repertoire of fruits primarily includes dates and figs, but also grapes, olives, almonds, pomegranates, and jujubes, i.e. plants originally from the Mediterranean that were also cultivated in the pre-desert in Roman times. In addition, there are some wild plants of local origin. Some of the fruits mentioned may have been cultivated in the nearby oasis in antiquity (see the remarks above on ostracon no. 2); however, it is difficult to estimate how many fruits were obtained from the region or from long-distance trade. The investigations in the area of the ULVS showed a comparable range of cereals and fruits as were found at Gheriat el-Garbia, as well as pulses (lentil, pea, grass pea) and herbs (pursline, dill, celery) (Van der Veen *et al.* 1996, 238, table 8.3). The authors demonstrated that crops such as barley, durum wheat and bread wheat could be grown in the pre-desert settlements thanks to the highly developed irrigation systems, although these plants otherwise required significantly higher amounts of rainfall than is usual in the pre-desert (Van der Veen *et al.* 1996, 254–56).

As far as archaeozoology is concerned, a few years ago Leitch (2014) compiled the evidence for the distribution of fish, fish products, and shellfish from the Tripolitanian frontier zone and Fazzan as part of a study of Saharan trade. She drew attention to the finds of shellfish (*dolium galea, murex brandaris*) from the area of the *principia* and the *vicus* of Bu Njem, which can be assigned to the third-century phase of occupation, and apparently were used as food there.[27] There is also evidence of the consumption of seafood in pre-desert settlements, such as oysters at Ghirza, while seafood seems to have already reached Fazzan in pre-Roman times.[28] Leitch (2014, 123–25) argued that fish products may, generally, have played only a minor role in ancient Libya, especially in the desert zones, and should be regarded as luxury goods. Nevertheless, the evidence of the amphorae and the customs inscriptions indicate that *salsamenta* and fish sauce were widely available along the *limes Tripolitanus* and other sections of the Roman frontier in North Africa. As already mentioned, some of these products may also have been delivered in skins.

Meat was also an integral part of the military diet. Rebuffat (2000, 240) referred to the consumption of poultry and small game as well as goat, sheep, and cattle on the basis of the bone finds from Bu Njem; likewise, camel seems to have been used as an animal for slaughter (Rebuffat 1977, 400; Marichal 1992, 105). Significant results can be expected from the analysis of the faunal record from Late Antique contexts at Gheriat el-Garbia by Nadja Pöllath. Of particular interest is the question of whether differences can be found between the forts on the

[24] Mackensen 2024 was published after this manuscript had been finalized, so it was not possible to reference the specific contributions in it on the archaeobotany and archaeozoology of Late Antique Gheriat el-Garbia.

[25] Van der Veen *et al.* (2018, 23–24, 28–30) noted a greater focus on local food plants and locally available rather than imported meat in the food supply of Roman settlements in the Eastern Desert of Egypt from the third century onwards, as a result of political and economic changes.

[26] Junkelmann 1997, 104; Coccoluto 2014, 30, 131; Vossen and Groot 2009, 94–96 (with regard to the north-western provinces); see also Van Limbergen 2018, 1057–58.

[27] Leitch 2014, 118; cf. Rebuffat 1969–70b, 155. For further shellfish finds from the fort and its surroundings, see Rebuffat 1974–75, 238; 1976–77, 75–76. Moreover, Anna Walas (2022, 50) referred recently to unpublished graffiti from the *vicus* with depictions of ships and a lighthouse, which she sees as confirmation of a 'conscious connectivity to the Mediterranean'.

[28] Leitch 2014, 118–20. See also Höpken 2014 on the preservation, transport, and consumption of oysters in inland regions of the northern provinces.

Table 7.3. Macro-botanical remains identified at Gheriat el-Garbia (after Morales and Mackensen 2020).

Chronology	Late Roman (c. 360-455 CE)						Libyan (c. 500-550 CE)			
Context	57	57	57	57	61	62	23	23	23	
date	05/04/2009	12/05/2010	13/05/2010	06/04/2009	07/04/2009	08/04/2009	11/05/2010	12/05/2010	15/05/2010	**total**
volume sediment (in litres)	2	10	10	hand picked	hand picked	hand picked	10	10	10	**52**
Cereals										
Hordeum vulgare subsp. *vulgare*, grain (barley)		22	52				2			**76**
Hordeum vulgare subsp. *vulgare*, rachis (barley)		72	263							**335**
Triticum aestivum/ durum, grain (wheat)		1	3							**4**
Triticum durum, rachis (hard wheat)		83	177							**260**
Triticum durum, ear (hard wheat)						2				**2**
Triticum aestivum, rachis (bread wheat)		7	5							**12**
Pennisetum glaucum, grain (pearl millet)		2	5							**7**
Pennisetum glaucum, inflorescence (pearl millet)			3							**3**
cereal culm node		16	37							**53**
Fruits										**0**
Capparis spinosa (caper)	2	3	1				2	2		**10**
Capsicum sp. (chilli pepper)		1	3							**4**
Ficus carica (fig)	62	11	4				23	8	3	**111**
Olea europaea (olive)	2	1					2	2	4	**11**
Phoenix dactylifera, seed (date)	8	23	42	6	1			1	1	**82**
Phoenix dactylifera, perianth (date)		7	22					2	2	**33**
Phoenix dactylifera, male flower (date)		3	3							**6**
Phoenix dactylifera, rachilla (date)		1	2	1						**4**
Punica granatum (pomegranate)	1	3	2				2	14	3	**25**
Prunus dulcis (almond)			1	1				1	1	**4**
Vitis vinifera, seed (grape)	14	3	2				9	12	12	**52**
Vitis vinifera, stalk (grape)							1	2	1	**4**
Ziziphus spina-christi (jujuba)	1	2	4				1	1	4	**13**
Wild plants										**0**
Beta sp. (beet)							1			**1**
Citrullus colocynthus (wild watermelon)		1	1							**2**
Pistacia atlantica (wild pistachio)	2									**2**
Raphanus raphanistrum (wild radish)							2			**2**
Retama sphaerocarpa (white broom)		2	5							**7**
Medicago sp., pod							1	2		**3**
Undetermined		4		1			5	3		**13**
total	**92**	**268**	**637**	**9**	**1**	**2**	**51**	**50**	**31**	**1141**

one hand and the open farms and qsur of the pre-desert on the other, where the combination of both sheep and goat husbandry and gazelle hunting turned out to be a general phenomenon throughout the ages (Van der Veen *et al.* 1996, 259). Furthermore, the find of ostrich eggs at Bu Njem and Gheriat el-Garbia should be highlighted.[29]

Conclusions

By establishing the oasis forts of Ghadames, Gheriat el-Garbia and Bu Njem, Septimius Severus brought the Tripolitanian pre-desert under direct Roman control. This resulted in the sudden presence of a large number of soldiers and *vicani* at these sites. An essential requirement for the functioning of the new military communities on the *limes Tripolitanus* was, as elsewhere, to ensure the supply of food, including foodstuffs such as wheat, oil, and wine. The supply of the troops in general probably followed a similar pattern as in other frontier zones of the Roman Empire, even though the military was confronted with particular challenges here due to the extreme natural environment. In this context, it is significant that a large part of the soldiers garrisoned on the African frontiers in Severan times were recruited from North Africans who might have been familiar with the natural landscape conditions (Guédon 2018, 249–50).

The integration into regional and supra-regional trade networks of the Tripolitanian oasis forts and their *vici* during the third century is reflected in the wide range of foodstuffs available, which can be inferred at least partly from the archaeological, epigraphic, archaeobotanical, and faunal evidence: the basic foodstuffs primarily included cereals, especially barley and hard wheat, as well as olive oil. In addition, there were other standard products of Roman military supply such as wine (probably also *posca* and *acetum*) and, to an indeterminable extent, also fish products. The latter seem to have been supplemented by (sporadic) dried or salted (?) seafood.[30] Meat also played a fundamental role in feeding the troops, including poultry, small game, goat, sheep, cattle and camel, as has been seen at Bu Njem. In addition, various fruits of African and Mediterranean origin, including dates, figs, grapes, olives, almonds, pomegranates and jujubes, were consumed at Gheriat el-Garbia, most probably as early as the mid-imperial period. The same is likely to be true for various legumes and spices found in the samples from open farms and qsur in the Libyan Valleys.

As far as the origin of the various foodstuffs is concerned, a fairly complex supply pattern of local, regional and long-distance trade emerges. The fruits found in the archaeobotanical evidence probably originated

[29] Bu Njem: Rebuffat 1976–77, 50; Walas 2022, 50. Gheriat el-Garbia: Schimmer 2011, 317 (backfilling of a Late Antique storage pit).

[30] Van Neer (1997, 146) assumed that the Roman stations along the desert routes in the eastern desert of Egypt may have been supplied also with fresh fish when temperatures were low in winter.

primarily from the Libyan Valleys or were cultivated in the oases of the military sites themselves (Morales and Mackensen 2020, 216–17). Likewise, the supply of (fresh) meat would have been organized, above all, on a local or regional level, if only because of how perishable it is, but the final results of the archaeozoological investigations at Gheriat el-Garbia are pending. According to the ostraca from Bu Njem, wheat and barley were probably also obtained, at least in part, from the immediate or wider surroundings (see above). In the case of Gheriat el-Garbia, Morales assumed that these cereals, attested in the Late Antique deposits, were imported to the site. Their almost complete absence in the post-Roman layers seems to indicate the end of the corresponding supply networks.[31] It is possible that the Wadi Sofeggin and the adjoining regions to the south were of particular importance here. Wheat from the large granaries on the coast (Lepcis Magna) would also have contributed to the supply of the *limes Tripolitanus* on the basis of the *annona militaris*, but we do not know in what quantities. The pearl millet from a Late Antique context at Gheriat el-Garbia is an exception that would have reached the site via trade from Fazzan or further south.

The amphora record of the oasis forts and their *vici* provides information on the supply of olive oil, wine, and fish products. Olive oil came, unsurprisingly, first and foremost from Tripolitania (especially from the Tarhuna area), as documented by the large number of Tripolitana 3 amphorae at Gheriat el-Garbia and Bu Njem (Bonifay 2007, 458). In addition, Gheriat el-Garbia, and maybe also Bu Njem, received Tunisian oil (Africana 1) in limited quantities.

A more nuanced pattern emerges in the case of wine, which also finds some confirmation in the customs tariff from Lambaesis. Regional products are attested at Gheriat el-Garbia (Dressel 2–4/Schöne-Mau 35); however, their precise proportions remain vague due to the question of how many of the Tripolitana 2 amphorae actually carried wine. The same applies to Bu Njem. On the other hand, a significant share of the wine was shipped to Gheriat el-Garbia via long-distance trade from Sicily (MRA 1a) as well as from Mauretania Caesariensis and Tunisia (Dressel 30) during the third century. In contrast, according to the current state of research, these products did not reach Bu Njem or Fazzan. Nevertheless, evidence documented at sites in the pre-desert indicate that at least Sicilian wine found some distribution in the region beyond the coastal area. In addition, the presence of a Kapitän 2 wine amphora recovered at Gheriat el-Garbia can be taken as further evidence that the site was connected to the Mediterranean market.

The quantities of the different fish products transported in amphorae of Tripolitana 2 and Africana 2A types are difficult to estimate. It should be noted that Africana 2A vessels are considerably more frequent at Bu Njem than at Gheriat el-Garbia, which can perhaps be explained by different supply routes (Mackensen *et al.* 2021, 192). However, fish sauce and *salsamenta* were most probably part of the regular supply of the garrisons, especially since there is evidence that seafood also reached the Tripolitanian frontier zone. Regarding the imports of Mediterranean fish products to Fazzan, where Tripolitana 2 amphorae are also attested (Leitch 2014, 122), further research on the small-sized 'desert amphorae' could provide important results.

Generally, it seems that certain products were specifically acquired by the military (see above the example of Aemilius Aemilianus), while others arrived at the forts and their *vici* through free trade. To what degree the Garamantes played a central role in supplying the garrisons, as suggested by Broekaert and Vanacker (2016, 105–12), remains a matter of debate. Merchants and suppliers were probably only granted limited access to the forts. In this context, the exact meaning of the verbs *introire* and *supervenire* on the Bu Njem ostraca has been discussed (Marichal 1992, 109; Guédon 2018, 170–71, 175; see also Walas 2020, 57–58). It was argued that in case of ostracon no. 71 the Garamantes and Egyptians were allowed to pass the gate (*introierunt*). The same applies to the Garamantes (?) delivering barley that are mentioned on ostracon no. 72 (Marichal 1992, 109; Guédon 2018, 171). However, neither the names of the suppliers nor the quantity of barley were specified. The Garamantes could therefore, as Stéphanie Guédon (2018, 171, 174) emphasized, also have voluntarily offered their goods for sale to the soldiers, without being involved in the regular military supply system. In contrast, the more general term *supervenire* on ostracon no. 73 in connection with the *suriacae* could mean that the (textile?) traders or convoy in question remained outside the fort (Guédon 2018, 175).

The Roman army usually took the regional conditions of the natural environment into account when supplying its permanent forts with food and fodder (Deschler-Erb and Groot 2019; see also Mattingly 1995, 152). In this respect, the significant regional component in the range of foodstuffs presented above is not surprising. However, even in the case of those goods that were produced within Tripolitania, such as oil, wine or fish products, longer distances sometimes had to be covered. It is striking that the roads through the pre-desert and desert areas, which were unsuitable for chariots, were no obstacle to the mass transport of amphorae, as both the evidence from the oasis forts and that from Fazzan show. At least large containers such as amphorae Tripolitana 1–3 may have been carried by dromedaries rather

[31] Morales and Mackensen 2020, 217; Mattingly 2023, 556. The high ratio of rachis segments in comparison to grains is interpreted as residues of cereal processing for consumption or as leftovers of fodder: Morales and Mackensen 2020, 215.

than donkeys or mules (Bonifay 2013, 552, note 102). Mattingly (2013b, 184–85) assumed that for caravans of a maximum of 50–100 animals, each camel was loaded with two large amphorae (maximum 150 kg). Based on the data from the Garamantian tombs in Wadi al-Ajal, he calculated this equated to several caravans or 187 to 250 loaded animals per year to have travelled from the Mediterranean coast to Fazzan during the first to fourth centuries CE. In the oasis forts and their *vici*, the supervision of the water points and water supply was of particular importance, not only for the soldiers and *vicani*, but also for the caravans. In this context, Guédon interpreted the term *statio camellariorum* (Bu Njem, ostracon no. 5), which has been intensely debated in recent times, as a facility near the fort in the sense of a caravanserai, where the military both registered the arriving caravans and goods, and also provided the infrastructure for unloading and supply.[32] The same can be assumed for the other oasis forts.

The question remains as to what effects the establishment of the Severan oasis forts had on the surrounding areas of the pre-desert and its inhabitants. It can be assumed that the new military infrastructure and regular army patrols to control the traffic routes, caravans, and goods ensured stable conditions and security in the region. On the other hand, the garrisons certainly had a considerable economic impact, as the *milites* and *vicani* represented a new market for the agricultural surplus of the wadi farmers (Mattingly 1995, 89). One aim of Severus' territorial expansion may have been to improve access to the most important north–south routes of the Saharan trade between Tripolitania and Fazzan (Guédon 2018, 223–24). The extension of these routes possibly made it easier for the inhabitants of the pre-desert to expand their range of trade and to better profit from supra-regional trade networks (Sheldrick 2021, 58). Whether or to what extent the Severan military sites had an immediate effect on the rural settlement in the pre-desert is not clear. A detailed analysis is problematic due the lack of precise chronologies of the individual sites and their developments (Sheldrick 2021, 26–34; see also Nikolaus and Sheldrick, Chapter 5); however, it is most likely that the new situation generally created favourable conditions for growth and prosperity.

References

Ahmed, M.A.M. 2019. *Rural Settlement and Economic Activity. Olive Oil, Wine and Amphorae Production on the Tarhuna Plateau during the Roman Period.* London: Society for Libyan Studies.

Ballet, P., Bonifay, M. and Marchand, S. 2012. Africa vs Aegyptus: routes, rythmes et adaptations de la céramique africaine en Égypte. In S. Guédon (ed.), *Entre Afrique et Égypte: relations et échanges entre les espaces au sud de la Méditerranée à l'époque romaine.* Bordeaux: Ausonius Éditions, 87–117.

Bonifay, M. 2004. *Études sur la céramique romaine tardive d'Afrique.* Oxford: Archaeopress.

Bonifay, M. 2007. Observations préliminaires sur les amphores africaines de l'oasis de Bahariya. In S. Marchand and A. Marangou (eds), *Amphores d'Égypte de la basse époque à l'époque arabe.* Cairo: Institut Français d'Archéologie Orientale, 451–62.

Bonifay, M. 2013. Africa: patterns of consumption in coastal regions versus inland regions. The ceramic evidence (300–700 A.D.). In L. Lavan (ed.), *Local Economies? Production and Exchange in Inland Regions in Late Antiquity.* Leiden-Boston: Brill, 529–65.

Bonifay, M. 2016a. Éléménts de typologie des céramiques de l'Afrique romaine. In D. Malfitana and M. Bonifay (eds), *La ceramica africana nella Sicilia romana – La céramique africaine dans la Sicile romaine. Volume II.* Catania: IBAM, 507–73.

Bonifay, M. 2016b. Amphores de l'Afrique romaine: nouvelles avancées sur la production, la typo-chronologie et le contenu. In R. Járrega and P. Berni (eds), *Amphorae ex Hispania: paisajes de producción y consumo.* Tarragona: Instituto Catalán de Arqueología Clásica, 595–611.

Bonifay, M. 2017. Can we speak of pottery and amphora 'import substitution' in inland regions of Roman Africa? In D.J. Mattingly, V. Leitch, C.N. Duckworth, A. Cuénod, M. Sterry and F. Cole (eds), *Trade in the Ancient Sahara and Beyond.* Cambridge: Cambridge University Press, 341–68.

Bonifay, M. 2021. African amphora contents: an update. In D. Bernal Casasola, M. Bonifay, M. Pecci and V. Leitch (eds), *Roman Amphora Contents. Reflecting on the Maritime Trade of Foodstuffs in Antiquity (in Honour of Miguel Beltrán Lloris).* Oxford: Archaeopress, 281–97.

Bonifay, M. and Capelli, C. 2013. Les Thermes du Levant à Leptis Magna: quatre contextes céramiques des IIIe et IVe siècles. *Antiquités Africaines* 49: 67–150.

Bonifay, M., Capelli, C. and Muçaj, S. 2010. Amphores tardives de tradition punique: observations sur le type Benghazi LRA 7. In C. Ebnöther and R. Schatzmann (eds), *Oleum non perdidit. Festschrift für Stefanie Martin-Kilcher zu ihrem 65. Geburtstag.* Basel: Archäologie Schweiz, 151–59.

[32] Guédon 2016, 254; 2018, 172–73, 178. For the discussion see also Marichal 1992, 112; Walas 2020, 58, with further references. According to Mattingly (2023, 553–54), the *statio* could have been located north of the main well and oasis, where an enclosure measuring c. 65 × 57 m can be seen in an aerial photograph.

Broekaert, W. and Vanacker, W. 2016. Raiders to traders? Economics of integration among nomadic communities in North Africa. In D. Slootjesand and M. Peachin (eds), *Rome and the Worlds Beyond its Frontiers*. Leiden-Boston: Brill, 96–122.

Brogan, O. and Smith, D.J. 1984. *Ghirza. A Libyan Settlement in the Roman Period*. Tripoli: Department of Antiquities.

Cagnat, R. 1914. A new Roman customs list. *Journal of Roman Studies* 4: 142–46.

Coccoluto, M. 2014. *Panis ad milites. L'approvvigionamento dell'esercito romano in Numidia da Augusto ai Severi*. Ancona: Affinità Elettive.

Deschler-Erb, S. and Groot, M. 2019. Think global, act local: regionalism and the supply of meat to the Roman army. In M.G. Allen (ed.), *The Role of Zooarchaeology in the Study of the Western Roman Empire*. Portsmouth, RI: Journal of Roman Archaeology, 53–72.

De Simone, R. 2018. Sugli ostraka da Gheriat el-Gharbia (Libia) e di una supposta 'südpunische Variante'. *Sicilia Antiqua* 15: 359–61.

Dore, J. 1996. The UNESCO Libyan Valleys Archaeological Survey pottery. In D.J. Mattingly (ed.), *Farming the Desert. The UNESCO Libyan Valleys Archaeological Survey. Volume 2: Gazetteer and Pottery*. London: Society for Libyan Studies, 317–93.

Dore, J., Leone, A. and Hawthorne, J. 2007. The Fazzan Project: the pottery type series. In D.J. Mattingly (ed.), *The Archaeology of Fazzān, II. Site Gazetteer, Pottery and Other Survey Finds*. London: Society for Libyan Studies, 305–431.

Dowler, A.D. and Galvin, E.R. 2011. *Money, Trade and Trade Routes in Pre-Islamic North Africa*. London: British Museum Press.

France, J. 2014. Normes douanières et réglementation des échanges. Trois questions simples sur le tarif de Zaraï (Numidie). *Antiquités Africaines* 50: 93–110.

Guédon, S. 2016. La statio camellariorum: circulation et transports caravaniers dans le corpus des ostraca de Bu Njem. *Journal of Papyrology and Epigraphy* 197: 249–56.

Guédon, S. 2017. Circulation and trade of textiles in the southern borders of Roman Africa: new hypotheses. In D.J. Mattingly, V. Leitch, C.N. Duckworth, A. Cuénod, M. Sterry and F. Cole (eds), *Trade in the Ancient Sahara and Beyond*. Cambridge: Cambridge University Press, 259–84.

Guédon, S. 2018. *La frontière romaine de l'Africa sous le Haut-Empire*. Madrid: Casa de Velázquez.

Höpken, C. 2014. Römische Austern aus Bonn und den Limeskastellen Zugmantel, Alteburg-Heftrich und Saalburg. *Saalburg Jahrbuch* 58: 89–103.

Junkelmann, M. 1997. *Panis militaris. The Diet of the Roman Soldier or the Basic Substance of Power*. Mainz: Philipp von Zabern.

Keay, S. and Williams, D. 2005. *Roman Amphorae: A Digital Resource*. University of Southampton: http://archaeologydataservice.ac.uk/archives/view/amphora_ahrb_2005.

Le Bohec, Y. 1989. *La troisième légion Auguste*. Paris: Éditions du CNRS.

Léquement, R. 1980. Le vin africain à l'époque impériale. *Antiquités Africaines* 16: 185–93.

Leitch, V. 2014. Fish and ships in the desert? The evidence for trans-Saharan trade in fish products. In E. Botte and V. Leitch (eds), *Fish & Ships. Production and Commerce of Salsamenta during Antiquity – Production et commerce des salsamenta durant l'Antiquité. Actes de l'atelier doctoral (Rome, 18–22 juin 2012)*. Aix en-Provence: Errance, 115–27.

Leitch, V., Duckworth, C.N., Cuénod, A., Mattingly, D.J, Sterry, M. and Cole, F. 2017. Early Saharan trade. The inorganic evidence. In D.J. Mattingly, V. Leitch, C.N. Duckworth, A. Cuénod, M. Sterry and F. Cole (eds), *Trade in the Ancient Sahara and Beyond*. Cambridge: Cambridge University Press, 287–340.

Leitch, V., Bonifay, M., Capelli, C. and Mattingly, D.J. 2018. Pre-desert Tripolitania: a new archaeological and archaeometrical examination or Red Slip Ware from the Ghirza excavations and the Libyan Valleys Survey. *Rei Cretariae Romanae Fautorum Acta* 45: 759–63.

Leitch, V., Bonifay, M. and Capelli, C. 2020. Chronologie de quelques établissements de la frontière romaine du Sud tunisien à partir de la céramique collectée sur les sites: une révision des données. In S. Guédon (ed.), *Vivre, circuler et échanger sur la bordure septentrionale du Sahara. Antiquité-époque moderne*. Bordeaux: Ausonius Éditions, 41–64.

Leone, A. 2017. Pottery and trade in North and sub-Saharan Africa during Late Antiquity. The distribution of North African finewares. In D.J. Mattingly, V. Leitch, C.N. Duckworth, A. Cuénod, M. Sterry and F. Cole (eds), *Trade in the Ancient Sahara and Beyond*. Cambridge: Cambridge University Press, 369–92.

Leone, A., Leitch, V. and Mattingly, D.J. 2013. Pottery from the excavations at Jarma. In D.J. Mattingly (ed.), *The Archaeology of Fazzān, IV. Survey and Excavations at Old Jarma (Ancient Garama) Carried Out by C.M. Daniels (1962–69) and the Fazzān Project (1997–2001)*. London: Society for Libyan Studies, 325–408.

Liverani, M. (ed.) 2006. *Aghram Nadharif. The Barkat Oasis (Sha'abiya of Ghat, Libyan Sahara) in Garamantian Times*. Florence: All'Insegna del Giglio.

Mackensen, M. 2008. Mannschaftsunterkünfte und Organisation einer severischen Legionsvexillation im tripolitanischen Kastell Gholaia/Bu Njem (Libyen). *Germania* 86: 271–306.

Mackensen, M. 2015. Zur spätrömischen Nutzung des Kleinkastells Vezereos am limes Tripolitanus (Südtunesien). In P. Henrich, Ch. Miks, J. Obmann and M. Wieland (eds), *Non solum... sed etiam. Festschrift für Thomas Fischer zum 65. Geburtstag*. Rahden: Marie Leidorf Verlag, 259–70.

Mackensen, M. 2016. Survey and excavation of the German Archaeological Mission at the Roman Fort of Myd(---)/Gheriat el-Garbia and its vicinity, 2009/2010. *Libya Antiqua* n.s. 6: 83–102.

Mackensen, M. 2021a. *Das severische Vexillationskastell Myd(---)/Gheriat el-Garbia am limes Tripolitanus (Libyen), I: Forschungsgeschichte, Vermessung, Prospektionen und Funde 2009–2010.* Wiesbaden: Reichert Verlag.

Mackensen, M. 2021b. Observations and results of recent excavations and surveys of Late Roman military fortifications in the province of Tripolitana. *Libya Antiqua* n.s. 14: 111–45.

Mackensen, M. 2022. Late Roman African red slip ware from central Tunisia in Tripolitanian forts and fortlets. *Libya Antiqua* n.s. 15: 179–96.

Mackensen, M. 2024. *Das severische Vexillationskastell Myd(---) und die spätantiken castra Madensia/Gheriat el-Garbia am limes Tripolitanus (Libyen), II: Ausgrabungen und Untersuchungen im Kastell, im Steinbruch, in den Heiligtümern und am Beobachtungsturm 2009–2010.* Wiesbaden: Reichert Verlag.

Mackensen, M., Schimmer, F., Schmid, S. and Weber, M. 2021. Keramik-Survey. In M. Mackensen, *Das severische Vexillationskastell Myd(---)/Gheriat el-Garbia am limes Tripolitanus (Libyen), I: Forschungsgeschichte, Vermessung, Prospektionen und Funde 2009–2010.* Wiesbaden: Reichert Verlag, 155–214.

Marichal, R. 1979. Les ostraca de Bu Njem. *Comptes rendus des séances de l'Académie des Inscriptions et Belles-Lettres* 123.3: 436–52.

Marichal, R. 1992. *Les ostraca de Bu Njem.* Tripoli: Department of Antiquities.

Marlière, E. and Torres Costa, J. 2007. Transport et stockage des denrées dans l'Afrique romaine: le rôle de l'oure et du tonneau. In A. Mrabet and J. Remesal Rodríguez (eds), *In Africa et in Hispania. Études sur l'huile africaine.* Barcelona: Publicacions i edicions de la Universitat de Barcelona, 85–106.

Mattingly, D.J. 1995. *Tripolitania.* London: Batsford.

Mattingly, D.J. (ed.) 2003. *The Archaeology of Fazzān, I. Synthesis.* London: Society for Libyan Studies.

Mattingly, D.J. (ed.) 2007. *The Archaeology of Fazzān, II. Gazetteer, Pottery and Other Finds.* London: Society for Libyan Studies.

Mattingly, D.J. (ed.) 2010. *The Archaeology of Fazzān, III. Excavations of C.M. Daniels.* London: Society for Libyan Studies.

Mattingly, D.J. 2011. *Imperialism, Power, and Identity. Experiencing the Roman Empire.* Princeton: Princeton University Press.

Mattingly, D.J. (ed.) 2013a. *The Archaeology of Fazzān, IV. Survey and Excavations at Old Jarma (Ancient Garama) Carried Out by C.M. Daniels (1962–69) and the Fazzān Project (1997–2001).* London: Society for Libyan Studies.

Mattingly, D.J. 2013b. To south and north: Saharan trade in antiquity. In H. Eckardt and S. Rippon (eds), *Living and Working in the Roman World. Essays in Honour of Michael Fulford on his 65th Birthday.* Portsmouth, RI: Journal of Roman Archaeology, 169–90.

Mattingly, D.J. 2022. Beyond barbarians: the Garamantes of the Libyan Sahara. In R.B. Hitchner (ed.), *A Companion to North Africa in Antiquity.* Hoboken, NJ: Wiley-Blackwell, 64–80.

Mattingly, D.J. 2023. *Between Sahara and Sea: Africa in the Roman Empire.* Ann Arbor, MI: University of Michigan Press.

Mattingly, D.J., Leitch, V., Duckworth, C.N., Cuénod, A., Sterry, M. and Cole, F. (eds) 2017. *Trade in the Ancient Sahara and Beyond.* Cambridge: Cambridge University Press.

Mazou, L. 2017. Nouvelles données sur les amphores d'Afrique vers la Cyrénaïque et l'Égypte. De la fin de l'époque romaine aux premiers temps de la conquête arabe. In D. Dixneuf (ed.), *LRCW 5. Late Roman Coarse Wares, Cooking Wares and Amphorae in the Mediterranean: Archaeology and Archaeometry.* Alexandria: Centre d'Études Alexandrines, 881–900.

Mitthoff, F. 2001. *Annona militaris. Die Heeresversorgung im Spätantiken Ägypten. Ein Beitrag zur Verwaltungs und Heeresgeschichte des Römischen Reiches.* Florence: Edizioni Gonnelli.

Morales, J. and Mackensen, M. 2020. Agriculture and food exchange at the late Roman Fort of Myd(---)/Gheriat el-Garbia (NW Libya): macro-botanical finds from the German Archaeological Missions of 2009 and 2010. In S. Guédon (ed.), *Vivre, circuler et échanger sur la bordure septentrionale du Sahara. Antiquité-époque moderne.* Bordeaux: Ausonius Éditions, 203–22.

Mori, L. (ed.) 2013. *Life and Death of a Rural Village in Garamantian Times. Archaeological Investigations in the Oasis of Fewet (Libyan Sahara).* Florence: All'Insegna del Giglio.

Morizot, P. 2009. Les échanges commerciaux entre la côte méditerranéenne et à l'intérieur du Maghreb au IIe siècle vus au travers du tarif Zaraï. In J.-R. Gaborit (ed.), *Circulation des matières premières en Méditerranée, transferts de savoirs et de techniques. Actes du 128e Congrès national des sociétés historiques et scientifiques, 'Relations, échanges et coopération en Méditerranée' (Bastia, 2003).* Paris: Éditions du CTHS, 158–71.

Noeske, H.-C. 2021. Fundmünzen. In M. Mackensen, *Das severische Vexillationskastell Myd(---)/Gheriat el-Garbia am limes Tripolitanus (Libyen), I: Forschungsgeschichte, Vermessung, Prospektionen und Funde 2009–2010.* Wiesbaden: Reichert Verlag, 229–34.

Pelling, R. 2013. The archaeobotanical remains. In D.J. Mattingly (ed.), *The Archaeology of Fazzān, IV. Survey and Excavations at Old Jarma (Ancient Garama) Carried Out by C.M. Daniels (1962–69) and the Fazzān Project (1997–2001).* London: Society for Libyan Studies, 473–94.

Rebuffat, R. 1966–67. Bu Njem 1967. *Libya Antiqua* 3–4: 49–138.

Rebuffat, R. 1969–70a. Bu Njem 1968. *Libya Antiqua* 6–7: 9–105.

Rebuffat, R. 1969–70b. Bu Njem 1970. *Libya Antiqua* 6–7: 107–66.

Rebuffat, R. 1974–75. Bu Njem 1971. *Libya Antiqua* 11–12: 189–241.

Rebuffat, R. 1976–77. Bu Njem 1972. *Libya Antiqua* 13–14: 37–78.

Rebuffat, R. 1977. Une zone militaire et sa vie économique: le limes de Tripolitaine. In A. Chastagnol, C. Nicolet and H. van Effenterre (eds), *Armées et fiscalité dans le monde antique. Actes du colloque (Paris, 14–16 octobre 1976)*. Paris: Éditions du CNRS, 395–419.

Rebuffat, R. 1989. Notes sur le camp romain de Gholaia (Bu Njem). *Libyan Studies* 20: 155–67.

Rebuffat, R. 1997. Les marques d'amphores de Bu Njem. *Libya Antiqua* n.s. 3: 163–73.

Rebuffat, R. 2000. L'armée romaine à Gholaia. In G. Alföldy, B. Dobson and W. Eck (eds), *Kaiser, Heer und Gesellschaft in der Römischen Kaiserzeit. Gedenkschrift für Eric Birley.* Stuttgart: Franz Steiner Verlag, 227–59.

Revilla, V. 2010. Ánforas africanas del primer cuarto del siglo III d.C. del Monte Testaccio (campañas 1998–1999). In J.M. Blázquez Martínez and J. Remesal Rodríguez (eds), *Estudios sobre el Monte Testaccio (Roma), V.* Barcelona: Publicacions i edicions de la Univrsitat de Barcelona, 397–413.

Schallmayer, E., Eibl, K., Ott, J., Preuß, G. and Wittkopf, E. 1990. *Der römische Weihebezirk von Osterburken, I. Corpus der griechischen und lateinischen Beneficiarier-Inschriften des Römischen Reiches.* Stuttgart: Theiss Verlag.

Schimmer, F. 2011. Nördliche praetentura des Kastells. In M. Mackensen, Das severische Vexillationskastell Myd(---) und die spätantike Besiedlung in Gheriat el-Garbia (Libyen). Bericht über die Kampagne im Frühjahr 2010. *Mitteilungen des Deutschen Archäologischen Instituts, Römische Abteilung* 117: 313–27.

Schimmer, F. 2012a. New evidence for a Roman fort and vicus at Mizda (Tripolitania). *Libyan Studies* 43: 33–39.

Schimmer, F. 2012b. Amphorae from the Roman fort of Gheriat el-Garbia/Libya. *Rei Cretariae Romanae Fautorum Acta* 42: 319–25.

Schmid, S. 2018. Gasr Isawi. Fortified farm and hilltop settlement in the Wadi N'f'd, Tripolitania. *Libya Antiqua* n.s. 11: 71–106.

Schmid, S. and Weber, M. 2010. Mittelkaiserzeitliche Sigillata. In M. Mackensen, Das severische Vexillationskastell Myd(---)/Gheriat el-Garbia am limes Tripolitanus (Libyen). Bericht über die Kampagne 2009. *Mitteilungen des Deutschen Archäologischen Instituts, Römische Abteilung* 116: 398–406.

Schörle, K. 2012. Saharan trade in Classical antiquity. In J. McDougall and J. Scheele (eds), *Saharan Frontiers: Space and Mobility in Northwest Africa.* Bloomington, IN: Indiana University Press, 58–72.

Sheldrick, N. 2021. *Building the Countryside. Rural Architecture and Settlement in Tripolitania during the Roman and Late Antique Periods.* London: Society for Libyan Studies.

Trousset, P. 2002–03. Le tarif de Zaraï: essai sur les circuits commerciaux dans la zone présaharienne. *Antiquités Africaines* 38–39: 355–73.

Van der Veen, M., Grant, A. and Barker, G. 1996. In G. Barker (ed.), *Farming the Desert. The UNESCO Libyan Valleys Archaeological Survey. Volume 1: Synthesis.* London: Society for Libyan Studies, 227–63.

Van der Veen, M., Bouchaud, C., Cappers, R. and Newton, C. 2018. Roman life in the Eastern Desert of Egypt: food, imperial power and geopolitics. In J.-P. Brun, T. Faucher, B. Redon and S. Sidebotham (eds), *The Eastern Desert of Egypt during the Greco-Roman Period: Archaeological Reports.* Paris: Collège de France, http://books.openedition.org/cdf/5252.

Van Limbergen, D. 2018. What Romans ate and how much they ate of it. Old and new research on eating habits and dietary proportions in classical antiquity. *Revue belge de philologie et d'histoire* 96.3: 1049–92.

Van Neer, W. 1997. Archaeozoological data on the food provisioning of Roman settlements in the Eastern Desert of Egypt. *Archaeozoologia* 9: 137–54.

Vaz Pinto, I., Morais, R., Fabião, C., Oliveira, C. and Gabriel, S. 2021. Lusitanian amphora contents. In D. Bernal Casasola, M. Bonifay, M. Pecci and V. Leitch (eds), *Roman Amphora Contents. Reflecting on the Maritime Trade of Foodstuffs in Antiquity (in Honour of Miguel Beltrán Lloris).* Oxford: Archaeopress, 183–204.

Vossen, I. and Groot, M. 2009. Barley and horses: surplus and demand in the civitas Batavorum. In M. Driessen, S. Heeren, J. Hendriks, F. Kemmers and R. Visser (eds), *TRAC 2008. Proceedings of the Eighteenth Annual Theoretical Roman Archaeology Conference (Amsterdam 2008).* Oxford: Oxbow Books, 85–100.

Walas, A.H. 2022. New perspectives on the Roman military base at Bu Njem. *Libyan Studies* 53: 48–60.

Weber, M. and Schmid, S. 2012. Supplying a desert garrison. Pottery from the Roman fort at Gheriat el-Garbia (Libya). *Rei Cretariae Romanae Fautorum Acta* 42: 327–35.

Wilson, A.I. 2012. Saharan trade in the Roman period: short-, medium- and long-distance trade networks. *Azania* 47: 409–49.

Wilson, A.I. 2017a. Trade across Rome's southern frontier. The Sahara and the Garamantes. In A.I. Wilson and A.K. Bowman (eds), *Trade, Commerce, and the State in the Roman World.* Oxford: Oxford University Press, 599–624.

Wilson, A.I. 2017b. Saharan exports to the Roman world. In D.J. Mattingly, V. Leitch, C.N. Duckworth, A. Cuénod, M. Sterry and F. Cole (eds), *Trade in the Ancient Sahara and Beyond.* Cambridge: Cambridge University Press, 189–208.

Zanker, P. 2008. Selbstdarstellung am Rand der Libyschen Wüste. Die Reliefs an den Häuplings-Mausoleen in der Nordnekropole von Ghirza. In F. Pirson and U. Wulf-Rheidt (eds), *Austausch und Inspiration. Kulturkontakt als Impuls architektonischer Innovation. Kolloquium vom 28.–30.4.2006 in Berlin anlässlich des 65. Geburtstages von Adolf Hoffmann.* Mainz: Philipp von Zabern, 214–26.

Ziegler, S. and Mackensen, M. 2014. Spätantike Ostraka aus Gheriat el-Garbia (al-Qaryāt al-Garbīyah) in der Provinz Tripolitana (Libyen). Belege für eine regionale Variante des Punischen. *Mitteilungen des Deutschen Archäologischen Instituts, Römische Abteilung* 120: 313–40.

Chapter 8

THE RELIGIOUS IDENTITY OF ROMAN SOLDIERS IN TRIPOLITANIA: ARCHAEOLOGICAL AND EPIGRAPHIC EVIDENCE

Sebastian Schmid

Introduction

Religion, religious ceremonies and cultic acts played an important role in the Roman army, but also in the lives of the individual soldiers. The worship of the same gods, the celebration of the same festivals and of the imperial cult by the legions and auxiliaries stationed across the Roman Empire expressed the loyalty of the troops towards Rome and the emperor as their supreme commander. The festivals and rituals celebrated throughout the Empire also led to a strengthening of the sense of togetherness, to the formation of a communal identity and to the disciplining of the troops.

In this 'official' army religion, which was binding for all parts of the Roman army, the imperial cult in particular played a decisive role, in addition to the worship of Roman state gods such as Mars or Jupiter. This is impressively shown by the so-called '*Feriale Duranum*' – a papyrus containing a festival calendar of the *cohors XX Palmyrenorum*, which was found in the 1930s at Dura Europos in Syria (see Haynes 2013, 198–206, with references). On the papyrus, which can be dated to the reign of Severus Alexander (222–35 CE), 27 of the 41 entries refer to the imperial cult. In addition to the reigning ruler and his family, numerous deified emperors and empresses were also commemorated with sacrifices. In addition, there are individual (Roman metropolitan) festivals such as the Quinquatria or the Vestalia. Of great symbolic importance for the Roman army were also the various insignia, especially the eagles of the legions.

Alongside the *Feriale Duranum*, inscriptions are the main source of information on religious practices in the Roman army. Inscriptions that can be referred to the official Roman army religion usually mention the respective units alone or together with their commanding officer. However, there is also a large number of inscriptions set up by individuals – ordinary soldiers, non-commissioned officers, and officers. These are to be seen as an expression of the personal need for protection and security by the gods and thus of the private cults of individual soldiers. The gods honoured in this way were in part local deities that were worshipped in the vicinity of the soldiers' stationing place. But soldiers also set up inscriptions in honour of gods from their regions of origin. These cults from their homeland were also important for entire units and defined their collective identity, as can be seen in particular in the case of some Syrian units. In addition, Roman state gods and emperors were worshipped by soldiers as private individuals. A clear distinction between official army religion and private cult is therefore not always possible.[1]

In Tripolitania, apart from a few auxiliary units, mainly detachments of the *legio III Augusta* were stationed, whose main fortress was at Lambaesis in Numidia. This chapter examines what sources are available to understand the religious identity of the soldiers stationed in Tripolitania, and whether differences between auxiliary and legionary soldiers can be ascertained. In addition, it explores whether (and to what extent) the worship of gods at Lambaesis and in the forts and fortlets on the *limes Tripolitanus* differed.

[1] On the religion of the Roman army, see in general Stoll 2007; Haynes 2013, 189–237, with further bibliography.

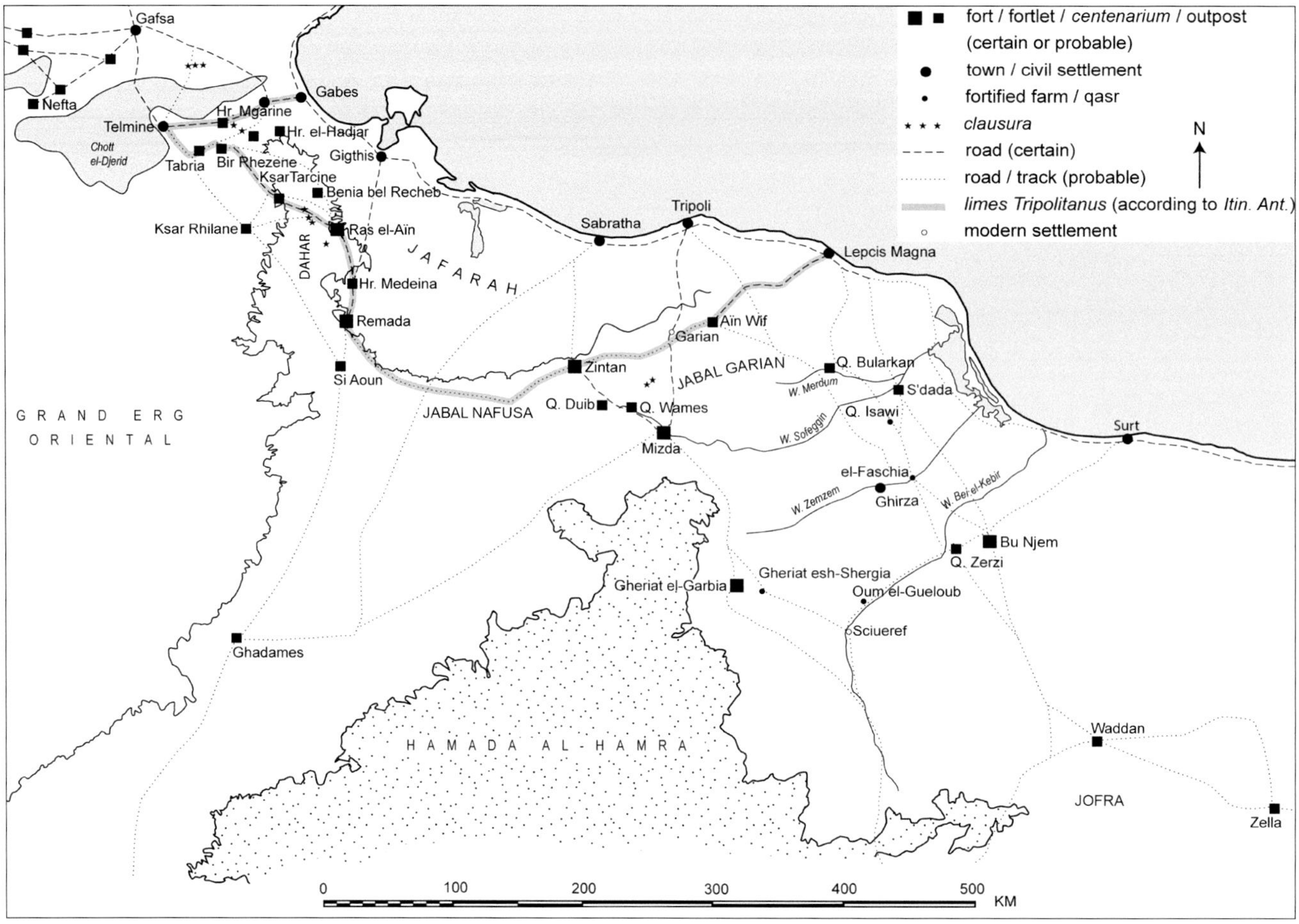

Fig. 8.1. Mid-imperial and late Roman military and civilian sites in Tripolitania (after Mackensen 2022, 182, fig. 1).

Evidence for the religious identity of Roman soldiers in Tripolitania

For the question of which deities the Roman soldiers stationed in forts and fortlets in Tripolitania worshipped, inscriptions are the most important source. Other artefacts which could be connected to the religious identity are missing. Excavations of sanctuaries in or around Roman forts, which would allow conclusions to be drawn about the gods worshipped there, as well as about their builders and worshippers, have hardly ever taken place. However, particularly worthy of mention are the investigations in the 1960–70s at Gholaia/Bu Njem by René Rebuffat, who uncovered not only several cult sites inside the fort, but also on the hills around it. Excavations were also carried out recently at Gheriat el-Garbia (2009–10), where several buildings to the east of the fort were investigated (on both sites see Mackensen, Chapter 6, with bibliography). Furthermore, the fortlet of Tisavar/Ksar Rhilane was excavated in the late nineteenth century. However, a building inside the fortlet that was referred to as a sanctuary is hardly known. There were other cult rooms outside the fortification, which have been described, but their ground plans are not known.

In Tripolitania, the Roman army built several forts, especially in the late second and third centuries CE, in which detachments (*vexillationes*) of the *legio III Augusta* were stationed (Fig. 8.1). These include the forts of Myd(---)/Gheriat el-Garbia, Gholaia/Bu Njem, and possibly Cidamus/Ghadames. However, the exact location and size of the latter site are not known, and it may have been only a fortlet. In addition to these vexillation forts, there were some forts that housed auxiliary units: Talalati/Ras el-Aïn Tlalet; Tillibari/Remada; Thenteos (probably Edref near Zintan); and Secedi, which is known from ostraca from Bu Njem but has not been yet located. Another fort is assumed because of its geographical location at present-day Mizda; however, it is unclear which unit might have been stationed here. So far, no inscriptions or other finds are known from Secedi, Talalati, Thenteos, and Mizda that would point to the deities worshipped by soldiers there.[2]

In addition to these larger forts, which ranged in size from 0.8 to 2.5 ha, there were several fortlets and outposts in Tripolitania, some of which were occupied by legionaries (for instance, Vezereos/Sidi Mohammed ben Aïssa near Bir Rhezene, and Tisavar/Ksar Rhilane), others by auxiliaries (probably Si Aoun). Other

[2] On these forts see Trousset 1974, 98–102; Mattingly 1995, 87–88, 95–98; Mackensen 2022, 190–95; Schimmer 2012.

inscriptions that provide clues about the religious identity of Roman soldiers come from smaller sites in the hinterland, such as Aïn el-Avenia, where fortlets or outposts are also suspected on the basis of inscriptions, and from the large coastal towns (for a general overview see Mackensen, Chapter 6).

Vexillation forts and auxiliary forts

Myd(---)/Gheriat el-Garbia

The largest, and therefore probably the most important, fort in Tripolitania was located at an oasis at Gheriat el-Garbia, about 280 km south of Tripoli. Only the initials Myd(---) are known of the ancient name of this place. Here, between 198 and 201 CE, a vexillation of the *legio III Augusta* built a fortification covering more than 2 ha (Fig. 8.2), which housed between 600 and 800 legionaries until 238 CE. The composition of the garrison after the dissolution of the legion is unclear. It is possible that soldiers of the *cohors I Syrorum sagittariorum milliaria* were stationed at Gheriat el-Garbia afterwards. It is assumed that from about 240 CE the fort was the headquarters of the regional commander for the *limes Tripolitanus* (*praepositus limitis Tripolitanae*). It was abandoned around 275–80 CE, but after a hiatus of about a century it was again occupied by the Roman military.[3]

Archaeological investigations carried out by Michael Mackensen in 2009–10 concentrated mainly on the excellently preserved fortifications. However, parts of the headquarters building (*principia*) were also uncovered inside the fort, including the central room of the rear row of rooms. This is to be regarded as the fort's shrine (*sacellum* or *aedes*). No inscriptions or statues have survived *in situ* in the *principia*, but an inscription on a statue base was found recycled into a Late Antique wall in the area of the main gate (*IRT2021* 1135). Its original setting is unknown, but it is possible that it came from the *principia*. The statue was dedicated by the commander of the unit, a centurion of the *legio III Augusta*, together with the soldiers of the vexillation of Myd(---) to the mother of the emperor Severus Alexander, Julia Mamaea. The soldiers refer to themselves in the inscription as devoted to their divine power and majesty (*devoti numini maiestatique eorum*). On the poorly preserved sides of the base are numerous names of the soldiers who may have taken part in the ceremony associated with the consecration. Among them are possibly also members of other (auxiliary) units (Mackensen 2010a, 441–47). It should be considered that the dedication of the statue took place in the second half of August, possibly in the year 222/223 CE, in honour of the birthday of the emperor's mother, which was celebrated throughout the Empire, as the *Feriale Duranum* (2.26) shows (on the dating of the inscription, see Mackensen 2010a, 444). No other references to gods worshipped in the fort are known.

As part of the UNESCO Libyan Valleys Archaeological Survey (ULVS), in 1981 a British team investigated not only the fort but also its surroundings. On a plateau about 220 m east of the fortification and about 17 m above it, they discovered five buildings labelled GG2–6 (Fig. 8.2), some of which were interpreted as sanctuaries (Mattingly 1996, 98–102, fig. 14.1). Of these, GG2 was excavated subsequently by the German mission in 2009–10, and GG4 was cleared of debris (see Mackensen 2016, 94–96). The best known building GG2 was 18 m long and about 14 m wide (Fig. 8.3). The eastern wall featured an apse; to its south, the remains of a small annexed building were documented. The main entrance to GG2 was to the west and led into a courtyard surrounded by columns or pillars (13.5 × 8.8 m). Between the outer

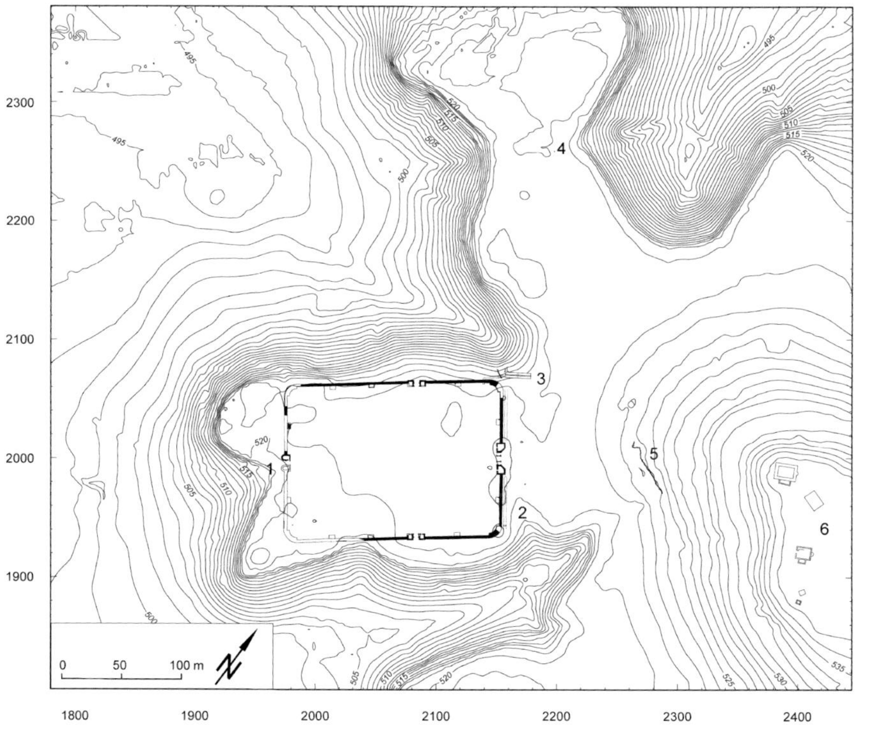

Fig. 8.2. Gheriat el-Garbia: Severan fort with sanctuaries on the plateau to the north-east of it. 1: South-west access; 2: East access; 3: Double cistern; 4: North access; 5: Limestone quarry; 6: Sanctuaries (after Mackensen 2016, 87, fig. 4).

[3] On the history of the fort see Mackensen 2021a, 257–58; 2022, 186–89; Mackensen, Chapter 6. On the sanctuaries see now Schmid 2024.

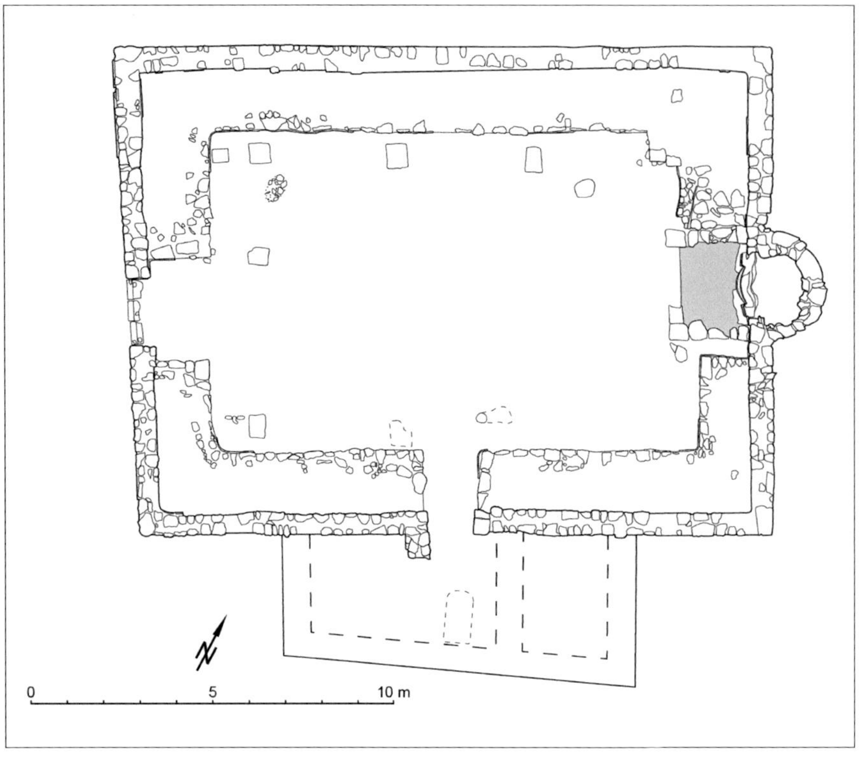

Fig. 8.3. Gheriat el-Garbia: temple GG2 (image F. Schimmer/S. Schmid, project Gheriat el-Garbia).

walls of the building and the columns, a surrounding podium (1.4–1.5 m wide and about 50 cm high) was recorded. This podium was interrupted at three points: at the main entrance to the west, at a pathway leading to the annex building, and in front of the apse. Here, another low podium was constructed, about 3 m long and 2 m wide and raised c. 20 cm above the level of the inner courtyard. Its western corners were formed by two of the columns or pillars of the surrounding colonnade. The apse itself was separated from the podium by a moulded stone, identified as a base. The apse consisted of solid masonry up to a height of 0.5 m. A statue probably stood on the base formed by this, although no remains have survived. In terms of its ground plan, building GG4 is very similar to GG2, being c. 13 m long and 10 m wide, and was also entered from the west. The building had an apse, an annex to the south and an open courtyard, which was surrounded at least partially by a podium. GG3, on the other hand, had neither an apse nor any annexed buildings. It could be entered from the south, but its interior structure is unknown. The two other buildings GG5 und GG6 are much smaller, with sides measuring 3 to 5 m. Of these, only the edges of the outer walls were documented.

Because of the position of GG2 and its orientation towards the main axis of the vexillation fort leading through the main gate (*porta praetoria*), it seems obvious that it was built when the fort already existed. Furthermore, small fragments of an inscription were found recently inside GG2, mentioning the emperor Septimius Severus. These chronological hints lead to the assumption that GG2 was built between 201 CE, when the fort was constructed, and 211 CE, when Septimius Severus died. The other buildings on the plateau cannot be dated, but a connection with the first occupation of the fort in the third century CE seems obvious. For how long GG2–6 were used is unclear. During a survey in 2009, small fragments of Late Antique Tripolitanian red slip ware and lamps were found, which prove that the plateau was at least visited during the second half of the fourth and the first half of the fifth century CE (Mackensen 2021a, 179–82).

Mattingly (1996, 98–102) interpreted the buildings GG2–4 as temples, and GG5–6 as possible funerary cairns. The location on a hill above the fort and the ground plans of the buildings GG2 and GG4 speak for an interpretation as sanctuaries, resembling other sacred buildings that can be clearly interpreted as such on the basis of epigraphic evidence or through the associated finds, for example at Ghirza (Brogan and Smith 1984, 80–92) and Bu Njem (see below). GG3, GG5, and GG6 have not been investigated in detail yet, but their location near GG2 and GG4 suggests that they also served a similar cultic function. Inside GG3, a large capital was recovered, which belonged to a column about 5 m tall. One could imagine a single honorary column set up on the plateau, perhaps with a statue on top of it. The orientation of GG2 towards the main gate of the fort and the chronology of the sanctuaries suggest that the temples were somehow linked to the fort. Furthermore, it seems hard to imagine that the army allowed civilians to construct buildings that towered above their fort. As a consequence, it is highly likely that the vexillation of the *legio III Augusta* at Gheriat el-Garbia was involved in the construction of the sanctuaries (a similar situation can be seen at Bu Njem: see below).

It is not clear which gods were worshipped in these sanctuaries. The ground plans of GG2 and GG4, especially the podiums or benches along their outer walls, are not a common feature of temples dedicated to gods of the Roman pantheon. However, some sanctuaries at Ghirza and Bu Njem have comparable structures. At least the temples at Bu Njem were dedicated to Mars Canappher and Jupiter Hammon, as inscriptions show. Vanammon was worshipped in another smaller sanctuary (see below). Apart from Jupiter Hammon, these deities – together with Mastiman and Gurzil – are interpreted as being of regional, Libyan origin (Mattingly

1995, 167–68). Due to the similar ground plans, it seems likely that these local gods were also worshipped at GG2 and GG4. Furthermore, on another fragmentary inscription found outside GG2, one can read the letters [---]POLITAN, which might indicate a dedication to a [*genius regionis Tri*]*politan*(*ae*), which is so far not attested elsewhere in the region. However, a dedication to Jupiter Heliopolitanus cannot be ruled out as a possible alternative.

Gholaia/Bu Njem

About 200 km east of Gheriat el-Garbia lies the fort of Bu Njem. As at Gheriat el-Garbia, a vexillation of the *legio III Augusta* built a fort here in 201 CE, but this was only slightly more than 1 ha in size. Until 238 CE, it housed a legionary detachment of about 300–500 men, occasionally reinforced by troops composed of various units (*numerus conlatus*). After the dissolution of the legion in 238 CE, the vexillation probably remained on site, but under the designation of *vexillatio Golensis* and with a changed status. The toponymic term *Golensis* refers to the ancient name of Bu Njem, Gholaia, which is attested on inscriptions (see, for instance: *AE* 1972, 679 = *IRT2021* 1058; *AE* 1976, 698 = *IRT2021* 1064; *AE* 1976, 700 = *IRT2021* 1066). The fort was evacuated in the early 260s CE, or perhaps as late as the 270s CE (Mattingly 1995, 95–97; Mackensen 2008). A few Late Antique finds prove that the site was also used in this period. However, there is no evidence for a new stationing of Roman military forces (Mackensen 2021b, 130; 2022, 186).

At Bu Njem, Rebuffat carried out excavations from 1967 to 1980. In particular, the buildings in the central part of the fort were investigated: the *principia*, the *praetorium*, the *horreum*, and the baths. Parts of the barracks in the front area of the fort (*praetentura*) and the fortifications were also uncovered. In addition, investigations were carried out in the civilian settlement around the fort. Outside this settlement, several buildings, mostly located on small hills, were identified as temples. A large number of inscriptions, graffiti, and ostraca were discovered during the excavations. These provide unique clues not only for the development of the fort and the organization of Roman border control in Tripolitania, but also about the gods worshipped on site. Several fragments of an inscription were found in the baths of the fort, among other places (*IRT2021* 1059; Rebuffat 1990, 149). Originally, however, it probably stood in the headquarters building (*principia*). It was erected in honour of the supreme god of the state, Jupiter Optimus Maximus, and for the health and safety of emperor Maximinus Thrax and his son. A centurion of the *legio III Augusta*, who was also the commander of the unit at Gholaia (*praepositus vexillationis*), and the vexillation consecrated this *ara cerei*. Consecrations of such altars are also known from Castellum Dimmidi (Algeria); according to the inscriptions there, they took place on 3 May, the end of the feast of Rosalia mentioned in the *Feriale Duranum*. Two other inscriptions from the legionary fortress of Lambaesis and from Menaa (the latter set up by a vexillation of the *legio III Augusta*) do not mention an *ara cerei*, but they do mention the date of 3 May. A connection is therefore obvious. The interpretation of this *ara cerei* is unclear; in some cases an interpretation as an altar of Cerus or Ceres has been suggested. More likely, however, it is a translation of the term *cereus*, referring to a candle that was placed on the altar and lit on the feast day of 3 May (Schmidt Heidenreich 2013, 56–58, with note 131).

About 20 m east of the *principia*, the fragment of an inscription was found on which the *genius vexillationis* is named and the remains of imperial titles (IMP AVG) are also preserved (*IRT2021* 1228; Rebuffat 1990, 150). The inscription may therefore have been set up for an unknown emperor and the patron god of the detachment stationed at Gholaia. In addition to these two inscriptions, a statue of a female deity wearing a helmet and a herm was also documented in the headquarters building. Furthermore, a small marble statuette of Venus *pudica* may have come from there (Rebuffat 1990, 157).

To the right of the *principia* was the house of the unit commander (*praetorium*), to which a smaller building with pedestals was attached. Besides a statue base, two altars with inscriptions were discovered in it, which is why the building was interpreted as a chapel. One inscription was dedicated by a centurion of the *legio III Augusta* to the *genius Gholaiae* and to the safety of the emperors on the day of the arrival of the Roman army at Bu Njem (*IRT2021* 1066; Rebuffat 1990, 138, 150; Brouquier-Reddé 1992, 178). Apparently, it was considered necessary to secure the protection of the local deity as quickly as possible. The second inscription dates from the time after the disbandment of the legion in 238 CE (*IRT2021* 1065; Rebuffat 1990, 138, 150; Brouquier-Reddé 1992, 178–79). It was erected by a *decurio*, an officer of mounted auxiliary units and commander of the fort during this phase. It is dedicated to the *numen praesens*, the divinity who is present. It is possible that this divinity is also the *genius Gholaiae*.

Numerous inscriptions were found in the baths on the left side of the *principia*. Particularly noteworthy is a limestone slab over 1.8 m high with an inscription of several lines in rhyme (*IRT2021* 918; Rebuffat 1990, 151), with which the commanding centurion Q. Avidius Quintianus consecrated the bath building to the goddess Salus – a deity that was responsible for personal health, but also for the welfare of the state (*Salus rei publicae*). Especially in the inhospitable environment of the Libyan pre-desert, the dedication of a bath building to this deity is self-explanatory. The inscription was placed in the *frigidarium*, and in another room a small niche was documented in which a small statue of Fortuna stood. An altar found there also names the *dea sancta Fortuna* (*IRT2021* 1230; Rebuffat 1990, 151–52; Brouquier-Reddé 1992, 179–82). In addition, a plaster plate with an inscription was discovered, which testifies to a partial restoration of the bath (*IRT2021* 1231; Rebuffat 1990, 152). On it the undefeated divinities (*numina invicta*) are invoked. The inscription was set up by a non-commissioned officer (*principalis*) with all the soldiers (*cum omne numerum militum*). Several fragments of an alabaster slab also mention a dedication to Jupiter Optimus Maximus and to the safety and security of the emperors (*IRT2021* 1322). Finally, an inscription was found in the baths, which was set up by the vexillation in honour of Septimius Severus and his sons (*IRT2021* 913).

A fragment of a bronze tablet was documented at the fort's east gate. On it were apparently written acclamations in honour of an emperor, probably Elagabalus, and of a *mater exercitus*, probably his mother Julia Soaemia (*IRT2021* 1063). The voussoir of an arch was also found in the fort, but without a more precise location, bearing a dedication to Sol Invictus (*IRT2021* 917; Rebuffat 1990, 152). The inscription was made by Peticius Pastor on the basis of a vow, but whether he was a soldier, an officer, or a civilian is unclear.

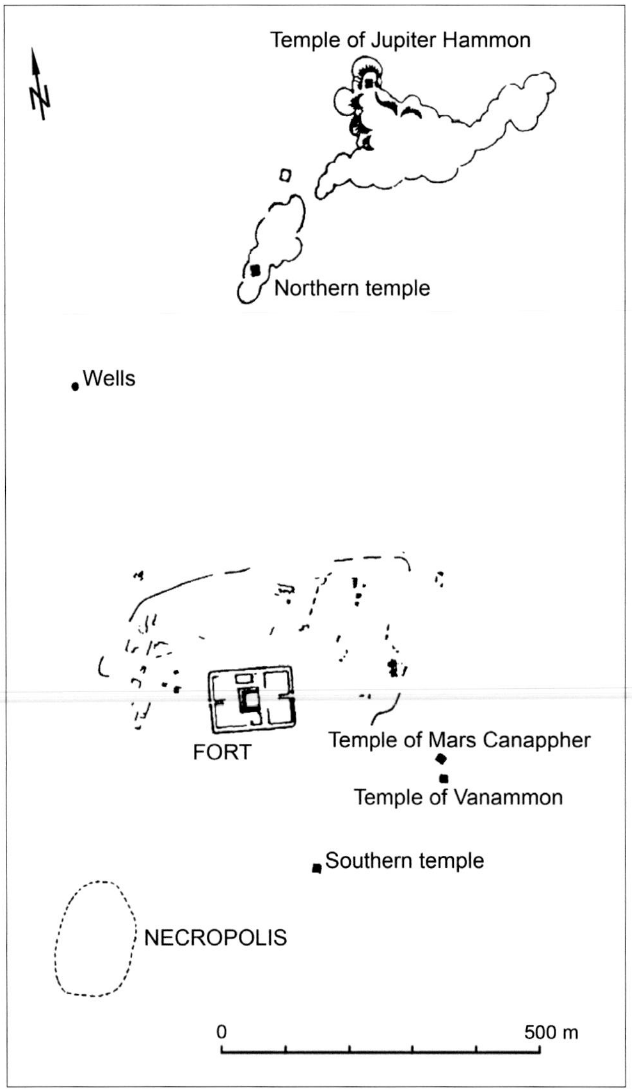

Fig. 8.4. Bu Njem: Severan fort with civil settlement and sanctuaries (after Brouquier-Reddé 1992, 149, fig. 83).

Outside the fort and the civilian settlement, c. 300 m to the south-east and c. 1 km to the north respectively, five temples were uncovered, most of which were situated on smaller mounds (Fig. 8.4). On the basis of the inscriptions found in these buildings, the gods to whom they were dedicated are known for three of these sanctuaries. To the south-east was the sanctuary of Mars Canappher (Fig. 8.5.1). It was built in 225 CE by the vexillation under the direction of the commanding officer in honour of this god and for the safety and security of the emperor Severus Alexander, his mother Julia Mamaea, and the whole imperial house. The temple has a roughly square ground plan of about 7.5 × 8 m and was entered from north-west. Opposite the entrance was a semicircular apse. Four masonry pillars supported the roof of the building; between two of these pillars and in front of the entrance to the apse, a masonry altar was documented. Inside the apse, an alabaster base was also found, probably for a (cult) statue. Between the pillars and the outer walls were masonry platforms 0.95 m wide. They could be accessed via stairs and served as a place for the worshippers to sit or lie down.[4]

Approximately 20 m south of the Mars Canappher temple, another small cult site was found, which – as an inscription shows – was dedicated to Vanammon (Fig. 8.5.2) (*IRT2021* 1092; Rebuffat 1990, 154–57; cf. Guédon 2018, 256). Once again, a centurion called Aurelius Varixen appears as the donor, but the troops he commanded are not mentioned. It could therefore be a private donation by this officer. The building was about 2.7 × 2.7 m in size and the eastern side had a semicircular apse. The interior was not accessible, at least on the ground floor. Rebuffat therefore assumed that it was a base on which a statue of a god could be placed, and it was probably protected by a kind of canopy.[5] A very similar sanctuary, measuring 4.2 × 4.2 m, was found slightly west of the two mentioned above and 200 m south of the fort. In contrast to the temple of Vanammon, it did not have an apse, but rather a niche on the west side (Fig. 8.5.3). Again, it was not accessible on the ground floor. Due to the lack of an inscription, it is unclear which deity the building was dedicated to. Rebuffat (1990, 129, 142, fig. 12; see also Brouquier-Reddé 1992, 159–60) called it 'Temple Sud' and referred to its form and that of the temple of Vanammon as 'temple-blocs'.

[4] Rebuffat 1976–77, 51–54; Brouquier-Reddé 1992, 156–59; Guédon 2018, 255. On the inscription, see *IRT2021* 1057; Rebuffat 1990, 154.

[5] Rebuffat 1990, 130, 142–43, fig. 13. See also Brouquier-Reddé 1992, 155–56; Guédon 2018, 255.

Fig. 8.5. Bu Njem. 1: Temple of Mars Canappher; 2: Temple of Vanammon; 3: Southern temple (after Rebuffat 1990, 129–30, 132, figs 12–13, 15).

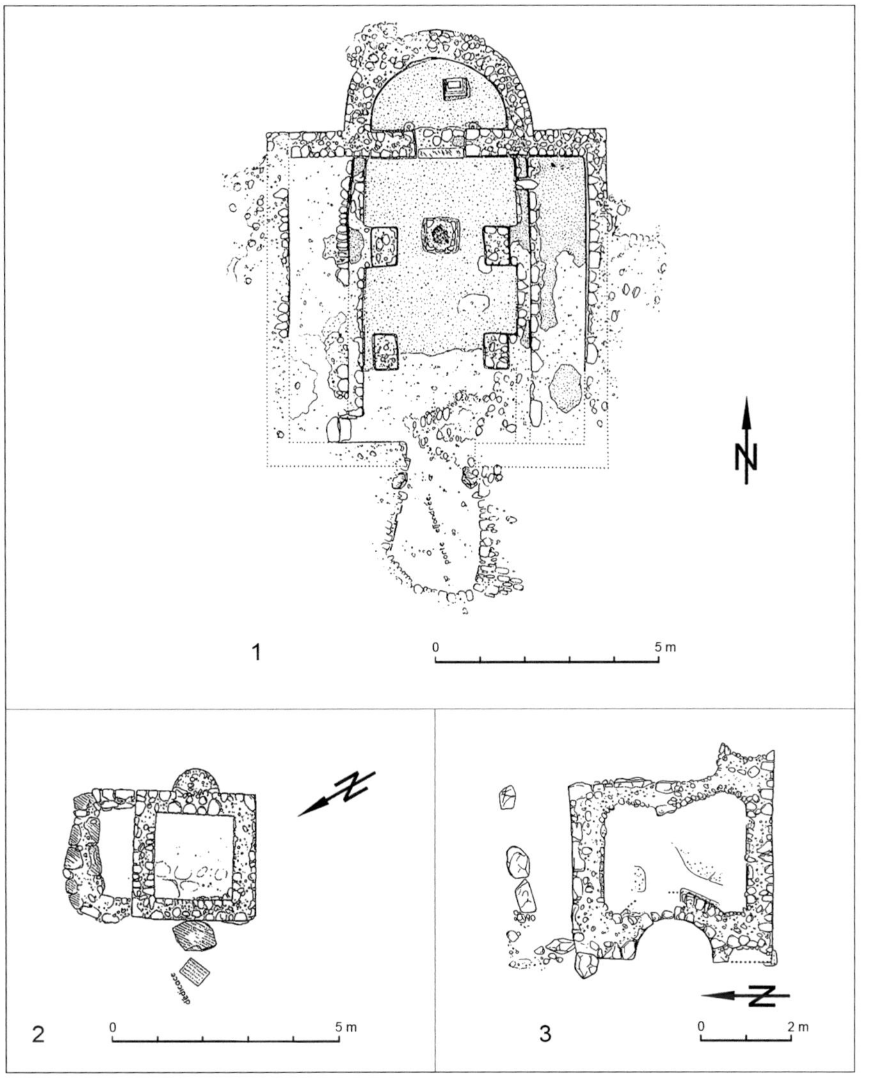

Another sanctuary was uncovered on a small hill about 1 km north of the fort (Fig. 8.6.1). There was a walled area measuring about 11 × 11 m, which could be entered from the south. Opposite the entrance on the north wall was the *cella* with a vestibule in front. The building was surrounded by a portico, which rested on masonry pillars. Between the pillars and the outer wall there was a raised pedestal, as in the temple of Mars Canappher. Outside the precinct, a masonry altar was uncovered. A little to the east of it, another building was found, which was probably used for the preparation of (sacrificial) food. The temple was built in 205 CE, as attested by an inscription at the entrance to the *cella* (*IRT2021* 1064). The vexillation of the *legio III Augusta* appears as the builder. Another inscription, which was not found *in situ* but on the slope of the hill, names the god to whom the temple was dedicated: Jupiter Hammon (Rebuffat 1990, 153–54; Brouquier-Reddé 1992, 151–54; Guédon 2018, 254). Furthermore, it names the centurion Tullius Romulus as the dedicator. Possibly the same officer is behind another fragmented inscription found at the foot of the hill with the temple of Jupiter Hammon (*IRT2021* 1054; cf. *AE* 2013, 1767). This was set up in honour of Geta and his mother and the entire imperial house, and it is likely that Septimius Severus and Caracalla were also originally named on the inscription. Unfortunately, the name of the dedicator has not survived. However, the rare designation of the dedicator with the rank *maioriarius*, which Tullius Romulus also bears on the inscription mentioned above (*centurio ex maioriarius*), the place of discovery, and the dating suggest that this inscription may also have been set up in honour (and for the security and safety?) of the Severan imperial house by Tullius Romulus. From the temple of Jupiter Hammon comes a coin of the period 330/331 CE and two Late Antique Tripolitanian lamps, demonstrating that the sanctuary was still visited in Late Antiquity. However, it is unclear whether it was still used as such at this time.[6]

Approximately 300 m south of the Jupiter Hammon temple, another sanctuary located on a hill was uncovered (Fig. 8.6.2). It consists of a 12 × 13.5 m walled area that was entered from the south. To the north, opposite the entrance, is a roughly square *cella* with a vestibule in front. A statue base was documented inside the *cella*. Once again, a narrow masonry pedestal ran along the outer wall of the precinct. No inscriptions were found in the temple or in its surroundings, and it is therefore unclear which deity was worshipped in it. Rebuffat called it the 'Temple Nord', and on the basis of the associated finds a date in the third century CE seems probable (Rebuffat 1976–77, 54–56; 1990, 126; Brouquier-Reddé 1992, 148–51).

Graffiti naming Neptune, Venus, and Victoria were found in the so-called 'Bâtiment aux Niches' in the civilian settlement. In addition, there are incised drawings of Victoria and Venus as well as a lightning bolt (Rebuffat 1990, 125–26). However, these inscriptions and depictions cannot be definitely linked to the Roman military. With regard to the numerous ostraca from Bu Njem, these give no indication of gods

[6] Rebuffat 1987, 85, 89, fig. 12; 1990, 147. On the use of the temples after the withdrawal of the garrison at Gholaia, see Guédon 2018, 256.

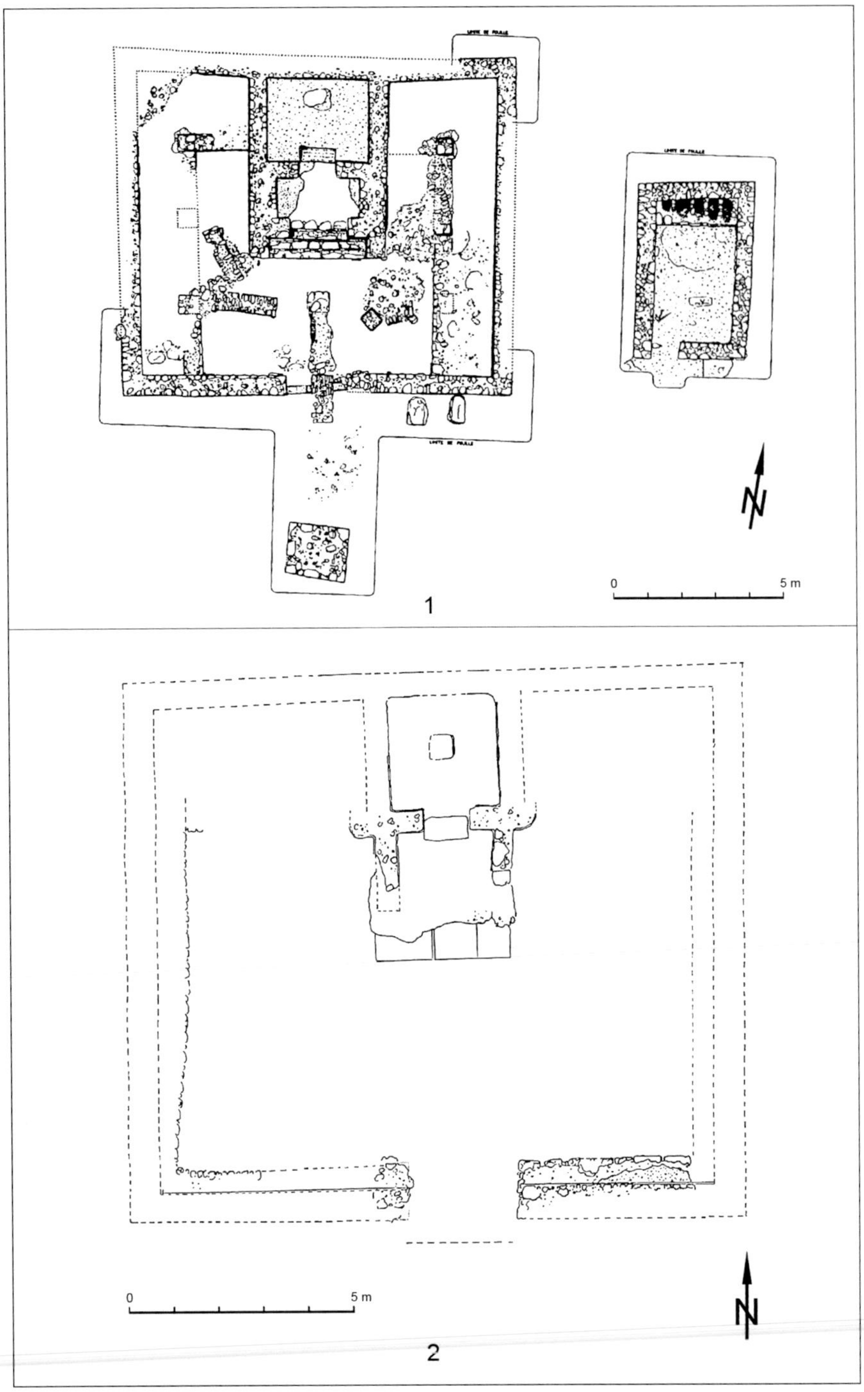

Fig. 8.6. Bu Njem. 1: Temple of Jupiter Hammon; 2: Northern temple (after Rebuffat 1990, 131, 133, figs 14, 16).

inscriptions attest to the presence of soldiers of the *legio III Augusta* in this place, which was called Cidamus in antiquity. However, it has not yet been possible to locate the fort they probably built in Severan times. Its size is therefore just as unknown as the number of legionaries stationed there. Whether it was a fort comparable to Gheriat el-Garbia, and especially Bu Njem, for perhaps 300–400 men, or only a fortlet remains an open question. However, the comparable position of the three forts on one of the main routes to the south suggests the presence of a larger number of soldiers.[7] An inscription from Ghadames mentions a tribute to Severus Alexander and his mother Julia Mamaea. It was set up by the vexillation of the *legio III Augusta* under their centurion (*IRT2021* 908). Another inscription gives information about the fulfilment of a vow by the soldiers stationed at Cydamae (*praetendentes Cydamis*) (*IRT2021* 907), but the deity to whom the vow was made is not preserved. Finally, an inscription by the centurion of the *legio III Augusta* M. Aurelius Ianuarius, also taking the form of a vow, names the goddess Fortuna Augusta (*IRT2021* 1109).

worshipped by the soldiers or cultic acts performed by them. Only the mention of a *laniarius*, a butcher, in a daily report for 31 August could be associated with celebrations in connection with the birthday of Commodus (Marichal 1992, 98–99; note that *IRT2021* 1510 translates *laniarius* with 'wool-worker'). An ox was sacrificed for the emperor on this day, as the *Feriale Duranum* (3.1) attests.

Cidamus/Ghadames

Another vexillation fort was located in the oasis town of Ghadames, about 400 km south of Gabes. Several

Tillibari/Remada

An auxiliary unit (*cohors II Flavia Afrorum*) was stationed in the fort of Tillibari, about 150 km south of Gigthis. This is attested by an inscription dated to the year 197 CE (*AE* 1975, 870), which refers to the reconstruction of a building that had collapsed due to age (*vetustate dilapsa*). The builder was the commander (*praefectus*) of the *cohors II Flavia Afrorum*. Archaeological investigations at Remada started as early as the nineteenth century and uncovered the defence walls and small parts of the interior construction. Several building phases could be distinguished, whereby according to Mattingly the shape of the

[7] On Ghadames see Le Bohec 1989, 450; Rebuffat 1994; Mattingly 1995, 97.

gate towers indicates that the fort was built in Hadrianic times. It was evidently rebuilt in the Severan period and was still occupied by the *cohors II Flavia Afrorum* in Late Antiquity (Trousset 1974, 114–18; Mattingly 1995, 90–92; Mackensen 2021b, 125). The building mentioned in the inscription is called *aedes* and should therefore be interpreted as a sanctuary. However, it is unclear whether this refers to a temple dedicated to a specific deity – in the fort or in the civil settlement – or perhaps to the shrine inside the fort (*sacellum/aedes*). The lack of mention of a specific deity could point to the latter possibility.

Fortlets

The majority of fortlets and outposts along the *limes Tripolitanus* have hardly been archaeologically investigated. Evidence for the worship of gods by the soldiers stationed there is largely lacking. Exceptions are Vezereos/Sidi Mohammed ben Aïssa and Tisavar/Ksar Rhilane. At least the ground plans of the fortlets erected there are known and there are some inscriptions (see also Mackensen, Chapter 6). Further inscriptions were found at Si Aoun and Aïn Wif, but the military buildings located there are almost unknown archaeologically.

Vezereos/Sidi Mohammed ben Aïssa

The fortlet of Vezereos, about 0.25 ha in size, is located c. 70 km south-west of Gabes. So far, only its defence walls are known, while the inner buildings are not. However, there are indications of an extensive civilian settlement around it. An inscription from the year 201 CE (*AE* 1909, 151) mentions repairs to the fortlet, and it is therefore assumed that it had been built under Commodus, perhaps even earlier. It was probably occupied, with alterations, until the first third of the fifth century CE (Mattingly 1995, 80–81, 100, 137, table 4.1; Mackensen 2015; 2022, 189–90).

There are two inscriptions from Vezereos which attest to the worship of gods and the emperor at the site. A dedicatory inscription was found south-east of the fortlet (Trousset 1974, 77; *EDCS* 103000026). It mentions the donation of an altar to Minerva, but is also dedicated to the safety of the Severan imperial house. The dedicator is Iulius Zeno, an *optio* of the *legio III Augusta*. A second inscription was found inside the fortlet (Trousset 1974, 76–77; *EDCS* 08201701). It was erected in honour of the emperors Septimius Severus and Caracalla as well as Julia Domna by the vexillation of the *legio III Augusta* stationed at Vezereos. What is remarkable about this inscription are the sides of the stone, where over 300 soldiers are listed by name. Due to the size of the fortlet, they were undoubtedly not all stationed at Vezereos. Apparently the soldiers came from surrounding outposts and took part in the ceremonies associated with the erection of the inscription.

Tisavar/Ksar Rhilane

The fortlet of Tisavar is located about 35 km south-east of Vezereos. It is only 0.1 ha in size, but still very well preserved. The fortlet has a rectangular ground plan with rounded corners and could be entered through an entrance from the east. Above this entrance was a gate tower. Inside the complex was a central building with a small courtyard, which can be interpreted as the *principia*. At a later date, another room was added to the east. The barracks, storage buildings, and also the accommodation for the commander of the small unit stationed in the fortlet, on the other hand, abutted the inner side of the defence walls. On the basis of a building inscription found here (*CIL* VIII, 11048), the construction of Ksar Rhilane can be dated to the period 184–91 CE. An extensive burnt layer suggests that the building was destroyed by fire. The most recent coin is from Maximinus Daia (305–13 CE). To the east of the fort, a small building and a series of rooms with different ground plans were documented, but their function is unclear. Also outside the fort, the remains of three other buildings with niches were noted in the late nineteenth century. In contrast to the fortlet and the buildings to the east of it, however, no ground plan is known of these (Mackensen 2010b).

Several altars were found in the buildings with niches, most of them without inscriptions (Mackensen 2010b, 465–66). One, however, did have one, mentioning a dedication by a centurion of the *legio III Augusta* to the *genius* of Tisavar (Trousset 1974, 94; *EDCS* 24100103). The officer commanded a vexillation, but it is uncertain whether this was the unit stationed at Tisavar. Since the necessary space was not available to accommodate a soldier of this rank in the fort, the vexillation stationed at Tisavar was probably commanded by an officer of lower rank (an *optio* would be conceivable here: Mackensen 2010b, 462). On the basis of the altars and the inscription, the three buildings outside the fort are probably to be regarded as sanctuaries, which were at least partly used by the Roman military. However, no information is available about their ground plan and layout.

Another sanctuary – besides the *aedes*, about which little is known – was found inside the fortlet. There, in the nineteenth century, an inscription was documented above the door that led into the room, which was subsequently added to the *principia*. It names the god Jupiter Optimus Maximus Victor, to whom this room was probably dedicated. In the twentieth century, the inscription was removed and used as a door lintel (Trousset 1974, 94, fig. 27b; Mackensen 2010b, 465–66, fig. 11).

Si Aoun

Little is known about the fortlet of Si Aoun about 40 km south of Remada. Judging from the descriptions, it seems to be a similar complex with a central building as at Tisavar. A building inscription attests to its construction in 198 CE and describes it as a *praesidium*. The *cohors II Flavia Afrorum* is named as the unit responsible for its construction. Together with a *numerus collatus*, it probably also provided the garrison (Trousset 1974, 118–20; Mattingly 1995, 102; Mackensen 2021b, 113–14). Another inscription on a fragment of an altar was found in front of the east gate of the fortlet (*EDCS* 10300008), attesting to the erection of this altar in honour of Jupiter. The dedicator was Aemilius Emeritus. The *decurio* mentioned on the fortlet building inscription bears the same name; it therefore stands to reason that this was one and the same person.

Thenadassa/Aïn Wif

At Aïn Wif, 80 km south of Tripoli, Mattingly (1982) assumed the existence of two Roman military camps. They were located to the south of an extensive civilian settlement on a slightly higher plateau. One of these camps could have been up to 0.5 ha in size and had rounded corners; the other was smaller and had rectangular corners. The two inscriptions from Aïn Wif, which name military units or soldiers, can be dated to the Severan period. Mattingly, however, did not want to exclude the possibility that a fort existed at Thenadassa as early as the second century CE, perhaps under Commodus. One of these inscriptions (*IRT2021* 868) was found within the civilian settlement, about 200 m north-west of the two forts postulated by Mattingly. However, it is unclear whether it might have been transported there at a later date, perhaps as building material (Mattingly 1982, 76–77; Brouquier-Reddé 1992, 173–75). The inscription is engraved on an altar to Jupiter Optimus Maximus Dolichenus and dedicated to the safety and victory of the Severan imperial house. The dedicator is a high-rank officer of equestrian rank who was commander of the *cohors II Hamiorum* and at the same time of a vexillation of the *legio III Augusta*. This unit is not otherwise attested for Tripolitania and may have been stationed in Numidia (Mattingly 1982, 77). The presence of such a high-rank officer at Aïn Wif is surprising. Perhaps he and the troops he commanded were not permanently stationed there, but might have come to the place in the course of a special mission.

Other sites

Auru (?)/Aïn el-Avenia

From Aïn el-Avenia, a small settlement east of Zintan, some inscriptions and also brick stamps are known that name the *legio III Augusta*. It is therefore assumed that there was a military outpost in the village. However, there is no archaeological evidence of this (Mattingly 1995, 102). One of the inscriptions is a dedication to Sol Hierobolus and to the safety of the Severan imperial house (*IRT2021* 1099; Brouquier-Reddé 1992, 206). A vexillation of the *legio III Augusta* and soldiers of the *cohors I Syrorum sagittariorum* are named as dedicators.

Lepcis Magna

In addition to smaller settlements or military sites in the Tripolitanian hinterland, a dedicatory inscription is also known from Lepcis Magna, which was set up by a Roman officer (*IRT2021* 292; Brouquier-Reddé 1992, 119–21). It was found on an altar that was discovered in front of the stairway of a temple on the south side of the harbour (on the temple see Mugnai, Chapter 3). The altar was dedicated to Jupiter Optimus Maximus Dolichenus on the birthday of Septimius Severus, 11 April, and to the safety and victory of the three *Augusti* and their return to their city (Rome or Lepcis Magna?).

Conclusion

The few references to the religious identity of the soldiers on the *limes Tripolitanus* show that the official Roman army religion played an important role there. There are 13 epigraphic records of the emperor's cult. Most of these inscriptions or altars were not only dedicated to the health, safety and security of the emperors, their son(s) and wives, but also to certain gods (nine examples). Three of these are the Roman gods Jupiter Optimus Maximus and Minerva, three are the oriental gods Jupiter Dolichenus and Sol Hierobolus, two are local deities (Mars Canappher, *genius Gholaiae*), and one is the *genius vexillationis*. The worship of Roman gods is attested eight times, with Jupiter Optimus Maximus dominating with four attestations. Local gods were worshipped with similar frequency (six records). On the one hand, these appear in anonymous form as *genius* of the place (*genius Gholaiae*, *genius Tisavar*, possibly also the *genius regionis Tripolitanae* at Gheriat el-Garbia). However, Mars Canappher, Vanammon, and the Libyan Jupiter Hammon are also attested at Bu Njem (on this latter god see Brouquier-Reddé 1992, 255–65; Mattingly 1995, 168). Based on the ground plan of the sanctuaries outside the fort at Gheriat el-Garbia, these buildings were probably also dedicated to local deities.

Evidence of the worship of oriental deities is much rarer. It is striking that the dedicators of the inscriptions for Sol Hierobolus at Aïn el-Avenia and for Jupiter Dolichenus at Aïn Wif both have connections to the Roman East. At Aïn el-Avenia, in addition to a vexillation of the legion, one finds the *cohors I Syrorum sagittariorum*, at Aïn Wif the *praefectus* named there commanded the *cohors II Hamiorum*. To what extent the dedicator of the inscription for Jupiter Dolichenus at Lepcis Magna had connections to the Near East is unclear, although the corresponding altar was found in front of the probable temple of this deity. At Gheriat el-Garbia, where the interpretation of an inscription for Jupiter Heliopolitanus is not certain due to its fragmentary state of preservation, the presence of (parts of the) *cohors I Syrorum sagittariorum* is expected after the disbandment of the *legio III Augusta* in 238 CE (Mattingly 1995, 83, 87; Mackensen 2010a, 448). Here, too, the worship of an oriental deity could be explained by the unit stationed in the fort. However, the inscription dates to the Severan period, when a vexillation of the *legio III Augusta* was stationed at Gheriat el-Garbia. Due to the lack of mention of a unit or the rank of the dedicator, it is unclear in the case of the inscription for Sol Invictus at Bu Njem whether it was set up by a soldier, by an officer of the troops stationed at the fort, or by a civilian.

Other deities are rarely attested on the *limes Tripolitanus*. The *genius vexillationis* is known once at Bu Njem, and the worship of such *genii* by units or parts of them is frequently attested elsewhere (see Stoll 2007, 462). The *numina invicta* also occur at Bu Njem. There are no references to the worship of gods popular in North Africa, such as Dea Caelestis or Saturn, or to Egyptian deities.

The dedicators are named on 20 inscriptions. Eleven times it is the commanding officer together with the unit he commands or the unit(s) themselves, without naming an individual. Nine times no unit is named, but an officer (usually a centurion) or a non-commissioned officer (*principalis*) is. Ordinary soldiers do not appear as dedicators. Collective regimental dedications mentioning the unit, or the commander and the unit, concern not only the imperial cult and Roman gods, but also local deities (Mars Canappher, Jupiter Hammon, *genius Tisavar*).

The collected testimonies mainly concern soldiers and officers of the *legio III Augusta*, who were detached from their main fortress at the Numidian site of Lambaesis to the various outposts along the *limes Tripolitanus*. A comparison of the epigraphic sources from Lambaesis and from forts on the *limes Tripolitanus* shows that the soldiers on outpost duty essentially worshipped the same gods as in the legionary fortress. Here as there, Roman gods such as Jupiter and Minerva and especially the imperial cult are frequently attested. North African deities (Saturn, Dea Caelestis, etc.) were hardly worshipped, while oriental gods such as Jupiter Dolichenus had more followers.[8]

The main difference between the situation at Lambaesis and on the *limes Tripolitanus* is the worship of local gods, as proven at Bu Njem and assumed at Gheriat el-Garbia. Their sanctuaries were erected outside the fort in both places. Obviously, their worship in temples or chapels within the fortifications was not permitted. To what extent such deities were also worshipped in other forts and fortlets is unclear. Corresponding temples would probably also be expected outside the fortifications, where, however, archaeological investigations are largely lacking. Le Bohec (2000, 224, note 137; see also Guédon 2018, 254) linked this deviation from the behaviour at Lambaesis to a greater independence of the soldiers stationed in the oasis forts. Rebuffat (1990, 143), in contrast, questioned whether the temples at Bu Njem were built at all for the soldiers but rather for the local population, whose goodwill was to be won. However, this was probably not the main reason for the construction of sanctuaries for local deities at Bu Njem and probably also at Gheriat el-Garbia. Rather, the invocation of local gods by the soldiers can be explained by their individual need for security and can also be observed in numerous other places across the Roman Empire (Stoll 2013, 85–94). Especially in such inhospitable places as Bu Njem and Gheriat el-Garbia, where – as an inscription from Bu Njem describes it – 'in the midst of the hills of sand [...] the burning flames of the southern sun' made life difficult for the soldiers (*IRT2021* 918), this protection was probably particularly needed.

References

Brogan, O. and Smith, D.J. 1984. *Ghirza: A Libyan Settlement in the Roman Period.* Tripoli: Department of Antiquities.

Brouquier-Reddé, V. 1992. *Temples et cultes de Tripolitaine.* Paris: Éditions du CNRS.

Guédon, S. 2018. *La frontière romaine de l'Africa sous le Haut-Empire.* Madrid: Casa de Velázquez.

Haynes, I. 2013. *Blood of the Provinces. The Roman Auxilia and the Making of Provincial Society from Augustus to the Severans.* Oxford: Oxford University Press.

Hilali, A. 2016. *Armée et religion dans le monde Romain. La Legio Tertia Augusta en Afrique.* Milan: Éditions Mimésis.

Le Bohec, Y. 1989. *La troisième légion Auguste.* Paris: Éditions du CNRS.

Le Bohec, Y. 2000. Le rôle social et politique de l'armée romaine dans les provinces d'Afrique. In G. Alföldy, B. Dobson and W. Eck (eds), *Kaiser, Heer und Gesellschaft in der Römischen Kaiserzeit. Gedenkschrift für Eric Birley.* Stuttgart: Franz Steiner Verlag, 207–26.

Mackensen, M. 2008. Mannschaftsunterkünfte und Organisation einer severischen Legionsvexillation im tripolitanischen Kastell Gholaia/Bu Njem (Libyen). *Germania* 86: 271–306.

Mackensen, M. 2010a. Das severische Vexillationskastell Myd(---)/Gheriat el-Garbia am limes Tripolitanus (Libyen). Bericht über die Kampagne 2009. *Mitteilungen des Deutschen Archäologischen Instituts, Römische Abteilung* 116: 363–458.

[8] Le Bohec 1989, 553–70. On the gods worshipped by the Roman army in North Africa (especially Numidia), see in general Hilali 2016.

Mackensen, M. 2010b. Das commoduszeitliche Kleinkastell Tisavar/Ksar Rhilane am südtunesischen limes Tripolitanus. *Kölner Jahrbuch* 43: 451–68.

Mackensen, M. 2015. Zur spätrömischen Nutzung des Kleinkastells Vezereos am limes Tripolitanus (Südtunesien). In P. Henrich, Ch. Miks, J. Obmann and M. Wieland (eds), *Non solum... sed etiam. Festschrift für Thomas Fischer zum 65. Geburtstag.* Rahden: Marie Leidorf Verlag, 259–70.

Mackensen, M. 2016. Survey and excavation of the German Archaeological Mission at the Roman Fort of Myd(---)/Gheriat el-Garbia and its vicinity, 2009/2010. *Libya Antiqua* n.s. 6: 83–102.

Mackensen, M. 2021a. *Das severische Vexillationskastell Myd(---)/Gheriat el-Garbia am limes Tripolitanus (Libyen), I: Forschungsgeschichte, Vermessung, Prospektionen und Funde 2009–2010.* Wiesbaden: Reichert Verlag.

Mackensen, M. 2021b. Observations and results of recent excavations and surveys of Late Roman military fortifications in the province of Tripolitana. *Libya Antiqua* n.s. 14: 111–45.

Mackensen M. 2022. Late Roman African red slip ware from central Tunisia in Tripolitanian forts and fortlets. *Libya Antiqua* n.s. 15: 179–96.

Marichal, R. 1992. *Les ostraca de Bu Njem.* Tripoli: Department of Antiquities.

Mattingly, D.J. 1982. The Roman road-station at Thenadassa (Aïn Wif). *Libyan Studies* 13: 73–80.

Mattingly, D.J. 1995. *Tripolitania.* London: Batsford.

Mattingly, D.J. (ed.) 1996. *Farming the Desert. The UNESCO Libyan Valleys Archaeological Survey. Volume 2: Gazetteer and Pottery.* London: Society for Libyan Studies.

Rebuffat, R. 1976–77. Bu Njem 1972. *Libya Antiqua* 13–14: 37–78.

Rebuffat, R. 1987. Lampes romaines à Gholaia (Bu Njem, Libye). In T.-J. Oziol (ed.), *Les lampes de terre cuite en Méditerranée. Des origines à Justinien. Table ronde du CNRS, tenue à Lyon du 7 au 11 décembre 1981.* Lyon: Maison de l'Orient et de la Méditerranée, 83–90.

Rebuffat, R. 1990. Divinités de l'oued Kebir (Tripolitaine). In A. Mastino (ed.), *L'Africa Romana. Atti del VII convegno di studio (Sassari, 15–17 dicembre 1989).* Sassari: Gallizzi, 119–59.

Rebuffat, R. 1994. Ghadames (Cidamus). In *Enciclopedia dell'arte antica, classica e orientale, II supplemento.* Rome: Istituto della Enciclopedia Italiana, 765–66.

Schimmer, F. 2012. New evidence for a Roman fort and vicus at Mizda (Tripolitania). *Libyan Studies* 43: 33–39.

Schmid, S. 2024. Die Heiligtümer GG2–6 auf dem sog. Tempelplateau. In M. Mackensen, *Das severische Vexillationskastell Myd(---) und die spätantiken castra Madensia/Gheriat el-Garbia am limes Tripolitanus (Libyen), II: Ausgrabungen und Untersuchungen im Kastell, im Steinbruch, in den Heiligtümern und am Beobachtungsturm 2009–2010.* Wiesbaden: Reichert Verlag, 475–518.

Schmidt Heidenreich, C. 2013. *Le glaive et l'autel. Camps et piété militaires sous le Haut-Empire romain.* Rennes: Presses Universitaires de Rennes.

Stoll, O. 2007. The religions of the armies. In P. Erdkamp (ed.), *A Companion to the Roman Army.* Oxford: Wiley-Blackwell, 451–76.

Stoll, O. 2013. Einheit und Vielfalt. Religionen und Kulte der römischen Armeen der Kaiserzeit (1.–3. Jh. n. Chr.). In F. Bertholet and C. Schmidt Heidenreich (eds), *Entre archéologie et épigraphie. Nouvelles perspectives sur l'armée romaine.* Bern: Peter Lang, 79–110.

Trousset, P. 1974. *Recherches sur le limes Tripolianus du Chott el-Djerid à la frontière tuniso-libyenne.* Paris: Éditions du CNRS.

Chapter 9

IN SEARCH OF THE ROMANS IN JABAL NAFUSA AND SURROUNDING AREAS

Isabella Welsby Sjöström

The Jabal Nafusa, also referred to as Jabal Gharbi or Western Jabal, corresponds to the western part of the chain of mountains that runs from west to east between the Jafarah plain and the Hamada el-Hamra. It is the least well-known part of Roman Tripolitania, as it has not benefited from the same amount of archaeological research as the Eastern Jabal and the Tarhuna Plateau. The reasons for this apparent neglect are first, that the Jabal Nafusa has none of the spectacular classical remains that dot the coastal area. Second, there is no late Roman settlement of the size of, for example, Ghirza (Brogan and Smith 1984) to warrant a larger project, nor the need to study the means by which the pre-desert was able to sustain surplus agriculture, which launched the UNESCO Libyan Valleys Archaeological Survey (ULVS) in the 1980s. The eastern end of the mountain range that tapers out into the richer agricultural land around Tarhuna is easier to access than the craggier western side. The Western Jabal rises to some 680 m asl (Fig. 9.1) and is cut by deep gorges and wadis, making its terrain ideal for avoiding invaders (Fig. 9.2). The population was originally wholly Berber, but Arab tribes have also settled in the area since the eleventh century CE (see the useful schematic map in Prevost 2016, map 2, and Prevost, Chapter 10, on the relationships between Jabal Nafusa and Jerba in the Islamic era). Despite sparse rainfall, with careful husbanding of the water resources, particularly through the use of wadi walls, the Western Jabal is nonetheless able to produce olives and grain, and has clearly done so from the pre-Roman period onwards with no significant interruption. While it is generally known that Jabal Nafusa was settled and subject to Roman administration, few sites dating to the Roman and Byzantine eras are published, or have received the attention of archaeologists. Fieldwork has been undertaken there by Barbara Barich and her colleagues on prehistoric sites (see, for instance, Barich *et al.* 2010), but this is not pertinent to the present discussion.

Little is known about the road network in Roman times in Jabal Nafusa, as no milestones have been found. The map published by Richard Goodchild (1949, fig. 3) shows a dotted line heading west from Thenadassa/Aïn Wif, tentatively passing Zintan and heading for Dehibat in Tunisia. Milestones have been found to the south of Zintan, in conjunction with roads leading to the pre-desert (*IRT* 963–69). A tantalizing statement by Renato Bartoccini (1926, 82) suggested that Sabratha was supplied by an aqueduct originating in Fassato, some 70 km to the south. While an aqueduct of such length would hardly have been beyond the means of the Romans, there is however neither much spare water in the Jabal nor any

Fig. 9.1. Jabal Nafusa escarpment, looking east from Tarmisa (photo I. Welsby Sjöström).

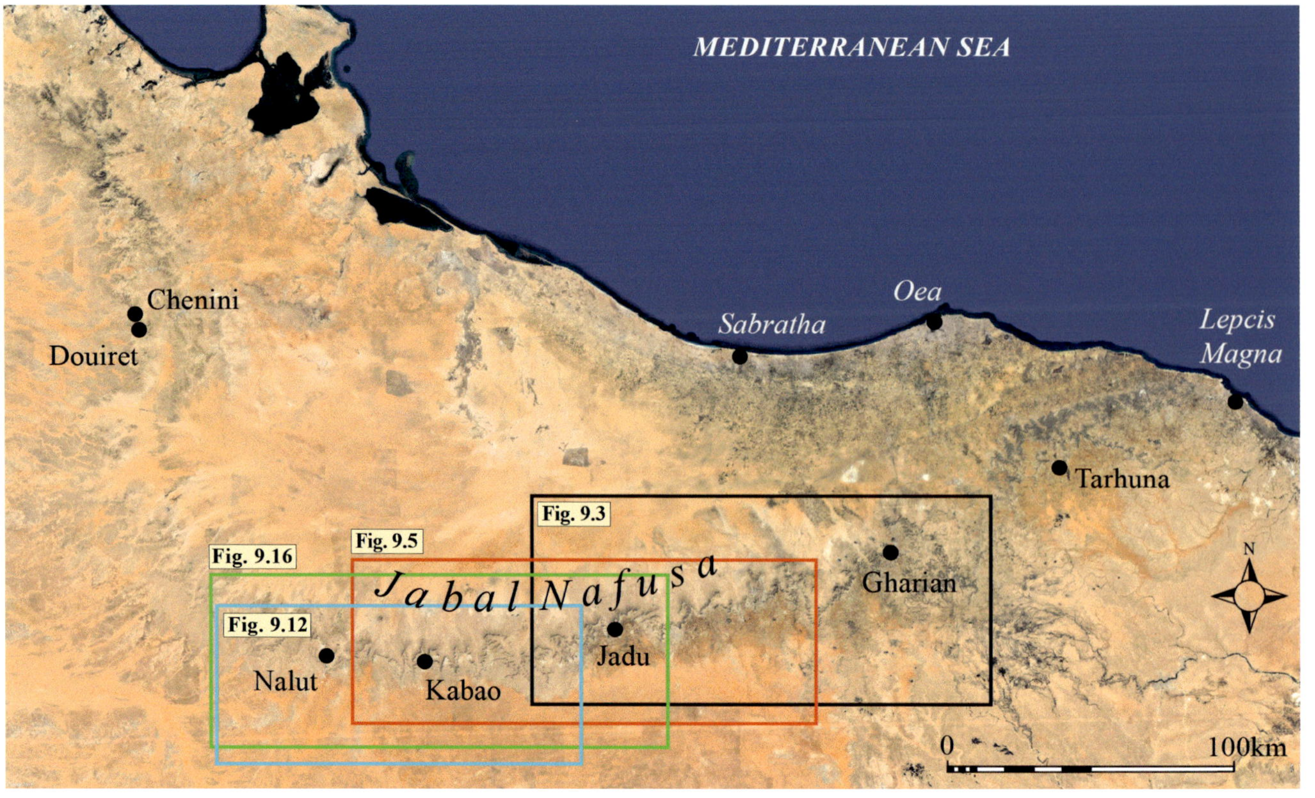

Fig. 9.2. General map of Tripolitania, showing Jabal Nafusa and the coastal cities (basemap Google Earth, data SIO, NOAA, US Navy, NGA, GEBCO, image Landsat/Copernicus, 14/12/2015).

material evidence of such a conduit. Years later Bartoccini (1964, 23) withdrew the aqueduct theory, attributing it to a local myth, while stating that there was no trace of such a structure ever having existed; the water required for the baths and fountains of Sabratha was by then understood to originate from wells dug in Roman times, not far to the south of the city.

A trawl through the more obscure published literature in conjunction with Google Earth (GE) does, however, reveal quite an extensive body of information including potential sites in the Western Jabal. The Eastern Jabal has been more intensively studied and will not be included in this brief overview.[1] In the attempt to expand and improve our knowledge of the area, the aim of this chapter is to draw together what information is already published, especially the sites described by Francesco Corò in the 1920s, focusing on the mountain area roughly demarcated by Nalut in the west and Gharian in the east, and taking into account the occurrence of classical-period spolia in mosques. Spolia may well have been used in private dwellings as well, but these have not been published in sufficient detail. The same geographical division between the two parts of the Jabal was also used by the authors of *The Inscriptions of Roman Tripolitania* (see Reynolds and Ward-Perkins in *IRT*, 204) and by Ward-Perkins and Goodchild (1953, 35–43) – both interregional studies.

The area of Jabal Nafusa is vast, some 180 km long and 23 to 30 km wide, including the foothills to the north. It is challenging to present a meaningful overview, given the size of the area involved and the relatively uneven quality of information available. It remains impossible to assess the density of settlement in the Roman period, as we do not know how much has been missed on the ground. Locating some of the sites from earlier published descriptions can be problematic, and some of the locations presented here are only approximate, especially in the case of Corò's work. In the present we are faced with a further problem, the need not to make the sites easy to find for looters of antiquities by publishing their coordinates. For this reason the sites under discussion are shown on maps in Figs 9.2–3, 9.5, 9.12 and 9.16, while the KMZ file with the locations will be logged at the Archive of the British Institute for Libyan and Northern African Studies (BILNAS). A team of the Department of Antiquities in Tripoli has launched a survey in the Jabal, and it is hoped that in future the collated information may prove helpful.

Previously known sites

Sites already published include the mausoleum and fortified farm at Henscir Suffit (Bartoccini 1926, 71, fig. 42; 1929, 106–10), and the remains of mausolea and the farms at Henscir el-Ausaf (Brogan 1965)[2] and Qasr el-Gezira (Brogan and Oates 1953) (Fig. 9.3).

[1] See Goodchild 1951; Oates 1953; 1954; Ahmed 2019.

[2] Henscir el-Ausaf, a few kilometres north-east of Tiji is not strictly speaking in the Jabal proper, but on the edge of the Jafarah plain.

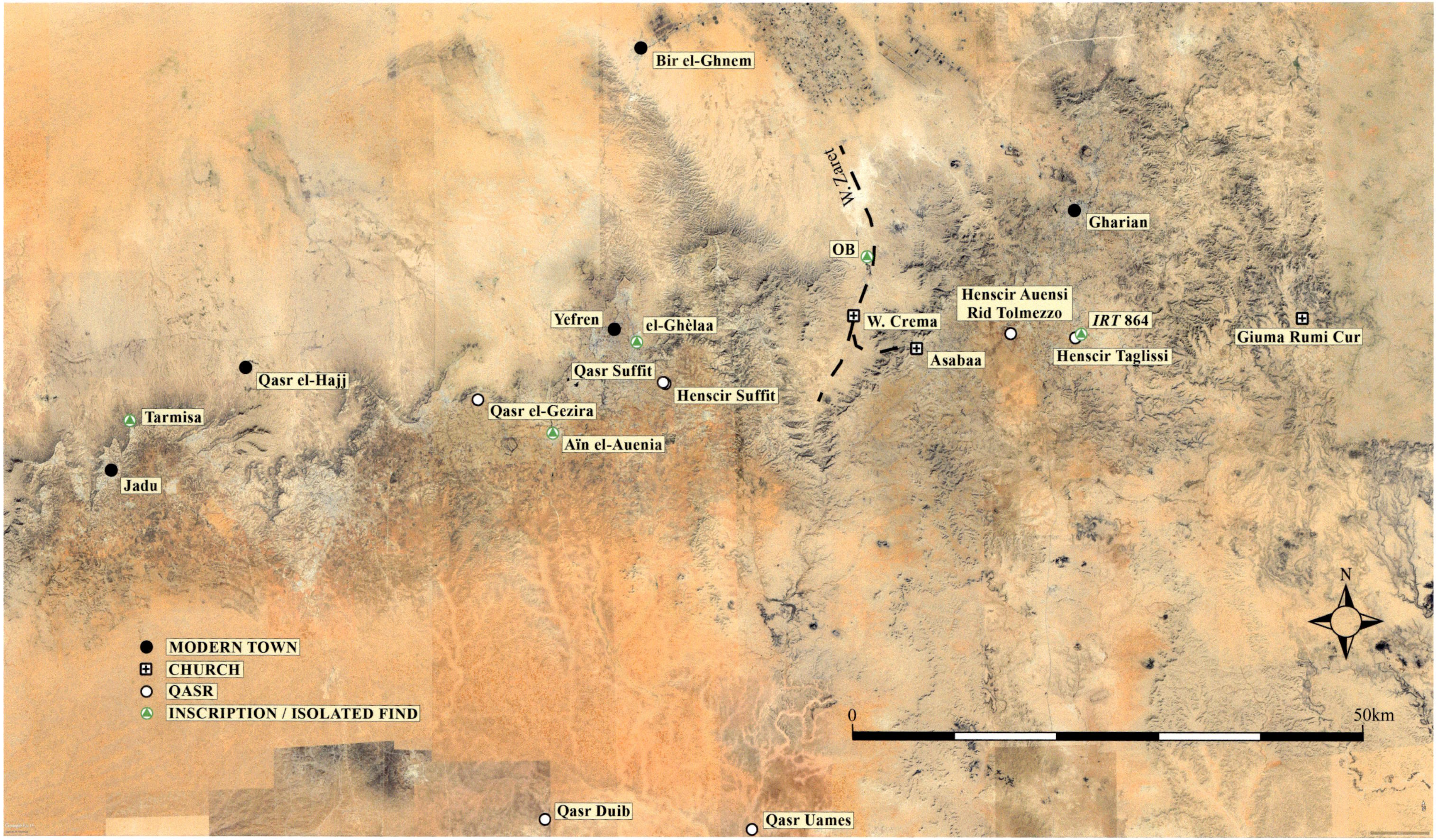

Fig. 9.3. Previously known Roman and Byzantine sites, not including Corò's (basemap Google Earth, data SIO, NOAA, US Navy, NGA, GEBCO, image Landsat/Copernicus, 14/12/2015).

Inscriptions: *IRT*

(Numbers and the location descriptions are taken virtually verbatim from the publication).

IRT 856–57: **Aïn el Auenia**, near Yefren (Auru on the *Tabula Imperii Romani*).

IRT 859: **el-Ghèlaa**, 4 km east of Yefren.

IRT 860: Sàniet el-Krèma, on a small hill 200 m east of the well.

IRT 861: *in situ* in the **church** 1 km south of Ras el-Uadi and 3 km north-west of the *mudariya* of **el Asabaa**.

IRT 862: Asabaa plain area, exact location unknown.

IRT 863: **Henscir Taglissi** a ditched ruin on the right bank of Wadi en-Nzasat, 500 m south-west of the village of el-Msufiin.

IRT 864: fragmentary inscribed block built into the wall of a small mosque at **el-Msufiin**.

Latin inscriptions on the whole are rare and have not been recovered further west than Qasr el-Gezira within the Jabal, found the year after the publication of *IRT*.[3] None have been found in the Jafarah plain. Corò (1928, 61) records an apparently nonsensical brief inscription in Latin characters on the plaster decoration at Qasr el-Girl; this could be in Berber, which is known on occasion to have been written using Latin characters: PONT / NOTA(?)O.

An additional contribution to the list of Roman-period sites in Jabal Nafusa is a 'tip' the author received from Olwen Brogan (then Mrs Hackett) many years ago:

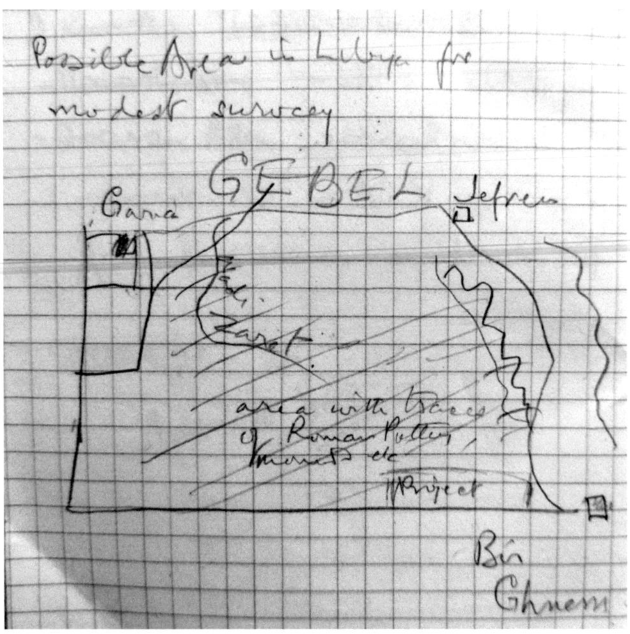

Fig. 9.4. Sketch plan by Olwen Brogan (photo I. Welsby Sjöström).

a '*possible area in Libya for a modest survey*', between Garian and Yefren, by the Wadi Zaret, '(*an*) *area with traces of Roman pottery, mounds, etc.*' (Fig. 9.4). A dam has been built 3 km downstream from Wadi Crema on the Wadi Zaret, near Rabta, but it is not clear if this may have disturbed the area indicated by Brogan, which appears to be to the west of Wadi Zaret, south of Bir Ghnem and east of Yefren, on the plain below the mountains. A mound found on GE in this approximate location is labelled 'OB' on the map in Fig. 9.3.

While looking for the above sites on GE, a number of qsur were located. No names are attached to them, and as far as the author is aware they do not feature in other publications. They are shown here in Fig. 9.5, and a qasr (no. 5) is shown as an example in Fig. 9.6.

Christian (Byzantine) sites

Archaeological evidence of Byzantine settlement is sparse, especially in the Western Jabal. This is not to say that the area was not settled in that period, but simply that not enough work has been carried out. A number of qsur mentioned by Corò and found on GE may well date to this period. Below is a list of Christian settlements/sites listed by Ward-Perkins and Goodchild (1953), with page references given in the text. The sites are marked on Fig. 9.3 (churches identified with a cross in a square).

From west to east:

- **el-Asabaa** (35–37, pl. 12a–c and e). The church is now in a very poor condition; note that the later fortified granary c. 3 km to the north-west (Kenrick 2009, 75), is called Qasr Asabaa al-Atiq according to GE.
- **Bir el-Cur Church** (37). Giuma Rumi Cur, as it is known locally, lies 24 km south-east of Garian, but was nonetheless included in the Western Jabal sites by the authors, and to retain consistency it is listed here. The original record was a letter in the archives of the Superintendency of Antiquities dating to 1934, without the orientation of the apse being stated. It is now located on GE, 1 km south-south-east of Bir Kur. The apse appears to be to the west (but if the curved wall that can be seen is indeed the apse, this is an internal apse, rather than a projecting one). The dimensions as given by Ward-Perkins and Goodchild are roughly compatible;[4] the outline is clear, and judging by the shadows, three arches in the south arcade are still standing, and one in the north. There are several modern buildings nearby that have not encroached on the church (Fig. 9.7).

[3] See Reynolds and Ward-Perkins' remarks in *IRT*, 204–8; Brogan and Oates 1953, 79–80, pl. 22b.

[4] 36.6 × 18.5 m as measured on GE, vs approx. 30 × 11.5 m – but the width measurement probably does not take into account the thickness of the walls.

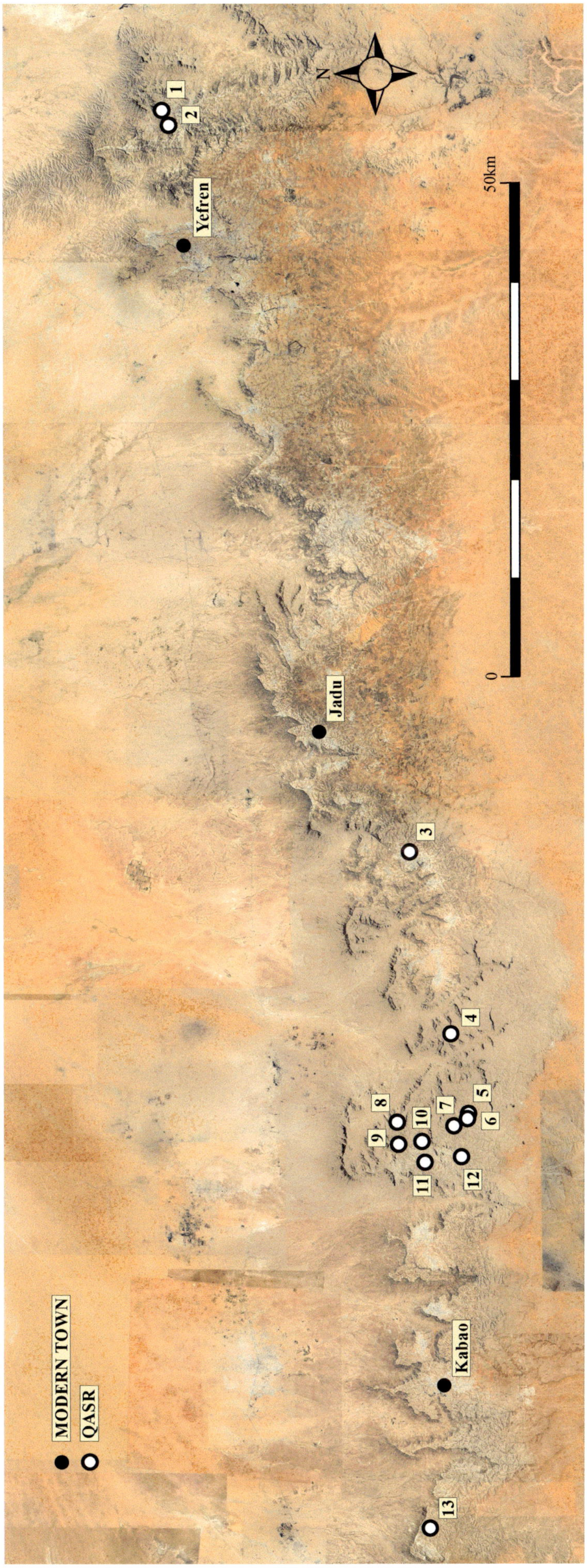

Fig. 9.5. Previously unknown (and so far nameless) qsur found on Google Earth, numbered 1–13 (basemap Google Earth, data SIO, NOAA, US Navy, NGA, GEBCO, image Landsat/ Copernicus, 14/12/2015).

Fig. 9.6. Close-up of qasr no. 5. Dimensions of building within the ditch: c. 22 × 20 m (Google Earth, image CNES/Airbus, 02/01/2019).

Fig. 9.7. Giuma Rumi Cur church (Google Earth, image CNES/Airbus, 05/10/2019).

- Wadi Crema (37). A church by the junction of **Wadi Crema** and **Wadi Zaret**, 6 km west-north-west of the church at el Asabaa. The junction is marked on the map; a possible location of the church is some 80 m to the east, now right on the bank of Wadi Zaret, an unlikely place to have built the church, even if the bank was some distance away 1500 years ago?
- Msufiin, **Henscir Taglissi** (37–43), one of a group of buildings on the right bank of Wadi Nzasat, west of and below the hilltop village of el Msufiin, 12 km south of Garian. Note a stone block from here found in the Usaden mosque 2 km to the north. It is impossible to make out any structural detail apart from what looks like filled-in trenches/rooms of the building, but the location seems accurate when comparing it with GE.
- Church near Tebedut (43). I could only find the nearby **Henscir Auensi** on GE, but not the church, which does not appear to be 500 m to the north, nor anywhere else in the vicinity. The distances given by Ward-Perkins and Goodchild of the Tebedut church from the Asabaa church also appear to be wrong (too low).
- **Tarmisa** (43). Limestone block with a chi-rho monogram, now in the Tripoli museum.[5] Note that the right-hand block of the arched lintel of the doorway of the mosque has carved decorative roundels, different in character to the block with the monogram, but reminiscent of other carvings, such as in the Breviglieri/el-Khadra church in the Eastern Jabal (pl. 17c–d). The fact that the carvings are only on one side of the entrance supports the possibility that the block was recycled (Kenrick 2009, 81) (Fig. 9.8). Inside the building there is what may be a blocked doorway (the whole wall is covered in several layers of white plaster) with various niches; the two at the bottom have a curious half-moon shape, one vertical and one horizontal, reminiscent of a carved stone in the mosque at Abu Ma'aruf in Sharwas, thought to possibly be part of an Islamic (but not Ibadi) gravestone (Warfalli 2007, 101–2, figs 131–33).

Fig. 9.8. Doorway of the mosque in Tarmisa: note the carved decoration on the upper right-hand side of the lintel (photo I. Welsby Sjöström).

[5] Bartoccini 1926, fig. 86; Ward-Perkins and Goodchild 1953, 43, pl. 13d; mentioned by Kenrick 2009, 80–81.

Francesco Corò's sites

Francesco Corò's brief monograph, *Vestigia di colonie agricole romane: Gebel Nefusa*, was published in 1928. Corò (1878–1975) was an officer in the Italian army, who in 1922 was put in charge of the Italian occupation of the western part of Jabal Nafusa, and in the course of this mission collected information on the archaeology of the area (see Corò 1928, introduction). The resulting book is a mine of information on Roman sites in the western Jabal Nafusa proper as well as in the northernmost parts of the Hamada el-Hamra and the southernmost parts of the Jafarah plain. Corò's military duties meant that he focused on the area between Kabaw and Nalut. The area between Nalut and Dehibat is virtually devoid of traces of Roman settlement, the reasons for which perplexed Corò. No qsur nor mosques are known west of Nalut; it is not a particularly fertile area, although wadi walls have been constructed across most wadis and siah, often with only one tree per terrace. Nor could Corò find information about Roman sites in this area, with the exception of Khascem el-Roman. According to a brief survey of the area between Nalut and Wazzen (Tancioni 1933–34, 186–89), there are many cave dwellings used by seasonal workers at harvest time here, which explains the lack of visible settlement on GE.

Corò mentions about 100 sites (if including individual mausolea) in varying degrees of detail, giving some idea of the range of Roman sites present. Although the impression given is that he was very thorough, constantly asking the locals about ancient remains, his work was not the result of a systematic survey, and therefore is hardly definitive. Corò was a keen observer of both the ruins and the surrounding areas, looking for both evidence of water cisterns as well as relief fragments from the mausolea. The book is illustrated with several sketches of architectural fragments as well as of occasional standing remains and the silhouettes of hills, but there are few photographs, not surprisingly given the date of the book. Corò's work has been referred to in passing by many scholars[6] as evidence for a Roman presence in the Western Jabal, but where exactly are the sites?

Locating the necropolises on GE with only the aid of Corò's descriptions of his route and the use of a map has generally proven impossible; only the general area can be indicated, a minor step forward, but ground-truthing is essential to find them. The qsur and *gusbet* he mentions are somewhat easier to locate, depending on whether the description begins from a fixed point (the approximate centre of a village, for example); when it is only stated that a qasr lies within the territory of a settlement, it becomes more difficult, unless some useful landmark is mentioned. Already in Corò's day (almost exactly a century ago) many of the sites – the tombs or mausolea in particular – were reduced to heaps or scatters of stones, used as convenient stone quarries by the locals. It is almost impossible to identify such small structures on satellite images, even when searching across large, still undeveloped empty spaces. In some areas the reverse is the case: along the southern edge of the Jafarah plain/foothills of the Jabal, some disturbance has been caused by modern farming and construction projects.

The spelling has changed considerably with different ways of transliterating the original Berber or Arab place names, and few of these are on GE. While it is possible to recognize a place name in Corò's Italianized Arab transliteration, the doubt then arises as to which form should be used. Except for the better known towns or villages, the spelling of place names has been left here as Corò wrote them down. The colonial-era maps are a helpful guideline: the 1 : 400,000 series from 1916 is clear enough and the spelling generally matches that used by Corò, but this early map is somewhat inaccurate and the scale is too small (in fact it is labelled '*schizzo dimostrativo*', demonstrative sketch). The author himself in 1922 may well have had access to a better map. Consulting the American Military Service (AMS) maps based on the later (post-1916) series of the Istituto Geografico Militare (IGM) maps at scale 1 : 100,000 provides more accurate information.[7] It has been possible to locate some of the structures/settlements Corò mentions by following his itinerary (often described), but this is also beset with problems, as the distances he gives (4 km, 500 m, etc.) are clearly approximates, and although he on occasion specifies whether he was riding, in a car or on foot, a statement such as '15 minutes' travel from el-Cherba' leaves a fair margin of error (and in this instance nothing could be found on GE within the range of any means of transport). Thus all that can be done is to mark the town and village names as well as any qsur in the vicinity, at least giving an idea of where the sites might be located. Ultimately ground-truthing is clearly essential. The purpose here is to draw attention to Corò's work, otherwise easily lost in a not easily accessible publication.[8]

In order to better appreciate the criteria by which Corò identifies structures as Roman or local, as well as to illustrate the kind of decorative architectural elements Corò found at many of the sites, see Figs 9.9–11, showing a wall in the Berber village of Tarmisa and an ashlar wall at Qasr Suffit, as well as a detail of the decoration on the nearby mausoleum of Henscir Suffit.

[6] For example: Reynolds and Ward-Perkins in *IRT*, 205; Mattingly 1995, xv; Sheldrick 2021, 12. Ward-Perkins and Goodchild (1953, 80) specifically reference some of the sculptural fragments Corò describes.

[7] These were the two sets of maps available while undertaking this research.

[8] However, an Arabic translation was published in 2003 by Maison Arabe du Livre and a new edition was made available in 2015 by Tawalt Cultural Foundation Archaeological Series.

Fig. 9.9. *(top left)* Wall in the Berber settlement at Tarmisa. This is the kind of masonry that Corò would have termed 'Berber' and in some instances suggested these structures were built by the local Berber population, contemporary with Roman buildings (photo I. Welsby Sjöström).

Fig. 9.10. *(top right)* Detail of the carved decoration on the mausoleum of Henscir Suffit, typical of what Corò found in other cemeteries (photo I. Welsby Sjöström).

Fig. 9.11. *(left)* Close-up of the external wall of Qasr Suffit, a good example of the first- and second-century CE ashlar masonry, easily identified as Roman (photo I. Welsby Sjöström).

Gazetteer of Corò's sites

Unless otherwise stated, all page references are to Corò 1928, as are the chapter titles in italics, translated from the Italian. The area between Kabaw and Nalut is covered from east to west (Fig. 9.12).

Kabaw

Ch. 1. *Gsur el-Berber (Cabao)* (7–22): c. 20 km south of Kabaw. On sheet 1670 of the USA map based on the IGM map there is marked a '**castello romano**' (but much closer to Kabaw, c. 10 km).

Ch. 2. *Siah el-Nakhla* (23–32): south-east of Kabaw, between Kabaw and Haraba, located on a rise, but not identified. At least eight Roman mausolea, with sculptural decoration.

Ch. 3. *The Roman eagle at Henscir ez-Zarizera (Cabao)* (33–37): c. 5 km east of Kabaw, on the bank (not clear whether right or left) of Wadi Zarizera. The name comes from a relief of an eagle on one of the fallen blocks of one of the mausolea, hence 'Henscir ez-Zarizera' (a kind of bird). Two mausolea at least and a farm, 200 paces east of the mausolea, which sit on the edge of the wadi. On a piece of broken architrave are a few almost illegible

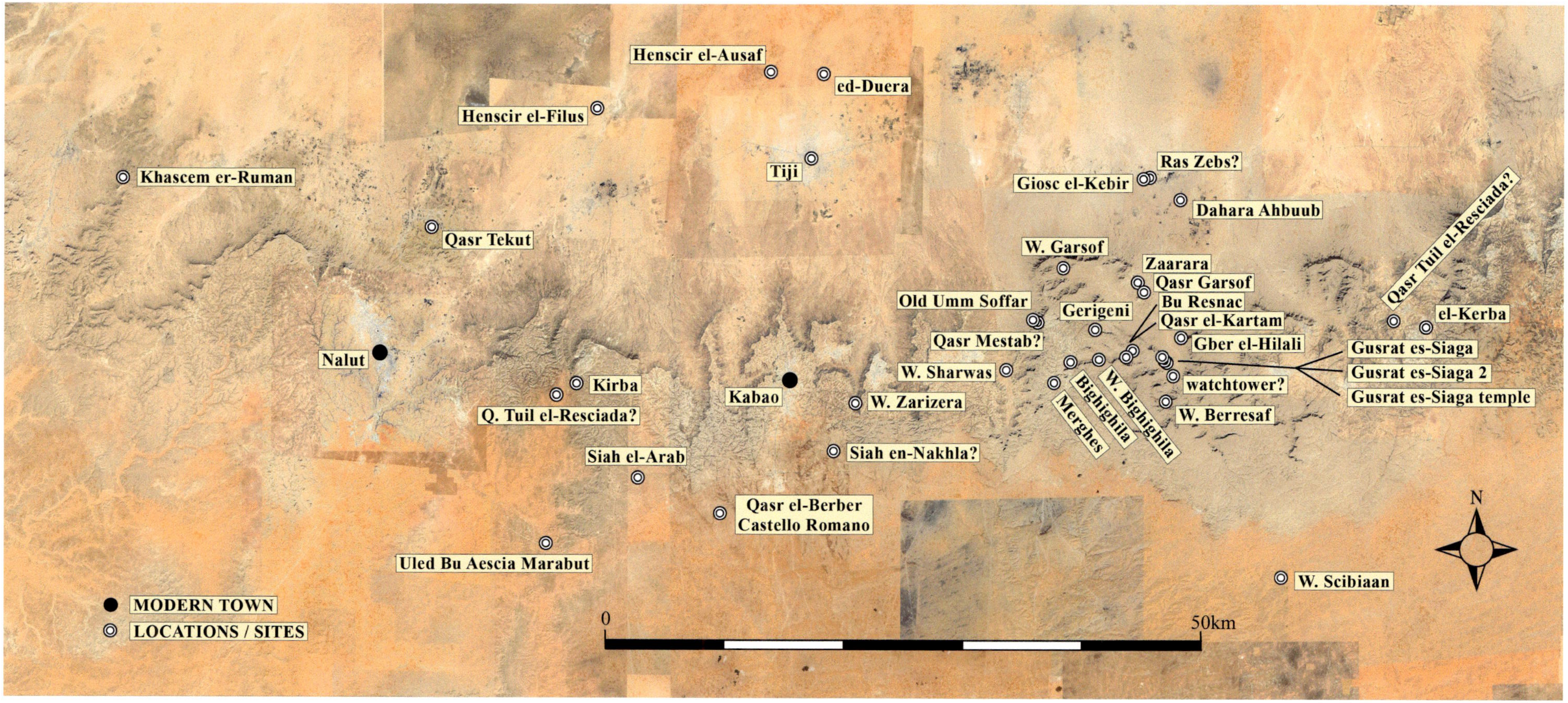

Fig. 9.12. Corò's sites: often only the nearby wadis or villages could be located (basemap Google Earth, data SIO, NOAA, US Navy, NGA, GEBCO, image Landsat/Copernicus, 14/12/2015).

Fig. 9.13. The mausoleum of Henscir Suffit in 2010, looking south. Qasr Suffit lies c. 250 m to the north-east of the mausoleum, on an adjoining hillock. Note the commanding views of the surroundings (photo I. Welsby Sjöström).

Latin characters (36); all the structures are in a state of collapse. Only Wadi Zarizera was located.

Haraba

Ch. 4. *The south of Haraba (the Roman farms of Giuemaat, Scibiaan and Senu Bellel)* (39–46): a little south of the caravan track from Kabaw to Jadu, 15 km (south-east) from Bighighila. Roman (open) farms of Giuemaat, Scibiaan (3 km from Giuemaat) and Senu Bellel (7 km west of Scibiaan), with accompanying mausolea in ruin, their vaulted subterranean chambers well made. Impossible to locate on GE; this area lies in the northern edge of the Hamada el-Hamra, and while it has been possible to locate Wadi Scibiaan, no structure could with any confidence be related to the farms or tomb monuments. The wadis in this area are shallow and a great deal of sand is present.

Ch. 5. *A large Roman centre at Gusrat es Siaga (Gber el-Hilali and the necropolis of Essnan el-Bagla* (47–58). **Gusrat es-Siaga**: almost certainly the four parts of this site have been located; see GE and map sheet 1671. However, Gber el-Hilali (possibly located) and the necropolis of Esnama el-Bagla, in Wadi el-Bagla, a tributary to the Wadi Berresaf, are impossible to locate, and the same goes for the Berber Qasr Legef. Along Wadi Bighighila, mentioned at the beginning of the chapter, the Berber (?) qasr **Bu Resnac**, according to local tradition built c. 1000 CE; Corò could see no sign of earlier walls or settlement. Further east lies **Qasr el-Kartam**, also Berber.

Ch. 6. *Agricultural colonies of Haraba (Roman remains of Kasr el Girl and Resciadet el Tual)* (59–64): between **Merghes**, **Umm Soffar**, **Tenzeghet**, **Gerigeni** (northern and eastern border); **Wadi Bighighila** is to the south and to the west lies **Wadi Sarus** (Sharwas). Qasr el-Girl and the Berber remains of Qasr Kusbet are in the territory of Gerigeni, and Qasr Kusbet is c. 2 km north of Qasr el-Girl, but unfortunately the location of the latter is not specified, beyond stating that it sits on a rise with a good overview of the surrounding area (like Henscir Suffit; see Fig. 9.13, which gives an idea of the dominant location of this and many other qsur).[9] Three unidentified qsur with surrounding ditches were found in the area on GE, and among these may be the site(s) described by Corò.

[9] Probably precisely because of its commanding viewpoint, Henscir Suffit became part of a battleground during the 2011 revolution. The monument was slightly damaged, but the area at the foot of the mausoleum is now the burial ground of many combatants.

The following qsur are not built with ashlar blocks, nor do they have any 'Roman' decoration: Qasr Mestab at Um Saffar, Qasr Iahia c. 500 m from Tenzeghet, and Qasr el Uast in the territory of Bighighila. Corò interprets them as Berber constructions contemporary with the Roman period (60). To these may be added the ruins of small inhabited centres, such as Taghlis (by Ibughturin, see below for description of the spolia in the mosque) where there are many remains of old buildings, vaulted underground rooms and large caves once used as dwellings or for storage, now partly filled in, such as Mazel Tarat in the territory of Gerigeni. Most of the above are Roman in date but probably of local construction, for the local inhabitants, even if some are built on earlier foundations. Corò thinks there is a *castrum* (Qasr el-Girl, with a watchtower) and an open farm, Tuilet er-Resciadet, of late Roman date in the territory of Haraba.

Ch. 7. *The Libyco-Roman necropolis in the Wadi Garsof (Haraba)* (65–70): the exact location of the necropolis, al-Essnan, could not be found in the **Wadi Garsof.** It is located on flat ground next to the mountain 'that closes the wadi off to the south'. Described as three Berber mausolea (built without ashlar masonry, and no worked stone in general), thought by Corò to be contemporary with the Roman period. On a height is a 'Berber' fortification, **Qasr Garsof.**

* There is also a brief description of a mine near **Zaàrara**, on the east side of the spur the old village is located on, according to local tradition used in Roman times. Apparently, in the last years under Ottoman rule a commission formed of three Europeans had examined the 'mine' and proclaimed it of Roman date (65).

Auamed

Ch. 8. *Remains of Roman farms at Siah el-Arab (Auamed)* (71–76): classical-period ruins in the territory of Auamed are particularly poorly preserved.

Siah el-Arab was located with the aid of AMS 1 : 1,250,000 sheet NH32-4 series P502, first edition, 1953. The three sites described by Corò could however not be found, particularly as the author does not specify where along the wadi the first site is located. Dafta Nethra necropolis: located on a slight rise in the terrain, apparently tumuli arranged on three lines, with five or six tumuli each, with only the central one having dressed blocks visible; no houses were found nearby. Dafta el Boggar on the right hand of the head of the small Wadi Boggar, four mausolea, large dressed blocks. Traces of buildings 50 paces to the east. Ras Siah Buzid lies 3.5 km west of Dafta el Boggar. There are two mausolea, made of ashlar blocks, one with a figure carved in a niche; some 50 m to the north are the ruins of a building.

Ch. 9. *Henscir el-Melia (the farm of abundance) (Auamed)* (77–83): Qasr Tuil el-Resciada (15 minutes from el-Kerba – unclear by what means of transport?) tentatively marked on GE. A farm or qasr heavily ruined but built with large dressed blocks. Henscir el-Melia – is a mausoleum with underground chamber, rather distant from the qasr and to the west of it; as no other building could be found in the vicinity, it has been associated with the qasr mentioned by Corò. Various sculptural fragments.

Nalut

Ch. 10. *Rodet Auled bu Aescia* (85–88). Roman remains (necropolis) within some 600 m west and an Islamic (?) qasr 1 km to the north. Only the marabout at the foot of Rodet could be located with some degree of confidence, although the resolution is clear and there has only been minimal modern activity. Wadi walls are however visible.

Seaan

Ch. 11. *The Roman colony of Giosc el-Kebir. The ruins of Kasr el-Lamir and the Roman tombs of Ras Zebs and el-Hagiar (Seaan)* (89–93): qasr and tombs near **Giosc Kebir** (west of?). Not possible to identify on GE, but there is a Roman presence in the area, as evidenced by the cemeteries at Ras Zebs (200 m from Giosc el-Kebir, tentatively marked on the map), and el-Hajar. Corò himself warns that 'soon no trace will remain of the tombs', their stone blocks used as building material for the Ottoman, and then the Italian, forts as well as burnt in lime kilns, some within the apogee themselves; no trace seems to remain of Kasr el-Hamir itself, which is surprising. According to the description given, Ras el-Zebs is 200 m from the village (direction not specified, but where it is marked fits with the fact that it is a narrow rise in the lime rich terrain); west of this (no distance given, and unclear how Corò travelled at this point) is the qasr (with a footprint of 120 × 100 paces), and 400 m west of this is the cemetery of el-Hajar.

Ch. 12. *The Roman remains of Dahara Ahbuub (Seaan)* (95–99): the (a?) mosque at **Giosc Seghir**, with Roman columns in arcade (99). Between Giosc and the Jabal, there are at least two groups of Roman tombs and Qasr Ahbuub along Wadi Teghluf, but nothing is visible along wadis on GE. To the east of the wadi that Corò most likely refers to there is a vast new agricultural project which may have further obscured the lone grave monuments, but the qasr is meant to have been on the west bank.

Ch. 13. *The agricultural colony of el-Duera (Seaan). The Roman remains of the qasr and of the necropoleis of el-Benia and el-Ruegia* (101–6): Qasr near Duera, tombs

1.5 km distant at Duera el-Benia, between 10 and 12 km north-east of Tiji. 2 km east of the qasr there is another necropolis, with at least 14 collapsed monuments; nothing could however be found on GE. An **el-Duera** is marked on the AMS 1 : 100,000 sheet 1569, Umm el-Far, sheet 1570, Tigi, but this is only c. 7.5 km from Tigi. Further out in the same direction nothing can be found either; the terrain appears flat and sandy, without any notable changes in altitude.

Ch. 14. *Henscir el-Ausaf. The farm of the figures. North of Tigi* (107–18): **Henscir el-Ausaf**, 7.7 km north of Tiji, Gefara of Seaan, on 1 : 100 000 map sheet 1570, Tigi, T699882. The main sculptural fragments were brought to the Tripoli museum in 1955 (Brogan 1965, 47), to the author's knowledge the only architectural fragments among all that Corò describes in his book to be rescued. The others are presumably still *in situ* or lost.

Ch. 15. *The Roman necropolis of Garaet el-Ahsan (Seaan)* (119–25): the Roman necropolis of Garaet (Henscir) el-Ahsan (Sèaan). 15 tumuli, only two with articulated masonry in the 1920s (119–23). Located on the same line as Henscir el-Ausaf and Henscir el-Filus, or so Corò says; unfortunately the maps do not help locate it in the almost featureless landscape (there is a 'Garaat el-Hsun' on the AMS map, but it is located c. 2 km south-south-west of Henscir el-Ausaf, and there is nothing visible there, but neither would we expect to identify the cemetery on GE).

Ch. 16. *Henscir el-Filus. The farm of the money (Seaan)* (127–33): **Henscir el-Filus**. Tumuli rather than grave monuments, finds suggested a date in the fourth century CE. Some 47 km east of Jawsh, in the Jafarah north of Nalut, at the head of Wadi Maghargar. Also evidence of an olive oil press and water tank, the former interesting because there were no olive trees further north than Nalut, 40 km to the south in this area in the early twentieth century.

Tunisian border

Ch. 17. *A Roman farm on the Tunisian border (Khascem er-Ruman)* (135–39): **Khascem er-Ruman** (approximate location, just within the Tunisian border). Corò found the remains of a Roman mausoleum here, following local information – some of the sculptured fragments were incorporated within the walls of Dehibat fort by the French in 1916–17.

Ch. 18. *The remains of the Libyco-Roman village of el-Ghorria* (141–44): Corò does not state where this is located beyond saying it lies within the territory of the Seaan tribe, and that according to local tradition it was originally inhabited by a Berber tribe from Tunisia. As the book more or less progresses from east to west, logically it should be near the Tunisian border, but for the present purposes it does not matter, as Corò writes that, although he believes it to be contemporary with the Roman-Byzantine period, he could find no trace or Roman architectural fragments, foundations or small finds. Again, according to local tradition, its origins go back to the Byzantine period; at the time of Corò's visit it had been uninhabited for a considerable time. There is a Ghorria marked on the Ufficio Politico Militare (UPM) 'sketch' map from 1916 (1 : 400,000, sheet III, Nalut-Ghadames), more or less where the village of al-Hawamid now stands. However, Qasr Tekut some 13 km to the west would fit better with the description that Corò gives; certainly al-Hawamid does not appear to have an old town.

Islamic sites with spolia in the Western Jabal

Another way of tracing ancient occupation in the Jabal is through the use of spolia from classical or Byzantine buildings in later medieval edifices, particularly in mosques. The use of ancient spolia is not limited to the Jabal, but is also amply documented in Tripoli (for instance, at the Arbaa Arsat crossroads in the medina, and in the Jamaa en-Naga, also in the medina: Messana 1977, 131–46, pl. 26), at the Dargouth mosque in Tajurah (alternatively Dragut Pasha, or Targut Reis in Turkish: Messana 1977, 124–31, pl. 24), at the mosque by Ras el-Hammam (see Zocchi in Munzi *et al.* 2014, 236, fig. 23), and at Ghadames (Pinna Caboni 2020), to name but a few instances. Spolia from Lepcis Magna have famously travelled as far as Virginia Water near Windsor (Lane 2004; 2012). Of course the practice is not confined to Libya: it occurs all around the Mediterranean, and elsewhere, as the motive is fundamentally practical and pragmatic. The following instances have been taken from publications (and a few personal observations). Note that as the publications do not principally deal with the occurrence of spolia, other sites published within them may also contain reused materials.

It should be stressed at this point that the intention here is not to discuss or take into account the date of the buildings in which the spolia occur, nor the exact date of the reused blocks, beyond qualifying them as of the Roman or Byzantine period where possible. The former is a difficult exercise, as the mosques in particular have been restored on several occasions and only few have inscriptions that give us some premise of date of construction as opposed to restoration: for example, Abu Ma'ruf at Sharwas (Prevost 2016, 97), Abu Mansur Ilyas in Tendemira (Prevost 2016, 91), and Tnumayat mosque (Warfalli 2007; Dell'Aquila *et al.* 2011; Prevost 2016, 58). Nor is the date of the original building from which the blocks were taken easy to assess. Instead, the simple fact that spolia blocks have been incorporated in a structure

Fig. 9.14. *(above)* Mitewnia mosque. In the centre of the arcade note especially the spiral column (photo A. Rahebi).

Fig. 9.15. *(right)* Jadu mosque before restoration. The mihrab niche is flanked by reused columns (photo A. Rahebi).

will be taken as an indication of earlier settlement in the area, whether of the Roman or Byzantine (Christian) period. To draw such a conclusion is possibly reckless, but deserves further investigation. In many cases there is no visible evidence (on GE; ground-truthing is clearly needed to assess each instance) of nearby ruins from which the blocks could have been reused, and the question will have to remain open as to over what distance the blocks could reasonably be expected to have been transported to enhance a new building project. For example, in the case of the Tmezda Kanisiyya mosque (see below), the mosque has 12 columns, no less than nine thought to have been reused from a Roman-period building (or buildings), and further architectural elements are also reused, such as column capitals and/or bases. However, looking at the site on GE, it is surrounded by olive groves and there is no sign of any buildings in ruin for kilometres around, nor of fields left unploughed, which tends to be the case where there is dense settlement, even if it cannot be seen clearly in satellite photographs. On the other hand, it is possible that there was a structure here in the same location in the Byzantine period and the building has subsequently been adapted for use as a mosque (the mihrab, while inset in the south-west wall, is made of smaller stones than the walls). Nonetheless, whoever built the structure must have quarried the stone from somewhere and brought it at a minimum across the c. 3 km from the nearest rocky outcrops at the plateau edge.

Although one of the main types of spolia are columns, recycled from earlier monuments (churches, mausolea, peristyle courtyards or temples) to support the arcades in mosques, it is not always easy to be certain that they are indeed reused and not purpose made (Dell'Aquila and Fiorentino 2014, 23). That said, some of the reused columns are clearly from Roman-period buildings or tombs, such as the Corinthian capital in Umm at-Tubul and the spiral column shaft in Mitewnia mosque, or the fluted and partially fluted columns in the mosque of Abu Mussa al-Tarmisi (Figs 9.14–15). While some spolia are usually more exotic than plain dressed or ashlar masonry blocks, for the purposes of the present chapter we will consider any reused classical or Byzantine building material as spolia.[10] There is

[10]When assigning plain blocks, such as ashlar, to the category of spolia, this may seem rather culturally prejudicial – surely the autochthonous population of the Jabal would have been capable of quarrying neat blocks? It does however remain the case that such masonry is rarely used in the local mosques and other older buildings, and when they are used, it is in such small quantities and so randomly that it is only logical to assume they were brought in from a limited source.

an obvious practical reason for reusing such items, but in some instances, fragments of friezes or other carved blocks have been used to decorate a secular building (for instance, the entrance to the home of Ahmed Ben Aberrahman in Tarhuna).[11] A reasonable supposition might be that the smaller and the more pleasingly carved a piece was, the farther it may have travelled, but when it comes to dressed blocks, followed by columns, the shorter the distance.[12] Fig. 9.16 shows the approximate locations of the sites with spolia.

Nalut

Nalut, Jami' al 'Ali (arch with regular stonework). In this case it would not be spolia but high-quality masonry contemporary to the arch (Allan 1972–73, 149, no. 2, pl. 51b). Also at Nalut, there were reused columns and capitals in the house of the '*caimacan*' (Laronde 1997, fig. 59). The capitals appear to be somewhat battered and of the Corinthian order.

Tanumayat/Tnumayat. A rock-cut underground mosque (Dell'Aquila *et al.* 2011, fig. 8; Prevost 2016, 55–59). One of the oldest in the Jabal, with an inscription dating it to 454 AH/1062 CE. The arches of the two arcades rest on short, rather rough, limestone columns, at least two of which (in the eastern arcade), may be classical spolia.

Kabaw (Kabao)

Forsetta Abu Yahya, niches for lights in the spandrels (Allan 1972–73, pl. 52b; Prevost 2016, 80–83). At least two reused columns are present (Allan 1972–73, 149–51, no. 4; Prevost 2012, 60).

Forsetta Hawariyyin. Reused limestone columns in the arcades, as well as a number of dressed blocks, some used as steps (Allan 1972–73, 151, no. 5; Prevost 2016, 72).

Tatauzin mosque (Dell'Aquila and Fiorentino 2014, 18, fig. 17; Prevost 2016, 76) has remarkably well-constructed arches in the arcade in front of the mihrab, with regularly cut stone blocks and open lamp niches in the spandrels. Note similarity in arches of the lower mosque at Nalut, albeit of inferior masonry (Prevost 2016, fig. 16). The arches rest on rough but slender columns.

Haraba

Abu Mansur Ilyas mosque at Tendemmira (Tandamira); the qibla wall and mihrab are made with (reused?) ashlar blocks (Prevost 2016, fig. 62).

Taghlis mosque at Forsetta. No visible spolia, but late Roman pottery was found outside the mosque (Allan 1972–73, 151, no. 7; Prevost 2016, 76–79).

Ibughturin/Bughtura Taghlis. Several dressed stone blocks are incorporated within the building; on the right upper corner of the exterior lintel there is a carving with a flower, possibly from a Roman mausoleum? Outside the building, also pottery sherds from the second to sixth century CE (Allan 1972–73, 151, no. 8, pl. 56b; Prevost 2016, 106–7).

Wighu. No direct evidence of spolia, but interesting use of small squared blocks in the houses, especially in the so-called 'House of the Mihrab', where especially the mihrab wall is of very fine masonry (Warfalli 2007, 115–18, figs 167–72). Warfalli describes the walls as having a clay core faced with small, squared blocks of stone. This construction style is similar to the masonry in the church at Suq el-Lhoti (Ward-Perkins and Goodchild 1953, pl. 24) and to some extent also in the church at Chafagi Aamer in the Wadi Sofeggin (Ward-Perkins and Goodchild 1953, 50–52, pl. 22; Mattingly 1996, 289–90, fig. 37.13). On the map, the location of the main mosque is indicated.

Abu Shayba mosque, in the territory of Dijji. It contains reused columns and capitals (Allan 1972–73, 154, no. 11).

Jadu

Jami' Sudga or al-'Amirat (alternative spelling: Shaykh Sidqa), west of Jadu, in the centre of el-Kerba. I could not find the exact location on GE; the marker is in the centre of the old town next to the modern mosque of **Jamaa el-Kerba** (Allan 1972–73, 155–56, no. 13; Prevost 2016, 178).

Mitewnia mosque (Rehibat). Two spiral columns as well as plain columns, all probably reused from Roman buildings (Abdulla Rahebi pers. comm.). Two columns appear to be horizontally banded. Also one column in the mosque in Jadu (below) has the same effect (see Fig. 9.13).

Tmezda Hawariyyin mosque, one ashlar block in the entrance doorway (right-hand side: Allan 1972–73, 157, no. 16; Prevost 2016, fig. 91).

Kanisiya mosque, south of Tmezda. A courtyard of the mosque with regular arcades, with ashlar blocks protecting the roof and several other ashlar blocks redeployed in the surroundings, as part of the courtyard wall, or protecting a cistern or well. In the interior there are several Roman columns used in the arcades, six with

[11] https://www.gettyimages.it/detail/fotografie-di-cronaca/entrance-to-ahmed-ben-abderrahmans-house-fotografie-di-cronaca/929555164.

[12] Alternatively, it might be that the decorative elements were chosen precisely *because* they were local and in fact gave greater gravitas to the modern house owner.

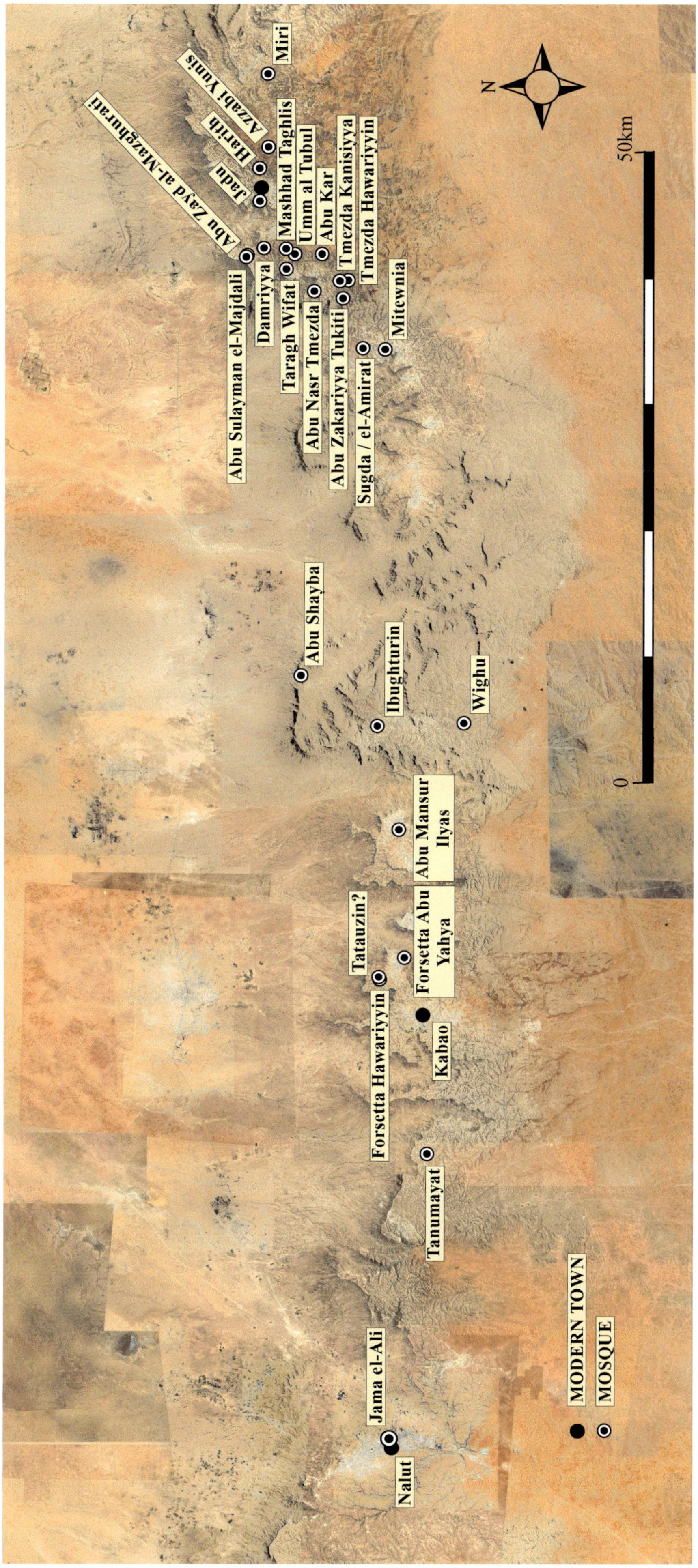

Fig. 9.16. Islamic-period sites (generally mosques) with classical spolia (basemap Google Earth, data SIO, NOAA, US Navy, NGA, GEBCO, image Landsat/Copernicus, 14/12/2015).

Roman bases, as well as three bases lying about inside the mosque (*sic*). According to Allan, nine of the 12 columns are probably Roman. On the whole, this is an unusually regular and well-built mosque, the inside of the entrance being reminiscent of that of a qasr (Allan 1972–73, 157–59, no. 17, pl. 64a–b; Warfalli 2007, figs 173–88; Prevost 2016, 118–24, see fig. 85 especially for the entrance doorway).

East of Tmezda **Buqar (Abu Kar)** mosque, a carved relief showing camel ploughing found nearby, and several ashlar blocks redeployed in the south-west wall, visible from the exterior (Allan 1972–73, no. 18, pls 64c and 65a; Warfalli 2007, fig. 207; Prevost 2016, figs 201–3, with plan at fig. 204).

Umm al Tubul mosque (or Tayishaqt, Ta Ishaq), 2 km north of Buqār (Abu Kar) and 1 km south-west of Mashhad Taghlis. Reused Corinthian capital and olive press upright used in restoration to support a vault. A spiral column has been inserted in the original arcade. A further column with a reused Corinthian-style capital and decorated base (Allan 1972–73, 160, no. 19, pls 65b, 66a–b; Warfalli 2007, figs 189–200; Prevost 2016, 133, figs 103–4).

Mashad Taghlis, two columns, a large ashlar block and part of a lintel (?) seen on exterior by the door (Allan 1972–73, no. 20, pl. 67c). A new mosque was built recently, according to Prevost (2016, 138) 'tout à côté'; the old one, a tiny building measuring 3.5 × 6 m, is difficult to make out on GE.

Tmezda mosque of Abu Nasr, double columns/pilasters in arcade of indeterminate date, but a single column (most likely spolia) has been inserted by the tomb (Allan 1972–73, 161, no. 21, pl. 68a; Prevost 2016, fig. 80).

Damriyya mosque, two squared (ashlar) blocks functioning as threshold. There are also two column bases, one built into the structure and one in the proximity. There are remains of a ruined Berber (?) settlement near this mosque, to the west (Allan 1972–73, 162, no. 22, pl. 69a; Prevost 2016, 139).

Taragh of Wifat mosque, four reused columns and one column capital (base?), used in a pier and in the north wall, visible on the interior (Allan 1972–73, 162, no. 23; Prevost 2016, figs 98–100).

Abu Zakariyya al-Tukiti mosque. There is a Roman stone block outside the mosque door, at the foot of the staircase leading down to the mosque (Allan 1972–73, 162, no. 24).

Abu Zayd al-Mazghurati. This mosque, with a Roman column base in the courtyard, is located in the centre of old Mezghura. It has now been entirely rebuilt (Allan 1972–73, 164, no. 25; Prevost 2016, 138).

Abu Suleiman al Majdali (Abu Sulayman el-Majdali) mosque in Mezghura has a column and base with a rope-effect decoration on the torus (Fig. 9.17). The exact location of this mosque could not be found; according to Dr Rahebi it is in Mezghura, but according to Allan and the historical sources there is only one other mosque in the village, that of Abu Mansur Ilyas. However, no mosque other than Abu Zayd is marked on GE.

Abu Mussa al-Tarmisi, near Tarmisa; it has not been possible to locate this structure precisely on GE. Several flat-fluted and partially fluted columns, as well as plain ones (Fig. 9.15). The mosque has recently been beautifully restored and is open to worship.[13]

Jami Shubat Miri. The mosque has an enclosure in front of the entrance. Several Roman stones have been used both in the original building and in subsequent repairs, including uprights from one or two olive presses (Fig. 9.18) (Allan 1972–73, 164, no. 26, pl. 71a).

Fig. 9.17. Column with decorated base in the (ruinous) Abu Suleiman al Majdali mosque in Mezghura (photo A. Rahebi).

[13] Abdulla Rahebi pers. comm. and post on Facebook: https://www.facebook.com/photo?fbid=4947881855300234&set =pcb.4947893838632369.

Fig. 9.18. Miri mosque. Note the fragment of an olive press upright used as a column, second from the far end (photo I. Welsby Sjöström).

Jami' Azzabi Yunis. A fluted column has been built into the south-west corner; all the columns are round (as opposed to being square pilasters) except for one, but as they vary in size and character, they most likely do not all come from the same structure (Allan 1972–73, 164–65, no. 27). Located on GE with the aid of AMS sheet 1672 (Giado), though confusingly on GE it is labelled as a synagogue.

Khirbet al-Harah/el-Harith mosque, near Jadu. Nine columns, two column bases and three-quarter capitals have been reused in the structure (Allan 1972–73, 165, no. 28).

Conclusion

The source material for this brief overview of the traces of classical (Roman) settlement in Jabal Nafusa is disparate in most aspects: the area covered, the periods focused on, and the lack of systematic coverage. Corò's research only covers the western part, between Kabaw and the Tunisian border; that of Ward-Perkins and Goodchild only the easternmost area of the Western Jabal (as well as the mention of a reused block at Tarmisa), while the mosques that are known to contain spolia range between the environs of Jadu in the east and Nalut in the west. The coverage is not consistent, affected by the research interests and the practical constraints placed on the authors. Corò's surveys were made while he was on active service in the Italian army and were limited by the remit of his official military duties; the listing of Christian antiquities was by default single-period, and the published mosques, while located throughout Jabal Nafusa, are focused on Ibadi structures.

One point that arises from looking at the evidence presented is that Roman sites are by no means concentrated only in the eastern end of the mountain range and among the gentler hills in the Tarhuna district. There are Roman-period sites throughout the whole Jabal, but it remains unclear what the density of Roman-period settlement was and to what extent there are Byzantine-era remains. Some sites are thus dated by Corò, but without visiting these with the expertise gained from a subsequent century of research it is not possible to say for certain. The still elusive terms *hawariyyin*, *taghlis*, and *kanisiyya* attributed to some mosques in Jabal Nafusa are still not fully understood, or rather no evidence has been found to definitively link them to Christian origins. The Christian cemeteries of Aïn Zara and en-Ngila near Tripoli have shown that there was a Christian community, at least in the coastal area, until the eleventh century, but whether the same was the case in the Jabal remains uncertain. The evidence presented here suggests that it is the absence of a multi-period approach that has resulted in this apparent gap.

Corò (1928, 18–19) suggests that there was a line of (fortified) farms along an east–west line both to the north (Jafarah) and south (Hamada el-Hamra) of the Jabal. He also mentions a large number of cisterns, mostly sanded in, which he, rightly or wrongly, attributes to Roman agricultural endeavours.

Another point that emerges from looking at the sites on GE is how few, if any, have been destroyed by modern agricultural, industrial or construction projects (but see Kenrick 2009, 74 regarding the church at Asabaa). Some sites are hard to locate, such as isolated mausolea, but there is no sign on GE that they may have been bulldozed to make way for new developments. Often new buildings can be seen near ancient qsur or churches, but the earlier structures have not been touched. In other instances, in the midst of good agricultural land the remains of a settlement of unknown date are still visible on GE, although disturbed. The traces of buildings visible near the mosques of Miri and Umm al-Tubul, not themselves affected, are examples of this.

The degree of preservation of the ancient sites can be explained by various factors. Nucleated settlement prevailed over to isolated farmsteads in the pre-modern eras because of the scarcity of water resources in the Jabal, and this has meant that ancient isolated farms/qsur have remained safe from destruction by looters or the construction of new buildings. As for destruction by farming, it is difficult to plough a field full of the stone walls of an abandoned settlement and were thus avoided. In antiquity, as in the present, settlements were founded away from arable land and potential flooding, leaving the sites largely untouched by the forces of nature. Finally, in some cases the ruins are respected for their own sake. Many were given names by the locals (Qasr el-Girl, Henscir el-Filus, etc.) and associated with local legends (Corò 1928, *passim*). Less so some of the mosques or Islamic shrines: the Metewnia mosque has written on it '*Hadim*' (must be destroyed), presumably by a passing salafist (Rahebi pers. comm.).

It must be stressed that, in the case of the hitherto unknown qsur (Fig. 9.5), this is in no way an exhaustive survey, and many more remain to be located, whether on GE or on the ground (on the use of GE and satellite imagery for archaeological surveys, see also Nikolaus and Sheldrick, Chapter 5). The same goes for the sites with spolia (Fig. 9.16), where the author has relied on publications and photographs whose primary purpose was not to illustrate this particular attribute. Much more remains to be discovered and documented through field research. The presence of Roman remains in the Jabal should be assessed within the context of the whole of Roman-period Tripolitania. More detailed research should give us a better understanding of how far the influence of Rome extended in the region, and how intensively the Jabal was settled, whether by Romans or the autochthonous populations. It will also allow us to trace not only the routes used in antiquity, but also the lines of contact, both economic and cultural, between the coast and the interior – not just between the coastal cities and the mountains, but also with the settlements beyond, such as Ghadames/Cidamus and parts of the pre-desert investigated by the ULVS in the 1980s and early 1990s.

Acknowledgements

I wish to thank Abdulla Rahebi for a journey through Jabal Nafusa many years ago and for the use of Figs 9.14–15 and 9.17, as well as for help identifying a number of photographs/sites, with the additional help of Abdulsalam Rahebi, Juma Gorsa, and Ayad Latrash. Mustafa Turjman and Philip Kenrick contributed very helpful information, and Derek Welsby gave deadline-beating assistance with the maps.

Maps consulted

Schizzo Dimostrativo della Tripolitania Settentrionale 1916, 1: 400,000, foglio no. IV, Giado-Mizda. Governo della Tripolitania – Ufficio Politico Militare.

AMS 1 : 100,000.

Tripoli 1 : 100,000 Sheets 1569 and 1570, Umm el Far and Tigi.

Tripoli 1 : 100,000 Sheet 1571, Scecsciuch.

Tripoli 1 : 100,000 Sheet 1572, Gasr el-Hag.

Tripoli 1 : 100,000 Sheet 1573, Gasr Iefren.

Tripoli 1 : 100,000 Sheet 1574, Gasr Garian.

Tripoli 1 : 100,000 Sheet 1670, Cabao.

Tripoli 1 : 100,000 Sheet 1671, Giosc.

Tripoli 1 : 100,000 Sheet 1672, Giado.

Tripoli 1 : 100,000 Sheet 1673, Gasr er-Resciada.

Goodchild, R.G. 1954. *Tabula Imperii Romani: Lepcis Magna (Sheet H.I.33)*. Oxford: Oxford University Press.

References

Ahmed, M.A.M. 2019. *Rural Settlement and Economic Activity. Olive Oil, Wine and Amphorae Production on the Tarhuna Plateau during the Roman Period*. London: Society for Libyan Studies.

Allan, J.W. 1972–73. Some mosques of the Jebel Nafusa. *Libya Antiqua* 9–10: 147–69.

Barich, B., Garcea, E.A.A., Giraudi, C., Lucarini, G. and Mutri, G. 2010. The latest research in the Jebel Gharbi (northern Libya): environment and cultures from MSA to LSA and the first Neolithic findings. *Libya Antiqua* n.s. 5: 237–52.

Bartoccini, R. 1926. Le antichità della Tripolitania. *Aegyptus* 4: 49–96.

Bartoccini, R. 1929. Scavi e rinvenimenti in Tripolitania negli anni 1926–27. *Africa Italiana* 2: 22–110.

Bartoccini, R. 1964. Il tempio antoniniano di Sabratha. *Libya Antiqua* 1: 21–42.

Brogan, O. 1965. Henscir el-Ausāf by Tigi (Tripolitania) and some related tombs in the Tunisian Gefara. *Libya Antiqua* 2: 47–56.

Brogan, O. and Oates, D. 1953. Gasr el-Gezira, a shrine in the Gebel Nefusa of Tripolitania. *Papers of the British School at Rome* 21: 74–80.

Brogan, O. and Smith, D.J. 1984. *Ghirza: A Libyan Settlement in the Roman Period*. Tripoli: Department of Antiquities.

Corò, F. 1928. *Vestigia di colonie agricole romane. Gebel Nefusa*. Rome: Sindacato Italiano Arti Grafiche.

Dell'Aquila, F. and Fiorentino, G. 2014. Moschee rupestri nel Gebel Nefusa occidentale (Libia). *Opera Ipogea* 1/2014: 9–26.

Dell'Aquila, F., Fiorentino, G. and Bencini, C. 2011. La moschea rupestre di Tnumayat (Gebel Garbi, Tripolitania, Libia). *Opera Ipogea* 1.2/2011: 263–70.

Goodchild, R.G. 1949. The limes Tripolitanus in the light of recent discoveries. *Journal of Roman Studies* 39: 81–95.

Goodchild, R.G. 1951. Roman sites on the Tarhuna Plateau of Tripolitania. *Papers of the British School at Rome* 19: 43–77.

Kenrick, P.M. 2009. *Libya Archaeological Guides: Tripolitania*. London: Silphium Press.

Lane, A. 2004. The ruins at Virginia Water (part 1). *Libyan Studies* 35: 67–94.

Lane, A. 2012. Emperor's dream to king's folly: the provenance of the antiquities from Lepcis Magna incorporated into the 'ruins' at Virginia Water (part 2). *Libyan Studies* 43: 67–80.

Laronde, A. 1997. *La Libye à travers les cartes postales 1900–1940*. Tunis: Alif les Éditions de la Méditerranée.

Mattingly, D.J. 1995. *Tripolitania*. London: Batsford.

Mattingly, D.J. (ed.) 1996. *Farming the Desert. The UNESCO Libyan Valleys Archaeological Survey. Volume 2: Gazetteer and Pottery.* London: Society for Libyan Studies.

Messana, G. 1977. *Originalité de l'architecture musulmane libyenne*. Tripoli-Tunis: Maison Arabe du Livre.

Munzi, M., Felici, F., Sjöström, I. and Zocchi, A. 2014. La Tripolitania rurale tardoantica, medievale e ottomana alla luce delle recenti indagini archeologiche territoriali nella regione di Leptis Magna. *Archeologia Medievale* 41: 215–45.

Oates, D. 1953. The Tripolitanian Gebel: settlement of the Roman period around Gasr ed-Dauun. *Papers of the British School at Rome* 21: 81–117.

Oates, D. 1954. Ancient settlement in the Tripolitanian Gebel, II: the Berber period. *Papers of the British School at Rome* 22: 91–117.

Pinna Caboni, B. 2020. Ghadames (Libya). Surveying data for a reconstructive proposal of the ruins locally known as 'el-Asnam', the idols. *DisegnareCon* 13.25: https://doi.org/10.20365/disegnarecon.25.2020.2.

Prevost, V. 2012. Les ibadites et leurs mosquées cachées. *Qantara* 82: 59–63.

Prevost, V. 2016. *Les mosquées ibadites du Djebel Nafūsa. Architecture, histoire et religions du nord-ouest de la Libye (VIII*[e]*–XIII*[e] *siècle).* London: Society for Libyan Studies.

Sheldrick, N. 2021. *Building the Countryside. Rural Architecture and Settlement in Tripolitania during the Roman and Late Antique Periods.* London: Society for Libyan Studies.

Tancioni, M. 1933–34. Ricognizione fra Nalùt e Uàzzen. *Bollettino Geografico* 5–6: 185–89.

Ward-Perkins, J.B. and Goodchild, R.G. 1953. The Christian antiquities of Tripolitania. *Archaeologia* 95: 1–82.

Warfalli, M.S.M. 2007. *Some Islamic Monuments of Jabal Nafusa in Libya*. Tripoli: Publications of the Department of Archaeology, Libya.

Chapter 10

SOME OBSERVATIONS ON THE CULTURAL PROXIMITY BETWEEN TRIPOLITANIA AND THE ISLAND OF JERBA

Virginie Prevost

It seems that relations have always been very close between Tripolitania (western Libya) and the Island of Jerba (southern Tunisia). This is of course explained by geographical proximity, the island being situated in the Gulf of Gabes, at the latitude of the northernmost extremity of the vast mountainous chain that includes Jabal Dammar in Tunisia and Jabal Nafusa in Libya (Fig. 10.1).[1] Indeed, Jerba and the surrounding area were part of the region of Tripolitania itself in Roman times (on Tunisian and Libyan Tripolitania see Mattingly, Chapter 11). The exchange of Berber populations and their early rallying to Ibadi Islam also brought together these two regions, which were opposed to the central Islamic power and which shared a rather similar fate for centuries. This chapter aims to highlight some of these relationships between the two areas from a historical and architectural standpoint.

Firstly, it is useful to present in a few lines the Ibadis who constitute, alongside the Sunnis and the Shiites, the third branch of Islam. Originally linked to Kharijism, they founded an independent movement during the first half of the eighth century in the Iraqi port of Basra. Fighting against the hegemony of the Umayyad and then Abbasid caliphs, they demanded that their leader, the imam, be chosen by virtue of his science and piety, regardless of his ethnic origin. The Ibadis defend a rigorous ethic based on moral purity, the importance of education and the transmission of traditions, and respect for the memory of ancestors. Their doctrine presents some particularities – the fate reserved for sinners, the dogma of the created Quran, the impossibility of seeing God – and some minor differences with the Sunni ritual, such as the position of the hands during the prayer. Ibadism quickly attracted crowds in many regions, but it only took root in the Maghreb and Oman, where it still dominates.

In North Africa, the Arab conquest was very painful and the Ibadi missionaries easily succeeded in setting the Berbers against the Umayyad governors. After the failure of a first attempt at imamate, a certain ʿAbd al-Raḥmān ibn Rustum founded the Ibadi dynasty of the Rustamid imams in Tahert, in the west of present-day Algeria, around 778.[2] The territory recognizing Rustamid authority was very vast: it extended northwards to the Mediterranean, included part of the Aurès, the Algerian oases of Wadi Righ and Ouargla, as well as Jerba and all of southern Tunisia. In Libya, Ghadames, Jabal Nafusa, Tripolitania and Fazzan are Ibadi. For these regions far from Tahert, however, the imam represents a spiritual guide rather than a real ruler or military leader. The reigns of ʿAbd al-Wahhāb (c. 784–823) and his son Aflaḥ (c. 823–71) constitute the apogee of the Rustamid imamate, whose trade flourished. Three major trade routes developed towards present-day Mali, Niger and Chad: the Ibadis exercised a real monopoly on trans-Saharan trade for several centuries, which brought them great wealth. But alongside these commercial successes, several schisms occurred and divided them. If the reigns of the first three imams were prestigious, the Rustamids then lost themselves in internal quarrels. Tahert was taken by the Shiite army of the Fatimids in 909 and many Ibadis took refuge in the region of Ouargla. In 969, after a vain attempt to refound an imamate, they gave up this idea and later set up religious councils, the *ḥalqa-s*, to

[1] Jerba is pictured as a star shining in the middle of the lunar crescent formed by the Dammar and Nafusa Jabals: pers. comm. Naceur Bouabid, former President of the Association for the Safeguarding of the Island of Jerba (Assidje), 23 January 2016.

[2] Unless otherwise stated, dates are to be intended as CE.

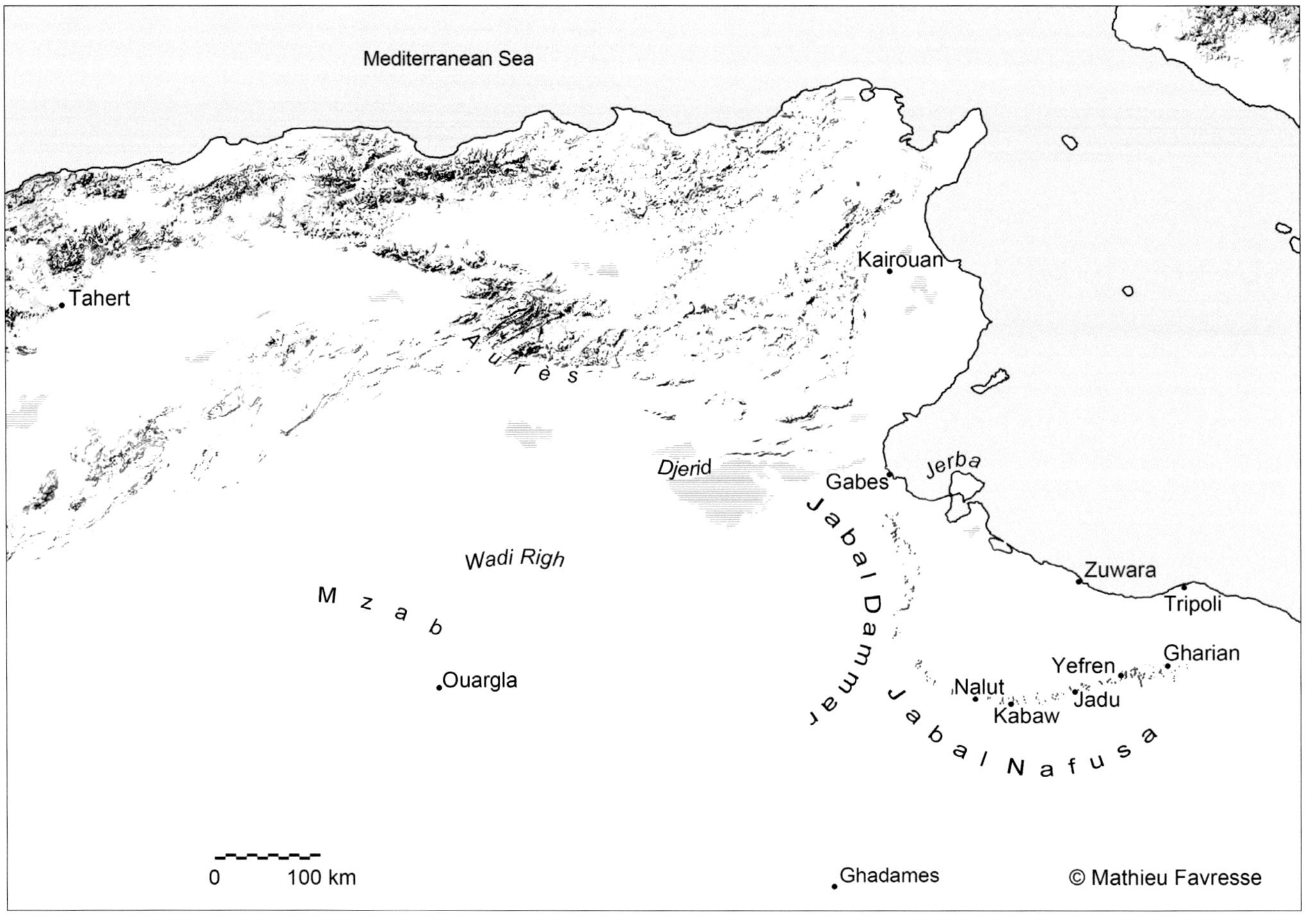

Fig. 10.1. General map, with key sites in the area between Tripolitania and the Island of Jerba (image M. Favresse).

which we will return. Some of the Ibadis settled in the Algerian Mzab valley, their last land of refuge, as their territory, once so vast, began to shrink ineluctably. Today, the Ibadis are concentrated in three regions of the Maghreb: in Jerba, in the Mzab and in Tripolitania, in Jabal Nafusa and the coastal town of Zuwara.

In the first part of this chapter, we will show, through the Ibadi written sources, how much the intellectual and religious life of the island was dependent on Tripolitania. It is not possible to be exhaustive in this chapter, and we will only give a few examples from among the oldest texts available. As the Jerbian Ibadi sheikh F. al-Jaʿbīrī (1975, 287–89) pointed out a long time ago, the history of the relations between these two regions would require extensive research, of which he himself had gathered the main leads in a few pages. In the second part, we will discuss some architectural similarities between Jabal Nafusa and the Island of Jerba.

The (modest) contribution of written sources

The first successes of Ibadism in Tripolitania cannot be precisely dated, but it appears that it had already largely conquered the Berber population by the middle of the eighth century. In 132 AH/749–50 CE, in fact, a leader from the Nafusa tribe, Ismāʿīl ibn Ziyād, was elected imam by the Ibadis of Tripolitania; he was, however, quickly defeated by the Umayyad governor of Ifrīqiya.[3] There is every reason to believe that Jerba, whose inhabitants are said by Ibn Khaldūn (1992, VI, 475) to have been converted to Kharijism since its appearance among the Berbers, adhered to this doctrine already at this time or in the decades that followed. Unfortunately, documents on this subject are lacking.

The father of Jerbian Ibadism, Abū Miswar al-Yahrāsanī, whose work on the island seems to have been decisive in the first half of the tenth century, is the best example of the close relationship between Jerba and Tripolitania. Abū Miswar belonged to the Banū Yahrāsan, a fraction of the Zānāta who lived in Tripolitania and south-eastern Tunisia. He studied in Sharūs (or Sharwas) in Jabal Nafusa, under Abū Maʿrūf and other famous scholars of his time, married in this region and then moved to Jerba with his wife.[4] Several factors may explain Abū Miswar's settlement on the island. The first is the terrible defeat that Jabal Nafusa suffered at the

[3] Ibn ʿAbd al-Ḥakam 1922, 225; Ibn Khaldūn 1992, VI, 135. On the beginnings of Ibadism in Tripolitania, see Prevost 2016, 20–21.

[4] Abū Zakariyyāʾ 1985, 239–40. Al-Darjīnī 1974, I, 158, insists on his wife's origin. Al-Shammākhī 2009, 778, mentions a certain ʿAqīla from Jerba who has an opposite background as she lives in Yefren in the Jabal.

hands of the Aghlabid army in 283 AH/896–97 CE at Mānū, south of Gabes. In this disaster, a good part of their scientific elite disappeared, which interrupted the tradition of teaching that they had been providing until then among the Ibadis; a transfer of some of the scholars to Jerba took place. Abū Miswar, who earned his living as a copyist, was undoubtedly able to provide the Jerbians with some of the books of the scholars who died on the battlefield, assembling a rich collection that would have served as the basis for the island's first libraries. The second factor is religious: the pious scholar would have chosen a land of adoption conquered by the dissident Ibadis (Nukkaris and Khalafis) in order to be able to impose Wahbi Ibadism there, i.e. the 'orthodox' Ibadism, which is in the majority and which remains faithful to the Rustamid imams of Tahert and to the original doctrine.[5] Thirdly, economic considerations were undoubtedly taken into account. Abū Miswar would have frequented the island as a merchant before settling there as a pious scholar: he would have been a fine connoisseur of Saharan trade networks (Barbū 2018, 351–52). To this we may add that the texts sometimes present Jerba as a land of easily accessible food, far more nourishing than the arid Jabal; this is to be qualified, however, since there is also talk of dearth and drought, necessitating the need to fetch date supplies from the Nafzāwa.[6]

Like Abū Miswar, many Tripolitanian inhabitants probably joined the refuge that the island provided after the defeat of Mānū. At the beginning of the tenth century, the fall of the Rustamid imams of Tahert, defeated by the Shiite Fatimids, marked the end of the only important Ibadi state that existed in the Maghreb; this event undoubtedly caused the arrival of new immigrants. Unfortunately, written sources provide little information on these population movements, the most documented being that of the Zawāgha. The Zawāgha occupied certain regions of south-eastern Tunisia and the Tripolitanian coastline; they were nomads who earned their living by grazing flocks of sheep and camels, particularly in the Jafarah plain (Ben Tanfous 1994, 16). Some of them were Khalafi dissidents, supporters of the son of the rebel Khalaf ibn al-Samḥ, others were Nukkaris. When Abū Manṣūr Ilyās (Fig. 10.2), the Rustamid governor of Jabal Nafusa,[7] came to fight Khalaf ibn al-Samḥ's son at the very end of the ninth century, the latter sought protection from the Zawāgha who obeyed him. The confrontation was very violent and the Zawāgha were put to flight; the survivors took refuge in

Fig. 10.2. Jabal Nafusa: the Abū Manṣūr Ilyās mosque in Tandamira, drowned out by the modern developments imposed by Colonel Gaddafi (photo V. Prevost, 2010).

[5] Gouja 2016, 89. For more details about Abū Miswar, see Prevost 2021, 68–71.

[6] Abū Zakariyyā' 1985, 189–90, 242–43. This is also recorded in the region of Tripoli, which involved going to Ifrīqiya (present-day Tunisia) for food: Al-Bughṭūrī 2017, 364.

[7] It seems that by the end of the ninth century the island was under the Rustamid governor of Jabal Nafusa and no longer under the governor of Gabes as had been the case previously, under imam 'Abd al-Wahhāb: Prevost 2007, 127–28.

Fig. 10.3. Jerba: the *jāmiʿ al-kabīr* (photo A. Derriks, 2010).

Jerba. This episode seems to be the origin of some of the Khalafi settlement that Abū Miswar fought against on his arrival on the island.[8]

From the ninth century onwards, there was a considerable expansion of rural settlement on the island, where the number of sites doubled by the tenth century and small farmsteads covered the landscape. There is a striking change in the location and type of sites from the Roman period onwards, which may be related to the arrival of Ibadi groups on the island. In Tripolitania, there is also a significant increase in the density of rural settlement from the late eighth century onwards, particularly in the coastal area near Lepcis Magna, where new fortified villages appeared in quantity.[9]

The Banū Yahrāsan quickly established themselves as the main Wahbi tribe in Jerba: Abū Miswar converted the Khalafis and then attacked the Nukkaris, against whom he succeeded in imposing himself after having received the support of the Zawāgha, the Banū Dammar and the Nafusa of the neighbouring regions (Al-Darjīnī 1974, I, 337–38; al-Shammākhī 2009, 522–23; al-Wisyānī 2009, I, 280–82). The Berbers of Tripolitania were thus involved in the establishment of Wahbi Ibadism in Jerba. Ibadi scholarly activity, previously concentrated in Tahert and Jabal Nafusa, moved to southern Tunisia and to Jerba, which became a refuge for the persecuted and an asylum for intellectuals.[10]

Faṣīl, Abū Miswar's son, took over his father's work, continuing the construction of the great mosque of Jerba, the *jāmiʿ al-kabīr* (Fig. 10.3), the first important centre of Wahbi Ibadism on the island and the seat of power of the Banū Yahrāsan. He maintained good relations with Tripolitania: for example, he is seen travelling to Tripoli with his son (Abū Zakariyyā' 1985, 343). But despite the influx of students to the island, he dreaded the gradual extinction of the Ibadi communities, geographically isolated from each other and subject to a regime with which they were in deep contradiction. Faṣīl was convinced that the era of the imamate was over and that his co-religionists had to resign themselves to living in clandestinity (*kitmān*). The scholar then envisioned the *ḥalqa* – an organization in which each geographical community elected from among its most pious members a council of men of religion called *ʿazzāba* (Cherifi 2005, 40–45). Ibadi texts report that in 409 AH/1018–19 CE, Abū ʿAbd Allāh Muḥammad ibn Bakr, the best disciple

[8] Abū Zakariyyā' 1985, 148 and al-Darjīnī 1974, 86. Despois 1935, 294–96, emphasizes the constant movement of people from Jabal Nafusa into Tunisia from the eleventh century.

[9] Fenwick 2022, 431. See also the details provided by Leone 2019, 266, 271–73.

[10] Gouja 2016, 94–95. Fatimid persecutions took place in the Jabal which may have caused a wave of migration to Jerba: see Prevost 2016, 25–26.

of Faṣīl, reached the region of Wadi Righ, settled with his followers in a cave and created the first *ḥalqa*, a system that later spread to other Ibadi communities (Al-Darjīnī 1974, I, 167–70; Abū Zakariyyā' 1985, 252–55). The *ḥalqa* is based on the tradition of the scholars of Jabal Nafusa, transmitted in Jerba by Abū Miswar to his son Faṣīl, and on the personality of Abū 'Abd Allāh Muḥammad ibn Bakr (440 AH/1048–49 CE), whose family came from Fursaṭā in Jabal Nafusa (Al-Shammākhī 2009, 569).

An important step in the development of the *ḥalqa* seems to have been the collective writing of the *Dīwān al-'azzāba*, a 12-volume legal encyclopaedia; it took place on the island, in the cave of Majmāj where the seven 'people of the cave' (*ahl al-ghār*) met. The editors were four scholars from the Mazāta tribe, as well as Abū 'Imrān al-Numaylī, Abū Muḥammad 'Abd Allāh ibn Mānūj al-Lamā'ī, and Abū Zakariyyā' Yaḥyā ibn Jūnān al-Nafūsī (Abū Zakariyyā' 1985, 284). The latter, whose name varies according to the authors although they agree on his Nafūsī origin, is presented in the texts as a scholar who rendered *fatwā-s* in Tripoli (Al-Darjīnī 1974, 393; Abū Zakariyyā' 1985, 343–44; al-Shammākhī 2009, 580). Of all the scholars in the cave, he is the only one who testifies to a collaboration between Jerba and Tripolitania, which is quite surprising when one considers the importance of this writing.

In the absence of political unity and of state framework, only the teaching of doctrine and the training of scholarly and religious elites within the context of the *ḥalqa* could ensure the continuity of the Ibadi tradition (Cherifi 2005, 44). The scholars set up a veritable travelling school and their travels multiplied, facilitated perhaps by the respect that the *'azzāba* commanded (Al-Darjīnī 1974, 380; Abū Zakariyyā' 1985, 264). These long journeys allowed for frequent exchanges between the scholars of the different communities, spread the news from the East, provided material aid to the needy, and above all revived the faith of the most isolated communities. The Ibadi sources are full of examples of these trips, which brought together students from all the Ibadi regions, including Tripoli (Abū Zakariyyā' 1985, 275). This organization undoubtedly contributed to strengthening exchanges between Jerba and Tripolitania, and in particular with Zuwara, west of Tripoli, which had close contacts with the island.[11]

Al-Bughṭūrī, whose work was completed in 1203, thus reports that, during the period evidently following the fall of Tahert, the Ibadis from Jerba, Tripoli, and Ifrīqiya gathered in a village in the Jabal called 'Imāsin' in numbers of about a thousand, sometimes more, sometimes less, requiring the presence of interpreters; they worshipped at shrines and sometimes also gathered in the desert that separates the Jabal from the Fazzan (Al-Bughṭūrī 2017, 105–6). According to al-Wisyānī, the people of Ifrīqiya, probably here the Ibadis of the Djerid, wanted to visit their co-religionists in Tripoli and the surrounding area and began their journey towards 'Tripoli whose border was at Gabes'; this formula confirms that for medieval chroniclers Tripoli referred not only to the city but also to its region, presumably to the coastline. They first passed through Jerba where they attended a scholarly meeting at which Abū Miswar was present.[12] Later on, we see scholars returning from the pilgrimage to Mecca first to Tripoli and then to Jerba (Al-Wisyānī 2009, 476). We also read that a group of *'azzāba* from the Jabal broke the Ramadan fast only with dates from Jerba (Al-Bughṭūrī 2017, 322). These intellectual and religious relations were certainly most often coupled with commercial relations, as many scholars were also merchants, and Jerba represented one of the outlets for trans-Saharan trade.[13]

For centuries, scholars from the Jabal came to study and teach in Jerba, and many Jerbian scholars were trained in the Jabal. This is the case of two important figures from the late tenth century, Abū Mūsā 'Īsā ibn al-Samḥ al-Zawāghī and Abū Ṣāliḥ Bakr ibn Qāsim al-Yahrāsanī, who twice underwent a lengthy apprenticeship there; two old mosques on the island still bear their names and are believed to house their tombs (Al-Shammākhī 2009, 434; Prevost 2023, 68–74, 200–4). In the fourteenth century, Abū l-Faḍl Abū l-Qāsim al-Barrādī, the author of *al-Jawāhir al-muntaqāt*, studied in the Jabal before pursuing his career in Jerba and the famous Ismā'īl al-Jīṭālī, a native of the Jabal, frequented the *jāmi' al-kabīr*.[14]

The examples of contacts provided here are all related to the Ibadis, but it would also be interesting to examine the links within the Jewish community, which had a whole network of settlements in Tripolitania, notably in Sharūs and Jadu in Jabal Nafusa, but also in Lebdah (Lepcis Magna), Tripoli, and Ghadames (Hirschberg 1974, 130–32; Abitbol 1982, 234). Around the mid-twelfth century, the documents of the Cairo Geniza concerning the island refer to the Jews captured during the

[11] Gouja 2016, 60. Several ancient poems in Berber language have been found in Jerba and in Jabal Nafusa, which explain in a simple way the main principles of the Ibadi doctrine, intended to spread knowledge of the dogma more easily. They arguably belonged to a vast poetic corpus, a sort of 'oral catechism', undoubtedly intended for a largely illiterate population. These poems, which had to be understood in all the regions populated by Ibadis, were obviously written in an 'Ibadi koine' used for religious teaching: see Brugnatelli 2005, 139–41.

[12] Al-Wisyānī 2009, 338. On the question of the designations of Tripoli and Tripolitania, see Abdouli 2019, 125–27.

[13] Fentress 2018, 247–48 notes that the slave trade, reported in Jerba during the medieval period, was probably much older; the Garamantes sold enslaved people, often children, acquired in sub-Saharan Africa to Lepcis Magna and it is likely that Jerba was another terminus of this trade, especially when the security of Lepcis Magna collapsed in the fourth century.

[14] Al-Ja'bīrī 1975, 208, 242; al-Shammākhī 2009, 806–7. There are many other examples of these scholarly exchanges in Prevost 2023.

Norman raid of 1135. Among the many pieces of information preserved is a letter that was sent from Tripoli to Cairo. The author of the letter signs 'Isaac, son of Rabbi Sedaqa, the cantor, captive among the captives of Jerba'. He describes the difficult times experienced by his family members, his father, brothers and nieces, who were in Tripoli at the time. It is not clear whether Isaac was a Jerbian whose family had found refuge in Tripoli or whether he was born in Tripoli and was only serving as a cantor, officiating at prayer, in one of the Jewish communities of Jerba at the time of the arrival of the Normans. In any case, he experienced dramatic events on the island (Valensi and Udovitch 2022, 16). Another letter, dated 1136, indicates that Isaac's father was forced, after a famine, to sell their house in Jerba to cover debts.[15]

Like the fate of the Ibadis, that of the Jews of Jerba and Tripolitania is linked, and they were probably victims in the same way, if we are to believe Ibn Ezra's elegy of the Almohad persecutions (Hirschberg 1974, 134–36; Abitbol 1982, 239). The Nafusa had two synagogues named Ghriba, as did the most famous synagogue in Jerba (Merimi 2020, 152). One of these synagogues, located in Yefren, is still in good condition and it is striking to note the resemblance of this building and its decoration with the neighbouring mosques and with those of Jerba.[16] Numerous comparisons can also be made between the traditional costumes and adornments worn by the Jerbian women and those of the women of Tripoli; it is clearly through the Jewish community of the island and especially through its jewellers that very ancient models of adornment from Tripolitania were imposed on Jerba (Ben Tanfous *et al.* 1978, 185–87).

The special links between Jerba and Tripolitania continue to this day. At the end of the nineteenth century, one of the villages on the island was called 'Nafusa' (Bertholon 1897, 582). The Jerbians have kept many property deeds originating from the Tamezda and Jadu region (Despois 1935, 239–40). Studying the similarities between the Nafūsī Berber language and that of Jerba, Vermondo Brugnatelli (2009, 357) insists on the fact that many Jerbian families of Guellala keep the memory of their origin from the Jabal and cites many family names that still attest to this: Jadoui, Ben Tanfous, Kebaoui, Fassatoui, etc. Today, exchanges remain very strong between these regions. Since the war in Libya, the island appears to be a sort of Eldorado where many Libyans come to rest, have fun and temporarily escape the distressing situation in their country. Relations are still very close within the Ibadi community between the island and the inhabitants of Jabal Nafusa. This can be seen on the website of the Berber Ibadi community of Jerba, where news from the Jabal, its mosques and a number of reports on the Ibadis of this region are regularly given.

The hypothesis of an architectural filiation: could the Abū Maʿrūf mosque have been a model for the *jāmiʿ al-kabīr* of Jerba?

In 2010, the photographer Axel Derriks and I made a study trip to Jabal Nafusa: this was a simple reconnaissance of this little-known region and several other trips were planned to study in detail the Ibadi mosques, which were poorly documented at the time. In 1969, 1971 and 1973, three archaeological missions under the auspices of the Society for Libyan Studies (now the British Institute for Libyan and Northern African Studies) had brought together British and Libyan archaeologists under the supervision of James W. Allan to study 29 places of worship (Allan 1972–73); Muhammad Warfalli, who had participated in the last two missions, subsequently devoted his doctoral thesis to some of these mosques (Warfalli 1981). A few rare publications complemented these two essential studies (on the recycling of classical-period spolia in some mosques of Jabal Nafusa, see Welsby Sjöström, Chapter 9). The war broke out a few months after our trip, and several years later, with no hope of continuing this research for a long time, we resigned ourselves to publishing the little material we had been able to gather on the spot (Prevost 2016).

Sobriety, even austerity, and the simplicity of the materials used are characteristics common to all the Ibadi regions without exception. At the time of writing the book, many common features between the mosques of the Jabal and those of Jerba, partly linked to this rigorous doctrine, already seemed obvious: the profusion of places of worship, which is mainly explained by their central role in the life of the Ibadis, the protrusion of the mihrab, whose niche is often extremely simple, the smallness of the prayer rooms and the maximum reduction of their openings, intended to preserve cool temperatures.[17] The absence of a minbar is almost systematic; there is traditionally no minbar in the Ibadi mosques of the Maghreb because since the fall of the Rustamids of Tahert, the Ibadis no longer have an independent imam at the head of their community and therefore no longer deliver the *khuṭba* – the Friday sermon delivered in the name of the sovereign in power. In Jerba, however, the

[15] Letter T-S 10J15.26, to be found at www.geniza.princeton.edu.

[16] Some photos of the decoration of the vaults, mixing Hebrew epigraphy and 'hands of fatma' are visible on archive.diarna.org/site/detail/public/1983 et sur udayen.com/yefren/.

[17] Prevost 2016, 153–81. On the other hand, other elements differentiate the mosques of the Jabal from those of Jerba; they rarely have a courtyard, and in several cases they have a very particular pointed arch shape. Most of the older mosques have given priority to a space reserved for women, by creating one or more bays for them, separated from the rest of the prayer room by a wall, to which a private entrance often leads. The mihrabs of the Jabal are distinguished by the large size of their niches and by the fact that their multiplication, both in the prayer room and outside, is rare.

Fig. 10.4. *(top right)* Jabal Nafusa: the main mosque in Nalut (photo A. Derriks, 2010).

Fig. 10.5. *(bottom right)* Jerba: the Bāzīn mosque in Mezrane (photo A. Derriks, 2021).

obligation to perform the Friday prayer was imposed on the Ibadis in the main mosque of Houmt Souk as early as 1079 AH/1668–69 CE and a minbar was therefore added in this mosque and in many others thereafter (for more details on the minbar issue, see Prevost 2016, 177–79).

The frequent absence of a minaret in the form of a tower can also be noted: as in early Islam, the call to prayer was in fact once made from outside the mosque or from the roof. Jabal mosques often have a *ṣum'a*, a kind of pinnacle, sometimes openwork, placed on the roof; its role would be limited to indicating the position of the building but this pinnacle is sometimes considered, rightly in our view, as a kind of miniature minaret.[18] The *ṣum'a* is present in the four mosques we have studied in Nalut, where it consists of three or four legs that meet and are surmounted by a cylindrical element (Prevost 2016, 43–44, 181) (Fig. 10.4). This element is abundantly found in a similar form in the mosques of the island (Fig. 10.5).

'Primitive decoration' is frequently seen in the sanctuaries of the Jabal and Jerba; it consists mainly of geometric motifs (sets of dots, chevrons, crosses inscribed in squares, triangles, six-pointed stars, circles, etc.) and appears in relief on the plaster covering the walls of the prayer room or is engraved on them. Rarely very abundant, it is generally limited to certain portions of the vault, to certain intrados of arches, especially in the bay parallel to the *qibla* wall – the wall that indicates the direction of Mecca (Prevost 2016, 188–93) (Figs 10.6–7). Another architectural element, a determining factor in Jerba, is sometimes present in the Jabal: the staircase-minaret, a few steps that allow the muezzin to place himself high up to call for prayer (Fig. 10.2).[19] It is said in southern Tunisia that Jabal Nafusa is the continuity of Jerba, and that Jerba is the open-air museum of Jabal Nafusa (*matḥaf jabal Nafūsa*).[20]

Today, after having gathered a great deal of information on the island's mosques (Prevost 2023), we are particularly struck by other connections, which concern in particular the Abū Ma'rūf mosque in Sharūs,[21] a set of ruins located between Kabaw and Jadu. We studied this mosque in 2016 but unfortunately did not have the opportunity to visit it (Fig. 10.8). Its name evokes a renowned scholar of the end of the ninth and beginning of the tenth century, master of Abū Miswar, whose biographers praise his great science and decisive role in the transmission of the Ibadi traditions (see, for example: al-Shammākhī 2009, 417–20; al-Wisyānī 2009, 240–45).

[18] The *ṣum'a* is the same as the *ṣawma'a* (rooftop pavilion) of some early mosques; the word persisted in North Africa as the name for the tower minaret in later times. I am very grateful to Jonathan Bloom for his insightful comments on this chapter.

[19] This element was recently studied in detail in Prevost 2022.

[20] Naceur Bouabid pers. comm. (23 January 2016).

[21] The photograph was taken in September 1971 by Anthony Hutt. I am very grateful to Felicity Crowe and Philip Kenrick for their help in finding the old photographs of the British Mission to Libya.

Fig. 10.6. *(top left)* Jabal Nafusa: decor of a mosque in Kabaw (photo V. Prevost, 2010).

Fig. 10.7. *(top right)* Jerba: decor of Sīdī ʿUmar mosque (photo A. Derriks, 2021).

Fig. 10.8. *(right)* Jabal Nafusa: the Abū Maʿrūf mosque in Sharūs in 1971 (photo The Khalili Research Centre Image Database).

Comparison of its plan with that of the *jāmiʿ al-kabīr* at Jerba shows several similarities, both buildings striking for their spaciousness and imposing, massive character (Fig. 10.9). The measurements of the Sharūs mosque, partly underground, are about 15.3 m twice, 12.9 m and 14 m, with five vaulted bays parallel to the *qibla* wall; there are five naves perpendicular to the *qibla* wall but they are in various places interrupted by walls (Warfalli 1981, fig. 113; Prevost 2016, 97). The Jerbian prayer hall also has five bays and five naves, is square and measures 15.3 m on each side. The entrance to both buildings is placed in the same place, in the third bay; the location of the second entrance, however, differs now;[22] apart from these two doors, the buildings originally had no other openings. At Sharūs, a partition wall separates the first three bays from the last two, which appear to have been reserved for women; this is a common arrangement in the Jabal. In the *jāmiʿ al-kabīr*, it is the fifth bay that is reserved for women, but this arrangement seems to be very recent. Both sanctuaries show traces of ancient decoration.

The Abū Maʿrūf mosque has a staircase of a few steps to the west of the second bay, which originally led to the roof to call for prayer; the opening was blocked during renovation work (Warfalli 1981, 128–29, figs 125–26). The great mosque of Jerba also includes a staircase-minaret that rises outside, parallel to the main façade, in the north-east corner below the minaret (Fig. 10.3). Moreover, in the buildings we compare, this north-east corner is isolated from the rest of the prayer hall: at the *jāmiʿ al-kabīr*, this enclosed space houses the staircase that provides access to the minaret and the roof of the mosque. At Sharūs, this small square room found in other shrines in the Jabal was clearly intended to store the mosque's possessions, presumably mainly manuscripts (Warfalli 1981, 137).

It is striking that in the Sharūs mosque the *ṣumʿa* is not openwork and dominates the roof exactly above the mihrab; this is also the case in the very old Abū Manṣūr Ilyās mosque in Tandamira (Fig. 10.2), which is still the object of pilgrimage (*ziyāra*) among the Ibadis of the region and those of Jerba (Gouja 2016, 68–69). The *jāmiʿ al-kabīr* has a minaret in the form of a low, squat tower at the north-east corner, surmounted by a solid lantern, which can be reached by a staircase from the hall. This

[22] It is likely that the entrance to the women's section of the Sharūs mosque was originally located in the middle of the north-west façade, as evidenced by an archway that has been blocked off: Warfalli 1981, 137. It thus occupied the same place as in the Jerbian building.

lantern, which is distinctive because it is not openwork, bears a strong resemblance to the *ṣum'a* of the two Jabal mosques just mentioned (Fig. 10.3).

Thus, these two key shrines share many similarities in plan and general appearance, although the geographical setting is not at all the same. The main difference, a priori, is the orientation: the *qibla* wall points much further south in Jerba and a niche for the minbar was added to it late in life, when the Ibadis on the island were forced to make the *khuṭba*. With regard to aesthetics, one may add that it seems that unlike the *jāmi' al-kabīr*, the Abū Ma'rūf mosque was never whitewashed.

Given the surprising scale of these two buildings and the many similar aspects that distinguish them within their respective regions, it is tempting to hypothesize that it was in the Abū Ma'rūf mosque that Abū Miswar studied and that this building may have influenced him when he much later began the construction of the *jāmi' al-kabīr*. However, and this is mostly the case with ancient Ibadi mosques, this proposal runs into the question of the dating of these buildings. The Jerbian mosque is fairly well documented in the written sources, through the biography of Abū Miswar, and it seems very likely that the prayer hall was built around the middle of the tenth century, with its large size justified by its role as the main centre of Ibadism and the Banū Yahrāsan.

The Sharūs mosque appears to be very old, being recorded in written sources to date to the ninth century but not explicitly associated with Abū Ma'rūf (Al-Shammākhī 2009, 461; al-Bughṭūrī 2017, 117). Warfalli (1981, 141) believes that the building, which has certainly been much altered, dates back to at least the ninth century and that Abū Ma'rūf may have restored it rather than founded it. It is certainly this place of worship that Ibn Ḥawqal refers to when he mentions the Sharūs minbar in the tenth century.[23] Nicholas Lowick (1974, 14, 16) has dated the inscription on the tympanum of the western entrance in a 'Kufic floriated provincial' to between the second half of the tenth century and the twelfth century. It should be noted, however, that these two lines, which are not a foundation inscription, but a formula inspired by the Quran, may have been added at a later date. Although it is very likely that there was an important mosque on this site as early as the time of Abū Ma'rūf, there is nothing to confirm that its prayer hall was already of this impressive size. Unfortunately, our investigation stops here, like many other investigations we have carried out on ancient Ibadi buildings; only new elements brought to light by archaeological excavations could allow us to continue it.

The question of underground mosques

What seems to us to bring the culture of Jabal Nafusa closest to that of Jerba is the importance of caves and underground mosques.[24] We can only launch a few lines of thought here, in the hope of being able to resume investigations in the Jabal in the future. From the Rustamid period, the Ibadis celebrated the cult of caves just as their Berber ancestors did before Islam. The numerous anecdotes reported in the written sources clearly show the different functions of the cave: it is the dwelling place of the jinns, a beneficial place in which miracles take place, and lamps lit by mysterious forces await the faithful. It can also be a simple place of devotion where pious people shut themselves up for long periods to pray and recite the Quran. Indeed, it was in a cave he had dug for this purpose that Abū 'Abd Allāh Muḥammad ibn Bakr is said to have founded the first *ḥalqa* and lived with his *'azzāba*. The cave favours study and concentration, it seems to be for the Ibadis the place of scholarly meeting *par excellence* and it is probably for this reason that the *Dīwān al-'azzāba* was written by the seven scholars in the cave of Majmāj. While Berber traditions

Fig. 10.9. Jerba: the great mosque, *jāmi' al-kabīr* (photo A. Derriks, 2018).

[23] Ibn Ḥawqal 1939, 94. On Abū Ma'rūf mosque see Prevost 2016, 96–102, and especially Warfalli 1981, 119–38, pls 112–46, who offers several illustrations.

[24] This phenomenon is present, perhaps to a lesser extent, in other Ibadi regions such as the Mzab and Ouargla, or in Djerid. For numerous examples of this cave cult, see Prevost 2012, 47–53.

remain particularly rooted, Islam also develops a special link with caves, whether it be the cave of Ḥirā' where Gabriel is said to have appeared to the Prophet or that of the Seven Sleepers.

Both Tripolitania and Jerba have a tradition of underground buildings: one thinks of the innumerable troglodytic dwellings in the Gharian region or, on the island, the tombs of the Punic period and the numerous underground oil mills. Some contemporary authors have tried to explain the abundance of underground places of worship by a desire on the part of the Ibadis to defend themselves or to hide from persecution (for example: al-Murābiṭ 1996, III, 178–79; Lauricella 2019, 37). This hypothesis has always seemed unconvincing to us because access to these places does not seem to have been concealed and because these so-called refuges would have been extremely dangerous to use in the event of an attack: the Ibadis would have been caught there like rats. In reality, it seems that the main reason for their construction is the almost constant and very pleasant temperature that these rooms offer. To this must be added the ease of construction: digging the cave does not require any materials and especially no water, which is very appreciable in these regions.

Alongside the caves there are real excavated mosques: we know of nine underground rooms with a mihrab in Jerba.[25] It is very likely that there were many more in the past, and older people sometimes remember that there was an ancient underground mosque in the very close vicinity of their modern mosque, now condemned, but whose location has remained in the collective memory.[26] As far as Jabal Nafusa is concerned, unfortunately, we have documentation (sometimes very briefly) for only six underground places of worship. There are certainly many more, as suggested by surveys conducted by an Italian team (notably Dell'Aquila *et al.* 2009; Dell'Aquila and Fiorentino 2014) and by medieval written sources: the *Tasmiyat mashāhid al-jabal* – a list of worshipped places in Jabal Nafusa dated between the fourteenth and sixteenth centuries – records, for example, five cave-related places of worship (Basset 1899, 372–73). As in Jerba, they are most often found right next to built mosques, probably because they preceded them. This is the case of an underground mosque, which the inhabitants called Ghazāla, a few metres from the great mosque of Wīghū, to which Warfalli (181, 144) makes a simple allusion. Unfortunately we do not know what it looked like.

Another entirely subterranean mosque, reached by a deep ramp cut into the ground with walls made of neatly arranged stones, is about eight metres from the Ḥawāriyyīn mosque of Fursaṭā, near Kabaw (Fig. 10.10). As we passed, this ramp, parallel to the mosque's façade on the north-west side, was too cluttered with litter to enter, but others were able to access a large, almost circular prayer hall with bare walls, a mihrab, and a very small room contained within the circular space that may contain the remains of a tomb.[27] In Jerba, in the Cedghiane region, there is still a mosque of this type, the mosque of Sa'īd ibn Ṣālah, with a similar access ramp, but one now has to crawl to reach the prayer hall, the floor of which is so covered with rubble that one can only stand bent in half (Fig. 10.11).

It seems that in the Jabal, simple underground prayer halls are in the minority.[28] Curiously, the reverse is true on the island, judging by the small number of preserved places of worship. Like Sīdī Bū

Fig. 10.10. Jabal Nafusa: the Ḥawāriyyīn underground mosque in Fursaṭā (photo V. Prevost, 2010).

[25] The Majmāj cave does not have a mihrab and is therefore considered a simple sacred cave, not a real mosque.

[26] In the garden behind the Sīdī 'Abd al-Qādir mosque in Khnensa, for example, a few stones and a saucer used to collect water for birds still indicate the former underground mosque, which was active around 1925.

[27] Allan 1972–73, 151; Dell'Aquila and Fiorentino 2014, 17–18 (with a plan); Prevost 2016, 72–76. The prayer hall has clearly remained as it was excavated. The underground prayer hall of the mosque of Abū 'Ubayda 'Abd al-Ḥamīd in Ijnāwun, on the other hand, was completely renovated in the 1970s: see Prevost 2016, 139–42.

[28] Dell'Aquila and Fiorentino 2014, 21–23 were also able to visit the mosque of Takūt, to the west of the Jabal, which appears as a long, more or less rectangular, room cut into the rock under the fortified granary.

Fig. 10.11. *(left)* Jerba: the underground mosque of Saʿīd ibn Ṣālah (photo A. Derriks, 2019).

Fig. 10.12. *(below, top)* Jerba: the Ben Mūmin mosque (photo A. Derriks, 2021).

Fig. 10.13. *(below, bottom)* Jerba: the underground prayer hall of Ben Mūmin (photo A. Derriks, 2020).

Saʿīd, Bardāwī and Sīdī Zakrī, Ben Mūmin and Luṭā have a single underground hall (Prevost 2023, 176–81, 184–88, 207–12). The Ben Mūmin underground mosque in Khnensa adjoins, in the same space bounded by a low wall, two built mosques, a small old mosque and a modern one. One can see very clearly the entrance to the underground hall on the left, an outer mihrab in the foreground, opposite the old mosque, and the new one on the right (Fig. 10.12). The prayer hall is rectangular, entirely carved out of the rock, with an extremely simple mihrab and a sort of high bench on which the faithful light candles (Fig. 10.13). The Lūṭā Mosque of Sedouikech is, like the previous one, clearly visible from the outside with its two large domes (Figs 10.14–15). It could date from the thirteenth century (Al-Murābiṭ 1996, III, 51). It is still the object of pilgrimage by sterile women who believe they can find a remedy for their illness by offering eggs there.

Underground mosques with several rooms are the most common in the Jabal, such as Tanūmāyt in the Kabaw area, which includes a prayer hall with three naves and a small annexed room, probably intended for women's prayer; the date 454 AH/1062 CE is engraved on the semicircular plaque over the entrance to the mosque (Warfalli 1981, 65–69, pls 18–34; Dell'Aquila *et al.* 2011; Prevost 2016, 55–59). Sīdī Abū Raghwa has a more elaborate plan. A long corridor in the form of a staircase, overhung by a small minaret, descends to the underground mosque and leads to a covered vestibule which opens on the left side into two passages; the first leads to the mosque and the second to a burial chamber in which the deceased are prepared before being buried. On the right, a partially walled passageway opens into a shapeless room. In several places the date 1321 AH/1903–4 CE is noted,

Fig. 10.14. *(above)* Jerba: the Lūṭā mosque in Sedouikech (photo A. Derriks, 2010).

Fig. 10.15. *(top right)* Jerba: the underground prayer hall of Lūṭā mosque (photo A. Derriks, 2010).

Fig. 10.16. *(bottom right)* Jabal Nafusa: the underground mosque of Abū Zakariyyāʾ al-Tūkītī (photo A. Derriks, 2010).

which may correspond to the addition of the minaret. The plan of this underground mosque and its long access corridor bear similarities to the older Tanūmāyt mosque, whose plan may have been copied (Dell'Aquila and Fiorentino 2014, 19–20; Prevost 2016, 59–61). In the same vein, the 'Tatauzin' mosque in the vicinity of Fursaṭā has a deep ramp leading to a vestibule giving access to the prayer hall framed by two rooms, one of which would be for women (Dell'Aquila and Fiorentino 2014, 18–19, with plan).

Another example of a more complex underground mosque is Abū Zakariyyāʾ al-Tūkītī (Fig. 10.16), next to which a modern mosque is built. The personage for whom it is named was a kind of spiritual leader of the Jabal in the first half of the ninth century. The entrance, made of a long flight of stairs, was refurbished a few decades ago. One enters a large rectangular room with no pillars, extended by two burial chambers, one to the west and the other to the east (Allan 1972–73, 162–63, pl. 70; Prevost 2016, 109–13). In Jerba we know of only three examples of underground mosques with a complex plan: Wilḥī and Sīdī Ya'īsh have been studied in detail (Prevost 2023, 74–89), the third is the Barrādī mosque of Wadi Zbib which is also called 'the white birds'. A long ramp, the steps of which were carved into the stone but have now disappeared, gives access to a first room with a bench, then to a long room with a mihrab. Although the ramp has recently been cleared by volunteers, it is still difficult to enter the prayer room. Next door is a small mosque (Figs 10.17–18).

Further research is needed, but here too it seems to us that Jabal Nafusa may have influenced Jerba. The fact that the underground mosques there often have a complex layout is explained in our opinion by the very large number of cave dwellings. Several thousand of them still existed in the 1930s, with very different structures and sometimes multiple rooms (Dell'Aquila *et al.* 2009, 6–12). Among these mosques, some are still important places of prayer for today's Ibadis, such as Abū Zakariyyā' al-Tūkītī in the Jabal or Ben Mūmin in Jerba. Associated with certain very ancient rituals, it seems exciting to us to try to document them better.

Ibadi texts show that the island's scholarly life drew its main resources from Tripolitania. Several historical events caused the intellectual activity to move from Jabal Nafusa to Jerba, but the Jabal remained a decisive centre of study for the islanders and many scholars from Tripolitania made their careers on the island. We tend to think that the same influence may have been exerted in the architectural field, in landscapes that are nevertheless very different. Only a few lines of thought have been developed here, concerning two of the most emblematic mosques and underground sanctuaries, but many other subjects could give rise to a comparison: this is the case of tombs for example. One area seems particularly promising, although our knowledge of Jabal Nafusa is still too sketchy to address it, and that is the use by the Ibadis of places of worship as part of their defensive system, both in the mountains and on the island.

Fig. 10.17. *(above)* Jerba: the Barrādī underground mosque (photo A. Derriks, 2019).

Fig. 10.18. *(right)* Jerba: the prayer hall of Barrādī mosque (photo A. Derriks, 2022).

References

Abdouli, H. 2019. Le déplacement de la capitale provinciale de la Tripolitaine de Leptis Magna à Tripoli: modalités et datation. In R. Bockmann, A. Leone and P. von Rummel (eds), *Africa – Ifrīqiya. Continuity and Change in North Africa from the Byzantine to the Early Islamic Age. Papers of a Conference Held in Rome, Museo Nazionale Romano – Terme di Diocleziano (28 February – 2 March 2013).* Wiesbaden: Harrassowitz Verlag, 121–35.

Abitbol, M. 1982. Juifs maghrébins et commerce transsaharien du VIIIe au XVe siècle. In M. Abitbol (ed.), *Communautés juives des marges sahariennes du Maghreb. Actes du colloque tenu en mars 1980 à Jérusalem.* Jerusalem: Yad Izhak Ben-Zvi, 229–51.

Abū Zakariyyā'. 1985. *Kitāb al-Sīra wa-akhbār al-a'imma*, ed. 'A. Ayyūb. Tunis: Al-dār al-tūnisiyya li-l-nashr.

Allan, J.W. 1972–73. Some mosques of the Jebel Nafusa. *Libya Antiqua* 9–10: 147–69.

Barbū, M. 2018. *Tanẓīm al-majāl wa-l-tawṭīn wa-l-ta'mīr bi-jazīrat Jarba fī l-'ahd al-wasīṭ.* PhD Thesis: Tunis, Faculté des sciences humaines et sociales.

Basset, R. 1899. Les sanctuaires du Djebel Nefousa. *Journal Asiatique* May-June: 423–70 and July-August: 88–120.

Ben Tanfous, A. 1994. Khalaf ibn Aḥmad aw Sīdī Yātī. *Jarīdat al-Jazīra* 87: 16.

Ben Tanfous, A., Mahjoub, N., Louis, A., Sethom, S., Skhiri, F., Sugier, C. and Zouari, A. 1978. *Les costumes féminins traditionnels de Tunisie.* Tunis: Maison Tunisienne de l'Édition.

Bertholon, L. 1897. Exploration anthropologique de l'île de Gerba (Tunisie). *L'Anthropologie* 8: 318–26, 399–425, 559–83.

Brugnatelli, V. 2005. Un nuovo poemetto berbero ibadita. *Studi Magrebini* n.s. 3:131–42.

Brugnatelli, V. 2009. La classification du parler de Jerba (Tunisie). In S. Chaker, A. Mettouchi and G. Philippson (eds), *Études de phonétique et linguistique berbères. Hommage à Naïma Louali (1961–2005).* Paris: Peeters, 355–68.

Cherifi, B. 2005. La ḥalqa des 'azzāba: un nouveau regard sur l'histoire d'une institution religieuse ibāḍite. *Bulletin of the Royal Institute for Inter-Faith Studies* 7.1: 39–68.

Al-Darjīnī. 1974. *Kitāb Ṭabaqāt al-mashā'ikh bi-l-Maghrib*, ed. I. Ṭallāy (2 volumes). Constantine: Maṭba'at al-ba'th.

Dell'Aquila, F. and Fiorentino, G. 2014. Moschee rupestri nel Gebel Nefusa occidentale (Libia). *Opera Ipogea* 1/2014: 9–26.

Dell'Aquila, F., Fiorentino, G., Polimeni, B. and Bencini, C. 2009. Insediamenti rupestri nel Gebel Nefusa occidentale (Libia). *Opera Ipogea* 2/2009: 3–18.

Dell'Aquila, F., Fiorentino, G. and Bencini, C. 2011. La moschea rupestre di Tnumayat (Gebel Garbi, Tripolitania, Libia). *Opera Ipogea* 1.2/2011: 263–70.

Despois, J. 1935. *Le Djebel Nefousa (Tripolitaine). Étude géographique.* Paris: Larose Éditeurs.

Fentress, E., 2018. An island in transition: Jerba between the fifth and the ninth centuries. In S. Panzram and L. Callegarin (eds), *Entre civitas y madīna. El mundo de las ciudades en la Peninsula Iberica y en el norte de Africa (siglos IV–IX).* Madrid: Casa de Velázquez, 241–52.

Fenwick, C. 2022. The Arab conquests and the end of ancient Africa? In R.B. Hitchner (ed.), *A Companion to North Africa in Antiquity.* Hoboken, NJ: Wiley-Blackwell, 424–37.

Gouja, M. 2016. *Une géographie humaine des espaces ibadites maghrébins au 6ème H./12ème s.* Paris: Ibadica Éditions.

Hirschberg, H.Z. 1974. *A History of the Jews in North Africa. Volume 1: From Antiquity to the Sixteenth Century.* Leiden-Boston: Brill.

Ibn 'Abd al-Ḥakam. 1922. *Futūḥ Miṣr, The History of the Conquest of Egypt, North Africa and Spain*, ed. C.C. Torrey. New Haven-London: Yale University Press.

Ibn Ḥawqal. 1939. *Kitāb Ṣūrat al-arḍ / Opus geographicum*, eds M.J. de Goeje and J.H. Kramers. Leiden-Boston: Brill.

Ibn Khaldūn. 1992. *Kitāb al-'Ibar wa-dīwān al-mubtada' wa-l-khabar fī ayyām al-'Arab wa-l-'Ajam wa-l-Barbar wa-man 'āṣarahum min dhawī al-sulṭān al-akbar* (7 volumes). Beirut: Dār al-kutub al-'ilmiyya.

Al-Ja'bīrī, F. 1975. *Niẓām al-'azzāba 'inda al-ibāḍiyya al-wahbiyya fī Jarba.* Tunis: Institut National d'Archéologie et d'Art.

Lauricella, A.J. 2019. Ibāḍī boundaries and defense in the Jabal Nafūsa (Libya). In A. Asa Eger (ed.), *The Archaeology of Medieval Islamic Frontiers. From the Mediterranean to the Caspian Sea.* Louisville: University Press of Colorado, 31–46.

Leone, A. 2019. Cultural transitions in archaeology. From Byzantine to Islamic Tripolitania. In R. Bockmann, A. Leone and P. von Rummel (eds), *Africa – Ifrīqiya. Continuity and Change in North Africa from the Byzantine to the Early Islamic Age. Papers of a Conference Held in Rome, Museo Nazionale Romano – Terme di Diocleziano (28 February – 2 March 2013).* Wiesbaden: Harrassowitz Verlag, 265–78.

Lowick, N.M. 1974. The Arabic inscriptions on the mosque of Abū M'arūf at Sharwas, Jebel Nafûsa. *Libyan Studies* 5: 14–19.

Merimi, M. 2020. *Juifs de Jerba et stratégies identitaires.* Paris: Ibadica.

Al-Murābiṭ, R. 1996. *Jawāmi' wa-masājid jazīrat Jarba fī l-'aṣrayn al-ḥafṣi wa-l-murādī. Dirāsa athariyya wa-tārīkhiyya.* PhD Thesis: Tunis, Faculté des sciences humaines et sociales.

Prevost, V. 2007. L'influence de l'État rustumide dans le Sud tunisien. *Acta Orientalia* 68: 113–33.

Prevost, V. 2012. Maǧmāǧ et les sept savants: la création du Dīwān al-'azzāba. *Acta Orientalia* 73: 35–58.

Prevost, V. 2016. *Les mosquées ibadites du Djebel Nafūsa. Architecture, histoire et religions du nord-ouest de la Libye (VIIIe–XIIIe siècle).* London: Society for Libyan Studies.

Prevost, V. 2021. The Banū Yahrāsan, political and sacred leaders in Ibāḍī Jerba. *Al-Masāq* 33.1: 66–84.

Prevost, V. 2022. Quelques remarques sur la diffusion du minaret-escalier et son lien avec les ibadites. In C. de la Puente and M. Meouak (eds), *Connected Stories: Transmissions of Knowledge between East and West in the Premodern Islamic World.* Berlin: De Gruyter, 194–216.

Prevost, V. 2023. *Résistance et dévotion. Anciens sanctuaires ibadites de Jerba.* London: British Institute for Libyan and Northern African Studies.

Al-Shammākhī. 2009. *Kitāb al-Siyar*, ed. M. Ḥasan (3 volumes). Beirut: Dār al-madār al-islāmī.

Valensi, L. and Udovitch, A.L. 2022. *Juifs de Jerba. Regards sur une communauté millénaire.* Tunis: Déméter.

Warfalli, M.S.M. 1981. *Some Islamic Monuments in Jabal Nafusa.* PhD Thesis: London, School of Oriental and African Studies.

Al-Wisyānī. 2009. *Siyar al-Wisyānī*, ed. ʻU. Bū ʻAṣbāna (3 volumes). Muscat: Wizārat al-turāth wa-l-thaqāfa.

Chapter 11

TRIPOLITANIA: CONCLUSIONS AND PROSPECTS FOR FUTURE RESEARCH

David J. Mattingly

The state of the field

The coastal lands of south-eastern Tunisia and north-western Libya saw initial urban development in the first millennium BCE, traditionally explained as the initiative of Phoenician 'settlers' – though our ancient sources describe the population of the zone as *Libyphoenices*. While designated as an outlying territory of the province of Africa in the first to third centuries CE, Tripolitana later became a separate province in the early fourth century, was conquered by the Vandals in the fifth century and reintegrated into the Byzantine African province in the sixth century, before being an early target of the Islamic raiders in the 640s. These dramatic shifts in political affiliation need to be contextualized alongside the evidence of regional wealth and high culture – exemplified in brilliant artworks (statuary, sculpture, mosaics) and monumental marble-adorned architecture. Tripolitania may have been climatically and geographically on the margins of the rich African provinces, but it was by no means inconsequential in the story of the Roman Empire – sending a string of men into imperial service as equestrians, senators and ultimately emperors, with Septimius Severus and his sons. The foundational study of this region was carried out by Italian archaeologists during the early twentieth-century period of colonial domination, with a long-term continuing impact into the post-colonial age.[1] The great urban monuments of the classical cities of Lepcis Magna and Sabratha have thereafter been a prime focus of study and conservation efforts.[2]

Tripolitania has also been an important component of my research throughout my academic career (Mattingly 2019, for some biographical notes). In the early 1980s I carried out PhD research on Tripolitania, while at the same time participating in the UNESCO Libyan Valleys Archaeological Survey (ULVS), whose results were published in Barker 1996; Mattingly 1996a. Two edited books relating to Tripolitania came out in the 1980s (Buck and Mattingly 1985; Mattingly and Lloyd 1989 = *Libyan Studies* 20, 1989) and this work was then further developed into a monograph (Mattingly 1995). That book attempted to provide an account in English of the history and archaeology of the region and later Roman province known as Tripolitana (often rendered as 'Tripolitania' in modern times). Nearly 30 years on, Niccolò Mugnai is to be congratulated in bringing together the present book, which provides an important opportunity to take stock on the progress of the field in some key research areas in the intervening years. With a number of broader English-language overviews of North Africa under Roman rule now available, it is worth reflecting further on the distinctiveness of Tripolitania.[3] The chapters of this volume certainly stand out as original contributions to these ongoing debates.

In the colonial era, archaeological work was concentrated at the major coastal cities (see below), and while this continued to a degree in post-colonial times there were fewer opportunities for major new projects by the foreign missions under the Gaddafi regime.[4] The situation for fieldwork and research in Libya has become even worse since 2011, due to the long-term political

[1] Merighi 1940; cf. Di Vita *et al.* 1999; Rizzo and Di Vita-Évrard 2015; Rizzo 2017. On the colonial context: Mattingly and Hitchner 1995; Munzi 2001; 2004; Mattingly 2011, 43–72.

[2] Kenrick 2009; Balice 2010; Di Vita 2010; Musso and Turjman 2022.

[3] Mattingly and Hitchner 1995; Mugnai *et al.* 2016; Hitchner 2022; Mattingly 2023, for a synthesis with many reflections on Tripolitanian specifics.

[4] Among important new fieldwork initiatives in Libya since the 1990s, I would highlight the work of Roma Tre University around Lepcis Magna (Musso *et al.* 1997; 1998; 2010; 2014); the German Archaeological Mission at Gheriat el-Garbia (Mackensen 2021a–b; 2024); and the French Archaeological Mission's excavation of the baths to the east of the harbour at Lepcis Magna (see essays in Michel 2015).

instability that has followed the Arab Spring and the overthrow of Gaddafi. Tripolitania is thus very distinct from many other parts of the former Roman Empire in terms of the pace, volume and character of new research.

Before going further it is worth asking what we mean by Tripolitania in geographical and historical terms. The name clearly relates to the three large ancient cities (emporia) of western Libya – Sabratha, Oea (Tripoli), and Lepcis Magna – but the ancient province extended into south-eastern Tunisia up to the eastern flank of the Chott Jarid and the port of Tacape (Gabes) (Mattingly 2000a, for an attempt to capture this cartographically). The coastal zone of western Tripolitania, along with the Island of Jerba, included a number of other important urban centres (Meninx, Tipasa, Gigthis, Zitha), as well as at least one inland oasis town at Telmine (Turris Tamalleni). Tripolitanian territory also technically continued around the Greater Syrtis, with the border with neighbouring Cyrenaica at the eastern end of the desert coastland (Mattingly 2000c, for mapping of sites in the Syrtica region).

A key aspect of my approach in my 1995 book *Tripolitania* was to reunite data on both the Tunisian and Libyan territories, but many studies before and since tend to align to one side or the other of the modern border – indeed the editor's introduction here (Chapter 1) acknowledges a greater focus on the Libyan part for the volume.[5] Edited volumes, such as the present one, are inevitably dependent on authors who are willing and able to deliver on promised contributions; many of the contributors here are British-based, German, or Italian researchers whose work relates primarily to Libya, though not all the active Italian Missions are represented. As the editor flags up in his introduction, it is unfortunate that no North African researchers feature among the final contributions, as they have helped advance research in important ways. The essays collected here do however succeed in advancing new ideas or providing a clear synthesis on aspects of the archaeology of Tripolitania, especially when read alongside both older and newer syntheses.

Most chapters in this volume focus on Roman-era archaeology, with the important exception of Prevost's essay on mosques on the Island of Jerba and their architectural links to the rural mosques of the Jabal Nafusa region (Chapter 10). The mosques of the latter zone are also mentioned in Welsby Sjöström's contribution and are noteworthy for their reused stonework from Roman-period sites (Chapter 9). Islamic Tripolitania is a subject that merits a larger and more focused study in its own right (see Leone 2019; Fenwick 2020). In order to contextualize the contributions to this volume within broader debates, my comments are structured beneath a series of themes.

The Roman garrison deployment and military community

The Roman army in North Africa is known primarily through epigraphic records rather than modern field investigation of military bases and installations (for summary accounts, see Mattingly *et al.* 2013a; Guédon 2018). Mackensen's masterful account of the Roman military garrison (Chapter 6) is an example of a chapter that does provide a broad overview of developments across time in both east and west Tripolitania. Building on his transformational fieldwork at the desert fort of Gheriat el-Garbia, the author is able to make significant revisions to previous knowledge – most notably with the now attested late reoccupation of that fort in the fourth-fifth centuries CE. This makes much better sense of the *Notitia Dignitatum* entries, which seem to imply that substantial elements of the third-century CE system of regional *limes* commands were still intact in Late Antiquity, rather than the prior assumptions of a very substantial shrinkage of the garrisoned zone (Mackensen 2021b; Mattingly 2023, 271–77; cf. 1995, 186–93). On the other hand, some elements of the overall presentation remain much as they were in the 1990s, reflecting the lack of significant fieldwork advances (with the obvious exception of Gheriat el-Garbia). While Mackensen rightly questions some of my more speculative suggestions in earlier works, there is equally a lack of conclusive evidence in some cases for alternative suggestions. For example, the argument that the *clausurae* (linear barriers) were purely a late Roman innovation in Tripolitania remains unproven and is unlikely to be resolved until and unless there is excavation of related installations, such as gates.[6] Likewise, for all periods, there are some notable gaps in the mapped distributions of epigraphically attested forts and we can speculate on the one hand that some locations were military bases (Mizda), and from another perspective there are a number of ancient toponyms related to garrison points where no certain modern location can be proposed (Thenteos, Secedi). The simple truth is that, in the absence of excavation, or indeed modern research, at many known Roman army bases or locations that may have been military positions (as Mackensen himself points out), we have a lacunous narrative and a threadbare distribution map. Even with known military sites, the occupation history may have been vastly different to what is established epigraphically. Where modern excavations have taken place, as at Gheriat el-Garbia and Bu Njem, these have revealed unexpected complexities of garrison units, phases of occupation and activities that took place there.

[5] Sheldrick 2021 has admirably clear maps of the entire territory from southern Tunisia to the border with Cyrenaica.

[6] Mattingly 1995, 106–15; 2023, 258–62 on a potentially longer chronology – backed up in part by my observation of surface pottery at some of these locations.

In my most recent work I have moved away from referring to Roman 'frontiers' as I think this gives a misleading idea of a Roman defensive line facing the desert, whereas forts and minor installations were spread across a broad and deep 'security zone', with the garrison equally involved with supervising peoples inside as outside the notional limits of Roman territory (Mattingly 2023, 247, 251). This has important implications for our understanding of the work of the garrison.

The other contributions on the military theme are more focused case studies: Schimmer (Chapter 7) on military food supply in the third century CE and Schmid (Chapter 8) on religious practices in the military community. Schimmer is particularly good in combining different sorts of data (botanical and faunal information, ceramic evidence and textual indications) to construct an overall picture that relates primarily to the two main excavated forts. The extent to which this picture applied across the entirety of the Tripolitanian Jabal and desert landscapes is debatable of course, but the significance of the existence of oases in the northern Sahara is at any rate clear. Schmid recapitulates the evidence from religious epigraphy and shrine/temple construction related to the army, with updates from the Gheriat el-Garbia work again underpinning some new insights.[7] What one could add to this picture is a consideration of how these military practices related to, or differed from, local religious behaviour. In my own recent work, for instance, I have argued for a clear separation between the military community and the rural populations of North Africa in terms of their religious preferences and behaviours.[8]

Urbanism

There is no overall chapter on urbanism in Tripolitania *senso lato*, though the two contributions on aspects of the urban history at Sabratha (Aiosa, Chapter 2) and Lepcis Magna (Mugnai, Chapter 3) are both insightful and novel in their arguments relating to those specific sites and specific phases of their development. The major Italian colonial-era excavations exposed a stunning suite of urban monuments at Lepcis Magna and Sabratha, which publication has only slowly been catching up on. Thus, while there have been important advances in knowledge in the last few decades, it needs emphasizing that some of these relate to the long delayed publication of old excavations from the time of the Italian colonial regime,[9] or the British military mandate and Libyan Kingdom that followed the Second World War.[10] Many of those early twentieth-century excavations had been essentially clearance and reconstruction programmes, with relatively little attention to finds beyond coins, architectural and sculptural elements, and inscriptions (the Sabratha excavations under Kathleen Kenyon and John Bryan Ward-Perkins are an important exception).[11] Although it is tremendously important to have (at last) monographic reports on many of the major monuments, the essentials of these monuments have been widely known for many years from preliminary reports and incorporated into the standard accounts (see Di Vita *et al.* 1999; Kenrick 2009). Moreover, with the exception of a few instances of modern sondages into surviving stratigraphy,[12] the sequences of construction, use and abandonment of these structures are often poorly established. The earliest phases of the Tripolitanian cities (often unreached by colonial excavations) and the latest occupation levels (generally removed with minimal record by the same) are the most elusive.[13] The epigraphic evidence is especially rich from Lepcis Magna, with a significant body from Sabratha, but drastically fewer texts from the many other urban centres (compare *IRT2021* with the known texts from Tunisian sites published in *CIL* VIII, *ILAfr*, and *ILT*). Thus, while we have two of the best studied 'Roman' cities in the region from an architectural perspective, the typicality of these in relation to the wider Tripolitanian urban pattern is frankly impossible to assess fully.[14]

Aiosa makes especially novel arguments about the second-century CE developments at Sabratha, while Mugnai gives a fresh and balanced account of Severan-period construction at Lepcis Magna that takes into consideration both the monumental schemes and minor building projects of that era. These will be important points of reference. Mugnai's chapter is an excellent complement to his recent reflection on Roman architecture at Lepcis Magna in the first and second centuries

[7] For a previous overview see Brouquier-Reddé 1992. See also relevant discussion of religion in the military community in Mattingly 2023, 310–14.

[8] Again, see discussion of Gaetulian religious practices among rural communities in Mattingly 2023, 505–16.

[9] De Miro and Polito 2005 (Lepcis Magna, Old Forum, including pre-Roman levels); Di Vita and Livadiotti 2005 (Lepcis Magna, north-west temples in the Old Forum); Tomasello 2005 (Lepcis Magna, fountains and nymphaea) and 2011 (Lepcis Magna, Temple on the *decumanus maximus*); Aiosa 2013 (Sabratha, Temple of Hercules); Montali 2015 (Sabratha, amphitheatre); Mazzilli 2016 (Lepcis Magna, Arch of Trajan); Livadiotti and Rocco 2018 (Lepcis Magna, curia); Ricciardi 2018 (Lepcis Magna, amphitheatre).

[10] Kenrick 1986 (Sabratha, excavations around the forum area and related material culture); Ward-Perkins 1993 (Lepcis Magna, Severan buildings).

[11] Sabratha finds: Dore and Keay 1989; Fulford and Tomber 1994; Allason-Jones and Greep 2023.

[12] For example: De Miro and Polito 2005; Tomasello 2005, 215–74; 2011, 119–80; Aiosa 2013, 101–60; Montali 2015, 161–84; Livadiotti and Rocco 2018, 395–402.

[13] Though see Kenrick 1986 (Libyphoenician levels at Sabratha and Lepcis Magna); Tantillo and Bigi 2010 (Late Antique Lepcis Magna). For a general reflection on Late Antique cities, see Leone 2013; 2019.

[14] Brouquier-Reddé 1992; Baratte *et al.* 2018; Mattingly 2023, 405–11 for a range of views on the nature of urban religious practices and architectural embellishment in the Roman era.

CE (Mugnai 2021); elsewhere, he has also contributed an important synthesis study on Roman urban architecture in North Africa (Mugnai 2022).

For a larger view of urbanism in the region across time one should look also at the sites in Tunisian western Tripolitania and on Jerba, where there has been much important work.[15] The chronological framework of the present volume understandably does not encompass the pre-Roman period, but one should point out the significance of work on the origins of the urban sites of Henchir Bourgou and Ghizène on Jerba, where the earliest phases are related to distinctive handmade pottery and extend back before the earliest imported pottery, indicating sedentarized or semi-sedentarized Libyan communities in the early first millennium BCE (Ben Tahar 2014; 2018; Ben Tahar *et al.* 2020; 2022). With other sites in western Tripolitania also yielding signs of early sedentarization of the local population groups, this changes our understanding of the nature of Libyphoenician societies.[16]

A separate issue concerns the nature and development of urban centres at oases such as Turris Tamelleni (Telmine) and Cidamus (Ghadames) (Mattingly *et al.* 2020b, 195–98, 202–5). There is no particular reason to think that these closely resembled the coastal cities in terms of their layout and monumentality, though both sites undoubtedly featured some monumental architecture by later antiquity (Mattingly 2023, 369–71).

Artistic works

Wootton's essay (Chapter 4) is an important summary of the rich evidence of mosaics, and to some extent the painted mural art, drawing out distinctive influences from the eastern and western Mediterranean. Perhaps more explicit consideration of the material from western Tripolitania would have been helpful as this might have highlighted some contrasts between the different parts of the territory. The chapter also points out the serious conservation issues relating to mosaics and the valuable remedial measures that have been taken as part of recent international programmes.

Sculpture features strongly in three chapters: that by Aiosa presents new ideas on the reliefs from the stage *pulpitum* of the theatre at Sabratha and comments on Severan-period sculpture from Lepcis Magna also feature in Mugnai's chapter, while the work of Nikolaus on rustic funerary reliefs from the pre-desert region features in the co-authored Chapter 5 (see also Nikolaus 2016; 2017; Mattingly 2011, 246–68). These chapters speak to very different cultural engagements. The cosmopolitan Roman artistic engagement of the leading citizens – evident in the exceptional quality of much of the mosaic and painted decoration and marble sculpture and statuary – cannot be denied, but there is also material evidence of more diverse cultural influences (for instance, in the painted decoration related to tombs: see Di Vita's papers collected in Rizzo and Di Vita-Évrard 2015, 363–92, 559–66, 819–34, 859–90). Art in Tripolitania was both extremely hybridized and reflective of a variety of influences, not simply from Rome but also from centres such as Alexandria among others, and this determined very specific, local idiosyncrasies. I return to this theme of cultural diversity below.

Rural settlement patterns

Rural settlement has been an area of considerable progress in Tripolitanian archaeology over recent decades, though there is a critical lack of excavations of sites recorded by survey.[17] The desert landscapes of Syrtica have revealed details of a mixed farming and certainly semi-sedentarized peoples (Reddé 1988; Longerstay 1999; Le Quesne *et al.* 2010). In eastern Tripolitania, the UNESCO Libyan Valleys Archaeological Survey recorded the remarkable landscapes of Romano-Libyan floodwater farming regimes and this work has been enhanced by recent remote sensing work.[18] The co-authored essay by Nikolaus and Sheldrick (Chapter 5) is another important update for this area, covering both settlement and funerary monuments. Important work by Muftah Ahmed (2019) has followed previous studies of olive oil production in the Tarhuna Plateau (cf. Mattingly 1988a). The immediate hinterland of Lepcis Magna has also been intensively explored.[19] The Jabal Nafusa area is to a degree a bit of a blind spot at present, which makes Welsby Sjöström's contribution in this volume (Chapter 9) all the more important (see also Nebbia *et al.* 2016 and ongoing survey in this area by Libya's Department of Antiquities). Western Tripolitania has also seen extensive survey under the Tunisian national mapping programme (Mrabet 2011; 2014), as well as through the systematic study of Jerba (Drine *et al.* 2009).

Perhaps the most significant change in perception of Tripolitania's landscapes in recent years concerns the relationship between this territory and its desert hinterland. The changing picture represents more a deepening

[15] See, *inter alia*, Drine 1991; Drine *et al.* 2009 (for surveys of various urban sites on Jerba); Fentress 2009; Ritter *et al.* 2018 (for excavation and geophysical survey at Meninx); Ritter and Ben Tahar 2022.

[16] Ben Tahar 2004; 2016. See also Mattingly 2016 for a first exploration of the Libyan contribution to the take-up of agriculture and urbanism.

[17] Mattingly 2023, 437–47. See also Sheldrick 2021 for the best current overview of data from all parts of the region.

[18] ULVS: Barker 1996; Mattingly 1996a; there are also numerous reports published in *Libyan Studies*. Remote sensing and updated synthesis: Sheldrick 2021.

[19] See, *inter alia*, Munzi *et al.* 2004; 2010; 2016; Zocchi 2018a, 139–75, 211–24; 2018b.

of understanding, rather than a radical reorientation. The Garamantes of the Libyan Sahara had already achieved a level of scholarly prominence through the work of Charles Daniels in the 1960s–70s, with indications of sedentary settlement and oasis cultivation from about 1000 BCE onwards (Mattingly 2010 provides a good summary of Daniels' main work). As a result of further work between 1997 and 2011, knowledge of the scale and sophistication of Garamantian oasis settlements has been dramatically enhanced (Mattingly 2003; 2007; 2010; 2013; Mattingly *et al.* 2020a). It is now clear that in the time of the Roman Empire, Tripolitania was bordered to the south not simply by a rag-tail assortment of 'nomadic tribes', but that the evolution of oasis settlements supported some really large population clusters, with the Garamantian kingdom most prominent among them and arguably displaying the hallmarks of a polity (Sterry and Mattingly 2020b; Mattingly 2022; 2023, 174–89). In recent publications I have proposed that we use the more neutral term 'peoples' rather than 'tribes' when describing the indigenous populations of North Africa to avoid some of the obvious colonial baggage of the latter term (Mattingly 2023, 115–16); it is good to see that the editorial policy in this volume has also followed this course. Although the Garamantes were perhaps the most successful and influential oasis society, it is clear that oasis settlement was becoming significant in many other parts of the eastern, central and western Sahara during the Roman era.[20]

The late Roman/Late Antique landscapes of Tripolitania have long been characterized by the presence of so-called fortified farms (qsur), though on occasion these have been confused or conflated with minor military installations.[21] That rural settlements came to emulate military style fortifications should come as no surprise. The late Garamantian rural landscape also contained many fortified villages, whose architecture evoked the form of late Roman *quadriburgi* from the Roman garrison zone far to the north (Sterry *et al.* 2011; Sterry and Mattingly 2013).

Funerary practices

The ancient burial practices of Tripolitania also varied greatly between coast and interior and between desert and settled communities. An important marker of the advanced societal development in pre-Roman times is the prestige funerary monuments clustered at multiple urban sites: Lepcis Magna, Sabratha and the centres on Jerba.[22] The tradition of subterranean hypogea and rock-cut burial chambers initially continued strongly in the early Roman period, with elite Lepcitanian families continuing the use of traditional Libyphoenician monuments.[23] Although these have tended to be conventionally presented as of Roman or Phoenician inspiration, there are aspects that clearly also evoke what seem to be Libyan identities and practices (Mattingly 2023, 427–29).

In the mid-late Roman period, there was a gradual rise of mausoleum culture, with striking above-ground monuments to the ancestors of elite families. This is evident both around the main cities, but also on estate lands in rural districts, extending well beyond the *territoria* of the coastal cities into the pre-desert zone (Zocchi 2018a, 87–108). The joint chapter by Nikolaus and Sheldrick presents an excellent discussion of the links between the evolution of rural settlement and society as manifested in these monuments. Recently, I have pushed further into speculation about the belief systems that lay behind the visible funerary practices and the associated iconographies, suggesting that in the pre-desert in particular we see the evolution of a distinctly Libyan tradition of ancestor worship related to the Gaetuli peoples (Mattingly 2023, 510–16).

Economy

Tripolitania was always a somewhat marginal part of Africa in the Roman Empire (see Mattingly 2023, 18–32). Rainfall across the territory was sparse and irregular, making agricultural productivity of even the better watered parts of the upland Jabal unpredictable (Mattingly 1995, 1–13). Much of the territory constitutes pre-desert or fully desert terrain. In light of this the achievements of the Roman period were considerable, especially if one starts with the largest and wealthiest cities, whose monuments attest to very significant local resources in olive oil.[24] Work on the mechanics and capacity of ancient olive oil and wine production have highlighted the potential scale of regional exports.[25] Studies of amphora production sites in both eastern and western Tripolitania confirm that this was a significant and long-lived industry and in some

[20] Garamantian Fazzan: Mattingly 2000b; 2003; 2007; 2010; 2013; Mattingly *et al.* 2020a (including the Wadi ash-Shati area surveyed by Merlo). Cf. Mattingly *et al.* 2020b for the oasis belt running from Libya to Algeria. For other work exploring the wider Saharan context of the Garamantes, see Mattingly *et al.* 2017 (trade); Gatto *et al.* 2019 (mobility, funerary practices and identity); Duckworth *et al.* 2020 (mobile technologies); Sterry and Mattingly 2020a (sedentarization, urbanization and state formation).

[21] Classic studies by Goodchild 1976; Brogan and Smith 1984; see also Mattingly 1989; 1995, 202–13; Mattingly *et al.* 2013b; Munzi *et al.* 2014.

[22] Lepcis Magna: Zocchi 2018a, 88–94; Sabratha: selected essays by Di Vita in Rizzo and Di Vita-Évrard 2015; Jerba: Akkari Werriemi 1985; 1995a–b; 2003; Ben Younès 1996; Drine *et al.* 2009, 100–28.

[23] Di Vita-Évrard *et al.* 1996; 1997; Zocchi 2018a, 66–81; Mattingly 2023, 419, 425–29. For other Tripolitanian hypogea of Roman date, see Di Vita's essays in Rizzo and Di Vita-Évrard 2015, 363–92, 819–34, 873–90.

[24] See Hobson 2015 and Ahmed 2019, following up earlier work by Mattingly 1988a–b.

[25] Mattingly 1988c; 1993; 1996b; Mattingly and Hitchner 1993; Ahmed 2019, 105–38.

cases amphora manufacture can be linked directly to olive oil production centres and to the region's leading families.[26]

There is also considerably more evidence now for the development of Saharan trade between the Garamantes and Rome (and also arguably between the Garamantes and people further off to the south and south-west).[27] Saharan trade was almost certainly another important area of economic activity that brought profit to the Mediterranean port cities. This changes our overall understanding of the regional economy and raises questions about the supervisory role of Roman garrison arrangements.[28]

Libyan population groups and culture

A major change in considerations of the cultural history of the region is the shift away from a colonial-era emphasis on external cultural groups, which had also tended to ignore or minimize local agency. To put it simply, where at one time the role of colonists from elsewhere in the Mediterranean was highlighted above all as lying behind politico-cultural advances and economic prosperity in classical antiquity, there is now a greater appreciation of the contributions of ancient Libyans to both Libyphoenican and Roman society in Tripolitania.[29] The colonialist discourse that lay behind the previous exaggeration of the achievements of outsiders has been deconstructed (Mattingly 2011, 43–72; 2016; 2023, 51–65). However, echoes of these interpretative tropes linger on to some extent in the scholarship.

In the first place, we need more explicit discussion of the cultural complexity of Libyphoenican society – this is still too much dominated by the idea of Phoenician colonists being of pre-eminent importance and a search for eastern parallels and origins of cultural and religious behaviours. The recognition of a pre-Phoenician commencement of sedentarization of the Libyan (Gaetuli) communities in northern Tripolitania necessitates reappraisal of their partnering role in the evolution of Libyphoenician society. Here as well as comparing and contrasting sites along the North African coastline that have been at various times been dubbed 'Phoenician' or 'Libyphoenician' emporia, we need to connect with wider arguments about the nature of the Punic western Mediterranean and the agency of North African populations they came into contact with (see Prag and Quinn 2013; Quinn and Vella 2014; Quinn 2018).

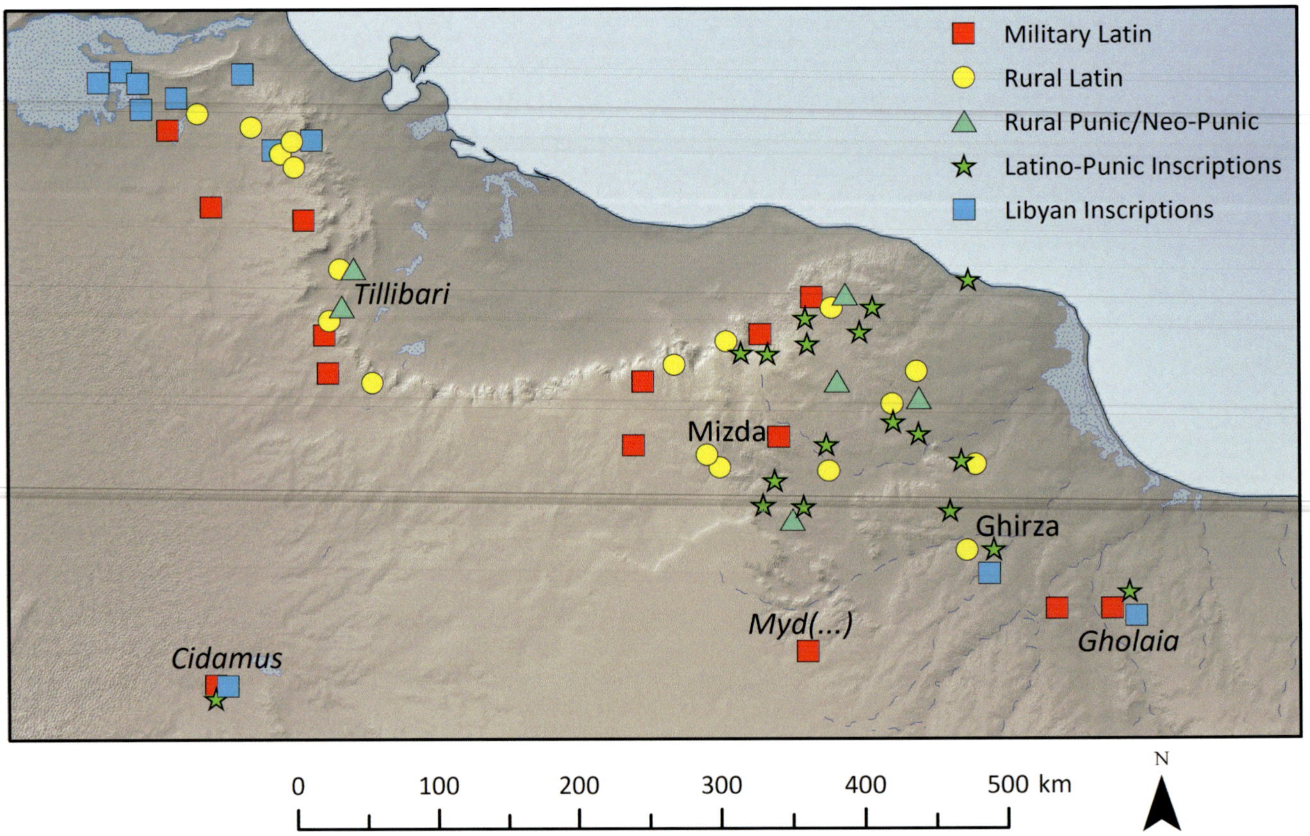

Fig. 11.1. Finds of rural inscriptions in Tripolitania (after Mattingly 2023, fig. 11.4).

[26] Hobson 2015, 119–23; Jerray 2015; 2016; Ahmed 2019, 145–71.

[27] See Mattingly *et al.* 2017 for a detailed exploration of the evidence for pre-Islamic Saharan trade.

[28] Mattingly 2017 (for a list of the probable commodities of trade); 2023, 208–9, 545–59 (on the links between garrison deployment and trade).

[29] Although the theme was explored already in Mattingly 1995, 160–70, the arguments are now much more developed theoretically in Mattingly 2023, 48–70.

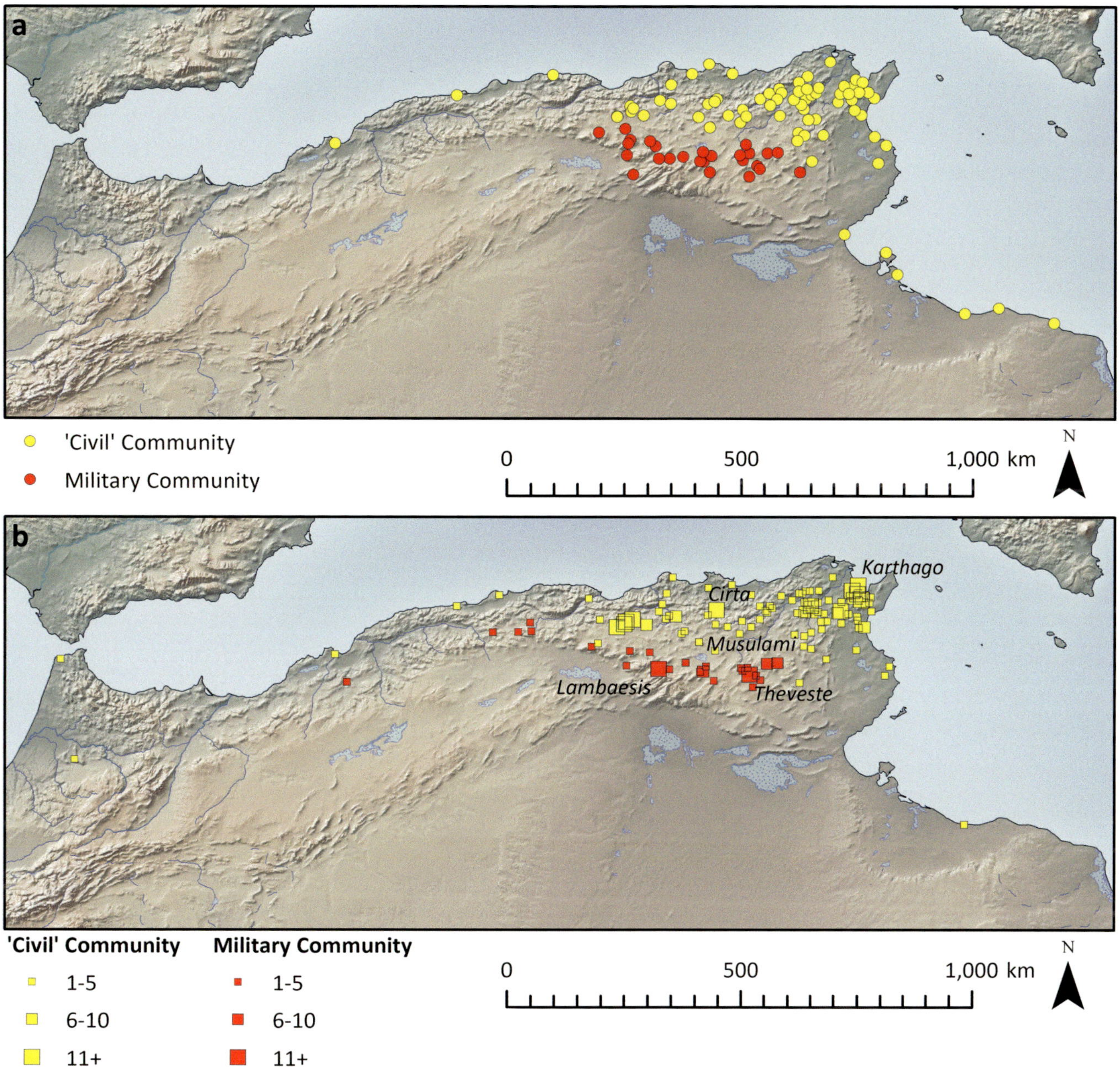

Fig. 11.2. Distribution of Saturn cult in North Africa. A: Saturn temples and stelae/statues; B: Saturn inscriptions (after Mattingly 2023, fig. 11.7).

In the Roman period, the process of sedentarization extended much further through the pre-desert zones. It has long been recognized in eastern Tripolitania that this was achieved by people of broadly Libyphoenician culture, given the prevalence of neo-Punic and Latino-Punic texts rather than Latin inscriptions at rural sites (Fig. 11.1).[30] As the map shows, this is not the whole story, as there is a hitherto somewhat underappreciated substrate of Libyan epigraphy across the region. The occurrence at the key site of Ghirza of Latin, Latino-Punic and Libyan texts illustrates the linguistic complexity of a rural society in which a few elite people could speak and write Latin, perhaps more were conversant in Punic and the majority were probably Libyan speakers (though this is the least represented language in terms of the epigraphic habit). While non-military related Latin inscriptions were rare throughout the region, we can also observe significant divergence between eastern and western Tripolitania, with Latino-Punic inscriptions essentially an epiphenomenon of the eastern pre-desert zone and Libyan inscribing tendencies more marked closer to the oases of Nefzaoua, Ghadames (Cidamus) and Bu Njem (Gholaia).

The cultural ramifications of these local patterns are clearest in terms of the practice of religion. The evidence of the archetypal African stelae cult of Baal (later Saturn) is essentially limited to a few of the coastal towns in Tripolitania (Fig. 11.2), and I have argued that the cult was most diffused in the core territory of

[30] On neo-Punic and Latino-Punic texts, see Kerr 2007; Wilson 2012; Barron 2020; Mattingly 2023, 484–90.

Carthage in northern Tunisia and in the neighbouring heartlands of the old Numidian kingdom and certainly among elements of the Roman garrison (Mattingly 2023, 497–504). The map shows an extremely low penetration of the cult among the Gaetuli (and Mauri) even at Libyphoenician towns associated with the Gaetuli. The nature of much excavation at the coastal cities to date (with its focus on the monumental and the elite end of society) and the lack of detailed examination of daily material culture also means our view is heavily skewed to the epigraphically attested cults, practices and behaviours that may well not fully represent the overall preferences of these communities. These maps really demonstrate some fundamental cultural differences between Tripolitania and other parts of the African provinces.

There are also remarkably few identified rural religious sites from Tripolitania – whether stelae finds, temples or churches, and this indicates a very distinctive pattern of religious behaviour among the rural majority of the Tripolitanian population. The most visible manifestation of religious behaviour among these rural communities appears to have been a form of ancestor worship focused on the elite burials.[31] While the patterns are striking, this is clearly an area where fresh archaeological investigation of rural communities could yield important additional data.

Finally, it is evident that improved knowledge of desert peoples like the Garamantes offers a window on the cultural outlook of ancient Libyans in contact with Mediterranean societies. Nonetheless, there is a need to amplify this with further investigation of identity presentation (based on analysis of material culture use and behaviours) across a wide range of sites.

Future prospects

At the time of writing Libya remains relatively unstable politically and though foreign archaeologists are starting to venture back into the field, this is predominantly focused on the relatively well-policed coastal cities. Southern Tunisia is archaeologically more active, but again with a focus on Jerba and the coastal zone. As and when more extensive field research becomes possible, I would identify the following seven priorities for further exploration.

1. Urban origins

A prime requirement is deeper excavations targeting the earliest phases of coastal sites by excavating beneath the open spaces of the Roman-era cities, following a model established by the Catalan-Tunisian team at Althiburos (Kallala and Sanmartí 2011). On Jerba, the site of Henchir Bougou is a key location, because of its less monumental Roman-period development (Ben Tahar 2014; 2018; Ben Tahar *et al.* 2020; 2022). This needs to be accompanied by a holistic study of pottery assemblages, including handmade wares, and radiocarbon dating, rather than a reliance on imported wares from other parts of the Mediterranean. Again, the work on Jerba has shown the way here.

2. Roman urbanism

While the urban monuments are a precious resource, to better understand their place within the local societies, we need more excavation on non-monumental elements of the cities. This can be achieved through application of modern geophysical survey techniques, including Ground Penetrating Radar (GPR), to extensive areas (as exemplified by Ritter *et al.* 2018), but ideally needs accompanying excavations of domestic and commercial quarters. The physical character of an oasis town needs establishing archaeologically (Turris Telmine, Cidamus or Tacape for instance) – at present, there is a strong sense that these were rather different sorts of urban community in terms of size, layout and monumentality.

3. Rural society

Knowledge of rural settlement can be enhanced by remote sensing and surface survey, but there remains a critical lack of excavations of rural sites. There are also myriad questions about the character, function and dating of many of the different forms of site recognized through survey work, not to mention their associated material culture. Again, only with widespread work will we be able to fill in the suspected picture of regional differences and distinctiveness. A major lacuna is the lack of proper excavation of one of the really large olive oil production facilities (oileries), to enhance our understanding of the organization and scale of production there.

4. The military community

The military garrison was a key institution of the Roman period, but due to modern colonial associations it is understandably uncherished by the national heritage services of Libya and Tunisia. Yet, a fuller knowledge of the nature of military occupation and supervision of provincial territory is essential to understanding the impacts of the ancient Roman Empire. A particular lacuna is excavation of the installations (gates and towers) associated with linear barriers (*clausurae*), which would elucidate their origin and history of use. For the moment the

[31] Mattingly 2011, 246–68; 2023, 513–16; see also Nikolaus and Sheldrick, Chapter 5.

third-century CE forts of Bu Njem (Gholaia) and Gheriat el-Garbia (Myd…) are by a distance the best-known sites, but with earlier and later garrison posts less well known and sites in western Tripolitania generally poorly investigated.

5. Desert societies

Priorities for future work should be the oasis-based societies of Fazzan, the Jofra, Ghadames and the Nefzaoua, but other minor oases could also repay investigation. Work on the funerary material culture of the Garamantes was interrupted in 2011 and needs completion when conditions allow. This material potentially has much to contribute to knowledge of Saharan trade.

6. Economy

As noted, there is a pressing need for excavations of the productive facilities at a major oilery and/or amphora production facilities on a rural estate in eastern Tripolitania. More focus on possible differences in amphora production between eastern and western zones could also amplify understanding of the rural economy. Relatively little is known in detail about urban production – at least for the eastern cities – and time is running out as the suburban areas (where much productive industry was located) around sites like Sabratha and Lepcis Magna are increasingly encroached on by modern development.[32]

7. Identity and material culture

Studies of ancient art and epigraphy need to be more broadly contextualized with improved recording and publication of the full range of material culture and ecofacts (especially dietary choices) across a wide range of site types and at different social levels. Much more attention needs to be paid to the more 'provincial' or local aspects of Roman-period communities, rather than simply noting the correlation with cosmopolitan Roman fashions and so on. Material identities can also be compared with biological identities established from the study of human remains (including aDNA). The present state of such palaeopathological studies in the region lags behind most other areas of the Mediterranean world.

Finally, it should be apparent from this volume that the most interesting research questions are often ones that cut across standard academic categories or areas of expertise. Roman Tripolitania requires a broad interdisciplinary suite of investigations to make fullest sense of its diverse and intertwined cultural history. And we should remember that that history is not simply a top-down perspective on the rich and successful within Roman provincial society, but also an evaluation of the range of experiences of diverse peoples (Libyans, Libyphoenicians, migrants from other parts of the Roman world or Africa) living as colonial servants, subjects or neighbours of the Roman Empire.

References

Ahmed, M.A.M. 2019. *Rural Settlement and Economic Activity. Olive Oil, Wine and Amphorae Production on the Tarhuna Plateau during the Roman Period*. London: Society for Libyan Studies.

Aiosa, S. 2013. *Il Tempio di Ercole a Sabratha. Architettura e contesto urbano*. Rome: 'L'Erma' di Bretschneider.

Akkari Werriemi, J. 1985. Un témoinage spectaculaire sur la présence libyco-punique dans l'ile de Jerba: le mausolée de Henchir Bourgou. *Reppal* 1: 189–96.

Akkari Werriemi, J. 1995a. La nécropole libyco-punique de Ghizene (Djerba-Tunisie). *Africa* 13: 51–74.

Akkari Werriemi, J. 1995b. Note préliminaire sur deux tombes phenico-puniques à Aggar au nord-ouest de Djerba (Tunisie). *Africa* 13: 77–82.

Akkari Werriemi, J. 2003. Sépultures monumentales d'époque romaine à Djerba (Tunisie): le mausolée temple de Henchir Ghardaya. *Africa: Séances Scientifiques* n.s. 1: 163–99.

Allason-Jones, L. and Greep, S. 2023. Excavations at Sabratha 1948–1951: the small finds. *Libyan Studies* 54: 76–98.

Balice, M. 2010. *Libia. Gli scavi italiani 1922–1937: restauro, ricostruzione o propaganda? Una nuova visione storica fra indirizzo scientifico ed intervento politico alla luce dei documenti inediti dell'IsIAO*. Rome: 'L'Erma' di Bretschneider.

Baratte, F., Brouquier-Reddé, V. and Rocca, E. (eds) 2018. *Du culte aux sanctuaires. L'architecture religieuse dans l'Afrique romaine et byzantine*. Paris: De Boccard.

Barker, G. (ed.) 1996. *Farming the Desert. The UNESCO Libyan Valleys Archaeological Survey. Volume 1: Synthesis*. London: Society for Libyan Studies.

Barron, C. 2020. Amator concordiae, ornator patriae. The Latinisation of Punic titles in early imperial Lepcis Magna. *Libyan Studies* 51: 10–23.

Ben Tahar, S. 2004. Quelques réflexions sur les autochtones de Gigthis à l'époque punique. *Reppal* 13: 45–59.

[32] See Drine *et al.* 2009; Stone *et al.* 2011, for comparative work on the productive areas of other African coastal towns.

Ben Tahar, S. 2014. Le site punique de Ghizène (Jerba): premiers resultats des fouilles 2008–2009. *Mitteilungen des Deutschen Archäologischen Instituts, Römische Abteilung* 120: 59–97.

Ben Tahar, S. 2016. Henchir Tawrirt (Jerba): un site libyque aux origines. *Antiquités Africaines* 52: 9–52.

Ben Tahar, S. 2018. Henchir Bourgou (Jerba) à la lumière des nouvelles recherches archéologiques. *Mitteilungen des Deutschen Archäologischen Instituts, Römische Abteilung* 124: 311–51.

Ben Tahar, S., von Rummel, P., Ritter, S., Aoudi, M., Dinies, M., Fassbinder, J., Mansel, K., Möller, H., Mukai, T., Peters, J., Reichmuth, S. and Trixl, S. 2020. Henchir Bourgou (Djerba), Tunesien. Die Arbeiten der Jahre 2017 bis 2019. *e-Forschungsberichte* 2020.1: 97–108.

Ben Tahar, S., von Rummel, P., Mansel, K., Möller, H., Mukai, T., Lappi, T., Peters, J., Trixl, S., Aoudi, M., Dinies, M. and Büchner, S. 2022. Henchir Bourgou (Djerba, Tunesien): Stratigraphie und Fundvorlage einer Sondage im Zentrum der antiken Siedlung (8. Jh. v. Chr. –2. Jh. n. Chr.). *Archäologischer Anzeiger* 2021.2: 1–178.

Ben Younès, H. 1996. Le Sahel et l'île de Djerba: les charactéristiques de l'architecture funéraire punique. *Africa* 14: 7–12.

Brogan, O. and Smith, D.J. 1984. *Ghirza: A Libyan Settlement in the Roman Period.* Tripoli: Department of Antiquities.

Brouquier-Reddé, V. 1992. *Temples et cultes de Tripolitaine.* Paris: Éditions du CNRS.

Buck, D.J. and Mattingly, D.J. (eds) 1985. *Town and Country in Roman Tripolitania. Papers in Honour of Olwen Hackett.* Oxford: British Archaeological Reports.

De Miro, E. and Polito, A. 2005. *Leptis Magna. Dieci anni di scavi archeologici nell'area del foro vecchio. I livelli fenici, punici e romani.* Rome: 'L'Erma' di Bretschneider.

Di Vita, A. 2010. L'università di Macerata: dieci anni di studi e restauri archeologici in Tripolitania (1998–2008). *Libya Antiqua* n.s. 5: 11–23.

Di Vita, A. and Livadiotti, M. (eds) 2005. *I tre templi del lato nord-ovest del foro vecchio a Leptis Magna.* Rome: 'L'Erma' di Bretschneider.

Di Vita, A., Di Vita-Évrard, G. and Bacchielli, L. 1999. *Libya: The Lost Cities of the Roman Empire.* Cologne: Könemann.

Di Vita-Évrard, G., Fontana, S., Allegni, F., Munzi, M. and Musso, L. 1996. L'ipogeo dei Flavi a Leptis Magna presso Gasr Gelda. *Libya Antiqua* n.s. 2: 85–133.

Di Vita-Évrard, G., Fontana, S. and Munzi, M. 1997. Le necropoli di Leptis Magna, 3. Une tombe hypogée de la nécropole occidentale: Laurentii ou Claudii? *Libya Antiqua* n.s. 3: 119–46.

Dore, J.N. and Keay, N. 1989. *Excavations at Sabratha 1948–1951, Volume II. The Finds, Part 1: The Amphorae, Coarse Pottery and Building Materials.* London: Society for Libyan Studies.

Drine, A. 1991. Note sur le site de Zitha (Hr. Zian) à Zarzis. *Reppal* 6: 17–30.

Drine, A., Fentress, E. and Holod, R. (eds) 2009. *An Island through Time: Jerba Studies, Volume 1. The Punic and Roman Periods.* Portsmouth, RI: Journal of Roman Archaeology.

Duckworth, C.N., Cuénod, A. and Mattingly, D.J. (eds) 2020. *Mobile Technologies in the Ancient Sahara and Beyond.* Cambridge: Cambridge University Press.

Fentress, E. 2009. The Punic and Libyan towns of Jerba. In S. Helas and D. Marzoli (eds), *Phönizisches und punisches Städtewesen. Akten der internationalen Tagung in Rom vom 21. bis 23. Februar 2007.* Mainz: Philipp von Zabern, 203–19.

Fenwick, C. 2020. *Early Islamic North Africa: A New Perspective.* London: Bloomsbury.

Fulford, M.G. and Tomber, R. (eds) 1994. *Excavations at Sabratha 1948–1951, Volume II. The Finds, Part 2: The Finewares and Lamps.* London: Society for Libyan Studies.

Gatto, M.C., Mattingly, D.J., Ray, N. and Sterry, M. (eds) 2019. *Burials, Migration and Identity in the Ancient Sahara and Beyond.* Cambridge: Cambridge University Press.

Goodchild, R.G. 1976. *Libyan Studies: Selected Papers of the Late R.G. Goodchild* (edited by J.M. Reynolds). London: Elek Books.

Guédon, S. 2018. *La frontière romaine de l'Africa sous le Haut-Empire.* Madrid: Casa de Velázquez.

Hitchner, R.B. (ed.) 2022. *A Companion to North Africa in Antiquity.* Hoboken, NJ: Wiley-Blackwell.

Hobson, M.S. 2015. *The North African Boom. Evaluating Economic Growth in the Roman Province of Africa Proconsularis (146 B.C. – A.D. 439).* Portsmouth, RI: Journal of Roman Archaeology.

Jerray, E. 2015. *La production d'amphores en Tripolitaine occidentale: les ateliers de Zitha et de sa région en Tunisie méridionale.* PhD Thesis: Aix-Marseille Université.

Jerray, E. 2016. Les ateliers d'amphores de Zitha et le potentiel économique de la Tripolitaine tunisienne. In N. Mugnai, J. Nikolaus and N. Ray (eds), *De Africa Romaque: Merging Cultures across North Africa. Proceedings of the International Conference Held at the University of Leicester (26–27 October 2013).* London: Society for Libyan Studies, 157–70.

Kallala, N. and Sanmartí, J. (eds) 2011. *Althiburos, 1. La fouille dans l'aire du capitole et la nécropole méridionale.* Tarragona: Institut Català d'Arqueologia Clàssica.

Kenrick, P.M. 1986. *Excavations at Sabratha 1948–1951. A Report on the Excavations Conducted by Dame Kathleen Kenyon and John Ward-Perkins.* London: Society for the Promotion of Roman Studies.

Kenrick, P.M. 2009. *Libya Archaeological Guides: Tripolitania.* London: Silphium Press.

Kerr, R.M. 2007. *Latino-Punic and its Linguistic Environment.* Göttingen: Universiteit Leiden.

Leone, A. 2013. *The End of the Pagan City: Religion, Economy, and Urbanism in Late Antique North Africa.* Oxford: Oxford University Press.

Leone, A. 2019. Cultural transitions in archaeology: from Byzantine to Islamic Tripolitania. In R. Bockmann, A. Leone and P. von Rummel (eds), *Africa – Ifrīqiya. Continuity and Change in North Africa from the Byzantine to the Early Islamic Age. Papers of a Conference Held in Rome, Museo Nazionale Romano – Terme di Diocleziano (28 February – 2 March 2013).* Wiesbaden: Harrassowitz Verlag, 265–78.

Le Quesne, C., Basell, L.S. and Sheibani, R. 2010. Archaeology in the Sirte Basin: preliminary results of mitigation surveys carried out for Shell 2007–2009. *Libyan Studies* 41: 7–32.

Livadiotti, M. and Rocco, G. 2018. *Exornata aedes. La curia del foro vecchio di Leptis Magna.* Rome: 'L'Erma' di Bretschneider.

Longerstay, M. 1999. Prospection archéologique dans cinq vallées de la région syrtique (Libye) et fouille d'un bâtiment antique de la vallée du Wadi Harawah: rapport préliminaire. *Bulletin archéologique du comité des travaux historiques et scientifiques: Afrique du Nord* n.s. 25: 53–68.

Mackensen, M. 2021a. *Das severische Vexillationskastell Myd(---)/Gheriat el-Garbia am limes Tripolitanus (Libyen), I: Forschungsgeschichte, Vermessung, Prospektionen und Funde 2009–2010.* Wiesbaden: Reichert Verlag.

Mackensen, M. 2021b. Observations and results of recent excavations and surveys of late Roman military fortifications in the province of Tripolitana. *Libya Antiqua* n.s. 14: 111–45.

Mackensen, M. 2024. *Das severische Vexillationskastell Myd(---) und die spätantiken castra Madensia/Gheriat el-Garbia am limes Tripolitanus (Libyen), II: Ausgrabungen und Untersuchungen im Kastell, im Steinbruch, in den Heiligtümern und am Beobachtungsturm 2009–2010.* Wiesbaden: Reichert Verlag.

Mattingly, D.J. 1988a. The olive boom. Oil surpluses, wealth and power in Roman Tripolitania. *Libyan Studies* 19: 21–41.

Mattingly, D.J. 1988b. Oil for export? A comparison of Libyan, Spanish and Tunisian olive oil production in the Roman empire. *Journal of Roman Archaeology* 1: 33–56.

Mattingly, D.J. 1988c. Megalithic madness and measurement. Or how many olives could an olive press press? *Oxford Journal of Archaeology* 7.2: 177–95.

Mattingly, D.J. 1989. Farmers and frontiers. Exploiting and defending the countryside of Roman Tripolitania. *Libyan Studies* 20: 135–53.

Mattingly, D.J. 1993. Maximum figures and maximizing strategies of oil production? Further thoughts on the processing capacity of Roman olive presses. In M.C. Amouretti and J.P. Brun (eds), *La production du vin et de l'huile en Méditerranée.* Paris: De Boccard, 483–98.

Mattingly, D.J. 1995. *Tripolitania.* London: Batsford.

Mattingly, D.J. (ed.) 1996a. *Farming the Desert. The UNESCO Libyan Valleys Archaeological Survey. Volume 2: Gazetteer and Pottery.* London: Society for Libyan Studies.

Mattingly, D.J. 1996b. Olive presses in Roman Africa: Technical evolution or stagnation? In M. Khanoussi, P. Ruggeri and C. Vismara (eds), *L'Africa Romana. Atti dell'XI convegno di studio (Cartagine, 15–18 dicembre 1994).* Ozieri: Editrice il Torchietto, 577–95.

Mattingly, D.J. 2000a. Tripolitana. In R.J.A. Talbert (ed.), *Barrington Atlas of the Greek and Roman World.* Princeton: Princeton University Press, map 35 and map-by-map directory, 529–44.

Mattingly, D.J. 2000b. Garama. In R.J.A. Talbert (ed.), *Barrington Atlas of the Greek and Roman World.* Princeton: Princeton University Press, map 36 and map-by-map directory, 545–51.

Mattingly, D.J. 2000c. Syrtica. In R.J.A. Talbert (ed.), *Barrington Atlas of the Greek and Roman World.* Princeton: Princeton University Press, map 37 and map-by-map directory, 552–57.

Mattingly, D.J. (ed.) 2003. *The Archaeology of Fazzān, I. Synthesis.* London: Society for Libyan Studies.

Mattingly, D.J. (ed.) 2007. *The Archaeology of Fazzān, II. Gazetteer, Pottery and Other Finds.* London: Society for Libyan Studies.

Mattingly, D.J. (ed.) 2010. *The Archaeology of Fazzān, III. Excavations of C.M. Daniels.* London: Society for Libyan Studies.

Mattingly, D.J. 2011. *Imperialism, Power and Identity. Experiencing the Roman Empire.* Princeton: Princeton University Press.

Mattingly, D.J. (ed.) 2013. *The Archaeology of Fazzān, IV. Survey and Excavations at Old Jarma (Ancient Garama) Carried Out by C.M. Daniels (1962–69) and the Fazzān Project (1997–2001).* London: Society for Libyan Studies.

Mattingly, D.J. 2016. Who shaped Africa? The origins of urbanism and agriculture in Maghreb and Sahara. In N. Mugnai, J. Nikolaus and N. Ray (eds), *De Africa Romaque: Merging Cultures across North Africa. Proceedings of the International Conference Held at the University of Leicester (26–27 October 2013).* London: Society for Libyan Studies, 11–25.

Mattingly, D.J. 2017. The Garamantes and the origins of Saharan trade: state of the field and future agendas. In D.J. Mattingly, V. Leitch, C.N. Duckworth, A. Cuénod, M. Sterry and F. Cole (eds), *Trade in the Ancient Sahara and Beyond.* Cambridge: Cambridge University Press, 1–52.

Mattingly, D.J. 2019. A road less travelled? The Society for Libyan Studies and the landscape archaeology of Libya's early civilisations. *Libyan Studies* 50: 35–46.

Mattingly, D.J. 2022. Beyond barbarians: the Garamantes of the Libyan Sahara. In R.B. Hitchner (ed.), *A Companion to North Africa in Antiquity.* Hoboken, NJ: Wiley-Blackwell, 65–80.

Mattingly, D.J. 2023. *Between Sahara and Sea: Africa in the Roman Empire.* Ann Arbor, MI: University of Michigan Press.

Mattingly, D.J. and Hitchner, R.B. 1993. Technical specifications for some North African olive presses of Roman date. In M.C. Amouretti and J.P. Brun (eds), *La production du vin et de l'huile en Méditerranée.* Paris: De Boccard, 439–62.

Mattingly, D.J. and Hitchner, R.B. 1995. Roman Africa: an archaeological review. *Journal of Roman Studies* 85: 165–213.

Mattingly, D.J. and Lloyd, J.A. (eds) 1989. *Libya. Research in Archaeology, Environment, History and Society 1969–1989.* London: Society for Libyan Studies (= *Libyan Studies* 20, 1989).

Mattingly, D.J., Rushworth, A., Sterry, M. and Leitch, V. 2013a. *Frontiers of the Roman Empire. The African Frontiers.* Oxford: Archaeopress.

Mattingly, D.J., Sterry, M.J. and Leitch, V. 2013b. Fortified farms and defended villages of Late Roman and Late Antique Africa. *Antiquité Tardive* 21: 167–88.

Mattingly, D.J., Leitch, V., Duckworth, C.N., Cuénod, A., Sterry, M. and Cole, F. (eds) 2017. *Trade in the Ancient Sahara and Beyond.* Cambridge: Cambridge University Press.

Mattingly, D.J., Merlo, S., Mori, L. and Sterry, M. 2020a. Garamantian oasis settlements in Fazzan. In M. Sterry and D.J. Mattingly (eds), *Urbanisation and State Formation in the Ancient Sahara and Beyond.* Cambridge: Cambridge University Press, 53–111.

Mattingly, D.J., Sterry, M., al-Haddad, M. and Trousset, P. 2020b. Pre-Islamic oasis settlements in the northern Sahara. In M. Sterry and D.J. Mattingly (eds), *Urbanisation and State Formation in the Ancient Sahara and Beyond.* Cambridge: Cambridge University Press, 187–238.

Mazzilli, G. 2016. *L'arco di Traiano a Leptis Magna.* Rome: 'L'Erma' di Bretschneider.

Merighi, A. 1940. *La Tripolitania antica. Dalle origini alla invasione degli arabi, I–II.* Verbania: Airoldi Editore.

Michel, V. (ed.) 2015. *De Leptis Magna à Derna, de la Tripolitaine à la Cyrénaïque. Travaux récents sur la Libye antique.* Paris: Riveneuve Éditions.

Montali, G. 2015. *L'anfiteatro di Sabratha e gli anfiteatri dell'Africa proconsolare.* Rome: 'L'Erma' di Bretschneider.

Mrabet, A. 2011. Identité de la Tripolitaine occidentale: de quelques signalements archéologiques. In C. Briand-Ponsart and Y. Modéran (eds), *Provinces et identités provinciales dans l'Afrique romaine.* Caen: Presses universitaires de Caen, 221–37.

Mrabet, A. 2014. Le territoire de Tacapes: essai de delimitation. In C. Briand-Ponsart (ed.), *Centres de pouvoir et l'organisation de l'espace. Actes du Xe colloque international sur l'histoire et l'archéologie de l'Afrique du Nord préhistorique, antique et médiévale (Caen, 25–28 mai 2009).* Caen: Presses universitares de Caen, 169–78.

Mugnai, N. 2021. A promenade at Lepcis Magna: experiencing buildings from the Augustan to the Antonine era. *Libyan Studies* 52: 87–118.

Mugnai, N. 2022. Architecture and art. In R.B. Hitchner (ed.), *A Companion to North Africa in Antiquity.* Hoboken, NJ: Wiley-Blackwell, 247–84.

Mugnai, N., Nikolaus, J. and Ray, N. (eds) 2016. *De Africa Romaque: Merging Cultures across North Africa. Proceedings of the International Conference Held at the University of Leicester (26–27 October 2013).* London: Society for Libyan Studies.

Munzi, M. 2001. *L'epica del ritorno. Archeologia e politica nella Tripolitania italiana.* Rome: 'L'Erma' di Bretschneider.

Munzi, M. 2004. *La decolonizzazione del passato. Archeologia e politica in Libia dall'amministrazione alleata al regno di Idris.* Rome: 'L'Erma' di Bretschneider.

Munzi, M., Felici, F., Cifani, G., Citelli, E., Gaudiosi, E., Lucarini, G. and Matoug, J. 2004. A topographic research sample in the territory of Lepcis Magna: Sīlīn. *Libyan Studies* 35: 11–66.

Munzi, M., Felici, F., Cirelli, E., Schingo, G. and Zocchi, A. 2010. Il territorio di Leptis Magna: ricognizioni tra Ras el-Mergheb e Ras el-Hamman (2007). In M. Milanese, P. Ruggeri and C. Vismara (eds), *L'Africa Romana. I luoghi e le forme dei mestieri e della produzione nelle province africane. Atti del XVIII convegno di studio (Olbia, 11–14 dicembre 2008).* Rome: Carocci, 723–46.

Munzi, M., Schirru, G. and Tantillo, I. 2014. Centenarium. *Libyan Studies* 45: 49–64.

Munzi, M., Felici, F., Matoug, J., Sjöström, I. and Zocchi, A. 2016. The Lepcitanian landscape across the ages: the survey between Ras el-Mergheb and Ras el-Hammam (2007, 2009, 2013). *Libyan Studies* 47: 67–116.

Musso, L. and Turjman, M.A. (eds) 2022. *Libia – Italia. Un'archeologia condivisa (Castello Rosso, Tripoli, 22 settembre – 22 dicembre 2021).* Rome: 'L'Erma' di Bretschneider.

Musso, L., Baldoni, D., Felici, F., Fontana, S., Mallegni, F., Masturzo, N., Munzi, M., Pentiricci, M., Severini, F. and Usai, L. 1997. Missione archeologica dell'Università Roma Tre a Leptis Magna, 1996. *Libya Antiqua* n.s. 3: 257–72.

Musso, L., Baldoni, D., Bianchi, B., Cilla, M., Di Vita-Évrard, G., Felici, F., Fontana, S., Mallegni, F., Masturzo, N., Munzi, M. and Usai, L. 1998. Missione archeologica dell'Università Roma Tre a Leptis Magna, 1997. *Libya Antiqua* n.s. 4: 176–218.

Musso, L., Baldoni, D., Bianchi, B., Calì, M.G., Davidde, B., Di Vita-Évrard, G., Munzi, M., Petriaggi, R., Pinna Caboni, B., Ponti, G. and Shebani, R. 2010. Missione archeologica dell'Università Roma Tre, 1998–2007. *Libya Antiqua* n.s. 5: 49–78.

Musso, L., Baldoni, D., Baroni, F., Bessi, B., Bianchi, B., Bruno, M., Buccino, L., Davidde Pietraggi, B., Felici, F., al-Hadad, M., Munzi, M., Petriaggi, R., Shebani, R., Sjöström, I. and Zocchi, A. 2014. Missione archeologica dell'Università Roma Tre (2009–2014). *Libya Antiqua* n.s. 7: 11–54.

Nebbia, N., Leone, A., Bockmann, R., Hddad, M., Abdouli, H., Masoud, A. and Khatab, M. 2016. Developing a collaborative strategy to manage and preserve cultural heritage during the Libyan conflict. The case of the Gebel Nāfusa. *Journal of Archaeological Method and Theory* 23.4: 971–88.

Nikolaus, J. 2016. Beyond Ghirza: Roman-period mausolea in Tripolitania. In N. Mugnai, J. Nikolaus and N. Ray (eds), *De Africa Romaque: Merging Cultures across North Africa. Proceedings of the International Conference Held at the University of Leicester (26–27 October 2013).* London: Society for Libyan Studies, 199–214.

Nikolaus, J. 2017. *Roman Funerary Reliefs and North African Identity: A Contextual Investigation of Tripolitanian Mausolea and Their Iconography.* PhD Thesis: University of Leicester.

Prag, J.R.W. and Quinn, J.C. (eds) 2013. *The Hellenistic West. Rethinking the Ancient Mediterranean.* Cambridge: Cambridge University Press.

Quinn, J.C. 2018. *In Search of the Phoenicians.* Princeton: Princeton University Press.

Quinn, J.C. and Vella, N. (eds) 2014. *The Punic Mediterranean: Identities and Identification from Phoenician Settlement to Roman Rule.* Cambridge: Cambridge University Press.

Reddé, M. 1988. *Prospection des vallées du nord de la Libye (1979–1980). La région de Syrte à l'époque romaine.* Paris: Presses de l'École normale supérieure.

Ricciardi, M. 2018. *L'anfiteatro di Leptis Magna.* Rome: 'L'Erma' di Bretschneider.

Ritter, S. and Ben Tahar, S. (eds) 2022. *Studies on the Urban History of Meninx (Djerba). The Meninx Archaeological Project 2015–2019.* Wiesbaden: Reichert Verlag.

Ritter, S., Ben Tahar, S., Fassbinder, J.W.E. and Lambers, L. 2018. Landscape archaeology and urbanism at Meninx: results of geophysical prospection on Jerba (2015). *Journal of Roman Archaeology* 31: 357–72.

Rizzo, M.A. (ed.) 2017. *Antonino Di Vita. La Tripolitania antica, scritti inediti.* Rome: 'L'Erma' di Bretschneider.

Rizzo, M.A. and Di Vita-Évrard, G. (eds) 2015. *Antonino Di Vita. Scritti Africani, I–II.* Rome: 'L'Erma' di Bretschneider.

Sheldrick, N. 2021. *Building the Countryside. Rural Architecture and Settlement in Tripolitania during the Roman and Late Antique Periods.* London: Society for Libyan Studies.

Sterry, M. and Mattingly, D.J. 2013. Desert Migrations Project XVII: further AMS dates for historic settlements from Fazzan, south-west Libya. *Libyan Studies* 44: 127–40.

Sterry, M. and Mattingly, D.J. (eds) 2020a. *Urbanisation and State Formation in the Ancient Sahara and Beyond.* Cambridge: Cambridge University Press.

Sterry, M. and Mattingly, D.J. 2020b. State formation in the Sahara and beyond. In M. Sterry and D.J. Mattingly (eds), *Urbanisation and State Formation in the Ancient Sahara and Beyond.* Cambridge: Cambridge University Press, 695–721.

Sterry, M., Mattingly, D.J., Ahmed, M.A.M., Savage, T. and Wilson, A.I. 2011. DMP XIII: reconnaissance survey of archaeological sites in the Murzuq area. *Libyan Studies* 42: 103–16.

Stone, D.L., Mattingly, D.J. and Ben Lazreg, N. 2011. *Leptiminus (Lamta): A Roman Port City in Tunisia. Report no. 3: The Field Survey.* Portsmouth, RI: Journal of Roman Archaeology.

Tantillo, I. and Bigi, F. (eds) 2010. *Leptis Magna. Una città e le sue iscrizioni in epoca tardoromana.* Cassino: Edizioni dell'Università degli Studi di Cassino.

Tomasello, F. 2005. *Fontane e ninfei minori di Leptis Magna.* Rome: 'L'Erma' di Bretschneider.

Tomasello, F. 2011. *Il tempio sul decumano maggiore di Leptis Magna.* Rome: 'L'Erma' di Bretschneider.

Ward-Perkins, J.B. 1993. *The Severan Buildings of Lepcis Magna: An Architectural Survey (published by P.M. Kenrick).* London: Society for Libyan Studies.

Wilson, A.I. 2012. Neo-Punic and Latin inscriptions in Roman North Africa: function and display. In A. Mullen and P. James (eds), *Multilingualism in the Graeco-Roman Worlds.* Cambridge: Cambridge University Press, 265–316.

Zocchi, A. 2018a. *The Periphery of Lepcis Magna. Suburban Topography and Land Use of a Roman City.* PhD Thesis: University of Leicester.

Zocchi, A. 2018b. The periphery of Lepcis Magna: new data related to the ancient road network and land partition. *Libyan Studies* 49: 51–79.

ويُختتم القسم ببحثين يتناولان المراحل التي أعقبت العصر الروماني. ففي الفصل التاسع، تقوم ويلزبي سجوستروم Welsby Sjöström بتجميع قائمة بالمواقع في جبل نفوسة حيث يمكن للمسوحات الميدانية المستقبلية أن تؤكد وجود بقايا أثرية رومانية/من أواخر العصور القديمة. ويشمل ذلك المواقع التي تم مسحها سابقًا، مثل تلك التي سجلها ضباط الجيش الإيطالي في عشرينيات القرن العشرين، والأماكن التي لوحظ فيها، في السنوات الأخيرة، وجود بقايا رومانية في المباني الإسلامية (وخاصة المساجد). وفي الفصل العاشر، تلفت بريفوست Prevost الانتباه إلى الروابط الثقافية بين جزيرة جربة (تونس) وطرابلس. وفي حين أنه من المعروف أن هذه الأراضي كانت جزءًا من نفس الكيان (شبه الإقليمي) في العصر الروماني، فإن البحث يسلط الضوء على الروابط العمارية المهمة بين بعض المساجد الإسلامية في جربة وأمثلة من جبل نفوسة، والتي تتحدث عن الترابط المستمر بين هذه المناطق في العصر الإسلامي. وأخيرًا، في الفصل الحادي عشر، يقدم ماتينغلي Mattingly سلسلة من الأفكار والتأملات حول علم الآثار في إقليم طرابلس في الأراضي الليبية والتونسية. ويستعرض بشكل نقدي الموضوعات التي تمت مناقشتها في الفصول المختلفة، في حين يتم الإشارة إلى التطورات الأخيرة وكذلك الثغرات في معرفتنا، التي يمكن استخدامها لتطوير مشاريع وأساليب بحثية مستقبلية.

إن الهدف الرئيسي للمجلد الذي يحمل عنوان إقليم طرابلس في العصر الإمبراطوري الروماني وما بعده *Tripolitania in the Roman Empire and Beyond* هو دراسة الإقليم في العصر الروماني ضمن محيطه الأوسع في شمال إفريقيا، ويحمل هذا معنيين مزدوجين، حيث يشير الأول إلى الإطار الجغرافي الذي يتوافق مع حدود المنطقة كما تم إنشاؤها تحت الحكم الإمبراطوري الروماني، بشكل أساسي أراضي المراكز الثلاثة (لبدة الكبرى وأويا وصبراتة) التي شكلت كيانًا فرعيًا لأفريقيا القنصلية Africa Proconsularis، قبل أن تصبح مقاطعة مستقلة حوالي عام 303 م؛ ولكن في الوقت نفسه، يمتد النقاش في بعض المقالات إلى مناطق خارج السيطرة الرومانية خاصة في منطقة الصحراء. أما المعنى الثاني فهو زمني، إذ يمتد الإطار الزمني الرئيسي قيد الدراسة من القرن الأول قبل الميلاد إلى القرن الرابع الميلادي، لكن تم تضمين فترات سابقة ولاحقة أيضًا. لقد أنبرى المؤلفون لمهمة صعبة متمثلة في كتابة عمل موثوق وميسر الوصول إليه، ويعكس هذا جمهور قراء المجلد الواسع الذي يسعى إلى أن يشمل طلاب الجامعات على مستويات مختلفة، والعلماء الأحدث سناً وأولئك الأكثر خبرة، فضلاً عن عامة القراء.

النوع الرئيسي من الأدلة قيد الفحص والبحث هو الجانب الأثري، إلا أنه تم أيضًا النظر إلى المصادر النصية والنقوش، ولا يُدّعى أن هذا العمل يغطي جميع جوانب علم الآثار في إقليم طرابلس القديم، وقد تأثر اختيار الموضوعات بخبرة المؤلفين الشخصية واهتماماتهم البحثية، مما أتاح تعدد الأصوات وظهور آراء مختلفة في بعض الحالات. وتجدر الإشارة أيضًا إلى أن التركيز الرئيسي كان على الجزء الليبي (الغربي) من إقليم طرابلس، في حين امتدت المنطقة في العصور القديمة إلى جنوب شرق تونس ناحية الغرب وما بعد سرت ناحية الشرق. يتعلق الجزء الأول من المجلد (الفصول 2–4) بالمواقع الحضرية والفيلات في المنطقة الساحلية من طرابلس. تقدم أيوسا Aiosa (الفصل 2) فرضيات جديدة حول التطور الحضري لصبراتة من فترة ما قبل الرومان إلى أواخر العصر الروماني. من خلال تحدي الآراء السابقة والتفسيرات التقليدية، فإن إعادة التقييم لمعظم الأدلة الأثرية الموجودة لها تداعيات بعيدة الأمد فيما يخص التسلسل الزمني أو تحديد المعالم الفردية وأحياء المدينة القديمة بأكملها. ينظر موغناي Mugnai (الفصل 3) في تحول لبدة الكبرى في العصر السيفيري، بدءًا بمراجعة المباني السيفيرية التقليدية التي كانت مركزية لدراسات وارد بيركنز Ward-Perkins، ويتناول البحث أيضًا مشاريع البناء الصغرى في المدينة التي تم تنفيذها جنبًا إلى جنب مع المشاريع الإمبراطورية الكبرى، إذ يتم فحص أدلة وافرة: ميزات التصميم والبناء ومواد البناء والزخارف العمارية والنحت والنقوش الأثرية التي وجدت على المباني. يقدم ووتون Wootton، في الفصل 4، نظرة عامة شاملة على الأرضيات المزخرفة والفسيفساء في إقليم طرابلس من العصر البونيقي/الهلنستي إلى العصر البيزنطي. يتم تناول مسائل الأسلوب والأيقونات والجانب الحِرفي، وفحص هذه المنتجات الطرابلسية في سياقها المتوسطي الأوسع، ومن المهم أن الفصل يتناول قضايا الحفاظ على هذا التراث الاستثنائي، الذي يعد في الوقت ذاته هشًا.

في الجزء الثاني (الفصول 5–10)، يتحول الاهتمام إلى المناطق الداخلية وتلك النائية والصحراوية من إقليم طرابلس. تقدم كل من نيكولاس Nikolaus وشيلدريك Sheldrick (الفصل 5) نظرة شاملة على المحيطين landscape الريفي والجنائزي في منطقة مشارف الصحراء، بناءً على نتائج مشروع مسح الوديان الليبية ULVS ودمج أحدث الأبحاث. يسمح الاستخدام الدقيق لمواد الأرشيف وصور الأقمار الصناعية أضافة إلى موارد أخرى للمؤلفتين بالتحقيق في حياة وموت أولئك الذين سكنوا هذه المناطق في العصر الروماني وأواخر العصور القديمة. هذا وتتناول الأبحاث الثلاثة التالية جوانب تكميلية للجيش على التخوم، من خلال تقييم مفصل للأدلة الأثرية، يحدد ماكينسن Mackensen (الفصل 6) تطور المنشآت العسكرية على حدود الإقليم من القرن الثاني إلى القرن الخامس الميلادي، ويتضمن هذا بيانات من الحفريات الأخيرة في حصن القريات الغربية، التي تسهم بشكل كبير في فهمنا لمنطقة التخوم في إقليم طرابلس. إن هذه المجموعات الجديدة من البيانات، إلى جانب الأدلة التي تم جمعها في الدراسات السابقة والعمل الميداني في المنطقة، تمكن شيمر Schimmer (الفصل السابع) من فحص إمدادات الغذاء للجيش، مع النظر بشكل خاص إلى محتوى الأمفورات وتداولها، والمصادر الكتابية، والأدلة الأثرية النباتية والحيوانية. في الفصل الثامن، ينظر شميد Schmid إلى المعتقدات والممارسات الدينية للجنود. يرتبط تخطيط المباني، التي تم تحديدها أثناء الأبحاث السابقة والحالية، باستخدامها الديني المحدد، في حين تُكمل النقوش هذه الصورة من خلال المعلومات التي تقدمها عن الآلهة المعبودة وهوية المصلين.

جزيرة جربة: Ritter and Ben Tahar 2022 ؛Drine *et al*. 2009. ويمكن العثور على تقارير الأنشطة والمشاريع الدولية المتعلقة بالحفاظ على التراث الثقافي الليبي في أقسام الموضوعات المخصصة للبحث في مجلة الدراسات الليبية، العدد 48 الصادر في 2017، وفي 2018 ,21 *Quaderni di Archeologia della Libya*. وأخيرًا، كانت الخطوة الرئيسة المتقدمة هو إنشاء نسخة متاحة مجانًا عبر الإنترنت من مجموعة النقوش الرومانية في إقليم طرابلس – *IRT*، والتي تضم مئات النصوص المكتشفة حديثًا: *Inscriptions of Roman Tripolitania (2021) – IRT2021*.

بالإضافة إلى هذه المنشورات، يجدر بنا أن نأخذ في الاعتبار تلك الأعمال التي قدمت لمحة عامة عن علم الآثار وتاريخ إقليم طرابلس لجمهور أشمل وأوسع نطاقاً، بدءاً من كتاب دينيس هاينز Denys Haynes الدليل الأثري والتاريخي لآثار ما قبل العصر الإسلامي في إقليم طرابلس *Archaeological and Historical Guide to the Pre-Islamic Antiquities of Tripolitania* (الطبعة الرابعة المنشورة عام 1981). كما يقدم كتاب صدر عام 1999 بعنوان ليبيا: مـــدن الإمبراطورية الـــرومانية المفقودة *The Lost Cities of the Roman Empire* (1999) ألفـه Di Vita صحبة علماء آثار بارزون وصفاً لعلم الآثار والتخطيط الحضري والفن والعمارة في ليبيا في العصر الروماني. وكانت الإضافة الأحدث والأكثر ترحيباً إلى هذه السلسلة من المنشورات هي كتاب فيليب كينريك Philip Kenrick أدلة ليبيا الأثرية: إقليم طرابلس المدن الثلاث *Tripolitania* (2009، والمتوفر أيضاً باللغة العربية) بتقييمه النقدي للعلماء والأدلة الأثرية التي يرجع تاريخها إلى العصر الفينيقي/البونيقي وحتى العصر الإسلامي المبكر الذي يعد مورداً لا غنى عنه لكل من القراء العاديين والعلماء المتخصصين، وقد ألهم هذا الكتاب بعدة طرق فكرة المجلد الحالي.

إقليم طرابلس: دراسة إقليمية جديدة

حتى وقت قريب جدًا، كانت الغالبية العظمى من الكتيبات والمنشورات التوليفية المجمعة syntheses والدراسات الجماعية حول شمال إفريقيا في العصر الروماني متاحة في الغالب باللغتين الفرنسية والإيطالية، في حين كانت الأعمال باللغة الإنجليزية تميل إلى أن تكون أكثر محدودية في نطاقها، أما الآن فالوضع يتغير بسرعة: كان نشر كتاب بروس هيتشنر Bruce Hitchner عام 2022 عن شمال أفريقيا تحت عنوان *Companion to North Africa in Antiquity* بمثابة علامة فارقة لبدء معالجة هذا الخلل من خلال تغطيته لمناطق مختلفة من المغرب وما وراءه، من الألفية الأولى قبل الميلاد إلى القرن الثامن الميلادي، وتلى ذلك عام 2023 نشر كتاب ديفيد ماتينغلي David Mattingly في الوقت المناسب بعنوان بين الصحراء والبحر: أفريقيا في العصر الإمبراطوري الروماني *Between Sahara and Sea: Africa in the Roman Empire* (2023)، وهو كتاب يقدم نظرة متجددة طال انتظارها لحياة المجتمعات الحضرية والريفية والعسكرية في جميع أنحاء شمال أفريقيا من القرن الأول قبل الميلاد إلى القرن الثالث الميلادي. إن هذه الدراسة تبتعد عن وجهات النظر القديمة (الاستعمارية) التي شكلت جزءًا كبيرًا من الدراسات السابقة وتقترح أفكارًا واتجاهات جديدة للبحوث المستقبلية.

وفي ضوء هذه التطورات، يبدو من المناسب أن نبدأ في التفكير في دراسات تركز على المنطقة يمكن أن تستكمل هذين العملين الأكثر عمومية وتأتي مكملة لها. ونظراً لغزارة التراث الأثري لإقليم طرابلس وتوافر البيانات الجديدة بفضل تقدم البحث، فإن الإقليم يمثل في هذا السياق حالة ملائمة للدراسة. وبالتالي، كان خيار تخصيص مجلدًا جديدًا حوله مدفوعاً بالرغبة في تقديم صورة حديثة لآثار هذه المنطقة المهمة في شمال أفريقيا، والبناء على مجموعة المؤلفات الرصينة التي نوقشت أعلاه والمحاولة على الأقل دمج بعض أحدث التطورات الأخيرة. وقد قُوبل هذا الاقتراح بحماس من جانب BILNAS، وتم تحديد سلسلة الدراسات المستقلة في شكل مونوغراف Open Access Monograph Series على أنه المكان المناسب للنشر لجعل المجلد في المتناول بيسر وسهولة. وإلى جانب هذا المجلد عن إقليم طرابلس، فإن النية هي تشجيع استمرار مشروع النشر من خلال مجموعات مستقبلية من الدراسات الأثرية والتاريخية عن إقليم برقة (شرق ليبيا)، وكذلك عن المناطق الواقعة قي تونس الحالية (بما في ذلك الجزء التونسي من إقليم طرابلس) والجزائر والمغرب.

البحوث والمنشورات الأثرية

تشكل علم الآثار في قطاع إقليم المدن الثلاث (إقليم طرابلس)، الذي يشغل حاليًا غرب ليبيا، إلى حد كبير من خلال التاريخ الحديث لهذه البلاد، حيث بدأت حفريات واسعة النطاق في ظل الحكم الاستعماري الإيطالي (1911–1943) أدت إلى الكشف عن بقايا رائعة من المعالم الأثرية القديمة، وخاصة في مواقع الحضر مثل لبدة الكبرى وصبراتة، وقد ترك هذا الإرث من الحقبة الاستعمارية أعمالاً حول بعض هذه المناطق، منها ما لم يبصر النور ومنها نشر جزء منها فقط، مع قضايا متعلقة بالحفاظ على هذه الآثار وصيانتها؛ ومع ذلك، اتسمت الفترة التي أعقبت مرحلة الاستعمار بوفرة الأعمال التي قام بها باحثون ليبيون وأجانب، اشتملت على تقارير العمل الميداني ودراسات لمبان ومواقع محددة. ويمكن لأولئك الذين بدأوا في التعرف على علم الآثار والتاريخ والتراث الليبي العثور على ثروة من هذه الأعمال في ثلاث مجلات مخصصة: الدراسات الليبية (نشرها المعهد البريطاني للدراسات الليبية وشمال أفريقيا British Institute for Libyan and Northern African Studies – BILNAS)؛ ليبيا القديمة *Libya Antiqua* (المجلة الرسمية لمصلحة الآثار الليبية – DoA)؛ و *Quaderni di Archeologia della Libya* (نشرته 'L'Erma' di Bretschneider)، ويمكن أيضًا العثور على معلومات مهمة في المنشورات القديمة أثناء فترة الاستعمار، مثل *Africa Italiana*، وفي المجلات الأكاديمية الحالية التي تركز على شمال أفريقيا وخارجها منها على سبيل المثال: *Antiquités Africaines*، و *Karthago*، و *Azania*، و *Journal of African Archaeology*.

ظهرت بانتظام منذ عام 1948 دراسات باللغة الإيطالية حول العمارة والفنون والتخطيط الحضري في ليبيا القديمة (إقليمي طرابلس وبرقة) من بين مواضيع أخرى في سلسلة كتب وأبحاث ليبية مستقلة معروفة باسم Monografie di Archeologia Libica ('L'Erma' di Bretschneider). ويمكن العثور على المزيد من الأعمال حول مواضيع مماثلة باللغة الإيطالية ولغات أخرى في سلسلة (متوقفة الآن) من الملاحق الخاصة بمجلة ليبيا القديمة Libya Antiqua. وينبغي أن يضاف إلى هذه الأعمال، الدراسات الأثرية التي نُشرت باللغة الإنجليزية في شكل دراسات مستقلة ومجلدات محررة في سلسلة منشورات BILNAS.

بُذِلت محاولات قيّمة لتقديم توليفات وملخصات لهذا الكم الغني من المواد ولإنتاج مجموعات من الدراسات يمكن للقراء استخدامها بمثابة نقطة انطلاق لبحثهم الخاص، ومن أمثلة ذلك المجلد المنشور تحت عنوان *Town and Country in Roman Tripolitania* (Buck and Mattingly 1985) الذي يجمع أوراقًا بحثية حول الآثار في إقليم طرابلس، من المراكز الحضرية في المنطقة الساحلية إلى المناطق الصحراوية النائية. وعلى نحو مماثل يجمع قسم حول موضوع مخصص للدراسة في مجلة الدراسات الليبية، العدد 20 الصادر في 1989، أوراقًا كتبها فريق دولي من العلماء الذين يرسمون العريضة لتطور البحث في ليبيا بين الأعوام من 1969 إلى 1989، مع التركيز على علم الآثار (من عصور ما قبل التاريخ إلى الفترة الإسلامية) والتاريخ والنقوش والفن والعمارة، وقد كانت هذه الأعمال بمثابة مقدمة لنشر كتاب ديفيد ماتينغلي David Mattingly *إقليم طرابلس Tripolitania* عام 1995 الذي يظل دراسة مرجعية أساسية لأي مهتم بهذا الموضوع.

وقد أحرزت الدراسات الأثرية حول إقليم طرابلس منذ ذلك الحين تقدمًا كبيرًا، فبعد النشر النهائي لمسح الآثار في الوديان الليبية التابع لليونسكو (ULVS) في عام 1996، تم تطوير مشاريع جديدة للبحث في المجتمعات القديمة، وخاصة الجرمنت على أطراف وخارج حدود الإمبراطورية الرومانية: مشروع هجرات الصحراء Desert Migrations Project ومشروع فزان Fazzan Project ومشروع إعمار الصحراء Peopling the Desert Project ومشروع عبر الصحراء Trans-Sahara Project. وقد أسفر النشاط الميداني للبعثة الأثرية الفرنسية في إقليمي طرابلس وبرقة عن نتائج علمية هامة (لمزيد من التفاصيل انظر Michel 2011–12; 2015). كما قدم العمل الميداني، الذي أجرته البعثة الأثرية الألمانية، (Mackensen 2021; 2024) بيانات جديدة قيمة حول المباني العسكرية في إقليم طرابلس في العصر الروماني والفترات المتأخرة. وقد نُشر مؤخرًا دليلًا مفيدًا للعديد من المشاريع الأثرية التي تم تنفيذها كجزء من الشراكات الليبية الإيطالية في مجلد ثنائي اللغة، الإيطالية والعربية (Musso and Turjman 2022). ومن المهم أيضًا أن نذكر العمل الأخير الذي قامت به فِرق البحث العلمي الدولية في القطاع التونسي من إقليم طرابلس، وخاصة في